LIBER ELIENSIS

LIBER ELIENSIS

A HISTORY OF THE ISLE OF ELY

FROM THE SEVENTH CENTURY
TO THE TWELFTH

COMPILED BY A MONK OF ELY IN THE TWELFTH CENTURY

TRANSLATED FROM THE LATIN,

WITH AN INTRODUCTION, NOTES,
APPENDICES AND INDICES BY

JANET FAIRWEATHER

THE BOYDELL PRESS

First published 2005
The Boydell Press, Woodbridge

ISBN 978-1-84383-015-3

Printed from camera-ready copy provided by the translator
Indices typeset by Chapman and Harvey, 29 Forehill, Ely

The Boydell Press is an imprint of Boydell & Brewer Ltd
PO Box 9, Woodbridge, Suffolk IP12 3DF, UK
and of Boydell & Brewer Inc.
668 Mt Hope Avenue, Rochester, NY 14620, USA
website: www.boydellandbrewer.com

A catalogue record for this book is available
from the British Library

This publication is printed on acid-free paper

CONTENTS

FOREWORD BY THE DEAN OF ELY

The *Liber Eliensis* was compiled by a monk of Ely at a time when the 500th anniversary of his monastery's foundation by St Etheldreda must have been very much on the community's mind. Janet Fairweather's translation of this important, but relatively little explored, chronicle of early medieval English history, centred on the Isle of Ely, was commissioned by my predecessor, Dean Michael Higgins, in 1999, when the end of the second millennium of the Christian era was provoking much historical stock-taking.

Remarkably, this is the first ever translation of the *Liber Eliensis*. Indeed, no printed edition of the complete Latin text was available before 1962. The translator would wish me to pay tribute to the immense labours of the late Dr E. O. Blake in producing that edition for the Royal Historical Society.

The monk entrusted with the compilation of the *Liber Eliensis* understood Old English, and his task included translation from that language into Latin which was, then, and for long afterwards, the standard medium of international communication in western Europe. English, falling into disuse as a written language in the twelfth century, has since staged its remarkable come-back, and it is fitting that the voice of an oppressed nation, as recorded in the *Liber Eliensis*, should, at last, be made available in the language that has even exceeded the international status of Latin.

It is with enthusiasm that I commend this translation of the *Liber Eliensis* to everyone interested in the spiritual heritage of Ely Cathedral, in the local history of eastern England, and in the tradition of freedom and the rule of law in the English-speaking world.

Michael Chandler

ACKNOWLEDGEMENTS

This translation of the *Liber Eliensis* has been produced as the result of a commission from the Dean and Chapter of Ely Cathedral, so I must begin by thanking the former Dean of Ely, Michael Higgins, together with the former Vice-Dean, John Inge, now Bishop of Huntingdon, and two successive Cathedral Bursars, David Smout and Stephen Wikner, for their work in administering the project and raising funds for it. To the funders of the translation, anonymous though they have chosen to remain, I must, of course, also express thanks.

As a Latinist with no particular expertise in medieval English history, I owe a particular debt of gratitude to Simon Keynes, who read and commented on, the first draft of my translation of *Liber Eliensis* i, introduced me to his bibliographical work, patiently answered many questions arising from my unfamiliarity with Old English, and very generously allowed me access to some unpublished work by himself and Alan Kennedy, most importantly, a draft translation of one of the major sources of the *Liber Eliensis*, the *Libellus Æthelwoldi*. I am further indebted to Alan Kennedy, now living in Sydney, Australia, for many helpful answers to enquiries, particularly about points of Anglo-Saxon law.

Rosalind Love of Robinson College, Cambridge, very kindly gave me, in advance of publication, a draft copy of her edition of the Latin of certain *Lives* of the early abbesses of Ely, now published in an Oxford Medieval Text. Access to this critical edition of texts hitherto only accessible in scattered manuscripts was an invaluable help to me over the interpretation and source-criticism of *Liber Eliensis* i.

Nicholas Karn of St Edmund Hall, Oxford, was very generous in allowing me to benefit from his researches, as yet unpublished, on the *Acta* of the earliest bishops of Ely.

With regard to liturgical matters, I am indebted to Alistair MacGregor of the Ushaw Library, Durham, for light thrown on many tricky details. I am grateful to my Ely friend Bridget Nichols for putting me in touch with him and for her general encouragement.

I am grateful also to Anne Holton-Krayenbuhl, John Maddison, Jane Kennedy, Roderick Regan and Quintin Carroll for information about the archaeology and architectural history of Ely. I owe to my sister and late brother-in-law, Pamela and Fraser Burrows, of Wareham, Dorset, my familiarity with the site of Bishop Nigel's unpleasant encounter with soldiers of King Stephen. Over miscellaneous points of detail I have benefited from discussions and correspondence with Kathy Bradney, Nicholas Denyer, Pat Easterling, Gillian Evans, Margaret Fox, Derek and Angela Helson, Francis

Jones' translation-workshop (6.6.05), Archimandrite Maximos Lavriotes, Hugh Morris, Marie Lovatt, John Parish, Peter Rex, Sophie Rixon, Canon Peter Sills, Theodosia Tomkinson, Tessa Webber and Cynthia Woodbridge.

It has been a great privilege, without which I could not have brought this work to satisfactory completion, to have had access to the Cambridge University Library and Faculty of Classics Library; the Wren Library of Trinity College, Cambridge; the Parker Library of Corpus Christi College, Cambridge, and the manuscripts room of the British Library.

The whole first draft of the translation was checked against the Latin, with great meticulousness and a welcome sense of humour, by Ann Webb, formerly of Millfield School, Somerset. Roger Lovatt, of Peterhouse, Cambridge, and Christine Pownall, of Ely, very kindly checked through the whole of certain later drafts. I am also indebted to other voluntary proof-readers from among my Ely friends and neighbours who, at yet other stages, corrected, and commented on, sections of the translation and its introduction and notes: John Baker, Sonja Baxter, Joan Cameron, Dorothy Clark, Paul Eyles, Peter Heald, Elizabeth Magba, Bill Marshall, Polly Perkins, Marilyn Pledger, Virginia Watkinson. Heartfelt thanks to Hilary Lavis and, once more, to Christine Pownall, for checking the index-entries against the text.

I recall with gratitude that the first suggestion that I should translate the *Liber Eliensis* was made by Roy Stubbings (senior), and that Pam Blakeman and John Maddison commissioned me to translate small portions of the text before translation of the whole became practicable. That I have been able to work from my own copy of E. O. Blake's edition of the Latin text I owe to the prescient kindness of Donald Russell, who presented me in 1998 with a copy from the library of the late Joy Russell. I am indebted to the generosity of Eric and Camilla Willner in providing me, at minimal cost, with the Macintosh computer on which the translation was typeset, and to the firm of Paragon, of Exning Road, Newmarket, for supplying a laser-printer compatible with it, after two others had ceased to function. I owe to the website of Cathy Ball my acquisition, with the help of Derek Wilcox, of an Old English font. I am much indebted to Mike and Jamey Harvey, who finalized the typesetting of the indices. I wish to thank Bill and Guy McCormack of Supercharge, Cambridge, my prompt and friendly suppliers of recycled printing-cartridges, and Michael and Simon Crunden for a gift of computing equipment which enabled me to regain ready access at home to the Internet after my modem had been struck by lightning. Many thanks, lastly, to everyone at the Boydell Press who has played a part in the publication of this book, and to Ken Hitch for the photograph used in the cover-design, showing a boss some sixty feet up in the presbytery vault of Ely Cathedral, above the final site of the shrine of St Æthelthryth.

Janet Fairweather, Ely, 2005.

DEO GRATIAS

INTRODUCTION

The *Liber Eliensis:* Themes, Sources and Context

The *Liber Eliensis*, alternatively referred to as the *Historia Eliensis,* and regarded by its compiler as a *History of the Isle of Ely,* was composed towards the end of the twelfth century. An ambitious work, recording the history of the monastery of Ely from its beginnings to the compiler's own time, it is for many reasons of national, and not just local, interest.

Its opening narrative, after a preliminary mention of the arrival of the Angles in Britain, is chiefly devoted to the genealogical background and life-story of that remarkable seventh-century saint, Æthelthryth, Queen of Northumbria and first Abbess of Ely, otherwise known as Etheldreda or Audrey. The compiler makes acknowledgement, indeed, of a tradition that there had been a minster on the Isle founded by St Augustine of Canterbury, no less, in the earliest days of English Christianity, when Æthelberht was King of Kent. But so great was the glorious reputation of St Æthelthryth, proclaimed by Bede and confirmed by recent recipients of miracles at her shrine, that he felt no need to lay any emphasis on this claim to origins before her time, and instead viewed her as the foundress, to all intents and purposes, of monastic life on the Isle. For him, St Æthelthryth was the doyenne (Lat. *primiceria*) of the monastery of Ely, and a well-beloved lady, worthy of his most fervent devotion. The *Liber Eliensis* presents a history of the successive religious communities which, after the earthly lifetime of its foundress, guarded and reverenced her shrine, and those of three of her kinswomen, St Seaxburh, St Eormenhild and St Wihtburh.

In its early days a double house for monks as well as nuns, subject to the rule of abbesses, the monastery was left in a ruinous state following depredations by the Danes in East Anglia round about 870, later becoming, for a short while in the mid-tenth century, a community of canons, and perhaps canonesses too, under non-celibate leadership. Then in 970, as part of the monastic reform movement spearheaded by Dunstan, Archbishop of Canterbury and Æthelwold, Bishop of Winchester in the reign of King Edgar, the house was refounded as a well-endowed Benedictine monastery and any canons unwilling to become monks were ejected. Both the abbey church and its associated domestic buildings were restored at this date, and were to outlast the upheavals of the Norman Conquest; but not for long. In the late eleventh and early twelfth centuries the minster was rebuilt on a grand scale, and became the seat of a bishop in 1109. This last development immediately caused serious financial problems, as the monks' resources had to be shared with an expensive episcopal establishment, but it was the minster's status as a cathedral that was ultimately to ensure the preservation of most of the medieval monastic buildings of Ely, including a good deal of the eleventh- and twelfth-century work, until our own day.

The Benedictine community founded in 970 was for men only. That is not to say that women in the Ely area feeling a call to the religious life were left entirely unprovided for: from the early eleventh century there was an abbey of nuns at Chatteris, only about ten miles away, for which Hervey, the first Bishop of Ely, was to take upon himself paternal responsibility (*LE* ii. 71; iii. 17). We also hear of the occasional isolated woman living a dedicated religious life in and around Ely, financed by her own, or if necessary the monastery's, resources. Benefactors to the house, and recipients of miracles at the shrines of the saints, were often women. And St Æthelthryth and her kinswomen, whose shrines were the focus of much heart-felt devotion throughout the Middle Ages, were indubitably female. But in its later stages, the *Liber Eliensis* is primarily concerned with monks, living in an all-male community, and with senior ecclesiastics all of whom, with the exception of the Abbess of Chatteris, were men.

Containing as it does records concerning the monastic estates, as well as the monastery itself, the *Liber Eliensis* preserves a wealth of data on the social organization, economics and government, national and local, of pre-Conquest England. It offers much treasure-trove for the art-historian and the liturgist. It records some rattling good tales about Hereward's resistance to William the Conqueror and another, later, anti-Norman conspiracy, and offers information about two figures of some importance in post-Conquest national politics, Abbot Richard and Bishop Nigel. It provides an insight, too, into the distinguished intellectual culture that flourished in Ely for several centuries before the foundation of Cambridge University, only seventeen miles away and within the same diocese. In view of all this, it is strange that this *History of the Isle of Ely* did not receive its first complete printed edition until 1962 – that of the late E. O. Blake – and is only now receiving its first English translation.

The compilation takes the form of a cartulary-chronicle, starting with the seventh century and ending in the twelfth. A cartulary-chronicle is not a fully integrated piece of historiography but resembles a modern source-book designed to present key primary texts as the basis of a course for students on some historical theme. It differs in approach from what a modern compiler of such a work would think suitable, in that it includes, alongside chapters which simply present charters or copy out some complete narrative text word for word, others in which the compiler combines data from several sources, working the material up, to a greater or lesser extent, in his own words. Thus, the monk responsible for compiling the *Liber Eliensis* saw his task as going beyond the duties of an archivist. But he disclaims, in his opening preface, any aspiration to be the ideal 'philosopher' or 'good historiographer' who, so he hoped, would one day treat the history of Ely as it deserved to be treated. By implication, he had a more modest end in view. His undertaking was a very large one, none the less: the task of synthesizing a mass of material about nearly five centuries of history, including material from the monastic archives that had never been adequately sorted or set out in chronological order. The compilation is set out in three books, each introduced by prefatory matter and lists of chapter-headings to guide the reader through the complex subject-matter.

The compiler's attitudes, in so far as they can be distinguished from those of his sources, suggest English ancestry rather than Norman, and his work includes many texts translated by himself or others from the vernacular, as well as material which had been written from the outset in Latin. Local sources available to him included: commemorations of abbesses, abbots, bishops and other benefactors to the monastery, both lay and clerical; detailed records of land-transactions and legal proceedings; the wills of private individuals; title-deeds; episcopal enactments; inventories; narrative accounts of the more troubled periods of Ely's history, and a rich and varied archive of miracle stories. Other texts drawn upon by the compiler originated elsewhere than in Ely: *Lives* of various notable saints, for instance. One document relating to Ely had been found in the archives at Bury St Edmunds; local traditions about St Æthelthryth had been collected by the compiler or some earlier writer of her life-story from Coldingham, Durham and north Lincolnshire. The charters cited include many which, while relating specifically to the monastery of Ely, were formulated far outside its confines, some of them setting out privileges granted by kings, others, mandates received from the Archbishop of Canterbury or the Pope.

Several works of local historiography can be recognized as having been embedded in their entirety, or nearly so, in the *Liber Eliensis*: at the end of book i, a remarkable tenth-century work by one Ælfhelm, entitled *An Exhortation of a Priest to his Archpriest*; at the beginning of book ii, a translation from the vernacular, commissioned by Bishop Hervey, of the *Book of the Lands of Bishop Æthelwold*, comprising records of the transactions whereby the monastery, thanks to the efforts of the Bishop of Winchester and the first Abbot of Ely, Byrhtnoth, acquired many of its estates; later in book ii, a little work commemorating seven notable benefactors ot the monastery who in the time of King Stephen were exhumed and buried together in a place of honour. This work is referred to in the footnotes to this translation as a *History of Seven Illustrious Men*, though its exact title is not known. Much of book iii seems to have been derived from the works of one Brother Richard.

For the life-story of St Æthelthryth the compiler tells us that he had an

English source to supplement Bede's *Ecclesiastical History*; he also had access
to several local hagiographical works in Latin, one at least of which provided
biographies of the other lady saints of Ely as well. For the canons, he had
Ælfhelm. For the lives of pre-Conquest abbots of the Benedictine foundation,
he had commemorative texts of some sort, and it seems likely, from internal
evidence, that efforts had already been made to assemble these into a
continuous narrative before the compiler of the *Liber Eliensis* set to work on
them. But, probably, in his time, there was still archival material, English and
Latin, recording benefactions to the abbey, which could usefully be
interpolated into any chronologically ordered account of the succession of
abbots that may already have existed. There are also a number of interesting
passages included in *LE ii* about visits by pre-Conquest royal personages to
Ely; given that the origin of these is not known, it was most likely local.

There had been a considerable flurry of historiographical activity
surrounding Hereward's resistance to William the Conqueror, in which the
monastery was implicated, and clearly the compiler drew on several different
sources for this episode, including a work about Hereward by the earlier of
two literary monks of Ely called Richard. The compiler's manner of
assembling his source materials may be faulted by critical historians, but we
must be extremely grateful to him for preserving a such a varied archive for
our attention.

The monastery's relatively hard times following the siege of Ely are
covered by more commemorations of individual abbots and of the custodian
Godfrey. We are presented with an inventory of the monastery's remaining
treasures; records of the meeting convened by King William's delegate, his
half-brother, Odo, Bishop of Bayeux, re-establishing the title of the Ely monks
to their estates; and finally copies of various charters granted by the
Conqueror. From the times of the two last abbots, Simeon, brother of
Walkelin, Bishop of Winchester, and Richard, son of Richard Fitz Gilbert de
Clare, there were preserved some wonderfully well written miracle
narratives, as well as texts commemorating the distinguished abbots
themselves. Abbot Richard had been the subject of an encomiastic work, and
the removal by him of the mortal remains of the Ely saints to new resting-
places had been afforded special literary treatment.

On the conversion of the abbacy into a bishopric there were available
certain local memoranda about Abbot Richard and Hervey, the first Bishop of
Ely, and also the papal, royal and archiepiscopal charters which documented
the founding of the new diocese. Bishop Nigel appears to have been the
subject of an expansive monograph by a member of the community who was
outraged by much that he did, namely, the second of the two literary monks
of Ely called Richard. Large stretches of this work are probably quoted word
for word, or lightly adapted, in the latter parts of book iii, together with a
lesser work by the same author, the history of a particular lawsuit concerning

the monastery's estate at Stetchworth. But the compiler was able to supplement the data provided by Richard's works, just as he had supplemented the memoranda on the abbots and on Bishop Hervey, with other texts, notably anecdotes taken from more than one collection of miracle-narratives. After a strangely confused assemblage of materials about the later years of Bishop Nigel, the *Liber Eliensis* concludes with a contribution to the hagiography of Thomas à Becket, recently martyred.

The general history of England which was used by the compiler as the continuous thread on which to string together the components of his *History of the Isle of Ely* in chronological order was a massive *Chronicle* composed at Worcester. Blake cites this work as by 'Florence of Worcester' whereas the editors of its Oxford Medieval Text credit it to another monk of Worcester called John. The truth of the matter seems to be that this Brother John took over a project on which a deceased colleague, Brother Florentius, had done a huge amount of ground-work. To avoid confusion, and to be even-handed to both its compilers, this work is referred to in the footnotes to the present translation as the *Worcester Chronicle*.

The Ely compiler's identity is unknown. There have long been attempts to attach a name to him – Thomas or Richard – but these almost certainly derive from unsafe inference from source-texts within the *Liber Eliensis* where these names appear. The ascriptions will be discussed in footnotes to the relevant passages (*LE* iii. 61, 96). The case for Thomas was cogently dismissed by Blake on stylistic grounds: that in favour of Richard has to be examined more seriously, but seems untenable. The main point to observe is that the compiler makes clear in his opening preface that the division of his work into chapters is to be seen as an integral part of his work and, in the chapter-headings, Brother Thomas is referred to as 'a certain monk of ours' (iii. 61) and the Brother Richard in question is referred to as 'our brother Richard' (iii. 101). Furthermore, this same brother Richard, Ely's second literary monk of that name, is praised more than once in the chapters themselves for his eloquence, learning and diligence (iii. 44, 101). So, whatever the meaning of a Latin phrase in iii. 96 which appears to say that Richard was the 'author of this work', it can hardly mean that he was the monk charged with the compilation of the *Liber Eliensis*. He might have been the 'instigator' of the project, but that is another matter.

Throughout this introduction and the footnotes 'the compiler' is referred to in the singular, on the supposition that there was a single monk in charge of producing the history. Certainly, whoever wrote the prefaces to the three books and the concluding chapter of the whole work, sometimes used the first-person singular when referring to his enterprise. However, we are free to imagine him working with assistants, and in the last twenty-five chapters of book iii the material is set out in such an irrational order, and there are such strange omissions from its record, that one is led to suspect that his guiding hand had finally been lost to the project, and the draft chapters left on his desk copied out by someone else, in a hasty and undiscriminating manner. Why are there two chapters about tenth-century events set out as *LE* iii. 119–20, amidst otherwise twelfth-century material? Why were the chapters about the foundation of Denny Abbey not included where they belonged, before the death of Bishop Nigel? Why is there no mention of the Templars, into whose hands Denny was almost immediately transferred? Why does our *Liber Eliensis*, unlike another text from medieval Ely, the *Chronicon Abbatum et Episcoporum Eliensium*, not quote Archbishop Becket's letter of reproof to Bishop Nigel? Why does it contain no reference to the earthquake which, according to Matthew Paris, shook Ely, Norfolk and Suffolk in 1165, throwing people to the ground and causing the bells to ring? All these are puzzling questions arising from the last part of book iii. That is not to say that the ordering of materials elsewhere in the *Liber Eliensis* is as fully comprehensive as the compiler, given his resources, could have made it, or that it invariably accords with what modern logicality would think sensible. The juxtapositions of sources telling the same story in different ways are not always happily executed. There are surprising oversights and some cases of deliberate obfuscation. But at least a semblance of order prevails throughout most of the work, and posterity must thank the compiler and his colleagues heartily for the richness and diversity of the materials which, for whatever reasons, they did choose to record and preserve.

It remains to consider what the motivation may have been behind the considerable labour of compiling this *History of the Isle of Ely*. Clearly, the work may be viewed as belonging to what has been termed the 'Twelfth-century Renaissance'. An interest in the past for its own sake may be discerned from the outset; a local patriotism that prompts people to glorify their home-towns is acknowledged as normal, and we find Ely writers imitating classical, as well as biblical, historiography. Whereas one writer on Hereward's resistance drew on the Books of Maccabees in the Vulgate Bible for many of his phrases (*LE* ii. 102), an account of a twelfth-century conspiracy plotted in Stretham Church (*LE* iii. 47, 51–2) features repeated allusion to Sallust's *Catiline* and an abstruse recollection of Horace. The compiler himself was the heir of a distinguished historiographical tradition going back to Thucydides, when he noted, in the second of his opening prefaces, that the coinage of past kings and metal artefacts found on a derelict site near Ely corroborated other evidence of former 'human habitation' in that place. There are signs of critical discrimination with regard to hagiography, and of empirical testing of evidence in the miracle-stories. Medical case-histories are described in unsparing detail. A classification of the fauna of the Isle of Ely is committed to writing in the context of the Hereward narratives: eight different mammals, nine varieties of fish and seven types of bird are distinguished (ii. 105).

The monastery of Ely was already, in pre-Conquest times, a place where learning was valued, and even, under Abbot Leofsige in the time of King Cnut, a precondition for entry there, if we may believe *LE* ii. 84. In Bishop Hervey's day, a schoolmaster from Dunwich called Ralph, formerly a married man, became a monk at Ely after recovery from an illness which he described graphically in an autobiographical narrative, and he brought with him to the monastery a considerable stock of abstruse erudition, at least a smattering of Greek, a distaste for the educational use of corporal punishment, and a dauntingly elaborate mode of writing Latin (*LE* iii. 35). Around 1140, about a hundred and forty years before the foundation of the first Cambridge college, the younger monks of Ely were being introduced to the latest methods of disputation by a learned Londoner called Julian, who had previously taught the liberal arts on the continent and the disciplines of rhetoric, philosophy and theology in what seems to have been an incipient University of London, before being obliged to flee to the sanctuary of Ely amid the anarchy of the civil war raging between the partisans of Stephen and Matilda (iii. 93). His enlightened teaching methods, based on amiable conversation, are described with appreciation. We seem not far away from the world of Erasmus.

The monks' involvement in lawsuits had taught them the value, against unlettered opponents, of a thorough knowledge of grammar, logic and rhetoric, and also the advantages of a mastery of elegant conversational Latin, particularly when on visits to the papal curia. The fact of these occasional travels to Rome by monks of Ely, and by Bishop Nigel, too, is worth noting as a feature of the cathedral's cultural history. This fenland establishment was not, in intellectual or artistic terms, a rural backwater.

It had been an outsider, Goscelin of Saint-Bertin and Canterbury, who provided Ely, in Abbot Simeon's day, with *Prosae* ('Sequences') on the life of St Æthelthryth for liturgical use (*LE* ii. 133). But the monks of Ely could boast hagiographers, and the occasional Latin poet, among their own number. In the early years of the bishopric, a monk called Gregory wrote a metrical *Life and Miracles of St Æthelthryth* which includes a wonderful description of Ely at the time when the remarkable beauty of the cathedral church had first become apparent, with painters, sculptors and metal-workers still busily at work and striving after a classical ideal of realism, amid the luxuriant orchards, fruitful vineyards, the resident peacocks and the teeming wild life of the Isle. It was almost certainly this same monk who translated the *Libellus Æthelwoldi* for Bishop Hervey and, in another verse-tribute, praised the grounds of the Bishop's Palace at Little Downham as a new Garden of the Hesperides. Bishop Æthelwold of Winchester was praised to the heavens by the same poet, too, in the Latin dactylic hexameters at which he was adept.

The Benedictines of Ely were not behind the times where part-singing and musical theory were concerned. The compiler of the *Liber Eliensis* could countenance the notion that King Cnut once improvised a secular song in concert with simultaneous chanting by the monks (*LE* ii. 85). Another local author whom he cites (ii. 148) could imagine the four lady saints of Ely as percussion-players hammering out a celestial tetrachord on the wood of the cross! Texts from Ely refer to the polyphony *(organum)* of the Holy Spirit and of the prophets. As for the visual arts, the monastery's extant inventories attest to the rich decoration of liturgical books, vestments and gold and silver vessels treasured in Ely and to a large extent manufactured there; they describe pre-Conquest statuary on a grand scale, overlaid with precious metals; sumptuous, jewelled decoration on the shrine of St Æthelthryth in the early days of the bishopric (ii. 114, 139; iii. 50). English embroidery was enjoying its long heyday. Silk vestments were not unknown in the monastic treasury, and gold-thread work, commonplace. And although disappointingly little is said in the *Liber Eliensis* about the processes of building and rebuilding the minster, the favourable verdict in *LE* ii. 143 on the judicious proportions of the architecture favoured by Abbots Simeon and Richard is one with which we are still in a position to agree.

Richard, the last of the abbots, sprang from the highest Norman nobility and had been educated at Bec at a time when that monastery, the spiritual home also of Archbishops Lanfranc and Anselm, was one of Europe's most distinguished intellectual centres. A power to be reckoned with in the nation's affairs in the time of Henry I, he held 'liberal' views on kingship, and once dared to eject from his residence one of the king's jesters, who was insulting him (*LE* ii. 142).

Later in the twelfth century (1133–69) came the long episcopate of Nigel, a man who came from a family of noted administrative reformers. For he was a nephew of Roger, Bishop of Salisbury, who, in the reign of Henry I, had revolutionized the nation's financial accounting by the use of counters on a chequered cloth, in accordance with the principle of the abacus. One of the boys educated in the monastery of Ely in Bishop Nigel's time (*LE* iii. 122) was his son, Richard Fitz Nigel, himself a future Bishop of London. This youth, remembered by the monks as a trouble-maker, was evidently schooled in politics and economics by his father, a former Treasurer of England, and he was later to write a *Dialogue on the Exchequer* which has, in our own time, been found worthy of publication in an Oxford Medieval Text and inclusion in many an undergraduate reading-list.

There had been much disruption of the economy of the monastery of Ely in the mid-twelfth century, but Bishop Nigel, who was blamed for most of its troubles, had at least seen to it that the Ely drachma remained a sound currency amidst all the demands for protection-money, minting of coinages by private individuals, and devaluations of the rate of exchange, which were endemic in the troubled times of Stephen and Matilda. The monastery, as the century drew towards its close, remained surrounded by its tall trees and rich orchards, first planted two centuries before by one Provost Leo (*LE* ii. 54). Neither the disruptions of the civil wars nor Bishop Nigel's depredations of the monastic resources had stifled the literary aspirations of the more highly educated monks. Indeed, paradoxically, the resulting hardships provided interesting material for would-be historiographers and were the context of a significant advance in the monastery's educational provision.

That the *Liber Eliensis* was intended to glorify the monastery of Ely, its founding saints and its subsequent benefactors, is obvious. We may also reasonably surmise that it was designed to inculcate into the monks' consciousness a knowledge of the historical foundations upon which the privileged legal standing of the monastery of Ely rested: how it had acquired its numerous estates; how, in some cases, it had lost control of them; what the legal basis was for the contentious division of the monastic revenues, introduced when Ely became a bishopric, between the prior and monks, on the one hand, and the bishop's establishment on the other. For lawsuits seem to have disrupted, with annoying regularity, the ability of at least the senior monks of Ely to engage in the quiet Benedictine round of daily prayer, labour and recreation, in cloister, workshop, garden and refectory. It would have been seen as of great practical value that all the monks should know their rights in law.

A theme uniting all three books of the *Liber Eliensis* is the veneration of St Æthelthryth, the monastery's foundress, whose posthumous reputation as an important heavenly personage through whose mediation miracles of the Lord were frequently performed, was the basis on which the success and wealth of the monastery rested. The triumphs belonged to the Lord, so the compiler was at pains to insist on a number of occasions, but He was perceived to act in and through His saints. This is the message of the concluding words of the book, following an account of the martyrdom of Archbishop Becket in 1170. As for the compiler's decision to devote the last chapter of his local chronicle to this nationally important event, thus ending his book with a bang, not a whimper, as one might say: it may seem a puzzling choice, but was in fact very apt. For a second major theme uniting all three books of the *Liber Eliensis* is the relation between Church and state: the counter-balancing of the interests of monastics and the Pope on the one hand, and, on the other, the kings of England and the secular magnates of the realm, aided and abetted by politically minded clerics. For centuries, so we see through the microcosm of Ely's history, the accumulation by monasteries of huge wealth, privilege and influence had been creating conditions almost bound to precipitate, sooner or later, the sort of clash between king and Church exemplified by Becket's assassination.

But that is to read the *Liber Eliensis* with modern hindsight and from a secular viewpoint. To its compiler it seemed that monasticism was unquestionably the highest mode of earthly living and that anything potentially detrimental to its welfare and security was unquestionably wrong. From his point of view, the great days of the monastery of Ely had been in the days of Kings Æthelred, Cnut, and Edward the Confessor, when its wealth was immense, its liberty promoted by royal patronage, when the monks were customarily men of nobility and learning, and offerings of gold and silver were shared out on the refectory tables (*LE* ii. 84). The Norman Conquest evoked in him thoughts of the biblical book of Lamentations (ii. 78), and he deplored the fact that, earlier in his own century, the founding of an episcopal see had diverted such a large proportion of the funds originally intended for the support of the monks (iii. 25). As for Becket's martyrdom, that was, as he saw it, not a setback for the Church, but, in the perspective of eternity, a triumph.

When, exactly, was the *Liber Eliensis* completed? No events at Ely later than the death of Bishop Nigel in 1169 are recorded in it. Work on the project might certainly have begun well before that date. But clearly the conclusion of book iii was not written until after a certain amount of hagiography had accumulated around Becket, who was martyred in 1170 and canonized in 1173. On the other hand, there is no reason to believe that it is to be dated later than the latter part of the twelfth century. The handwriting of its oldest extant manuscript has been assigned by experts to that period.

Something to bear in mind in speculations about dating is that Nigel's successor, Geoffrey Ridel, Bishop of Ely from 1173 to 1189, had been Becket's archdeacon, and no friend to him. It might be suggested that the unusual idea of concluding Ely's local chronicle with the praises of Becket's martyrdom would hardly have been reckoned tactful during his episcopate. However, the monks of Ely were not noted for deference to their bishops' opinions, and Ridel, immediately before taking office as Bishop of Ely, had formally cleared himself of any involvement in the archbishop's murder. There is, in fact, some evidence in favour of the supposition that book iii of the *Liber Eliensis* dates from very early in his episcopate. We happen to know the date when Richard, the former sub-prior, took office as prior, namely: 1177. Now, the following wording is used in *LE* iii. 101 of the brother Richard who represented the monks at Rome in the Stetchworth case: 'It is indeed the case that the Brother Richard referred to, someone worthy of all veneration, has performed good and faithful service in all his duties: wise steward that he is, he has distributed the communal wealth in a fitting and discerning manner, as he has known it to be expedient for each person, in accordance with the need of the particular individuals; as a result he is the recipient of favour and gratitude.' Clearly, this monk was a high office-holder in the monastery, and the supposition that he was at the time sub-prior, and in line for election as the next prior, seems entirely consonant with the evidence. But he can hardly yet be prior, seeing that he is referred to as plain 'Brother Richard', and even granted that 'Richard' was a common enough Norman name, and one particularly associated with a family which had a long-standing connection with Ely (*LE* ii. 142), it is improbable that there would have been two high office-holders of the same name in the monastery at the same time. So the evidence seems to favour identification of Prior Richard with the monks' former advocate in the Stetchworth case, and it would suit the evidence to suggest a date for the completion of the *Liber Eliensis* before 1177, when Richard was still sub-prior and when Becket's martyrdom was very much on people's minds: perhaps even 1173, the year when Ridel was enthroned at Ely on Ascension Day, and when, coincidentally, the monastery was celebrating the 500th anniversary of its foundation by St Æthelthryth, and the feast of the newly canonized saint, Thomas à Becket, was to be celebrated for the first time on December 29th. The disorder in the latter chapters of book iii of the *Liber Eliensis* is suggestive of a rush to a deadline.

The Translation: Principles, Background and Bibliography

The present translation, besides being intended to bring the contents of the *Liber Eliensis* to the attention of the general public, has been designed to be used by scholars in conjunction with the Latin printed edition of E. O. Blake, *Liber Eliensis*, Camden Third Series, vol. xcii (Royal Historical Society: London 1962), which provides a detailed textual apparatus, together with much historical annotation.

The translator was trained as a classical scholar, not as a medieval historian, and it will be for others to publish the new, definitive edition of the *Liber Eliensis*, complete with exhaustive historical commentary, which needs, of course, one day, to be produced. Meanwhile, this translation, its notes, appendices and indices, are offered as a serious contribution to the large scholarly endeavour required as a preliminary to the eventual publication of such a work. For the moment, Blake's notes and bibliography should be the places where the serious student of the chronicle initially looks for historical guidance, together with H. C. Derby, *The Medieval Fenland* (Cambridge 1940, repr. Newton Abbot, 1974); E. Miller, *The Abbey and Bishopric of Ely* (Cambridge 1951); Dorothy Owen, *The Library and Muniments of Ely Cathedral* (Cambridge 1973); R. B. Pugh, *The Victoria History of the County of Cambridge and the Isle of Ely*, vol. iv (London 1967) and P. Meadows and N. Ramsay eds., *The History of Ely Cathedral* (Woodbridge 2003), a collaborative history, the first essay in which is a study by Simon Keynes of the monastery up to the foundation of the bishopric. Canon J. Bentham's pioneering *History and Antiquities of the Cathedral and Conventual Church of Ely* (second edition, Norwich 1812) still deserves the antiquarian's attention.

The translator's initial sources of general information about medieval England have been the three volumes of the Oxford History of England covering the relevant period: J. N. L. Myres, *The English Settlements* (1986); F. M. Stenton, *Anglo-Saxon England* (third edition, 1971) and A. L. Poole, *Domesday Book to Magna Carta* (second edition, 1955). For an up-to-date and wide-ranging bibliographical guide to English history up to the eleventh century, the reader is referred to Simon Keynes, *Anglo-Saxon England: A Bibliographical Handbook for Students of Anglo-Saxon History* (Department of Anglo-Saxon, Norse and Celtic, University of Cambridge, 2001), an earlier edition of which (1998) is available on the Internet, courtesy of John Chandler of Western Michigan University (www.wmich.edu/medieval/rawl/keynes1/index.html). Another valuable resource for historians, again instigated by Simon Keynes and accessible on the Internet, is *The Anglo-Saxon Index* (www.trin.cam.ac.uk/sdk13/asindex.html).

The Footnotes

The footnotes to this translation present, mainly, two types of information: source-criticism and detailed observations about the Latin text.

Each chapter, or series of related chapters, is provided with an initial note on the compiler's likely source or sources for it. These notes chiefly summarize the findings of Blake, whose footnotes provide meticulous detail about specific borrowings from extant sources, should the reader require it. In the case of charters, the notes to this translation present the datings suggested by Blake with a few references to alternative views, including some caveats suggested by Nicholas Karn on the basis of his study of the *Acta* of the earliest bishops of Ely. Where the translator has made independent speculations as to the character of the underlying source of a chapter, these are not to be regarded as more than provisional suggestions. The reader is warned that much more research is called for, particularly, into the exact relationship of the *Liber Eliensis* to other medieval narrative texts from Ely, some of them still only accessible in the original manuscripts.

The textual notes are intended to alert readers to the fact that there seemed to the translator to be many problems in the text presented by even the oldest Latin manuscript. For the principle has been adhered to that it is better to acknowledge bafflement than to gloss over problems. The translator's hope is that the conjectures offered may be of some assistance to scholars struggling with detailed points of interpretation, and to any future editors of the Latin text of the *Liber Eliensis*.

As a means of forestalling the need for annotation of other kinds, there will be an attempt, later in this introduction, to explain various problems of translation and technical terms recurrent in the *Liber Eliensis*, and to suggest sources where the reader might look for further information on specialized topics.

The Latin Text behind the Translation

In the textual footnotes, Blake's *sigla* are used in references to manuscripts of the *Liber Eliensis,* the *Libellus Æthelwoldi* and Ely cartularies, but with reference the *Lives* of St Æthelthryth and her saintly kinswomen, the *sigla* used are derived from Rosalind Love's *Goscelin of Saint-Bertin and the Lives of the Female Saints of Ely,* (Oxford University Press, 2004).

Blake's sigla

E   Trinity College, Cambridge, MS O.2.1
F   Cambridge University Library: Ely Dean and Chapter MS: *Liber Eliensis*
O   Bodleian Library, Oxford, MS Laud. Misc. 647
A   British Library, London, MS Cotton, Vespasian A xix (*LE* iii and *Libellus Æthelwoldi*)
B   British Library, London, MS Cotton, Domitian A xv (*LE* i and ii, *Chronicon, Book of Miracles*)
G   British Library, London, MS Cotton, Titus A i (*LE* ii and Cartulary)
C   Trinity College, Cambridge, MS O.2.41 (Cartulary and *Libellus Æthelwoldi*)
D   British Library, London, MS Cotton, Tiberius A vi (Cartulary)
M   Cambridge University Library: Ely Diocesan Registry, Liber M (Cartulary).

Rosalind Love's sigla

T   Trinity College, Cambridge MS O.2.1 (= E in Blake's edition of *LE*) fos. 215r–228r
A   British Library, London, MS Cotton, Caligula A viii, fos. 108r–228r
C   Cambridge, Corpus Christi College MS 393, fos. 3r–9v
D   Trinity College, Dublin MS 172 (B.2.7), pp. 259–64.

For the most part, the Latin text presupposed in this translation is identical with that set out by Blake, and his order of chapters is followed. The translator acknowledges huge indebtedness to Blake's stupendous labour of textual collation. However, it has not proved practicable to translate the text exactly as it stands in his edition, for the following reasons.

The two oldest manuscripts of the *Liber Eliensis* are: Trinity College, Cambridge, MS O.2.1 (twelfth century) known as E, and Cambridge University

Library: Dean and Chapter of Ely MS: *Liber Eliensis* (thirteenth century), known as F. On the reasoning that F presents a fuller text than E, Blake's editorial policy was to reproduce the text of F almost unmodified. For the most part, readings in E are only noted by Blake in his *apparatus criticus,* along with textual variants in certain later manuscripts containing all or part of the *Liber Eliensis,* cartularies, and other historical narrative texts from Ely.

Sadly, however, there are places scattered all through the text where the readings of F do not make good sense. An editor, having made the decision to give priority to a particular manuscript, may legitimately think it best to let obscurities in its text stand: a translator has no such option. And so, whereas very few textual conjectures were admitted by Blake, the present translator has felt obliged to think of many more, with the simple, pragmatic objective of making sense of the Latin. The same objective lies behind a decision to attach more importance to the text of E, in this translation, than Blake did in his edition: often, its readings simply make more sense than those of F, which is unsurprising, given that it is the older of the two manuscripts. It has also emerged from the translator's checking of textually doubtful passages that some important readings in E are not recorded in Blake's apparatus. These have been recorded in bold type in the footnotes to the translation. They have eliminated the need for conjectural emendation in a number of passages. Would that this desperate expedient could have been dispensed with altogether!

To allay possible misunderstandings, it seems desirable to explain here what sorts of error we are to presuppose in places where it is indicated in a footnote that a conjectural reading has been translated. Latin textual emendation normally has to do with mistakes that have arisen in the course of many centuries of copying and recopying, but in some places where the Latin of the *Liber Eliensis* has seemed to the translator to need elucidation by educated guess-work, it may well be the case that the original compiler wrote exactly what we find in manuscript E. However, he probably did not intend to. Given that the usual standard of Latinity in the *Liber Eliensis* and its sources seems to be highly competent, we cannot simply attribute unintelligible, or obviously corrupt, readings to the fact that we are dealing with a post-classical work. We have to suppose, rather, that errors crept even into the E-text, either through miscopying of the sources used in it or though misreading of some earlier draft of the compilation itself. We also have to countenance the possibility that, even when engaged in free composition, the compiler could sometimes inadvertently have written down words other than the ones he meant to write – a very human thing to do.

The hypothetical Latin text of the *Liber Eliensis* presupposed in the translation is more like E than F, then, in points of detail. The aim has been that the text translated should approximate to what the first compiler intended to write, back in the twelfth century. It has been with this end in view, also, as well as for pragmatic reasons, that this notional Latin text has been tidied up by conjectural means – as an interim measure.

We await, of course, the ideal edition of the Latin text of the *Liber Eliensis*. For this, a completely new collation of E would be a prerequisite, and if the decision were made, as it surely should be, to place E in the foreground of such an edition rather than F, it would be appropriate for the text of the cartulary-chronicle to be prefaced by the Ely Kalendar that precedes it in E, and to be followed by the items which follow it in that manuscript in an appendix: the *Inquisitio Eliensis* – the Domesday listing of the monastic properties – and a set of *Lives* of the saintly kinswomen of Abbess Æthelthryth. It emerges from the listing of the chapter-headings of *LE* iii in the E manuscript that the *Inquisitio* and these *Lives*, which usefully supplement the surprisingly brief treatment in *LE* i of St Æthelthryth's successors, were envisaged as forming a necessary appendix to the main cartulary-chronicle.

However, any future editor of the *Liber Eliensis* will have to admit that E has its failings, and in one important respect presents a less rich historical record than F. There is a long series of chapters, early in book ii, where F reproduces word for word the text of the *Libellus Æthelwoldi*, an amazingly detailed account of the acquisition in the late tenth century, by Bishop Æthelwold of Winchester, of a vast acreage of estates, in order to provide the monks of Ely with their livelihood. The E manuscript provides only an epitome of what is set down in the *Libellus*, and presumably the systematic epitomizing represents the original compiler's intention. One can see sound reasoning, for instance, behind his elimination from the early chapters of *LE* ii of all references to events later than King Edgar's time. On the other hand, no one would have thanked the present translator if the policy of giving priority to E had been rigidly adhered to in the case of the chapters which have the *Libellus* as their source. Consequently, this translation includes the whole of the Latin text that Blake chose to print. It has, however, been made clear by means of square brackets which passages the E text omits. Thus, the English rendering of *LE* ii. 7–49, taken together with the passages and poems translated in its Appendix A, constitutes an almost complete translation of the *Libellus*.

Elsewhere in the *Liber Eliensis* too, useful supplements in F are included in the translation within square brackets. In the few chapters where E and F differ radically, both variants have been translated. There are a few chapters which are not to be found in E at all. Again, square brackets are used to mark material extraneous to its text.

In Appendices A and B to this translation there will be found English versions of the Latin passages cited in Blake's appendices: those portions of the *Libellus Æthelwoldi* not cited in full even in the F text of the *Liber Eliensis*, and an extract from the *Book of Miracles* in British Library MS Cotton Domitian A xv. Appendix C contains a translation of poem from another part of that same manuscript, which is cited by Blake, pp. 235–6, note *g*. Also translated, in footnotes, are certain passages from a later, expanded version of the *Liber Eliensis,* that of the Oxford manuscript, O (Bodleian Library: MS Laud. Misc. 647), where these are cited by Blake in his edition.

Almost no notice is taken, otherwise, in the present translation or its footnotes, of this Oxford manuscript, on which see Blake, Introduction, pp. xxiv–xxv, or of any other later continuator or adapter of *Liber Eliensis.* A number of later manuscripts, presenting texts which expand, adapt, epitomize or are otherwise related to the *Liber Eliensis,* are described in some detail by Blake. The only full, printed edition of any of them appears to be Henry Wharton's edition in *Anglia Sacra* i, pp. 591–688, of Lambeth Palace Library MS 448, a *Chronicle of the Abbots and Bishops of Ely,* concluding with the episcopate of Thomas Thirlby (1554–59). Blake describes this manuscript in his Introduction, p. xxvi. Further research is needed into its exact relationship with the *Liber Eliensis.*

Editorial Conventions

Abbreviations, on the lines as *LE* for *Liber Eliensis,* should be readily intelligible on the basis of the introduction and bibliography. The three successive prefaces of *LE* i are cited as i pr. H, i pr. S and i pr Æ respectively.

Where scholars might wish to make detailed cross-reference to the Latin in E. O. Blake's edition of the *Liber Eliensis,* references are given by page and line number, thus: p. 271.16, ed. Blake.

Where the translator has been obliged to resort to conjecture to make sense of an obscure passage, footnotes are always given. Where it has seemed impossible to guess the intended Latin text, the obelus is used to mark out the problematic word or words, thus: 'Earl William of Warenne, whose brother Hereward slew † some time before†'.

Angle brackets, e.g. '<and>' or '<et>', indicate that the Latin text seems to lack something, and that the translation presupposes a supplement, either wholly conjectural or derived from some extant source other than the *LE* manuscripts.

Square brackets, e.g. in 'The brothers of the church [also] bought from Byrhtlaf a farm at Cambridge built upon in the best manner . . .' enclose material which is found in F, the second oldest manuscript, but not in E, the oldest. The aim has been only to translate divergent readings of F when they are of high quality such as, for example, when they preserve the full text of the *Libellus Æthelwoldi.*

Double square brackets, e.g. in [[A charter of the king about *Estona.*]] enclose material, printed in Blake's text, which was not included by the first scribe of either E or F, but was later added by another hand.

Curly brackets are used for two purposes: (1) to indicate that a gloss, explaining rather than directly translating the Latin, has been incorporated in the translation for clarity's sake, e.g. '{Friday}, the sixth day of the week' or (2) in conjunction with the word *'recte'* (Latin for 'rightly'), to correct factual inaccuracies in the text, e.g. 'thirty {*recte* twenty} shillings'.

Where bold type is used in the footnotes, this indicates that the translation renders a reading in the E manuscript, or in B *(Book of Miracles)*, which is not recorded in Blake's edition.

A dating formula set out as follows in the footnotes: '1133 X 1169', indicates the timescale within which an uncertain date might fall.

The Translator's Tools

The translator's two most frequently used reference-books have been: C. T. Lewis and C. Short, *A Latin Dictionary* (1879, reprinted Oxford 1980), valuable for including usages of the Christian writers of late antiquity alongside those of earlier classical authors, and R. E. Latham's *Revised Medieval Latin Word-List from British and Irish Sources* (Oxford 1965). Occasional forays have also been necessary into the more detailed and wide-ranging lexicography of C. du Cange, *Glossarium Mediae et Infimae Latinitatis*, ed. L. Favre (Niort and London 1884–87), its incomplete successor, *Novum Glossarium Mediae Latinitatis* (Copenhagen 1957–) and the excellent, but also as yet incomplete, *Dictionary of Medieval Latin from British Sources*, another project initiated by R. E. Latham (London and Oxford 1975–). In moments of despair, various dictionaries of Romance languages, including Norman French, have been consulted. Roget's *Thesaurus* (ed. R. A. Dutch, 1962, frequently reprinted) has more than once provided a cure for translator's block. Word-searching of the authors in J. P. Migne's *Patrologia Latina* (Paris 1844–64) by means of the *CETEDOC* programme has occasionally been employed as a means of discovering the meaning of rare expressions or obscure allusions; likewise the Google search-engine on the Internet.

General Principles of Translation

The Latin used by the compiler and his sources in the *Liber Eliensis* was rich and varied, with a very large vocabulary. The English translation has needed to range equally widely. Moreover, because many concepts deployed by the medieval Christian thinker are no longer in common currency, some of the vocabulary drawn upon must seem somewhat archaic, just as the expression of ideas is often long-winded by modern standards. However, the translator is satisfied, on the strength of the response to readings presented to the general public in Ely, that the idiom employed is one capable of being appreciated by a contemporary English-speaking readership. One general principle adhered to has been that any vocabulary recognized in the 1933 edition of the Shorter Oxford English Dictionary has been deemed acceptable. Any newer coinages in English have been deployed only with caution.

In the treatment of proper nouns, this translation follows the conventions of the Oxford Medieval Texts (OMT) series: place-names are given in their modern form where this is known with certainty; otherwise, they are printed in italics as they appear in the Latin text or, for the sake of consistency or ease of reading, in some other Old English form. For the identification of places, Blake's index has normally been followed, or an unpublished draft for an edition of the *Libellus Æthelwoldi*, made available to the translator by Simon Keynes and Alan Kennedy. Other important aids are the publications of the English Place-name Society, particularly those of P. H. Reaney, *The Place-names of Essex* (Cambridge 1935) and *The Place-names of Cambridgeshire and the Isle of Ely* (1943). The index to the Penguin translation of the *Domesday Book*, published in 2002, is useful in listing concisely the principal place-names of the whole of England. Also now available is: V. Watts, *The Cambridge Dictionary of English Place-names* (Cambridge 2003).

Again in line with established academic practice, Old English forms of personal names are retained, except in the case of certain well-known, royal names, such as Alfred, Edmund, Edgar, Edward and Edith, which are firmly ingrained in public awareness in a particular form. Usually the forms of names used, whether Old English or Anglo-Norman, correspond to those in the index to Blake's edition, the most notable exception being St Etheldreda whom, in deference to the advice of Old English specialists, the translator has referred to throughout as Æthelthryth.

The rhetorical principles of the more elevated stylists cited in the *Liber Eliensis* demanded that they should never use the same word for the same thing twice in the same passage; frequent use was made, too, in both narrative and documentary Latin, of words meaning 'aforesaid' or 'often-mentioned'. The translator has made a conscious decision to defer to the authors' sense of proper style and not to modernize. Liberties have, however, been taken with comparative adjectives and adverbs: they have often been translated by the superlatives to which they appear to have been equivalent in sense.

Particular Problems of Translation

Medieval Latin letter-writers had a way of using flowery, third-person forms of address to one another, not just 'Your Majesty' to the king, but 'Your Amiability', 'Your Fraternity' to lesser worthies. Sometimes it has seemed unacceptable to translate these titles exactly as they stand and, for reasons of clarity, periphrases have been substituted, such as 'your amiable self', 'your fraternal self'.

The term *locus*, literally 'place', is frequently used in *LE* as a synonym for 'monastery' and the translation takes account of this fact. The term 'vill' is used for Latin *villa*, to designate a settlement with the land belonging to it. Latin *ornamenta*, a term which covered all the moveable accoutrements of a church, whether vestments, church-furnishings or plate, is usually translated simply as 'ornaments', this being still a standard term amongst liturgists, even though it has fallen out of common use. The term *prepositus*, 'a man placed before others', the word for an abbot's deputy in the *Rule of St Benedict*, is used in the *LE* as the title of a variety of monastic and secular office-holders: in this translation it is rendered by its English derivative 'provost' in most contexts, but by 'reeve' where a financial administrator is clearly meant.

The term *cirographum*, from the Greek for 'handwritten', is used in the *Libellus Æthelwoldi*, with reference to a number of charters conveying the ownership of land. Not all of them were of the kind referred to in modern technical parlance as 'chirographs', that is, documents written in duplicate or triplicate with the word CIROGRAPHUM written in large capitals between the copies and cut through transversely on completion of the transaction. Hence *cirographum* is only translated as 'chirograph' where it is explicit that the document had this special form, or where the document referred to is someone's will. In the case of title-deeds of properties the translation 'charter' is preferred.

The Latin term *virtus*, with its semantic field ranging from 'virtue' to 'miracle', presents the modern translator with particularly intractable problems. For, although, in pre-Reformation times, its English derivative, 'virtue', used to cover an equivalent range of meanings, it has not done so since then. The Shorter OED lists amongst the archaic and obsolete connotations of 'virtue': 'the power or operative influence inherent in a supernatural or divine being' and 'an act of superhuman or divine power'; a 'mighty work'; a 'miracle', in addition to what we chiefly understand as 'virtue', that is, 'conformity of life and conduct with the principles of morality'. The notion implicit in the medieval understanding of *virtus* seems to have been that a saintly person, by cultivating moral virtue and leading a life of prayerful discipline, builds up a power which enables him or her, during life and after it, to be a channel for performance of God's mighty works; these mighty works themselves could be called *virtutes*. Since the Reformation, with its devastating attack on the cult of the saints and their relics, this kind of thinking has been utterly eliminated from the Protestant English consciousness, and the vocabulary attached to it has correspondingly fallen into total disuse. Hence it is that *virtus* is translated variously in different contexts, while there is sometimes reference to the Latin in a footnote, for the sake of anthropological honesty. One further observation: the use of *virtutes* to mean 'mighty deeds' was derived from the Vulgate Bible, where, in 2 Corinthians 12.12, it translates the plural of the Greek word from which 'dynamism' is derived.

Technicalities, Background Information, Specialized Bibliography

Modes of Dating

Some modes of dating employed in the *Liber Eliensis* will not be familiar to all readers. In one respect the dates have been modernized: Roman-style calculating of the days of the month backwards from the Kalends, Nones and Ides, has been replaced by the straightforward modern mode of dating: thus, '28th June', rather than 'the fourth day', by inclusive reckoning, 'before the Kalends of July'.

Dating by 'indiction' is sometimes used, a mode of reckoning by fifteen-year periods dating back to Roman times and explained by Bede in a treatise *De Temporibus* (*Opera de temporibus*, ed. C. W. Jones, Cambridge, Mass. 1943, pp. 268–9). The term 'indiction' might be used to mean the fifteen-year period itself, or, as normally happens in the *Liber Eliensis*, a year within that period. To calculate a year's indiction-number, one took the number of years since the Lord's incarnation, added three (because it was reckoned that the Lord was born in the fourth year of an indiction) and divided by fifteen; any remainder gave the year's number in the indiction. To avoid confusion, a dating such as *quinta indictione* has been translated not as 'in the fifth indiction', but as 'in the fifth year of the indiction'.

Dating by lunar month is sometimes found, and this is explained by Bede in the same work. The term 'epact', used in this connection, means 'addition' and refers to the fact that, in relation to dating by non-lunar months, the fifth night of the Moon one year will be the sixth in the following year, and will not be the same until nineteen years have elapsed. To calculate epacts, one took the number of years since the incarnation and divided it by nineteen; the number left over gave the number of epacts.

A 'concurrent', according to the OED, after Webster, is: 'one of the supernumerary days of the year over fifty-two complete weeks – so called because they concur with the solar cycle, the course of which they follow'.

The term *synodus*, translated as 'conjunction', derived from ancient Greek astronomy and could refer specifically to the state of the heavens immediately before the New Moon.

Money

The property transactions of the *Liber Eliensis* are conducted in pounds, shillings, mancuses and marks. Pennies are also occasionally mentioned. The reckoning: 20 shillings = 1 pound, which was to remain in use until the year 1970, is already clearly in evidence in records from the tenth century. That 12 pence = 1 shilling is not made explicit in the *Liber Eliensis,* but may be presupposed. There were 8 mancuses to the pound, so that, like the more recent half-crown, a mancus was equivalent to 2 shillings and 6 pence. A mark was two-thirds of a pound: 13 shillings and 4 pence.

The Ely drachma of Bishop Nigel's time presumably consisted of one drachm of pure silver, that is, probably, one eighth of an ounce.

The minting of unofficial money-equivalents by landowners in the fens (*LE* iii. 73) has persisted, at times of shortage of copper coin, into quite recent times. (Information from Hugh Morris, pers. comm.)

Weights

A system of weights sometimes used in inventories of the monastic treasury, with reference to precious metals, is identifiable as the 'Troy weight' system, originating from the market at Troyes, according to which: 20 pennyweights = 1 ounce; 12 ounces = 1 pound.

A 'skep' was a measure of dry goods, e.g. grain, its name being derived from an Old Norse word defined by the OED as 'basket', 'bushel'.

A 'tray' was a measure equivalent to one-fifth of a quarter; a quarter being, in recent years at least, reckoned equivalent to 28 pounds (weight) or 8 bushels (capacity).

Measures of Length

The *Liber Eliensis* contains references to a 'foot', *stadia*, translated as 'furlongs' and a 'mile'; otherwise the only designation of length is *longitudo hominis* – 'the length of a man' or, as we would prefer to say, his 'height'.

The starting point for an understanding of what *stadia* and a 'mile' might have meant for the compiler is the Roman system of measurement. A 'mile' was originally a thousand paces (*milia passuum*), while a 'pace' consisted of five 'feet'. A 'pace', then, as the Romans understood the term, is not to be equated with a modern yard, but evidently consisted of what we would count as two normal walking 'paces'. Presumably the primary unit in this system, a 'foot', had been the length of the actual foot of a Roman soldier of average build, and the available evidence suggests that a Roman mile consisted of 1,618 (modern) yards. Our own mile is slightly longer, at 1,760 yards.

A *stadium* was one eighth of a Roman mile, just as a 'furlong' (which denoted 'the length of a furrow in the common field') is an eighth of a modern mile.

Measures of Area

An 'acre' (Lat *acra*) was originally 'as much land as a team of oxen could plough in a day; later limited by statute to a piece 40 poles long by 4 broad (= 4,840 square yards)' (OED). Its exact extent in the days when the source-texts of the *Liber Eliensis* were written is unknowable, but probably not greatly different. Already, surveying-methods of considerable precision were in use.

A 'hide' (Lat. *hyda*) in the *Liber Eliensis* is used to mean 120 acres, calculated as 12 x 20 (twelve-score) acres. The reference in *LE* ii. 97 to forty hides as the property-qualification for a nobleman is apparently unique in medieval literature (Simon Keynes, pers. comm.), though it is remembered in so recent a source as J. C. Newsham, *The Horticultural Notebook*, revised by W. E. Shewell-Cooper (fourth edition, London 1950), a work which preserves details of a wide range of pre-metric weights and measures.

A 'virgate' was a unit of perhaps 30 acres, though its meaning varies in different texts.

Designations of Social Rank

Particularly in the section of the *Liber Eliensis* derived from the *Libellus Æthelwoldi*, there are many references to people of some high standing in local affairs. In this translation they are described variously as 'the better men', 'loyal men', 'the foremost men' (of a place), 'men of rank', the principle being to keep as close to the Latin as possible without introducing anachronistic concepts into pre-Conquest texts. It is acknowledged that women landowners feature amongst the participants in public meetings recorded in the *Liber Eliensis*. Nevertheless, the word 'men' is sometimes preferred to 'people' even where the Latin does not specify gender, because of the likelihood that the words underlying the Latin would have been exclusively male designations, and that the groups referred to would have consisted mainly, if not exclusively, of men.

It is not possible to be sure which precise OE terms of social rank underlie the rather vague expressions used in the Latin of the *Libellus Æthelwoldi*. (Information from Simon Keynes, pers. comm.) The article by A. J. Duggan on 'The Old English Vocabulary of Nobility' in *Nobles and Nobility in Medieval Europe*, ed. J. Roberts (Woodbridge 2000), surveys the available range of words.

Most usually, the Latin term *comes* is translated by 'earl', exceptions being a few continental nobles who are referred to as 'counts'. In one narrative of very early times, derived from Bede (*LE* i. 23) where the reference is known to have been to a *gesith*, the man is referred to simply as a 'high-ranking retainer' of his king.

Old English Legal Terminology

Certain OE legal terms repeatedly figure in grants to the monastery, even after the Normal Conquest. A detailed explanation of them is set out in F. E. Harmer, *Anglo-Saxon Writs* (Manchester 1952), pp. 73–85, and from this the following brief summary is derived.

Sake and *Soke*: 'cause and suit'. These terms referred to the right to hold a private court or, at all events, to receive profits from jurisdiction within the estate to which the grant refers.

Toll and *team*: 'toll' was 'the right to take toll on the sale of cattle and other goods within an estate', while 'team' related to the holding of a court in which men accused of the wrongful possession of cattle or goods could prove their honesty, either meaning the right to hold such a court or the right to receive profits from its justice.

Infangentheof: literally 'thief captured within'; the right to try a thief caught within the estate and to take the profits.

Forfeitures arising from the following offences were normally rights of the king, sometimes granted to specially favoured subjects. The amount of the fine is in some cases stated to have been five pounds.

Hamsocne: 'forcible entry or an assault on a person in a house'.

Grithbryce: 'breach of *grith*', *grith* being the king's special peace or protection given to particular persons, whether by the king's own hand, by writ and seal, or by the king's deputy.

Fihtwite: 'the fine imposed for fighting'.

Fyrdwite: 'the fine imposed for neglect of military service.'

Other OE terms left untranslated in this version of the *Liber Eliensis* are:

Mund: 'Special protection' or 'peace', similar to *grith,* but of wider application. (For more detail see Harmer, *Anglo-Saxon Writs,* p. 80.)

Wergeld: 'the price set upon a man according to his rank, paid by way of compensation or fine in cases of homicide and certain other crimes to free the offender from further obligation or punishment' (OED).

Feudal Terminology.

Any readers of this translation unfamiliar with the workings of the feudal system introduced to England by William the Conqueror are referred to the opening chapter of A. L. Poole's *Domesday Book to Magna Carta,* the third volume of the Oxford History of England. Explanations will be found there of this system in which the king's tenants-in-chief – 'all the barons, all the bishops' (with one exception) 'and all the older and greater abbeys' – held their land by knight-service – the amount of which was arbitrarily imposed, 'without any exact relationship of the size or value of the holding'.

Knights were required to be properly trained and equipped with a coat of mail, helmet, shield and lance. They might remain part of their lord's household, or alternatively could be 'enfeoffed', that is, provided with a land-holding, known as a 'knight's fee'. Substitution for a knight's actual service on the field by money payments, 'scutage', was a possibility from early days. Poole describes the complications which arose from the division of knight's fees into smaller holdings, so that several tenants might perform the military service in rotation or, alternatively, contribute 'scutage'. He also describes the situation where a monastery, such as Ely, was required to contribute towards the guard of a castle somewhat remote from it.

The *Liber Eliensis* contains some references to Anglo-Norman judicial procedures, and the reader is referred to Poole, chapter 12, for an explanation of these. In particular note the principle: 'No one may be convicted of a capital charge by testimony'; instead: 'Proof depended not on human evidence, but on purgation or ordeal or combat, the judgement of God.' Poole observes that: 'Compurgation, the method by which the defendant swore his innocence supported by oath-helpers, was still the regular procedure in the church courts' and in some other places. 'In the criminal trials of this period, however, the normal mode of proof was . . . the ordeal of cold water' – a test to see if the trussed victim would sink or float in hallowed water. 'We hear of few carrying the hot iron except women who were, it seems, never subjected to the ordeal of water.'

Theology and Liturgy

The translator's first port of call, when baffled by a piece of unfamiliar medieval Christian thought, has been F. L. Cross, *The Oxford Dictionary of the Christian Church* (second edition, revised 1983). The edition used for citations from the Latin Vulgate Bible in footnotes has been *Biblia Sacra iuxta Vulgatam Versionem*, ed. R. Weber and R. Gryson (fourth edition, Stuttgart 1994). Otherwise, biblical chapter and verse numbers correspond to that found in any derivatives of the Authorized Version, e.g. the Revised Standard Version, which has been cited in addition to the Vulgate in the case of references to the Psalms. Migne's *Patrologia Latina* is cited in footnotes as *PL* and *Patrologia Graeca* as *PG*.

The bibliography by Simon Keynes cited above (p. xxii) includes a section devoted to liturgical sources. Fundamental to an understanding of life at the monastery of Ely is the *Rule of St Benedict*, of which there exist many translations. See especially: Timothy Fry OSB, *The Rule of St Benedict in Latin and English with notes* (Collegeville, Minnesota 1981), the translation from which is reprinted in Esther de Waal, *A Life-giving Way: A Commentary on the Rule of St Benedict* (London 1995). In the new *History of Ely Cathedral*, ed. Meadows and Ramsay, the chapter by Joan Greatrex (pp. 77–94) is entitled: 'Benedictine observance at Ely: the intellectual, liturgical and spiritual evidence, considered'. In the same collaborative work (pp. 157–168), Nigel Ramsay surveys 'The Library and Archives 1109–1541', looking back, too, at the evidence for Ely's earlier holdings of manuscripts. For background to the veneration of St Æthelthryth see S. J. Ridyard, *The Royal Saints of Anglo-Saxon England: a study of West Saxon and East Anglian cults* (Cambridge 1988).

Ecclesiastical Art

The *Liber Eliensis* records several inventories dense with technical terms for liturgical 'ornaments'. Definitions, discussions and illustrations of these, together with useful bibliography, are supplied in Janet Mayo's *A History of Ecclesiastical Dress* (London 1984) and C. E. Pocknee's *The Christian Altar* (London 1963). Readers are warned that although most of the terminology in this field is still in current ecclesiastical use, the vestments and altar-trappings referred to in medieval texts were not necessarily of quite the shape and style of their modern namesakes.

General resources for the student of Anglo-Saxon art are included in the bibliographical handbook, *Anglo-Saxon England*, cited above (p. xxii) and John Maddison's *Ely Cathedral: Design and Meaning* (Ely 2000) supplies bibliography of relevance specifically to the art and architecture of Ely.

The illustrations in J. Beckford's *Early Medieval Art: Carolingian, Ottonian, Romanesque* (London 1969, reprinted 1996) are very helpful in giving a general impression of the styles and compositional devices likely to have been used in the lost artefacts of early medieval Ely. Likewise, Richard Morris, *Cathedrals and Abbeys of England and Wales* (London 1979), has been a source of enlightenment to the translator.

A. G. A. Christie, *English Medieval Embroidery* (Oxford 1938) remains the standard work on its subject. It features an astonishing range of fine black and white illustrations of embroidery-fragments, and even whole vestments, from our period.

C. R. Dodwell, *Anglo-Saxon Art: A New Perspective* (Manchester 1993) draws extensively on the *Liber Eliensis* for evidence about pre-Conquest works of art. It also contains an important discussion of the meaning of the term *purpura*, which occurs frequently in the inventories of the monastery of Ely. This appears to have referred not to a colour but to a particular type of rich, iridescent, silk cloth which could be of a variety of different colours, some of them far removed from what we understand to be 'purple'. The term 'orphrey' which also occurs frequently in the Ely inventories, translates a Latin word which originally meant 'Phrygian gold-work' and came to mean a strip or band of rich embroidery attached to a vestment.

The *History of Ely Cathedral* includes articles by Eric Fernie on 'The architecture and sculpture of Ely Cathedral in the Norman period' (pp. 95–112) and John Maddison on 'The Gothic Cathedral: new building in a historic context'.

Archaeology

David Hall, *The Fenland Project, Number 10: Cambridgeshire Survey: The Isle of Ely and Wisbech* (East Anglian Archaeology Report no. 79, Cambridgeshire Archaeological Committee, Cambridge 1996) provides an admirably detailed archaeological survey of the whole area, though sadly the parishes of Wilburton, Stretham and Little Thetford – an area where one might wish to look for early Saxon settlement or evidence of Norman military activity – are not scrutinized as rigorously as other districts.

The Benedictine Monastery of Medieval Ely by Anne Holton-Krayenbuhl, a booklet published by the Ely Society in 1988, is an archaeologist's brief account of the monastic buildings; John Maddison's *Ely Cathedral: Design and Meaning*, also has an archaeological dimension. There is a chapter by the archaeologist Philip Dixon in the *History of Ely Cathedral* (pp. 142–155), on

INTRODUCTION

'The Monastic Buildings at Ely.'

Reports on recent excavations in Ely are held by the County Archaeologist's department at Castle Court, Shire Hall, Cambridge. The most important ones for the period covered by the *Liber Eliensis* are those concerned with the excavations along West Fen Road conducted by the Cambridge Archaeological Unit (University of Cambridge), notably on Cotmist Field, by Richard Mortimer (April, 2000) and Cornwell Field, by Roderick Regan (January, 2001). These reports show that a new secular settlement near the present Cathedral was established at a date not far removed from 673, but indicate that it started on low ground and spread up the hill, rather than being founded initially on the high ground, as one might have expected from the *LE* i pr. S. There was no evidence, either, of catastrophic destruction of the town in 870.

The settlement close to West Fen Road cannot have been *Cratendune*, as it was still occupied in the twelfth century, when the settlement in a place of that name is stated to have been derelict. Nor have excavations at Angel Drove discovered *Cratendune*. A more likely site lies slightly further south, near the Anglo-Saxon cemetery discovered during the construction of the now disused Witchford aerodrome, on which see Hall, pp. 39 and 71.

The report of Paula Whittaker, *Archaeological Excavation at the King's School, Ely* (December, 1999) has some relevance to the issue of where St Æthelthryth's spring was situated. A problem of 'rising water levels' was encountered in the vicinity of a pre–fourteenth century wall near, and aligned with, the former stables of the Old Bishop's Palace.

Excavations adjacent to Broad Street have revealed Ipswich ware (produced c. 680–850) at the lowest level (Quintin Carroll, pers. comm.). The discovery of Saxon settlement at low levels within the present city of Ely has been a surprise, but ties in with evidence that from 800 onwards, and not before, the rising of water-levels caused many fenland settlements to be abandoned, so that fifth–seventh century sites may be covered by a metre of silt.

The Broad Street excavations revealed a system of artificial cuts at right-angles to the present river-front: evidently part of the medieval port of Ely. The question of when exactly the channel was cut which allowed the landing of travellers and goods closer to the monastery of Ely than Turbotsey is still unresolved. The channels excavated were full of pottery, but had been cleaned out too often for their original date to be accurately determined. The excavations have since been covered over.

Several further small excavations have taken place near the river at Ely recently and it remains to be seen whether the archaeologists' findings will provide further information on the city's medieval port or fortifications.

Latin and Old English Authorities for the History of the British Isles cited or paralleled in the Liber Eliensis: Printed Editions

Abbo, *Passio S. Edmundi,* in *Memorials of St Edmund's Abbey,* ed. T. Arnold (Rolls Series xcvi. i, London 1890), pp. 3–25.

    Printed also as '*Life of St Edmund* by Abbo' in *Three Lives of English Saints,* ed. M. Winterbottom (Toronto 1972).

Adelard, *Vita S. Dunstani* in *Memorials of St Dunstan,* ed. W. Stubbs (Rolls Series lxiii, London 1874), pp. 53–68.

Ælred, *Vita S. Edwardi:* Ailred of Rievaulx, *Vita S. Edwardi regis et confessoris,* Migne *PL,* cxcv, cols. 737–796.

    J. Bertram, trans. *The Life of St Edward, King and Confessor, by blessed Aelred, Abbot of Rievaulx* (Southampton 1990, rev. 1997).

Anglo-Saxon Charters, second ed. A. J. Robertson (Cambridge 1956).

    For subsequent work on Anglo-Saxon charters (vernacular and Latin), see bibliography in S. D. Keynes, *Anglo-Saxon England,* (Cambridge 2001), pp. 34–6, and the website: <http://www.trin.cam.ac.uk/chartwww/

Anglo-Saxon Chronicle, ed. B. Thorpe, 2 vols. (Rolls Series xxiii, London 1861).

    Later editions: C. Plummer, ed., *Two of the Saxon Chronicles Parallel* (1892–99, repr. Oxford 1952), 2 vols.; D. Dumville and S. D. Keynes general editors: *The Anglo-Saxon Chronicle: A Collaborative Edition* (Cambridge and Woodbridge 1983 onwards).

    Translations: Dorothy Whitelock et al., *The Anglo-Saxon Chronicle: A Revised Translation* (London 1961); M. J. Swanton (London 1996).

Anglo-Saxon Wills, ed. and trans. D. Whitelock (Cambridge 1930).

Annales Radingenses, ed. F. Liebermann, in *Ungedruckte Anglo-Normannische Geschichtsquelle* (Strassburg, 1879).

Battle of Maldon:

    The Battle of Maldon, ed. E. V. Gordon (1937), with a supplement by D. G. Scragg (Manchester 1976)

    The Battle of Maldon, AD. 991, ed. D. G. Scragg (Oxford 1991). This comprises an edition and translation of the Old English poem of that name, together with passages relating to the battle in other sources, and interpretative essays.

INTRODUCTION

Bede:

Bede's Ecclesiastical History of the English People, ed. and trans. B. Colgrave and R. A. B. Mynors (OMT, Oxford 1969, rev. edn. 1991).

Venerabilis Bedae Opera Historica ed. C. Plummer (1896 repr. Oxford 1946), with introduction and commentary.

J. M. Wallace-Hadrill, *Bede's 'Ecclesiastical History of the English People': a Historical Commentary* (OMT, Oxford 1988).

Translations:

L. Sherley-Price, rev. by R. E. Latham and D. H. Farmer, *Bede: Ecclesiastical History of the English People* (Harmondsworth 1990);

J. McClure and R. Collins, *Bede: The Ecclesiastical History of the English People* (Oxford World's Classics 1994).

Bede, *De temporum ratione*, ed. T. Mommsen, *Monumenta Germaniae Historica: Auctores Antiquissimi* xiii, *Chronica Minora* iii (Berlin 1898), pp. 247–327.

Chatteris Cartulary:

The Cartulary of Chatteris Abbey, ed. Claire Breay (Woodbridge 1999).

Eadmer, *Vita Wilfridi* in *Historians of the Church of York*, ed. J. Raine (Rolls Series lxxi, London 1879–94) pp. 161–226.

Eadmer, *Vita Sancti Wilfridi*, ed. and trans. B. J. Muir and A. J. Taylor (Exeter 1998).

Eddius Stephanus, *Vita Wilfridi*, is included in the Rolls Series volume, *Historians of the Church of York*, cited above.

The edition cited by Blake is: *The Life of Bishop Wilfrid*, ed. and trans. B. Colgrave (Cambridge 1927, repr. 1985).

English Episcopal Acta: Ely 1133–1197, ed. N. Karn (British Academy: OUP, forthcoming).

English Historical Documents i, c. 540–1042, ed. D. Whitelock (second edition London and New York 1979).

Essex Charters: *The Early Charters of Essex*, ed. C. Hart (University of Leicester, Department of English Local History, Occasional Papers, nos. 10 and 11, Leicester 1957).

Felix, *Life of St Guthlac*, ed. and trans. B. Colgrave (Cambridge 1956).

Flores Historiarum, ed. H. R. Luard (Rolls Series xcv, London 1890).
Florence of Worcester, see *Worcester Chronicle.*

Gesta Herwardi Incliti Exulis et Militis, in Gaimar, *Lestorie des Engles,* ed. Sir Thomas Duffus Hardy and C. Trice Martin (Rolls Series xci. i, London 1888), pp. 339–404.

 There also exists a translation by W. D. Sweeting of a transcript by S. H. Miller of the *Gesta Herwardi* (typescript edition: Peterborough 1895), and another by M. Swanton, printed in *Medieval Outlaws: Ten Tales in Modern English* ed. T. H. Ohlgren (Stroud 1998) and in Swanton's own *Three Lives of the Last Englishmen* (New York and London 1984). An OMT with translation, eds. P. G. Schmidt and J. Mann, is forthcoming.

Gesta Stephani, eds. K. R. Potter, R. H. C. Davis (OMT, Oxford 1976).

Goscelin of Saint-Bertin, *Vita S. Ivonis Episcopi Persae,* in Migne *PL* clv, cols. 81ff. For Goscelin's probable contributions to the hagiography of Ely saints see below, entry on *Vitae S. Ætheldrede, S. Sexburge, S. Ermenilde, S. Werburge, S. Wihtburge.*

Inquisitio Comitatus Cantabrigiensis, ed. N. E. S. A. Hamilton (London 1876).
 See also *Regesta regum Anglo-Normannorum, Acta of William I,* ed. Bates, no. 117, for the *Inquisitio Eliensis.*

Gregory of Ely, *Vita et miracula S. Etheldrede metrice*: Latin text edited with notes by P. A. Thompson and E. Stevens, 'Gregory of Ely's Verse Life and Miracles of St Æthelthryth', *Analecta Bollandiana* 106 (1988), 333–90.

John of Worcester, see *Worcester Chronicle.*

Lanfranc, *Constitutions: Decreta Lanfranci Monachis Cantuariensibus Transmissa,* ed. and trans. D. Knowles, London 1951.

Matthew Paris: *Chronica Maiora,* ed. H. R. Luard (Rolls Series lvii, London 1872–83).

Orderic Vitalis: *The Ecclesiastical History of Orderic Vitalis,* ed. and trans. Marjorie Chibnall (OMT, Oxford 1969–80).

Osbern, *Vita Dunstani,* in *Memorials of St Dunstan,* ed. W. Stubbs (Rolls Series lxiii, London 1874), pp. 3–161.

INTRODUCTION

Osbert of Clare:
: *The Letters of Osbert of Clare*, ed. E. W. Williamson (Oxford 1929).

Papal Letters: *Papsturkunden in England* ed. W. Holtzmann, 3 vols. (Göttingen 1932–52).

Passiones S. Thomae:
: J. A. Giles, *Patres Ecclesiae Anglicanae* (London and Oxford 1843–48) vol. xxxvii, pp. 157–80.
: *Materials for the History of Thomas Becket*, ed. J.C. Robertson (Rolls Series lxvii. iv, London 1876) pp. 431–41.

Ramsey Cartulary: Cartularium Monasterii de Rameseia, ed. W. H. Hart and P. A. Lyons (Rolls Series lxxix, London 1884–93).

Ramsey Chronicle: Chronicon Abbatiae Rameseiensis, ed. W. Dunn Macray (Rolls Series lxxxiii, London 1886).

Regesta Regum Anglo-Normannorum: The Acta of William 1 (1066–1087), ed. D. Bates (Oxford 1998).

Theobald, Archbishop of Canterbury, ed. A. A. Saltman (London 1956).

Vitae S. Ætheldrede, S. Sexburge, S. Ermenilde, S. Werburge, S. Wihtburge.
: For texts and translations of Latin *Vitae* and *Lectiones* concerned with Saints Æthelthryth, Seaxburh, Eormenhild, Wærburh and Wihtburh, see *Goscelin of Saint-Bertin and the Lives of the Female Saints of Ely*, ed. and trans. Rosalind C. Love (Oxford 2004).
: Old English materials relating to the Ely saints are published in F. Liebermann, *Die Heiligen Englands* (Hanover 1889); *Leechdoms, Wortcunning and Starcraft of Early England* ed. T. O. Cockayne (Rolls Series xxxv. iii, London 1864–66), pp. 422–32; M. J. Swanton, 'A fragmentary Life of St Mildred and other Kentish royal saints', *Archaeologia Cantiana* xci (1975), 15–27.

William of Malmesbury, *De Gestis Pontificum Anglorum*, ed. N. E. S. A. Hamilton (Rolls Series lxx, London 1870).
: Trans. David Preest, *The Deeds of the Bishops of England* (Woodbridge 2002).
: *Historia Novella*, ed. K. R. Potter (London 1955).

William of Poitiers, *The Gesta Guillelmi of William of Poitiers*, ed. and trans. R. H. C. Davis and Marjorie Chibnall (OMT, Oxford 1998).

Winchester Annals:

Annales de Wintonia in *Annales Monastici,* ed. H. Luard (Rolls Series xxxvi. ii, 1–125, London 1865).

Annals of the Church of Winchester, trans. J. Stevenson in *The Church Historians of England,* vol. iv, part 1 (London 1870).

Worcester Chronicle:

Florence of Worcester, *Chronicon ex Chronicis,* ed. B. Thorpe (London, 1848), the edition cited by Blake.

The Chronicle of John of Worcester (OMT, Oxford 1995, 1998): vol. ii (450–1066), ed. R. R. Darlington and P. McGurk, trans. J. Bray and P. McGurk; vol. iii (1067–1140) ed. and trans. P. McGurk.

Wulfstan of Winchester: *The Life of St Æthelwold,* ed. and trans. M. Lapidge and M. Winterbottom (Oxford 1991).

BOOK I

Here begins a prologue about the history of the Isle of Ely.[1]

As I was considering the excellence of the Isle of Ely and turning over in my mind the things which have been collected and written down on account of the merits of the holy virgins laid to rest there – the wonderful achievements and successes of the Isle and the actions of great men – my attention lighted upon past events which, because of the passage of years, of epochs, of kings and of rulers of the Isle, are not at all well known, or which were committed to writing in English in a variety of different places or in a disorganized manner, and I set about an attempt to unfold into a history, in sequential order, the good deeds and miracles of the saints, male and female, who have fought battles for God in that place.

For up to now we have not had in our house writings of this kind, assembled in an orderly fashion and at the same time in historical sequence, with the exception of an account of the lives and miracles[2] of the lady saints who rest there. This was derived from histories, chronicles, English and Latin writs, wills and the reports of the faithful. I have undertaken to set down some material from this work, my object being that matters which deserve to be made the subject of preaching should not be left unwritten as if unknown, or wasted away and effaced by old age. For when the philosopher, or good historiographer, who has long been awaited, attempts to take up his pen, there will be many places in which he will not find raw material. And if by any chance someone ventures to reproach this little work, we pray that he may place upon it the hand of myrrh-distillers[3] and grant it acceptance as the work of a poet, so that, if he sets it forth for future generations, it may be preserved for their remembrance. For the rest, I beg that no one may find fault with the meagreness of my style and the prolixity of my treatment,

---

[1] Source: the compiler's own composition, with a borrowing (in paragraph 3, on the multiplicity of kingdoms) from Abbo, *Passio S. Edmundi*.

[2] Perhaps read conjecturally at p. 1.9, ed. Blake: *vitae et miracula* instead of *vita et miracula*. The reference is likely to be to the set of *Lives* appended, with the exception of its *Life* of St Æthelthryth, to the E manuscript.

[3] Lat. *manum myrrham distillantium adponat* – exact meaning obscure. This is not a direct allusion to the Vulgate Song of Songs, but compare 5.5: *manus meae stillaverunt murra*; also 5.13 *labia eius lilia distillantia murram primam*, which shows that 'myrrh' could be understood to mean perfume in general. The reference could either be to gatherers of myrrh-resin (used in incense), or to individuals perfumed with myrrh like the lovers in the Song of Songs, or perhaps (nearer to home) to people involved in perfume-manufacture, e.g. in the extraction of scented oil from the herb sweet cicely, used in culinary sweetening, medicines or polish.

knowing that the actions and times of large numbers of people cannot be summarized briefly and succinctly without causing the reader very great disgust and annoyance.

Now, although the territory of the English is a single land, there have at various junctures been several rulers in it, spread out over several provinces, and it has turned out that the task of ruling one and the same Britain has provided sufficient work first for a plurality of chieftains and later for a plurality of kings. But unless the reader sedulously pays attention to the narrator as he recounts variously the winding sequence of events, now concerning one kingdom, now another, and the names of the kings, he will not easily grasp the way in which they were ordered. For this reason I have approached my history by dividing it clearly into three parts and into separate chapters, and by narrating separate events in their proper places and as contemporaneous with the people in whose times they happened.

The first book, in fact, comprises an account of the situation of the Isle and of the glorious Queen Æthelthryth and the holy virgins who succeeded her; otherwise it recounts what misfortunes the Isle was subjected to in the period up to the arrival of the monks in Ely. The second book is about the times of the monks of Ely and about the liberty of the place, and how the church was rebuilt and about the siege of the Normans, up until the time of the bishops. The third is about the times of the bishops – which is now.

And since the solicitude of the brothers and their graciousness have prompted me to turn my attention to a narrative of this kind, I consider it a matter of obligation to commend to book-form a memorable work of love and the endeavours which we have undertaken. My object is that in this way the purity of love incorporated in the work may shine forth all the more readily for being distinguished by a beautiful variousness. And thus I will attempt a beginning by invoking God, who is everyone's collaborator.

Here ends the prologue.

Here begins {a preface} about the situation of the Isle of Ely.[4]

All people of distinction and nobility feel the urge to glorify and honour their own town to the utmost, and not a few make it their aim to commend to writing the affairs of their region and those deeds of their forebears that have

---

[4] Sources: Bede, *Hist. Eccl.* iv. 17 (19); Richard I of Ely, *Gesta Herewardi* (the presumed chief source of both the extant *Gesta Herwardi* and the Hereward narrative in *LE* ii); hagiography of Saint Æthelthryth, cf. *Vita S. Ætheldrede* CD ed. Love (that is, the Latin *Life* of St Æthelthryth found in Corpus Christi College, Cambridge MS 393 and Trinity College, Dublin MS B.2.7, and now edited by Rosalind Love in *Goscelin de Saint-Bertin and the Lives of the the Female Saints of Ely*, Oxford 2004); William of Malmesbury, *Gesta Pontificum* iv. 184; monastic archives (e.g. charter of Edward the Confessor, as cited in *LE* ii. 92); local tradition, including archaeological observation.

been worth remembering. They are right in doing so, and, concerned though we are to relate in sequence the deeds of our forebears, it seems an appropriate way of ordering things for us to begin, before the history gets further under way, with the name of the place.

For Ely, which we begin by declaring undoubtedly worthy of renown, is the largest of the islands of the fens. It is magnificent in its wealth and its towns; equally praiseworthy for its woods, vineyards and waters;[5] exceedingly rich in all fruit, livestock-breeding and crops.[6] We call it in English, † 'Elge't,[7] that is, it has taken its name 'from the abundance of eels which are caught in these same Fens', as Bede, the most eloquent of Englishmen, tells us.[8] It is now called 'Ely', the name being changed by way of improvement, the implication being that it is a house worthy of God, whose name it worthily bears. Among the cities of the realm of England it is of the greatest beauty and renown, famous for its miracles, glorious for its relics. It is recognized as providing a satisfactory, peaceful dwelling-place, and, to give a true account of the facts, it is guarded by a garrison of strong and warlike men, prepared to resist their enemies with courage and armed force.

But, for fear that it would bore the listener excessively <if>[9] we were to speak about the domestic animals, the wild beasts of the woods, the birds, the numerous and large fish which are frequently caught in the waters round about called meres, and saying what an abundance of them there are: these are referred to, each in turn, in the second book of the series,[10] where we read that the island was conquered by the Normans. What more shall I say? In its interior, the island is satisfactorily fertile through the richness of its soil, very pleasant in the beauty of its gardens and groves, richer than average in its pasture for cattle and horses, and surrounded on all sides by very large rivers full of fish. It is not actually an island in the sea but, inaccessible as it is, owing to the overflowing of ponds and marshes, the means of approach used to be by boat. However, now that a causeway has been built, because at one time it was dangerous for people wishing to go there in boats, an approach by

---

[5] Cf. *Gesta Herwardi*, pp. 380–1.

[6] Tentative interpretation of Lat. *omni fructu, fetu ac germine uberrimam* (from *Gesta Herwardi*, p. 382). This phrase presents difficulties of interpretation not least because *fetus* can be used with reference both to the young of animals and to plant-growth. In Pliny, *Nat. Hist.* xvii. 17.1, the only other passage I have yet discovered where *germin-, fet-* and *fruct-* are juxtaposed, *germinatio* refers to a tree's budding season, *fetus* to its summer growth and *fructus* to its mature fruit.

[7] Conjectural, but in line with Bede, *Hist. Eccl.* iv. 17 (19) and a parallel passage in *LE* 1.15. The mss. have: *Ely* (p. 2.9, ed. Blake).

[8] *Hist. Eccl.* iv. 17 (19).

[9] Reading conjecturally at p. 2.16, ed. Blake: *ne auditorem nimis fastidiret <si> de domesticis animalibus . . . diceremus, in libro . . . secundo singula memorantur.*

[10] I. e. in *LE* ii. 105.

foot is possible through the reed-swamp.

The Isle[11] stands at seven miles long from *Cotingelade* to Littleport or to *Abbotesdelf* {'Abbot's Ditch'} – which is now, however, called *Biscopesdelf* {'Bishop's Ditch'} – and four miles wide, that is, from *Cherchewere* to Stretham Mere with the islands nearby encircling it, in addition to Doddington, part of an island[12] on which there are cottages and groves, with islanders belonging to them and other inhabitants – not without progeny – together with very rich pastures. Also assigned to the aforementioned Isle is Chatteris, where there is an abbey of nuns,[13] and the district of Whittlesey and the abbey of the monks of Thorney.

The Isle is now reckoned to be in Cambridgeshire and to consist of two hundreds;[14] but this is a unit comprising additional lands which are outside it. It is within the boundaries given here that from ancient times the Isle has been reckoned to exist, namely: from the middle of Tydd Bridge[15] as far as Upware, and from *Biscopesdelf* as far as the river near Peterborough which is called the Nene, in the region of the Gyrwe.[16] The Gyrwe are all the South Angles who live in the great fen in which the Isle of Ely is situated. But to speak more truthfully, in accordance with the testimony of Bede, it belongs to the province of the East Angles, being situated at the gateway to that province.

In times of old, so it is said, there was a vill[17] situated at *Cratendune*, that is, in Latin, *vallis Cracti* {'the down of Cractus'}[18] a mile away from the city which now exists.[19] There, one frequently finds implements of iron-

---

[11] For the details that follow cf. *LE* ii. 54.

[12] Taking *ex* in Lat. *ex insula* to have a partitive sense. See *LE* ii. 2f. on exchanges of land at Doddington, but a much later stage in land-ownership is referred to in this preface.

[13] Cf. *LE* ii. 71; iii. 17.

[14] Cf. *LE* ii. 54, 105.

[15] Lat. *pontis de Tid*: perhaps better, 'Tydd causeway'.

[16] Lat. *Girvii*.

[17] Lat. *villa* can mean anything between a farmstead and a town.

[18] Reading with E: *vallem cracti*: the other mss. have *vallem crati*. The interpretation is dubious. *Vallis* has to mean 'valley', 'down', but a 'down' may be perceived as an upland, as in the case of the 'South Downs'. *Cracti / Crati* was maybe thought of as a personal name attached to the 'down' (cf. the ancient British name *Caratacus*) thus: 'the down of Cractus'; or maybe a version of *crasseti/craceti*, 'of the fattening pasture'. For modern identifications of *Cratendune*, see Hall, *Fenland Survey*, pp. 36ff., 71.

[19] Note that it is not stated in *LE* in which direction it lay, in relation to the later city; it was Bentham who located a 'Cratenden' field to the south of it. The evidence of the Ely Coucher Book, in which *Cratendune* is listed next to Grunty Fen (information from Anne Holton-Krahenbuhl, pers. comm.), would tie in with this evidence. On the other hand, there is also a reference to *Cratendune* together with Chettisham in the 1251 survey (see Hall, *Fenland Survey*, p. 39).

work and the coinage of past kings,[20] and the fact that it was for a long time a place inhabited by men is clear from various pieces of evidence. But after Æthelthryth, beloved of God, chose to dwell there[21] – having come into possession of the Isle through the legal settlement upon her of a marriage-portion from Tondberht, her first husband[22] – she sited her living-quarters near the course of the river, on higher ground. When the city was built in that place[23] subsequently, living conditions were better and more decent.

In the early Church, when the Christian faith was in its infancy, a monastery had been built there,[24] in honour of the ever-virgin Mary, by the blessed Augustine, apostle of the English. King Æthelberht[25] was the first founder of this institution: he established in it clergy performing the service of God. The army of King Penda afterwards drove them out from there, when it was devastating the country and its neighbourhood, and reduced the place to an uninhabited wilderness. Thus it was at an early date, and with founders such as these, that the monastery of Elge[26] was founded. And yet, given that a long period of desolation elapsed, the blessed Æthelthryth deserves, as a result of it, the position of primacy which is hers in this place where, with

[20] Or 'ancient kings': Lat. *regum nummisma . . . antiquorum.*

[21] *Lat. illic* here is ambiguous: it could be interpreted as 'on the Isle of Ely', rather than 'in *Cratendune*', though the latter was probably the meaning in the source-text.

[22] See Tacitus, *Germania,* 18.2, on marriage among the ancient Germans: 'Wife does not bring a dowry to husband, but husband to wife.'

[23] *Illuc,* lit. 'thither'; a move of location being implied.

[24] Lat. *ibi:* again, this does not have to mean specifically 'in *Cratendune*' and in a parallel passage, in *Liber Eliensis* i. 15, St Æthelthryth's new monastery, with the same dedication, is represented as a restoration of the one destroyed by Penda. However, in the *Chronicon Abbatum et Episcoporum Eliensium* (ed. H. Wharton, 1695, in *Anglia Sacra* i, p. 594), we read that: 'In the year of the Lord 607, the blessed Augustine, in the 9th year from his arrival in England, constructed a church in Ely in honour of the blessed Virgin Mary in the place which is called *Cradundene* . . . There was no church in the whole Isle except the one church founded by Augustine.' Note that the *Chronicon,* in its extant form, is later in date than *LE* and is judged by Blake to be in general a derivative from it. However, its very specific datings here are not derived from *LE* and it seems likely that its foundation-narrative is closer to its source-text than the near-parallel in *LE* i. *pr. Æ.* The *Chronicon* goes on to say that: 'in the year 673 the virgin Æthelthryth constructed a monastery in a higher place near the course of the river'. Again it looks probable that this was what the source text said, and that the compiler of *LE* has obscured matters.

[25] King of Kent at the time of Augustine's mission to England; his kingdom is said by Bede, *Hist. Eccl.* i. 25, to have extended as far north as the Humber.

[26] For this alternative name of the place see also *LE* i. 15, where an etymological connection with Hebrew is postulated. One might more appropriately cite Greek *ge,* 'earth'. Stenton, *Anglo-Saxon England* (third edition), p. 293, remarks: 'An archaic *ge,* "district", cognate with the German *gau,* forms the second element of the names Surrey and Ely, each of which is called a *regio* by Bede . . .' The modern Welsh *helig,* meaning 'willow', has suggested to some local historians an ultimately Celtic origin for the name. Note, however, by way of caution, the name 'Heligoland', given to an island near the homeland of the Angles, and 'Helgeland' on the Norwegian seaboard.

Christ as its Preserver, there has been a church right up to the present, a place which we know subsequently was made the seat of a bishop and was to be the chief city of his diocese.

The Isle is absolutely free from anyone's jurisdiction and power, with the consequence that neither a bishop nor any tax-official may enter without the invitation of the monks, or may presume to disturb the property of the lady saint.[27] We will be including a fuller treatment of this, recounting its privileges and charters in their proper places. We think it appropriate to relate first the history of the famous Isle, which has flourished and flourishes now – Christ, through His presence, being its patron – thanks to good works and miracles brought about by the saintly women, namely Æthelthryth, Wihtburh, Seaxburh and Eormenhild, on whose assistance it happily congratulates itself. Also contained there are the relics of very many holy men and women who had succeeded these saints as servants of Christ in the church, up to the time of the Danes, specifically, the pagan King Inguar and his allies, who thoroughly ransacked the place, having killed some of the women living there and put to flight the rest.

In the bosom of the Isle there are twelve churches, together with farmland settlements and the smaller islands, and from ancient times these have been attached to the monastery, as chapels are attached to their mother church. No graveyards were created adjacent to these churches, as opposed to within the monastery, except at a late date; instead, the bodies of the deceased from the whole Isle used to be buried at Ely.[28]

Here ends {the preface} about the situation of the Isle of Ely.

Proem[29] to the life of Æthelthryth, holy virgin and queen.[30]

We have learnt from reports from the early days of history-writing that there flourished among the people of long ago individuals devoted to various arts. Thanks to the subtlety which belongs to a lively intellect, these people have had the power to live right up until today, so as to acquire immortal fame as a

---

[27] This assertion of the monastery's liberty is much harped on by the compiler; it is to be found in a charter of Edward the Confessor cited in *LE* ii. 92. With the phrase *rem sancte* compare *possessiones sancte* in *LE* ii. 54 (p. 126.4, ed. Blake).

[28] Lat. *apud Ely*: 'at the (monastic) house of Ely'. With reference to the question of the site of Cratendune and the monastery reputedly founded by St Augustine, note the existence of a large early Anglo-Saxon cemetery on the Isle of Ely between Witchford and Little Thetford.

[29] The translation here follows E.

[30] Sources: the style of this preface is indistinguishable from that characteristic of the compiler of *LE*, but the content reads as if it were copied or adapted from the hagiographical work referred to in the first preface (p. 1.9ff., ed. Blake). Blake notes borrowings in this third preface from Eadmer, *Vita Wilfridi*; Jerome, *Commentary on Ezechiel*.

reward for their work. Another outcome has been this: there have emerged a great many people, of exceptional powers in various branches of knowledge, whose reputation for certain things some people have extolled to the heavens in highly coloured language, whereas in reality their habits of life are found to be unworthy of such fulsome praises. But we decline to take upon ourselves the praising and remembrance of people who passed away as their transitory epoch passed away. Our intention is to set forth with our pen proclamations of the merits of the holy virgin Æthelthryth, whose glory rests on her conveying of blessings, and whose memory shall not recede. It is our aim that by our endeavour they should be conveyed to the written page, as is fitting, and should not be allowed, as changing circumstances intervene, to slip away beyond easy recall.

And the things which Bede reports about her in the *History* of our people are not invariably all-sufficient: it is a proven fact that notable things which Æthelthryth had done in her life are found scattered in various authors, not just in a single one. Impelled by devotion to the most holy mother herself, we have been able, not without effort, to gather into a unity the things which have been recorded up to now in the English language or in the testimonies of truthful people, our aim being that they should become known to posterity, made resplendent by the light of truth. And no would-be listener or reader will find anything which cannot be corroborated by their authority:[31] I am confident that what I am going to say will not be at all contradictory[32] but, word for word, in accordance with what Bede set forth, except that I have admitted as requiring inclusion, along with Bede's data, any facts concerning her father and mother, her life and her death which we are able to surmise from the testimony of some written source. For, to be sure, our ancestors used to tell innumerable stories relating to this dulcifluous mother; but given that the monastery has so frequently experienced disasters, now massacres and fires, now barbarian invasions, it could well have perished amid the upheavals, and scarcely any of the accounts which had been written about her life are discoverable, having either been burnt or taken away. But let it be sufficient to have touched upon these matters briefly. Should anyone, however, perhaps draw attention to the little book written in English about her life, there are many things in it which are not to be found mentioned here at all.

May the Holy Spirit be with us by the merits of His holy virgin – He who inspires and instructs each one of us as He wishes and as much as He wishes

[31] Repunctuating with a colon after *inveniet* (p. 6.18, ed. Blake).

[32] Perhaps read conjecturally at p. 6.19ff., ed. Blake, with transposition of clauses and one supplement: *sed verbum ad verbum sicut Beda edidit de ortu eius, licet aliqua his conserenda admisi <que> de patre et que de matre eius, de vita atque de obitu, alicuius scripti testimonio conicere possumus* (presupposing an omission in the archetype corrected in the margin, and wrongly reinserted). At least, the word order, as it stands, is very contorted.

– so that with His consent we may complete with a truthful pen what we have begun for His glory. Let no bearer of ill-will, therefore, touch this little work of our little self: let him bear in mind that we have passed by the dogs of Scylla with our ears stopped up.[33] Certainly I have related things exactly as I have discovered and read and learnt them from truthful people.

For what has armed me has not been a yearning for human fame – that on completion of this work, I might seem to acquire glamour from a distinguished reputation. No, rather, Æthelthryth – the glorious and simple etymology of whose name is plain to hear – the praiseworthy queen, I say, my patroness and advocate, whose merit before God is greater than can be declared by any eloquence: love of her and frequent remembrance urge the undertaking of this task and enfold my soul with the joy of devotion and, whenever the grief of desolation comes rushing upon my mind, the cloud, once its darkness has been dispersed, has disclosed brighter weather for my soul. Indeed, feeble though I am in sensibility and poor in speech, nevertheless, with her patronage, I am confident, in any writing I may venture upon, of successful completion – even though I do not shine in splendour of vocabulary. And, even granted that the words produced by our mouth are not at all adequate, may she, in her indulgence, deign to assist our tongue, out of the loving-kindness in which she excels – she who cured a dumb youth, the plectrum of his tongue making music beneath his palate.[34] What follow, therefore, are the very famous deeds of the virgin, by hearing which we can profit, and by relating which we can benefit others.

Here begin the chapter-headings.

1. From what ancestors the virgin Æthelthryth was descended according to the flesh, and how her father, Anna, became King of the East Angles.

2. That the father and mother of the holy virgin Æthelthryth became the parents of a holy progeny.

3. That Æthelthryth began to live a holy life in infancy.

4. How Æthelthryth was first given to a husband, who lived only for a short time.

5. On the fact that Bede cited precedent with regard to the blessed Æthelthryth and her betrothed, Tondberht.

---

[33] Blake notes (p. 7, n. 2) that this classical allusion (cf. Homer, *Odyssey* xii. 73ff., 222ff.; Virgil, *Aeneid* iii. 420ff.) resembles one in Jerome's *Commentary on Ezechiel*.
[34] See *LE* i. 45.

BOOK I

---

[35] The Latin reads simply: *in Ely*, which hereafter will for simplicity's sake be rendered 'in Ely', in acknowedgement of the fact that the modern city had now been founded – but the Isle as a whole may be meant where it occurs.

a journey to Rome but on his return learnt that she had died.

20. That when she fell ill she repented in the presence of all.

21. How, weighed down by very great sufferings, she gave up her spirit to Heaven on the third day.

22. About the holy priest Huna.

23. That a certain retainer of the blessed virgin could not be held in chains, because of the sacrifice of the mass with its saving power.

24. That Wærburh, virgin of the Lord, was taken from Ely and put in charge of certain churches.

25. After the death of St Æthelthryth, her sister Seaxburh was made abbess in Ely and, divinely inspired, conceived a desire to remove her bones from the tomb.

26. Seaxburh sent some of the brothers to search for stone for her tomb.

27. That she found the body of the most holy virgin undecayed and – a miraculous thing – the wound in her dead flesh cured.

28. That the sepulchral stone of the virginal corpse was fitted together by divine agency and, when the cover was put on, the join was not visible.

29. That benefits were conferred by virtue of the shroud-cloths of the virgin Æthelthryth.

30. Miracles are reported concerning the coffin in which she was buried.

31. That a spring arises from her burial-place.

32. A prayer of the author to his lady, Æthelthryth.

33. And what Bede set forth initially in the manner of historical narrative he also expressed in verse.

34. What Bede wrote not only in his *History of the English People*, but also in a book which he published *On Times*, out of his *History*.

35. On the death of the Abbess Seaxburh.

36. That Eormenhild was made abbess after her and entrusted the church of Sheppey to Wærburh, her daughter.

37. That Wærburh, virgin of the Lord, after the death of her mother, Eormenhild, took charge of Ely and where she chose her place of burial to be.

38. That devotion to God's work flourished at Ely under the rule of holy women until the place was laid waste by the Danes with fire and iron weaponry.

39. In whose times it was that the Danes sacked England; and concerning their downfall.

40. That, on landing at Ely, they [the Danes] burned down the monastery and had all those they came upon put to death.

41. That a pagan made a hole in the virgin's sarcophagus but, by the vengeance of God, was soon struck down.

42. About the victory of the kings of England and about the birth of King Edgar.

43. A priest's exhortation to his archpriest, relating to him the miracles which follow, from a desire to shake him out of his temerity.

44. About a certain married woman.

45. About a young man unable to speak.

46. About a blind girl.

47. About a certain young man.

48. About a priest's maid-servant.

49. That the judgement of God came down with anger upon the aforesaid archpriest and his colleagues.

50. The manner in which King Edgar ruled.

[Here end the chapter-headings.]

1. The text of the little book that follows begins with the life of the holy virgin Æthelthryth, relating from what ancestors she was descended according to the flesh, and how her father became King of the East Angles.[36]

Well then, according to old histories, the English arrived in Britain, which is now called *Anglia* {England}, in the time of the Emperor Marcian,[37] a hundred and fifty-six years before the arrival of blessed Augustine and his companions. They had come from three very mighty tribes of Germany: the Saxons, the Angles and the Jutes. The people of Kent are descended from the Jutes; the people of Essex, from the Saxons, but the East Angles originated from the Angles, that is, they were from a homeland called *Angulus*.[38] They gained possession of the eastern part of the island, title to it having been assigned to them by lot, and they kept possession of it by means of a continuous line of hereditary succession. Right up till now it is called in the language of the English: *Estangle* {East Anglia}. It was from the ancestral stock of the future parents, according to the flesh, of the exalted virgin Æthelthryth that the royal house of many provinces derived its origins. She shone out as one as remarkable for her outstanding sanctity as she was prominent in her royal dignity. The latter appears a thing all the more exalted when we set about retracing the origin of the blessed virgin, verifying particular details from Bede or the histories, and listing the kings of the province.

Now, there was a King of East Anglia, Rædwald by name, who long before in Kent had been initiated in the sacraments of the faith, but in vain. For, having been led astray by his wife, he had latter years inferior to his earlier ones. Moreover, although he was ignoble in his behaviour, he was noble in his birth, being the son of Tytel, whose father was Wuffa, because of whom they call the kings of the East Angles the *Wulfinges*. Now, the person who succeeded the aforementioned Rædwald was Eorpwald, his son. It was Eorpwald who for the first time adopted, together with that same province, the faith and sacraments of Christ, on the persuasion of Edwin, King of Northumbria, but not long afterwards he was killed. His brother, Sigeberht was a man in all respects most Christian and learned. When he took possession of the kingdom, he brought the province, which had been

---

[36] Sources: *Worcester Chronicle* on the years 616, 632, 636; Bede, *Hist. Eccl.* i. 15; ii. 1, 15; iii. 18, 19. A close relation may be assumed between the whole portion of *LE* i devoted to the life of St Æthelthryth and the local hagiographical work referred to in *LE* i. pr. H, probably to be identified with that preserved – without the *Vita S. Ætheldrede* – in the appendix of ms. E (Trinity College, Cambridge O.2.1).

[37] See J. N. L. Myres, *The English Settlements* (Oxford 1986), pp. 9ff. on the likely antiquity of the tradition. Marcian: Roman Emperor (of the East) A. D. 450–7.

[38] Lat. 'angle', 'corner', 'nook', 'a retired, unfrequented place': roughly, then, the name would suggest, to a reader of Latin, the 'Outback'.

embroiled in error for three years, to a correct faith and the works of righteousness. He did this through the agency of the holy Bishop Felix.

This Felix had become a friend of Sigeberht when the latter was in exile in Gaul, and after the death of Eorpwald he came to England with him and was made Bishop of East Anglia, taking up his see in the city of *Dummoc*,[39] which he freed by his preaching from long-standing wickedness and infelicity – in accordance with the sacred significance of his name.[40]

Meanwhile this same King Sigeberht, retiring from affairs of state and entrusting them to his kinsman Ægeric, who previous to this was already in charge of part of the kingdom, entered a monastery which he had brought into being for himself and having received the tonsure, proceeded to serve the eternal King devotedly for a long time. While he was doing this, it came to pass that the tribe of the Mercians, under the leadership of King Penda, went forth to war against the East Angles. Seeing they were being worsted in the war, they asked Sigeberht to come with them into battle as an encouragement to the soldiery. Indeed, as he was unwilling and refused, they extracted him against his will from the monastery and led him into battle, hoping that the soldiers' spirits would become less panic-stricken, and less inclined to flee, in the presence of a chieftain who had once been very strenuous. But the holy man, mindful of his profession, all the time that he was surrounded by the massed ranks of the conquering army, refused to hold anything but just a staff in his hand, and he was killed, along with King Ægeric and as the pagans kept on attacking, their whole army was massacred and routed. These things happened in the 637th year from the incarnation of the Word of God.[41]

Now, the successor of Sigeberht and Ægeric was Anna to whom we referred earlier, the son of Eni. He was an excellent man descended from the royal line and the father of an excellent family: he was the father of the aforesaid Æthelthryth and her sisters, as chapters yet to follow relate. After his accession Anna, as king of the province, adorned with buildings and a great many gifts the monastery which Fursey, a man of God about whom one reads wonderful things, had been given by the aforementioned King Sigeberht, sited within the castle which is called, in the language of the English, *Cnobheresburch*.

---

[39] *Dummoc* is the reading of E: Bede has Dommoc; the form Dunuuoc preferred by Blake (after ms. F), suggests identification of the place with Dunwich, an important place in the Middle Ages, though submerged in the sea now. But it cannot be assumed that this was the compiler's view, and the identification is not now regarded as certain. See M. Gallyon, *The Early Church in Eastern England* (Lavenham, Suffolk 1973) p. 61.

[40] Latin: *iuxta nominis sui sacramentum*: a pun on the name *Felix*, Latin for 'happy', 'fortunate'. Source: Bede, *Hist. Eccl.* ii. 15.

[41] Adopting the reading of E.

2. That the father and mother of the holy virgin Æthelthryth became the parents of holy progeny.[42]

So then, King Anna, some years before receiving his kingdom, to his glory acquired a wife worthy of a husband such as he; she being his equal in lineage and outstanding in moral character. God endowed their life and their habits of living with a blessing so abundant that, through progressive increases of their virtues, they were for ever raising their souls to the heights above. Sedulously carrying out the work of Christ with regard to the poor, they were tenacious in ministering to them and, dedicated as they were to such practices, they were given the riches of a legitimate succession of offspring, the issue of their bodies. There were born to them children whose praiseworthy living and no less precious dying serve as a commendation of them.[43] Yes indeed, there were two sons, Aldwulf and saintly *Jurminus*, and four daughters, namely Seaxburh, the first-born, an incomparable woman, Æthelburh, Æthelthryth and Wihtburh, who by rejecting the enticements of the flesh for the Lord's sake, earned the right to have oil in their flasks among the wise virgins.[44] That Aldwulf was the son of King Anna – an inference adopted in the present work – is shown by several pieces of evidence, and receives confirmation, if we are attentive, from parallel accounts in Bede and the histories. *Jurminus*, moreover, whose holiness of life and meritoriousness with regard to justice commend him as blessed, as one reads in the *Gesta Pontificum Angliae*,[45] is said to have been the brother of the virgin Æthelthryth. But the questions which need now to be investigated carefully are these: what were the origins of the women just mentioned?; what were their later careers like and what was their end?

In point of fact, the mother to whom this important family owed its birth was the daughter of Hereric, the *nepos*[46] of Edwin, King of the Northumbrians, and her name was Hereswith. This, certainly, is what one reads in the life of the holy virgin Milburh. The eldest daughter of King

---

[42] Sources: hagiography. Phrases in common with *Vita S. Ætheldrede* CD, ed. Love. Borrowings from Bede, *Hist. Eccl.* ii. 8; iii. 8; iv. 21 (23); William of Malmesbury, *Gesta Pontificum* ii. 74; a *Vita S. Milburge*; *Vita S. Wihtburge* TC, ed. Love (i.e. the *Vita* from Trinity College, Cambridge ms. O.2.1 and CCCC 393). *Worcester Chronicle* on the year 640. This chapter opens the *Libellus breviter comprensus in quo continetur Genealogia et Vita S. Etheldrede et sororum suarum . . .* etc. which takes the place of *LE* i in the *Chronicon Abbatum et Episcoporum Eliensium*, as printed in Wharton, *Anglia Sacra* i, pp. 595–604.

[43] Blake, p. 2, discusses this genealogy in relation to other sources, not all of which accord exactly with it.

[44] Cf. Matthew 25.4.

[45] William of Malmesbury, *Gesta Pontificum* ii. 74, where this 'Germinus' is said to be entombed at Bury St Edmunds.

[46] *Nepos* can mean either 'nephew' or 'grandson'. It appears that our author took it in the latter sense, but Blake (following Plummer, *Bede*, vol. ii, p. 244) believes this to be wrong.

Anna, Seaxburh – sister of the holy virgin Æthelthryth, whose mother was called Hereswith – was given in marriage to Eorconberht, king of the people of Kent. Nor is there in all the history of the English of that time – to be more precise, neither in English chronicles nor in Latin – any other woman found who is enlisted under a name like Hereswith, except this mother of holy women, whom Bede undoubtedly calls 'the mother of King Aldwulf'.[47] Concerning her we read the following, written in the annals:[48] 'When Æthelwold, King of the East Angles died, his successor was Aldwulf, whose mother was Hereswith, the sister of the holy Abbess Hilda, whose father was Hereric, whose father was Eadfrith, whose father was Edwin.' Hereswith herself, indeed, as Bede attests,[49] 'had another daughter, called Sæthryth, by another husband'; she remained a holy virgin. Seaxburh, on the other hand, in the fifth year of the reign of her father, married a husband, Eorconberht, King of the Kentish people, as has been stated previously, whereas another daughter, Æthelburh, preserved the lovely glory of perpetual virginity in great continence.

Now, at that time there were not many monasteries built in the region of the Angles: many people from Britain used to go to the monasteries of the Franks in order to live the monastic life: moreover,[50] they even sent their daughters there to be educated and to become brides of the celestial Bridegroom, particularly to Brie, Chelles and the monastic community at Les Andelys. Among these was Sæthryth, mentioned above, the daughter of the wife of Anna, King of the East Angles, begotten by another husband, and Æthelburh, the same king's own daughter, serving the Lord in the place which is called Brie. But Wihtburh, the youngest of the daughters, despising kings' sons and her parents' honours, chose, after her father's violent death, a humble place in his province at Dereham, her desire being to live in solitude. We are only setting out these facts briefly by way of supplementation, in so far as the sequence of our narrative coincides with them, but the reader will find information enough about the separate individuals through perusal of the books particularly concerned with them.

3. That Æthelthryth began to live a holy life in infancy.[51]

The blessed and glorious virgin Æthelthryth was born among the East Angles at a well-reputed place called Exning, of the noblest parents, as Bede, the

---

[47] Bede, *Hist. Eccl.* iv. 21 (23).

[48] That is, in the *Worcester Chronicle*.

[49] *Hist. Eccl.* iii. 18

[50] Lat. *sed et* is frequently used in *LE*, apparently with this meaning.

[51] Sources: hagiography with parallels in *Vita S.Ætheldrede* CD, ed. Love, chapter 1; reference to Bede, *Hist. Eccl.* iv. 17 (19).

venerable teacher and most truthful writer of history, testifies. She was the daughter of Anna, King of the East Angles, born of a mother called Hereswith, as has already been said. Well then, being nobly exalted by her lineage, she adorned the nobility of her mind by the glory of sanctity. For being a good girl even in her infancy, she grew better and better in the sight of all, giving notice in advance that something was to happen to her by God's gift. Æthelthryth, pre-elected by God was growing up, having passed her adolescence in a home of good breeding, in the manner customary for a girl of that age with her parents' wealth. She was always pleasant, sweet and gentle to everybody. But something very wonderful and laudable is that, favouring sobriety and chastity from the very earliest stages of her infancy, she used to keep making her way to the thresholds of churches, sometimes following in her parents' footsteps, sometimes alone, and was happy to pray to God assiduously, while neglecting the pastimes of girls. Her parents were amazed that their daughter was delighted by such pursuits, realizing perfectly well[52] that, by the grace of God, she was to have a very great endowment of the mighty powers of the virtuous[53] bestowed upon her. For she did not embrace the lasciviousness of the World. No, rather, she chose to complete the course of her present life in virginity, living in a manner that was pious, saintly and devout, and she made efforts that, even when she was of tender years, the saying of the wise man should be clearly exemplified in her: 'An unblemished life is maturity of age.'[54]

4. How Æthelthryth was first given to a husband, who lived only for a short time.[55]

When, in the progress of a praiseworthy life, the blessed virgin had passed the years of childhood and, now being adult, seemed ripe for marriage, report of her spread: her holiness of mind and beauty of body became famous far and wide; many people came, were amazed by the excellence of the virgin's appearance, and honoured with high praise the glories of her virginal purity. For indeed her beauty pleased innumerable princes, and her pretty face prompted girls to embrace her. She was sighing for the bridal-chamber of God alone, singing for Him solemnly a virgin's epithalamium. She was constant in her song and full of ardour for the sacrifice of her marriage-yoke as a whole-offering before God. Meanwhile, under the prescient gaze of the

---

[52] Lat. *potius*: interpreted as comparative for superlative, a very frequent idiom in *LE*.

[53] 'The mighty powers of the virtuous': Lat. simply: *virtutum*.

[54] Wisdom of Solomon 4.8.

[55] Sources: hagiography, with some parallels in *Vita Ætheldrede* CD, ed Love, chapter 2; Bede, *Hist. Eccl.* iv. 17 (19); local tradition for reputed evidence of Tondberht's gift of the Isle of Ely to his bride.

BOOK I

supernal Judge, the virgin Æthelthryth was made ready for speedy wedlock and the marriage-bed, to the accompaniment of diverse kinds of music-making, amid pomp and ceremony.[56] And this was not taking place in order that her chastity should be harmed: rather, so that, the more her endurance was put to the test in this conflict, the greater and more precious would the victory of martyrdom be, with which she would be crowned.

At length, she was asked for in marriage by Tondberht, Ealdorman of the Southern Gyrwe. It was his intention to cast his whole spirit into love for the virgin, and he asked her father, the king, that she be given in marriage to him. King Anna gave his assent to the longed-for object of the young petitioner's desire and, being a trustworthy king, made it his aim to give him satisfaction. Æthelthryth, hearing this, was very horrified, resisted for a long time, said 'no' for a long time, as she wished with all her desire to live her whole life out in virginity. But the authority of her parents was victorious – no, rather, what changed her mind was Divine Providence, prescient of the fact that she was to be crowned with a glorious laurel-crown of chastity all the more glorious in view of the encumbrance of her marriage. She was therefore betrothed, with the greatest ceremoniousness, two years before the violent death of her father. She was bound by a marriage-bond, even though against her will, and, as has been discovered in writing,[57] she received the Isle of Ely from this same betrothed, Tondberht, as a marriage-gift. After this happened, she remained a virgin for evermore. See! This is something out of the ordinary in this World, something by which everyone is astonished: that any virgin betrothed to a husband should remain immaculate! But let this be a matter of doubt to no one: <what is very difficult> in the thought of mankind is very easy before God, no matter what sort of apparent difficulty He may have chosen.[58]

Well then, Æthelthryth, betrothed as she was, earned the right to imitate the Mother of the Lord and thus, unconquered by carnal desire, to be holy in body and spirit. Thus, as an uncorrupted virgin amid the documents of a marriage-settlement, she was oppressed by the difficulties of this corruptible life, but at the same time she was being crowned every day with an ineffable martyrdom by virtue of her heavenward yearnings, even though she was being given in marriage to a husband – if, however, one may give the name of husband to a man who does not inflict loss of chastity. And, devoting their attention to frequent prayers and the fruits of mercy, they spent their days in all righteousness and the pursuit of holiness rather than in unchaste actions or the arrogance of this life, for they both knew that their marriage-promises made in accordance with law would be holier by virtue of a shared vow.

---

[56] Reading conjecturally at p. 14.24, ed. Blake: *sollempniter et festive*, rather than *festivum*.

[57] Source: unidentified; cf. *LE* i. 15 (p. 32.6, ed. Blake).

[58] This attempt at translation rests on a conjectural supplement (p. 15.6, ed. Blake): *in cogitatu hominum <difficilimum> apud Deum fieri facillimum.*

But, as Bede attests,[59] Tondberht died not very long after he had received Æthelthryth in marriage and, as a reward for chastity, received from the Lord the crown of life. Yet, as was reported by truthful people, he lived almost three years in the marital state in companionship with the virgin. In their union they were not one body through the conjunction of the flesh, but, so it is believed, they were one spirit in Christ, while each abided by the advice of the apostle,[60] and dissension and discord never came between them. And, however much the virgin devotedly wept for the destruction of their companionship, she rejoiced all the more that she was free in the liberty of Christ from the yoke of marriage, and she hoped that thus she had escaped from the encumbrances of the World.

From then onwards she made herself an incense-offering to God with prayers and gifts of alms, consigned to the flames tears and fragrant spices, and sent forth echoing invocations to Christ and the heavens. And although one can scarcely, or [n]ever at all, find a woman who is not unequal to the lures of desire, this woman went, conspicuously, all the way to marriage and yet, being without knowledge of the marital act, succeeded, by tireless prayers before God, in ensuring that He would keep her immaculate. But one should not disbelieve that it was possible for something to have been done in our age which reliable histories report as having sometimes been done in days gone by.[61]

5. On the fact that Bede cited precedent with regard to the blessed Æthelthryth and her betrothed, Tondberht.[62]

Some people ask the question in what document or history there is found reference to what Bede, bearing witness in favour of Tondberht and his spouse Æthelthryth, mentioned, 'as having sometimes been done in the past, as reliable histories report'.[63] That is, specifically, they ask: 'How ever had a man and a woman living in wedlock persisted in remaining unstained by one another?'

We first note that the blessed Mother of our Lord – blessed before, and

---

[59] Bede, *Hist. Eccl.* iv. 17 (19).

[60] Among relevant texts are 1 Corinthians 7.1: 'It is good for a man not to touch a woman'; Galatians 5.22: 'The fruit of the Spirit is love, joy, peace, patience, kindness, goodness, faithfulness, gentleness, self-control . . .'

[61] This last sentence is a quotation from Bede, *Hist. Eccl.* iv. 17 (19), acknowledged as such in the following chapter.

[62] Source: research, apparently conducted at Ely, in which a text named as *Collationes Patrum*, identifiable as *De Vitis Patrum Liber Quintus sive Verba Seniorum* (Migne *PL* lxxiii, col. 1006) was adduced to illustrate Bede, *Hist. Eccl.* iv. 17 (19).

[63] I assume we should understand, and punctuate, the Latin thus: *quod Beda . . . 'factum aliquotiens' asseruit, sicut 'fideles narrant historie'* (p. 16.3f., ed. Blake).

above, all other women – that unique woman, the virgin Mary, maintained chaste wedlock with her husband, according to the testimonies with which the holy Gospels provide us; and so did others whose memory the Church venerates. However, some people, faced with assertion of this fact, are mightily zealous to hear of proof from elsewhere. Hence, out of a desire to cite a precedent for Tondberht and Æthelthryth, we have sedulously investigated volumes of books, but most particularly, we have made studious investigations in our usual way in a book which is called *Collationes Patrum*,[64] and it has come to pass that we have found in our hands something long desired and sought after! We add this as a supplement to the sequence of the narrative, as is appropriate.

'Two of the fathers asked God to indicate to them the standard to which they had measured up. And a voice came to them saying that: "In the village †*Illa*†[65] which is in Egypt there is a layman whose name is Eucharistus and his wife is called Maria. You have not, for sure,[66] <yet> succeeded in measuring up to their standard." Those two old men arose and came to that village and, while staying there, found the man's one-roomed cottage.[67] And he, on seeing those old men, prepared a table and poured water into a bowl to wash their feet. And they said to him: "We will not taste anything unless you reveal to us what it is that you do." He then said with humility, "I am a shepherd and this is my wife." But since those aged men persevered in asking him to inform them of everything and he was unwilling to talk, they said to him: "God has sent us to you." And, hearing their words, he was afraid and said, "See here. We have these sheep from our parents, and whatever income God may have given to us from them we regard as made up of three parts: one belonging to the poor, one for receiving travellers and one for our own use. And all the time since I received this wife I have not been polluted and nor has she. No, she is a virgin, and we sleep separate from each other and, moreover, at night we put on sackcloth garments, but in the day, our own clothes. And up until now, no one of mankind has known this." On hearing what he said, those fathers were amazed and made their departure, glorifying God.'[68]

Well then, in view of the antiquity of this precedent, with its literary authority, it is not without utility to cite it for the benefit of those who read that Tondberht and his betrothed, Æthelthryth, according to the information

[64] St Benedict, *Regula* 42, had recommended works of this sort (*Collationes vel Vitas Patrum*) as after-supper reading for monks of his order.
[65] So also in the Migne text.
[66] Reading with E, *enim* and with E and Migne, <*adhuc*>.
[67] 'One-roomed cottage': Lat. *cella*.
[68] Reading with E and Migne: *recesserunt glorificantes Deum*.

19

given by Bede, continued to wear the long robe of chastity[69] into marriage and afterwards, and that, as has been said, this was sometimes the practice among the people referred to. May it serve to ensure that they know without doubt that 'God is no respecter of persons.'[70] Rather, in every race and in every order, in every social class, in every rank, the Lord knows the people who belong to him, and he justifies those whom he has fore-ordained, so that neither poverty nor riches may take away sanctity, and nor may obscurity make perfect nor distinction make blameworthy.

6. About the passing away of Bishop Felix, and where he lay buried.[71]

Now, previous mention has been made of Felix, Bishop of the East Angles. When he had taken charge of this same province with his pontifical leadership for eighteen years, he departed this life in peace at *Dummoc*[72] in the twelfth year of King Anna's reign.

Carried from there, he was buried at Soham[73] which is a vill by a mere.[74] This place, moreover, is said to be at the approach to the Isle of Ely. There used to exist there a large and well-known monastic house, in which a considerable community of monks, assembled by a venerable prince called Lutting, observed the order of a holy rule under an abbot, Wæreferth. Indeed, one reads in an English source[75] that St Felix was the original founder of the old monastery of *Seham* and of the church at *Redham*. But a cruel and impious tribe of pagans, coming from Denmark and running wild over all the regions of England, devastated the aforesaid monastery – and everything in the vicinity – encircling it with iron weaponry and fire, and reduced it thereafter to an unpopulated waste. Hence, after the place had been for a very long time without divine worship, in the time of King Cnut the remains of the most holy confessor Felix were translated to the monastery of Ramsey, and reburied with the honour that befitted them.

That we should write about this confessor of the Lord was, moreover,

---

[69] Cf. 2 Samuel 13.18.

[70] Cf. Acts 10.34.

[71] Sources: Bede, *Hist. Eccl.* ii. 15; William of Malmesbury, *De Gestis Pontificum* ii. 74; local traditions concerning Soham and Ramsey.

[72] *Dum'oc* BE; cf. their reading, *Dummoc*, at p. 11.4, ed. Blake. Again F has *Dunuuoc*. Bede, *loc. cit.*, gives the length of the pontificate of Felix as seventeen years.

[73] The form given is: *Seham*, meaning: 'The village by the lake'. Identification with Soham, Cambridgeshire, is assumed by our author, as by William of Malmesbury. On the archaeology of Soham see Hall, *Fenland Survey*, pp. 72ff. On the possible importance of a foundation at Soham for the mission of Felix, see Gallyon, *Early Church in Eastern England*, p. 61.

[74] Lat. *iuxta stagnum*, words of William of Malmesbury, ii. 74, p. 147 ed. Hamilton. For Soham Mere see Hall, *Fenland Survey*, pp. 72ff.

[75] Not extant.

something that the sequence of our narrative had itself demanded: as histories relate, it was Bishop Felix who washed clean with the water of baptism King Anna and all his household along with the province of East Anglia, and taught them the proofs of salvation.[76]

7. About the death of King Anna, and that his brothers ruled after him.[77]

In the period that followed, the aforementioned King Anna, though pre-eminent in England for renown and dignity, did not adopt the high and mighty stance of human pride. Rather, with a profound recognition of God's goodness towards himself, he sedulously made it his purpose not to think exalted thoughts. And although he was a king, exalted upon a throne, he presented himself to his servants as their equal; to priests, as a humble man, and to the people, as someone agreeable. He was a man of amazing devoutness with regard to the worship of God, amazing solicitude for the building of churches. For he had been 'the father of orphans and the judge of widows',[78] and a strong defender of his homeland, to whose protection all those who could not withstand ambush and enemy invasion took refuge. My aim, in deciding to write this account, has been to make plain the magnanimity of this very great king, as a way of approaching more general history.

Now, it happened that Cenwalh, who was the successor to the throne of his father Cynegils, refused to accept the faith and sacraments of the heavenly kingdom, with the consequence that not long afterwards he lost command over his earthly kingdom too. After repudiating the sister of Penda, King of Mercia, to whom he had been married, he took a second wife, and consequently he was harried in war and deprived of his kingdom by Penda. Finding no protection from anyone, he took refuge with the King of the East Angles, whose name was Anna. Spending three years in exile in his household, he came to a recognition of the faith and received the truth. For the man in whose household he was spending his exile was a good king and happy in his good and holy progeny, namely, being the father of the blessed women who are the principal subject of this book.

King Cenwalh was baptized in this same province by Bishop Felix, and King Anna received him from the holy font. With King Anna's assistance, Cenwalh returned after a while to Wessex, and successfully wrested his

---

[76] Reading conjecturally: *salutaria* for *salutaris* (p. 17.17, ed. Blake), for agreement with *documenta* or, as an alternative, simply: *salutis*; or maybe we should mark a lacuna thus: *salutaris* < . . > *documenta*, and assume the loss of some such word as *fidei* or *evangelii*.

[77] Sources: Bede, *Hist. Eccl.* iii. 7, 21–4; iv. 17 (19), 21 (23); *Worcester Chronicle* on the year 654; Felix, *Life of St Guthlac*, p. 146, ed. Colgrave.

[78] The Vulgate version of the Septuagint Psalter is translated here: *patris orfanorum et iudicis viduarum* (Psalm 67.6, cf. 68.5 RSV).

father's kingdom from his enemies. Report of this was frequently repeated and became public knowledge to the whole English world, as some people marvelled at King Anna's zeal and love for God and others praised his sanctity. From all around people entered into alliance with him. Mercia alone, still puffing and panting for death, began to threaten the destruction of the East Angles and, with the support of troops of warriors marched out on an expedition to oust them. Anna, hastening to meet them, was killed by the same King Penda of the Mercians, in the nineteenth year of his reign, the 654th year from the incarnation of the Lord. His brother Æthelhere succeeded him as king. He became friendly with King Penda, then accepted his overlordship, with a view to reigning under him. There is in the same province a place called Blythburgh[79] in the vernacular, in which the body of the venerable King Anna is buried, and to this day is venerated by the pious devotion of faithful people. In that place,[80] too, his son *Iurminus*, God's chosen one, was buried, but afterwards he was translated to *Bederichesworthe*, which they now call *Sanctus Edmundus* {Bury St Edmunds}, and given honourable burial.

As the affairs of East Anglia were in such upheaval, the queen, after her king's death, travelled to Gaul, despising this World, and retreated to the convent of Chelles and there, subjected to the disciplines of a rule, she awaited the eternal crown. Later, her saintly sister, Hild, came to join her, leaving her homeland in emulation of her example. It was her wish to live as an expatriate, in that same convent of Chelles, for the Lord's sake, but she was called home after a year by Bishop Aidan, and afterwards lived the monastic life with great abstinence.

The year after these events, the unbelieving King of Mercia, Penda – the killer of Sigeberht, Ecgric and Anna, Kings of East Anglia, and also of Edwin and Oswald, Kings of Northumbria – supported by thirty legions and the same number of most noble commanders, went up to Bernicia,[81] to wage war against King Oswiu. Oswiu, along with his son Alhfrith, came to meet him. He had only one legion, but had placed his reliance upon Christ's leadership.[82] For Oswiu's other son, Ecgfrith, was at that time detained as a hostage in the province of Mercia in the household of King Penda's queen, Cyneswith. It was Ecgfrith who was to receive as his consort the holy virgin Æthelthryth, about whose life and mighty works this book, fittingly, is being composed.[83] But, to resume: even the son of King Oswald, Odilwald, who

---

[79] Near Southwold, Suffolk.

[80] Reading with E: *illic* (p. 18.18, ed. Blake).

[81] In the north of Northumbria. See Stenton, *Anglo-Saxon England,*pp. 74ff.

[82] Bede, *Hist. Eccl.* iv. 24, mentions the 'thirty legions' but records a more sober estimate of the disparity of the two sides, namely that Oswiu's forces were outnumbered three to one.

[83] The verb used is *texitur*, meaning literally: 'is being woven' or 'braided'.

ought to have been assisting Oswiu and Alhfrith on that occasion, was on the side of their enemies. He had become a commander, and was to fight for them against his homeland and his uncle. On this particular occasion, although he had kept apart from them, he was awaiting the outcome of the battle in a safe place. And when battle was entered, the thirty pagan commanders of King Penda were put to flight and slaughtered, and those who had come to his aid were almost all killed. Amongst the slain was the very person who had instigated the war, Æthelhere, the brother of Anna, King of the East Angles, who became ruler in succession to him. Then King Oswiu, in return for the victory conferred upon him, made an offering to God of twelve properties for the construction of monasteries and his daughter, Ælfflæd, to be consecrated in perpetual virginity. King Oswiu brought this war to a close in the thirteenth year of his reign, to the great benefit of both populaces. For he freed his own people from the hostile pillaging of the pagans, and the people of Mercia and the neighbouring provinces, now that its unbelieving head had been cut off, he converted to the grace of the Christian faith.

But in the fourth year after this event the leaders of that people rebelled against Oswiu. They set up Wulfhere, son of Penda, as king, having kept him in hiding And thus they served Christ joyously with a king of their own. Wulfhere received as his wife the daughter of King Eorconberht and Seaxburh, sister of the venerable virgin Æthelthryth. Her name was Eormenhild, and by her he became the father of the holy virgin Wærburh. And he reigned seventeen years, as we read in Bede.

And now that Æthelhere, King of the East Angles, had been killed, as mentioned previously, a third brother called Æthelwold received the kingship, a good man and a true worshipper of God, whose ways with regard to the faith and holy works were in conformity with those of his brother Anna. The King of the East Saxons, Swithelm, often came up to visit him, because of their common interests and so, when this happened, Æthelwold exhorted him with friendly and, so to speak, brotherly advice to abandon the vanity of idols for belief in the Lord Jesus Christ. With the support of his friends, Swithelm became a believer and was baptized by Ceadda, Bishop of the Mercians, who at that time had arrived in the province of the East Angles. The King of these self-same East Angles, the brother of their King Anna, received Swithelm from the water of baptism, and he reigned for five years. We have mentioned before Aldwulf, the son of King Anna, the brother, that is, of the virgin Æthelthryth. It was he who received the kingship after Æthelwold. His daughter Eadburh, an abbess [at Repton], sent across a sarcophagus of lead and linen for Guthlac, the servant of God, after his death, to be laid and wrapped in.

8. How Æthelthryth was once again given to a husband, namely the King of the Northumbrians; also, the people who went with her and how she lived in a holy manner.[84]

Now, the Ealdorman of the Gyrwe, Tondberht, mentioned earlier, departed from this transitory life not very long after he had received Æthelthryth as his wife, and soon afterwards she went down to her own home in Ely, as if reaching the shore after a shipwreck. Then, right on this very island, remote from encounters with visitors, she made great efforts to serve Christ the Lord for the rest of her life. She fled from the empty honours of the World, in pursuit always of silence and a truly inglorious life, as afterwards became apparent. That place, moreover, was surrounded by difficult terrain for access and by trees all around. It had springs from the brow of the hill, small but providing water. As if in a desert, she began to live by herself, and the people she particularly attached to herself in friendship were those whom she knew to be of exceptional piety. For she was beginning to make her body thinner by vigils and abstinence from food; she was striving after heavenly things with constant psalmody and complete mental concentration. Exercised in observances of this kind, Æthelthryth's premiss was that there was nothing sweeter, nothing more delightful than to rejoice in the Lord and to please Him for whom she was making herself acceptable. Her reverential devotion was increasing daily and her holy yearning was rising to ever greater heights, fired by the Holy Spirit. Thus, in her case, habit had instructed nature to keep carnal desires in check[85] by the halters of parsimony. What more is one to say? Now that her first ordeal was ended by the judgement of God, for the second time a conflict was assigned to the blessed virgin, more severe than the first, so that her palm of virginity might appear to the World all the more excellent.

At that time, however, holding sway among the English over the northern territories was Ecgfrith, whose city of York had the position of capital of the kingdom. This noble and distinguished king was enflamed with love for the virgin and he brought with him measureless wealth and promised many marriage-gifts. Being all the time aimed at conferring transitory honours upon her, the petition of the prince[86] became most assuredly a burden to her rather than an honour. He next assailed her parents

---

[84] Sources: hagiography with parallels in *Vita S. Ætheldrede* CD, chapter 4, ed. Love; Bede *Hist. Eccl.* ii. 9; iv. 3, 17 (19); *Worcester Chronicle* on the year 660; Eddius Stephanus, *Vita Wilfridi*; Eadmer, *Vita Wilfridi*.

[85] Reading, with BE, *cohiberet*.

[86] *Petitio principis*: perhaps our author has in mind the logical term *petitio principii*, meaning 'an attempt to demonstrate a conclusion by means of premisses that presuppose that conclusion'; cf. *intenderet* above, which seems to mean: 'she had as her premiss'.

with earnest pleas, as a result of which, since she could not find the strength to struggle against their will any longer, she eventually acquiesced in the wishes of the petitioners, even though with reluctance. So it was that, contrary to her hopes, in the sixth year after the death of her father, by the united will of her kinsfolk, in the time of her uncle Æthelwold, who reigned after the blessed Anna and his other brother, called Æthelhere, she was given in marriage a second time, to another royal husband, namely Ecgfrith, son of Oswiu, King of the Northumbrians, whose father was Æthelfrith, whose father was Æthelric. This Æthelric acceded to the kingship after Ælla, who ruled the kingdom of the Deiri most energetically for thirty years. It was on his name that the blessed Gregory made a pun, when he discovered boys of English birth on sale in the Roman forum: 'Alleluia!' he said. 'The praise of God the Creator ought to be sung in those regions.' And this same King Oswiu had a brother, Oswald, a holy martyr of God, who held the kingdom for nine years before him; other brothers whom a chronicle enumerates, and a sister called Ebba, under whose magisterial authority Queen Æthelthryth, pleasing to God, afterwards put on the habit of holy religion, having laid aside her royal crown, and both observed and learnt the rules of the monastic life. Moreover, the aforesaid King Oswiu was the father of sons and daughters, as the *History of the English* relates, and he set up his son Ælfrid as king over the province[s] of the Deiri [and Bernicii], whereas Ecgfrith, a younger son for whom he had felt a deep love, he appointed as his sharer in the kingship over the province of York, since, being oppressed by bodily illness, he was finding difficulty in maintaining secure jurisdiction over the kingdom. Ecgfrith, in fact, was a young man about thirty years old, pleasant in speech, civil in his ways, a man strenuous in arms and bound with strong ties of friendship to the blessed Wilfrid.[87] And, as we read in the fourth book of the *Histories of the English*, King Ecgfrith took a wife named Æthelthryth, the daughter of Anna, King of the East Angles. Her father was a very religious man, and one outstanding in all respects, in thought and in deed; she herself had had another husband before him, to be precise, the Ealdorman of the Southern Gyrwe of whom we have made mention before. But she would have prevented this, if she had been able to put up resistance against it.[88]

So then, a virgin daughter of Zion was led to the citizens of Babylon, but she was not at all burnt by the fire of this furnace. A day was named for the consecration with solemn nuptials of the act whereby the king betrothed himself to a king's daughter. Æthelthryth, therefore, was married, with

---

[87] The statement about Ecgfrith's age is wildly at variance with Bede's report in *Hist. Eccl.* iv. 24 (26), that he was forty when killed in battle in 684, which, if correct, would mean that he was only about fifteen at the time of his marriage.

[88] Tenses in the Latin, *obstaret . . . posset* (p. 21.13, ed. Blake): imperfect subjunctives for an unfulfilled condition in the historic present.

multifarious splendour and diverse celebratory dances of joyous people, to a king deserving of reverence – while sighing rather for the nuptials of the Heavenly Bridegroom. And indeed, celestial Love preserved her sacred intent from the desire of the flesh and, if royal glory brought her any not inglorious mode of making her, as a king's daughter, seem more glorious,[89] it was more on account of her rank rather than as a result of luxury and pride which might be her downfall, that fine linen and *purpura* were pleasing to her. Indeed, at court, a place where other virgins, while in residence, usually seethe with carnal desires, she was being consumed in the fire of Him upon whom angels yearn to look. Consequently, though pledged to a royal marriage for many years, she always, thanks to the protecting shadow of God, remained inviolate.

Now, in this period, King Ecgfrith, devoted to holy works along with his Queen, Æthelthryth, became, together with her, obedient in all matters to Bishop Wilfrid. There followed[90] peace and joy among their peoples, and successful years and victories against their enemies, God being their helper. So one reads in the *Life* of this same confessor of the Lord, Wilfrid.[91] But, in addition, the soul of the queen was soon drawn to the holiness of God in the love of Christ and she took care to give Him a share of the things which belonged to her by virtue of her marriage. For having received[92] Hexham from God's beloved, Queen Æthelthryth herself, he built a house for the Lord in honour of the blessed Apostle Andrew, raised upon variegated columns and many pillared aisles, which is more fully appreciated from seeing it than from hearing of it.[93] But by wandering off rather a long way after particular details, we are being rather slow to reconstruct the matter which is the intended subject of our work. However, in the interests of general knowledge, we communicate discoveries, as the subject-matter recommends.

There had come with Æthelthryth some noble men and women from the province of the East Angles, among whom there was a distinguished man of particular authority, Owine[94] by name, a monk of great merit. Leaving as he did the secular World with the pure aim of receiving heavenly recompense, he was a person worthy of being in a special way the recipient of revelations from the Lord of His mysteries, and he was worthy to receive the attention of listening ears when he recounted his faithful testimony. Now he, too, had come with the same Queen Æthelthryth from the province of the

---

[89] Cf. Psalm 44.14 Vulgate = 45.13 RSV, on the glory of a king's daughter.

[90] Lat. *subsecute sunt*: strictly speaking, *subsecuta* (n. pl.) would be grammatical.

[91] That of Eddius Stephanus.

[92] *Augustaldense adepta*, lit. 'Hexham having been received': a non-deponent variant on *adipiscor* is presupposed, as elsewhere in MedLat (p. 21.29–22.1, ed. Blake).

[93] See Richard Morris, *Cathedrals and Abbeys of England and Wales* (London 1979) p. 255 for bibliography on Hexham Priory, where the crypt of Wilfrid's church still exists.

[94] Reading with E, at p. 26.8, ed. Blake: *Owinus*, the form used in all mss. for the parallel passage in *LE* i. 23. Bede (*Hist. Eccl.* iv. 3) gives the name as Ouinus.

East Angles, and was the first of her ministers and the head of her household. It was fitting that she should have as her guardian and provider a man of such character and distinction, whose life in public was one of amazing sanctity and, as viewed by one who witnessed him in private, a man of great merit, who knew that <he>[95] was in the midst of the unstable honours of the World, yet, thanks to his spiritual life, was never absent from the celestial mysteries. For after the adoption by Æthelthryth, this distinguished queen, his lady, of the monastic life, he so completely stripped himself of worldly things, after which people used to think he hankered, that he approached the monastery of Ceadda, Bishop of the Mercians, clothed solely in a habit, and with a hatchet and an adze in his hand, and made it clear that he was not entering the monastery for an easy life, as some do. There, on the strength of the reverence of his devotion, he was accepted among the brothers and became a great friend of the saintly bishop, and heard above him the arrival of the heavenly host before Ceadda's death. I am passing over in silence very many things, for fear that I may go beyond the limits of my subject-matter by the narrating of details.[96]

To return to my theme, let me say this too: King Ecgfrith was full of joy at his marriage with the queen. He was for ever speaking coaxingly to her, but did not soften her in favour of his desires. Observing her pious behaviour and devout life, he was amazed that now she was in her exalted position on a royal throne she did not in the least alter the gravity of demeanour to which she had accustomed herself. For, indeed, she often spent the night sleepless, and the day without taking food, and – let me avow the truth – she used to spend days and nights continually in prayer. And on occasions when she had retired to take her rest on the royal couch in the manner of those joined in wedlock, she with difficulty fended off sleep and fled to her usual saying of prayers; nor had it been her custom to return again to bed, as one learns afterwards from Bede's words. For the Holy Spirit, who had prepared her heart as his abode, kept free from all corruption the home of his indwelling. Hence the courageous virgin stood firm and fearless amid adversity and prosperity, and so violence did not break her and nor did the love of princes keep her from the duties owed to the Highest King, for love of whom Queen Æthelthryth proposed to spend her whole life under a vow of virginity rather than be violated by the sensual desire of another. She was married to him by the law of wedlock – not, however, by the conjoining of the flesh.

But the wicked Despoiler[97] groaned at having been left prostrate in their very first combat, with the consequence that he subsequently rose up to fight against her all the more fiercely. He therefore spurred on Ecgfrith more

---

[95] Supplying conjecturally (p. 22.13, ed. Blake): *noverat* <se> *esse*.

[96] See the fuller account in Bede, *Hist. Eccl.* iv. 3.

[97] That Satan is meant, not Ecgfrid, becomes clear from the next sentence.

eagerly than ever and vehemently inflamed his fierce passions and attempted
by a cunning strategem to seduce this woman whom he could not violate
through her publicly recognized married state. His aim was that a woman
who was incapable of being swayed by the conjugal bond of common usage,
would deviate towards the snares of the flesh under the cover of discipline.
But God benignly arranged a glorious outcome for what His ancient Enemy
was striving to turn in the direction of ruin and, just as the virgin had won
the first victory thanks to Him, so, in view of her virginal bodily state, He
considered she was also winning a second one.

**9. How the king was not able to consummate marriage with the virgin; how,
with St Wilfrid as intermediary, he tried to entice her to change her mind,
but how Wilfrid put before the queen exhortations in favour of chastity.[98]**

And lest anyone, doubtful about the queen's self-restraint, should disparage
her supreme virtue, let him be assured that in those times it was something
well known and believed throughout the whole of England, as many people,
certain about the fact, avowed. The king, I say, restraining himself by some
heaven-sent power – so it is our religious duty to believe – was stupefied in
terror, and did not touch the most blessed queen in an unchaste manner, nor
cause her misery nor inflict any harrassment on her, and he revered her in
all respects, not as his queen or his consort but as ruler over him. He became
her husband where his mind was concerned, not his flesh; in name alone,
not in deed. He did wish, however, for his due from his wife – but neither by
prayers nor by promises could he bend her resolve in favour of his desire.
Finally, he approached St Wilfrid both in person and through his friends, and
quite frequently had meetings with him, begging and beseeching him, and
trying to entice him with the promise of very great things, to induce him to
persuade the queen to set aside her resolve concerning virginity – something
which it is incumbent upon me to describe later in the words of Bede also. He
saw her assiduous friendly relations with the bishop, <for> she[99] kept
receiving instruction from the latter's exhortations; she was emulating him
in the love of Christ. Consequently, the king kept wearying God's herald
with rewards – vainly. For Bishop Wilfrid was never willing to urge marital
relations upon the virgin, and she was never willing to give her acquiescence
to the king. 'Although she fulfilled the rôle of his consort for twelve years,' as
is written in the *Book of Sermons* of Bede the Priest, 'she nevertheless

[98] Sources: hagiography with parallels in *Vita S. Ætheldrede* CD, chapter 5, ed. Love; Bede,
Hist. Eccl. ii. 9; iii. 11, 14, 21, 24; iv 3; iv (17) 19; Eadmer; *Vita Wilfridi*; Eddius Stephanus,
Vita Wilfridi; tradition concerning an embroidered stole and maniple preserved at Durham.
[99] Here there seems need of e.g. <nam> after *familiaritatem* (p. 23.24, ed. Blake): perhaps
it is lacking from E because of its position at the page-turning and at the beginning of a section
where the text has evidently been revised.

remained glorious in the perpetual inviolateness of virginity.'[100] wonderful thing! A wonderful instance of God's grace! She remained a virgin within marriage! Only in the secret awareness of God was knowledge of this amazing thing accessible: how Queen Æthelthryth reduced the virile strength of her first husband to femininity and by what devising of the Holy Spirit she evaded the perilous desires of her second. Truly, God did not allow a temple consecrated to Himself in a virgin's body to be violated by what is the lawful norm in marriage, nor did innocence devoted to righteousness suffer defeat and consent to defilement. In view of this, we append here something which we are aware that many people report.

It happened once that the most blessed queen entered the bed-chamber at a quiet time of the night; and the king sent a message that he would quickly be following her. And when she learnt of this, she began to be ineffably saddened and grief-stricken, for fear of being robbed of the desired object of her resolve. And, opening up her inner self in prayer accompanied by groaning, she said to God, 'O good Jesus, Lord and Master, remember thy mercies and the sweetness of thy beloved Mother and, by virtue of her pious intercessions, help me at this hour!' There was no delay and the king, in a state of high excitement, arrived at his threshold, looked inside and – behold – the house in question was all lit up inside, as if it were on fire! As a result he was seized by very great terror and retreated in astonishment, calling out to her: 'Do not, do not imagine, good woman, that I wish to make sport of you any more. The Lord God is your protector and your mighty helper.' And thus the royal virgin of the Lord, Æthelthryth, shines forth, renowned in God's sight, and, furthermore, in the sight of the World a queen.

For Wilfred, being a supporter of her vow of virginity, ensured, thanks to the wisdom of his vigilant sensibility, that the virgin would not deviate from her intention through any inconstancy of the feminine mind and would not change her way of thinking, being defeated some day by worldly snares. Moreover, he dissimulated – with foresight and prudence – pretending to be favourably disposed to the king and promising an effective outcome of his own yearning to persuade the queen.[101] For he was afraid that, as the result of such a business as this, he would cause offence to the king – as in fact happened. And the saintly pontiff, all the time that he was intending – so it was thought – to talk about such matters to the queen, set about discoursing earnestly on the sweetness of the life of Heaven, and thus

---

[100] The words are exactly paralleled in a sentence in the *Hist. Eccl.* iv. (17) 19. The manner of citation seems an extreme example of attention to the rhetorical principle of *variatio*, unless, for some reason the author responsible was using a book of *excerpta* at the time. He again refers to Bede as a priest (using the word *presbyter*, Bede's own description of himself at the opening of *Hist. Eccl.*) in chapter 21 (p. 39.22, ed. Blake). In chapter 23 (p. 42.9, ed. Blake) he describes himself as taking material *de Bede opusculis*.

[101] Reading conjecturally a t p. 24.16, ed. Blake : *persuadendi* for *persuadendum*.

Æthelthryth, endowed with God-given courage as a result of the holy bishop's advice, absolutely refused assent to the king. Moreover, the blessed man brought it about on his own initiative that she should seek a divorce, so that she could leave the World, gaining her liberty, and could happily cling to the nuptials of the Eternal King.

Obeying Bishop Wilfrid's admonitions and promptings, Æthelthryth, best-beloved virgin of Christ, stood by immediately to carry out his longed-for plan. For he was someone whom the true love of religion had bound to herself, deservedly so. Moreover it was by God's design that she had come to that place, this being of assistance to many people: she made it her earnest concern to bestow help on all in a spirit of piety and mercy. Throughout the time she resided in that place, she used to admit ministers of holy religion – men and women – to friendly association with her. Her thinking was that by consultation and confederacy with them, she would advance to all sanctity, and that she would be well fostered under the guardianship of her own merits. She used to assert that one should gather into one's circle of friends – as particularly suitable for a venture such as this – people from the monastic orders and communities because of their cleanness of life and honourable behaviour, and among them the most holy Bishop Wilfrid, with whom we are concerned at present. She also advanced into her grace and favour another man distinguished by the glory of his life of sanctity, the most blessed hermit Cuthbert, when, in point of fact, he was not yet a bishop, and she supplied him with much assistance from out of the abundance of her private resources. In addition, being skilled in handiwork, she made with her own hands, so it is reported, by the technique of gold-embroidery, an outstanding and famous piece of work, namely a stole and maniple of matching materials, of gold and precious stones, and she sent this work to be offered to him as a blessing in recognition of a deep-seated affection. These are kept at the church of Durham, as a sign of the pious devotion of both him and her, and they are [still] shown to people on request, as a great honour, and quite frequently some of our number have seen them. In terms of righteousness and piety it was fitting that she, in an act of self-abasing devotion such as this, should pledge a gift to him, beloved virgin to beloved virgin, so that subsequently he might use it standing in the presence of our Lord and King, [and] would with the greatest ease be able to display a reminder of her amidst the holiest of holy ceremonies of the mass and placate the Lord of Majesty with pious supplication on her behalf. We do not find any mention of this in Bede, but we have thought it essential for us to write of it in view of all the people who have borne witness to it up to now.

Moreover, it was not only the individuals whom we have mentioned, but innumerable people far and wide, who recognized that the blessedness of the saintly queen was <no> less[102] than the rumour in circulation reported.

---

[102] Reading conjecturally (p. 25.5, ed. Blake): *beatitudinem sancte regine <non> minorem esse*

Innumerable people longed for the opportunity to make her acquaintance and at the same time to talk with her, and they honoured her with a diverse profusion of guest-gifts. She was amiable to all, pleasant in her manner of talking, beautiful in appearance, of exceptional modesty and adorned with the virtue of extreme chastity; a lover of what was right, caring for no sweet delights except those of Heaven. She made frequent visits to the church of God; she continually found time for prayer, and hence her life became an education for many. For it was to this end that nature gave her birth, will-power kept her in action and grace preserved her.

10. That Queen Æthelthryth, instructed by the exhortations of the blessed bishop, had for a long time pleaded for divorce from the king but, on obtaining this with difficulty, entered a convent and received [from him] the veil of holiness.[103]

Who is there, in truth, who might give an adequate account of the excellence of the good works carried out by the virgin Æthelthryth while she lived beneath the yoke of marriage, sufficiently tested, yet not overcome, by the temptations and surging passions of the flesh? She found wedlock an excessively heavy burden and wished to dissolve it and be with Christ. And so she reckoned that all glory was a slippery thing and, recognizing by the spirit of understanding[104] that the life of Heaven was the only thing that endures, she became most eagerly desirous of living in solitude. For she knew that it was rare for anyone who seeks liberty of the soul amongst the riches of the World to be able to remain self-consistent, and the soul which does not go on its way free from burdens when amidst lower things, finds it difficult to arrive at higher things.

Hence, with numberless sighs, she began to attempt to cut herself loose from the yoke of the kingdom in an ardent desire to fly away to Christ and rest in Him. And now that she had been bound by the law of marriage for so many years, she refused to delay further something which she had long before decided upon in her mind. Instead, taking note carefully of the day and the hour, she petitioned her husband, the king – not in secret but publicly, not on rare occasions, but frequently – for permission to leave the cares of secular life and to serve Christ the King and Him alone in a monastic house. The king, when he heard this, resisted and did not easily acquiesce. Moreover, he said that he would be bound to grieve deeply if ever it came about that he should endure divorce from his beloved wife, even though he

quam fama disperserat . . .
[103] Sources: hagiography, cf. *Vita S. Ætheldrede CD,* chapter 7, ed. Love; Eadmer, *Vita Wilfridi.*
[104] Lat. *spiritu intelligentiae,* cf. Isaiah 11.2: *spiritus sapientiae et intellectus.*

had never been united with her in the customary way of married people. The queen petitioned once again for what she had requested, with tears, and in a long series of petitions she kept pressing her case all the more importunately the more difficulty she believed there would be over obtaining consent for her request. For in a burning passion she had transferred all her yearnings towards the powers above, for love of the celestial Bridegroom. She demanded His protection – appropriately – and the more burdensome was the state from which she yearned to be rescued, the more firmly and fervently she resolved to win over by prayers Him by whom she knew she was to be rescued. The obliging deference of servants every day, the trappings of pomp, the grand opulence of her circumstances: none of these things could recall her from her resolve.

In fact, the king was eventually defeated by her importunate prayers and, though reluctant, nevertheless let her go, invincible as she was. She, of course, rejoiced greatly at the king's yielding and granting of permission, difficult and slow though it had been to obtain. After a great number of endowments had been provided to go with her, the noble virgin and mighty queen entered the monastic community of the holy Abbess Ebba, who was the aunt of King Ecgfrith and the sister of King Oswald the martyr and King Oswiu. The monastic house was situated in the place which they call the city of *Coludus* {Coldingham}. She received the veil of the religious life from Bishop Wilfrid, whom we have mentioned earlier.

Many men and women from the kingdom followed after her, and settled beneath the shelter of churches for the Lord's sake, in the same way that Owine, her major-domo, a man deservedly dear to God and the hearer of celestial mysteries, followed in his mistress's footsteps and returned to the monastic life, as we have related before, not having forgotten what manner of man he was. But, in addition, many people far away, on learning of the religious profession of this most important virgin and queen, renounced the World or exerted themselves more fully in good works.

So, entering a monastic community, Æthelthryth offered herself to God as a living sacrifice. She left behind, spurned, and ejected utterly from her heart, all the things which belong to the world; moreover, in place of a diadem, she covered herself with a humble veil and, in place of fine linen and *purpura*, a coarse, black habit enfolded her. Truly, the first time that the famous queen believed that she was exerting royal power was when she made her exit from her royal position, free for the service of Christ, doing this in such a way that she not only brought her whole being to God, on laying aside the insignia of royalty, but, by adopting the rule of monastic religious life for the love of Christ, subjected her own will and body to holy obedience.

In the place to which she had come, all the time that she was being tested in her frailty, she was found perfect. Deservedly blessed, deservedly glorious: having been put to the test, she was glorified by the suffering of obedience and, making the observance of religion her sole activity, as one appointed for holy discipline, she delighted in being cut off from human social relations for the sake of the sweetness of divine contemplation, so that she might live apparently like Martha, but devote herself utterly to the quietude of Mary.[105] Her reputation for goodness increased, and equally there increased in her a religious devotion beyond all her fellow-nuns belonging to that congregation. There she learnt for the space of a year that the 'yoke' of the Lord 'is easy and' that His 'burden is light'.[106] In that place, also, she attained to such a high level of holy living and presented a demonstration of such perfect humility that, if anyone were in search of an illustration of holy discipline, he would realize that its mastery was expressly exemplified in her life. And truly, I say, the happy virgin was now adorned by two triumphs. For she was given in marriage to two husbands – specifically, the first time to an ealdorman and latterly to a king – but yet, by the power of God, she made her marriage-union with both of no validity. And behold, it came to pass that, because she always upheld a soul unconquered in its determination upon virginity, she could never be defiled by the violence of two husbands. Thus He who rescued the three boys from the fiery furnace of Babylon[107] protected Æthelthryth from the flame of defilement.

11. That King Ecgfrith made efforts to remove her forcibly from the convent, but that she was kept safe, by the mercy of God.[108]

Now, Queen Æthelthryth, as has already been established, was already subject to the rules of monastic discipline, but King Ecgfrith, who had long been dedicated to chaste marriage with her, did not take kindly to divorce from his beloved spouse, and soon began to be immeasurably sorrowful and grief-stricken. Hence, at the suggestion and instigation of his people, he began attempts to remove her forcibly from the convent, despite the fact that she was under the protection of the veil of holiness. Without delay, he went up to the convent where the holy virgin was living, with fury and hullabaloo, and in a great hurry. On hearing him coming, the mother of the community, Ebba, advised her that the only means of safety lay in escape. And, impelled by the Spirit of God, Æthelthryth resolved to take action whereby she might remain a virgin for the rest of her life; nor must she rest until she reached

---

[105] See Luke 10.38ff.

[106] Matthew 11.30.

[107] See Daniel 3.23ff.

[108] Sources: hagiographical tradition about Coldingham, associated with local topography, and independent of the tradition represented by *Vita S. Ætheldrede* CD, as well as from Bede. Blake notes no direct allusion to other sources, apart from the Bible, though, for instance, the *Worcester Chronicle* reports Wilfrid's expulsion and Eadmer knew of Ecgfrith's remarriage.

her home in Ely. She decided that there she could, by God's power, avoid the Charybdis of incontinency. Forthwith, this woman who, the day before yesterday, had been mistress over a kingdom, in contempt of earthly sovereignty, entered the monastic life. She now became a maid-servant of the handmaidens of Christ, taking upon herself the lowest of servile duties. For this virgin dedicated to God took delight in such things, always having before her eyes the saying: 'The greater thou art, the humbler thou shouldest make thyself in all things.'[109] But though, by God's generosity, favourable conditions for the peace which she longed for were granted to her, she did not lack enemies determined to trap her. Hence the testimony of the apostle, that 'all who wish to live piously in Christ suffer persecution',[110] was most truly confirmed in her case. For the king, wishing to take her back as his wife, went into action, not failing to set out in pursuit, in the hope that he might perhaps be able to catch her. But the holy woman, groaning and anxious now with redoubled fear, fled under compulsion from her pleasant hiding place and went forth, commending her chastity with great earnestness to the Lord. Having secretly made a circuit of the place, she came, accompanied by two handmaidens of God, Sewenna and Sewara, to a high hill nearby called *Coldeburcheshevet*, which means 'Coldeburch's Head' – and climbed up it.

But God, who 'commands the winds and sea and they obey Him',[111] does not desert those who trust in Him. We believe it came about by His decree that the sea, leaving its bed and now pouring forth its waters in many directions, surrounded the place up which the holy virgins had climbed, and, as we have learnt from the local inhabitants, kept them hidden for seven days on end, without food or drink, as they took their stand together in prayer, and that – wondrous to relate – it forgot how to ebb back in the usual manner, so long as the king remained there, or near the place. And thus the water stood still, to make clear to everyone the merit of the virgin, and the water served as a means of help and protection and was, as it were, not water, with its propensity to harm or destroy. The handmaid of Christ, protected in this manner by this defence, evaded the threats of the king and did not suffer any harm from him. For God, who has pity on the needy, brought help and protected His betrothed, unarmed as she was, with the shield of His merciful right hand. For, in a moment, the place became set apart and, all of a sudden, shielded by the grace of God, so that on one side of the eminence there was to be found a high rock-face cleft in the middle, and <on the other>[112] the waves of the sea, the embrace of which had been slightly withdrawn, presented an unbroken level surface, so that the empty solitude of the desert

---

[109] Ecclesiasticus 3.18.

[110] 2 Timothy 3.12.

[111] Luke 8.25.

[112] Reading conjecturally (p. 27.35, ed. Blake): *ex uno latere . . . rupes haberetur et <ex altero> equam planitiem maris fluctus reducto paululum sinu ostenderent . . .*

place should not be accessible even for the purpose of escaping an enemy.[113] Report of this matter, and of the remarkable miracle, spread rapidly, and people who had seen it, or heard about it, were awe-struck, recognizing that God was everlastingly their Protector.

Now, for a long time they had been on top of the summit of the rock and surrounded on all sides by a multitude of waves, and yet the king had found it quite impossible to find any direction from which to approach them. In the end, however, he retreated from the place marvelling at what had happened, and reduced to stupefaction. He returned to York and thereafter did not regard the confessor of the Lord, Wilfrid, favourably in confidential matters, nor with affection, as he had before, but instead for a considerable while harboured anger against him in his breast, and having bided his time, ejected him – the reason being such as we have described – from his episcopal see. Eventually, when he was deprived of all conviction that there could be a return to marriage with the holy queen, he took Eormenburh to himself in wedlock.[114]

Now, the time came when the nuns on the summit of the rock were beginning to suffer, being exceedingly feverish because of the dryness of thirst, so Ebba, the venerable abbess, urged Æthelthryth to pray to the Lord Christ that He who gave drink from a rock to His people in the desert, might provide them with a taste of water in this crisis of thirst. And as she was most earnestly pouring out her prayer to God with the deepest devotion of mind, a spring of water straight away broke forth close to her, sparkling clear, and, in answer to her prayers, by the grace of God, the dry rock gushed forth what it did not naturally contain: water, which was sufficient for the nuns' use and did not fail to supply their needs. And it flows without ceasing now and for ever more. Taking a drink from it, they gave thanks to God – and it is available still as a most effective cure for the sick. In addition, something worthy of record and incomparably wonderful is that the foot-prints that Æthelthryth made when going up and coming down were moulded in the side of the cliff as if in hot wax and are even now pointed out in glorification of our Lord Jesus Christ.

Now, if we carefully pay attention, we can ponder on four things inherent in this occurrence, all worth recalling as sufficiently deserving of our amazement. One is that God mercifully protected them from violent seizure by the king. Another is that the sea poured out its waters for their defence as if in place of a wall. The third: that a rugged rock provided water at

---

[113] Lat. *ut nec ad evadendum hostem vasta heremi solitudo peteretur*. The highly rhetorical notion here is that, whereas this desert place had just proved a refuge for some people escaping from an enemy, it was inaccessible now even for such people.

[114] Cf. Eadmer, *Vita Wilfridi*, p. 186.

the time of their thirst. The fourth: that the hardness of rock altered its usual character, as if forgetting its nature, and was able to become soft when the sole of one of her feet touched it.

We have not taken this from the writings of Bede, but all those who know the locality of Coldingham are witnesses to this fact by their affirming of it. For it had not been within the capacity of the blessed man, Bede, to remember, or hear, or imprint on his pages,[115] all the things, one by one, which were being done throughout England by all the saints in his time. Rather, he had made it his plan to commend to writing only those things[116] which had been long and frequently reported by devout and truthful people.[117] Having just done likewise, we return to our proposed themes. Truly, from what follows one may obtain firm attestation of the extent to which the blessed virgin after this was dogged by troubles and wearisome experiences up until the time when she reached the destination of her journeying: Ely.

12. A remarkable testimonial to her virginity.[118]

Therefore, let no one have doubts about Æthelthryth, this woman dedicated to God, feeling qualms about the assertion that after her royal husbands she remained an untouched virgin. This was the Lord's doing but, because these days one scarcely, if ever, has positive evidence of this happening among people who are married, we are astonished and it is a miracle in our sight. Also, what the sainted Bede wrote was in accordance with what he had learnt from the spoken evidence of Wilfrid, the most holy Archbishop of York, the physician Cynefrith and other truthful people, and the testimony of the general public, as well. Bede also had a remarkable piece of evidence for her untouched state which he committed to writing as follows. He stated that: 'although the truth about this virgin betrothed of Christ has been called into question by some people, the pontiff Wilfrid of blessed memory, when I personally made an enquiry, as to whether this was the case, told me that he was the most certain witness to her standing as *virgo intacta*, in as much as Ecgfrith had promised to give him many estates and many gifts of money, if he would persuade the Queen to consummate his marriage with her, because he knew that she loved no man better than him.'[119]

The chastity of this virgin – so very holy as she was – is something fit to

---

[115] *Cedis inprimere* (p. 28.25, ed. Blake).

[116] Reading conjecturally (p. 28.26, ed. Blake): <*non*> *nisi*.

[117] Reading: *et veridicis* for *a veridicis* (p. 28.27, ed. Blake)

[118] Source: expostulations by the compiler, or the author of his hagiographical source, on the foundation of a specific statement by Bede.

[119] Bede, *Hist. Eccl.* iv. 17 (19).

be the subject of preaching: it was her ally in adversity and her inseparable companion in prosperity. Never mind how people may take this: I have myself discovered from the testimony of the faithful, and it has come about that I know on the basis of written evidence, that in her lifetime she cured the lame, gave sight also to the blind and healed innumerable people in the name of Jesus. For she is a most highly sanctified virgin, and one of the number of the wise ones, having not known a sinful bed and having not departed with Dinah,[120] the daughter of Jacob, to visit the women of a region not her own, and having not at any time been overpowered by Shechem, son of Hamor, and given way to defilement – because her foundations were built on firm rock.

Nothing whatsoever of earthly substance pleased her by its appearance: rather, she despised a worldly kingdom and temporal splendour for the sake of the love of the Lord Jesus Christ, whom she loved above all things with her mind and with a pure heart, and by whom now she is given in return the crown of righteousness. And although she did not endure martyrdom, as it was a time of peace, nevertheless she is adorned with the glory of martyrdom, since, being in conflict with vices and desires, she continually carried the cross of the Lord in her bodily condition. I hope most confidently and trust that she is entirely acceptable to those who have washed their garments in the blood of the Lamb and for ever sing a new song most sweetly before the throne of God. Because, if she had been permitted to fight her battle in those days, under Nero[121] or Diocletian,[122] it is unquestionable that she would have climbed up on to the torturers' rack of her own accord, would have thrown herself into the flames of her own accord, would never have been afraid to have her limbs severed by threshing-wheels or saw-blades, and would by now certainly have been standing unmoved, not recanting her acknowledgement of the Lord in the face of all the punishments and torments to which human weakness usually gives in, so that she would have laughed in the midst of any tortures whatsoever, happy in her sores, rejoicing in her agonies. As it was, though she did not endure these things, she none the less achieved a bloodless martyrdom. For what sufferings from among the miseries of mankind did she not endure for her hope of the eternal? She suffered in hunger, in vigils, in nakedness, in care for the sick, in concern for those in danger, the reason being that it was only the sweetness of Heaven that she had loved upon earth, so that, in comparison with this, all the adversity and prosperity of the World became of little account.

---

[120] See Genesis 34.1ff.

[121] Roman Emperor, A. D. 54–68.

[122] Roman Emperor, A.D. 284–313.

13. How Æthelthryth set out for Ely, and what happened to her on the way.[123]

This is a well-known matter, related by our forefathers and so conveyed to us; it is something which the whole district in which it had happened remembers and recounts as if it were news of yesterday.

Well then, the hostility of King Ecgfrith, her former husband, was compelling Æthelthryth, the betrothed of the Lord, to move from the place where she entered seclusion for Christ's sake and to seek a dwelling-place elsewhere. And, taking with her the handmaidens of God who have been mentioned before, Sewenna and Sewara, she departed from the place and from the region, bearing in mind the teaching of the Lord: 'If people have persecuted you in one city, flee to another.'[124] Arriving at the river which is called the Humber, she made the crossing of its channel, thanks to the blowing[125] of a light breeze, and arrived successfully at the port of Wintringham. But, about ten furlongs[126] on from there, she turned aside for a little village called *Alftham*,[127] more or less surrounded by marshes, like an island, and, accompanied by the aforementioned girls, she sought and found lodgings. Staying there for a few days, she could not be inconspicuous because of the signs of her merits: she constructed a church for the Lord, in which, through her intercessions, many benefits are brought to the people who live there. From that place, the blessed virgin hastened on her way in humble attire, like one of Christ's pilgims, and so,[128] humbling herself for the Lord's sake not only in mind but also in clothing, she did not walk on the direct highway towards her destination: rather, she made her journey aside from the road, and so that she would not be caught by the would-be captors in pursuit of her[129] she made her way clandestinely. For she did not wish to reveal her secret to anyone or explain to anyone the reason for her journeying.

There came a time when she was walking in the burning heat of the

---

[123] Sources: Blake indicates no precise parallels in other sources for the data in this chapter. However, the opening paragraph proclaims the antiquity of the hagiographical material in it, which comprises local traditions from Coldingham and particular places in Lincolnshire. The story of 'Etheldreda's sprig' is still circulating in the oral tradition of Ely.

[124] Matthew 10.23.

[125] 'Blowing': *in pulsu* is interpreted here (p. 30.1, ed. Blake) as *impulsu*.

[126] Lat. *sed inde quasi stadiis decem ad viculum devertens* . . .

[127] Evidently this is West Halton, which has a church dedicated to St Etheldreda, and within whose boundaries, at Flixborough, archaeological excavation has shown the existence of a monastery from about 670.

[128] Here (p. 30.7, ed. Blake) *ut* may be a mistake for *et;* at any rate the *ut*-construction has been forgotten by the time *gradiebatur* is reached.

[129] Here (p. 30.9, ed. Blake) either *prosecuta* is understood as passive, as if *prosequor* were not deponent, or we should emend to *prosecutis.*

Sun, and exceedingly weary as the result of her unaccustomed exertion, she could scarcely stand. She therefore sought intently a shady, pleasant place, so that they might cool their bosoms, drenched as they were with sweat, and reinvigorate their weary limbs with new strength. And her prayer was not unavailing: no, its swift effectiveness yielded the desired result, and, as she continued on her way at a slow pace, it was arranged by God's grace that she happened upon[130] a place nearby, suitable as a stopping-place for travellers, a remarkably flat meadow – you would have thought it had been levelled deliberately – sprinked all about with flowers of various colours. She made for the longed-for place, saw it to be agreeable, was delighted that it was possible to stop there, to breathe in with pleasure wonderful, flower-scented draughts of air.[131] The saintly traveller, delighted by the pleasantness of the place, desired to stop there for a little while, refresh herself for a little while, so that, once the strength of her weary limbs was restored, she might complete the remainder of her journey. Then she settled herself down and fell asleep. And there she slept for a while in the place where tiredness had compelled her to sleep.

My narrative now, the matter of which I desire to inform you, is miraculous: no one of those who hear it doubts its truth. When, after a little while, she woke up from her sleep and rose to her feet, she found that her travelling-staff, the end of which she had driven into the ground, dry and long-seasoned, was now clothed with green bark, and had sprouted and put forth[132] leaves. Seeing this, she was stupefied with amazement and, along with her companions, she praised God and blessed him for this most extraordinary happening from her innermost heart.

Yet you should not by any means[133] reckon this a fiction: all the people of the district in fact know about it, and attest that it is perfectly true. Certainly we have not discovered this in history books, but compelled by such unassailable evidence, we are not omitting it from our compilation. Likewise, all the things which Jesus did which are not in the books of the Gospels: supposing they should be recorded later by someone, can they for this reason be proved not to be true?

The wooden staff grew, then, and became the biggest ash tree of all the trees in that region and to this day there are many of our people who have seen it. The place is called to this day *Ædeldrethestowe*, which means 'the resting-place of Æthelthryth'. A church was constructed there in honour of

---

[130] Reading with EB: *offendit*.

[131] Strange Latin: a rhetorical rhyming effect – *videt delectabilem, iuvat pausabilem* – seems to take precedence over normal syntax.

[132] Reading (p. 30.26, ed. Blake): *prodidisse* for *prodisse*.

[133] Taking *nequamquam* (p. 30.28, ed. Blake) to be equivalent to, if not a mistake for, *nequaquam*.

the blessed virgin, to the glory of our Lord Jesus Christ, who is a source of wonder among the saints.

14. That the church at Coldingham was destroyed by fire after her departure.[134]

Not long after the departure of the venerable Æthelthryth, the monastic community of virgins which had been situated at Coldingham, in which she received the habit of the religious life, went up in flames. Carelessness was to blame. However, everyone who knew the place could easily recognize that it had happened as the result of the ill-nature of those who dwelt in it, and particularly those who seemed to be the more important of them – a fact which we are certainly not passing over without comment. But those who were to be punished did not lack a warning from the Divine Pity, and as a result of this rebuke they were in the position to avert anger from themselves, by fasting, weeping and prayer, in a manner reminiscent of the righteous judge of the people of Nineveh.[135]

There was, you see, in the monastery in question a man from the race of the Scots, Adamnan by name, living a life of great devotion to God in chastity and prayerfulness. When occupied, one night, in vigils and psalms, he suddenly saw standing before him someone with a face he did not recognize, who, because Adamnan was terrified at his presence, told him not to be afraid and, speaking to him in what seemed a friendly voice, said: 'You do well not to yield to sleep at the time of nocturnal rest, and instead to persist in vigils and prayers and in sedulously making intercession to God. While making a systematic survey of the whole of this monastery, I have just inspected the beds of individuals and I have found no one except you alone occupied to the benefit of the health of his soul. Instead, without exception, all the men and women are either sleeping – idle and unconscious – or else they are awake for sinful purposes. Even the virgin women dedicated to God, in contempt of the solemnity of their profession, are adorning <themselves> like brides[136] – thereby endangering their status – or acquiring the friendship of men outside the walls. Hence, with good reason, vengeance from Heaven with fierce flames has been prepared for this place and its inhabitants.' Adamnan soon took it upon himself to tell this to the mother of the congregation, whose name was Ebba. It was she, as we have said, who had received the God-deserving Æthelthryth into the religious life and had nurtured and educated her as an adopted daughter. But, perturbed for good reason by a prophecy such as this, she said: 'Why have you not wanted to

---

[134] Source: almost entirely from Bede, *Hist. Eccl.* iv. 23 (25).

[135] See Jonah, chapters 3–4.

[136] Reading, in line with Bede, *Hist. Eccl.* iv. 23 (25): <*seipsas*> *ad vicem sponsarum in periculum sui status adornant*. Note that mss. EB are closer to Bede than F.

reveal this experience to me sooner?' He answered, 'I was afraid for the sake of Your Reverence, fearing that you would be excessively troubled. But yet, you will have the consolation that this blow is not to be inflicted in your time.'

When this vision became general knowledge, the residents of the place were a little afraid for a few days and began to chastise themselves, giving up their misdeeds. But, after the death of the abbess herself, they went back to their former filthiness; no indeed, they committed even worse crimes. And at a time when they were saying, 'Peace and security',[137] all of a sudden they were smitten by the punishment of the vengeance to which we have referred. Alas! Undoubtedly the revelation of their overthrow had come upon them swiftly because they did not deserve to be viewed favourably[138] for their association with a most beloved virgin. Frustrated by her presence, they had remained incorrigible in their wicked and perverse activities. As a result, we recognize that, just as Bede relates, these people who had neither been prompted by a divine warning to change their ways, nor pricked by contrition at the devout conduct of the venerable Æthelthryth, brought both themselves and the place to perdition, because of the enormity of their crimes. But bear this in mind, readers and listeners: I have not written this without very great pain and fear. For the setting apart of good people is always the downfall of those who are utterly bad.

15. That the blessed Æthelthryth on {the Isle of} Ely, returned to her own estate, and there assembled a community of both sexes, subject to a monastic pattern of life; also, who the people were, with whose aid she founded the church there.[139]

Meanwhile, Æthelthryth, virgin of the Lord, a year after she had taken the veil of sanctity, returned, by way of many travelling difficulties and a variety of hardships, to Ely, that is,[140] to her own estate. She arrived at Ely, and her own estate, which she had received from Tondberht, her first husband, predestined for her, and to be held by her in perpetuity, by virtue of the legal settlement on her of a marriage-gift – no, rather, by divine agency. Together with her were the handmaids of the Lord previously mentioned. They remained by her side, sharers in her sweated toils, both throughout the time when they were in the king's realm, and throughout the time they were

---

[137] 1 Thessalonians 5.3.

[138] Taking *suffragari* as passive in meaning, as if it were not a deponent.

[139] The chapter-heading as in E is translated. Sources: hagiography with parallels in *Vita S. Ætheldrede* CD, chapter 7, ed. Love; Bede, *Hist. Eccl.* iv. 17 (19); Bull of Pope Victor confirming earlier privileges (see *LE* ii. 93); chronicles, e.g. *Anglo-Saxon Chronicle* and *Worcester Chronicle*, on the year 673; local tradition.

[140] Reading, with E, *videlicet*.

travelling through many out-of-the-way places, and they endured many dangers along with her.

Well now, it fell to the lot of Æthelthryth, servant of Jesus Christ, to dwell in this same place {Ely}, and there, after being received with due honour, she took possession of the Isle and had free disposal of it as her lawful property – and for evermore, with Christ as her Bishop, she illuminates it and keeps it in her embrace by the bestowal of gracious gifts. There followed her a praiseworthy man by the name of Huna, a holy priest who gave her advice pertaining to salvation and talked to her about the teachings and deeds of the saints. There will need to be mention of him at a later stage. But now it is a good moment to give a preliminary account of the status and name of the place, so that the reader may more readily observe in what ways, or by what people, it was in need of restoration.

Elge does not, in fact, as some people reckon, belong to Cambridgeshire. Rather, it is in fact called, in accordance with Bede's information, 'a region[141] of the East Angles, by virtue of its importance and size, consisting as it does of about six-hundred hides. It is surrounded like an island by marshes and stretches of water called 'meres', and moreover it is from the abundance of eels which are caught in these same marshes that it took its name.'[142] Now that this name has been changed by way of improvement, it is called 'Ely',[143] on the reasoning that it is a dwelling worthy of God, for which His name is appropriate, or, as some people assert, from two Hebrew words, 'el', 'ge', since 'el' means 'God', and 'ge', 'land', and the compound has the resonance, 'God's Land'. It is appropriate, you see, that such a name should be used to designate an island which at the beginning of Christian faith in England soon began to believe in the Lord Jesus and worship Him.

Æthelthryth, the aforementioned handmaid of Christ, wished to have a monastic community there, since her descent, according to the flesh, was from the province of these same East Angles, as we have said earlier.[144] Furthermore, her life there became well known to all the people living over a large area, thanks to her spirit of prophecy and all her great miracles, because the Lord, the 'Sun of Righteousness',[145] illuminated her with the splendour of His brightness and He had placed perfection upon the mountain of her virtues, so that she should shine forth to all. As her felicitous merits became manifest, a great many people vied to live under her rule; they also handed over their daughters to be educated by her. Many people of both sexes made their way to her, and, as they did so, they began to be kindled with a

---

[141] Lat. *regio*.

[142] Bede, *Hist. Eccl.* iv. 17 (19).

[143] See above (p. 3) on the text at p. 2.11, ed. Blake.

[144] From Bede, *Hist. Eccl.* iv. 17 (19).

[145] Malachi 4.2.

yearning for eternal life – following her example in this – and subjected themselves to the service of the almighty Lord under her instruction. Amongst them there arrived Wærburh, virgin of the Lord, the daughter of Eormenhild who was the daughter of her sister St Seaxburh, and she received and learnt from St Æthelthryth the rule of the religious life. And so the blessed mother, seeing that lay-people were hurrying eagerly to come to her, praised the Lord and urged them all individually towards spiritual advancement, saying that the pattern of this life was passing away, and that the true life was the one which was purchased by hardship in the life of today.

At that time, I should explain, there had not yet been any church on the island other than one founded by the blessed Augustine, the apostle of the English, but later demolished right to ground level by the army of the unbelieving King Penda. This church Æthelthryth, lover of God, laboured with all her might to renew and rebuild after its prolonged desolation. And as soon as it was rebuilt, dedicated, as of old, in honour of Mary, the holy Mother of God, it became a shining light, through innumerable signs and miracles, as God carried out His work every day. She then adorned the grounds of the place most handsomely with monastic buildings. In point of fact, the remains of the previous foundation had been demolished, and so the buildings provided were all new. But so great is the liberty and free status which the place perpetually commands that it was not challenged by any of the kings of England, nor by any king of a neighbouring tribe, nor falsely alleged to be subject to any legal obligation whatsoever: rather it was considered, and consistently remained, a free 'region'. The only person, moreover, who at that time exercised episcopal jurisdiction there was the pontiff Wilfrid, whom the virgin, when queen, had favoured and singled out above all other people in her realm, and employed in those days as the supplier of her needs. It was by Wilfrid, as one reads in Bede, that she was made abbess.[146]

It was decreed, therefore, in the proper manner, by all the people who were the lay and ecclesiastical leaders of England at that time – that with regard to[147] the Isle of Ely, which the same consecrated woman, Æthelthryth, had taken possession of as a marriage-portion but now had assigned for the service of God – the liberty of the place should not be diminished or destroyed in future by either king or bishop. That this was confirmed by the authority of a great many popes is proved by the authority of the Bull of Pope Victor,[148] as we shall relate, inserting a full account in the appropriate places. But first, we need to attend to the full exposition of the history on which we

---

[146] This is not specifically stated by Bede, in *Hist. Eccl.* iv. 17 (19), where, however, it is recorded that it was from Wilfrid that she received the veil.

[147] The Latin is loosely constructed: *ut insulam . . . libertas loci diminueretur . . .* (p. 33.17, ed. Blake).

[148] For the text of this Bull see *LE* ii. 93.

have started work.

Well, after a little while, Æthelthryth, being a woman of extreme devotion to God, built there, with the help of her brother mentioned earlier, King Aldwulf, a good-sized[149] monastic house of female virgins dedicated to God, and she began to be a virgin mother, both in the exemplary character of her life and the guidance she gave, and she made a settlement assigning the island in its entirety for their purposes, and, with the help of her beloved Wilfrid, sent it to be confirmed by the approval of the Apostolic Father in Rome, to the end that those living their lives in Ely in the service of God should remain living in accordance with a rule, free from all financial hardship, without the harrassment of any tax official.

How just are the arrangements of God the Creator! A virgin woman was placed in charge of virgins – in line with the fact that, at the passion of Christ on the cross, a virgin was entrusted to a virgin – so that, living by a vow, they should reign together with the virgin Lord, having garnered a hundred-fold harvest. Nor, indeed, are you to think there was[150] less power for good in the large community of women living there who for God's sake had been victors over the nature of their sex and over worldliness, than that which you recognize as having been possessed by the people who in ancient times removed themselves from human social relations. For all of them in that place held to one and the same rule: outstanding virtue, and their priorities were: obedience, a love of divine worship and the guarding of the beauty of the house of God with all watchfulness.

The information is found in English and Latin chronicles that, in the 673rd year from the incarnation of the Lord, Æthelthryth began building-works in Ely and in a short while collected a community of God-fearing people of both sexes living subject to the direction of a rule. So Bede wrote, saying that, on the occasion of the translation of this same godly virgin, 'all the congregation – brothers on one side, sisters on the other – singing psalms, stood around'[151] her burial-place. From this, one understands that men and women were living a celibate life together in the same monastery at the same time, and we recognize that the same arrangement as had been decreed by her was maintained in the church for a very long time, until the Danes ransacked the monastery and the land. That the same was also the practice at Coldingham and in many churches of the English in that period the *History of the English People* attests.

---

[149] The Latin adjective used, *maiore*, which might mean 'largish', 'larger' or 'very large' is, unlike the surrounding sentence, not from Bede, *Hist. Eccl.* iv. 17 (19).

[150] At p. 33.30ff., ed. Blake, *esse* etc. have to be interpreted as historic presents, because of the use of the feminine gender.

[151] Bede, *Hist. Eccl.* iv. 17 (19).

BOOK I

16. How Æthelthryth was made abbess in Ely by St Wilfrid.[152]

Now, Wilfrid, holy man of the Lord, did not forget the blessed virgin, and did not exclude himself from the reciprocation of her love. On having heard that she had gone down to Ely, he went flying to her side in all haste. He talked about[153] things beneficial for her soul, the health of her mind, what characterizes a turn to the religious life. Then he consecrated her, in the office of abbess, and also consecrated the community which had been brought together there.[154] He established the place with its own constitution, and showed himself solicitous in every respect, and there for some time he spent his life, in a way useful not only to himself but to all those also resident there, and Æthelthryth herself received from him a great deal of advice about rulership, and solace in her life.

The blessed virgin was intoxicated with heavenward meditation, stretching forth a hand generous in almsgiving, delighting in long periods of continuous prayer and practising frequent vigils, as one finds more fully expounded in the words of Bede. And yet the fact is that, from the time that she became a monastic postulant, she never wished to wear linen clothing, only woollen, and refused to bathe in hot baths except when the major festivals – specifically, Easter, Pentecost and Epiphany – were imminent, and when she did, she was last of all to bathe, after the other handmaids of Christ who were in that place had been washed with her assistance and that of her serving-women. For it was not necessary for one whose heart was washed clean to have her body washed. She also used to protect the congregation committed to her with continuous prayers, and used to urge it on heavenward by most salutary counsels and, what is more, she herself gave, by her actions, an exemplary lead as to what ought to be done. And so the pious mother nurtured her sweet children with the sweetness of Christ amidst perpetual loving-kindness. In her great fervour she led them all on in her company to the crown of glory. She personally displayed to them an exemplar of humility and kindness, and her life of service provided an admonition to practise the virtue of abstinence. For rarely, except in the case of major festivals or particularly pressing need, would she have eaten more than once a day, for she fled from immoderate satiation of the belly as if from a dreadful plague and, unless a particularly serious illness had prevented this, she would have remained in church after the night office, intent on prayers, from the time of the service right until sunrise. How many bendings of the knee, how many contrite confessions of her innermost heart she offered up, is

[152] Sources: Bede, *Hist. Eccl.* iv. 17 (19); hagiography with parallels in *Vita S Ætheldrede* CD, chapters 7, 8, ed. Love.
[153] *Tractatur*: deponent.
[154] See Blake p. 34, n. 2, questioning the reliability of this tradition.

known to Him who is the receiver of prayers, the possessor and helper of untouched virginity.

17. That, under her, Wærburh, virgin of the Lord, received the habit of the religious life in Ely.[155]

Now, at that time Wulfhere, King of the Mercians, the son of Penda, had departed this life. It was he who first received the faith and baptism of holy rebirth in that kingdom, and overthrew the worship of demons everywhere among his people, and ordered that the name of Christ be preached everywhere throughout his kingdom, and built churches in many places. In addition he made that famous monastery *Medehamstede*, now called *Burc* {Peterborough}, very rich in estates and ornaments,[156] through the intermediacy of Seaxwulf, who was the first abbot and founder of the place, and afterwards Bishop of the Mercians, likewise under his kingly rule. King Wulfhere's queen, Eormenhild, the daughter of Eorconberht, King of the Kentish people, and Queen Seaxburh, bore him a daughter, St Wærburh, a virgin endowed with great virtues.[157] After her father's death, Wærburh renounced the World and, with a view to receiving the habit of the holy life, entered the monastery of her great-aunt – the blessed Æthelthryth, that is – where through God's action, she performed many miracles.

Now, the brothers of King Wulfhere were: Æthelred, who in succession to him wielded the sceptre of the kingdom; another was Peada, who held the kingdom of the Southern Angles, but he was very foully murdered, through treachery on the part of his wife, at the very time of the Easter festival; a third was Merewald, who held a kingdom in the western part of Mercia. His queen, St Eormenburh, the daughter of King Eormenred, bore him three daughters, namely St Milburh, St Milgith and St Mildrith, and one son, called Merewine, a boy of outstanding holiness.

18. About the arrival of the blessed Seaxburh in Ely.[158]

Many people, indeed, of varying dignity and age, had come to gather around the venerable Abbess Æthelthryth in that monastic community, desiring to

---

[155] Sources: hagiography with parallels in *Vita S. Werburge* and *Lectiones in festivitate sancte Werburge virginis*, ed. Love; *Worcester Chronicle* on the year 675, supplemented by extra material on Peterborough.

[156] Lat. *ornamenta*, comprising church plate, vestments, hangings, soft-furnishings and statues.

[157] Lat. *magnarum virginem virtutum*.

[158] Sources: unidentified local source on Huna, cf. *LE* i. 22; hagiography, with parallels in *Vita S. Sexburge* AT, chapters 14, 15, 18, 19, ed. Love.

live under her rule. And when any distinguished men, noble women, or anyone at all of younger age, renounced wordly activities and asked to be received, the statutory requirements of the church that were set before them were very demanding, and they recognized that the exertions of monastic discipline were heavy, this being a place where discipline was particularly fervent in its severity. Nevertheless,[159] the men and women who were received there had not asked[160] to live under easier rules, discouraged by these terrors, but rather would eagerly grasp at total obedience, so as[161] never to escape anything by refusal, however arduous and difficult it might be. Among them was St Huna, her priest, a man of great humility. He made his vows there and in a short time he became outstanding in his exercising of the mighty powers of virtue: being someone with a great capacity for fasting, conspicuous in humility and steadfast in faith, he had easily come to equal the monks of antiquity in their religious ardour. Hence he was considered by a good many people, including even the mother of the community herself, as worthy of the greatest honour and love.

Furthermore, even Seaxburh, the mother of saints and the sister of the same most blessed mother Æthelthryth, contemplating the desolation which, according to an oracle which she had received from an angel of God, was to come about in her kingdom, made up her mind to adopt a life of very great poverty and to put herself under another person's authority, considering it incongruous that she should be ruling over others when she had not previously herself learnt to be a subordinate.

Accordingly, in her capacity as a mother, she summoned her daughters, her companions in Christ, [as an abbess she summoned her nuns],[162] and announced to them her desire and resolve, saying, 'My daughters, I leave you, as your guardian, Jesus, and the holy angels attendant on the Bridegroom. I also appoint my daughter Eormenhild to be your mother, so that your hearts may be encouraged by her advice and educated with celestial things in view by her salutary practices of discipline. As for me, I <wish>[163] to visit East Anglia, within the borders of which I was raised, in order to be educated under the instruction of my glorious sister Æthelthryth, to receive an initiation into the principles of her monastic rule, to participate, certainly, in her labours, intending also to be a sharer in her rewards.' Then, when she had provided for them in beneficial and honourable ways, she travelled all

---

[159] The complexities of the sentence, 'Et cum quidem . . . diffugerent', have had to be dismantled and reconstructed for the purpose of English translation: 'nevertheless' here compensates for the omission of anything equivalent to licet (p. 35.28, ed. Blake).

[160] Reading (at p. 35.31, ed. Blake), in line with the reading of E: poposcerunt or poposcerant.

[161] Following the reading of E: ut, as opposed to at (p. 36.1, ed. Blake).

[162] An explanatory addition by F.

[163] A necessary supplement <volo> is here (p. 36.14f., ed. Blake) supplied by a second hand in the margin of E.

the way to Ely and the whole Isle rejoiced at her arrival. Queen greeted queen; sister conducted sister within, amid festive dancing. They wept profusely for joy, and, as there was true love between them, a double happiness resulted. For these women were full of delight in the sweetness of Heaven and each in turn was providing the other with solace. That wealthy woman, Seaxburh, came from a position of authority to one of subjection, from the position of teacher to that of disciple, seeking from her blessed sister a pattern of discipline and humility, as St Paul sought learning at the feet of Gamaliel.[164] The blessed sisters, allied to one another in unity of faith, following in all things the way of God's commandments, made it their aim to complete the course which was God's pleasure, and they set about progressing and growing in holy virtues[165] until their life's end.

19. That St Æthelthryth had a prophetic inspiration, and that Wilfrid went on a journey to Rome but on his return learnt that she had died.[166]

From this time onwards, miracles became more frequent, signs became more numerous, and the hand of the Almighty was stretched forth so as to demonstrate at a higher level the merits of the virgin Æthelthryth. Meanwhile, as she exercised herself day by day in progressively greater feats of virtuous strength, she became endowed with incredible power and so began to work every day unheard-of miracles involving the casting out of demons from possessed bodies. She did this not only when personally present, and not only by her word, but also, sometimes, in her absence, upon the invocation of her name. Every day, numerous people were rescued from diverse deaths and, in a wonderful manner, she was visited by throngs of people, was revered by all and was loved by everyone. And it is a fact that, by virtue of prophetic inspiration, she had foretold even the plague by which she herself was to die, and she had announced,[167] in the presence of all, even the number of people who were to be snatched from her own monastic community and from the World. And she gave counsel to their souls that they should spurn the things of the World more fervently and seek after those of Heaven. Nor was the virgin's assertion proved vain, when the particular women whose own departure she had foretold to them in the monastery, after a little lapse of time found rest in the sleep of peace.

[164] See Acts of the Apostles 22.3.

[165] That they were acquiring miraculous powers too is implied by this reference to the 'virtues'.

[166] Sources: Bede, *Hist. Eccl.* iv. 13 and 17 (19); *Worcester Chronicle* on the year 679; material of unknown origin, including, maybe, the compiler's unsupported inferences.

[167] The compiler, adapting Bede, *Hist. Eccl.* iv. 17 (19), replaced *praedixerit* (perfect subjunctive) *with praedixerat* (pluperfect indicative), but then evidently by mistake kept *intimaverit* unaltered; the translation assumes that he meant *intimaverat* (p. 37.4, ed. Blake).

Last of them all, in point of fact, the most blessed Æthelthryth, who had sent virgin servants ahead to her heavenly home to be reinstated there, was overcome by very grave sickness, so that she might follow after them, to be crowned with an immortal diadem in the heavens. And she it was who founded the monastery of Ely, in which, as we have said, she directed choruses of virgins under the discipline of a rule in a most honourable manner for seven successive years. And so, instructed by the Holy Spirit, the bountiful virgin, who was to bring forth for God a progeny of virgins, undertook to rule a monastery which for evermore stands consecrated by her presence, and just as in the body she was illustrious thanks to the holiness of her life, so she is now too after her death thanks to the power of God. Many remarkable miracles of hers are reported, certainly, and it has not been possible for them to be hidden. For indeed, in the course of avoiding ostentation, she concealed some of them, and did not allow them to reach people's notice, being a woman who, having transcended the human condition and concentrated her mind on virtue alone, was content with Heaven alone as her witness, trampling underfoot the glory of the World. We are able to reckon this the truth, assuredly, on the strength of the things which we have discovered and which could not be concealed.

Archbishop Wilfrid had been suffering exile for the previous three years,[168] as Bede writes, for, because of the rise of disagreement between him and King Ecgfrith, he was expelled by him from his episcopal see. During this time he stayed at Ely with the most blessed Æthelthryth, where as long as he lived – at that time and whenever there had been pressing need which called for it – he exercised the rights of his episcopal office. From there, having been provided with assistance for the journey, he travelled to Rome, where, by the judgement of Pope Benedict[169] and many others, he was found to be worthy of a bishopric. He returned to Britain and converted the province of the South Saxons to belief in Christ. Moreover, he brought from Rome privileges for the protection of certain communities which, having been carefully and attentively preserved until our own time, are recognized as bringing great stability to the places in question. He received also from the same Pope, in accordance with his wishes and with a request which the distinguished mother Æthelthryth had made, a privilege relating to the monastery of Ely, so that by the authority of St Peter, it might be established more securely against the assaults of wicked men. And this was done.

It was that same year, while Wilfrid was staying there, as one reads in the chronicles, that Æthelthryth, who had long been prophesying her end, is

---

[168] Caution: see Blake, p. 37, n. 3, on the chronology of this part of Wilfrid's life. According to Bede (*Hist. Eccl.* iv. 13), he wandered 'through many places' during his exile.

[169] Caution again: see Blake, p. 37, n. 4. Bede and Eddius Stephanus state that the pope in question was Agatho (678–81). The source being used here is the *Worcester Chronicle* on the year 679. The dates of Pope Benedict II were 684–5.

reported to have departed this life. For he heard of her falling asleep a few days afterwards, upon the arrival of a messenger.

20. That when she fell ill she repented in the presence of all.[170]

Well then, as the time was approaching when the Lord would raise up His beloved betrothed to the ineffable joy of the celestial homeland, rescuing her from the snares of this woeful life, she was afflicted with a swelling of the jaw, and pain in the neck, the reason being that she had a very large tumour underneath her jaw. And, as the discomfort of her intensifying pain increased, her body was laid on a bed in order for it to be treated with more liquid foods. For that swelling was inflicting upon her to a greatly increased extent stabs of severe pain. But, nevertheless, intent on her customary praying, she gave thanks to God, who scourges and corrects everyone whom He loves.[171] The household grieved; everyone groaned. The populace was afraid of losing its lady; the band of virgins, its distinguished mother; the poor, a generous distributor of alms; the clergy, a prolific worker of miracles. And, at the time when she was afflicted by the aforesaid swelling, it is related that she took great delight in the fact that her illness was of this kind, embracing it with all alacrity, as if it were an object of delight and a glorious adornment, and she was accustomed to say, 'I know with the greatest certainty that it is deservedly that I carry the weight of suffering upon my neck, on which I remember when I was very young I used to wear the futile incumbrances of necklaces. For youthful years induced in me the habit of adorning my neck with necklaces: hence I give praises and thanks to the Divine Pity that my pain is coming from the place where I was accustomed to arrange a delightful glitter. And I believe that the Supernal Pity has wished me to suffer from neck-pain, so that I may be absolved from the accusation of vain levity, so long as the redness and inflammation of the swelling protudes from my neck in place of gold and pearls.'

21. How, weighed down by very great sufferings, she gave up her spirit to Heaven on the third day.[172]

And so, as a result of the fact that the most precious virgin, amid the most splendid triumphs of her precious life, gave the glory to God and was fervently desirous of seeing the most serene face of her Maker, her obedience

---

[170] Sources: Bede, *Hist. Eccl.* iv. 17 (19); hagiography with parallels in *Vita S. Ætheldrede* CD, chapter 8, ed. Love.

[171] Hebrews 12.6.

[172] Sources: Bede, *Hist. Eccl.* iv. 17 (19); *De Temporibus* (cf. *LE* i. 34 below); hagiography, cf. *Vita S. Ætheldrede* CD, chapters 9–10, ed. Love; *Worcester Chronicle* on the year 679; allusion to Pseudo-Ambrose, *Sermones* 20.6.

was not defrauded of its prize, nor her long waiting, of its heavenly reward. But now, as the discomfort of her bodily parts increased more and more, people were keen to seek the aid of a medical practitioner, or, if they could, to assuage and remove the discomfort of the pain. In actual fact, a certain medical practioner called Cynefrith was summoned from among the people standing around her, the aim being that the virgin's pain might be relieved by him, and he was ordered to lance that swelling, so that the harmful liquid which was in it might flow out. While[173] he was doing this, she seemed for two days to feel somewhat relieved, with the result that many people thought she could be cured of her illness and could now avert death by this sort of remedy. For indeed, the swelling issued forth liquid, and the inflammation lessened a little for two days. All rejoiced, but the providence of God unexpectedly put an end to their sudden rejoicings. To resume: it is usual for the third day to be particularly serious for people with wounds and to give rise to more extensive sufferings for those afflicted,[174] and the Lord wished His virgin to reign with Him in the heavenly kingdom. So it was on the third day that, being overwhelmed by her earlier sufferings and sensing that her temporal death was imminent, she instructed the whole congregation to come to her, signalling now the time and hour of her summoning, just as before she had foretold the particular day. Moreover – as far as the severity of her illness allowed – she even poured forth the sweetness of the heavenly teaching in which she abounded, and the words of life eternal. Her advice to them[175] was that they should never let their souls despair of things supernal, and that, while sighing, they should taste the sweet food of celestial happiness in the love of Christ, which, while they were living in the flesh, they had not been able perfectly to apprehend. Indeed, in giving such counsels of salvation, she did not allow herself now to hear or say anything except what constitutes the love of Christ. For, presenting herself before the face of Christ, her beloved betrothed, with all her soul and might, she made urgent entreaties with hymns and psalms, demanding that her spirit be taken up by the holy angels. Then she fortified herself for departure with the body and blood of the Lord, and most earnestly besought Him to be propitious for evermore, and a guardian in perpetuity over the inhabitants of the place. While this was going on, she was suddenly snatched from the World, entrusting her spirit to the hands of the Creator and, as is written in the *Book of Histories* of the priest Bede, 'she exchanged all her pain and death for perpetual salvation and life'.

When[176] she departed this life, it came to pass that the monastery of Ely turned to face an exceedingly sad state of desolation and grief. For there arose

---

[173] Reading with *LE* mss. *dum* (p. 39.3, ed. Blake), whereas Bede *(loc. cit.)* has *cum*.

[174] E has *affectis* (p. 39.8, ed. Blake) as opposed to *afflictis* (F). Both mean much the same.

[175] The feminine plural pronoun *eas* is used.

[176] Reading at p. 39.24, ed. Blake: *cum* (E) rather than *dum* (F).

great mourning and weeping of brothers and sisters who, not without cause, could bewail their mistress and patroness most bitterly, for a long time. But the holy and glorious virgin, led forth from the prison-house of the flesh, was conducted into the heavenly bridal chamber to the embraces of the eternal King, following in the footsteps of the Lamb amongst the troops of virgins. Now that the fires of the flesh had been defeated, this[177] blessed soul – to whom the ethereal heights lay open and who deservedly acquired the ability to know in advance, and prophesy, the joys to come – rejoices with the angels. For away from the desert of the present age, with choruses of angels accompanying her on this side and on that, she ascended, wholly beautiful, wholly immaculate, and the daughters of Zion, seeing her, declared her most blessed and glorious, and queens praised her. The virgin Æthelthryth was snatched away to the Lord, in the midst of her own people, on 23rd June, seven years after she had received the rank of an abbess, and equally she was buried, as she had ordered, in the midst of her own people, following the order in which they had passed away, in a wooden coffin. She passed away, then, from 'the muddy turbulence of this World'[178] to the joys of the Kingdom of Heaven, in the 679th year from the incarnation of the Lord, when her brother Aldwulf was ruling as King of the East Angles, and Hlothhere, the son of her sister St Seaxburh, as King of the people of Kent. And happily positioned at the right hand of Christ, her beloved Espoused, she is present in the sight of the most sublime Father as a constant intermediary on behalf of all of us.

How happy [[art thou]], blessed virgin, who, living without corruption, knowest not corruptibility even when entombed! Now there shines out in thee the glory of the Resurrection! In thy changed state, thou hast a share in the risen Christ! For the sign of the divine miracle whereby the woman's buried flesh, as Bede attests,[179] was incapable of decaying, is additional evidence that she remained throughout uncorrupted by masculine contact.

Consequently, after her death, during the time that her bones remained in the coffin of her burial, she did not refrain idly from the giving of signs: no, truly, she shone forth brightly and was soon famous all around for the frequency of her miracles. For various people suffering from bodily illness, when they asked in faith at her tomb for assistance, vied with one another in praising the mighty works of Christ, as their health had been restored. Some people, indeed, when they were in the grip of some particularly severe illness, were advised in dreams to go with haste to her burial-place and, when they with all speed arrived there, they earned the reward of receiving the benefits of celestial healing. As the result of this, various sufferings and

[177] Reading conjecturally (p. 39.29, ed. Blake) *ea* in place of *et* before *beata anima*.
[178] Reminiscence of Pseudo-Ambrose, *Sermones* 20.6.
[179] Bede, *Hist. Eccl.* iv. 17 (19).

demons were put to flight and suppliants had their prayers answered, through our Lord Jesus Christ, who with God the Father and the Holy Spirit lives and reigns throughout all ages. AMEN.

22. About the holy priest Huna.[180]

In this period, there was a holy priest, Huna, who was from the order of monks and is said to have been the priest of the bountiful Æthelthryth. He it was, so it is reported, who celebrated the funeral of the holy Mother, along with that venerable community, amid tears and the greatest lamentation; and, in addition, a throng of lay-people of differing stations in life and differing ages had assembled, who had received many benefits from her in her lifetime. And he it was who buried her, not in carved stone or with a covering of gold-bedecked arches, but, in accordance with an order received from her, in the cemetery of the church, next to her own people. And, after the awesome[181] demise of Æthelthryth, Huna did not remain at the church, but retreated to a certain smallish island in the fen near Ely which is called *Huneia*[182] from his name, choosing the solitary life, and fought out his fight for God, devoting his time entirely to silence. And there, so long as he lived, he led a glorious life, something which was well known to everyone over a wide area. Numerous witnesses testify that, on going to his tomb with the aim of regaining their health, many people made a recovery thanks to his merits. Recognizing this, some people secretly transported his body, in a coffin which was later broken, across to Thorney and reburied it, hoping, with the help of his intercession, to obtain grace and mercy from the Lord.

23. That a certain retainer of the blessed virgin could not be held in chains, because of the sacrifice of the mass with its saving power.[183]

In the year when the Lord promoted his worshipful virgin Æthelthryth to the everlasting glory of the life of Heaven from this corruptible life, something miraculous and amazing happened which concerned a retainer of hers, and Bede realized that it ought to be recounted for the salvation of many.

---

[180] Source: local traditions about St Æthelthryth and the priest Huna, from sources unidentified by Blake, are specifically localized at *Huneia* and Thorney.

[181] The adjective used is *venerabilis*.

[182] Blake p. 41, n. 1, citing Reaney, *The Place names of Cambridgeshire and the Isle of Ely*, p. 249, identifies this with Honey Hill, Chatteris. But note that 'Honey Hill' is a name found six times in Cambridgeshire (Reaney, *op. cit.*, p. 166).

[183] Source: the main narrative (paragraphs 2–5 of this translation) epitomizes Bede, *Hist. Eccl.* iv. 20 (22), adding one detail unattested there; para 6: local traditions on Huna (cf. *LE* i. 22); Bede, *Hist. Eccl.* iv. 3 (on Owine); miracle narrative on *Ælgetus*, related in *LE* ii. 94 and included also in ms. B *(Book of Miracles)*.

There was, in point of fact, a grievous battle fought near the River Trent between Ecgfrith, King of the Northumbrians, long previously the husband of this same virgin, and Æthelred, King of the Mercians; Ælfwine, the brother of King Ecgfrith – whose sister Osthryth, was the wife of King Æthelred – was killed in it. From Ælfwine's army there fell, among others, a young man called Ymma. He lay for a day and the following night as if dead, but eventually revived, getting his breath back, and bound up his own wounds as best he could. Then he stood up and began to walk, but he was quickly captured by men from the enemy army, and was brought to their lord, that is, a high-ranking retainer[184] of King Æthelred.

Now, the king's retainer, receiving him, took care of his wounds, and when he began to recover, gave orders that he should be held in chains, so that he would not run away. But he could not be kept chained. No, as soon as the men who had chained him had begun to walk away his chains were unfastened. Meanwhile, the king's retainer became amazed and started to ask questions as to why he could not be chained. He replied, 'I have a brother, called Tunna, a priest and the abbot of a monastery in a city which is called *Tunnacester* after him, and <I know>[185] that he is celebrating frequent masses for me, believing me to have been killed, and, if I were now in the other life, my soul would be released from punishments there by his intercession.'

Well, as he could not be held in chains, the king's retainer sold him to a certain Friesian bound for London,[186] but, when he was being taken there, he could in no way be kept chained by the Friesian either; instead, at the hour when masses were being held, <the chains> would be unfastened.[187] And when the man who had bought him saw that he could not be kept bound, he gave him the opportunity of ransoming himself, if he could. Then Ymma, swearing an oath to return or send the Friesian money in place of himself, came to Kent and approached King Hlothhere, who was the son of the holy Queen Æthelthryth's sister, while Ymma was himself a former retainer of the queen, that is, her butler.[188] And he sought and received from him the money required for ransoming himself and, as he had promised, sent it to his master in place of himself.

Afterwards, returning to his brother, he recounted one after the other all the consoling things which had happened to him in the course of his hard times, and he realized from his brother's reports that his chains had been

---

[184] 'High-ranking retainer', 'king's retainer': Lat. simply *comes*, usually rendered in the OE version of Bede as *'gesith'*. To an Anglo-Norman readership the term would have meant 'earl', 'count'.

[185] Reading et <*scio*> *quia* (p. 41.25, ed. Blake), in line with Bede.

[186] *Lundoniis* mss.: *Lundoniam* Bede.

[187] Reading <*vincula*> *solvebantur* (p. 41.29, ed. Blake), in line with Bede.

[188] This detail is not in *Hist. Eccl.* iv. 20 (22). According to *LE* i. 23, p. 42.9, ed. Blake, the story of Imma as a whole was taken *de Bede opusculis*, whatever that may imply.

unfastened at exactly the times when masses had been celebrated for him. Moreover, he also came to recognize that other advantageous and propitious things <which>[189] had happened had been granted to him from Heaven, when he was in danger, through his brother's intercession and the offering of the Host that brings salvation. Many people, hearing of these things, experienced, thanks to the aforesaid man, the kindling of an ardent zeal for faith and religious devotion, either directed towards prayer, or almsgiving or the offering of sacrifices to God for the saving <of those related to them>[190] who had departed this life. For they[191] understood that the saving sacrifice was effective for the everlasting redemption of soul and body.

And we shall not think it at all surprising that we have seen fit to insert into the present work this item from Bede's *opuscula*, if we pay attention to the fact that the grace of God has been in many ways brought to bear in respect to the holy queen. This man Ymma, having contemplated her devotion while doing her service, as a result knew what to guard against and what, on the other hand, to do, <and>[192] became zealous to become all the more devoted to God. And it was not only Ymma, with whom the present story is concerned, but innumerable men and women, who, living in her company – whether this was when she was on her royal throne or when she was in the religious life – came to be pleasing to the Lord through their moral conduct, following her example and advice and spurning the delights and snares of the World. For example there was her priest and monk St Huna from the previous chapter, outstanding for the sanctity of his life,[193] and another, Owine by name, a monk, her tutor[194] and the chief official of her household, the hearer, in company with another, of heavenly mysteries, as we have related above; moreover, as was recently revealed in a divine vision, there was a man who, thanks to the merit of extreme sanctity, was the steward of her farmlands, St *Ælgetus* by name;[195] his body rests at *Bedericesworthe* which is the town of the blessed martyr Edmund, and we ought certainly not to be silent about him in our subsequent narrations.[196]

---

[189] Lat. < *que*> supplied by Blake (p. 42.3) from Bede.

[190] Lat. <*suorum*> supplied from Bede by Blake (p. 42.3) following an anonymous modern corrector in F.

[191] Following Bede: *intellexerunt*, though the *LE* mss. have *intellexit*, meaning: 'he understood' (p. 42.7, ed. Blake).

[192] Reading conjecturally (p. 42.12, ed. Blake): *novit*, <*et*> *ut Deo devotior existeret, emulabatur*.

[193] Deleting *et* before *sanctitate* (p. 42.16, ed. Blake).

[194] Lat. *pedagogus*.

[195] The words, *sed et vir merito sanctitatis egregie custos agrorum ipsius erat* (p. 42.19, ed. Blake) have to be taken as referring to Ælgetus, not to Owine.

[196] Cf. *LE* iii. 94.

24. That Wærburh, virgin of the Lord, was taken from Ely, and put in charge of certain churches.[197]

Already under the rule of Æthelthryth as abbess in Ely, Wærburh, a very well-known virgin of Christ who, as we have recounted above, once dedicated to the service of God, came to excel all the serving community of the monastery, to present herself as inferior to all, and to put the utmost effort of self-sacrificing love[198] into the supplying of everyone's needs. When King Æthelred, her uncle, who has been mentioned earlier, heard of her holiness, he took her from there, and put her in charge of certain monastic communities of virgins in the office of abbess, namely Hanbury[199] and Threekingham.[200]

25. After the death of St Æthelthryth, her sister Seaxburh was made abbess in Ely and, divinely inspired, conceived a desire to remove her bones from the tomb.[201]

Well then, after the time when the blessed and glorious Æthelthryth, desiring to be set free and be with Christ, passed away and departed from this wretched life of mortals to her immortal Espoused, in whose sight the death of His saints is always precious, it came about by the providence of God, which provides for the salvation of mankind in a salutary manner, that her sister Seaxburh, a woman dedicated to God, was installed in her place as the director of souls in the monastic community of Ely, subject as it was to observance of a disciplined life. This woman, whom Eorconberht, King of the Kentish people, had married, was Æthelthryth's sister as much by her imitation of her good work as by bodily kinship. By God's dispensation, after the death of her sister, chosen and beloved as she was by the sisters, she deservedly came to rule over them as their superior. In the office of abbess she followed the precedents of her sister in submission to the way of righteousness. And at the time when <she was exercising leadership>[202] over the Lord's flock by her own example and that of her sister – who, though dead

---

[197] Source: hagiography, cf. *Vita S. Werburge*, ed. Love; last sentence from *Worcester Chronicle* on the year 675.

[198] Lat. *vulnerate caritatis viscera*.

[199] In Staffordshire.

[200] In Lincolnshire.

[201] Sources: Bede, *Hist. Eccl.* iv. 17 (19); hagiography, cf. *Vita S. Sexburge*, chapter 20, ed. Love, though this is much more concise.

[202] Reading conjecturally, with preference for E over F (p. 43.7ff., ed. Blake): *Cumque gregi dominico suo et sororis sue exemplo, que carne mortua apud eum vivebat, bonorum operum attestatione <preesset>, ac magis prodesse satageret et studeret quam preesset . . .* E has *vivebat* so the omission of final 't' in Blake's edition is presumably a modern misprint.

according to the flesh, was alive among this flock, as was testified by good works – and was not so much exercising leadership as working hard and striving eagerly to be of benefit to them, Seaxburh was moved and stimulated to action by a God-sent zeal: she thought the matter over for a long time and decided to exhume the bones of the glorious virgin Æthelthryth from the place where they had previously been entombed. For her burial-place was not well known. Hence, given that the frequency of miracles was increasing and, as it were, demanding action, she fixed a day with her people when they would be able to see again so great a treasure and place it more honourably and fittingly in the church of Mary, the blessed Mother of God, and transfer her to be laid to rest once more, more gloriously, in a new tomb, at a time when she had already been buried for sixteen years. The celibate women praised what they heard her say and bystanders displayed joy at the solemn intent.

26. Seaxburh sent some of the brothers to search for stone for her tomb.[203]

The aforesaid abbess therefore decided, as has been said, to collect reverentially from the earth the relics of her sister, as Christ made it clear by the evidence of many miracles that she ought to be proclaimed to the World in glory and reverence. And she ordered certain of the brothers to look for stone from which they could make a tomb, and directed them to look outside for stone suitable for the second burial of this most important virgin, because within the Isle they could not obtain by any means what was suitable for this kind of need. For the region of Ely, because of[204] the nature of its position, is surrounded on all sides by stretches of water and marshes, and does not have stones of any considerable size on it, unless they have come from elsewhere.

Straight away, the brothers boarded a boat, and they came to land at a little city, not far from there, at that time in ruins, called in the English language *Grantecester*,[205] and, while they were walking around it, in a state of great distress, they soon discovered by the walls of that town a sarcophagus of white marble most beautifully equipped with a cover, in the place which to this day is called *Ærmeswerch*, that is: 'the work of a poor wretch'.

They marvelled, one and all. The people of the vicinity said that they had not possessed, nor had ever seen, such a stone in that place and, as they approached more closely, they kept expressing the view that it had not been placed there by just anyone, but rather had been brought there from Heaven by the command of God for their very own use. For stone of such a nature

---

[203] Sources: Bede, *Hist. Eccl.* iv. 17 (19); hagiography, with parallels in *Vita S. Æthelrede CD*, chapter 11, ed. Love.

[204] Reading with E: *ex*, as opposed to *et* (p. 43.24, ed. Blake).

[205] Probably the Roman riverside settlement on what is now Castle Hill, Cambridge. See Reaney, *Place-names of Cambridgeshire and the Isle of Ely*, p. 36.

and size was not found there: it was possible, indeed, for it to be named, but not to be seen. But indeed, in those times the whole territory of England appeared to have been prior to this completely without marble-stone:[206] now, in our days, however, all around us construction works on conspicuous buildings demonstrate both that it does possess it and that marble can be found in abundance in this country.

They also found a cover, very similar to the sarcophagus, made of material of similar colour and of the appropriate size and kind, without any difference or discrepancy of the matching parts: here as well, the gleaming of the white colour which has been referred to, was brilliant. They rejoiced beyond all measure at this discovery and also realized, as the result of it, that their journey had been made a success and their business rapidly brought to its conclusion by the Lord. Giving thanks to God for all His kindnesses, they returned to the monastery in the fastest possible time, with the wind behind them. Seaxburh, to be sure, overjoyed at the kindness of the divine gift, blessed God 'who alone worketh great marvels'.[207] At length they relieved the boat's keel-timbers of their pleasant load and transported the longed-for and quickly found sarcophagus to its place. The hour – of celebrated memory – is well known, and there is exultation in the heavens, as we believe, when honour to the saints is manifested on Earth. The people came running; most of the sick from all around came flooding in. People worn out by fevers and suffering from all manner of indisposition were overcome at her tomb by a gentle sleep, and on receiving good health through the intervention of her merits, they rejoiced. She kept coming to the relief of the various distresses of other people whose prayers were accompanied by purity of faith. This, really, was what most of all encouraged the blessed Seaxburh to exhume her from her old burial place and to rebury in the church this lady, whom the goodness of Christ saved and preserved, in a manner contrary to nature, while for a very long period she was buried in the earth.

27. That she found the body of the most holy virgin undecayed and – a miraculous thing – the wound in her dead flesh cured.[208]

And when, on a stated day, the body of the holy virgin and the bones of the betrothed of Christ were to be raised from the grave, after so many years, and entombed more fittingly in the basilica, the majority of the devout laity had come thronging together for the holy rites of this translation. Moreover, because a matter of this kind needs to be confirmed by the testimony of a great

---

[206] Lat. *marmor*.

[207] Cf. Psalm 71.18 Vulgate = 72.18 RSV.

[208] Sources: hagiography, with parallels in *Vita S. Ætheldrede* CD, chapters 12, 13, ed. Love; Bede, *Hist. Eccl.* iv. 17 (19), including reports of the autopsy of Cynefrith.

many people, Bishop Wilfrid of blessed memory, whom we have mentioned before, was present. He was a very close associate of the blessed Æthelthryth all the time she was married – in name alone, not in conjugal practice, even though within the true sacrament of marriage – to Ecgfrith, King of the Northumbrians, and he was a most veracious witness to her perpetual virginity; it was he who placed the consecrated veil of a nun's habit upon her, under the magisterial authority of King Ecgfrith's aunt, the Abbess Ebba, at the city of Coldingham; and when she had been established in her position as ruler of souls in the monastic community of Ely, as Bede asserts, he had been her helper, attentive and solicitous to her every need, in continual close association with her. He was also present at this spectacle, a splendid one which it was right should be displayed to public view, and was someone who brought to this unusual miracle a great weight of credibility by his presence and authority. In addition, countless people who knew and were present witnessed this particular happening; and, moreover – making the fact more certain and the truth more evident – among others present there was the medical man Cynefrith, who was at her side when she was raised from the tomb, just as he was when she was dying, so that he might be[209] a witness to that miracle, so marvellous and precious for its rarity. He was a witness, then, who retained a recollection of the incision[210] which he had once made in her body, and who had been accustomed to report that when she was ill she had a very large swelling beneath her jaw.[211]

'So, a tent-awning having been fixed up and arranged in a seemly manner over the place, <as>[212] the whole congregation, brothers on one side, sisters on the other, were standing around the grave singing psalms, a trench was dug, a heap of earth being removed, and her coffin was raised from the dust. And the holy Abbess Seaxburh, after the casket-lid had been opened,[213] went in with a few people, as if to raise the bones and shake them apart,[214] and after there had been a short pause, we suddenly heard her call out from inside in a loud voice: "Glory be to the most high name of the Lord!" And so that these things might be made public in the confirmatory presence of witnesses, a little while later, they called me inside too, and I saw, raised from the tomb and placed on a couch, the body of the holy virgin, looking like

---

[209] Reading conjecturally (p. 45.9, ed. Blake): *existeret* for *existerat*. E has *existet* with an abbreviation sign above the second 'e'.

[210] Here the unwieldiness of the Latin sentence has demanded some recasting. At p. 45.9, ed. Blake, the insertion of *ille* before *incisure* is probably not appropriate.

[211] What follows, as in Bede, is a first-person report, evidently from Cynefrith.

[212] 'As': translating *cum*, supplied by Blake (p. 45.11) in line with Bede.

[213] Deleting conjecturally: *ab* before *aperto sepulture hostio* (p. 45.14, ed. Blake).

[214] Lat. *dilutura*. Cf. the description of Seaxburh's exhumed remains (*LE* ii. 145), stating that bones and dust were separated and wrapped in silk.

someone asleep. And when her body had been brought out from the open tomb into the light, it was found as undecayed as if she had died or been buried that same day.'

A stupendous, extraordinary miracle, and one to be proclaimed for all eternity! Truly, the most holy Æthelthryth, at God's command, made nature unavailing: because she had in life kept her flesh untainted by lust, after her death she was found untainted by decay. And although she had lain hidden in the dust of the Earth for a period of sixteen years, she blossomed forth, all alive again, as if from resurrection, and presented the appearance of one sleeping sweetly in bed, being exempt from the customary process of decay which belongs to mankind: no rather, she was found to be entirely beautiful, fully formed, all complete!

'And when the covering of her face was removed, they showed me also that the wound of the incision which I had made, had been healed, in such a way that instead of the open, gaping wound with which she was buried, there appeared at that time the slightest traces of a scar.'

Who ever heard of such a thing or saw anything similar to this? So long as she lived, the wound had putrefied in her jaw: prolonged burial rendered it free from putrefaction, and whole! The flesh of other deceased persons putrefies when buried: in the case of this woman, flesh which was putrefied by a swelling when she was alive is repaired after burial! The bodies of others are destroyed: surgery on this woman is mended after death! The natural existence of others is consumed by putrefaction: heavenly healing is applied to this woman's gaping wound in the jaw! Truly, those present stood in awe at the marvels of the Lord. They found no rottenness in the wound, but †an apportionment of new glory joined together by grace.†[215] For the power and might of God had made whole again that glorious throat which they had expected to have vanished into dust. Nor does it seem astonishing or something to be wondered at, if we consider the omnipotent grace of the Lord, whereby He does whatever He has decided upon in Heaven and on Earth, and mercifully granted to the virgin's merit, not only that for love of Him, she should turn aside from things which are illicit, but she also spurned things which she could legitimately practise, that is to say, a marital relationship with an earthly, carnal husband. Most glorious and worthy to be proclaimed, therefore, is the power of God and his pity in all things! He it was who kept the burning bush from destruction by fire and who kept Daniel in the lions' pit unharmed by their bites: likewise, in the case of the virgin Æthelthryth, by some preferential prerogative, He glorified corruptible flesh in a way contrary to the customary lot of the human condition, by the bestowal upon her now of incorruption of the flesh.

---

[215] Reading conjecturally *gratia* instead of *gratie* at p. 45.37, ed. Blake, thus: *federatam gratia nove glorie portionem.*

28. That the sepulchral stone of the virginal corpse was fitted together by divine agency and, when the cover was put on, the join was not visible.[216]

Now, finally, they washed the body with great reverence and, carefully clothing it in new garments suitable for the preservation of such a great treasure , they brought it into the church with great and multifarious festal dancing by people devoutly rejoicing, and placed it in the sarcophagus which had been brought there. In this sarcophagus she awaits the return of the Lord, her betrothed, so that He may transform her body in[217] its humbleness into the likeness of His body in its glory. And, it is a fact certainly not to be passed over in silence, but to be proclaimed frequently, with solemnity and without cease, that in a wonderful way the grace of God gave the funerary casket in question such fittingness and congruent equivalence of proportion, and the sarcophagus was found to be as well suited to the virgin's body as if it had been specially prepared for her, with the result that the size of the stone was such as not to exceed in its capacity[218] the size of the holy body, and not to cramp it disadvantageously within itself through being smaller. The place set apart for the head also appeared most suitably configured. For indeed[219] its shape was foreordained by God's provision, and its dimensions were made not dissimilarly equivalent. And the stone placed on top shows what a precious pearl is concealed within. It does not project either on the near side or on the far; it does not sit incorrectly either at the head or at the foot, rendering the join, such a felicitous one, unstable. You will find no point of connection in which stone is joined to stone with cement. Nowhere does there appear a fissure where you would have the opportunity to search out any fastening. The cover is united with the receptacle belonging to it, in such a way that there is nothing resembling a join. One stone is produced from two, and thus becomes a reconstituted whole, in testimony of her virginal integrity. It is never natural to cut two stones from a single stone; moreover we have never heard of a craftsman having joined two together by natural means. And besides, God it is who is the Wonderful Craftsman. All nature is subservient to His rule, and by His will even things which are out of the ordinary are not inharmonious. For He himself, who in the desert produced streams of water from a rock for the children of Israel,[220] ordered one stone to be made of two in obedient consideration of the virgin. This stone, which the hand of the Celestial Craftsman polished and made solid with indissoluble

---

[216] Source: Bede, *Hist. Eccl.* iv. 17 (19); hagiography, cf. *Vita S. Ætheldrede* CD, chapter 13, which, like *LE*, includes allusion to the *Martyrium Sancti Clementis* (Migne, *PG* ii, col. 632).

[217] Lit. 'of': *corpus humilitatis eius configuratum corpori claritatis illius* (p. 46.15, ed. Blake).

[218] Reading, **with word division as in** E: *in continentia* (p. 46.19f., ed. Blake).

[219] Interpreting *nanque* as *namque* (p. 46.22, ed. Blake).

[220] Exodus 17.6f.

cement – as material evidence bears witness – was incapable of being opened or destroyed by any means whatsoever.

What a delightful and splendid bridal-chamber it was that God prepared in that sarcophagus, in which the incorrupt virgin in her blossoming flesh awaits the day of the heavenly nuptials! This is that treasure of the incomparable wisdom of God, which His creative omnipotence protected with a seal, enclosed and untouched, so that it should no longer be made open to human view. And not undeservedly so. For what woman anywhere, given to a husband under the law of marriage, defeats the flame of bodily desire, in the way that the most blessed virgin Æthelthryth, having been allotted husbands twice over,[221] preserved the modest demeanour of chastity perfectly intact?[222] She also makes manifest innumerable other benefits of piety to those believing in her, through the mercy of Him who once prepared the dwelling place of His martyr Clement in the shape of a marble temple – Clement, whose obsequies, so we read, were celebrated with the reverent assistance of the angels,[223] The shape of his body conforms exactly to the shape of the tomb. <We believe>[224] that the prerogative of the most blessed virgin Æthelthryth was much the same: a tomb, prepared for her through the munificence of Christ, was unexpectedly discovered, so we trust, under the patronage of the angels. And since it is held to be unknown by what masons it was made, and by what craftsmen it was polished, there is nothing to prevent one from believing, with one's faith intact, that these were the works of helpers from Heaven.

So then, the remarkable body of the most precious and distinguished virgin and queen, Æthelthryth was translated in the 679th {recte 695th) year from our Lord's incarnation,[225] on 17th October, and was placed in the church of the blessed, ever-virgin Mary, which she herself had built from its foundations. And there, right until now,[226] it is held in the greatest

---

[221] This translation presupposes deletion of *est* before *geminos* (p. 47.2, ed. Blake).

[222] Here the translation presupposes a full stop after *custodivit* (p. 47.2, ed. Blake).

[223] Tradition derived from the Latin translation of the Greek *Martyrium Sancti Clementis*, as in Migne *PG* ii, col. 632.

[224] Inserting conjecturally <*credimus*> before *cui* (p. 47.7, ed. Blake).

[225] A mistake! 679 was reckoned the year of Æthelthryth's death, but it is said that she died 'on the ninth day before the Kalends of July'. Apparently our author forgot to add the sixteen years which had elapsed since then, though the day and month presumably conformed to previous records of her translation. The dating 694 instead of 695 might be arrived at by inclusive reckoning on the same lines as the calculation (*LE*. i. 19, p. 37.11, ed. Blake) that St Æthelthryth's abbacy from 673 to 679 lasted seven years. But see *LE* ii. 147 for non-inclusive reckoning by the compiler of *LE*.

[226] The clause, *ubi usque hodie in maxima veneratione habetur*, translated as 'and there, right until now, it is held in the greatest veneration', is an almost exact quotation from Bede (*maxima*, 'the greatest', being substituted for *magna*, 'great'). Note that the body had in fact been translated again by the time the *Liber Eliensis* was compiled (see *LE* ii. 144).

veneration, to the glory of our Lord Jesus Christ, who chose her and pre-elected her to be a temple and dwelling-place of the Holy Spirit.

29. That benefits were conferred by virtue of the shroud-cloths of the virgin Æthelthryth.[227]

Further remarkable things, as well, were reported about her at that time – glorious occurrences, as a written account attests – and it is not out of place to add material from that source. Truly, all the linen wrappings with which the venerable corpse had been enfolded appeared so whole and so new that they seemed to have been wrapped around her chaste limbs that very day. It came to pass, moreover, as a consequence of contact with these same garments, both that demons were put to flight from bodies beset by them and that sicknesses were sometimes cured. Dropsy-sufferers came and were cured, and people afflicted by diverse illnesses were freed through her merits. And this was not contrary to her deserts: seeing that she had triumphed over instinctual powers[228] in her flesh, it was right that she should cure bodily infirmities in the sick.

30. Miracles are reported concerning the coffin in which she was buried.[229]

Moreover, a number of people report that the wooden coffin in which the precious virgin had been buried has been the source of healing whereby sufferers have had eyes restored.[230] For after they had prayed, placing their head against that same coffin, they soon put away the discomfort of pain or darkness from their eyes.

31. That a spring arises from her burial-place.[231]

Moreover, from the place in which the body of the virgin had first been buried, a spring of water arises, shining very brightly, and for evermore continues ceaselessly to flow. If any sick people take a drink from this spring, or have been sprinkled with its water, it is reported that they subsequently recover their original vigour. Indeed, the things which we ourselves have been privileged to observe will be described in the appropriate place.[232]

---

[227] Source: Bede, *Hist. Eccl.* iv. 17 (19), with inference also from iv. 18 (20) on dropsy-sufferers.

[228] Lat. *spirituales . . . potestates.*

[229] Source: again, Bede, *Hist. Eccl.* iv. 17 (19).

[230] Here (p.47.27ff., ed. Blake) the compiler is again quoting from Bede; the addition of *redditos* to his wording makes the Latin awkward.

[231] Source: local traditions associated with a spring cf. *LE* iii. 116–18.

[232] *LE* iii. 116–18.

32. A prayer of the author to his lady, the most blessed Æthelthryth[233]

Now, therefore – since we are briefly making a pause in the setting forth of our subject-matter, and since the labour of literary activity is extremely heavy for those who are weak – this work is demanding the conclusion which is its due.[234] Since we have, with the aid of God's grace, completed the toil of the promised work, it is permissible to put down our pen. And may the uncultivated style of the writer merit pardon, even if it has not merited the hope of reward. Even if there has been no resounding verbal elegance, nevertheless we have fulfilled our avowed desires. And, as for anyone who shall read through the work dedicated to thee, or shall give a sober hearing, glorious virgin, to someone else who reads it: have compassion upon the wretched lot of these people, whom thou understandest, blessed mother, to be thy devotees; assist them with thy prayers and let future immortality be the outcome of the good fight. May the efforts of thy poor reverencer, whose intellect has been exerting itself in sweated labour for thy glory, be dedicated to Christ through thy intercessions. The tongue of that exile shall sound forth thy praises so long as it remains an expatriate sojourner in this body: may thou, for thy part, at least guard over him at the last judgement, so that he may rejoice in a share of the glory of Heaven. No, indeed,[235] extend thy fortifications to protect all people in situations of affliction, and may thy faithful people merit the joys of eternal life through thy holy intercessions, through Him who assigned thee to himself as a bride, Jesus Christ, Son of a virgin and the Bridegroom of virgins, Redeemer of the World and its Lord, who with the Father and the Holy Spirit lives and reigns as God throughout all ages, for ever and ever. AMEN.

33. That what Bede set forth initially in the manner of historical narrative he also expressed in verse.[236]

Well then, we have made it our endeavour, by an effort of care and solicitude, to satisfy the desire of our brothers: we have woven together, so far as the limitations of our intellect have allowed, in the form of a history, the written accounts which have been found in our house, in Bede and[237] in English or Latin writings, concerning our glorious lady and patroness, Æthelthryth.[238] It is now right to add also the estimate which Bede himself

---

[233] Source: adaptation of the prayer concluding *Vita Sexburge* AT, chapter 27, ed. Love.

[234] Stronger punctuation seems required after *postulat* (p. 48.7, ed. Blake).

[235] Reading *quin immo* (E) rather than *quinnimmo* (p. 48.18, ed. Blake).

[236] Source: Bede, *Hist. Eccl.* iv. 18 (20).

[237] Reading conjecturally: *que<que>* (p. 48.25, ed. Blake).

[238] Punctuating strongly after *curavimus* and after *texuimus* (p. 48.25 and 27, ed. Blake).

set out in verse concerning her. For he wrote as follow
opportune to insert in this history additionally a hymn concern.
which very many years ago we composed in the elegiac metre[240] in pr.
proclamation of this same queen and betrothed of Christ, and to imitate ..
manner of Holy Scripture, in whose history-writing songs are included, † and
it is well known that they were written in metre and in verses.†[241]

> Trinity, bountiful God that rulest the ages eternal,
>> Smile now upon our attempts, Trinity, bountiful God.
> Virgil may sound forth wars: the gifts of peace be our theme-
>>> song.
>> Sing we the gifts of Christ: Virgil may sound forth wars.
> Chaste be the songs I sing: away with the rape of foul Helen.
>> Lust shall allure the depraved: chaste be the songs I sing.
> I tell of heav'nly gifts,[242] not Troy's calamitous warfare:
>> I tell of heav'nly gifts, whereby the Earth knows joy.
> See! God above draws nigh to the womb of a much-honoured virgin,
>> Bringing salvation to men. See! God above draws nigh.
> Virgin woman gives birth, in awe, to the Father of all things:
>> Mary the gateway of God, virgin woman, gives birth.
> Friends of the Thund'rer[243] unite in joy at the Virgin Mother:
>> Splendid in virginal state, friends of the Thund'rer unite.
> Honour of her has fathered from Virgin pure[244] many offspring.
>> Fathered by honour of her, virginal flow'rs spring forth.
> Burnt in the raging fires, the virgin Agatha's steadfast;
>> Eulalia triumphs too, burnt in the raging fires.

---

[239] All the remainder of this chapter is from Bede, *Hist. Eccl.* iv. 18 (20).

[240] The version given here is an attempt to render Bede's lines into an accentual derivative of classical elegiacs while keeping reasonably close to the Latin. The frequent repetitions of phrases are a feature of the original, each couplet of which begins with a different letter of the alphabet, from A to Z – X being represented by the Greek *chi* of *Xriste* – and then, in conclusion, with the letters which make up AMEN.

[241] In the obelized section, for the sake of clarity, the translation renders what Bede's manuscripts have here: *et haec metro ac versibus constat esse composita*, referring back to the songs (neuter plural) in the history-writing of the Bible, whereas *LE* (p. 48.31f., ed. Blake) has: *et hoc metro ac versibus constat esse compositum*, which does not make good sense but cannot be emended away simply.

[242] *LE* has *loquor* where Bede has *loquar*, 'Gifts of heav'n be my tale . . .'

[243] Here an epithet associated with Jupiter is applied the Christian God.

[244] 'Fathered' for *genuit* (p. 49.15, ed. Blake), because the word *honor*, in Latin, is masculine. Where *LE* has *casta de virgine*, 'from virgin chaste', in Bede the reading is *casto de germine*, 'from scion chaste'.

Thecla conquers the beasts: chaste she, as much as high-minded,
  Euphemia, chaste too, conquers the hastening[245] beasts,
Swords are a laughing stock to Agnes, stronger than iron;
  Joyful, Cecilia laughs, faced with an enemy's swords.
Many a triumph is won on Earth by hearts that are sober:
  Love of sober restraint mightily triumphs on Earth.
Our times too a noble virgin has graced with a blessing:
  Now Etheldreda shines, noble our virgin as well!
Born of a royal father, sprung from illustrious forebears,
  Daughter she was of God, nobler in parentage thus.
Thence she attained the rank of a queen and a temporal sceptre:
  Heavenly things she preferr'd; glory was hers from above.
Why seek a husband, my dear, when betrothed to the Heavenly
                                              Bridegroom?
  Christ, the Bridegroom, draws nigh: why seek a husband, my
                                                        dear?
Following now, I believe, the Mother of Him who rules Heaven,
  Thou too may'st be as if mother of Him who rules Heaven.
Twice six years she had reigned, promised betrothed of her God,
  Then in[246] a convent, too, plighted her troth to her God.
Wholly devoted to Heav'n, she blossom'd with actions supernal,
  Gave up the ghost also, wholly devoted to Heav'n.
Buried the virgin's dear flesh remained for sixteen Novembers,
  Nor would the virgin's dear flesh deem that it lay in the tomb.
Christ, 'tis a work of Thine that she and her clothing together
  Shine without trace of stain: Christ, 'tis a work of Thine!
Poisonous blackness departs[247] in honour of sanctified clothing.
  Sicknesses flee away: poisonous blackness departs.
Envy, Eve's conqueror once, stirs up in the Devil great fury:
  Virginal triumph ensues: furious the Devil remains.
Wedded to God as thou art, see how great on Earth is thy glory,
  And what awaits thee in Heav'n, wedded to God as thou art!
Joyful, receivest thou gifts that shine in the festive torch-light,
  See! The Bridegroom comes: joyful, receivest thou gifts.

---

[245] *LE* (p. 49.20, ed. Blake) has *rapidas,* where Bede has *sacras* 'holy'.

[246] Reading with Bede mss.: *inque,* as distinct from the unmetrical *in quo,* read by the *Liber Eliensis* tradition (p. 49.36, ed. Blake). The force of the latter reading would be to imply that Æthelthryth's life as a queen constituted a 'monastery'.

[247] 'Poisonous blackness departs'. The Latin, *Ydros et ater abit* means 'the black (water-) serpent departs' or 'the black poison of a (water-)serpent departs'. The word *ydros* does not come from any reference to the serpent the Eden narrative in the Vulgate Genesis: it was chosen, rather, because of Bede's need for an initial word beginning with 'y'. The compiler of the *Liber Eliensis* evidently took it to be equivalent to *ydrops,* 'dropsy' (*LE* i. 29).

BOOK I

Plucking sweet sounds on the lyre, thou singest new music,
  In a sweet hymn for thy Lord, joyful in new-married bliss.
No one avails to remove from the friends of the Lamb high-
                                                    enthronèd,
  Thee whom no one's desire lured from the high-throned Lamb.

34. What Bede wrote not only in his *History of the English People*, but also in a book which he published *On Times*, out of his *History*.[248]

We have set out in order what Bede, that most learned man, wrote in the book of the kings of England whether in prose or in verse, on the subject of the most sanctified Queen Æthelthryth: now it is not appropriate, either, that we should omit mention of what[249] he reported regarding her, concisely, it is true, but to the same effect, in the book *On Times*, which he composed for the furtherance of many purposes. Well then, in the 678th year from the Lord's incarnation, according to Bede's information: 'a universal synod was held at Constantinople in the times of Pope Agatho, under the Emperor Constantine, at which envoys of the Apostolic See and a hundred and fifty bishops were present < . . . >.'[250]

In that year, so one may see, <. . .>[251] 'the holy and constant virgin of Christ, Æthelthryth, who was daughter of Anna, King of the Angles,[252] and was married first to a very noble man and, after him, to King Ecgfrith – she who for twelve years kept the marriage-bed unstained,[253] after having been a queen, became a nun, taking the holy veil, and without delay also the mother and pious nurse of lady saints, having received a place called Elge for the building of a monastic house.[254] Even her dead flesh testifies to her lively

---

[248] Sources: (paragraphs 1 and 2) Bede, *De Temporibus*, ed. T. Mommsen, *MGH: Chronica Minora*, iii, pp. 314–15; (paragraphs 3 and 4) Bede *Hist. Eccl.* iv. 15 (17).

[249] In this sentence (p. 50.14–18, ed. Blake) there is redundant repetition of *quid,* and the verb in the indirect question is given as indicative: there may, or may not, be textual corruption. Perhaps delete the first *quid* and substitute *quod* for the second.

[250] It seems from *de qua nunc diximus* (p. 50.32, ed. Blake) that the compiler had meant there to be some previous reference to the heresy under discussion: supply here, perhaps, from the text of *De Temporibus*: <*et convicti sunt qui unam voluntatem et operationem astruebant in Christo, falsasse patrum catholicorum dicta perplurima*>, 'and those who assumed will and operation in Christ to be one were convicted of having falsified many sayings of the Catholic Fathers'.

[251] The text lacks any indication that the date of Æthelthryth's death is being given.

[252] So also the text of *De Temporibus*.

[253] Here, Blake's punctuation (full stop after *maritalem,* p. 50.25) needs to be weakened, or a supplement needs to be introduced, if the sentence is to have a verb. The translation presupposes the former course of action.

[254] According to other data in *LE*, the 679th year was the date of her death.

merits: it was found, along with the shroud in which it was wrapped, undecayed after sixteen years of burial.'

But indeed, as we have been calculating, with great care and maximum effort, the chronological order of our history, we have also found in Bede that the said year of the burial of the bountiful virgin was the one in which Theodore, Archbishop of Canterbury, 'hearing that the faith of the Church at Constantinople[255] was greatly disturbed by the heresy', about which we have now spoken,[256] 'was desirous that the churches of the English, of which he had charge, should remain untouched by anything of this sort'.

This was at the time when there ruled in the territory of England: Ecgfrith, <King>[257] of the Northumbrians, that is, the former husband of St Æthelthryth; Æthelred, King of the Mercians; Aldwulf, King of the East Angles, the brother of the aforesaid woman dedicated to God; and Hlothhere, King of the Kentish people, her nephew. In their presence[258] a gathering of very many bishops and learned men was assembled, in response to a command of Pope Agatho, mentioned earlier, to make sedulous enquiries into the question of what belief each of them individually held and he discovered unanimous agreement in favour of the Catholic faith.

35. On the death of the blessed Abbess Seaxburh.[259]

When, finally, St Æthelthryth had, in a sudden transmutation, been carried away from this fragile body, her sister Seaxburh, a virago of great worth, became her successor in ruling the monastery, as has already been said, and there she instructed the Lord's flock in the doctrine and form of true religion. It certainly contributed greatly to the advancement of her potency for good,[260] that she discovered the body of the aforesaid virgin Æthelthryth, which she had reckoned to have been rotten and completely decomposed in the course of very many years, to be whole and undamaged, as if it had been buried that same day. And when, after the circling course of many years had rolled by, this tireless woman was beginning to yearn for the Kingdom of Heaven, she

---

[255] Bede, *Hist. Eccl.* iv. 15 (17) has *Constantinopoli* where *LE* (p. 50.20 and 31, ed. Blake) has *Constantinopolim*.

[256] Evidently there has been a lacuna, see above, n. 3.

[257] Supplying *rege* before *Northanimborum* (p. 50.34, ed. Blake), cf. *Hist. Eccl.* iv. 15 (17).

[258] The presence of the kings is not actually specified in Bede, *Hist. Eccl.* iv. 15 (17), where their names and regnal years are given for chronological purposes only.

[259] Source: hagiography on St Seaxburh, with parallels in the *Vita S. Sexburge* from the appendix to the *LE* in Trinity College O.2.1 (E in Blake's edition: C in Rosalind Love's), fos. 215–28. Suddenly the narrative becomes markedly less expansive once the compiler leaves the subject of St Æthelthryth.

[260] Here 'potency for good' translates Lat. *virtutis*.

fell seriously ill and foresaw that the day of her summoning was imminent. Placed in the midst of her people, she obtained protection for her departure from the sacred mysteries of Jesus Christ, commended her spirit into the hands of the Creator in purity of faith and thus brought her last day to a close at a good, late age. She was buried, in a suitable position, behind[261] her most blessed sister, where the merits of her mighty powers do not cease to flower and plaudits in praise of her are for ever receiving amplifications, as is related in the book of her *Gesta*.

36. That Eormenhild was made abbess after her and entrusted the church of Sheppey to Wærburh, her daughter.[262]

Now, thanks to the providence of God who arranges all the affairs of mankind with gentleness and to salutary effect, the monastery of Ely was not long destitute of the solace and help of a mother, for, by the unanimous wish and the consent of all the congregation, after the death of blessed Seaxburh, St Eormenhild succeeded to her place. Setting aside ambition for any position of power whatsoever, she commended to Christ the virgins of whom she had charge, and then followed her most holy mother into the poverty of Christ which she had chosen. She became poor herself and, by fleeing from being honoured in the sight of mankind, achieved a glory which was greater in the sight of God and in the sight of mankind. When she had been given a suitable welcome by everyone, she became mother of the entire congregation.

In an English source, additionally, we read that Seaxburh received the veil of holiness from the blessed Archbishop Theodore in the church of Sheppey, which she had built, and that her daughter Eormenhild afterwards adopted the rule of the religious life under her in that same place, spurning the exalted standing of her royal rank. When she had prepared for her journey to Ely, she installed her daughter Wærburh to serve as abbess in place of her – something that she had long wished to do.

Well then, Eormenhild passed away to the heavenly realms, full of righteousness and sanctity. She rests buried together with her saintly aunt, that is, Æthelthryth, and next to her mother. Her precious death was

---

[261] Lat. *post beatissimam sororem suam*. After Abbot Richard's translation of her remains into the new minster, she lay at her sister's feet, and to the east of her (*LE* ii. 145, p. 231.9; iii. 50, p. 290.8, ed. Blake); previous to that, she and Seaxburh had lain north and south in the 'tower' (*LE* ii. 146, p. 231.28), and in *LE* ii. 133, p. 214.28, in a narrative referring to Abbot Simeon's time, all the lady saints are said to be buried 'around the high altar'. There seems to be recollection in the present passage (*LE* i. 35, p. 51.16f.) of an earlier burial position in 'St Mary's Church' (*LE* i. 28, p. 47.10ff.) The compiler of *LE* believed that there had only ever been two translations of St Æthelthryth's remains, but this was not necessarily so.

[262] Sources: hagiography, cf. *Vita S. Sexburge*, chapter 24; *Lectiones de S. Ermenilda*, chapter 7, ed. Love; an 'English' source is mentioned by the compiler of *LE*.

testimony to the greatness of her sanctity and piety, as the book of her *Life* recounts more fully.

37. That Wærburh, virgin of the Lord, after the death of her mother, Eormenhild, undertook to rule over the monastery of Ely; and where she chose her burial-place to be.[263]

Thereupon, Wærburh, betrothed of the Lord, though she was in charge of certain churches, as has been said before, after the death of her beloved mother also took charge of the monastery of Ely as its lawful superior. However, in accord with the prescience and will of God, she chose that her bodily resting-place should be at the monastery of Hanbury. And in that place of God the pearl was entombed with due reverence and by the testimonies of many miracles provides proof that she is alive in the glory of Heaven. And from there she has been translated to Chester, where she now rests.

And, assuredly, after her death blessed women, whose names are unknown to us and the knowledge of God alone knows, kept the place of Ely in honour and the promotion of sanctity, and subject to observance of life under a rule, until the devastation brought about by the Danes.

38. That devotion to God's work flourished at Ely under the rule of holy women until the place was laid waste by the Danes with fire and iron weaponry.[264]

Certainly, after the passing away of St Æthelthryth, St Seaxburh, St Eormenhild and St Wærburh, the church of Ely was by no means left devoid of the work of God: no, the potency for good that belongs to divine worship[265] flowered under the rule of blessed women. Their fervour for the discipline of their rule and their observance of their monastic profession did not grow cool, but waxed ever more passionate, as the circling course of many years rolled by. Furthermore, even though different kings were ruling different regions, and as the result of various circumstances, frequent wars kept following one after the other, the grace of the Supernal Mercy preserved churches[266] and monasteries, wherever they were in England, in peace and security and the increased observance of Christian law. But the evil Enemy of the human race could not abide times of such great serenity. It was because he

---

[263] Source: paragraph 1: hagiography, with parallels in *Vita S. Sexburge* 24, *Vita S. Werburge* 4, 10, 11, ed. Love; paragraph 2 is paralleled in the *Book of Miracles* (B).

[264] Sources: hagiography, with parallels in *Miracula S. Ætheldrede Virginis*, chapter 1, ed. Love; also, Abbo, *Passio Sancti Edmundi*.

[265] Here, 'the potency for good that belongs to divine worship' translates: *virtus divini cultus*.

[266] Reading conjecturally (at p. 52.24, ed. Blake): *ecclesias* for *ecclesie*.

lacks an appetite for good-will, and does not cease to feel malice towards the good that, stained as he was with his customary blackness, he stirred up a dire[267] and gloomy storm in all the regions of England.

39. In whose times it was that the Danes sacked England; and concerning their downfall.[268]

Well then, in the 866th year from the incarnation of the Lord, when King Æthelred was ruler of the Western Saxons, there arrived in Britain a great fleet of pagans from Denmark under King Inguar, together with his two brothers, Eowils and Halfden, and a man called Ubba, his colleague in all his trickery and malice and very like him in all respects, having as companions those three kings, Hæsten, Bagseg and Guthrum and their forces, together with a very large contingent of chieftains and nobles, tiresome to enumerate, though they are fully listed in the chronicle. They were accompanied by an immense multitude of bold warriors and they spent the winter in the kingdom of the East Angles, called *Estangle*, where the king holding sway was Edmund, approved by God, an adherent of the Christian faith.

All these men were persecutors of Christians, so cruel in their inborn ferocity that they did not know how to become gentle in the face of the miseries of mankind but,[269] without any pity, they fed on people's agonies and, in accordance with the oracular statement of prophecy that 'all evil comes from the North',[270] this same wicked race came leaping forward as the North Wind blows, from the cold climes of its birth; it breathed forth whirlwinds, sudden and deadly, into all the regions of Britain, encircling it now by sea, now by land, laying it all waste with flames and the sword and, had this not been prevented by the mercy of God, it attempted to bring the whole of Britain's territory to annihilation and, because it knew that they were observers of the law of God, it made repeated efforts to destroy them utterly and subjugate them to slavery. This race refused to keep peace with Christians: hence it devastated all the monasteries, demolishing them from the very foundations, with massacres and conflagrations – this being permitted by God's judgement.

These things were done in the first year of the reign of the

---

[267] Reading with E: *diram*, as opposed to the reading of F: *Dei iram* (p. 53.1, ed. Blake).

[268] Sources: *Miracula S. Ætheldrede Virginis* chapter 1, ed. Love (a rhetorically elaborated version of Ælfhelm, *Exhortatio*,the original text of which is the source of *LE* i. 43–49); Abbo, *Passio Sancti Edmundi*; *Worcester Chronicle* on the year 867, including the supplement on the year 870 found in ms. Bodley 297 (Bury St Edmunds interpolations).

[269] Reading with E: *sed* (p. 53.14, ed. Blake).

[270] Jeremiah 1.14.

aforementioned King Æthelred, son of Æthelwulf. Then, in the second year, the aforementioned atrocious and irreligious race moved on from the territory of the East Angles to the city of York, and from there, roughly speaking, the vast majority of the communities of the Northumbrians were destroyed and met their end, their two kings, Osberht and Ælla, having been put to death. Those people, indeed, who escaped, made peace with the pagans. And afterwards, in the third year, leaving the territory of the Northumbrians, the aforesaid army of pagans came to Mercia and went to Nottingham and wintered there. On their arrival at that place, Burgred, the King of the Mercians, entered into a pact with them. †After seven yearst,[271] in breach of the pact, they forced[272] him to abandon the kingdom and go, against his will, to Rome, and they subjected the kingdom of the Mercians to their domination. They burnt down the places of the saints and the monasteries of the handmaidens and servants of the Lord, plundering everywhere, and in the fourth year they returned for a second time to York and stayed there for a year. In the fifth year, however, they went through Mercia to the territory of the East Angles and spent the winter in the place which is called Thetford. There too, in the same year, Edmund, the glorious king of this same province was martyred by the aforesaid pagan King Inguar, as one reads in the chronicle. And thus, following the murder of the king, the pagans became exceedingly arrogant, and subjected that whole region to their domination. In that year also, as subsequent chapters relate, the church of Ely was consumed by fire, all the people who were within it being put to death.

These things having happened thus, the aforesaid King Æthelred, supported by God's aid, was the one man of all those ruling in England at that time to be capable of resistance. Gathering a good-sized army, he attacked the enemy at Ashdown,[273] where a battle was fought with ferocity on both sides. In that place, the pagans, by divine judgement, failed to withstand the attack of the Christians, and one of the two pagan kings, namely Ubba <and Bagseg>,[274] and five earls were struck down dead. There fell, then: King Bagseg, Earl Sidroc the elder, Earl Sidroc the younger, Earl Osbert, Earl Frene and Earl Harald; and all their army was routed.

But, that same year, King Æthelred departed this life, and his brother Alfred succeeded him. He was an intellectually acute man, so well educated by the most learned monks Grimbald and John that, in a short while, he had a knowledge of all books and translated the whole New and Old Testament into the high style of the English people. If anyone should wish to have a

[271] Problematic, but note that in the 'siege of Ely' narrative too the compiler is led astray by his own, or someone else's, fondness for seven year periods.
[272] Note the correction in E: *coegerunt* for *coegit* (p. 54.6, ed. Blake).
[273] In Berkshire.
[274] Reading conjecturally (p. 54.19, ed. Blake): *Ubba scilicet <et Bagseg>*.

fuller knowledge of these things, he will find the separate events set out in order in the *Chronicle*.

40. That the Danes, on landing at Ely, burned down the monastery and had all those they came upon put to death.[275]

Well then, with God's permission, the aforesaid race of barbarians, in a hostile, wide-ranging invasion, pillaged, devastated and burnt down all the possessions of the English, and defiled the precincts of monasteries with diabolic frenzy and, after this, they finally came to know of the people residing in Ely. All around, people of every age and condition, and of both sexes, guided by their love of being alive, decided to suffer the loss of their property, taking flight in one direction or another, in preference to confrontation with their enemies' fireballs of ferocity.[276]

Now, the Isle of Ely was by no means exempt from this common tribulation and misery, especially as the marshes and waters by which it is surrounded stretch out into a mere, and there is easy access to the Isle for any boats even from the waves of the tidal sea. At some time, this same Danish race sailed to this Isle with many boats, thinking to occupy the place once it had been emptied of defenders. It pressed on with the destruction of the place by pillaging-raids and ambushes, the intention being either to inflict defeat on the inhabitants or to receive their surrender when they had been exhausted by a siege, or to compel them to leave the place. Against them, the more warlike native Englishmen from among the inhabitants strove to offer resistance. For it so happened that when the Danes subjected the neighbouring region to their control, many of the English nobility gathered on the Isle. However, they had been afraid to provoke a war against such large numbers, in case some calamity should befall them, although they wielded a right hand lively for warfare[277] and it was trusted to be enough and sufficient for these operations, and they were sometimes victorious over other barbarians. Nevertheless, sending out envoys to all the surrounding areas, they summoned their neighbours to their aid, and gaining the assistance of a choice band of armed men for the slaughter of the enemy, they quickly laid the Danes low and inflicted far-reaching damage on them. In this way, consequently, they seemed to have a breathing-space for a little while, freed from oppression, but they did not have enough strength to exult in this freedom. In fact, the aforesaid gang of evil men gathered an army which was

---

[275] Sources: extensive use of *Miracula S. Ætheldrede Virginis*, chapter 1, ed. Love; another unidentified source with classicizing touches.

[276] Lat. *feritatis hostium globis*, an idiom derived from classical historiography; cf. Sallust, *Jugurtha* 85, *ex illo globo nobilitatis*.

[277] Reading at p. 55.12, ed. Blake, with the first hand of E, *vividam*, the idiom being Virgilian, cf. *Aeneid* x. 609: *vivida bello | dextra*.

stronger from being more courageous: they were accompanied by their king and a very numerous, dense-packed, column of warriors. And they came rushing upon them, maddened by a spirit of blood-thirsty carousing, broke their ranks and laid them low. Many of the inhabitants were hit on the head with crowbars,[278] and their bodies were kept from being handed over for solemn burial, and were cast out to be the food of beasts and birds. Moreover, on arriving, finally, at the community of virgins which Æthelthryth – the glorious virgin betrothed of Christ – had built – alas! – they broke in, defiled the holy places, trampled over them and pulled them down. The sword of madmen was thrust into milk-white, consecrated necks. The band of nuns was slaughtered, like an innocent sacrificial victim, and wherever they found brothers and sisters of the holy desire, they put them to death without any regard for humanity, in a headlong massacre. And thus the monastery, which God's true Christian, Æthelthryth, had built, was set on fire, along with its virgins and its ornaments and relics of saints, male and female. The city too was sacked and burnt down. Made richer by an abundance of plunder, taking away all the furnishings and utensils of the place, the enemies of the Lord returned to their own domains.

41. That a pagan made a hole in the virgin's sarcophagus, but, by the vengeance of God, was soon struck down.[279]

There was, even amongst the phalanxes of these most ferocious enemies, someone more outrageous and cruel than the rest, a henchman of the Devil, a breather of murder and bloodshed, a devotee of avarice, a truculent seeker after other people's property. When he saw the tomb of God's beloved virgin Æthelthryth, he thought there was treasure stored within it. He brooked no delay, but immediately, with the axe which he was carrying in his blood-drenched hands, struck on the side with repeated blows the marble receptacle in which the virginal corpse was resting. His aim when it had been broken open, so one may suppose, was to seize greedily the money which he falsely believed to be hidden within. The unfortunate man was unaware that the swift moment of divine punishment was imminent, when he would be seized in a wretched state from the midst of things, so as to pay the penalty.

O most pitiable pirate! Ignorant of the worship of the Deity, lusting after worldly gain! Doomed to ruination in an ill-fated downfall! While fatally burning with ardour for money – something corruptible – he was not afraid to disturb a treasure which was virginal and incorruptible. By dint of the

---

[278] Latin: *vectibus*. The term *vectis* usually denoted a strong pole used for carrying, leverage or demolition, rather than a killing-weapon.

[279] Sources: *Miracula S. Ætheldrede Virginis*, chapter 2, ed. Love.

assailant's full force, a breach was made in the sepulchral stone in which the eternal betrothed of Christ was resting as if in a marriage-chamber. The blows were multiplied: a hole was made which remains visible to this day. Once this was done, there was no delaying of vengeance from Heaven, but quickly, in the very act, he met the end of his sacrilegious life, his eyes being torn from his head by divine agency.

When the others saw this, they did not presume to disturb the bountiful corpse of the virgin any further. In the end, they overwhelmed everything with sword and fire, and nothing could remain which the impious band of barbarians did not destroy. Almost all the clerics were massacred; anyone remaining was taken away into captivity.

And thus the place lay in a miserable state, totally deprived of the observance of the divine office and of the fear of God. No one remained to carry out ministry. The singing of praise and rejoicing was taken away: the voice of gloom and misery sounded forth all around.

In the end, there returned after some years eight of the very clerics who were despoiled, and some of them remained, after the lapse of many years,[280] in decrepit old age until the time of King Eadred.[281] Patching up the aisles[282] of the church as best they could at a time of such calamity, they carried out due observance of the divine office.

But other clerics who were their successors, being given to pride and avarice in the manner of the wicked, and living their life not according to canon law but irreligiously, fell into error and foolhardiness, in contempt of the reverence of honourable behaviour. With wondrous indignation God overthrew their insolence, on account of the merit of the holy virgin and, after a just weighing of the facts, condemned it. About these clerics it will be necessary to speak in the context where they belong.

These things too[283] happened in the 870th year from the Lord's

---

[280] The mistaken forms, *transcursa . . . curricula*, are corrected in B to *transcursis . . . curriculis*; an easier correction would be *transcurso . . . curriculo* (p. 56.19f., ed. Blake).

[281] Most likely a false inference from statements by Ælfhelm of Ely cited in chapters 43 and 49 below (p. 60.16ff., ed. Blake). Eadred, a grandson of Alfred, reigned from 946 to 955. It seems improbable that any clerics from the first foundation would have survived so long. The source stated that canons and canonesses were installed in Eadred's time in former monasteries, and that Ely was no exception; it records also that certain of the first-foundation clerics survived to decrepit old age, but the man who had spoken to them had been a young lad (*adulescentulus*) at the time, whereas he was an 'old' priest when Ælfhelm knew him.

[282] The Latin term used is *porticus* (4th declension, accusative plural), cf. the compiler's use of *porticus* in his description of the church at Hexham (chapter 8; p. 22.2, ed. Blake) for his conception of the whole of a church building of consisting of a collection of *porticus*; the term was used variously to mean: 'porches', 'chapels', 'aisles'.

[283] Reading, in line with E (p. 56.26, ed. Blake): *Hec* (not *Nec*) *quoque gesta sunt . . . Hec* has to refer to the contents of the earlier part of chapter 42; the implication of *quoque* would seem to be that the damaging of Æthelthryth's sarcophagus and the sack of Ely monastery were contemporaneous.

incarnation, one hundred and ninety-six years from the time when Æthelthryth was made abbess in Ely.

42. About the victory of the kings of England and about the birth of King Edgar.[284]

Well then, King Alfred, whom we have mentioned above, held the kingdom after his brother most energetically for twenty-eight and a half years, but he was under attack in a most wearisome way, that is, by the same[285] pagan race as was his brother. He and his sons, assisted by Heaven, wore it down and brought about its destruction.[286] In fact, ever since this King Alfred, England has been expanding, under the government of one king, right up until now.[287] And it was his son, Edward, called the Elder, who ruled in succession to him. King Edward made the territory of the kingdom much more extensive than his father had done, since indeed he gained and held possession[288] of towns and cities and very large provinces which the Danes had held for a long time, and received the surrender of several kings. In addition, many years later, he slew two kings, namely Eowils and Halfden, the brothers of King Inguar, and many thousands of pagans fell, slain along with them. However, when, after many outstanding achievements he departed this life in the twenty-fourth year of his reign, he bequeathed the government of the kingdom to his son Æthelstan; Æthelstan held the kingdom most energetically for sixteen years and, after him his brother, Edmund succeeded him. Edmund's queen, Edith, bore him two sons, Edwy and Edgar. And when she had given birth to Edgar, St Dunstan heard voices of heavenly beings singing psalms and saying, 'Peace of the English in the time of the boy now born and of our Dunstan.'

This is the genealogy of the most noble King Edgar, High King[289] of the English, the famous founder and restorer of many monasteries, who restored

---

[284] Sources: unidentified source on the royal succession, differing from the *Worcester Chronicle* over length of reigns; Adelard, *Vita Sancti Dunstani*; Ælfhelm of Ely, *Exortatio sacerdotis ad archipresbiterum suum* (copied in *LE* i. 43–9).

[285] Lat. *ea* (p. 56.31, ed. Blake), if not a mistake for *ea<dem>*, is apparently equivalent to it.

[286] This sentence translates a clause which has singular verbs, as if the subject were Alfred alone (p. 56.32, ed. Blake); the reference to his sons looks like an afterthought.

[287] Here ms. O, adds further material on Alfred (quoted by Blake p. 56, n. *g*): 'For his father, Æthelwulf by name, King of the West Saxons, sent the aforesaid Alfred, his son, to Rome, and Pope Leo, at the behest of his father, anointed him as King of England in the year of the Lord's incarnation 853. Of him it is written: 'Alfred, King of the English and foremost monarch, / Unconquered warrior, learned also in letters, / Alfred, so righteously ruling that there might be / No other king like him and none his equal.'

[288] Reading at p. 57.3: *possedit*.

[289] The term used is *basileus*, classical Greek for 'king', and applied notably to the Great King of Persia.

the church of Ely most gloriously and made it rich in possessions – a fact which, with a view to posterity, it is not fitting to pass over in silence.

The aforesaid King Edmund, too, after holding the kingdom in a magnificent manner for seven and a half years, was killed, and carried to Glastonbury and there buried by the blessed Abbot Dunstan. And, soon afterwards, King Edmund's nearest heir, Eadred succeeded his brother and held the kingdom for nine years and six months.

Well now: in his time, something marvellous, and most astonishing to people who heard of it, happened at Ely concerning the priests living there, which one of them, called Ælfhelm, who had been complicit in their error and crime, owned up to and set down in writing, referring to himself covertly in the third person.[290] And this we are not passing over in silence here.

43. A priest's exhortation to his archpriest, relating to him the miracles which follow, from a desire to shake him out of his temerity.[291]

A short space had elapsed[292] following this period in the history of the English race.

In the reign of Eadred, as the zeal of loving-kindness was growing cool and the yoke of iniquity was growing hot, all the monasteries of the British world[293] were either lying flat, laid waste almost from their foundations up, by the vengeance of almighty God, their enclosing walls – oh, the sacrilege! – having been half demolished, or, if any had remained intact in ancient cities, they had been occupied for a very long time by persons of both sexes who were 'canonical' by name, not by worth. It came to pass also that the monastery of Ely, which is situated on the Isle – the monastery in which the virgin Æthelthryth rests with her sister called Seaxburh, and her venerable niece, Eormenhild – passed under their control. Their archpriest, superior and master, goaded by a deception of the Devil, had the audacity to violate the tomb of the holy virgin. He did not do this with impunity, but this is the way in which he did it.

---

[290] Lat. *sub persona alterius de se . . . asseruit et scripsit*. See chapters 43–9: there were in fact two *personae* involved: the anonymous third-person narrator of the narrative frame, and the 'old man' who issues his warning to the archpriest, backed up by miracle stories. The former may be regarded as Ælfhelm's *persona*.

[291] Source for chapters 43–9: after the link words in first paragraph, Ælfhelm's *Exortatio sacerdotis* is probably transcribed word for word up until p. 61.24, ed. Blake: 'humility of heart'. Internal evidence indicates that the text cited is of pre-Conquest date, and there seems to me no good reason for doubting that it is by a cleric who knew the minster at Ely before the arrival of the Benedictines. He may subsequently have joined them.

[292] Reading with E : *transactis eminus etatis huius temporibus in Anglorum gente. . .* (p. 57.34, ed. Blake). The Latin term *eminus* means 'a spear's throw away'.

[293] Lat. *Britannici orbis*.

When, on one occasion, the feast-day of the aforesaid most blessed lady saint was approaching, he called together the other priests and clerics of whom he had charge and, after entering the basilica in their company, he said to them: 'I wish to know without the slightest doubt, if the venerable virgin Æthelthryth remains even now whole in body, as the sacred writings of the venerable Bede relate in the *History of the English People,* or if anything whatsoever of her remains in the monument, in which long ago, she, with her little body, was entombed, since it does not seem to me probable, but rather I believe that there is nothing in the sarcophagus.' They, in response, said to their benighted master: 'How have you dared to conceive of such a great sin as to think of opening up in any way the sarcophagus of the untouched virgin? Is it not inevitable that we should swiftly cut short our life with a guilty death unless you very quickly cease from such unlawful presumption?' Straight away he said in answer to his questioners: 'I believe that if a virgin so holy were at this present time lying in the basilica as of old, God would have performed very many miracles here through her.' Then one of the priests said to him: 'Master,[294] the reason why you are advancing disputatious notions[295] of this kind is that, recent newcomer as you are to the Isle from another province, you have scarcely seen the miraculous acts of power which the Creator of things brings about, in numbers beyond counting, through the merits of this holy virgin. From among these, I will relate to you a very small number among the many which were performed a little while before you arrived here.

44. About a certain married woman.

There lodged in a certain village near to here a certain married woman who for about six years was so constrained by an unbearable paralysing illness, all the coordination of her limbs being loosened, that in no way was she able to bring her hands to her face nor[296] imprint the venerable sign of the saving cross upon her own forehead, nor rise from her bed without the help of maid-servants. After she had paid out a great deal of money to physicians and had not received from them any healing from a cure, she came to this hall, out of reverence for the Supernal Clemency, with eight attendants bearing her and, through spending a vigil in it, that very night she earned recovery of her health, and returned home, walking on the soles of her own feet, praising and glorifying the omnipotence of God.

---

[294] The Greek term *didascale*, 'teacher', is used.

[295] 'Disputatious notions', Lat. *sermocinationes*.

[296] Reading with E (p. 58.28, ed. Blake): *nec* rather than *hec*.

BOOK I

45. About a young man unable to speak.

'In addition, there was a certain adolescent in a certain vill which the inhabitants of the place call *Bradeford* who, throughout the course of seven years, lived his life without speaking. In similar fashion, on his being brought to this shrine by his parents, immediately the fetters of his tongue were loosened and he spoke in correct phrases, saying in the presence of all the people who were standing round about him, "Brothers, let us return to the lodging-house since, through the merit of the blessed virgin Æthelthryth, by the generosity of God, the Creator of all things, I have been cured."

46. About a blind girl.

'A certain girl, moreover, blind from the first moment of her birth, was brought in those days to the walls of this church, after the elapse of ten years, with a happy outcome. As soon as she entered the basilica, she received the healing of her eyes, and began to marvel at the light-suffused, resplendent workings of this World, and the fiery radiance of the Sun which she had never seen before, and she acknowledged the greatness of God, the Author of things, who had created all the wonders which she could see.

47. About a certain young man.

'And, moreover, a certain young man, who had a withered hand, came to the most sacred tomb of this bountiful virgin: immediately, the muscles of his arm having stretched out as I was standing near, he gained the strength, with restored powers, to open his hand. When they saw this, the people who were present blessed God who created all things.

48. About a priest's maid-servant.

'And furthermore there was a certain priest staying in this monastery who compelled his servant-girl to gather vegetables in the garden before the third hour on a Sunday. She had seized a huge stake in order to fulfil her master's order, when her hand became firmly stuck to the piece of wood which she was eagerly clutching and with which she was bent on uprooting the herbs illicitly. So firmly was it stuck that no one of the human race had been able by any endeavour to pull the stake out of the woman's hand. As she was tormented by a great agony they cut the stake on either side of her hand, being unable to give the wretched woman any other help, and she remained in this state for five years. When, with the revolving of Heaven's axis, those years were complete, it happened that we who were to help her met one day at the house of the aforementioned priest. When we saw her being tormented beyond all measure, we were very grieved that a creature of God should be perishing in this way, and said with united voice to the priest with whom we were sharing a meal: "Before we take our food, let us take this poor little woman to that church of yours, humbly beseeching the Maker of all created things to deign to have mercy upon her through the glorious intervention of the holy virgin Æthelthryth." He, in reply, said in joy to all the brothers: "For such beneficial advice may God almighty give you a place in the Kingdom of Heaven, where the saints enjoy perpetual light!" They entered the basilica and as soon as they had made their request to the Lord, the servant's hand opened up and out sprang the wood, which was now adhering to the joints of the bones, as the flesh was wasted away! And so, the woman received divine healing, and the gathering of clerics returned[297] for the shared meal, giving thanks and praises to Christ the Saviour.

'In view of this, I advise you, master, to cease from your audacious and unlawful undertakings with all speed. If, on the other hand, you refuse to believe my words, you shall die forthwith a fully deserved death, condemned to everlasting punishments, and in a state of misery you shall lie subject to perpetual torments, the worms of Hell and the fires of the underworld.'

Having been warned twice or three times by the wise old man, the archpriest refused to desist from his most wicked undertaking, but called together four young men from the order of clerics, whom he led with ease to ruin and condemnation by the crime which he perpetrated.

49. That the judgement of God came down with anger upon the aforesaid archpriest and his colleagues.

For there was in the casket in which the holy virgin was reposing a little fissure which had been made by pagans who were destroying the worship of Christ, as a certain old man told us[298] who learnt it from the very priests who witnessed it. For long ago the Northmen,[299] cruel peoples as they were, plundered the Isle of Ely no whit the less than they plundered very many provinces of the English and of the Franks. With iron weaponry and fire they depopulated it of all the clergy, nuns and lay-people, putting the boys and old men cruelly to death; afterwards they took the adolescents and young men to regions elsewhere. One of them, a fearsome Northman, dared to approach the tomb of the distinguished virgin. Carrying in his hand a tiny little axe,[300]

---

[297] Reading conjecturally at p. 59.34, ed. Blake: *regressus <est> ad convivium . . .*

[298] Repunctuating thus at p. 60.6, ed. Blake: *quedem rimula que, nobis ut senex quidam retulit qui a sacerdotibus qui hoc viderunt didicit, a paganis . . . facta fuerat.*

[299] Lat. *Normanni*, the word regularly used also for 'Normans'. The use of this word, rather than '*Dani*' or '*Daci*', supports a pre-Conquest date for the work ascribed to Ælfhelm.

[300] Lat. *exiguam . . . bipennulam*: contrast chapter 41, above, where the smallness of the axe is

he was striking the marble chest, in which she lay, three times and four times again, hoping to discover an immense amount of money when, as soon as he made a little window, he lost his eyes and his life. In the end, after some years, eight of the clerics who had been driven out of the monastery of Ely, made their way back to that very same place. Some of these, who had reached decrepit old age, now that the course of many years had elapsed, reported the facts just as set out in this little book,[301] to the aforementioned old man, who was then a young lad.

Why need I continue further with superfluous words? The unlucky priest approached this opening with his partners in crime. Taking stalks of the fennel with which the surface of the whole pavement had become adorned, and sticking them into the opening of the sarcophagus, all of them, following their dreadful master, had the audacity to prod the little body of the holy virgin. Then the priest said: 'Now I know without doubt and without the slightest bit of ambiguity that the holy virgin still rests in this tomb, remaining as she does with her flesh thus entire.' Then the old man who previously told him not to do it, said to him: 'You are bound to know more, forthwith, when you lie struck down by the vengeance of God.' And again the priest said, treating the old man's prophetic words as worthless: 'Now I wish to see if her coverings, too, even now remain in their entirety.' And he poked a candle stuck to a twig through the opening of the little casket which contained the blessed body-parts of the saintly woman, but he could see no more within than if he had been blinded in both eyes. But the burning candle, so they maintain, fell on top of the saint and remained burning upon the holy coverings until it was entirely burnt out, the flame being afraid to touch them. However, all the people who were present kept looking at the light of the candle which was coming out of the tomb through the hole and, being very afraid that whatever was hidden below would be burnt, they said to the priest, the instigator of the whole crime: 'It would be better for you not to have been born rather than that you should commit such an evil deed.' Not even thus did he withdraw from the evil design of his abominable mind. For, taking a piece of twig, he sharpened it at one end, and splitting it again with the blade of a little knife, he poked it into the grave-clothes of the most holy virgin, winding it round in circular motion, four times and four times again, and, with the combined effort of all who were present, he pulled it right to the hole and through; and he began to marvel because the grave-clothes were undamaged. In haste, he snatched up a massive dagger and, under the influence of demons, cut from it a tiny little piece, while the rest of his comrades, that is, the four young men mentioned earlier, dragged the

not admitted, being contrary to the narrator's rhetorical purpose, and the 'Dane' uses his full force to wield it.

[301] The reference is to Ælfhelm's little tract.

shroud upwards and held it with all their strength. Once it had been violated by the touching of wicked men, it was withdrawn from their filthy hands – as the priest who was party to the crime related – as if, within the tomb, two most mighty warriors were dragging it back, and as if the holy virgin, still alive, were saying to them: 'May you have neither God's favour nor mine, because you have dared to damage my muslin!'

Need I say more? Soon, a great plague seized the household of that priest, striking his wife and all his children with rapid death, and it utterly extirpated all his progeny; the priest himself moved to another place, but after a few days it also took him to Hell, because he did not wash away the crime he had committed by penitence. Moreover, of his four accomplices, divine vengeance very quickly killed two. A third, who was trained in the scribal duties which belong to the Church and its priesthood, was immediately driven mad; he forgot all his knowledge, as if he had learnt absolutely nothing. He paid the penalty for his great crime while still alive since, month after month, he lost his reason, as his mind's vigour ebbed and the Moon claimed back the remainder of his years. Now, the fourth was Ælfhelm, the aforementioned priest, who likewise was seized by a severe illness and for almost eight months remained paralysed until his parents, whose only son he was, in grief and sorrow took him, along with very many gifts, to the body of the blessed virgin. That very night, while they were keeping vigil there, promising restitution through the sacraments, he won the restoration of his health through the intercession of the bountiful virgin Æthelthryth, and in the morning they joyfully returned to their lodging-place, glorifying the Redeemer of the Universe.

Behold what was engendered by the blind presumption of one who doubted in an infidel manner! Behold the just deserts of an unrighteous action! May any unworthy touchers of the relics of the holy virgins consider it certain that they ought not to venture on this presumption without cleanliness and humility of heart.

But the church did not even thus cease to be under the control of wicked priests: no, it tossed upon the waves under their shipwreck-bound helmsmanship until the tenth year of the reign of the glorious King Edgar.[302] We recall these things briefly; they are narrated fully in the *Book of Miracles*[303] of the blessed virgin.[304]

---

[302] That is: 969/70. Here, ms. O adds: 'That was the year in which Æthelwold, Bishop of Winchester, expelled the clerics from there with the authorization of the aforesaid King, and restored the church – after it had been destroyed by the pagans and for a hundred years desolate and deprived of royal finance – and introduced monks, as is more fully explained in book 2, chapter 3.'

[303] Not the *Book of Miracles* in ms. B; probably the reference is to the rhetorically inflated work cited as *Miracula S. Ætheldrede Virginis*, ed. Love.

[304] Here ms. O draws attention to King Eadred's gift of the manor of Stapleford to the Church of Ely (see *LE* ii. 28).

50. The manner in which King Edgar ruled.[305]

Eadred, the distinguished King of the English people to whom we have referred earlier, fell sick in the tenth year of his reign and died. A prince who was his nephew succeeded him as king, namely Edwy, the son of King Edmund and his saintly queen, Edith, and, when the four years of his reign had run their course, he died and was buried at Winchester in the new minster. His own full brother, Edgar, succeeded to the kingship, when in the sixteenth year of his age, chosen by the whole people of England, he also being of the family of Cynegils, the distinguished king who received the faith of Christ from St Birinus, the first of the kings of the West Saxons to do so. King Edgar, having been properly instructed by the blessed Dunstan, enacted just laws for the kingdom of the English and kept control, all the time, over a kingdom that was in a most tranquil state. He restored and enriched the churches which had been destroyed. The complainings of the clerics were cast out of the monasteries,[306] and then he gathered together companies of monks and nuns for the praise of God, as will be set forth in the work that follows.

By concluding this work now, we avoid excessive prolixity. For it is time for the beginning of the next book to be put in order and for our powers of speech to be refreshed for a while through silence.

Version of E

Here ends the first book about the history of the Isle of Ely,
relating to the life of the most blessed Æthelthryth
and how she built a church there
and by whom, on the other hand, it was destroyed.

Version of F

Here ends the first book about the history of the Isle of Ely,
and about the glorious virgin Æthelthryth
and the holy virgins who succeeded her
and the misfortunes to which the church was subjected
up until the arrival of the monks in Ely.

---

[305] Source: *Worcester Chronicle* on the years 955–975; also on 654 (cf. chapter 7, above).
[306] Lat. *abiectis ex cenobiis clericorum neniis.*

BOOK II

Prologue of the second book in the history of the Isle of Ely, and how the church was restored or, more specifically, by whom it was endowed.[1]

In the previous work, it has been set forth in what manner St Æthelthryth, and afterwards her successors, engaged in building-work in Ely, or lived their lives in that place in a way pleasing to God and, on the other hand, the identity of the people by whom that place had been destined to be laid waste becomes clearly apparent. Certain of our number have urged me importunately not to take leave of my undertaking, but rather pursue to the end the doings of our Isle,[2] as I had promised. So now, at last, even though I shall be found inadequate in so great an undertaking, feeble as I am in strength and sensibility, I am placing my trust none the less in the solace of my lady advocate, Æthelthryth, and, having shaken off for once my sluggishness, I am making haste to carry out their behests and to combine into a single whole, within a comprehensive volume, matters of greater or lesser importance, as the subject demands. This subject is, primarily: the people who restored the monastery, and their wills. It has been with difficulty and with the greatest effort that I have sought these out and translated them from the vernacular into Latin, but eventually I have collected together the separate items, scattered though they have been in a variety of places. Such items as are familiar even to us, being not at all uncertain and witnessed to by many people, we offer to others in abridged form. For often it is a sweet and pleasant mental exercise to re-read even things which are well known and which the spirit delights to have repeated in the ear.

And given how we see the fictions of the Gentiles, or the ravings of the Stoics, set down with the greatest studiousness and celebrated publicly,[3] it is a worthwhile enterprise to record the deeds of saints by whose merit sanctity shines forth. From among their company, Æthelwold, confessor of the Lord – the man who restored our church after its destruction by the Danes – was outstanding in learning and holiness; he achieved great and noteworthy

---

[1] Source: presumably the compiler's free composition, though parts of this preface, as of chapters 1–4, and the whole text of chapters 7–49, are derived from the *Libellus quorundam insignium operum beati Æthelwoldi* (*LibÆ*), an early twelfth-century translation, commissioned by Bishop Hervey, of an earlier record in Old English of the acquisition of the monastery's lands, no longer extant (see Blake, Introd., p. xxxiv).

[2] Reading with E: *gesta nostre insule*, rather than *gesta nostra insule* (p. 63.7, ed. Blake).

[3] Borrowing from the *LibÆ*, prologue, quoted in Blake, Appendix A, pp. 395ff., which specifies that 'the fictions of the gentiles' etc. were 'celebrated publicly *in schools*'.

things which were not fully set down in the book of his *Life*.[4] These were the things which Hervey, the first Bishop of Ely, a distinguished and prudent man, discovered to be worthy of retelling, and caused them to be translated from English into Latin. And so, when the work was complete, he gave it the title: *Liber de terris Sancti Æthelwoldi*.

This present book comprises the time of the monks, reporting their affairs in full, whether successful or calamitous.

Here ends the prologue of the work to follow.

Here begin the chapter-headings.

1. How the church of Ely was restored by St Æthelwold on the instructions of King Edgar.

2. How King Edgar refused to give the monastery in question to certain men who asked for it.

3. That Bishop Æthelwold, at the command of King Edgar, ejected the clerics from the church of Ely and introduced monks there, and who it was that he made the first abbot there, and what ornaments he donated.

4. How the blessed Æthelwold bought the whole Isle of Ely from King Edgar.

5. A privilege of King Edgar about the liberty of the monastery and about its jurisdiction of seven-and-a-half hundreds, that is, of the two hundreds within the Isle and five-and-a-half in the province of the East Angles, with the addition of Melbourn, Armingford and Northwold; moreover he also assigned a quarter of the revenue of the common wealth of Cambridgeshire, to be given to the brothers of Ely as a perpetual right.

6. About the industriousness of Abbot Byrhtnoth.

7. How King Edgar gave Hatfield to St Æthelthryth.

8. How the blessed Æthelwold bought Linden with its appendages, Hill and Witcham and Wilburton, and the privilege of the king on this vill.[5]

9. The privilege of King Edgar about the same matter.

---

[4] The wording here again is closely related to *LibÆ*, prologue. The *Life* referred to is Wulfstan, *Vita Æthelwoldi*.

[5] The wording translated is that of E.

10. [How the blessed Æthelwold bought eight hides in] Stretham.[6]

11. About Downham.

[11a. About the same matter.][7]

12. About Witchford.

13. About Wold.

14. About Witcham.

15. About Sutton.

16. About Hill and about Haddenham.

17. About Wilberton.

18. About Stonea.

19. About Cambridge and about Dullingham.

20. About Cambridge.

21. About Doddington and Wimblington.

22. Again[8] about Doddington and *Wæremere*.

23. Again about Wimblington, and how much they owned in the fens as a result of purchase.

[24. About Stonea.]

25. About Bluntisham.

26. About Toft.

---

[6] E has simply: 'about Stretham'.

[7] Square brackets in this list of chapter-headings indicate that either the heading or, as in this case, the whole chapter, is lacking from E. For further details, see source notes on the chapters themselves and Blake's edition.

[8] Following the reading of E.

49. [About Horningsea.]

49a. [About Kensworth.]

49b. [About Armingford.]

50. What ornaments King Edgar brought to the church of Ely.

51. That the [holy] cross of Christ gave forth utterances in defence of monks.

52. At what time the church was dedicated and [on the other hand by whom.

53. That Abbot Byrhtnoth translated the body of the bountiful virgin Wihtburh to Ely.

54. By what boundaries the Isle is encircled and how great the authority is on which it places reliance.

55. About those who made benefactions to the church [of Ely] and those who did it harm.

56. In what sort of manner our first abbot, Byrhtnoth, was martyred.

57. After the death of the first abbot, who was appointed in his place.

58. A privilege of King Æthelred about the vill of Littlebury.

59. About Thaxted.

60. About Kingston, the Rodings, Undley, Whittlesey [and] Cottenham and about land at London called *Abboteshai*.

61. About Bridgham, Hengham, Weeting, Rattlesden, and Mundford, and [also] the fisheries around Thetford.

62. About the venerable Ealdorman Byrhtnoth, who gave to St Æthelthryth Spaldwick and Trumpington, Rettendon and *Hesberi*, Soham, Fulbourn, Teversham, Impington, Pampisford, Croxton and Fimborough, Thriplow, Hardwick and Somersham with its appurtenances.

63. [About] the Lady Æthelflæd {recte Ælflæd}, the wife of the aforesaid ealdorman, who gave us the vill of Rettendon, and [of] Soham and [of] Ditton

[of] Cheveley.[9]

64. About Hadham and Kelshall.

65. About Bishop Æthelstan of blessed memory, who gave us Drinkstone.

66. About Willingham.

67. About Stetchworth and March and Kirtling and Dullingham and one virgate in Swaffham.

68. About Chedburgh.

69. [About the vill of Hoo.]

70. About Hitcham.

71. About Bishop Eadnoth.

72. About Ælfgar, a confessor of the Lord.

73. Who it was gave the vill of Wratting.

74. That the properties specified here were handed over to the church of Ely along with Leofsige, the future abbot: Glemsford, Hartest, Barking, Feltwell, [Shelford] and Snailwell.

75. These properties were given to the church along with Bishop Ælfwine: Walpole, Wisbech, which constitutes a quarter of a hundred of the Isle, and Debenham, Brightwell and Woodbridge.[10]

76. That Abbot Ælfsige brought to Ely the relics of St Wendreth the virgin, and that he obtained, by purchase from King Æthelred, Hadstock, Stretley, and both of the Lintons.

77. Hence this charter of the same king.

78. That the church of Ely holds by custom a position of service at the court of the king.

---

[9] Lat. *de*, used in F's supplements and translated as 'of' could equally mean 'about'.

[10] E adds: *et Bramdune*, but there is no mention of the place (Brandon, Suffolk?) in the heading or text of the chapter itself.

79. How the relics of the bountiful virgin Wendreth were removed [from this place]; and that Queen Emma, just as she had promoted this church with honours under King Æthelred, similarly under King Cnut, her second husband, adorned it with beauty of vesture.

80. About the passing away of Abbot Ælfsige, who was succeeded by Leofwine, and he by Leofric, both consecrated, in the period that followed, by Bishop Ælfwine [of Elmham].

81. About Easter, Fambridge and Terling.

82. A privilege of King Cnut about the exchanging of Cheveley and Ditton.

83. About Barking.

84. Who it was by whom Abbot Leofsige of Ely was consecrated and what good things he did for this church,[11] and that at the behest of King Cnut, an annual levy of food-rent for the church is instituted.

85. With what [great] difficulty King Cnut arrived at Ely for its festival, and, hearing the monks from afar, composed a song.

86. That Bishop Ælfwine installed monks for the first time at *Bedericesworthe* {Bury St Edmunds} and afterwards, having relinquished his bishopric, returned to us and chose to be buried here.

87. How, [or, specifically, when and by whom,] the body of Wulfstan, confessor of the Lord, was translated.

88. About Balsham and Wetheringsett and Stetchworth.

89. About Ditton and *Burch* and Knapwell and the other properties which are named in that writ.

90. In what a nefarious way Prince Alfred, the brother of the glorious king Edward, was betrayed.

91. How Edward became king, and with what devotion he endeavoured [[as king]] to repay the good things done for him by the church in his infancy.

92. His charter about all the properties that the church owns.

---

[11] The variant of E is translated here. F has: 'what good deeds he did there'

93. A privilege of Pope Victor about the liberty of the place and of all things that appertain to it.

94. How Wulfric became abbot.

95. The stability of the place confirmed by the king.

95a. <Again, on the same matter.>[12]

96. That the church of Ely granted the vill of Easter to a certain person to hold temporarily.

97. How Abbot Wulfric granted certain properties of the church to his brother, without the knowledge of the community; and about his death.

98. How Archbishop Stigand held the position of abbot of Ely; and the grand scale of his gift of ornaments to that place.

99. About Bishop Osmund.

100. About the death of King Edward; and that, after him, Harold became king [and was the person who installed Thurstan as abbot in Ely].

101. That King Harold, a year later, was killed by William, Duke of the Normans, who obtained the right of kingship by war.

102. That, in fear of the new king, the nobles of the country fled to Ely and, having been defended for a long time by the strength of its position, rebelled against him, with the result that the king, moved by great indignation, ordered all the properties of the church to be seized.

103. That [Archbishop] Stigand, fleeing from before the king, came to Ely and how the relics of St Alban were conveyed there.

104. That King William caused a full account of the whole of England to be written; that he imposed intolerable taxation upon the English; and about the enormous severity of a famine such as never was from the beginning; and that the king's fellow-countrymen were slaughtered at the river through the trickery of Hereward.

---

[12] Chapter-heading supplied by Blake from the text where the chapter occurs.

105. With what a great tribute of praise a knight set free by Hereward extolled the magnificence of the place before the presence of the king.

106. How Hereward, disguising himself as a potter, gained information that evil was being devised against him.

107. How Hereward, cautiously on the attack, subverted and set fire to the siege-works of the king; and about a conspiracy of very many people against their lord, the king.

108 With what violence the monastery of Eynesbury was taken from the church of Ely.

109. That the monks of Ely made an approach to the king's clemency; and about the atrociousness of the journey of his army and horses.

110. That, with the departure of Hereward from the Isle, the king finally made his entry.

111. How cruelly the king took vengeance on his enemies for the injury done to him; and that the monks secured a firm treaty with him, giving him considerable amounts of money, to pay which in full everything outstanding by way of gold and silver was removed from the church.

112. About the passing away of Abbot Thurstan.

113. How the king appointed as abbot [in Ely] Theodwine, who would have been unwilling to take on the position, had not the king restored to that place everything that had been taken away, and who, having arrived there, was after a short while taken from this World's light without a blessing of his appointment, and left the position vacated by himself to a distinguished and prudent man, Godfrey.

114. [What items from the treasury of the church there were found to be after the death of Abbot Theodwine.]

115. [About the death of Abbot Theodwine; and that he left Godfrey as custodian in his place.]

116. In the sight of which prominent men the possessions of the church were ratified.

117. Charter of the king about the liberty and dignity of the monastery.

118. That King William moved Godfrey to Malmesbury from Ely[13] and appointed there [in place of him] Simeon, Prior of Winchester, who, contrary to custom and the dignity of the place and the instruction of the king himself, received consecration from the Bishop of Lincoln, without the knowledge of the sons of the church.

119. How William, Earl of Warenne, after his death, was damned [in respect to his soul].

120. A charter of the king about the giving back of the church's properties by their usurpers.

121. Again, another instruction about the same matter.

122. [Another charter of the king about the giving back of the church's properties.]

123. A charter of the king about the five hundreds in Suffolk.

124. The king's order prohibiting the Bishop of Lincoln or the secular judiciary from suing for customary rights within the Isle.

125. That King William gave instructions that the Abbot of Ely be blessed by an archbishop according to the ancient usage of the Church; and that he gave orders that the place's lesser and greater properties be listed in full.

126. An instruction of the king that the original customary rights arising from the liberty of the former church be preserved undiminished.

127. That the king was keen to discover by detailed enquiry how firmly based the foundation of the place is.

128. [[A charter of the king about *Estona*]][14]

129. About a certain brother who had gone out of his mind but was cured by the merits of St Æthelthryth.

130. About two dumb men.

---

[13] E adds: *nondum sacratum*, 'not yet consecrated', as if Godfrey had been appointed as abbot.

[14] This chapter, found neither in E nor in the first hand of F, is a later addition.

131. About Picot the sheriff, who brought[15] many discomfitures upon this church.

132. About Gervase, who was extremely hostile to the people of St Æthelthryth, and used to torment them.

133. That the Lord God, placated by the prayers of the holy virgin Æthelthryth, averted His indignation and anger from this place.

134. That King William harassed the church severely a second time; and about his decease and where he lies buried.

135. That, when Abbot Simeon was failing in strength, a certain retainer of his took possession of the estate of Witcham, and some other people, of other properties of the church.

136. That a certain Ranulf, at the command of the king, instituted an allowance for the monks, but a meagre one.

137. How Abbot Simeon cast off human mortality.

138. [The depredations which monks from elsewhere inflicted upon the church of Ely.][16]

139. [What manner of things Ranulf found in the treasure-chests of St Æthelthryth.][17]

140. How the abbacy was given to Richard, a monk of Bec.

141. That Abbot Richard refused to accept a blessing from the Bishop of Lincoln, and made it his endeavour to convert the abbacy into a bishopric.

142. How King Henry, at the instigation of men of ill-will, expelled Richard from the abbacy; and Richard himself went on a journey to Rome.

143. That Richard, coming back from Rome, was reinstated in his post and built the new work of the church, begun by his predecessor.

---

[15] Presumably *iessit* is equivalent to *gessit* (p. 71.16, ed. Blake).

[16] This whole chapter is lacking from E.

[17] This chapter is differently placed in E and its original title is lost.

144. About the second translation of the body of the holy virgin, which the same abbot brought about.

145. How he found the other lady saints and in what manner he translated them.

146. That before the solemn enactment of this translation, with a view to the enlargement of the building, he moved the sepulchres of St Seaxburh and St. Eormenhild from their former place, where the blessed Æthelwold had placed them, similarly removing the sarcophagus of the blessed Wihtburh, but careless servants accidentally broke it.

147. How the abbot provided a new sarcophagus, but its size was more or less than that of the form of Wihtburh's body; and that he opened to view her sacred body and reburied it in the old sarcophagus, which had been restored by divine agency.

148. In what year that translation came about, and with how much feeling Abbot Richard endeavoured to venerate the bountiful virgin Wihtburh.

149. How this same abbot established a title to Hadham.

150. How, when Abbot Richard was dying, he saw the blessed Wihtburh standing before him.

[Here end the chapter-headings of the second book.]

1. How the church of Ely was restored by St Æthelwold on the instructions of King Edgar.[18]

Now it remains to write about the restoration of the church of Ely which, as we have said, was privileged to have the virgin Æthelthryth as its first holy and venerable teacher of monastic discipline. Frequent upheaval when, long ago, the pagans attacked it, rendered the place destitute of worship, the upholders of its rites having been massacred. The wreck of this place, presenting visible evidence of the complete extermination of past religious practice there, had passed from celestial liberty into human servitude, and right until the times of glorious King Edgar was subservient to the royal treasury. In his time, also, blessed Æthelwold, an outstanding bishop, like a lamp aflame and spreading light, began to shine forth among the people of God. This man was endowed with the adornments of all the virtues and with an exemplary series of good works, and had made an undertaking to rule over the Church of God. He emerged subsequently not only as an energetic leader but also as the founder of a great many monastic communities. To be precise, he initiated some from the laying of their foundations; others, which had been destroyed or left deserted, he rebuilt by painstaking restoration, carrying the work right through to the finishing touch; and he placed the household of the Lord, the most high Paterfamilias, in all respects under the rule of holy living. One of those which he restored was the monastic community of Ely, which used to be open to every wayfarer, not as a monastic community but as a public minster, lacking ceremonial and reverence.

2. How King Edgar refused to give the monastery in question to certain men who asked for it.[19]

However, at that time, two of the king's magnates, Bishop Sigewold, a Greek by nationality,[20] and Thurstan, a Dane by race,[21] having seen the state of the

---

[18] Source: this chapter includes material from *Libellus Æthelwoldi* 1, paralleled also in B (*Book of Miracles*). For translations of the relevant texts, see Appendices A and B below.

[19] Source: chapter-heading and several quotations from *LibÆ* 2. See Appendices A and B.

[20] On the possible identity of this bishop, see M. Lapidge, 'Byzantium, Rome and England', in *Settimane di studio del centro italiano di studi sull' alto medioevo* XLIX, *Roma fra oriente e occidente*, Spoleto 2002, pp. 363–400, who observes that 'Sigewold' is the OE equivalent of the Greek 'Nicephoros', and that one Nicephoros, Bishop of Herakleia, incurred the displeasure of the Byzantine Emperor in 956 (from evidence in *Ioannis Scylitzae Synopsis Historiarum*, ed. H. Thurn, Berlin and New York 1973, p. 244).

[21] The *LE* mss. describe Thurstan as *Danus*, whereas *LibÆ* and B have *Dacus*, an epithet regularly used in MedLat to mean 'Dane', though originally meaning 'Dacian'. Thurstan's name is Old Norse.

place, asked the king for it, more out of greed than devotion. And as they were contending for it with identical ambition, a certain man called Wulfstan of Dalham, who was a privy counsellor[22] of the king, intervened, so that neither should trample over the other in contempt, nor be envious of the other on his acquisition of the property. He was motivated by divine approval rather than guided by human feeling. To prevent the king from granting them the objectives of their petition, he approached him with this speech: 'Lord King, whereas we are duty-bound to make provision for your safety and honour and for the whole kingdom, none of us has advised that the request of these men be complied with. For the place is holy and famous and undeserving of owners such as these, and, so that you may not be pressed unwittingly into sinning against its ancient dignity, I will, if you command it, not hesitate to supply you with a brief account of it.' And he gave the king an ordered account of the dignity of the monastery and the sanctity of its relics and whatever other things, hitherto unknown to the king, had either been written down by Bede or spread around by word of mouth. The king, on hearing this, was enflamed by divine fervour,[23] and he not only repeatedly refused to give the aforesaid men what they had requested, but kept on saying that he would add to the greatness of the place in question.

3. That Bishop Æthelwold, at the command of King Edgar, ejected the clerics from the church of Ely and introduced monks there, and who it was that he made the first abbot there, and what ornaments[24] he donated.[25]

Now that these presumptuous individuals had had the expectation of gaining their objectives cut from under them, the glorious King Edgar forthwith summoned the blessed Æthelwold and conferred with him about the restoration of the monastery of Ely, saying that his inward desire was for the gathering together in that place of brothers by whom the most high Lord and the holy relics might be revered with worthy veneration. And, promising that he would endow the monastery in question with lands and gifts and a privilege of eternal liberty, he asked that man of God to be his colleague in the accomplishing of this very important undertaking, and to make a concerted effort with him regarding the establishment of monks in that place. The man of God, consequently, understood that the Holy Spirit was at work in the king and, giving thanks to God, in whose hand are the

---

[22] Lat. *a secretis*; Bishop Æthelwold is also so described (p. 77.12, ed. Blake) in *LE* ii. 5.

[23] Reading with E and AC: **fervore**.

[24] Lat. *ornamenta*, 'adornments', 'trappings': a technical term covering all sorts of moveable church equipment, e.g. vestments, hangings, plate.

[25] Sources: this chapter includes quotations from *LibÆ* 3, for which see Appendix A, and has parallels with the *Book of Miracles*, in the passage translated in Appendix B.

hearts of kings,[26] he made no delay in bringing the good work to maturation, but carefully built anew the aforesaid monastery, having expelled the clerics who had been living there in an unworthy fashion for a considerable time and, as the previous book makes clear, were masters over it. He installed monks, to applause noised in various ways,[27] and appointed a religious man called Byrhtnoth, his own provost, as their abbot, and adorned the site of the place in a distinguished manner with monastic buildings. And thus, in accordance with God's ordinance, a band of monks, which in every place and at every time provides its own harmoniousness and supplies grace and mercy to anyone who wants it, arrived in Ely with much honour and reverence in the 970th year from the Lord's incarnation. It was, moreover, in the 297th year from the time when the virgin Æthelthryth began building-works there; in the hundredth year, in fact, from the sack of the monastery <as>[28] one reads, following the chronicle.

Specifically, he admitted into monastic life the clerics who consented to receive a monk's habit,[29] and expelled those who refused, something which he is recorded as having done in other churches also.[30] He also granted in their entirety to God and St Æthelthryth many lands – not only some bought by himself from the king, but also others received *gratis* from the king – these lands being accompanied by various gifts and ornaments and confirmed by a privilege having royal authority. Furthermore, buying a great many lands from other people, he gave these also to the church: these are entered in a book of their own elsewhere, but we have thought fit to allow each a brief entry here. The blessed bishop also contributed a number of ornaments for the glorious enactment of the divine office. Some of these have been diligently preserved in the church throughout the passage of a remarkable number of years until now, namely, a number of copes, one of them of outstanding workmanship, suitable for the office of the precentor on major festivals, encircled, as befits such a garment, with an excellent orphrey of precious *purpura* all around. He gave, furthermore, a great many grand and precious objects in silver and gold, but amidst the havoc of times of misfortune they have been removed from the church and completely destroyed The sacred altar, moreover, had been adorned with royal cloths and vessels, being itself decorated with gold and precious stones.

---

[26] Cf. Proverbs 21.1.

[27] Lat. *multimodo sonorum plausu* (p. 74.19, ed. Blake), or should we emend to *multimodo suorum plausu*, 'with manifold applause from his supporters'?

[28] Reading conjecturally <ut> *iuxta cronicum legitur* (p. 74.26, ed. Blake).

[29] Lat. *habitus*, translated first as 'pattern of life' and secondly as 'habit', covers both meanings.

[30] So E; the text printed by Blake means: 'in a number of other churches as well'.

4. How the blessed Æthelwold bought the whole Isle of Ely fr Edgar.[31]

Not long afterwards, the blessed Bishop Æthelwold – a man worthy to be mentioned by name frequently and with reverence – was filled with the Holy Spirit and, as he had foresight and foreboding for the future, with regard to the evils of treachery which on Earth have a way of being spawned and of rising up, he approached King Edgar a second time and, at a meeting held with him, bought from him the whole neighbouring region of the aforesaid Isle, namely twenty hides of land which the king possessed within the Isle and additionally the honour and soke of seven-and-a-half hundreds:[32] specifically, two within the Isle and, on the other hand, five-and-a half in the province of the East Angles, and five hides at Melbourn and three-and-a-half hides at Armingford and twelve hides at Northwold. In exchange {Bishop Æthelwold} gave sixty hides which he had held at Harting[33] as a gift from his lord, King Æthelstan, and, in addition, the sum of one hundred pounds, together with a golden cross, embellished with marvellous workmanship and filled with relics. The glorious king made a free-will offering of this cross, along with a wonderful gospel-book,[34] upon the altar of St Æthelthryth in Ely, as a safeguard for his grants and in furtherance of the liberty of the place. And thus St Æthelwold offered to God and St Æthelthryth the lands mentioned above, bought from the king with all customary royal rights, and confirmed with a privilege of eternal liberty, as the following privilege of the king will make clear. It needs to be set down here in order that it may be clear to all with what stability the house of God rests upon its foundation.

5. A privilege of King Edgar about the liberty of the monastery and about its jurisdiction of seven-and-a-half hundreds, that is, of the two hundreds within the Isle and five-and-a-half in the province of the East Angles, with the addition of Melbourn, Armingford and Northwold; moreover he also assigned a quarter of the revenue of the common wealth of Cambridgeshire, to be given to the brothers of Ely as a perpetual right.[35]

By the governance of God Almighty, who rules over the sceptres of all

---

[31] Source: the chapter-heading and parts of the chapter are from *LibÆ* 4. See Appendix A.

[32] I.e. the jurisdiction over this area.

[33] In Sussex.

[34] The first of seventeen gospel-books listed in the inventory in *LE* iii. 50.

[35] Source: monastic archives, cf. cartularies CM; British Library, MS Add. 9822; Stowe charter 31. Ostensible date: 970. This charter is not included in *LibÆ* and its authenticity is denied by Blake, Introd. p. 1. It probably derives from the same source as data in *LE* ii. 8–9 and 39 concerning charters of King Edgar.

kings,[36] nay, who equitably controls the reins of the whole secular Universe and of all creation, by indissoluble rule – supported by His assent and grace, I Edgar, High King[37] of the beloved Isle of Albion – enjoying as I am an untroubled peace, now that the sceptres of the Scots, Welsh and Britons[38] and all the surrounding regions have been rendered subject to us – am eager and earnestly occupied in increasing the praises of the Creator of all things, lest, by our[39] inactivity and in our days, His service might seem to be becoming more luke-warm than is right. Rather, in this our time, with the assistance of Him who deigned to promise to remain with us to the end of time, in view of the fact that everywhere in our kingdom the service of God, deficient in the monasteries deserted in former times, is now reviving, we are desirous that congregations of monks and nuns should arise, living under the rule of St Benedict the Abbot, so that by their prayer and lively religious observance of the service of God, we may be able to have the Ruler Himself at peace with us. Hence, pondering in our heart the frequent admonitions of the venerable Bishop Æthelwold, I desire to honour with this privilege and with abundant goods the monastery which is identified as situated in the region of Ely,[40] dedicated of old in honour of St Peter the Prince of the Apostles,[41] and adorned with the relics and miracles of the bountiful virgin Æthelthryth, whose venerable life is presented to the people of our time in the *History of the English People,* and who even now endures, concealed in a white marble sarcophagus. The aforesaid place, eventually, with the lapsing of the service of God had been, in our era, surrendered to the royal revenue. But our privy counsellor Æthelwold, lover of God, Prelate of the diocese of Winchester, having given us sixty hides in the vill which is called by its inhabitants Harting, has purchased[42] the aforesaid place with its appurtenances. And I have added to his purchase three vills which are called by these names: Melbourn, Armingford, Northwold, and he has, on my advice and with my aid, there, in Ely, established a large number of monks,

---

[36] Repunctuating at p. 76.15f., ed. Blake: *Omnipotentis Dei cunctorum sceptra regentis moderamine regum, immo totius seculi creatureque cuncte indissolubili regimine eque gubernantis habenas* . . .

[37] Lat. *basileus,* the term used in Greek for the Great King of Persia.

[38] Lat. *Scottorum, Cumbrorumque ac Brittonum.*

[39] Indiscriminate alternation between first person singular and plural forms is a feature of the Latin of this privilege.

[40] The form *Elig* is used in the Stowe transcript of this charter.

[41] However, other passages in *LE* (pp. 4.8; 33.3–7; 367.7–10, ed. Blake) state that the dedication both of St Æthelthryth's monastic foundation and its predecessor, destroyed by Penda, was to St Mary; cf. also the privilege of King Edgar, *LE* ii. 9, which makes a grant to the Lord, the Virgin Mary and St Æthelthryth.

[42] Lat. *mutuavit:* originally 'borrowed', 'leased', but also used of sale in MedLat.

serving God faithfully under the guidance of a rule, in charge of whom I have appointed Byrhtnoth, a wise and well-conducted man. I, sharing very much in the joy at this outcome, rejoicing for love of Christ and of St Peter, whom I have chosen as my patron under God, and of the holy virgin Æthelthryth, beloved of God, and her holy progeny resting there, and on behalf of the souls of my forefathers, the former kings, wish generously to augment that purchased with these gifts, my counsellors being witnesses: specifically, I grant the ten thousand eels which are rendered every year instead of military service in the vill which is called *Wellen*[43] for the provisioning of the monks now and henceforth, and I grant within the marshes the secular judicial proceedings of two hundreds, and outside the marshes I bestow the five hundreds in Wicklow in the province of the East Saxons {*recte* East Angles}[44] in kindness, reserving them by sanction for the needs of the brothers; also indeed all judicial proceedings or chastisements of breaches of the rightful law in respect to secular pleas relating to all lands or vills duly pertaining to the aforesaid monastery and those which the providence of God shall generously grant to the aforesaid place, for a future age, whether by purchase, or donation or any just acquisition: let secular judicial proceedings be permanently subject to the examination – so[45] merciful a one – of the brothers residing in the monastery, as a source of revenues necessary for their food or clothing. Over and above the foregoing, I assess every fourth coin of the public wealth in the province of Cambridge as due to be rendered to the brothers as a perpetual right. And let this be a free privilege – our gift being, as it were, devoutly offered to God and His aforementioned saints for the healing of our souls, as we have said previously, so that no one from among kings or princes, or anyone at all, of any rank, holding, in the future. pre-eminent power through persistent maintenance of a tyranny, may presume to contravene any of these things, if he does not wish to have the curse of almighty God and of His saints and of me and of my fathers, on behalf of whom we wish all the things mentioned to be kept free for evermore in eternal liberty. AMEN. We have caused this privilege consisting of this grant and liberty to be written in the 970th year from the incarnation of our Lord Jesus Christ, in the thirteenth year of the indiction, in the thirteenth year, likewise, of my reign,[46] in the royal vill which is known by tillers of the soil by the popular appellation of Woolmer.[47] {We have done so} not secretly in a corner, but openly, beneath Heaven, and most conspicuously, with the knowledge of all the foremost

---

[43] *Wellen* comprised Upwell and Outwell, Cambridgeshire.

[44] They were situated in Suffolk.

[45] Reading with EF: *tam*, not *tamen* (p. 77.31, ed. Blake).

[46] Other authorities state: 'in the thirteenth year equally of my reign.'

[47] Woolmer, Hampshire.

men of my kingdom.[48] We have also ordered that these our ordinances be written out in the language in customary use, so that they may sound in the ears of the common people, lest they might seem to contain any admixture of pettifoggery: rather let all contradiction be utterly nullified by the royal authority or power given to us by God.

6. About the industriousness of Abbot Byrhtnoth.[49]

Now, Byrhtnoth, servant of the Lord, on having received this gift from the aforementioned king, was consecrated as abbot of the church of Ely by the blessed Archbishop Dunstan and by Æthelwold, Bishop of Winchester. Then, with discernment and care, he organized a congregation of the Lord under the governance of a rule. Nor did he reckon the care of souls entrusted to him as a matter of little importance, and take more trouble over transitory matters doomed to obsolescence. No. For he was a man of exceptional prudence and the greatest self-denial, and one who was eagerly intent on carrying business through to its conclusion. On this occasion he was laying new foundations in a monastery, and assigning to it, in addition, considerable estates. Forthwith, the faithful steward whom the Lord set up over his household, 'to give them in season their measure of wheat',[50] both began to deny himself sleep while fulfilling the word of God with the works of his piety, and similarly, in his administration of worldly affairs, he began to work himself into a sweat in accordance with the teaching of the apostles, and, as for the sons of the Church living in community under him, he faithfully made apportionments to each according to his need. His mind's eye certainly did not become blinded to the contemplation of eternal things by reason of his immediate worries: rather, the more ample the means became whereby the church was supported, the more he yearned for the joy of the heavenly country, where he happily arrived by way of the palm of martyrdom, as is established later on. Moreover, he loved the glory and beauty of the house of God, which he sought to make resplendent with diverse ornaments. For he made statues of the blessed virgins and, at very great cost, overlaid them with gold and silver and jewels and set them up near the high altar, two to the right and two to the left. They presented to the

---

[48] The *LE* omits the list of witnesses, but this is known from elsewhere and printed by Blake, p. 78, n. *f*.

[49] Source: unidentified local source, commemorating Abbot Byrhtnoth, perhaps a work on the succession of abbots. There is further evidence, later in book ii, for the availability to the compiler of such a work, a precursor of the extant *Chronicon Abbatum et Episcoporum Eliensium*.

[50] Luke 12.42 Vulgate.

people much splendour in the glory of the temple of the Lord. They were stripped of their covering in the surrender to King William the Great – moreover, all the better and larger of the ornaments of the church were removed – and it is only as bare wood that they can be seen to this day.

7. How King Edgar gave Hatfield to St Æthelthryth.[51]

After the blessed Æthelwold, as has been said, had restored the aforementioned monastery, the glorious King Edgar, just as he had promised, set about venerating and enlarging the place and, wishing to fulfil his vow, made an offering to God and St Æthelthryth, with a charter, of forty hides of land in the district which is called Hatfield[52] which a certain powerful man called Ordmær and his wife Ælde bequeathed to him on their death. His intention was that, given that the region was wooded in that place, the brothers would be able to have timber from it for the building of the church and enough firewood to satisfy their needs.

[So then, as long as the king had been alive, the brothers held this land without claim against them. But after the king's death, when the government of the kingdom was in disorder and the legal tenure of the land disrupted, there arose powerful men, specifically, Æthelwine, styled Ealdorman, which means 'chieftain' or 'earl',[53] and his brothers, and they laid claim to the land, saying that their father, Ealdorman Æthelstan, had acquired the land in exchange for his inheritance, which was in the region called Devon, but that King Edgar had forcibly deprived him of it. When, therefore their claim had been set forth in narrative and demonstration, the claimants prevailed and, ignoring the respect due to Holy Church, they seized the land and appropriated it for themselves. The brothers, however, seeing that they could in no way be deprived of that land without great loss, in view of the fact that they did not have forest elsewhere from which they could meet their needs, made a request to the aforementioned Æthelwine and, when agreement with him had been reached, bought from him the land to which we have been repeatedly referring, namely Hatfield. They gave for it

---

[51] Source: *LibÆth* 5, word for word. Here begins the long section of *LE* (ending at ii. 49b) which is almost entirely derived from *LibÆ*. This translation follows, except where otherwise stated, the Latin text of F, which presents the *LibÆ* almost complete, whereas E shortens it drastically. Material within square brackets is that omitted in E. The epitome, which excludes most material from the period after King Edgar's reign, probably represents the intended text of the compiler of *LE*, witness the treatment of Hatfield in *LE* ii. 55.

[52] Hatfield, Hertfordshire. Monastic estates named in chapter titles in *LE* were situated in Cambridgeshire unless otherwise stated. Cambridgeshire, at the time of the compilation of *LE*, was understood to include the Isle of Ely (see *LE* i *pr.* S).

[53] Lat. *princeps sive comes.*

two pieces of land which Wulfstan of Dalham gave to St Æthelthryth when he died, namely thirty hides at Hemingford, and six at Wennington, adding, as well, five hides at Yelling[54] which Wulfwine *Cocus*[55] and his wife Ælfswyth forfeited for their wrongdoing, on many counts and with the public as witness. These proceedings were transacted in the place which is called Slaughter,[56] in the presence of Ealdorman Ælfhere and Æthelwine and Ælfric *Cild*, meaning *puer* {child},[57] and in the presence of the whole retinue accompanying them. In order, moreover, that this agreement should be fixed and incontestable, Æthelmær *Cild* and Ælfwold, two of the highest-ranking men[58] of England, were guarantors and witnesses of this matter.][59]

8. How the blessed Æthelwold bought Linden[60] with its appendages, Hill and Witcham and Wilburton, and the privilege of the king on this vill. [61]

[Since, as Truth bears witness, anyone wishing to build a tower first sits down and calculates the expenses which are inevitable – whether he has what is needed to complete the work – lest after he has laid the foundation and cannot complete it, all who see it will begin to ridicule him, saying, 'This man began to build and could not complete his work,'[62] so] the venerable Bishop Æthelwold, the disciple of Truth, having faith [not in gold or in silver but] in the Lord Jesus Christ, sought diligently to complete the work which he undertook and, in order to expand the aforementioned monastery, took pains to acquire many[63] properties. For, specifically, from Leofric of Brandon, the son of Æthelferth, he bought twelve hides, namely the estate which is called Linden, with its dependencies, namely Hill and Witcham and Wilburton, making a payment of one hundred mancuses and a very fine horse, and giving him the land at Bishampton[64] which Leofric's wife, called Æthelflæd, had previously sold to him. This purchase and agreement was

---

[54] Hemingford Abbots, Wennington and Yelling, formerly in Huntingdonshire (now Cambridgeshire).

[55] *Cocus* = 'cook'.

[56] Slaughter, Gloucestershire.

[57] *Puer*: 'boy', 'child'.

[58] Lat. *optimates*.

[59] Like E , the F version here omits some moralizing from *LibÆ*.

[60] Linden End, Cambridgeshire.

[61] Source: *LibÆ* 6, with some extra material added at the end probably from a local compilation of charters of King Edgar, cf. *LE* ii. 5, 39. The title is given here in the version of E, which is an expansion of that in *LibÆ*.

[62] Cf. Luke 14. 28–30.

[63] E substitutes: 'properties all around'.

[64] In Worcestershire.

thus effected in the place called Cambridge, in the presence of the better people[65] of the district. But when time had elapsed and King Edgar had died, that same Leofric endeavoured with crafty cunning to annul, if he could, the whole of the agreement which he had made with the bishop. But the lawmen Eadric *Rufus*[66] and Leofric of *Berle* and Siferth *Vecors*,[67] who had been involved in this matter and had been witnesses, declared him to be guilty.[68]

But as for the provision that the aforementioned king had made for posterity by means of the privilege which follows, the provision which he desired to have set down in writing not only in Latin but also in the language of the people and to be reinforced by a fearful curse, and which it has been decided to set down in both versions in the present volume:[69] in view of the fact that leave used not to be given for the royal charter to be shown to everyone and it ought not to be hidden away from everyone, it has been needful that there should be made public, through this present work, information about that charter which it has not been possible to obtain by means of the charter itself.

9. The privilege of King Edgar about the same.[70]

All inheritances of worldly goods are bequeathed to the uncertain heirs of one's descendants, and all the glory of the World, when the end of mortal life approaches, fades away, having been reduced to nothing. By means of our earthly holdings of transitory things, therefore, let us always profit by acquiring the enduring rewards of the heavenly country, the Lord being our advocate. On this reasoning, I, Edgar, High King[71] of all Britain, have bestowed a certain small country estate, namely ten hides in the place which is known by the commonly used name of Linton, upon the Lord and His Mother, Mary, and the ever-virgin Æthelthryth, too, at the monastery which is situated in Ely,[72] for the use of the monks living there, as an everlasting

---

[65] Lat. *melioribus*.

[66] *Rufus*: 'Redhead'.

[67] *Vecors*: 'the Mad'.

[68] The rest of the chapter is extraneous to the *LibÆ* material. The floweriness of its prose suggests derivation from the same source as non-*LibÆ* material in chapter 39, evidently a collection of the monastery's charters of King Edgar.

[69] It seems that the *LE* compiler is quoting word for word; the English version of the charter, which his source evidently gave, is not included in *LE*.

[70] Source: monastic archives, cf. cartularies C, E and G. Not part of *LibÆ*.

[71] Lat. *basileus*.

[72] The form *Elig* is used in C and G (first hand).

inheritance, so that it may belong to it for evermore with all its easements, namely meadows, grazing lands, woods. Moreover, there belong to this land many hides from various surrounding vills, honoured by perpetual liberty. Let the aforesaid country estate, moreover, be free of all imposition of earthly service, with three exceptions, namely: military service, repair of bridges or fortifications. If anyone, therefore, should wish to transfer this gift of ours to any purpose other than the one we have laid down, let him be punished, destitute of association with the Holy Church of God, in the eternal, gloomy fires of the Abyss, together with Judas, the betrayer of Christ and his accomplices, if he does not make amends with appropriate satisfaction for the delinquency which he has committed against our decree.

10. How the blessed Æthelwold bought eight hides at Stretham.[73]

About the same time, Leofric and Æthelflæd, mentioned earlier,[74] were endeavouring by their entreaties to obtain the consent of the bishop to dedicate their church at Brandon. At the time, therefore, when its dedication had come to pass they offered him a forty-shilling silver bowl, for the love and honour which he had shown towards them, with very many other fine things. When these things had been given to him, the bishop said to them: 'Most dear people, I do not want your silver, nor those gifts, but they are all yours. Merely grant, most dear Leofric, that I may be permitted to buy the land belonging to two sisters, namely eight hides at Stretham which their brother Leofric bequeathed to them on his death.' In consequence of this, when he heard the wish of the bishop, Leofric freely gave his permission, and the sisters of the man in question,[75] called Æthelflaed and Æthelgifu, likewise acceded. The venerable bishop did indeed buy the land from the one sister, namely Æthelflæd, giving her thirty pounds for her four hides and the stock which was held on the land, and to the other of them, namely Æthelgifu, he gave the same amount in silver for her four hides and her share of the stock. This money, moreover, was given and paid in full to the sisters in the town which is called Cambridge, at the same time [as the bishop bought Linden from the aforesaid Leofric for one hundred mancuses, as was related in an earlier chapter.[76] When the small son of Wulfsige and Æthelflæd was brought to that place, the bringers of the boy and his aunt Æthelgifu received thirty pounds and took the money, with the boy, to his mother, that is, Æthelflæd.]

---

[73] Source: LibÆ 7–9, word for word, except that certain passages of moralizing are omitted.

[74] I.e. in the preceding chapter of LibÆ = LE ii. 8.

[75] Lat. eius, referring to the other (deceased) Leofric.

[76] LE ii. 8 = LibÆ 6.

The space of a year having elapsed after these events, the blessed Æthelwold bought a hide and two weirs at this same place, Stretham, from Ælfwold of Mardleybury for twenty mancuses in the presence of the whole populace of the city of Cambridge, and two brothers with the same name – that is to say, two Ælfhelms, one of whom had the additional name *Polga* – were the sureties for this matter. But, after the death of King Edgar, this same Ælfwold broke the whole agreement, saying that he had been forced to do this, and that violence and pillage had been inflicted upon him. He said, too, that he wished to keep the land and return the money which he had received. Then Abbot Byrhtnoth set out and took proceedings against him at Hertford and, in the presence of everyone at a General Meeting, put it to him how his wife and sons had been estate-born slaves[77] on land belonging to St Æthelthryth at Hatfield and how it had been in order that he might have them free and without claim on them that he had sold the land to the bishop on receipt of twenty mancuses from the bishop. Consequently, after this explanation had been given a hearing, Ælfwold ceased his impudence and, at length, in the final agreement that was made, Abbot Byrhtnoth added forty shillings to the aforementioned gold and gave it to him. Ælfwold's two sons, Ælfwine and Æthelmær, came to Cambridge for this money, and Ælfweard and Wine of Witchford brought it to them there on behalf of the abbot. And the witnesses of this matter were Oswi and Oscytel of *Beche*[78] and Osulf of Gretton and many other prominent men[79] of that region.

In the same Stretham a certain widow, called by the name of Wulfflæd, the relict of Siferth, sold twenty-four acres to the aforesaid prelate of Ely on the same day that she became a nun consecrated to God. [Her father Wulfstan had acquired the land in the time of King Æthelstan and after the death of her father she held the land continuously without claim and the whole hundred knew this].

11. About Downham.[80]

[handwritten: ✓ land]

This is an account of how the blessed Bishop Æthelwold acquired six hides at Downham, a vill which is very fertile and close to the monastery. First, for two hides he agreed to pay fifteen pounds to Leofsige and his wife Siflæd at Cambridge. [Then, Provost Leofwine and Wine of Witchford and all the best men of Ely brought him part of the money, namely ten pounds. The witnesses of this transaction were Seaxferth and Oscytel and Oswi of *Beche*

---

[77] Lat. *innati*.

[78] *Beche* comprised Landbeach and Waterbeach, Cambridgeshire.

[79] Lat. *proceres*.

[80] Source: *LibÆ* 10–13.

and Uvi and many other loyal men.[81] Moreover, as for the remaining five pounds, a payment-date was agreed between them. Meanwhile] on a second occasion, they made another agreement [between themselves], to the effect that the aforesaid Leofsige and his wife should, with the fifteen pounds, buy from the bishop five hides at Clayhithe, [but on condition that the bishop should give them as well a silver cup worth forty shillings which Byrhtsige, the father of Leofsige, bequeathed to the bishop on his death. And so, by making this agreement, they brought about the exchange, or transfer, of the whole of the live stock and dead stock[82] which was on the two pieces of land, that is, at Downham and Clayhithe.]

Meanwhile, before Leofsige and Siflæd had handed back, in payment for Clayhithe, the ten pounds mentioned above, King Edgar died. Upon the king's death, the aforesaid Leofsige – an enemy of God and deceiver of men – and his wife, made void the whole agreement which they had with the bishop, [and sometimes offered him the ten pounds they had received from him, but at other times denied that they owed him anything at all. Furthermore, they reckoned that in this way they would recover through trickery the land which they had sold, but we continually refuted them in all respects with our witnesses. During that tempestuous time, moreover, when the king, as we have said, had died, and they were keeping us waiting and wearing us down over a long period, that deceiver {Leofsige} heaped evil upon evil and trickery upon trickery and by forcible means seized Peterborough and Oundle and Kettering from God and St Peter.] For this reason it came about that nobody ploughed those lands for two years, nor sowed or cultivated them in any way, and so all the arable land was going to waste. And then, seeing with what great injuries and tribulations that inveigler was burdening his servants, the Lord God had pity on their hardships. Through his mercy, Holy Church[83] recovered what it unjustly lost. For a General Meeting was convened in London where, it being a time when commanders, chieftains, governors, orators and advocates[84] had gathered from every region, the blessed Æthelwold summoned the aforesaid Leofsige to justice. Before them all, he gave an orderly exposition of his case and the damage and violence which Leofsige had inflicted on Holy Church. When the matter had been discussed by everyone, thoroughly and properly and openly, they all, by their judgement, restored Peterborough and Oundle and Kettering to God and the blessed Æthelwold. They ruled also that

[81] Lat. *fideles viri.*

[82] The term 'dead stock' is still in current use at farm-sales to denote inanimate farming equipment (personal recollection, confirmed by Derek and Angela Helson).

[83] Or: 'the holy church', that is, Ely monastery.

[84] Picturesque Latin here: *duces, principes, satrape, hretores et causidici.* For the equivalence of *dux* to *ealdorman*, see the witness-list to King Edgar's charter *(LE* ii. 9) quoted by Blake p. 82, n. *n.*

Leofsige should make amends to the bishop for his whole loss, and pay compensation to the value of his *mund,* and for the violence pay compensation to the king to the amount of his *wergeld.* After this, they met again,[85] within eight days, at Northampton, the whole of this region or shire having been gathered there, they again set out the aforementioned claim before them all. When it had been set out and made clear, the people at Northampton, too, gave the same verdict as had previously been given in London. This done, all the people, with oaths on the cross of Christ, restored to the bishop, free from challenge, the lands which were his, namely Peterborough, Oundle and Kettering.

In the mean time, as a result of [the boiling up of] divine vengeance, the aforesaid Leofsige, [who so greatly afflicted the servants of God], died shamefully and miserably. When he was dead, the blessed Æthelwold [and Æthelwine, styled Ealdorman, with the magnates of the shire of Northampton and the most prominent men of the East Angles, held at Wansford a meeting in respect to eight hundreds. Among other matters, it was there decided that Siflæd, the widow of Leofsige, and her heirs, ought to pay compensation for the aforesaid violence to God and the bishop, just as Leofsige himself would have had to do if he had lived, and they assessed the amount of the damage that he had done to the bishop at more than a hundred pounds. Then the aforesaid woman, supported by the advocacy of all the prominent people there, humbly asked the bishop to have pity on her for the love of God, so that she might pay the compensation which was due from her, in addition to what her sons owed, with the hundred shillings[86] which the bishop had been going to give her for the two hides at Downham, with respect to which he had received a completion-date from them, as we have said above. The renowned bishop, accordingly, granted what they had sought and, moreover, acted more mercifully than they were hoping for themselves. For he remitted the whole of the damage which had been awarded against her and, in addition, said to her that she should come to Ely within eight days and collect the hundred shillings from Abbot Byrhtnoth. And so she did, and the money was given to her before the witness of two hundreds. The bishop, moreover, gave her seven pounds for her corn which was on the land at Downham. This matter, therefore, having been concluded in this manner, the blessed Æthelwold] took possession of the two hides at Downham and his land at Clayhithe, with all the stock which was on them.[87]

Not long afterwards Siferth of Downham, incapacitated and declining

---

[85] Reading with the *LibÆ* mss: *convenerunt,* as in p. 85.12, ed. Blake.

[86] Equivalent to five pounds.

[87] Here *LE* omits 22 lines of hexameter verse in praise of the delights of Downham, translated in Appendix A from Blake, pp. 398f.

into the feebleness of old age, was seriously afflicted by a disease of the feet [which is called gout]. At the time when [the blessed] Æthelwold had brought with him to Ely Æthelred, the future king but at that time an earl, and his mother, Queen Ælfthryth,[88] [and Ælfric *Cild*] and many of the senior[89] men of England, this man, with his wife, Wulfflæd [by name], came to the bishop. In the presence of the people already mentioned, he informed him that on his death he would give the two hides which he possessed at Downham to God and St Æthelthryth for the sake of his soul, and said that he had chosen the place of his burial there,[90] and asked all who were present to be witnesses to this matter.

[On another occasion also, after the death of Goding of Gretton,[91] the same man, Siferth, came a second time to Ely, where he knew he had been buried, and asked the brothers to take him to his burial place. For he used to be a very dear friend to him. When they arrived there, he called the abbot to him, and Eadric, and Leofric of *Berle*, and Lyfing of Trumpington, and made it known to them that his most dear and faithful friends were buried there, and that he himself, weighed down by his extreme infirmity, was coming close to death. 'And therefore,' he said, 'most dear people, I desire that my agreement be renewed before you, namely how I have chosen the place of my burial here, and have given to God and St Æthelthryth, after my day is over, the two hides which I have at Downham, and how I give to my daughter two hides at Wilburton. And I beg, my friends, that you do not cast this into oblivion, but rather, when it becomes necessary, acknowledge it.' Similarly, on his return home that day, he renewed this agreement in the presence of the better people of his region beyond Upware, in the place which is called *Hyravicstowe*.

Then, when this same man Siferth of Downham, with sickness overpowering him, had come to feel that the hour of his death was approaching, and had taken to his bed at Linden without hope of recovering his health, he sent for Abbot Byrhtnoth and for the brothers of the church. And there were present: Ælfric of Witcham, Ealdstan and his son Wine, Leofric, Byrhthelm, Ælfhelm of *Redewinclen* and Eadric, one of Ealdorman Æthelwine's high-ranking men, and the priest Oswald, and Seaxferth with his son. Then Abbot Byrhtnoth arranged for the will of Siferth to be written down in a tripartite chirograph, in the presence of his wife and his daughter and all the people mentioned above, and had it read out before them all. When it was read, he had it cut, and Siferth kept one part of the chirograph, giving the second part to the abbot. The third part he sent at once by the

---

[88] The queen's name is found in E alone of the mss.

[89] Lat. *maiores natu.*

[90] Evidently at Ely, not Downham.

[91] Gretton, Northamptonshire.

110

aforesaid Byrhthelm to Ealdorman Æthelwine, who at that time was dwelling at Ely, and asked him to allow his will to stand, just as the abbot had written it and set it down at Linden in the witness of the aforementioned men. And so, when Ealdorman Æthelwine had heard this and saw the chirograph, he sent Wulfnoth of Stowe back there to him with Byrhthelm and asked him what it was he wanted concerning his will and with what conditions. Siferth soon sent the reply to Æthelwine through Wulfnoth and Byrhthelm, that he wanted his will to stand, free from challenge or alteration, just as the aforesaid abbot had set it down in the chirograph. When Ealdorman Æthelwine heard this, he granted that it should stand in its entirety, in accordance with the attestation that Siferth himself gave.

After this, Bishop Æthelwold and Abbot Byrhtnoth with repeated requests besought two brothers, Ælfric and Leofwine, the sons of a certain earl[92] called Hereric, to sell them two hides which they had at Downham for gold or silver, or to exchange them for other land of a similar value. But so long as the brothers held the land jointly, they were in no way able to bring the matter to a conclusion. At length, however, Ælfric, the elder brother, exchanged lands with his younger brother and, in return for the two hides at Downham, gave him land at Chippenham which their mother bequeathed to them.]

After some time it happened that Ælfric[93] was burdened with a heavy imposition of tax. Since he did not have the money demanded of him, he came to Bishop Æthelwold and Abbot Byrhtnoth and offered them his two hides at Downham in exchange for three hides which they had at Chippenham, [on condition they gave him, in addition, a sum of money, the amount to be decided by them. Æthelwold and Byrhtnoth acted accordingly, that is: exchanged the lands and gave Ælfric four pounds in addition.] This agreement and exchange was made between them and Ælfric was paid the money close by Cambridge to the south, in the presence of the whole populace of that region. [Ælfric accordingly first granted the land directly to Abbot Byrhtnoth before twenty-four judges in the aforesaid place, and then, in addition, did the same in the presence of the law-worthy witnesses Eadric and Ælfhelm *Polga*, and Leofsige, the son of Ælfwine, and Osulf and Lyfing, and Ælfnoth and Uvi, and Oswy and Grim, and Wulfnoth and Ælfric and Wynsige, and Leofsige and Ælfnoth, the son of Goding. With all these present and bearing witness, Ælfric, the son of Earl Hereric, gave Abbot Byrhtnoth the two hides at Downham, in their entirety, in respect to lands, woods, marshes, on terms just as full and free as those on which his father ever held the land, with the exceptions of one marsh close to Cambridge and five acres of land which Ælfric himself retained. Furthermore, when all this

---

[92] Lat. *comes.*

[93] E modifies the transition here.

was done, the renowned Bishop Æthelwold gave him ten shillings and Abbot Byrhtnoth gave him twenty shillings-worth of sheep and a horse worth ten shillings. And so, with the hand-over of these shillings and shillings-worth of property, Ælfric received, in exchange for his two hides at Downham, six pounds[94] and the three hides at Chippenham. The abbot and Ælfric moreover exchanged cattle and the grain which was in storehouses in the two places, that is, Ælfric surrendered fifteen cart-loads of grain at Downham to the abbot and the abbot for his part gave up the same amount at Chippenham. Ælfric also handed over to the abbot thirty acres of sown land and the abbot surrendered the same amount at Chippenham, and gave him forty-eight as a gift. And the witnesses present at this transaction were Leofsige, the son of Goda, and Uvi and Wacher of Swaffham, and Bondo, and Brunstan, a man of the same Ælfric.]

[11a. About the same matter.[95]

This matter of itself provides encouragement, it seems, for us to say how the three hides at Chippenham were acquired which had been given to Ælfric, the son of Earl Hereric, in exchange for two hides at Downham. In the first instance, a certain man called Wine bought at Chippenham from Leofsige of Freckenham eighty acres and five farms with houses built on them for a hundred shillings. He also bought from Ælfric of Witcham twenty acres and one plot with houses built on it, for twenty shillings. He bought from Wulfhelm, the brother of Wulfwine, ten acres for ten shillings. And all this was done in the witness of the whole hundred.

Then Ælfwold, who was called *Grossus*,[96] and his wife, offered to sell to Abbot Byrhtnoth all the land belonging to them which they had in that village, namely Chippenham, and accordingly they came to him at Horningsea. When they were there, the abbot asked them how many hides they had at Chippenham and at what price they had valued them. Accordingly, they said and affirmed that they had three hides there. At length, therefore, they agreed that the abbot would give them a hundred shillings for each hide, and they arranged a completion-date, namely eight days hence at Chippenham, when the wife of Ælfwold would go there to receive fifteen pounds and hand over to the abbot the three hides, in their entirety and free from claims, for it was she who had the greater right to that land, through her marriage to another husband. So the abbot came on the appointed day, and the aforesaid woman was there, and, along with her,

---

[94] That is, the £4 of the original agreement + twenty shillings-worth of sheep = £1 + ten shillings and the ten-shilling horse = a further £1.

[95] Source: *LibÆ* 14 . This chapter is not included in E.

[96] *Grossus*: 'the Fat'.

Othulf of Exning, and Sigemund and his nephew[97] Tucca, and Æthelweard and Osbern of Soham and Ælfstan of Fulbourn and the priest Æthelstan and his brother Bondo, and Wulfhelm and almost all the better people there were in that vill. When these people were gathered together, the abbot, before them all, produced fifteen pounds and, in so doing, poured them out.

Straight away, two men stood up, namely Brunstan of Soham and Glor, and, on behalf of Ulf, prohibited the woman from selling, and the abbot from buying, seventy-five acres of the land. They also prohibited the sale of seven acres to two villagers. Then one of the people standing there said: 'The land which is at issue, even supposing there were no claim against it, and might be granted whole all at once to one party – in no way were there three whole hides there; much less, while they are subject to a claim, do they split into parts for the purposes of the claim.' When he heard this, the abbot called all the better and wiser people who were there to him and, taking their advice, gave the woman half the money. He retained half until, according to the agreement, she could present him three hides intact and without claim. But if she were not able to do this, she would be awarded a sum of money corresponding to the value of the land. And the men previously mentioned were made sureties and witnesses in this matter for both sides. When morning came, therefore, a large number of men were chosen from both sides, that is, from the supporters of the abbot and the supporters of the woman. These people first went round and measured the land which was free from claim, and found the extent of the land which rightfully belonged to the woman to be only one hide of one hundred and twenty acres and, in addition to the hide, twenty-four acres; as for the land subject to claim, they found eighty-two acres of it.

Ulf, without delay, ordered his men to cultivate at once his seventy-five acres. Meanwhile, this same Ulf owed the abbot thirty-seven acres, as a supplementary payment additional to two hides at Milton which he had exchanged with the abbot for two hides and thirty-seven acres at Fordham. He also owed a debt to the abbot for twenty shillings which he had supplied to him and sent through Ælfric, the son of Eadwine. Accordingly, the abbot asked him to release to him the land at Chippenham mentioned previously – that is, the seventy-five acres to which he had laid claim – in exchange for the thirty-seven acres which he owed him and the twenty shillings which he had supplied to him, with the stipulation, however, that Ulf deliver the land, with establishment of the title, in a free and peaceable state without challenge. But, if he were unable to do this and the woman were awarded title to the land, the abbot would buy the land from her, just as they had agreed, and just as their witnesses would wish to affirm the agreement.

When, however, Ælfwold and his wife found out that they were going

---

[97] Lat. *nepos*, which could also mean 'grandson'.

to lose the land through the claim which Ulf had brought forward, as we have said above, they disregarded all advice, and nullified the whole agreement. And they went to their lord, Ælfwold, the brother of Ealdorman Æthelwine, and told him that the abbot had circumvented them by deceit, and that Ulf had claimed the land at his instigation. They said, moreover, that the abbot had agreed upon fifteen pounds for the land, be there more or less.

In order to settle this matter, therefore, Ealdorman Æthelwine and his brother Ælfwold and the Abbot of the monastery of Ely, and with them all the older men of East Anglia and Cambridge, went to Freckenham,[98] and from there they set out for the village called *Hegenetune*,[99] where three hundreds were assembled. And so there the abbot produced, as witnesses and guarantors between him and the woman, the men whose names we have recorded above. When the witnesses were brought before the three hundreds, they corroborated the testimony of the abbot, namely that, at a certain time, in the presence of three assembled hundreds and also the wife of Ælfwold, Ulf had maintained title to the land before them all, six months before the abbot sought to buy the land from her. They affirmed further that they were witnesses and guarantors, between the abbot and the woman, that the abbot would give her fifteen pounds if she would release to him three whole hides at Chippenham, but that, if she were not able to do this, a sum of money would be given to her by the abbot according to the value of the land.

Seeing therefore that the abbot was adjudged to be in the right by the testimony, Ealdorman Æthelwine asked him, for love of him, to increase by a little the amount mentioned above, namely seven-and-a-half pounds. At his request, the abbot gave her thirty shillings and sent it to her by Wine of Ely, the son of Osmund. Wine took this money to Cambridge in person and there on behalf of the abbot, gave it to the woman whose land it was, in front of her husband and publicly before everyone.

Oh, the sacrilegiousness of the age! Oh, the deviousness of the World! It never ceases to hunger after the possessions of the Church, to tear them to pieces by hungering after them, and to diminish them by tearing them to pieces! See how unfair this commerce is! The abbot gave this woman nine pounds and has for the money no more than a hide and twenty-four acres of arable land which is without claim, and six and a half farms bare and laid waste. That hide, therefore, cost a hundred shillings and the twenty-four acres, twenty shillings, and the six and a half farms cost sixty shillings, which nobody with any sense would value at more than twenty shillings!]

---

[98] Freckenham, Suffolk.

[99] Identified by Blake with the Hinton whose name is recalled at Hinton Hall, Haddenham, Cambridgeshire. Cherry Hinton, near Cambridge might seem another possibility, but Alan Kennedy (pers. comm.) finds Blake's identification persuasive.

BOOK II

12. About Witchford.[100]

Then Abbot Byrhtnoth, in the witness of the whole hundred, bought two hundred acres at Witchford from Sumerlida for eleven pounds in the time of King Edgar. [But when the king died and the affairs of the kingdom were in turmoil, that same Sumerlida resorted to tricks and annulled the agreement which he had had with the abbot and said that he, Sumerlida, had done what he had done under compulsion, and wished many times to return the money which he had received. Meanwhile, Ealdorman Æthelwine came to Ely and held a meeting with the whole hundred within the churchyard at the northern gate of the monastery, and there adjudicated upon the action and suit which existed between the abbot and Sumerlida in this way: that the abbot gave Sumerlida thirty {*recte* twenty}[101] shillings there and so paid him in full the twelve pounds for the two hundred acres.]

In the same vill the abbot exchanged sixteen acres with Osmund *Hocere*, giving him the same amount of land at Cambridge for them, on condition, however, that after the death of Osmund the abbot would have both properties.

The abbot also in the same vill exchanged seven acres which he had bought from Ælfnoth in Wilburton.

13. About Wold.[102]

Not far away from there, Æthelstan, the son of Manne, on his death, gave to St Æthelthryth a hundred acres in Wold.

14. About Witcham.[103]

At Witcham there are fifty acres which Ædward[104] and Byrhtferth used to have on lease. With these acres included, St Æthelthryth has three whole hides in Witchford and Wold and Witcham.

15. About Sutton.[105]

A certain Wulfsige and Mawa and their son, Ælfsige by name, gave to God and the holy [virgin and queen] Æthelthryth, three hides in Sutton and they

---

[100] Source: *LibÆ* 15–17, slightly abbreviated.

[101] Lat. xxx *solidos* appears to be a mistake for xx *solidos*, 'twenty shillings'.

[102] Source: *LibÆ* 18.

[103] Source: *LibÆ* 19.

[104] Following the reading of the *LibÆ* mss. and E, *Ædwardus*; F has *Æthelwardus*.

[105] Source: not from *LibÆ* as preserved in extant mss.

put Abbot Byrhtnoth into possession of it in the presence of the hundred so that remembrance of them would be kept with the brothers of the church.

16. About Hill and about Haddenham.[106]

At Hill and Haddenham, Provost Leofwine bought from Wulfheah of Hill a farm for sixty shillings and seventy acres for ten shillings in the witness of the whole hundred.

In the same vill, the brothers of the church bought almost all the land belonging to Ælfsige and very many acres from the poorer villagers there.

In the same vill, Haddenham, that is, the abbot bought from Æthulf and his wife Burgflæd a farm with buildings on it and seventy-six acres, according to the measurements of the priest Manne, and the abbot gave for that land seven pounds, at Thetford. [So then,] the witnesses of this matter were: [Oslac, the son of Appe, and Folcard, and the priest Kenelm, a kinsman of Bishop Æthulf, together with a great many other high-ranking men[107] and] all the citizens of Thetford and the better men of Ely, [namely Ælfstan and Eama and Godere and Wine of Witchford and Ælfric. The abbot and the brothers of the church leased these seventy-six[108] acres, and twenty others, which had previously been bought at Haddenham, to Grim, the son of Wine, so that he might have the income from them so long as he served them well.]

17. About Wilburton.[109]

In Wilburton, the abbot bought two hides of two hundred and forty arable acres, in addition to meadows, from Ælfwine and his wife Siflæd for ninety mancuses and, in addition, five farms with buildings on them. And all this gold was given to him at the monastery at Ely in the presence of [Oswy, the brother of Ulf, and in the presence of Wine and another Wine and] all the better and older men of Ely.

Bishop Æthelwold bought seventy acres there from Oppele. The abbot exchanged eighty acres there with Ælfric of Sutton, giving him land at Witcham.

The brothers also bought there seventy acres from Eading, and from others, whose names are not committed to writing, they bought there many acres, so that five whole hides are held there and the whole hundred bore witness to each purchase.

---

[106] Source: *LibÆ* 20–2.

[107] Lat. *barones*.

[108] The figure *lxxvi*, consistent with the measurement earlier in the chapter, is found in *LibÆ* ms. A, and is here adopted as a correction of the reading of EF: *lxxvii* (p. 93.3, ed. Blake).

[109] Source: *LibÆ* 23–6.

18. About Stonea.[110]

Long before Bishop Æthelwold had formed the community of monks at Ely, Wulfstan of Dalham went there with many men of rank[111] and, when the people of the two hundreds had been gathered there, at the entrance to the minster towards the north, he held a meeting. Then a certain widow, called Æscwyn of Stonea, came to him, and with her came many of her kinsmen and neighbours. In front of them all, she gave to Wulfstan Stonea and the fishery which she had there. Similarly, Ogga of Mildenhall arose and when silence had fallen he said: 'Most dear people, I want you to know that [after my death] I give to St Æthelthryth one hide of land at Cambridge.' On hearing this, Wulfstan arose and, before them all, gave to St Æthelthryth the land and the fishery which the aforementioned widow had given him. [Then he summoned Ogga and said to him: 'Most dear man, seeing that you have undertaken to honour the most glorious virgin Æthelthryth, do not delay in doing what you have undertaken to do. The wish you have conceived is good, certainly, but a more felicitous option is that you should carry it out while life is your companion.'] Ogga, [not failing to give] his advice[112] [due weight, did as he said, and] gave to St Æthelthryth the aforementioned hide in front of them all, [free from every claim. And the church at Ely was in possession or tenure of that land free from claim for many years, that is, so long as Ogga was alive. But, on his death, a kinsman of his, called Uvi, made a claim on that land. Accordingly, people came from all over the place to Cambridge and Wulfstan of Dalham was present there. When the claim which Uvi made had been heard, they discussed the suit this way and that, and judged that Uvi must give four marks as penalty, because he was claiming land to which he had never laid claim while Ogga was alive.

And after the death of King Edgar, that same Uvi, unwilling ever to desist from his impudence, but in fact, even adding trickeries to trickeries and claims to claims, behaved like the man who already had a fatal wound in his body and, after medical treatment, produced scar-tissue from the wound, but after its healing made the scar into a wound again through his own foolishness, so that, through his own lack of self-control, he prematurely brought about a death from which he could have been saved by the help of others. This Uvi, then, came to the abbot after the death of King Edgar, as we have said, and brazenly laid claim to the land and in this process laid traps with his tricks and lies. When the abbot saw this, he took counsel with the two hundreds and Oswi and Oscytel of *Beche*. By their testimony, the abbot was adjudged the possessor, on the grounds that Ogga had lawfully bought

---

[110] Source: *LibÆ* 27–8.

[111] Lat. *barones*.

[112] E adapts the wording slightly: 'the aforesaid Ogga, on his advice . . .'

the land from Uvi and held it unchallenged while he lived.]

19. About Cambridge and about Dullingham.[113]

At the same time, Oslac, [so it happened], was accused before King Edgar, and [the king] ordered that he be dispossessed of all his land and deprived of all the possessions which he had. In these circumstances he humbly asked Bishop Æthelwold to be his defender and to deign to intercede for him with the king. The bishop did so and the king restored everything to Oslac for love of Bishop Æthelwold and at his entreaty, on condition that Oslac give him – the king – one hundred mancuses. Since he did not have such an amount of gold, he borrowed forty mancuses from the bishop and, because the bishop kept coming to his rescue, he promised that he would give him forty acres of land at Cambridge, and a farm and the third part of a wood at Dullingham. And he sent Haward, his kinsman, to Ely and, in front of everyone, this man gave the land to the bishop on behalf of Oslac and made clear the gift which he had given him. [But after the death of King Edgar that same Oslac annulled the whole gift which he had given to the bishop. Then the Abbot of Ely sent Wine to him and to Ordhelm and his sons and asked them to appear against Oslac by the bridge at Cambridge. They did so. The abbot therefore enquired of Oslac what he intended to do about the gift which he had made to the bishop and how he would do it. And Oslac replied saying, 'I am not aware that I gave him what you say, but I know well that I owe him forty mancuses and I desire and agree that our friends who are here should view and assess the forty acres which you have from me and the farm and the third part of the wood at Dullingham. Then, in line with the valuation which they make, accept these properties in place of the equivalent sum, and I will pay the remainder.' Well, the properties were assessed without delay at twenty-six mancuses and Oslac was to pay the fourteen mancuses remaining. And so the matter was approved and settled on these terms and Ordhelm was witness and guarantor of this purchase for both parties.]

[20. About Cambridge.][114]

The brothers of the church [also] bought from Byrhtlaf a farm at Cambridge built upon in the best manner, together with thirty arable acres and a meadow, giving him for these properties a good farm at Witcham with houses built on it and a part of seventy acres, these acres and the farm being purchases which they had previously made from Burghelm.

They also bought there, that is, at Cambridge, seven acres from the son

---

[113] Source: *LibÆ* 29, apart from the title, which has no counterpart there.
[114] Source: *LibÆ* 30–1.

of Bishop Æthelmær, and seven acres from Siflæd, and each acre cost sixteen pence. And they bought there[115] five acres from a certain widow called Hungeva. She in addition gave to St Æthelthryth ten acres and the fishing rights of a weir, with the proviso that she, Hungeva, could have an income from the monastery so long as she lived.

21. About Doddington and Wimblington.[116]

The abbot also made an exchange with Wine, the son of Osmund: he gave him sixty acres at Doddington and Wimblington and a weir[117] yielding a thousand eels, which he bought from Gunulf for a hundred shillings, and Wine granted the abbot fifty-three acres at Cambridge and a weir worth a thousand eels, which Eanflæd left in part to Wine on her death and which in part he himself bought from his kinsmen. This same Eanflæd on her death gave to St Æthelthryth five acres. Wine moreover gave to St Æthelthryth eight acres at Hill. And the brothers of the church also bought five acres there from the son of Ælfstan.[118]

22. Again about[119] Doddington and *Wæremere*.[120]

Thurcytel, Abbot of Ramsey {*recte* Bedford}, sold to Bishop Æthelwold a hide at Doddington and a half-share of *Wæremere* and all the marshes which belong to *Wæremere*, on condition that on account of their friendship he be permitted to enjoy and hold the land at Beeby[121] which Bishop Oscytel on his death left to Bishop Æthelwold. [So it was that the abbot and the whole community at Ely presented that hide at Doddington to Wine so that it might provide him with clothing.]

23. Again about Wimblington, and how much they owned in the fens as a result of purchase.[122]

The Abbot of Ely bought from the monks of Ramsey for twenty shillings ten acres at Wimblington and two fisheries. So then, if one takes all the lands

---

[115] Reading, with ACE, *ibi* (p. 96.1, ed Blake).

[116] Source: *LibÆ* 32.

[117] Lat. *gurgo*, 'weir', 'whirlpool', artificially produced by blocking a stream or river.

[118] Accepting here (p. 96, 11), the reading of F.

[119] Following the reading of E.

[120] Source: *LibÆ* 33.

[121] Beeby, Leicestershire.

[122] The first sentence only = *LibÆ* 33. The rest derives from the end of *LibÆ* 34.

together which the blessed Bishop Æthelwold acquired within the waters and fens and the marsh of Ely, and gave to God and to St Æthelthryth, the total is found[123] to be sixty hides.

[24. About Stonea.[124]

We have recorded above how the widow Æscwyn had given Stonea and the fen belonging to it to Wulfstan of Dalham, and how Wulfstan afterwards gave the same land and fen to St Æthelthryth. Now one needs to say what happened about the fen.

The clerics who were in the monastery of Ely at that time leased the aforesaid fen belonging to Stonea to certain kinsmen of the aforementioned widow for two thousand eels. These people held the fen with that agreement for nearly fifteen years before Bishop Æthelwold took possession of Ely, and afterwards they did likewise under him, up until the time after King Edgar had died. But, following the king's death, Beahmund of Holland and the kinsmen of the widow, mentioned above, who had held the said fen and fishery on lease, unlawfully deprived St Æthelthryth of the land at Stonea without adjudication or the legal consent of the citizens and the hundred-men. Then Ealdorman Æthelwine came to Ely, and Beahmund and the others had been called and summoned for this suit to a meeting of the citizens and the hundred-men once, twice and, indeed, many times, but they were never willing to come. However, the abbot did not cease on that account and, at meetings within the city and outside it, kept renewing and restating this same suit many times, and so kept making this complaint before the people. In the end, Ealdorman Æthelwine came to Cambridge and held there a great meeting of the citizens and the hundred-men before twenty-four judges below *Therningefeld* near *Maideneberge*.[125] Whereupon the abbot related, in the presence of them all, how Beahmund and the kinsmen of the abovementioned widow unjustly deprived St Æthelthryth of Stonea, and how often they had been summoned to a meeting for that suit and never chose to come. Then those passing judgement decided that the abbot should have his land, namely Stonea, together with the marsh and fishery. They decided further that Beahmund and the kinsmen of the said widow should pay to the abbot his fish for six years, and pay full compensation, and pay a fine to the king. They decided also that if they were unwilling to pay this voluntarily, they should be distrained and punished by seizure of their property. Accordingly Ealdorman Æthelwine decreed that Oscytel and Oswy of *Beche* and Godere of Ely should go round the land and take the abbot over

---

[123] A text (as in E, first hand) without -*que* after *invente* is presupposed (p. 97.5, ed. Blake).

[124] Source: *LibÆ* 34. This chapter is not included in E.

[125] See Reaney, *Place-names of Cambridgeshire and the Isle of Ely*, p. 39.

it and put an end to the whole business. They did so, and in this way all was concluded. And so, if one takes together all the lands which the blessed Bishop Æthelwold acquired among the waters and fens and the marsh of Ely, and gave to God and St Æthelthryth, as has been related above,[126] there are held there sixty hides.]

25. About Bluntisham.[127]

On an occasion when the most glorious Bishop Æthelwold and Wulfnoth had met at Taunton, they discussed there for the first time a plan that the bishop should buy Bluntisham[128] from him. When the agreement had been made, therefore, and a purchase-price settled, namely thirty pounds, Wulfnoth [sent his elder son to Ely for the money, and there he received a hundred shillings from Abbot Byrhtnoth; the twenty-five pounds which remained were given to him afterwards] in the presence of King Edgar and his wise men. [When this had been transacted in the presence of these men, Wulfnoth] granted Bluntisham to the bishop with the charter. [When this had been done, Abbot Byrhtnoth, in addition, gave to Wulfnoth, in their presence, seven pounds for all the holdings on the land at Bluntisham, that is, the men, the stock and the grain.

But afterwards, when King Edgar died, the sons of a man called Boga of Hemingford laid claim to that land at Bluntisham, saying that their uncle, called Tope, ought to have the land by right of inheritance. This was on the ground that Tope's grandmother, being then in the flower of her virginity, had gone across from Bluntisham and petitioned King Edward at Cambridge at the time when Earl Toli had taken possession of Huntingdonshire against the king by force and, for this reason, she should by right have held the land as her own. The wise and old men of that district, who well remembered the time when Earl Toli had been killed at the River Thames, pronounced all of this spurious. They said, in addition, that King Edward had conquered Huntingdonshire and brought it under his control before he took control of Cambridgeshire. They asserted further that there was no land so free in the whole of Huntingdonshire that it could not be lost through forfeiture, apart from two hides at Bluntisham which Ælfsige *Cild* held, and another two near Spaldwick. And they decided that Wulfnoth should give peaceful possession of the land at Bluntisham to Bishop Æthelwold or give back the money he had received.

After this, the whole of Huntingdonshire was called together by

---

[126] The words translated as 'as has been related above' are found in F, but not in AC.

[127] Source: *LibÆ* 35.

[128] Bluntisham, formerly in Huntingdonshire.

Ealdorman Byrhtnoth and Ælfwold and Eadric. Without delay, a very great assembly was held. Wulfnoth was summoned to the meeting, as were the sons of Boga. When they had come, Wulfnoth brought there with him many loyal men, namely, all the better people of six hundreds, and the monk Leofsige of Ely produced there the charter of Bluntisham. They explained the claim to the assembled people and aired and discussed the case. And when the truth of the matter had been determined, they took Bluntisham away from the sons of Boga by their judgement for two reasons. The first of these reasons is that they had lied in all they had said about Tope and his grandmother. The other reason is that the person who had the charter was nearer to having the land than the one who did not have it. Then Wulfnoth produced more than a thousand loyal men in order to establish his claim to this same land through their sworn testimony, but the sons of Boga would not accept the oath. Everyone decided, therefore, that Wulfnoth should have Bluntisham, and faithfully promised him they would support him in this matter as sureties and witnesses, as to what they had done there, if ever at another time he or any of his heirs had need. And when all this was done, Bishop Æthelwold gave Wulfnoth forty shillings and a war-horse worth three marks, because he had worked hard on this action and because he was about to cross the sea in the service of his lord.]

26. About Toft.[129]

In the same year in which Bishop Æthelwold had bought Bluntisham from Wulfnoth, this same Wulfnoth offered the bishop his ten hides on sale at Toft. Hence, after a completion-date had been given and accepted, Abbot Byrhtnoth came [to Cambridge within eight days] and, in the presence of the whole city, gave Wulfnoth forty pounds for his ten hides at Toft. Wulfnoth himself, however, kept aside from it all his live-stock and dead-stock. This done, the abbot asked him for sureties for the purchase of this land and everyone said, in reply, that Cambridge, Norwich, Thetford and Ipswich were possessed of such great freedom and dignity that if anyone bought land there, he did not require sureties.

When Goding was dying, a monk, he bequeathed to St Æthelthryth one hide of land in the same village, that is, [in] Toft, [something which his son Ælfnoth wished afterwards to change; but the abbot gave him twenty shillings at Cambridge in the presence of an assembly of the citizens, and Ælfnoth himself conveyed to the abbot a full hide by way of arable land, pasture and woodland, with the exception of his own farm which he had left out of the transaction.]

---

[129] Source: *LibÆ* 36–7.

27. About Hauxton and Newton.[130]

[Eadric *Longus*[131] of Essex, on his death, left Hauxton and all the stock which was on it to King Edgar and, while life was still his companion, sent the king a chirograph of his will. After his death, however, many people asked the king for the land in question, and among them was] the venerable pontiff Æthelwold.] The bishop, [prudent and painstaking in all matters as he was, came in advance of the others and] bought from the king four-and-a-half hides at Hauxton and three hides at Newton in furtherance of the work of God and of St Æthelthryth. He gave two hundred mancuses to the king. Then, however, within one month, King Edgar departed this life, before the bishop and the abbot had obtained the charters relating to Hauxton and Newton [and before the heriots[132] had been provided in respect to those properties].

[Then Ælfwold, the brother of Eadric, and some of his kinsmen, sought to separate the three hides at Newton and alienate them from Hauxton, land which without doubt – acre after acre of it[133] – belongs to Hauxton. As a result of this, a lawsuit and quarrel of huge proportions arose, and it went on between them for many years. Yet the fact is that Ealdorman Æthelwine said, and brought it to the attention of many witnesses, that both properties, that is, Hauxton and Newton, had been given to the king as one manor and thus the bishop was the holder of both properties as though they were joined together. However, the bishop and abbot found it a serious difficulty that Ælfwold and the other kinsmen of Eadric were in possession of the charters of Hauxton and Newton. For they feared that claims and deceptions could arise at any time on account of this. The abbot accordingly asked Ealdorman Æthelwine to obtain the charters for the aforementioned lands from Ælfwold, the brother of Eadric, and make the lands, that is, Hauxton and Newton, peaceful and without claim against him. So that Æthelwine might be more willing to do this, the abbot promised to give him three hides at Wangford. When he heard this, Ealdorman Æthelwine took Wangford, all

[130] Source: *LibÆ* 38.

[131] *Longus*: 'the Long', meaning 'Lanky', 'Tall'.

[132] Lat. *relevationes*. The Normans used *relevium/relevatio* to translate the OE 'heregeatu' ('heriot') because the Anglo-Saxon legal concept which it denoted seemed akin to relief. The 'heriot' seems to have originated in an obligation by a man to return the weapons which his lord had given him, hence the original meaning 'war-gear'. Although regularly paid in military kind, and defined in military terms in legislation, it became a kind of death tax, payable to the lord of the deceased, and, at this level, survived into the thirteenth century. Information from Alan Kennedy (pers. comm. 27.3.04).

[133] Lat. *acra sub acra*: interpretation uncertain.

the time undertaking and promising that he would do what the abbot had sought, but his promise was without effect, for, in fact, the matter was the vexed subject of litigation for many years.

During this period Ealdorman Byrhtnoth came to Ely.] The abbot and the whole congregation of brothers approached him[134] then, and asked him, for the love of God and St Æthelthryth[135] to buy the aforementioned charters from Ælfwold, brother of Eadric, for the work of their church. And they said that, for the charters, they would give Ælfwold the charter relating to Ramsey and Sproughton in Essex, a charter which he greatly wanted, and they promised him thirty mancuses in addition. Ealdorman Byrhtnoth then did as he had been asked. For he indeed took the charter relating to Ramsey and Sproughton which the brothers of Ely used to possess and gave it to Ælfwold. And, in addition, he gave him thirty mancuses from his own gold and received from him in return the charters of Hauxton and Newton and sent them to St Æthelthryth at Ely.

28. The privilege of King Eadred on the manor of Stapleford.[136]

All things between Heaven and Earth which are the objects of active discernment are temporal, and the unseen things in the heavenly realms which are the objects of contemplation are to be believed in on the basis of the Catholic faith, and to the bottom of one's heart. Consequently, the ancients long ago decreed that things which are eternal and celestial should be endowed with earthly and transitory goods. Therefore, aspiring to this with all the effort of his mind, Eadred, King of *Angulsexana*,[137] and Overlord[138] of Northumbria, Governor of the Pagans and Defender of the Britons – and with him Eadgifu, the effectual mother of kings[139] – gives, with a generous hand and freely, things which are his own by God's consent – in accordance with what is written, with God as witness, 'Freely you have

---

[134] E names Ealdorman Byrthnoth here.

[135] Here E adds words, not paralleled in *LibÆ* mss., meaning: 'whom he loved with all his soul'. Other additions in E elsewhere in this chapter are substitutions for material omitted in its radical abbreviation of the text.

[136] Source: monastic archives. The text of this charter, not in extant cartularies or in *LibÆ*, is in part given only in summary, together with comments on its historical context probably by the compiler of *LE*. At any rate, the second paragraph refers to, and must be later than, the treatise of Ælfhelm cited in *LE* i. 43–9. Alan Kennedy comments (pers. comm. 1.8.02): 'The Stapleford charter is a fake, but such a messy fake that it probably derives from an authentic one, presumably in favour of Wulfstan of Dalham.' Ostensible date of the charter: 956.

[137] Assuming, at p. 102.6, ed. Blake, that *Angulsexana* is to be taken to mean *Angulsexane*.

[138] Lat. *imperator*, 'commander', 'emperor'.

[139] The parenthesis has ben transferred, for clarity, from later in the complex sentence.

received: freely give!'[140] – granting the vill which is called Stapleford to God and St Peter the Apostle,[141] and also to St Æthelthryth the virgin and the progeny of this saint reposing in the church in Ely, for the purposes of those serving God in that place by the inspiration of the Paraclete, this vill to be enjoyed by them in perpetuity. Thereby Wulfstan, a minister of the aforesaid king, has full power to speak publicly, with promptitude and plain utterance, concerning the intended use of the fifteen hides at Stapleford.

Accordingly, Eadred, a king noted for his triumphant standard-bearing for the faith, in the 956th year from the Lord's incarnation and in the ninth-recorded year from when the said overlord took up the sceptres belonging to his crowns – Eadred, in whose time one reads that wonderful things happened concerning the priests in Ely, <gave> this land <with>[142] the things great and small duly belonging to it in perpetuity. This same king adds to this estate part of a wood, specifically one of the three hides at Bardfield and a mill at Dernford[143] with not inconsiderable pastures. The witnesses of this grant, to be sure, were Archbishop Odo, Prince Edwy and his brother Edgar of blessed memory, both of whom earned the right to wield the sceptre of the kingdom and others whose names it is a long task to enumerate. This land, indeed, was in church hands before the monks were brought to that place, and it is to this day properly for the provision of their victuals.

29. About Eynesbury.[144]

It remains, therefore, to tell the story of Eynesbury,[145] which St Neot originally founded as a monastic establishment but which, after the iniquitous invasion of the Danes, had for a long time lain miserably doomed to desolation. After the passage of a very long period of time, however, the venerable father Æthelwold made it his endeavour to raise up again the monastery in question, like other venerable monasteries throughout

---

[140] Matthew 10.8.

[141] This dedication is attested elsewhere for 970 (Benedictine re-foundation); here we are given to understand that it went back to the days of the canons.

[142] Supplementing conjecturally e.g. <dedit cum> after tellurem (p. 102.13, ed. Blake).

[143] Both these names belong to the district of Stapleford, Cambridgeshire

[144] Source: not LibÆ as now extant, though the narrative part of the chapter is indistinguishable in style from that work. The last paragraph is obviously of post-Conquest date, and may, or may not, be entirely by the compiler of LE, who was certainly responsible for the last few words of it.

[145] Eynesbury, formerly in Huntingdonshire. Blake explains that there were two manors there, one of which became a separate parish known as St Neots.

England, to the former glory of its divine service. Taking monks from Ely to that place, he once more established them under a prior, in subjection to a rule.

For when Leofric, a man devoted to God, and his wife, named Leofflæd, attended the dedication of the aforementioned basilica, they consulted with him and Abbot Byrhtnoth, begging them earnestly to establish monks there. The abbot and Bishop Æthelwold, moreover, embraced this desire of theirs[146] and arranged to send to that place some men from Ely and some from Thorney. Then, in the presence of all, Leofric and Leofflæd humbly implored the bishop and the abbot, for the love of God and for reverence of holy religion, to make provision for these men, just as they would for their own people, and to consult their interests so that they might maintain the religious life in a worthy manner, and so that the place would be subject to the church of Ely and to all his successors; and the prior, on the other hand, would always be from the church of Ely unless a man of a kind suitable for the office in question could – with the consent and on the advice of the brothers of Ely – be found from among their own number. In fact, for their food and clothing they designated from the outset eighteen hides, usefully providing for their needs: that is, two hides in the aforesaid vill of Eynesbury and six at Waresley and nine at Gamlingay. The witnesses of this were Bishop Æscwig,[147] who dedicated the church on that occasion, Ealdorman Æthelwine, Eadric *Pape*, Ælfhelm *Polga* and others who had congregated for that dedication; and it is a generally acknowledged fact that this was confirmed by three documents written in English. Bishop Æthelwold had one, which is kept to this day in the church as evidence; Bishop Æscwig had another; they themselves retained a third.

And that place for a long time belonged to Ely, up until the present when England is subjugated by the Normans, but the church, groaning in its oppressed circumstances, lays claim to that property along with many, great possessions taken away from it unjustly and, with the Psalmist, continually makes complaint to God against those who said: 'Come let us cut it off from being a nation, and let the name of Israel not be remembered in it any more!'[148] For later, when the Normans conquered England, one of them, Gilbert de Clare, laid claim to the place for himself and expelled the Ely brothers, as living there on his property. Three of them, however – whom he was incapable of driving out either by hunger or by the whip – he sent over the sea into custody at Bec. He brought monks from that place and installed them at Eynesbury, the indigenous ones having been forcibly driven out, as is explained in later chapters.

---

[146] Omitting *multipliciter* (p. 103.5, ed. Blake) as not in E or the first hand of F.

[147] Bishop of Dorchester, Oxfordshire, 975 X 979 to 1002.

[148] Psalm 82.5 Vulgate = 83.4 RSV.

30. About Wangford.[149]

On another occasion, when they were at Eynesbury at the dedication of the church of Leofric, the abbot asked Ealdorman Æthelwine to give him the land at Wangford,[150] or pay for it in some other way, because he, Æthelwine, had in no way fulfilled the agreement which he had made [with him], the abbot, about that land. In consequence, Æthelwine recognized that the abbot had spoken the truth, and promised, with the witness [of Ælfstan and Eadnoth and Ælfwine], that he would give him thirty mancuses for that land. [A long time after these things had been thus transacted, Æthelnoth, the brother of Leofric, laid claim to Wangford and to Abington, and said that they were part of his inheritance. Ealdorman Æthelwine replied to the effect that he had bought those lands and that no opposition had been made public to him, that is, neither claim nor the voicing of objections, whether consisting in the protection of rights by lord or by kin.]

31. Concerning Fordham and Milton.[151]

Then Abbot Byrhtnoth – that venerable man approved by God and by men[152] – and Wine bought two hides and thirty-seven acres at Fordham from Grim, the son of Osulf, giving for the land eleven pounds with the witness of the vill and the hundred. Since this land was in a handy position for a certain man named Ulf, and that man had possessed two hides at Milton which the abbot greatly wanted, for the sake of ways of access in and out, they exchanged properties. The abbot accordingly granted him the two hides of twelve-score acres, and thirty-seven acres at Fordham, and in return Ulf granted to the abbot the two hides of twelve-score acres at Milton.

In the same vill, [moreover], Abbot Thurcytel[153] had four-and-a-half hides. At the time when he had been expelled from Bedford, he asked from Ælfstan, Bishop of London, and the clergy there, that he might have rights in common with them and membership in the monastery where he had earlier bought for himself a place in the presbyterate. The bishop, however, and the whole community refused him. At length, [however, prompted] by the [advice and] advocacy of his friends, he bequeathed to St Paul the four-and-a-half hides which he had at Milton [so that he might join their community.

---

[149] Source: *LibÆ* 39. In Blake's edition this chapter is printed as chapter 30, in conformity with the order of chapters in F, but in E it occurs before the chapter on Eynesbury.

[150] The land at Wangford, Suffolk has been mentioned previously in *LE* ii. 27.

[151] Source: *LibÆ* 40–41. Translation of the title as in E.

[152] The comment on Abbot Byrhtnoth is as in E, as against *LibÆ* mss. and F.

[153] Abbot of Bedford.

This done, he held the land from the brothers, that is, the clergy, for as long as he lived, giving them each year twenty shillings from its revenue. After his death, indeed, the clerks had the use of that land, but with the most vexatious difficulty. As they were enduring many troubles there, Abbot Byrhtnoth eventually conceived a desire to have the land from them, either for money or in exchange, if perhaps he had an equivalent amount of land close to them, within the shire. In the mean time, it so happened that Eadgifu, the grandmother of King Edgar, when she died, bequeathed to a noble married woman called Ælfthryth five hides at Holland in Essex which she had bought from Sprow for twenty pounds]. Then the aforesaid married woman, that is Ælfthryth, gave the land to St Æthelthryth.[154] But Bishop Æthelwold [and Abbot Byrhtnoth] and the whole community of monks at Ely gave the land to St Paul and the clergy of London for the four-and-a-half hides at Milton. They also made an exchange of stock. However, there was an excess at Holland of a hundred sheep, and fifty-five pigs, and two men, and five head of yoked oxen.

32. About Horningsea.[155]

In the time before the madness of the pagans on the rampage in East Anglia had boiled over all around Cambridgeshire and given the land over to waste and desolation, there was a minster of royal standing at Horningsea where a not insignificant community of clerics existed. At the same time, in fact, as an army went on the rampage in that place,[156] there was a priest Cenwold exercising his priestly office there. The people of the place, who had come rushing together in a flood-tide from paganism to the grace of baptism, then gave the aforesaid minster five hides at Horningsea and two at Eye.

Cenwold, however, having died, the priest Herolf succeeded to his position. Since he had been a retainer of King Æthelstan, he held the position under his guardianship and protection. However at that time Wulfric the reeve, who was a kinsman of Cenwold, forcibly and unjustly deprived the minster of two hides mentioned above at Eye {recte Horningsea}.[157]

[154] Here E gives a summary of the material omitted.

[155] Source: LibÆ 42.

[156] The information here must have been deduced from the wording of a charter in which Cenwold was mentioned, and, belonging as it does to a period considerably earlier than LibÆ, the chronology is disconcertingly vague. Key dates: traditional date of the sack of Ely, 870; the Cambridge area was reconquered from the Danes in the time of Edward the Elder (901–25); reign of Æthelstan, 925–40.

[157] It emerges from later parts of this narrative that there is a deep-seated error in the tradition here. Someone at an early stage, perhaps a copyist even before the text was translated into Latin, perhaps the translator, made the false inference that the two hides referred to here could only be the 'two hides at Eye' just referred to, and miscorrected an

BOOK II

Then in the days of King Edgar, the priest Æthelstan, a kinsman of Herolf, acting in Herolf's place and on his behalf in the minster, obtained the incumbency.[158] In those days, it so happened that certain people stole countless, grand possessions of one Thorth, the son of Earl Oslac. When they were breaking open his chests, they took out a very fine dagger, decorated with gold and silver. They also removed many garments made of precious fabrics. Carrying these things away with them, they brought them all to the priest Æthelstan and entrusted them to him. He took them and put them into chests belonging to Herolf. After these dealings had thus taken place, the stolen property was by chance discovered. Without delay, Thorth was there with hundred-bailiffs, trithing-bailiffs and appraisers,[159] and, when the chests belonging to Herolf had been unlocked, he brought to light the stolen goods in the custody of Æthelstan.

Æthelstan was seized at once, put in chains, and made to appear before Bishop Oscytel.[160] In the mean time, Herolf arrived and, having learnt of Æthelstan's plight, took all the ornaments of the church which good men devoted to God had in early times, for the sake of their souls, bestowed upon the minster. He went to Wulfstan and gave some of them to him on condition that he have pity on him and that he might have charge of the minster all the days of his life. He also gave some ornaments to the bishop to prevent the priest Æthelstan from being put to death or stripped of his position.

Not long afterwards, the priest Herolf passed away and Æthelstan replaced him. Now that these matters had been concluded thus, the blessed Æthelwold went as soon as possible to King Edgar and bought Horningsea from him for fifty mancuses. [Then Wulfstan ordered that the blessed Æthelwold should measure the land which the priest Æthelstan held, specifically, three hides of twelve-score acres. On hearing this, Æthelstan set about seizing Eye for himself and giving testimony that it was rightfully his own property. However, as he realized that he would not prevail against the bishop with his own resources, he sought out Wulfstan and gave his allegiance to him and promised that he would sell him Eye at whatever price he chose to put on it, provided that he support him against Bishop Æthelwold, because the bishop was laying charges against him regarding the treasures of the church, which he and Herolf had sacrilegiously removed. In this manner Wulfstan acquired Eye through the mendacity of a priest and for a small sum of money, and thus he held it for his lifetime in opposition to God and the blessed Æthelwold.

---

original reading equivalent to 'two hides at Horningsea'.

[158] Lat. *sacerdotium*.

[159] Guesswork for *centurionibus et triumviris ac preconibus*.

[160] Bishop of Dorchester (Oxfordshire) and Archbishop of York.

But after the death of Wulfstan, the bishop set about making a claim with regard to Eye and with regard to Æthelstan, who had appropriated the treasures of the church. The priest, therefore, realizing that he could in no way succeed if he were to oppose the bishop, sought patrons, namely Osulf and Goding and Ealhferth, and many other thegns, to plead his case with the bishop. At their request, the bishop then withdrew the claim against Æthelstan, at least where the treasures were concerned, on condition that he hand Eye over to God and St Æthelthryth. Accordingly, the priest went with the bishop to Ely and swore upon the holy altar and the body of St Æthelthryth that neither he nor any of his successors, during his lifetime or afterwards, would ever seek to regain Eye or make a claim upon it.

Four years before this, Wulfric the reeve departed this life and bequeathed to his nephew,[161] the priest Leofstan, the two hides which, as we have explained before, he had forcibly and unjustly seized from God and the minster at Horningsea. In the mean time, certain traders from Ireland landed at the little city which is called Cambridge with various wares and cloaks, and, when their wares had been put on display, it happened that the aforementioned priest Leofstan stole their cloaks. When this came to light, he sought the protection of the citizens, who interceded for his life and property. When this had been done, the said priest gave to Wulfstan the two hides which Wulfric the reeve had bequeathed to him, together with the charter; Wulfstan gave the land with the charter to his kinsman, Æthelstan *Chusin,* and, after the death of Wulfstan, Bishop Æthelwold bought it from him for eight pounds.]

33. [About Horningsea.][162]

Then, after the death of King Edgar, [the aforementioned] Leofstan and the son of Wulfric,[163] suddenly appeared and forcibly seized the [aforesaid] two hides at Horningsea, and the priest Æthelstan took Eye with violence, breaking the oath which he had sworn to God and St Æthelthryth. [And the priest shared the land with his two brothers in this way: first, he halved it and, after taking the half-share, took another third. For he received the larger share on the reasoning that the land belonged to him rather than the others. And he gave Æthelstan, the son of Manne, two marks of silver and a similar sum to Osmund and his brothers. He also gave a great deal to other prominent men, so that, in despite of law, human and divine, they would give him protection.] In view of the fact, therefore, that the priest Æthelstan

---

[161] Or 'grandson': Lat. *nepos.*

[162] Source: *LibÆ* 43–4. No title is given here in E.

[163] The abbreviator responsible for E, having omitted the end of the previous chapter, finds it necessary to specify here that this was the reeve Wulfric.

had afflicted the bishop and the abbot with many injurious actions, [after the elapse of many years they took counsel with their friends and at length arranged matters so that the priest and his brothers, Bondo and Ælfstan, would be treated together as one, and they arranged a hearing-date at Horningsea. On the day there came, accordingly, the abbot, and Ælfnoth, the son of Ona, Uvi and his brother Oswi, Wulfnoth of Stow, Grim the son of Osulf, Seaxferth and his son Oscytel, Oswi of *Beche*, Ælfstan, Clac of Fulbourn, Osmund and his son Simund, Uvi, Wacher of Swaffham and Ælfnoth the son of Goding.] Before [these][164] witnesses the abbot then gave Æthelstan, for his share of Eye, a farm and a hide of twelve-score acres at Snailwell, which he had bought from Wedwine, the son of Ealdstan, for six pounds. And he further gave him another farm and seventy-five acres which he had bought from Hugh and Ælfric. And the abbot also gave to Æthelstan's brothers, Bondo[165] and Ælfstan, at the same place, four pounds and eighteen pence, and thus, totally amicably and in the witness of the people, the abbot and Æthelstan and Bondo and Ælfstan were satisfied in every respect, that is to say, concerning the land, the marsh and the stock.

[Afterwards, certain brothers, Leofsige and Ælfstan and Wulfgar, and Oslac, their kinsman by marriage,[166] went to Ealdorman Byrhtnoth and gave him a hide which they had acquired, on condition that he give them a hand in obtaining certain land in East Anglia. When he did this, Wulfgar and Oslac made over to him their share of the hide, just as they had promised. But the others completely broke the agreement with him. From those who had broken the agreement, moreover, the abbot and Eadric bought their share in the hide for four pounds, in the witness of the people.

After these transactions, the priest Leofsige mentioned previously bought from the priest Leofstan a hide and a field for a hundred shillings. Even though he had previously broken the agreement which he had had with Ealdorman Byrhtnoth, once more he offered him one hide as a gift, and another for sale. But, just as before, it was now proved that he was telling a complete pack of lies. When, therefore, Ealdorman Byrhtnoth realized that the priest had deceived him with the lies and treacheries with which he was replete, he ordered him to be summoned and, coming to Ditton, he there proceeded to set out and explain the actions and claims, agreements and broken compacts which he held against him, by means of the testimony of many lawmen. As Leofsige denied and contradicted all the charges brought against him, they decided that he might clear himself with an oath. Since he could neither do this nor produce those who ought to swear with him, it was decreed that he should be evicted and Ealdorman Byrhtnoth should be given

---

[164] E says 'many' witnesses and names *LibÆ* as his source.

[165] Reading with the *LibÆ* mss: *Bondoni*.

[166] Lat. *gener*: usually 'son-in-law', but, clearly, not here.

possession of both hides, that is, the one which he had promised to give to him and the one which he had promised to sell. This same was decreed a second time on another occasion, at Cambridge. When it was done, Ealdorman Byrhtnoth granted these lands to St Æthelthryth.][167]

34. About Swaffham and *Berlea*.[168]

King Edgar bought Swaffham[169] and *Berlea*[170] from Æthelwine, the son of Æthelweard of Sussex, for eighty mancuses. Then Bishop Æthelwold bought both lands from the king, giving him the equivalent number of mancuses.[171] But after the death of King Edgar, certain evil men, by means of the violence of their kin, made an attack upon Berlea and took it by force. [However, because of a theft, that land had been made forfeit for wrongdoing during the time of King Edgar, when Wulfstan was exercising the office of reeve. Well, then, it came about, at a certain date, that a Great Meeting was held at Whittlesford and there gathered there Ealdorman Æthelwine, and his brothers Ælfwold and Æthelsige, and Bishop Æscwig, and Wulfflæd, the widow of Wulfstan, and all the more highly regarded spokesmen[172] of Cambridgeshire. And so, when they were all seated, Wynsige, the kinsman of Wulfric, rose and made a claim to the land at Swaffham, saying that he and his kinsmen were being unfairly deprived of the land, because they had had nothing for it, that is, neither land nor the money-equivalent of land. When this claim had been heard, therefore, Ealdorman Æthelwine asked whether anyone among the people there knew how Wulfstan had acquired the land referred to. In reply, Ælfric of Witcham said that Wulfstan had bought that land – that is to say, the two hides at Swaffham – from the Wynsige mentioned before, for eight pounds. And so that what he had said might be believed, he brought in, for purposes of testimony, eight hundreds from the southern part of Cambridgeshire. He said, furthermore, that Wulfstan had given Wynsige the eight pounds in two instalments, but sent the last part of the money and the last penny to him through Leofwine, the son of Æthulf, who gave him the aforesaid money wrapped in a glove, in the sight of the eight hundreds in which the land referred to had, perchance, been situated. Accordingly, once these matters had been heard about, they made the

---

[167]In place of the last section of this chapter E substitutes the following summary: 'Ealdorman Byrhtnoth, indeed, afterwards obtained the two hides which remained of Horningsea and handed them over to St Æthelthryth.'

[168]Source: *LibÆ* 45.

[169]Swaffham Prior or Swaffham Bulbeck, Cambridgeshire.

[170]Possibly identifiable with Barley, Hertfordshire.

[171]E summarizes these opening sentences.

[172]Lat. *concionatores*: 'speakers at assemblies'.

decision that the bishop and abbot should have the two hides at Swaffham free from any claim and might have lordship over them in accordance with their desire. If, moreover, Wynsige or his kinsmen had been wishing to exact money or other, additional, payment for the land, they should have exacted it from the heirs of Wulfstan and not from anyone else. For the land was now in the fourth hand and, even if it were in the third or second hand, they ought to have done the same. Afterwards, Bishop Æthelwold and Abbot Byrhtnoth granted these two hides, and the seventy acres which the bishop had bought, to Eadric, on the condition that, when he died, he should give the land in question to St Æthelthryth with all its stock and equipment and all the goods which he had acquired during his lifetime. And the witnesses of this matter were Ealdorman Æthelwine and the whole gathering which had assembled at that time at Cambridge.]

35. About Brandon and Livermere.[173]

[On his death, Ælfgar of *Multune* bequeathed to Wulfstan of Dalham five hides at Brandon and Livermere.[174] Wulfstan gave this land to his kinsman Wihtgar many years before the end of his life. But after the death of Wulfstan], on a certain occasion when the spokesmen of England[175] had gathered at London, that same Wihtgar offered the land for sale to Bishop Æthelwold. When they had heard of this, the bishop and abbot gave him fifteen pounds for the land in the witness of Leofric, the son of Æthelferth, and Uvi of Willingham. They afterwards sent him a hundred shillings [by Provost Leofwine and Wine of Witchford, who gave him the aforementioned money] at Brandon in the witness of the whole hundred in which the land is situated. [In addition, they bought from Wihtgar all the stock which was on the land, in accordance with the valuation of it which had been made.] At the time when King Edgar died, however, a certain man named Ingulf forcibly and unjustly took Brandon away from God and St Æthelthryth. But in demonstration of the power of God and the merit of the blessed virgin Æthelthryth, from that day on which he thus usurped the property of the church he tasted no food or drink, for without the slightest delay his heart suffered rupture. And so it came about that he who, when living, unjustly seized what belonged to God, on meeting death, was unable to keep it, but simultaneously lost himself and the property. After he died, his wife and sons also took possession of the same land similarly, but, just as they did not honour God and did not spare their souls, so, correspondingly, the Divine Vengeance burst upon them and they all perished miserably

---

[173] Source: *LibÆ* 46. The chapter heading is lacking from the extant *LibÆ* mss.

[174] Brandon and Livermere, Suffolk.

[175] Lat. *concionatores Anglie*.

within one year. At this point, Siferth the brother of Ingulf, fearing that things would turn out similarly for himself,[176] gave the land which was his to the bishop, against the will of Ealdorman Æthelwine and very many others.

36. [About Brandon and about Livermere.[177]

Ælfgar bought every eighth acre in Brandon and three hides at Livermere from a certain earl called Scule, for two war-horses and two back-hangings of pall-cloth and fifty mancuses.

Bishop Æthelwold added ten mancuses to the twenty pounds mentioned above and gave this to Wihtgar on account of the friendship there was between them.][178]

37. About Sudbourne.[179]

King Edgar and {Queen} Ælfthryth gave St Æthelwold an estate[180] called Sudbourne,[181] together with the charter for the land, [which the earl who was called Scule had once held], on condition that he, Æthelwold, translate the

---

[176] The last phrase, translated as 'fearing . . . himself', is in E, but not the extant LibÆ mss. Is this merely an addition by the compiler of LE or evidence of a fuller LibÆ text?

[177] Source: LibÆ 47–8. This chapter as it occurs in the LibÆ mss. appears to consist of supplementary material omitted (accidentally?) from LibÆ 46 = LE ii. 35. The title and first sentence (with the fuller form of Ælfgar's name) ought to stand at the opening of LE ii. 35; the second sentence seems to have dropped out from the report, in the same chapter, of Ælfgar's sale of land to the bishop and abbot.

[178] Tentative reconstruction of archetype of LibÆ 46 init.:

<De Brandune et Livermere>

Ælfgarus de Muletune <emit omnem octavam acram in Brandune et iii hydas apud Livremere a quodam comite, qui dicebatur Scule, pro duobus dextrariis et duobus dorsaliis de pallio et l aureis.> Ælfgarus cum moreretur, dimisit Wlstano de Delham v hydas apud Brandune et Livermere. Wlstanus vero dedit eandem terram cognato suo Wihtgaro multis annis ante finem vite sue. Post obitum vero eius quodam tempore, cum convenissent concionatores Anglie ad Lundoniam, idem Wihtgarus Æðelwoldo episcopo eandem terram optulit venum. Quod cum audissent episcopus et abbas, dederunt ei pro terra xv libras coram testimonio Leofrici Æðelferthi filio, et Uvi de Wivelingeham. Centum vero solidos miserunt ei postea per Leofwinum prepositum et Wine de Wicceford. Qui dederunt ei eandem pecuniam apud Brandune coram testimonio totius hundreti in quo illa terra iacet. Emerunt etiam ab eo omnem pecuniam que erat in illa terra secundum quod appretiata fuerat. <Æthelwoldus episcopus addidit supradictis xx libris x aureos et dedit Withgaro pro amicitia que inter eos erat.> Ea vero tempestate, qua rex Ædgarus de hac vita decessit etc.

[179] Source: LibÆ 49.

[180] Lat. manerium.

[181] Sudbourne, Suffolk.

Rule of St Benedict from Latin into the English language. And he did so. But then the blessed Æthelwold gave the land in question, with the charter of this same land, to St Æthelthryth.

38. About Woodbridge.[182]

The blessed Æthelwold bought three hides at Woodbridge,[183] and the appurtenances which belonged to them, from Wulfflæd, the widow of Wulfstan, for fifteen pounds, in the witness of the whole hundred.

39. About Stoke.[184]

A woman called Ælfthryth pleaded with King Edgar that he sell to the blessed Æthelwold ten hides at Stoke, which is near Ipswich,[185] and two mills which are situated in the southern part. Her entreaties availed with him. For the bishop gave the king one hundred mancuses for that land and the mills, [and] he afterwards presented [the same land and mills] to St Æthelthryth.

King Edgar, also,[186] realizing that it was a God-given position of dignity that had passed to him, counterbalanced the glory of his power with graciousness of demeanour. And the power of this graciousness was an amplification of his kingship, its authority was a defence of the church, its life, an instrument of virtue, its works, a public asset. Hence, adding this third gift of his generosity to the church, on the model of the preceding privilege[187] – this gift resembling the former one in having the same motivation[188] – he set his seal on it in both languages and, bringing this undertaking to a consummate conclusion, planted for himself the seed of eternal remembrance.

The sins, lamentable and mightily to be detested, of today's seductive World, set about as they are by the dire yelping-noises of foul and horrible death, present a challenge ot us, who are not secure in the country of guiltless peace,

---

[182] Source: *LibÆ* 50.

[183] Woodbridge, Suffolk.

[184] Source: the chapter-heading and first paragraph only = *LibÆ* 51. Thereafter, the introduction and charter are probably from the same source as *LE* ii. 5, 8 (last section) and 9.

[185] Stoke, near Ipswich, Suffolk.

[186] The use here of *Lat. quoque*, 'also', is one of several features in the material in this chapter that supplements the brief *LibÆ* entry, which shows that this material originally formed part of the same document as did *LE* ii. 5, 8 (last section) and 9.

[187] The reference is to the privilege quoted in *LE* ii.9.

[188] This is an attempt to render Latin which is brief to the point of opaqueness: *ea qua illud causa* (p. 112.9, ed. Blake).

but, as it were, about to fall into a whirlpool of fetid corruption, and they thereby warn us to flee from them, in their descents upon us, with the total exertion of our mind – not merely despising them, but regarding them even with abomination like a disgusting eructation of black bile – while turning our attention towards that famous prophetic saying: 'If riches come flowing, do not set thy heart upon them.'[189] Wherefore, casting off the foul off-scourings of filthiness, choosing heavenly things as resembling precious necklaces, fixing our soul upon eternal joys, with a view to the acquisition of a mercy whose sweetness is of dripping honey, and the enjoyment of the bliss of infinite felicity, I Edgar, raised up by the right hand of the Almighty upon the throne of the kingdom of all Britain, have, with a view to the recompense of eternal beatitude, bestowed as a perpetual inheritance upon the holy church of God dedicated to the reverencing of the blessed Peter, Prince of the Apostles, and also the blessed ever-virgin Æthelthryth, in the place which is called by the popular appellation of Ely,[190] a certain small piece of countryside, namely ten hides in the place which is called by the popular appellation of Stoke, so that the aforesaid country estate may serve dedicatedly the purposes of the monks who live in that place, as a consequence of what Bishop Æthelwold has obtained by his own service. Let the aforesaid land, with all its easements, namely its pastures, mills and town-outskirts,[191] indeed be perpetually made subject to the above-mentioned church. Moreover, let the aforesaid country estate be free of all subjection to the yoke of worldly service, with three exceptions: military service, repair of bridges and fortifications. If anyone, then, shall have conceived the desire to transfer this our gift to a purpose other than that which we have laid down, let him be deprived[192] of association with the Holy Church of God, let him be punished in harness with Judas, the betrayer of Christ, and his accomplices, in the eternal, murky fires of the Abyss, if he does not make amends with appropriate satisfaction for the offence which he has committed against our decree.

40. About Dereham.[193]

Among other magnificent things, Æthelwold, confessor of the Lord, gave

---

[189] Psalm 61.11 Vulgate = 62.11 RSV.

[190] The form of the name given in EF is *Heli*, but the original reading was probably the archaic *Elig* (so CG) or *Helig* (see p. 113.3, ed. Blake).

[191] Lat. *suburbanis*.

[192] Here (p. 113.10, ed. Blake) the reading of EF, *privetur*, 'let him be deprived', is translated, though probably the reading of CG, *privatus*, 'deprived', represents the original.

[193] Source: this chapter is not in extant mss. of *LibÆ*.

additionally to the church of Ely and freely offered to St Æthelthryth, Dereham,[194] which he had asked for from the king, along with everything which belonged to that same vill.

41. [About Sudbourne and Woodbridge and Stoke and the six hundreds.[195]

The bishop and the abbot and Ealdorman Æthelwine at one time made an agreement among themselves that Æthelwine should hold from them Sudbourne and Stoke and Woodbridge and the six hundreds which belong to Sudbourne.[196] He did so, and paid them ten pounds for these lands every year at the appointed date of Rogationtide.]

42. [About Northwold.[197]

Thurferth took twelve hides at Northwold[198] from God and St Æthelthryth by force. For this land was among the lands which the blessed Æthelwold bought from King Edgar, giving him Harting in exchange for them.][199]

43. About Pulham.[200]

[The same Thurferth also seized from God and St Æthelthryth] Pulham,[201] [which] Bishop Æthelwold had bought from King Edgar for forty pounds.

Because of a crime, Waldchist lost possession in the time of King Edgar of these lands, that is, Northwold and Pulham, and all that he owned, and they were in the possession of King Edmund and Æthelred {recte Eadred}, until Æthelred {recte Eadred} gave them to his mother Eadgifu. After her death Wulfstan acquired these lands from King Edgar. In addition, Eadgifu and Wulfstan acquired and bought more lands and more goods than ever Waldchist had owned, and added them to the two estates just mentioned.

These, then, were the two estates which the aforesaid Thurferth took by force and held.

---

[194] East Dereham, Norfolk.

[195] Source: LibÆ 52.

[196] Blake, following H. M. Cam, *Liberties and Communities of Medieval England* (1944) p. 101, identifies the 'six hundreds belonging to Sudbourne' with the 'five- and-a-half hundreds of Wicklow' mentioned in Edward the Confessor's charter, LE ii. 92.

[197] Source: LibÆ 53.

[198] Northwold, Norfolk.

[199] Cf. LE ii. 5.

[200] Source: LibÆ 54.

[201] Pulham, Norfolk.

44. About Weeting.[202]

Bishop Æthelwold bought three hides at Weeting from Æthelweard for six pounds. [Subsequently a man by the name of Steapa brought about by his good offices merely this: that the bishop was deprived of both of two things, that is to say, the land as well as the money.

45. About Horningsea.[203]

The bishop also bought two hides at Horningsea from Æthelstan, the brother of Æthelweard, for eight pounds. But now we are without both the land and the money.]

46. About Gransden.[204]

Bishop Æthelwold bought Gransden from Heanric of Wantage for two hundred mancuses in the witness of King Edgar [personally present, and Ealdorman Ælfhere and Æthelwine and Byrhtnoth and Ælfric *Cild* and Ringulf and Thurferth] and the other councillors who were present at that time. [And the agreement was made before them all, with the stipulation that, if anyone ever at another time wished to lay claim to that land, Heanric and his heirs would pay two hundred mancuses to the bishop, and would themselves take responsibility for the dispute with the claimants. In spite of the fact that this agreement had been made on such terms, the church of Ely nevertheless lacks both that land and the money.]

47. About Marsworth.[205]

King Edgar and Ælfthryth gave to St Æthelthryth land at Marsworth[206] which Ælfgifu bequeathed to him on her death.

48. About Kelling.[207]

Bishop Æthelwold bought from Eadric *Dacus*[208] for twenty pounds his land

---

[202] Source: *LibÆ* 55.

[203] Source: *LibÆ* 56.

[204] Source: *LibÆ* 57.

[205] Source: *LibÆ* 58.

[206] Marsworth, Buckinghamshire.

[207] Source: *LibÆ* 59.

[208] *Dacus*: 'the Dane'.

at Kelling,[209] and he bought the stock which was upon it for eleven pounds. [Accordingly, Eadric received a hundred shillings from the bishop at Ely in front of the hundred, and Æthelsige, who was at that time the bishop's reeve, took to him the fifteen pounds which remained] and gave them to him in the public view of the three hundreds within which Kelling lies. And present there were Wulfstan of Dalham and Ringulf and nearly all the better people of those parts. [And the money was given to Eadric there in the witness of the three hundreds.]

49. [About Horningsea.[210]

But after the death of King Edgar, when King Edward and almost all his counsellors were at Kingston,[211] Ealdorman Æthelwine asked Bishop Æthelwold to let him have Kelling, on the understanding that, in exchange, Æthelwine would give him the equivalent amount of land, which would be closer to him and more fertile; with regard to the stock that was on the land, of course, they would have done as they pleased. After the bishop and the abbot had agreed to this, Ealdorman Æthelwine handed over the land to Ringulf. Then the bishop and the abbot asked Æthelwine to settle the transaction with them, and to arrange for them to hold, free from claim from of the sons of Wulfric, the two hides at Horningsea which, as we have said before, the bishop had bought from Æthelstan. On hearing this, Æthelwine began for ever making fine promises to do this, but his words had no weight to them, and his promises never came to fruition.

49a. About Kensworth.[212]

Bishop Æthelwold bought two hides at Kensworth[213] from Leofsige, one of his highest-ranking men,[214] for four pounds. This land is in Bedfordshire and belongs to Houghton. Abbot Byrhtnoth accordingly gave Leofsige the first part of the money, that is, sixty shillings, at Hatfield in the witness of Ælfweard[215] of Stodham. Later, indeed, on Leofsige's death, the abbot arranged that the twenty shillings which remained should be given to and shared among the clerks for the good of his soul. But the heriot of Leofsige

[209] Kelling, Norfolk.
[210] Source: LibÆ 60. The chapters from LibÆ printed as LE ii. 49, 49a, 49b in Blake's edition are found in F but had not been included in E.
[211] Probably Kingston, Suffolk.
[212] Source: LibÆ 60 (continued).
[213] Kensworth, Bedfordshire.
[214] Lat. optimatum.
[215] The OE form of the name is deduced from the LibÆ manuscripts rather than those of LE.

went unpaid and had not been given to the bishop. In this way, the bishop bought the land, but it was taken from him through pillage and violence.

49b. About Armingford.[216]

Another hide and a half were lost to Æthelwold at Armingford,[217] which had been made subject to forfeiture on the grounds of fighting and theft.]

50. What ornaments King Edgar brought to the church of Ely.[218]

Furthermore, by performing large numbers of most generous and distinguished actions of this sort, not only at Ely but in many monasteries of the English, the venerable King Edgar and the godly Bishop Æthelwold were enabling the church to take root and providing it with light. Moreover, if the human intellect is capable of inditing anything that is honorable or glorious, let it discourse upon the praiseworthy enterprises and munificence of this beneficent king, to the greater glory of the Highest King, all of whose gifts are good works. Let it, in congratulatory mode, shout acclamation to the king with plaudits, in deference to the King[219] whose eternal governance brings about changes of kingship at will, and the transference of empires.

Recognizing himself to be the bond-servant of this King, the aforesaid King Edgar, by dutiful actions, raised up His Bride everywhere throughout England, but the church of Ely most especially. He protected it by privileges, to prevent any ruinous incursion from ever causing havoc to its estates; he also adorned it in a distinguished fashion with repeated generous bestowal of gifts and, so that he might provide a lavish exemplar of good works for everyone else, far and wide, he spread abroad in many ways the sentiment of pious devotion.

For, to be specific, he contributed his cloak of striking *purpura*[220] in the style of a hauberk, embroidered with gold all around, from which a chasuble was made and has been preserved to this day in the church, as good as new.

---

[216] Source: *LibÆ* (continued).

[217] See Reaney, *Place Names of Cambridgeshire and the Isle of Ely,* p. 50.

[218] Sources: maybe entirely the compiler's independent composition, maybe only partly so and related to the source of *LE* ii. 52. At all events this commemoration of King Edgar as one of the founders of Ely Monastery is a local product, referring to various material objects donated by him, which are referred to in later inventories.

[219] 'In deference to the King': the Latin has simply *in rege*.

[220] On *purpura*, a type of rich, shining, cloth which could be of a range of colours, apart from what we understand as 'purple', e.g. blood-red or black or even green, see C. R. Dodwell, *Anglo-Saxon Art: a New Perspective*, pp. 145ff.

He also gave, from his own chapel, caskets and amulets with the relics of a number of saints, for the sanctification of the monastery, and all the finest sorts of furnishings for the glory of the house of God. The church, thronging with a community of monks, accordingly, by the grace of God, embarked, free from care and at peace, on its voyage into the great and spacious sea of today.[221] Only the party of the wicked, which was ousted long ago, kept striving to oust it by their insistent complainings. But the Lord guards devotedly and mercifully all those who love Him, and will bring all sinners to perdition, as is implicit in the following chapter.

51. That the holy cross of Christ gave forth utterances in defence of monks.[222]

Now, in the time of glorious King Edgar, the order of clerics was in some places in such a state of disarray that not only did it have nothing more excellent about it than the life of the laity, but, through its evil doings, it was even, in its abject state, inferior to it by a long way. Those exercising pastoral care of the churches were dismayed by this state of affairs: most particularly, however, Æthelwold, Bishop of Winchester, and Wulfstan {recte Oswald} of Worcester, approached[223] Dunstan as their own primate, gave an account of the malpractices and sought guidance concerning their correction.

Now Dunstan, issuing the verdict pronounced by his authority against the abominable offenders, said: 'One must either live in accordance with canon law[224] or depart from the churches.' As a consequence of this, it came about that clergy of a great number of churches were expelled by the authority of the archbishop[225] for declining to be corrected in accordance with the condition proposed to them, and monks were brought in.

These clerics, having approached the king[226] or those whom the king's favour had made his closest associates, accused Dunstan of injurious actions, pronounced themselves lovers of virtue and begged for an assembly to be held in the presence of the king. Dunstan, therefore, not wishing to oppose demands reasonably made, came to Winchester, where an assembly had been convened, and there, by the decision of the whole council, he won victory

---

[221] Interpreting *navigabat* as inceptive imperfect, and *hoc mare* as an allusion to a present, as distinct from a past, state of affairs.

[222] Sources: miracle narrative also included in B (*Book of Miracles*). Blake notes extensive borrowings from Osbern, *Vita Dunstani* and the *Worcester Chronicle* on the year 969.

[223] Reading with E and Osbern mss.: *adeunt*.

[224] 'In accordance with canon law': Lat. *canonice*.

[225] Lat. *pontificis*.

[226] Lat. here and in the source: *rege adito*, with *adire* treated as a transitive verb.

over his adversaries. Present at this highly important debate was Byrhtnoth, the first abbot of the holy church of Ely, along with the rest of the multitude of monastics. They waited for aid from Heaven, not from Earth; from God, not from men. And when the enemies of the Lord saw that they had nothing further in their favour on legal grounds, they turned to entreaties, taking advantage of the support of the king and princes. In their entreaties they demanded of the bishop that the persons who had been appointed in their place should be expelled, and that those expelled should be restored. Well then, as the man of God was hesitating and giving no answer to the petitions, something happened which was miraculous and unheard of in any age. See! A representation, carved in stone, of the body of the Lord, fixed upon the ensign of the cross and positioned on the upper part of the house, displayed human characteristics, and silenced everyone's voices, saying: 'Far be it from you that this be done! Far be it from you that this be done!' On hearing this voice, the king and all the elders were frightened almost into giving up the ghost, and filled the courtyard with clamouring and, at the same time, praise of God.

Then the most blessed Archbishop Dunstan and the holy Æthelwold, father and patron of the monks, had ejected[227] the individuals in question, the one from his cathedral and the other from Ely, and in both cases had installed[228] monks – also the holy Oswald, Bishop of Worcester, who similarly ejected clerics from his cathedral and established monks.[229] There arose against them very strong opponents, and Ealdorman Byrhtnoth, of honoured memory, and Æthelwine, Earl of East Anglia, with his brother Ælfwold, put up a sustained resistance, under the king's purview, and said that they could in no way tolerate the ejection from the churches of the monks who upheld the whole of religious devotion in the kingdom. In this way, the hostile faction of those with malign feelings towards the good was ousted by the mighty power of God, so that in them there should be fulfilled what one reads in a Psalm: 'But the face of the Lord is over those who do evil deeds, to remove the remembrance of them from the Earth.'[230] But, by contrast, concerning those of your number[231] there is a blessing.[232] 'The

---

[227] Following the mss. reading (without *qui*) at p. 119.4. The sentence is loosely constructed, certainly, but tolerable if we mark a strong break after *instituit* (line 5).

[228] In the Latin text the verbs meaning 'had expelled' and 'had placed' are, problematically, given in the singular.

[229] Following Blake, at p. 119.6, in reading *monachos* for *monachis* (EF).

[230] Psalm 33.17 Vulgate = 34.16 RSV.

[231] 'Concerning those of your number': Lat. *de istis*. The author had his monastic readership in mind.

[232] What follows is a free paraphrase of parts of Psalm 106 Vulgate = 107 RSV. The wording used here is directly from any published translation.

righteous have cried aloud and the Lord hath heard them and will free them from all their tribulations, so that they who are in the house of God in times of prosperity and in times of adversity may learn to have a firm hope in the Lord.' For 'He who maketh eloquent the tongues of the speechless'[233] and ensures that 'all things work[234] together for good', gave orders to this motionless elemental substance to give forth utterances in protection of His faithful people for the glory of the name of Him who has done all things – whatsoever He has willed – in Heaven and on Earth, and arranges all things agreeably.

And so, in response to the unheard of and unhoped for event, all around each one of them, individually, extolled God with praises and joined in glorifying Him. Eventually, they all hastened to return to their own places of residence, and everywhere gladly proclaimed what they had seen and heard. Abbot Byrhtnoth too, being one who shared in the knowledge of this wonderful event and was a hearer of the Heaven-bestowed utterances, became a faithful witness of it, when he returned to his own people in Ely. They blessed God in His works – God, who 'deserteth not those who put their trust' in Him 'and casteth to the ground those' who glory in their own 'might',[235] when the name of Him 'who alone worketh great marvels'[236] has been called down upon us.

52. At what time the church was dedicated and, on the other hand, by whom.[237]

Meanwhile the abbot, [Byrhtnoth], supported by the generosity of the king and the assistance of the holy bishop, set about the material reconstruction of the church: not like an idle workman but with the utmost effort, he kept striving to raise the church, once reduced to ruins by the Danes, to a state of completeness. For, as the church was in a state of partial collapse, it was not without the greatest effort that he repaired it and, despite the very long period of time that had elapsed, he nevertheless finished it quickly, its completed state being as good as new. And then, when the roofs, which had

---

[233] Wisdom of Solomon 10.21

[234] Here, *cooperari* is apparently used as a deponent verb, with the meaning 'cause to work together'; this is not the case in Romans 8.28 Vulgate, to which, however, this seems to be an allusion.

[235] Cf. Judith 6.15.

[236] Psalm 71.18 Vulgate = 72.18 RSV.

[237] Source: local tradition commemorating the dedication of the church in 970, perhaps from a work on the succession of abbots; no source is identified by Blake except for the final paragraph, which abridges material found in *LE* ii. 144.

been destroyed by fire, had been restored, the rebuilt place of worship appeared no less fine nor less lofty than previously.

Finally, in response to the brothers' entreaties, the abbot and Bishop Æthelwold together secured a dedication-date from the most blessed Archbishop of Canterbury, Dunstan, the time arranged being the day after the Purification of St Mary. In company with the archbishop, many bishops and pastors of churches assembled to celebrate this most solemn rite. First, they filled the domestic buildings[238] of the monastery with blessings, and by their authority, in a written charter, jointly set a seal upon the place and whatever gifts had been brought there, thanks to the generosity of any of the faithful, adducing the privileges of the most excellent King Edgar, with which they confirmed them all. Next, they began the consecration with the 'blessings of sweetness',[239] establishing at the head of the church the titular altar[240] of the blessed Peter, Prince of the Apostles, and in the southern part a memorial chapel of the Holy Mother of God, the ever-virgin Mary, and, celebrating the day of exultation with solemnity, they blessed God with hymns and professions of faith in accordance with the order for the dedication of a church. And thus, following holy and awesome celebrations of the mass, they feasted for seven days on end, eating and drinking, and then, in great joy, each returned to his own domain. Thanks to the operation of the Divine Clemency, that place was purged of all the filth of squalor and neglect. Every day, an immaculate sacrifice to God was offered there, to produce an odour of sweetness; hence in the heavens the angels, too, rejoiced together, and the archangels were exultant and united in praises of the Son of God.

And the venerable father Æthelwold found the body of the most blessed virgin Queen Æthelthryth in the church near the high altar, in the place to which St Seaxburh had translated her, and he left her with the greatest certitude unexamined and uninspected, not in concealment beneath the earth but raised up above it. And indeed it accrued to her greater glory that no one presumed to open her tomb and look inside. Indeed, those who did ever try to look upon her, as one reads in the account of her miracles, perished miserably without delay, their eyes being torn out of their head.

---

[238] Lat. *officinas*.

[239] Lat. *benedictiones dulcedinis*. These were blessings pronounced at the dedication of parts of a church or of objects belonging to it in honour of particular saints (Alistair McGregor, pers. comm. 8.1.02).

[240] Given that St Peter was the dedicatee of the Benedictine minster, Lat. *titulus* must mean the high altar and its sanctuary (Alistair McGregor, pers. comm. 8.1.02). There is a roof-boss representing St Peter in Benedictine garb in the presbytery vault of the present cathedral, to the right of the high altar.

53. That Abbot Byrhtnoth translated the body of the bountiful virgin Wihtburh to Ely.[241]

In the reign of God's beloved Edgar, the most shining-white of the kings of Albion, to whose blessed time we ascribe the translation of the holy virgin Wihtburh, the healthy state of the churches once more put forth blossom and the splendour of the saints again shone out. Then clearly there was splendid validation of that oracle from Heaven which Dunstan, the jewel of the English people, had heard earlier at Glastonbury, on the subject of this same Edgar, now the peaceable bearer of the sceptre, at that time a new-born infant. It was this: 'Peace for the Church of the English in the time of the boy now born and of our Dunstan.' Never have the secular affairs of England seen happier times than this prince's reign, when there was monarchy throughout Britain, that of one very powerful and excellent king in company with that of the neighbouring kings of the islands. Truly, since the most blessed arrival of Augustine, our founding-father in the Gospel, and his colleagues, as far as anyone can remember, there have never shone out so many constellations of saints as under this prince.

Amongst them, Dunstan and Æthelwold illuminated this their sphere most brilliantly, like a latter-day Peter and a latter-day Paul. The former occupied the see of the capital of Kent, and the other, while holding the bishopric of Winchester, was active in the founding and repair of monasteries, thereby carrying out a campaign, as it were, of the Lord's warfare and the stationing of His troops. Among the large number of building-enterprises of this visionary architect was the restoration of the royal monastery, once powerful with its holy community of virgins, which had been founded of old on the Isle of Ely by the glorious Queen and perpetual virgin Æthelthryth. With a view to its restoration, he ennobled it with wealth old and new, fortified it with a community of monks, and instituted Dom Byrhtnoth, his own provost, as its first abbot.

Now, among other magnificent gifts solicited from King Edgar, Bishop Æthelwold added the monastery of Dereham with its most precious treasure, Wihtburh: what was being prepared for, in all that was done, was the favour of translating her. As a consequence of this, both the most holy bishop and the most devout abbot, of one accord in their intention, set about planning how, without a tumult, that most famous adornment[242] of the church, that most splendid pearl of a virginal corpse, to this day untouched by putrefaction, might pass into a more exalted bridal-chamber; how a more

---

[241] Source: narrative copied from *Vita S. Withburge* CT, chapters 9–14, ed. Love; also copied in B (*Book of Miracles*). Date: 8th July, 974.
[242] Lat. *monile*, lit. 'necklace'.

suitable hall might give her honour on a higher level and how she might give it greater lustre by the adornment and splendour of her presence. And when he had acquired the grace and favour of the benevolent king, it was decided above all to pray for the goodwill of the Most High and the willing assistance of the virgin herself, to the end that they might carry out the sacred plan without uproar.

Byrhtnoth, therefore, a pirate in the cause of the Faith,[243] coming before the face of the Lord with confessions, psalms and abstinence, along with the more sagacious of the brothers, came at the prearranged time to the aforesaid church of Dereham with a band of soldiers. He came to an inheritance given over into his hands; he was received into his own house; no one made enquiry as to any other reason for his arrival. Though he was empowered by royal authority to act with might and violence, he preferred to carry out his intention with reverence and prudence, in order to prevent sedition or tumult from arising from the common people. He invited the townsfolk to generous convivial festivities; he exercised his jurisdiction over the people.

To them he left the hall – a place of commerce: for himself he laid claim to the church – a place of seclusion.[244] He was a man well suited to holy sacrilege, to theft in furtherance of the Faith, rapine in pursuance of salvation, to Jacob's obtaining of a blessing by supplantation.[245] So now Night was summoning to their lodging-places and to their beds those who had eaten their fill and, with her great wings, was giving concealment to God's pirate as he kept watch, together with his monks and clerics, for the purposes of their sacred misdemeanour. Speech becomes inadequate to recount how many, at that time, were the bendings of the knee, how many the fomentations of prayer with which he implored the bountiful virgin to be his companion. In the end, armed with faith, they mounted their assault with thuribles of prayers and incense-offerings; they unsealed the sarcophagus and, finding Wihtburh fresh as Spring, with her body entire, like one reposing in sweet sleep, they greeted her with appropriate trepidation and wonderment. The cover was replaced and she was removed manually and by means of rollers and levers. Wagons having been made ready, they took her on board with due reverence and carried her off with assiduous singing of psalms and with triumphal rejoicing, as victors exult over captured booty. As forces in reserve, soldiers and attendants met them and surrounded them, at the ready with their arms and their courage, in case they should encounter

---

[243] 'Byrhtnoth, therefore, a pirate in the cause of the faith', expansion of the Latin, *fidelis predo*, 'faithful pirate', an example of the rhetorical figure *oxymoron*.

[244] 'The hall, a place of commerce . . . the church, a place of seclusion': a free rendering of the rhetorical antithesis expressed in Latin by *meritoriam aulam . . . secretariam ecclesiam* (p. 122.2, ed. Blake).

[245] Lat. *ad Iacob benedictionem supplantandam*. This is an odd expression but the reference is presumably to Genesis 25.24ff.

any opposition.

Thus, journeying for twenty miles by an over-land route, they came to the river at Brandon, went on ship-board with their life-saving cargo and then applied themselves energetically to their oars and nautical tackle. Something which, assuredly, it would not be fitting to leave unmentioned was the remarkable portent that during their journey, almost all through the night, an exceedingly bright star shone red above that most splendid corpse, near at hand, and, issuing forth clear rays of light, all the time accompanied them or led the way.

For indeed, as they were journeying on by water – see! – the people of Dereham, with neighbouring folk as their allies, were up in arms and in pursuit, as they fled. For the parishioners of Dereham, although everyone was already sluggish with sleep, investigated the abbot's lodgings in the house of prayer, for suspicions about these had belatedly been aroused. They found its entrances unlocked, a deep silence – from there being no one there, the sarcophagus of their blessed mother Wihtburh moved from its place, and Wihtburh herself taken away at the same time by the trickery of their hosts. There arose a dreadful clamour of people weeping; a blaring of trumpets reverberated, as if the fatherland were ablaze or an enemy army were perpetrating carnage and arson. The object of their quest was the sole glory of the district, removed by cunning and trickery, and taken captive away, like the Ark of God from the Philistines. Immediately, they all leapt to take up arms and, with a unanimous impulse, went rushing off to retrieve the booty by force. And so, divided for the march into two contingents, they occupied the river-bank to the right and to the left and, as if in an ambush, strove to block every route, apart from the one by river. They flung abuse, they aimed arrows, they reproached the tricksters for perfidious sacrilege; they filled the air with shouts, menaces, threats and insults. They scarcely spared the abbot or the virginal corpse itself, which no decay had touched. But the attempted quest of the desolate failed and vanished like insubstantial smoke. What deterred them was the greatness of the virgin, previously neglected, to whom the heavens were showing favour by means of such a bright star, and, at the same time, the resourcefulness of the Father Superior[246] of Ely. Like a deaf man, he did not hear them as they kept up their clamour, and he gained divine assistance by his repeated prayers; he urged on sailors and ship by his words of encouragement, as a knight urges on a horse with his spurs. And with God's protection, they escaped, while their pursuers, thwarted, returned home wearily.

---

[246] Lat. *preceptor*. This term, used e.g. as the official title of the superior of the Templars and Hospitallers, is here used merely for rhetorical variation as an alternative to the usual word for 'abbot'.

Consequently, when twenty miles had been completed by water, as far as Turbutsey – that is, the Island of Tidbyrht – they conveyed the sweet and pleasant burden, now in triumphant safety, over land, in the wagon which had been made ready and they sang praise and glory to the Lord. So, as the glorious new arrival[247] approached the funeral-rite prepared for her by Heaven, it would be a long task to relate how great was the gathering of various groups of people by which she was greeted, how great the reception she was given, with what concerted singing of monks and clerics she was greeted, with what joy and triumph on the part of all. Every Christian soul from among you may be sure that Æthelthryth, her most blessed sister and doyenne of the monastery and also her other most exalted sister, Queen Seaxburh, with her royal daughter Eormenhild as her mother's companion, along with all the chorus of holy souls, children to the Lord, whom these mothers bore to Him – that they went out to meet her, and gathered the newcomer with their sweet arms and embraces, and invited her into her new bride-chamber and laid her down in her place so that she might rest there for ever. The angels, fellow-citizens and friends to the sisterly chastity of the virgins, joined in the rejoicing and praised the Bridegroom of Glory in solemn assembly. The gladsome Wihtburh introduced this solemn festivity of her translation to the region of Elige, specifically 8th July, when Edgar was supreme ruler over the English Ocean with the valour of David and the peace of Solomon, when truly Dunstan, at the helm in Canterbury, was shedding light over all his homeland, and the blessed Æthelwold, Bishop of Winchester, engaged in his founding of churches, was darting to and fro magnificently, like a golden eagle.

54. By what boundaries the Isle is encircled and how great the authority is on which it places reliance.[248]

Holiness befits the house of God, and thus it was that the church was established for the length of its days under a community of monastics. Already, moreover, the resources of the church had begun to be increased and Abbot Byrhtnoth on his own had not been equal to all the plans for expansion. Hence, with the common consent and support of the brothers, he put in charge of external affairs a man of good character from amongst them,

---

[247] 'So, at the coming of the glorious new arrival': paraphrase of Lat. *veniens . . . nova gloria* (p. 123.3, ed. Blake).

[248] Source: this chapter seems to present the compiler's own synthesis of local traditions; in part he is repeating data also in *LE* i. pr. S; one of his sources seems to have belonged to the days when *Abbotesdelf* still bore that name; he may have used documentation from the inquest into the abbey's liberties in 1080 (see Blake pp. 124–5, n. 4.); a letter of Henry, Archdeacon of Huntingdon, a contemporary of Prior Alexander, is specifically cited.

named Leo, as his colleague in the campaign, a man prudent and painstaking, certainly, in business-matters, to whom he entrusted the administration of his household. Leo was also, in particular, a cultivator of the soil, and he took charge of the raising of cuttings and seeds of various fruits. Like Martha, he was 'troubled with regard to a great many things'[249] and, ready for any good work[250] from the moment he had taken up the assignment of Him who gave him his orders, he also provided his abbot with no little support in his undertakings. For, to be specific, by his own effort, he undertook the task of measuring the boundaries of the region of Elge, and prepared it for blockade, as it were, by means with fortifications, guarding against treacherous stratagems in times to come, for fear that anyone uncircumcised or unclean, in quest of property in excess of his own possessions, might wickedly and perversely cross their borders, harassing with unjust tax-exaction the servants of God in the freedom from labour which they enjoyed for the sake of quietude. This was something which, he recalled, had happened on numerous occasions.

As an outcome of this, the people living nearby were summoned all at the same time from this side and from that. After the share of each of the two neighbouring populations had been investigated and determined, he made, for perpetual recognition, right in the inaccessible and watery middle of the marshes, a cut marking the boundary of the possessions of the church, which in the English vernacular is called to this day *Abbotesdelf* and in Latin *Abbatis fossa* {'the Abbot's ditch'}. The aim was that there should be, as it were, a firm fixture in the mud of the waters, so that no one should incautiously pull down, or set fire to, the boundary-signs of either side. Moreover, with the authority of King Edgar, he defined the limits of the Isle by a pre-adjudged boundary line encircling it, and throughout all ages it is absolutely invalid to infringe his statutory provision.

The brother to whom I have been referring worked hard at the increasing of profits and, if he had exacted any payment, he handed it over in its entirety for communal use, keeping always before his eyes the well-known, terrifying case of Ananias and Sapphira;[251] for they held all things in common, just as is reported to have been the case in the earliest period of the nascent Church. Moreover, he made a silver cross, which is the cross of Provost Leo, in which the figure of the body of Christ, made hollow by the skill of the craftsman, contained relics of St Vedast and St Amandus. This Bishop Nigel removed – and more things too, of which we will tell in the chronologically appropriate place. Provost Leo, indeed, carried out another

---

[249] Cf. Luke 10.41. Provost Leo is probably identifiable with the *prepositus* named Leofwine in *LibÆ*.

[250] Reading with E *ad omne opus bonum* (p. 123.24, ed. Blake).

[251] Acts 5.1ff.

special and beneficial undertaking which, we believe, deserves to be reported in honour of him: he also planted gardens and orchards of newly propagated stock over a wide area around the church, and he did this personally, being a man of expertise, and one who considered that a distinguished and venerable monastery looked more comely with a surrounding of trees. These gardens and orchards contribute much in the way of pleasantness and profit and would that you might see all that was planted and sowed by him – such as the timber of woodlands standing high – and that it is all very soon filled with all richness of fruit. With these not inappropriate additions to our history, we now return to our original theme.

Well then, the extent of the region of Elge is seven miles long, namely from *Cotingelade*[252] to Littleport or to the Abbot's Ditch, which is now called the Bishop's Ditch, and four miles wide, from *Chirchewere* to Stretham Mere, but the boundaries of the two hundreds which from ancient times have belonged to Ely, are acknowledged to be understood as of wider extent, that is, as is related in the context of the opening of book one: extending from the middle of Tydd Bridge all the way to Upware, and from the Bishop's Ditch as far as the river near Peterborough which is called the Nene.

And the honours and customs of the church of Ely granted and confirmed for St Æthelthryth by King Edgar and all subsequent kings of England up until today, within the Isle and within the two hundreds of the Isle, are as follows: meetings and law-courts which pertain to the king's crown, and all the people of the two hundreds of the Isle must assemble fortnightly[253] at Ely or at Witchford, which is called the capital of the Isle, or at *Modich*,[254] which is a ferthing of the hundreds, for the judicial business of St Æthelthryth. And no one has land or any jurisdiction within the Isle except St Æthelthryth, and none of the king's barons has his court within the two hundreds of the Isle, but the person with a claim to make and the person against whom a claim is made are to come to the places mentioned above and be judged there; likewise in the five-and-a-half hundreds of Wicklow and the one-and-a-half hundreds of Dereham and the trithing of Winston. And if anyone in the land of St Æthelthryth – no matter whose man he is, no matter whether he is an outsider or locally-born – has had a charge brought against him, and has been judged by ordeal of fire and of water, he shall receive what God has mercifully granted to him in no other place but in Ely, and no secular or ecclesiastical personage is to demand the right to present him for trial, but recompense in full is payable to the church alone though

---

[252] Cf. *LE* i. pr. S, on the boundaries of the Isle. *Cotingelade* (cf. the modern name Cottenham Lode) seems to have been a mere in the region of the Old West River.

[253] Lat. *de quindecim in quindecim diebus* . . . Cf. Tacitus, *Germania* 11.1, on the holding by the ancient German peoples of meetings 'on fixed days, when the Moon is new or full'.

[254] The reading of E.

the hands of the sacrist, who fulfils the role of an archdeacon[255] with respect to the Isle. Hence, a highly competent writer, deserving respect for his age and white hair, is cited as witness. The text, to be precise, is as follows:

Henry, Archdeacon of Huntingdon, sends greeting to Alexander, Prior of Ely, venerable master and most beloved friend. May your Amiability know that neither Nicholas, Archdeacon of Huntingdon nor his predecessors ever exercised power, or received anything from any defendant who had undergone ordeal by water or fire, within the Isle of Ely, so far as my memory recalls and so far as I have ascertained from those whom I have painstakingly called to a meeting on the matter in question, and who have knowledge of it. Farewell.

On the contrary, neither bishop nor judge to this day has foisted himself upon the Isle, or presumed to disturb the business of the lady saint.[256] It appears that this is prohibited on the authority of popes and kings. Rather, it has been for them to choose to have their affairs ordered or sanctified by whichsoever bishop they please.

I gathered these facts from writs and official letters possessed by the church, and not from myself, as fabrications. But I speak, as it were, tearfully, warning and pleading that no one should presume to take away from the church the possessions of the lady saint, or lay claim to her honours. For the man who does so, whoever he is, shall have judgement laid upon him. God is my witness, as to the severity of the punishment with which those who have so presumed are inflicted every day! And not only they: on the contrary, it is known that the anger of the Lord's rage threatens the fourth and fifth generation! And now the very degenerates who seek to despoil God's sanctuary[257] of its heritage, not in the least content with the innumerable lands of their possessions, are being compelled to leave their own properties to strangers, and to endure grave poverty – thanks to Christ the Avenger.

55. About those who made benefactions to the church of Ely and those who did it harm.[258]

†Well then, King Edgar and God's pontiff Æthelwold, who reverenced the monastery of Ely most with honour and dignity – there is now a clear record,

---

[255] Reading conjecturally (p. 125.12, ed. Blake): *archidiaconi vices.*

[256] Here I assume strong punctuation after *presumit* (p. 126.1, ed. Blake) as a way of coping with the anacoluthon in the sentence, '*Sed neque . . . videtur*'.

[257] Correcting the typographical error at p. 126.9, ed. Blake, thus: *ipsi nunc degeneres.*

[258] Source: inferences from *LibÆ* by the compiler, who, as ms. E shows, had excluded references to events after the reign of King Edgar.

...ily of them but also of a group of people consisting of all, whoever they might be, who were donors or vendors, and of the sum of money involved – and there were other beneficent men, too, who generously donated[259] properties which they owned.† Among them, Wulfstan of Dalham, a man worthy of respect, and Ealdorman Byrhtnoth, beloved of God and men, contributed many benefactions to the place in the course of the restoration and afterwards. But everything that these people lavished out of piety to build up the standing of the church, certain evil-minded men were not afraid to seize, if not by force, then by trickery. In particular, Æ{the}lwine, the founder of the monastery of Ramsey, had the presumption to harass the monastery of Ely with claims and diminish its resources by lawsuits, with no regard for the reverence due to God and the lady saints reposing there, as one reads in the book of lands which is called *The Book of St Æthelwold*. His aim was to misappropriate an offering. In so doing, he was showing little regard for the saying of the wise man that one who helps himself to an offering is 'like one who sacrifices a son in the presence of his father.'[260]

For instance, after the death of King Edgar, the aforesaid Æ{the}lwine, styled Ealdorman, and his brothers, laid claim to the estate of Hatfield.[261] When, however, his claim had been narrated and made clear, they entered this estate and took possession of it for themselves. But the brothers of the church saw that they could in no way [either abandon or] manage without that land, without incurring great loss, given that they did not have woodland elsewhere from which they could cater for their needs, so they sought out the aforesaid Æ{the}lwine once again and, making an agreement with him, bought the aforementioned estate from him, and gave in exchange for it the two estates which Wulfstan of Dalham, on his death, gave to St Æthelthryth, namely thirty hides at Hemingford and six at Wennington, as a consequence of which the church is to this day deprived of these lands; moreover, in return for such an agreement he received from the abbot three hides at Wangford and five at Yelling, making guarantees and promises that he would always do things needful for the church; but his promising was to no effect. This man also caused the church to waste[262] much gold and silver on the buying of lands.

---

[259] The Latin here (p. 126.13–15, ed Blake) is confused, probably due to clumsy conflation of two drafts.

[260] Cf. Ecclesiasticus 34.24 Vulgate = 34.20 RSV.

[261] This claim was related in *LibÆ* 5, and in the F version of *LE* ii. 7; but note that the E version omitted all but the account of Æthelwold's initial acquisition of the estate. See Blake *ad loc.* for speculation on the relationship of the account in *LE* ii. 55 with that in the *LibÆ*, which gave Æ(the)lwine's name in the fuller form. It also contained no reference to Wangford.

[262] Something is wrong with the Latin at p. 127.14, ed. Blake. I am translating as if the reading were *qui etiam pro emendis terris aurum et argentum multum ecclesiam perdere fecit.*

BOOK II

56. In what sort of manner our first abbot was martyred.[263]

Well then, one day it so happened that, in the interests of the church, the holy Abbot Byrhtnoth set out on a journey to the court of King Æthelred, on this side of *Geldedune*, through the woodland which is called the New Forest. There, so the report goes, he went in search of remoter surroundings in response to the call of nature and, being an ingenuous man and one of great modesty, he looked all around him and by chance came upon Queen Ælfthryth[264] beneath a tree, engaged upon her concocting of noxious potions. [For it was as if, by her fantasies and magical art, she had been changed into an equine beast: to those who looked at her she used to give the impression of being a mare, not a woman, her aim being to satisfy the unquenchable intemperance of her seething lust. Running around hither and thither and cavorting with the horses, she indecently exposed herself to them, in contempt of the fear of God and the honour of her royal dignity, and in this way brought reproach upon her good name.]

At the sight of him, she groaned, not without tremendous sorrow and fear, at having been observed engaged in such activities by a holy man. She was, to be sure, considered very adept in the art of machination, so the story goes. But the godly man, exceedingly troubled by such happenings, retraced his steps from that place as quickly as possible and, arriving at the king's court, was received with magnificence, and carried out the business of his church with all speed. And so, having enjoyed the king's munificence and been cheered by it, he sought once more to return to his own domains and, so as not to shun the queen through his abhorrence of her, he went down to her hall, which he found, as it happened, completely deserted within.

However, his arrival quickly became known to the queen. In fact, she made the request that he should come to her on his own with all haste, and gave instructions that she had to discuss some matters concerning the salvation of her soul with him in private. On his entering, she spoke to him in an exceedingly cajoling and immodest way, uttering a number of lustful enormities. By means of entreaties and promises, she, shameless women as she was, meant to entice him to herself, like holy Joseph,[265] by the entanglements of a breach of continence. She was reckoning, by means of an ill-intentioned trick, to involve God's saint along with herself in wrong-doing, since she had been afraid that, through him, the cover would be

---

[263] Source: local commemoration of Abbot Byrhtnoth, perhaps forming part of a work on the succession of abbots; in *LE* ii. 57; for bibliography on the subject-matter of the narrative, see Blake, p. 127, n. 4.

[264] Second wife of King Edgar, who was succeeded first by his elder son, Edward 'the Martyr' (975–9) and then by his younger son, Æthelred 'the Unready' (979–1016). On the reputation of the dowager Queen Ælfthryth, see Blake, p. 127, n. 4; p. 128, n. 4.

[265] The allusion is to the wiles of Potiphar's wife, Genesis 39.

153

removed from the vice which he found her to be practising. He put up physical and verbal resistance, refused and shrank back.

As a result she was roused to fury, summoned the serving-women from her evil household and, because she 'conceived affliction' she 'gave birth to iniquity'.[266] She gave orders for the blessed man to be put to death, not wishing that a man should live on, whom she distrusted as one who would some day be the betrayer of her wrong-doings. She devised a way to put an end to him while keeping his body unscathed by a wound, and with no apparent damage. She instructed them to heat a couple of daggers in the fire and to thrust them into the abbot's arm-pits until they forced the life out of him. When this had been done, her attendants cried out [mournfully within], as if seized by terror at such a mischance. As a consequence the abbot's servants and the monks who had accompanied him came running; they heard from the women that he had been overcome by a sudden death and they groaned to hear it. But, deeply grieved though they were at what had happened and emitting mournful cries, they placed the body of their master on a wagon and conveyed it to their church at Ely and, discovering on him no indication of a wound, consigned him to burial.[267]

The first abbot of the holy church of Ely was martyred, therefore, deprived of breath by the machinations of one little woman, as it was his choice to succumb to human hands rather than to abandon God's law. His soul shall reign for ever with all the saints and has earned the everlasting joys which are in Heaven.

But concerning the queen: no one presumed even to mutter anything sinister about her, or to direct any evil report against her. And what has been said could have remained hidden from everyone for longer, had it not been that she herself, by God's mercy conscience-stricken, made a confession about her wrong-doings: about her sorceries and abominable activities, and particularly about the death of the glorious King Edward, her step-son, whom she openly entrapped by all her trickeries and unlawfully killed, so that her own son Æthelred should be raised up to the throne. In recompense for this, she founded the nunnery of Werwell from her own resources, and there she remained, all the days of her life, in sorrow and penitence, and with groans and trepidation she revealed – as has been described already – by what manner of death she had killed Byrhtnoth, Abbot of Ely. And in that place she was subsequently the donor of many benefactions, consisting both in material objects and in estates.

---

[266] Job 15.35 Vulgate.

[267] Date of Abbot Byrhtnoth's death: 996 X 999. See Blake, Appendix D, on the impossibility of dating the abbots of Ely exactly; the dating given in the *Chronicon* cannot be relied upon.

57. After the death of the first abbot, who was appointed in his place.[268]

Motivated as we are by the precedents of the ancients, we are refusing to allow memories to fade away, particularly where they concern certain holy abbots, in whose charge our community made progress in respect to holy religion, and where they concern kings and mighty men[269] as well, by whose munificence our place has flourished and by whose benefactions it has enjoyed increase. Rather, we have it in mind to single out particular items from the historical records with suitable brevity, our object being, on the one hand, that prolixity should not cause anyone tedium, and, on the other, that the full truth should be sufficiently known.

The reading[270] previous to this has, to be sure, indicated in what way the first abbot of Ely departed this life – the abbot to whom St Dunstan, Archbishop of Canterbury and St Æthelwold, Bishop of Winchester, gave their blessing on the orders of King Edgar. On his death, the aforesaid Æthelwold, on the orders of King Æthelred, appointed another man, named Ælfsige, in Byrhtnoth's place, and Æthelwold himself blessed him. Moreover, in the time of King Æthelred, the said church of Ely expanded enormously and, despite the fact that this king experienced frequent outbreaks of warfare, he renewed the generosity of his father, Edgar, towards that church and he, too, desired to promote remembrance of himself within it by means of munificence. So it was that, inspired by his father's probity, he set about aggrandizing it with estates, and in the privilege which follows he confirmed his grant with respect to it.

58. A privilege of King Æthelred about the vill of Littlebury.[271]

All patrimonies of secular wealth are left to the indeterminable heirs of one's progeny, and all the glory of the World, as the end of this life approaches, is reduced to nothing and fades away. As it is said by a certain sage, 'This transitory World is growing feebler every day, and all its beauty is fading like a flower of the hay.'[272] In view of this, one should, with the Lord as one's Defender, by means of earthly possessions consisting of impermanent things,

---

[268] Source. Ostensibly, this is the compiler's own introduction to *LE* ii. 58–99, chapters chiefly about benefactions to the monastery. But there is reference back to the death of Abbot Byrhtnoth, as well as mention of the appointment of his successor, and thus the chapter could be based on an earlier text commemorating abbots in succession.

[269] Here *vir* has apparently some such connotation as 'hero', in line with classical usage.

[270] Lat. *lectio*. Note this indication that the chapters either of the *Liber Eliensis* or of its source here, were conceived of as a series of 'readings'.

[271] Source: monastic archives, cf. cartularies CDM. Date: 1004.

[272] Unidentified quotation alluding to a phrase from the Vulgate Bible: see James 1.10; 1 Peter 1.24, cf. Isaiah 40.6–7.

acquire the never-failing joys of the heavenly country. Therefore, I Æthelred, High King of all Britain and the rest of the peoples residing round about it, have granted, by way of perpetual inheritance, a certain country estate, namely 20 *mansae* in the place which is called by the commonly known name of Littlebury,[273] to the Lord and His mother Mary and the blessed Peter, Prince of the Apostles, not excluding the distinguished virgin St Æthelthryth and the other virgins akin to her at the monastery – specifically, the one at Ely – for the purposes of the monks living there, so that it may belong to that monastery in perpetuity, along with all its easements, namely: meadows, pastures and woods. May the aforesaid rural property, moreover, be free from all imposition of earthly service, with the exception of three types of work, namely: military service, repair of bridges and fortifications. If anyone, therefore, should wish to divert this our grant to a purpose other than the one which we have established, let him be deprived of association with the Holy Church of God, let him be punished [continually] in the everlasting fires of the gloomy Abyss with Judas the betrayer of Christ and his accomplices, if he does not make amends for his offence against our decrees by appropriate satisfaction. This charter, in very truth, was written in the 1004th year from the Lord's incarnation.

59. About Thaxted.[274]

A woman worthy of respect called Æthelgifu gave to God and St Æthelthryth and that saint's blessed progeny who rest at Ely, land at Thaxted, with everything belonging to that vill and whatsoever relics of the saints she possessed. There were, indeed, many witnesses of this gift who had gathered around her at the time of her death, in particular, Ælfsige, Abbot of Ely, and a monk of his, Leofsige, and the notables of the district, and Byrhtsige the son of the woman in question, and her daughter, called Edith, and others who are included in her will, written in English, which is still kept in the church as evidence.

60. About Kingston, the Rodings, Undley, Whittlesey and Cottenham and about land at London called *Abboteshai*.[275]

Then a certain very wealthy man called Leofwine, the son of Æthulf, with an

---

[273] Littlebury, Essex.

[274] Source: will of Æthelgifu of Thaxted, cf. cartularies CDM. Dates of abbacy of Ælfsige: from 996 X 999 until a date before 1016 (see Blake, p. 411).

[275] Source: presumably a pre-existing local commemorative text relating to grants by Leofwine, son of Ædulf; also his actual will, written in English. Date: abbacy of Ælfsige, after 1002 (see Blake, p. 131, n. 1).

acknowledged reputation for pleasantness, charity and hospitality and especially for his devotion to the worship of God at Ely, came to regard the place with great reverence. But it is reported that he committed a lapse into the greatest sin; that, however, he did not remain in that state for long: no rather, by the grace of God, he returned to his senses again very quickly, and then he became extremely afraid. To explain: there had arisen at one time a quarrel between Leofwine and his mother, as a consequence of which he was scarcely able to restrain the passion of his raging spirit, driven as he was[276] by the goads of anger. As the saying goes: 'Anger prevents the spirit from being able[277] to recognize what is true.' Instead, before long he gravely wounded his mother, striking her with a log which he had seized. Crushed, she suffered pain for a considerable time, and such was the plight she was in that she expired as the result of the wound-damage.

Leofwine was, no wonder, exceedingly afraid of what he had done, and sought advice from priests and wise men. Their response to him was that he ought to have a personal consultation with the apostolic lord at Rome, who knew how to enjoin upon every individual a remedy consisting of appropriate and suitable penance, according to the nature of the fault. After this, he made his way to Rome, weeping and wailing, and making supplication in the presence of the blessed Peter and the relics of the saints also in that place, that they through their merits might avert the judgement of the Lord from him, in accord with the experience of the people of Nineveh.[278] Then in sorrow he revealed to the lord Pope the enormity of his sin, just as he had committed it. The Pope ordered that in penance he should give his first-born boy to a poor little church somewhere, as a monk, and richly endow this church from the abundance of his possessions and, for the good of his soul, bestow his wealth with the greatest liberality upon the poor people of Christ.

And, when he returned home, he brought to completion what he had in salutary fashion begun, and bestowed generous gifts of alms upon needy people everywhere. He distributed a very large amount to monasteries whose poverty was great and, most of all, he desired to direct his munificence towards the church of Ely, where he most devoutly offered his first-born son Æthelmær, with the properties which are listed here, on the evidence of a chirograph written in English, that is to say: Kingston,[279] the Rodings,[280] Undley,[281] and the fisheries which belong to it, and the land in

---

[276] Reading with E: *exagitatus* (p. 131.10, ed. Blake).

[277] Reading with E as well as BG: *ne possit* (p. 131. 11, ed. Blake).

[278] Cf. Jonah 3.5ff.

[279] Kingston, in south-east Suffolk.

[280] In west Essex.

[281] Undley, Suffolk.

Lakenheath[282] which people call *Oswaradala,* and a third part of Whittlesey, and land at Eastrea,[283] and Cottenham,[284] and land, forming part of London, which to this day is called *Abboteshai,*[285] and Glemsford[286] and the fishery[287] at *Upstaue,* and an annual food-rent from the royal estate of Hatfield, and he made more grants, which are written in it, and further munificently endowed the place, within and without, by bestowing very generous gifts.

After this, he called upon Abbot Ælfsige, servant of the Lord, and the brothers who had been[288] with him, in the presence of Archbishop Wulfstan and the bishops and abbots and an assembly consisting of a great number of other men and women, to swear that they would never alienate from the church, or exchange, the properties which he had donated and granted to God and his holy mother Mary and the blessed virgin Æthelthryth and the family of that saint, for the redemption of his soul and the souls of his wife and parents, not for gold, not for silver, not for any kind of benefit, but that, as a memorial to them, they would remain and stay in the church in a state of firmness and stability. The brothers, indeed, for their part, pledged to celebrate masses for him for ever on Mondays, and for his wife and children and his kindred on Tuesdays, and to feed the needy and clothe the naked, as one reads in his will written in English. Leofwine, approved by God, then added yet further to the good work on which he had begun, and began to enlarge the walls of the church, and build them at a wider distance away to the south and he brought them to a state of completeness, at his own expense, in which they were united with the rest of the building. He also made in one *porticus*[289] an altar to the honour of the most blessed Mother of God and, above it, a throne the height of a man,[290] on which was seen a

---

[282] Lakenheath, Suffolk.

[283] Whittlesea in the Cambridgeshire fens; Eastrea was the eastern part of the island of Whittlesea.

[284] Cottenham, Cambridgeshire.

[285] A much later marginal note in E explains that this was 'in Holborn, not far from Ely Palace'.

[286] Glemsford in Suffolk, further west than Kingston.

[287] Reading with E: *piscationem.*

[288] The mss. have *fuerant* (pluperfect) 'had been' (p. 132.6, ed. Blake), but this could be a mistake for *fuerunt* (perfect) 'were'.

[289] Lat. *porticus:* 'porch', 'aisle', 'side chapel'.[289]

[290] Lat. *ad longitudinem hominis.* As the name Eadric *Longus* illustrates (*LE* ii. 27), 'long' could mean 'tall' in OE thinking; hence also Lat. *longitudo* in the sense, 'height'; see Latham *et al., Dictionary of Medieval Latin,* s.v. *longitudo,* where Bede is cited for a a description of a wall as *altior longitudine stantis hominis.*

statue of her holding her son in her lap, fabricated to an exceptionally high standard from gold and silver and jewels, beyond price, such was the immensity of its value. King William took this statue and broke it to pieces, along with very many ornaments of the church, upon subjecting the Isle to his dominion by war.

And the praiseworthy man to whom we have been referring completed his days in ripe old age, and his body was carried to Ely and buried in the church of the holy virgin Æthelthryth, whom he had made the inheritor of his goods. For him, O God, may there be life and remission of sins. AMEN.

61. About Bridgham, Hingham, Weeting, Rattlesden, and Mundford, and the fisheries around Thetford.[291]

There was a certain widow, named Ælfwaru, who was noble by birth and extremely rich. However – and this is more important – she had grown eminent as much by the increasing of her virtues as by her riches. When she was dying, she had her will confirmed in the presence of many people in a chirograph written out in the language of the common people. And she gave to God, and the holy virgin Æthelthryth and her holy family, properties and gifts in abundance from her riches, her object being that she should offer back thankfully to God as an eternal possession, what He in his mercy had for a time granted to her, namely: Bridgham, with all things belonging to that vill, within the settlement and outside it, consisting in lands and waters, in woodland and field; she further added Hingham and Weeting, and Rattlesden and Mundford, and a shrine with relics which they called a 'stepped reliquary',[292] and two crosses wonderfully crafted[293] from gold and silver and precious jewels, which Bishop Nigel later removed and broke up. She also laid down, moreover, that land at Thetford[294] and fisheries around those marshes and all that she had – apart from those items of which she made an exception in her chirograph, which is still in our possession today – should be handed over to the church. Her body, having been brought to Ely, is, in fact, buried here, and her name has a perpetual memorial in the church, having been inscribed above the holy altar with the names of the brothers.

---

[291] Source: English will of the widow Ælfwaru. Material evidence: recollection of a particular reliquary and two crosses (since destroyed by Bishop Nigel) as her gifts, and of a memorial inscription over the altar in the church, including her name, along with those of monks. The chapter-title is given as in E.

[292] Lat. *gradatum feretrum*. See Dodwell, *Anglo-Saxon Art*, pp. 220–1 and 324.

[293] Translating the reading of E. The word for 'wonderfully' is lacking from F.

[294] The reference is thought to be to Little Thetford near Ely, where the monastery is known to have held land.

62. About the venerable Ealdorman Byrhtnoth, who gave to St Æthelthryth Spaldwick and Trumpington, Rettendon and *Hesberi*, Soham, Fulbourn, Teversham, Impington, Pampisford, Croxton and Finborough, Thriplow, Hardwick and Somersham with its appurtenances.[295]

What follows is a noteworthy account concerning Byrhtnoth, an outstanding and famous man whose righteous[296] life and deeds English histories commend with no small praises. From these, begging the reader's pardon, we have extracted a few items, irrespective of the character of our style. For indeed, the subject is a great one and our ancestors' account of it, one of the utmost dignity, and it is with some shame that we narrate it, insignificant and inarticulate as we are, in our dry style.[297]

This most noble man was indeed a very valiant leader of the Northumbrians[298] who, on account of the marvellous wisdom and physical fortitude with which he manfully defended himself and his people, was given by everyone the title of *Ealdorman*, in the English language, that is, 'elder' or 'leader'. He was fluent in speech, robust in strength, of huge physical stature, indefatigable in soldiering and warfare against the enemies of the kingdom, and courageous beyond all measure, being without respect for, or fear of, death. In addition he honoured Holy Church and the servants of God everywhere and bequeathed the whole of his patrimony to their use. On behalf of the religious communities, too, he used always to place himself as a bulwark against those who attempted to disturb holy places. For that religious man, while present at a synod, resisted with great firmness the greed and madness of certain prominent men, who wanted to expel the

[295] Source. The material in this chapter, seems to have been copied or adapted from what will be referred to (on no medieval authority) as *A History of Seven Illustrious Men*, a lost work commemorating a group of worthies whose remains have been, from early times to this day, buried and commemorated together, most recently in Bishop West's chapel. The compiler drew upon this same source for *LE* ii. 65, 71, 72, 75, 86, 87, 99, thus probably preserving nearly the whole of the work, but reordering its contents so as to present the seven worthies in chronological order rather than in order of ecclesiastical rank. In addition, brief quotations in this chapter from the *Worcester Chronicle* on the year 975 (Byrhtnoth's support of monks against secular clergy) are noted by Blake. On the Ely tradition regarding Ealdorman Byrhtnoth in relation to that in the *Ramsey Chronicle*, which corroborates it, see Blake p. 422. On Byrhtnoth's will, see Whitelock, *Anglo-Saxon Wills*, pp. 106–7. Date of the death of Byrhtnoth: according to the *Worcester Chronicle*, 988, but according to *LE*, 991.
[296] Translating *iustam*, the reading of E.
[297] Blake casts doubt on the historicity of the subsequent narrative. But it is not necessary to assume that the OE poem on the Battle of Maldon is more accurate than the *LE* tradition: its epic narrative might have conflated elements from more than one battle for poetic effect.
[298] Lat. *Northanimbrorum dux*. Byrhtnoth is nowhere else but in the Ely tradition associated with Northumbria; rather he was Ealdorman of Essex.

monks and recall to the churches those who had previously been ejected by Edgar and Saint Æthelwold. He said that he could in no way tolerate the expulsion from the kingdom of the monks who upheld all religion in the kingdom. As long as he lived, moreover, he devoted his life to defending the freedom of his native land, so totally committed to this desire that he would rather die than tolerate an unavenged injury to his country. At that time, indeed, frequent raids were being made by the Danes upon England, and they wreaked serious devastation upon it, arriving as they did in various places by ship. And all the foremost men of the provinces loyally bound themselves to Ealdorman Byrhtnoth, as to an invincible protector, because of his great worth and reliability, so that under his protection they might defend themselves against the enemy nation more confidently.

Accordingly, on one occasion, when the Danes had come ashore at Maldon, on hearing report of this, he[299] confronted them with an armed force and slaughtered †nearly all of them on a causeway above the water†.[300] It was only with difficulty that a few of them escaped and sailed to their own country to tell the tale.

After this victory, Ealdorman Byrhtnoth returned in good spirits to Northumbria. However, the Danes, very much saddened by the news that they had heard, fitted out a fleet again,[301] made haste to England and in the fourth year landed at Maldon again to avenge the killing of their men, with Justin and Guthmund, the son of Stectan, as their leaders. On having reached the harbour they learned that it was Byrhtnoth who had done these things to their men, so they sent word straight away that they had come to avenge them, and that he would have to be numbered among cowards if he would not dare join battle with them. Incited to daring by their messengers, Byrhtnoth summoned his former comrades together for this venture and, led on by the hope of victory and his exceedingly great courage, he set out on his way to battle with a few warriors, both taking precautions and moving fast, lest the enemy army should occupy so much as one foot of land in his absence.

When, during the march, he approached the abbey of Ramsey and sought hospitality and provisioning from Abbot Wulfsige for himself and his men, the reply was given to him that the place had not resources sufficient for such a multitude, but that, so that he should not go away entirely rejected, Wulfsige would provide what he was requesting for Byrhtnoth himself and seven of his men. To this, Byrhtnoth is said to have made the elegantly

---

[299] Reading with G: *ipse.*

[300] Problematic Latin at p. 134.20, ed. Blake. I translate as if the reading were *omnes super pontem aque interemit*, and take *pontem aque* to mean 'causeway above water'. D. G. Scragg, *The Battle of Maldon, 991 A.D.*, discusses the topography.

[301] Assuming the reading of GO, *reparant*, to be correct.

phrased response, 'Let the lord Abbot know that I will not dine alone without the men you refer to, because I cannot fight alone without them.'

And so, departing, Byrhtnoth turned his march to the church of Ely, sending word in advance to Abbot Ælfsige that he was about to pass [through] the Isle with forces of no great strength[302] on his way to battle and that, if this were acceptable to him, he would dine at this monastery with his army. The abbot replied to him, with the agreement of his community, that in the exercise of charity he was in terror of no multitude: rather he was delighted at their arrival. Welcomed, therefore, with all his men, Byrhtnoth was provided with hospitality fit for a king, and, as a consequence of the unremitting attentiveness of the monks, he was fired with a great love of the monastery. It seemed to him that he would never have had any success, if he had left this act of goodwill on the part of the monks unrewarded.

Thinking to himself, therefore, that those monks had been not a little burdened on his account, the next day he came into the chapter-house to receive membership of the fraternity,[303] and, giving thanks to the abbot and the community for their charity – so liberal was it – gave to them, there and then, in recompense for their generosity, these capital estates: Spaldwick and Trumpington, Rettendon and *Hesberie*, Soham and Occold. Explaining the business which was the objective of his journey, he granted other estates too, namely: Fulbourn, Teversham, Impington, Pampisford, Croxton and Finborough, Triplow, Hardwick, and Somersham with its appurtenances, and, in addition, thirty mancuses of gold and twenty pounds of silver, on the condition that, if by chance he should die in battle, they should bring his body here and give it burial. In addition, by way of investiture of this gift to the church of Ely, he supplemented it with two golden crosses and two borders of his cloak, woven with costly work in gold and gems, and a pair of skilfully made gloves. Then, commending himself to the prayers of the brothers, he hastened with his men to battle.

On arrival there, he was neither perturbed by the fewness of his men, nor fearful of the numerical strength of the enemy, but attacked them straight away and fought them fiercely for fourteen days. On the last of these days, few of his men being still alive, Byrhtnoth realized that he was going to die. He was not fighting any the less energetically against the enemy, but in the end, after he had inflicted great slaughter on his adversaries and almost put them to flight, they were encouraged by the small number of Byrhtnoth's supporters, made a wedge-formation, and, grouping together, rushed with one resolve upon him and, with a great effort, only just successful, cut off his head as he fought. They took it with them, fleeing from the place to their native land. But the abbot, on hearing the outcome of the fighting, went with

---

[302] Reading with E, *imbecillis*, where F has *bellicis*.

[303] Lat. *suscipiende fraternitatis*: cf. du Cange, s.v. *fraternitas* 5.

some monks to the battle-ground and found Byrhtnoth's body. He brought it back to the church and buried it with honour. And in place of the head he put a round lump of wax.[304] Long afterwards, in [our own] times, he was recognized by this sign, and was honourably entombed among the others.[305] But it was in the days of Edgar, Edward (king and martyr), and Æthelred, Kings of the English, that this pious and energetic man had his being, and he died in the fourteenth year of the reign of the same Æthelred, in the 991st year from the incarnation of the Lord.

63. About the Lady Æthelflæd {*recte* Ælfflæd}, the wife of the aforesaid ealdorman, who gave us the vill of Rettendon, and those of Soham and Ditton and Cheveley.[306]

This man's wife, indeed, the Lady Ælfflæd by name, at the time when her husband was killed and buried, gave to this church an estate at Rettendon, which formed part of her marriage-portion, and land at Soham, which is by a mere adjoining Ely, and Ditton, and a hide at Cheveley, and a golden torque, and a hanging woven upon and embroidered with the deeds of her husband, in memory of his probity.

64. About Hadham and Kelshall.[307]

Her sister, moreover, the wife of Ealdorman Æthelstan, whose name was Æthelflæd, was a very wealthy woman by virtue of her estates, her marriage-portion and the inherited patrimony of her family. Hence she seemed the noblest among her kinsfolk. However, while she seemed to cling to the uncertain riches of the World, she was devoutly scrupulous about the observance of holy religion and, after the death of her husband, remained perpetually in widowhood, following the example of the blessed Anna.[308] Moreover, she frequently sought out our saints with heartfelt love and veneration, and devoutly used to attend vigils at their shrines.[309] Hence, when in good health and sound condition, she had a meeting with Abbot Ælfsige and the brothers of the church, accompanied by the lavishing of

---

[304] Accepting Blake's conjecture (p. 136.8) *rotundam* for *rotunda* EF.

[305] That is, the other six benefactors commemorated in the source-text.

[306] Source: monastic archives – will of the Lady Ælfflæd, made after her husband's death; see Whitelock, *Anglo-Saxon Wills*, no. xv. It is not made clear whether the material objects mentioned as donated to the monastery were still extant.

[307] Source: monastic archives – will of the Lady Æthelflæd; see Whitelock, *Wills*, no, xiv. Date: abbacy of Ælfsige (see Blake, p. 411).

[308] Luke 2.36ff.

[309] Lat. simply: *ad eas.*

many gifts and, as a result of the exceptional favour of their close association, she was drawn to a great love of the place. [Moreover] she gave them Ditton and Hadham and Kelshall, and in her will in English she had these things confirmed, except that she made the proviso that her sister, Ælflæd, who has been mentioned earlier, should keep the vill of Ditton while she lived.

65. About Bishop Æthelstan of blessed memory, who gave us Drinkstone.[310]

A further witness to the extent to which this place was the object of veneration in the old days is Æthelstan, Bishop of Elmham, a man outstanding in his devotion in church matters, and a donor of outstanding liberality with regard to this particular church. Drawn towards love of this place by the manifold miraculous powers of the lady saints resting here and the religious devotion of the brothers, he had a meeting with Byrhtnoth and Ælfsige, that is, the first and second abbots of this place, and a full assembly of the community of the brotherhood, on the subject of the burial of his body, a long while before his death, being up to that time still in good health and sound condition. This meeting was accompanied by much bestowing of gifts. And both abbots granted to him the receiving of the professions of monks, and the granting of holy orders, and other episcopal rights in their house, on account of the exceptional favour of their close association. For the liberty of this church was of such a kind that they used to summon whomsoever of the bishops they might prefer to do these things. For this reason they would rather call upon bishops other than Lincoln's to exercise episcopal functions, lest the church of Lincoln, in whose diocese this diocese of Ely is situated, might be able at some time to burden it with vexatious exactions because of its subjection to the bishop's power. In consequence, as evidence of its ancient dignity, there have been preserved to this day in our archives written professions of former brothers which were made in the presence of the lord Æthelstan, Bishop of Elmham, but none made in the presence of any Bishop of Lincoln.

Æthelstan indeed, very greatly heartened and delighted by such an honour, gave the whole estate at Drinkstone, bought in free purchase with his own money, as his charter testifies, to the community at Ely for eternal possession by right of inheritance. And so that the munificence of this gift might be made the more secure, he augmented it with other magnificent gifts as well, and confirmed the enlarged endowment under the scrutiny of[311] many witnesses. It will not be without benefit to give an itemized account of

---

[310] Source: copied or adapted from the lost *History of Seven Illustrious Men*. Æthelstan was Bishop of Elmham from c. 995 to 1001.

[311] Lat. simply *sub multis testibus*.

these gifts in his own words: 'In addition,' he said, 'I grant to you, for the salvation of my soul, all the fine objects of my chapel-equipment, that is: my episcopal cross and very large pyx, assessed at twenty pounds, partly of gold, partly of silver' – which Bishop Nigel afterwards took and broke up along with many other things which will be referred to again in the place where they belong[312] – 'and my chalice with paten of silver assessed at ten pounds' – but this was taken away a long time later by the malpractice of the clerk Goscelin, surnamed 'of Ely' – 'and my better priestly vesture and a thurible worth five pounds, and one cantor's cope, and one good pall and forty mancuses of gold and, each year, five pounds for the clothing of the monks and whatever else of benefit of which I am capable I will do for you, so that my association may be the more pleasing to God and this holy church and my memory may be the more eagerly observed among you.'

When he died, a long time afterwards, he was brought here and received the place of burial which had been arranged and, having subsequently been removed from there, and translated into his place next to the others,[313] he reposes in felicity. And he was a contemporary of the blessed Æthelwold under the most pious King Edgar – the men who assigned this place to the monastic order and filled it with monks and riches.

66. About Willingham.[314]

There follows next a good man, Uvi by name, who sought to dispose of the riches entrusted to him in such a way that, after the course of this life was run, they would cause him not loss, but gain. And he gave to God and to His bountiful virgin Æthelthryth the vill of Willingham and land at Cottenham to possess as a perpetual right, with all things whatsoever which belonged to it. To other churches as well, moreover, he gave generous endowments consisting in properties and gifts, and caused these gifts to be confirmed with a will in the language which he customarily used, to prevent the endless, visible tearing apart of a gift presented to the Lord Christ in exchange for eternal glory. This agreement, in fact, was written in chirograph-form before the presence of a great many witnesses, and is retained for safe-keeping in the church [of Ely] right up to this time. Of these the first was Ealdorman Leofsige and Abbot Ælfsige and the brothers of the church of Ely and many others who are named in the chirograph.[315]

---

[312] Cf. *LE* iii. 89.

[313] That is, along with the other six honoured benefactors.

[314] Source: documents recording the donations of Uvi of Willingham. Date: abbacy of Ælfsige; see Blake, p. 138, n. 7.

[315] This sentence is likewise faultily constructed in the Latin original (p. 138.24f., ed. Blake).

67. About Stetchworth and March and Kirtling and Dullingham and one virgate in Swaffham.[316]

There was also a brother of the man just referred to, Oswi by name, whose generous alms and gifts to churches and poor people revealed his character, proven as it was before God and the World, honourably disposed in every respect and agreeable to every rank of society. Nor was his mind concerned about anything else apart from his aim of pleasing God and being second to none in his benefactions. He had a wife called Leofflæd who, applauding all the works of her husband, and herself longing for the rewards of beatitude, was habitually engaged in the generous bestowal of alms. God had given them offspring of both sexes whom, as a consequence of the abundance of their goods and properties, they had made rich and of high rank. One of these, Ælfwine by name, they offered to God and St Æthelthryth as a monk. They assigned the vill of Stetchworth for his clothing, so that[317] it would be an additional property for the church in perpetuity after his lifetime. In addition, they brought about the advancement of the church of Ely in many ways, and desired to enlarge it with the following properties, namely: March and Kirtling and Dullingham and one virgate at Swaffham. The witnesses of these things were Ælfric, Archbishop of Canterbury, and Æscwig, Bishop of the Mercians – whose seat, which now is at Lincoln, had been at Leicester[318] – and Æthelstan, Bishop of the East Angles, whom we recalled above, and Oswi's two brothers, Uvi, mentioned earlier, and another, Æthelric, and a number of people who are recorded in his chirograph [written out in English].

68. About Chedburgh.[319]

Well then, in the same way that mention has been made of two of the brothers, we ought likewise by no means to omit reference to the third. Moreover, this man approved by God, Æthelric by name, gathered in his goods, resembling in this a most prudent bee, and distributed what he had gathered to churches and the poor. He was, moreover, stirred by the example

---

[316] Source: documents recording the donations of Oswi and Leofflæd, parents of the monk Ælfwine. Date: see Blake, p. 139, n. 4.

[317] Reading conjecturally (p. 139.11, ed. Blake) *ut* for *et* before *post vitam eius*, to account for the subjunctive *adiaceret*.

[318] However, Bishop Æscwig was officially Bishop of Dorchester.

[319] Source: documents recording the donations of Æthelric, father of the monk Æthelmær; including an English will preserved in the monastic archives.

BOOK II

of his brothers, and conceived the desire[320] that his most blessed lady
Æthelthryth be venerated[321] with the complete devotion of his mind and
adorned with a great lavishing of wealth. And he handed over his most
beloved son, Æthelmær, for the life of religion in that place, and with him he
desired to add shoe-land,[322] namely Chedburgh, as a perpetual right so that,
with their offspring, he and his wife might deserve a blessing from the Lord.
This also was written in English, in his will, and preserved in our possession
to this time as a protection of the privilege – another item which, among
others, we have endeavoured to translate into Latin.

69. [About the vill of Hoo.[323]

Now again, it was in the days of the most blessed martyr King Edward that
the lord of the vill of Hoo, called Godwine, was struck down by an illness
affecting his whole body and was so greatly oppressed by the extent of his
disease that he had very little hope of recovering a healthy state of life. But
this man who, as a result of the infirmity of his body, had most beneficially
been fortified for hope of a better kind, sent for Dom Ælfsige, Abbot of Ely. He
requested and received from him the status of monk and, along with his own
person, gave an offering by way of payment, namely the aforementioned
property of Hoo, as a blessing upon St Æthelthryth, and confirmed it with the
security of a chirograph in the witness of many people, so that thereafter
nobody of future generations should be permitted by purchase or exchange to
take away from the brothers what he had given in that place to God and His
saints for the redemption of his soul. Then, not long afterwards, he died, and
he is buried in the cemetery of the church.

70. About Hitcham.[324]

Then, after a short time had elapsed, the brother of the said Godwine,
Ælfmaer by name, bestowed upon God and upon St Æthelthryth with her
fellow virgins, in an act of freely given generosity, a certain part of the land in
his lawful ownership, customarily called Hitcham, of which he had been the
possessor through inheritance from his father. And he prescribed in a

---

[320] Taking *cupiebat* as inceptive in sense.

[321] Taking *venerari* as the passive of the rare, but classical, *venerare*.

[322] Lat. *terram calciatoriam*, equivalent to an OE technical term *scohland*, ostensibly meaning
land for the provision of the monks' footwear, but actually of wider application.

[323] Source: monastic archives – will of Godwine of Hoo. Date: abbacy of Ælfsige, who,
however, cannot have been abbot as early as King Edward's reign; see Blake, p. 140, n. 3.

[324] Source: monastic archives – will of Ælfmær, brother of Godwine. Date: 995 X 1001
(episcopate of Æthelstan); abbacy of Ælfsige.

chirograph, in the witness of Æthelstan, Bishop of the East <Angles>,[325] and a great many people, that the lord Abbot Ælfsige and the brothers of the church of Ely might in perpetuity make arrangements with regard to it in such a way as to provide for their needs the more beneficially.][326]

71. About Bishop Eadnoth.[327]

Here follows Eadnoth, a man famed in Christ and an outstanding supporter of the religious life of monastics, who was raised by the blessed Oswald, Archbishop of York, and the glorious Ealdorman Æthelwine from the position of a monk at Worcester to the office of abbot in the church at Ramsey, which they had built. While he was flourishing there in all honour under Christ, and guiding the flock of the Lord safely with faithful care, a divine revelation was made to a certain smith[328] concerning the body of the blessed Ivo and his companions who were reposing along with him in the village of Slepe. For, appearing to the smith in the form of a bishop, the blessed Ivo explained that both he and his companions had lain in that village from a very ancient date, and he commanded him to tell this to Eadnoth. And, waking up immediately, the smith revealed his vision to the man of God, and brought him great delight, because of the gracious gift which had been conferred upon his time. Eadnoth did not allow the glory of the saints in all its great magnitude to remain concealed in the earth any longer but, calling together the clergy and people, hastened to dig out the heavenly treasure to the accompaniment of ecclesiastical ceremonies, and carried the blessed Ivo with his own hands right to Ramsey, while other people carried the others, and afterwards, in Slepe itself, he built a church in the name of the same saint.

Not long afterwards, the Bishop of Lincoln {recte Dorchester} died and Eadnoth was raised up to be the bishop. He did not, as a consequence of this position of power, become at all less strict in his religious observance. Rather, the higher the level at which his work was carried out, the better it became: he kept pressing on assiduously with the building of churches and the enlargement of communities. Among these he built one at Chatteris for love of the holy Mary, Mother of God, and for love of his sister Ælfwyn, styled 'the Lady', with a view to the establishment of nuns there in her company, and he made it rich with the necessary resources. Fired by piety and armed with

---

[325] Supplement from Keynes and Kennedy, draft translation. The Latin would be: *Orientalium <Anglorum> episcopi* (p. 140.21, ed. Blake).

[326] These last two chapters are not included in E.

[327] Source: lost *History of Seven Illustrious Men*; *Worcester Chronicle*; Goscelin, *Vita S. Ivonis*. For detailed source-criticism, see Blake, pp. 140–1, n. 5; p. 141, n. 2.

[328] The most likely interpretation of *faber*, though other craftsmen might be so designated.

faith, he also in person collected the body of the blessed Ælfheah,[329] martyr and archbishop, stoned by the Danes at Greenwich, and buried him at London.

In the end, indeed, Eadnoth became worthy of being adorned with the glory of martyrdom for his glorious conduct: he was killed, with Abbot Wulfsige,[330] by Danish comrades of Cnut, in the battle between King Edmund and Cnut at Ashingdon, while he was chanting mass. First Eadnoth's right hand was cut off for the sake of a ring, then his whole body was cut to pieces. According to the chronicle, Bishop Eadnoth and Abbot Wulfsige had come together to pray to God on behalf of the army waging war.[331]

His body was brought by his people to this church of Ely, with the intention that he should be taken from here forthwith to Ramsey, where he had been abbot. But the holy man Ælfgar, who at that time had retired from the bishopric at Elmham and had given himself over entirely to this monastery, buried the body, with the object of increasing the glory of this house,[332] in a secret place, when its guards were drunk. He did this for two reasons: because he knew that Eadnoth had loved our lady saints greatly and also because he believed he was a martyr. Translated with the others from his old burial-place, Eadnoth is now held in great honour among us. And he was martyred in the 1016th year from the incarnation, and had his being during the days of King Æthelred and King Edmund.

72. About Ælfgar, a confessor of the Lord.[333]

Concerning the aforesaid Ælfgar, there is available a report which runs as follows: that he was once the priest and confessor of the blessed Dunstan, Archbishop of Canterbury. With regard to him, the fact that he was taken up into so great an office by so great a man will suffice for praise of his holiness. What kind of merit he possessed in God's sight, while engaged in this service, one is given to understand by the following vision.

For, according to what one reads in the *Life of Saint Dunstan:* in the year when the saint went to the Lord, at the break of dawn on Ascension Day – which occurred three days before his passing – the aforesaid priest was keeping vigil all through the night in the church of the Saviour during the

---

[329] Otherwise known as St Alphege, martyred 1012.

[330] Abbot of Ramsey.

[331] *Worcester Chronicle* on the year 1016.

[332] In this sentence, for the sake of clarity, the expressions *hic* and *huius loci* are rendered as 'to this monastery' and 'of this house' (p. 142.2f., ed. Blake).

[333] Source: lost *History of Seven Illustrious Men*, the central portion being taken from Osbern, *Life of St Dunstan* (Rolls Series, vol. lxiii, pp. 120–3). Episcopate of Ælfgar: 1001 X 1020.

sacred offices and fixing his mind upon the contemplation of Heaven. In the course of this, he was caught up into the highest places in a remarkable vision and saw the blessed Dunstan sitting on an episcopal throne declaring the laws of the Church to the clergy. Suddenly he saw rushing through all the doors of the church a multitude of angels in their white robes and golden crowns suffused with rosy light, proclaiming themselves to be cherubim and seraphim, and bringing what seemed to be messages from God. And as they were standing in their ranks before the bishop, proffering words of greeting, they said, 'Accept our salutations, Dunstan, our dear friend, and, if you are prepared to come to us, be joined to our fellowship, as one enjoying favour.' In reply to them he said, 'You know, O blessed spirits, that it was on this day that Christ ascended into the heavens, and that today's office is an obligation which we owe to a day of such importance, and the people of God need our service, so that at this juncture I am not able to go with you.' Then they said, 'Be prepared, therefore, the day after the Sabbath to pass over [to Rome][334] with us, and sing the *Sanctus* before the holy of holies for ever.'[335] Replying to them, he readily agreed to this, and straight away, the beings who had manifested themselves disappeared.

But the priest, recipient as he was of a vision of such great things, awaited silently the outcome of the matter, until the saint, during the celebration of solemn mass on Ascension Day itself, preached, after the Gospel, about this most solemn feast, and foretold that his presence was soon to be taken from them. Then, finally, having recognized the truth of the vision, Ælfgar revealed openly to all, with great lamentation, what he had seen. Afterwards this man, made Bishop of Elmham on account of his distinguished life, followed the example of Æthelstan, his predessor, in giving such particular devotion, so long as he lived, to the monastery of Ely, that he resigned from his bishopric and stayed in this community for the remaining period of his life. Considering him worthy of honour, we translated him reverently from his former tomb, along with the others.

And it was during the times of Æthelred, Edmund and Cnut, Kings of the English, that the holy man Ælfgar lived, and he died in the year from the incarnation of the Lord 1021, in the reign of King Cnut.

73. Who it was gave the vill of Wratting.[336]

To resume, a long way back in time, there was a certain knight possessed of

[334] So F, in conformity with Osbern mss.
[335] Cf. Isaiah 6.3.
[336] Source: monastic archives – will of Ælfhelm Polga; see Whitelock, *Anglo-Saxon Wills* no. xiii, pp. 30–4, and 133f.

much wealth, called Ælfhelm, who observed from afar that the church of St Æthelthryth was prospering in the observance of true religion and also positively coruscating with miracles and mighty works in accord with the merits of that lady saint. As a result, he was attentive and full of good will in conferring benefactions and honour on it, frequently visiting its thresholds, fulfilling his obligations with various kinds of guest-gifts, loyally upholding with his advocacy its legal rights, business transactions and litigation – as if on the reasoning that he was going to receive due recompense as the result of this. Perhaps he had heard that famous proverb: 'He who honours God's saints appeases God Himself.' Moreover, when the time of his death was imminent, and he was providing for the well-being of his people on a spiritual level, he recommended himself more intimately to the prayers of the holy virgin by means of a particular pledge, granting to her, as alms-giving, the vill of Wratting to hold in perpetuity, apart from two hides, fulfilling that divine admonition: 'Make friends for yourself by means of the mammon of iniquity, so that, when you lose your strength, they may receive you into everlasting tabernacles.'[337]

74. That the properties specified here were handed over to the church along with Leofsige, the future abbot: Glemsford, Hartest, Barking, Feltwell, [[Shelford]][338] and Snailwell.[339]

That was surely the epoch when, as a boy of good character, Leofsige, the future abbot, was received to be educated for the monastic life. In connection with him, moreover, his parents, well-endowed with the abundant supplies of riches which accompany worldly nobility, made their petition for his admittance[340] in an honorific manner, and thus, offering up their most beloved son in the monastery, although he was still of a tender age, they set him free for the service of God, and certainly not unmeritedly. For they desired to present, for the expense of keeping him, a gift from the estates with which they were endowed. Specifically, the estates named were: Glemsford, Hartest, Barking, Feltwell, Shelford and Snailwell.[341]

---

[337] Luke 16.9.

[338] A marginal addition in F.

[339] Source: monastic archives – grant by the parents of Leofsige, the future abbot. Date: assigned by the compiler to the abbacy of Ælfsige probably by inference from Leofsige's likely age when abbot (1029–44).

[340] Lat. *postulationem fecerunt*, cf. du Cange s.v. *postulatio*.

[341] The name 'Sneillewelle' is lined through in E.

75. These properties were given to the church with Bishop Ælfwine: Walpole, Wisbech, which constitutes a quarter of a hundred of the Isle, and Debenham, Brightwell and Woodbridge.[342]

At the same time as Ælfgar, Bishop of Elmham, of whom we have made mention above, was translated to the realms of Heaven, Ælfwine, a monk of the church of Ely from his boyhood, dignified by the holiness of his life and the graciousness of his manners, succeeded to the ministry of that same bishopric. Now, along with him, when he was made an oblate in the church, a gift was made by his noble parents, in the presence of respectable witnesses, consisting of: Walpole, Wisbech – which is a quarter of a hundred of the Isle – with its appendages, and Debenham, Brightwell and Woodbridge. And, despite his having been as yet of a tender age, he began to prepare himself with a ready will to adopt the habit of the monastic life. And thus, now that he had grown older, he appeared by no means to make poor use of the instruction, long ingrained in him, which, for the advancement of his soul, he began to receive in his younger days. Hence the text which one reads in Jeremiah, 'It is good for a man, when he has carried his yoke from his youth,'[343] was faithfully fulfilled in his case. And he conducted the whole course of his life with the greatest prudence and the modesty which belongs to a serious outlook, right up to the age of manhood. As a consequence, on the strength of his reputation for religious devotion, he was raised to the elevated rank of bishop by order of King Æthelred, who has been mentioned earlier. And he was incapable of forgetting the church of Ely, his mother: rather, now that he was made bishop, he took care to make a great many additions to the properties first granted to the place on his behalf when he was a boy, as is explained later.[344]

76. That Abbot Ælfsige brought to Ely the relics of St Wendreth the virgin, and that he obtained, by purchase from King Æthelred, Hadstock and Stretley and both of the Lintons.[345]

The aforesaid Abbot Ælfsige, indeed, was distinguished by his generosity of mind, and lacked neither nobility of birth nor integrity in worldly matters. As

---

[342] Source: lost *History of Seven Illustrious Men; see also LE* ii. 88; monastic archives – grant by the parents of Ælfwine, later Bishop of Elmham. For the dating of Ælfwine's episcopate see Blake, p. 144, n. 7.

[343] Lamentations 3.27.

[344] See *LE* ii. 86.

[345] Source: local commemoration of Abbot Ælfsige, or the compiler's own inferences from traditions about a reliquary and a royal charter associated with him.

a result, he had been cherished and honoured not a little by the aforementioned king. But it was most of all with regard to the worship of God that he had been assiduous in his exertions. For how greatly he aspired to the promotion of the interests, and the raising of the status, of his whole church, is plain to the perceptive intellect. For, desiring to raise the importance of the monastery to a still higher level, he also brought the relics of the holy virgin Wendreth from the vill of March to Ely and placed them fittingly in a shrine adorned with gold and jewels. Furthermore, to cap it all, he had a meeting with the king and, for an assessed price, bought the estates here mentioned from him, as is intimated by the present charter.

77. Hence this charter of the king.[346]

In view of the fact that the supreme and ineffable Disposer of things rules for ever, people of all ranks who, between the four cardinal points of the universe, make it their concern, through the life of contemplation, to arrive at the joy of the never-failing beatitude of Heaven, must exert themselves with all the eagerness of their mind and unhesitatingly, with a freely willed impulse of devotion. For a certain wise man, on the strength of the deliberations of his perceptive mind, says by way of trustworthy promise: 'I judge, moreover, that a man who is good voluntarily is better and nearer to God than one whom inevitability compels.'[347] For this reason, casting away base things as the filth of off-scourings, choosing the things above as resembling jewellery of great worth, and concentrating attention upon joys everlasting, with a view to obtaining mercy of a mellifluous sweetness and attaining full enjoyment of the joy of infinite felicity, I, Æthelred, raised up to the throne of the entire realm of Britain by the right hand of the Accomplisher of all things, have bestowed upon our Lord Jesus Christ and Saint Peter, Prince of the Apostles, the chaste virgin Æthelthryth and her sanctified sisters who repose together with her, for the use of the monks residing in the monastery of Ely, by way of eternal inheritance, a certain little piece of countryside, namely nineteen hides in three places which are called in the commonly used nomenclature: Hadstock, Stretley and both of the Lintons. Moreover, two of the same nineteen hides are in the estate which is called Hadstock, ten in Stretley, and seven in Linton, and for ownership of these estates the abbot, named Ælfsige, has given to the aforesaid king a payment of nine pounds of the purest gold in accordance with the great measure of the Northmen. In very truth, the aforesaid estates with all their easements, namely meadows, pastures, mills and woods, are to be free from all imposition of earthly service, with three exceptions, namely: military

---

[346] Source: monastic archives, cf. cartularies G and M. Date: 1008.

[347] Unidentified quotation, not traceable in Cicero, Seneca or Migne, *PL*.

service, repair of bridges and fortifications. If anyone, therefore, should wish to transfer this our grant to a purpose other than the one we have laid down, let him be deprived of the fellowship of the Holy Church of God, and let him be punished in the eternal gloomy fires of the Abyss along with Judas, the betrayer of Christ, and his accomplices, if he does not make amends with appropriate satisfaction for the sin which he has committed against our decree. This little charter was written in the 1008th year from the incarnation of our Lord Jesus, in the sixth year of the indiction.

78. That the church of Ely holds by custom a position of service in the court of the king.[348]

The glorious king therefore acted further to adorn the church of Ely with renown and honour, just as he had promised when St Æthelwold had taken him there with his mother and the nobles of the kingdom, during the reign of King Edward, his brother, when, before a crowd of people, at the tomb of the blessed virgin, to whom he had been entrusted with affection and much love, he pledged that from henceforth he would be her servant. When afterwards, on attaining to the kingdom, he realised that he was the servant of another King, he observed in royal fashion the commands of his King and elevated that King's bride, the Church, as, so to speak, his Mother, with gifts and services, and tied them down with the rope of charters. And fulfilling his intention in this way, he established a perpetual memorial to himself, so that his end would be one without end, and that he would arrive at the end which has no end. Let the pious eye, therefore, transfer its gaze from present circumstances to things to come and, contemplating with suitable attentiveness a succession of deeds rather than of words, let him join the joyful King in his rejoicing, thanks to this most well-ordered benevolence of his!

In point of fact, he laid down and granted that the church of Ely, both then and always, would fulfil the office of chancellor[349] in the royal court. This is something which he also established for other churches, namely St Augustine's and Glastonbury, with the intention that the abbots of these communities should divide the year into three, succeeding one another at specified times, performing service with the reliquaries and other ornaments of the altar. The abbot of the community of Ely, moreover, would always proceed to his work of service on the day of the Purification of St Mary at the very beginning of the month of February, and thus the abbot, or whichever one of the brothers he appointed, reverently fulfilled his office there with the utmost diligence for however much time was available to him for a period of

---

[348] Source: local traditions about King Æthelred, unattested elsewhere. See Blake *ad loc.* for a cautious assessment.

[349] Lat. *cancellarius*.

four months, that is, a third part of the year; then the others whom we have mentioned[350] used to see out the remainder of the year, for the periods assigned to them. It is recorded, moreover, that this item of customary practice existed at the church from the time of its restoration, that it brought about great advancement of the monastery and great freedom, that it was not allowed to be assailed or suppressed by outside agencies, until England, pitifully weighed down under the Norman yoke, was despoiled of all her former glory, so that the church of Ely – once most famous, and a beauty among the daughters of Jerusalem – she who had been free – has now been overwhelmed by the bitterness of disaster, and a 'princess among the provinces has been made subject to tribute'.[351]

79. How the relics of the bountiful virgin Wendreth were removed from this place; and that Queen Emma, just as she promoted this church with honours under King Æthelred, similarly under King Cnut, her second husband, adorned it with beauty of vesture.[352]

King Æthelred had made many benefactions to the churches of the English everywhere, even though amidst frequent outbreaks of war. This was in order to avert from himself the anger of the Lord which he had incurred through the death of his brother, the most gentle King Edward, and to obtain God's mercy. Then he died at London after the great struggles and many tribulations of his life, which St Dunstan in prophetic inspiration had foretold to him, after his crowning, on the day of his consecration as king. 'Since you have aspired to the kingdom,' he said, 'through the death of your brother, whom your mother has killed, hear, as a consequence, the word of the Lord. Thus says the Lord: "The sword will not hold back from your house, raging against you all the days of your life, wreaking slaughter upon your progeny, until your kingdom shall be transferred to the rule of foreigners, whose culture and language are unknown to the people over whom you preside. Nor shall your sin, the sin of your mother and the sin of the men who were complicit in her wicked plot, be expiated except by a long punishment." '

Well, Æthelred's body was buried with honour in the church of St Paul. In succession to him the citizens of London and the part of the nobility who were at that time resident in London raised up Edmund, surnamed Ironside,

---

[350] Following the reading of F, with *quos* rather than *quod*.

[351] Lamentation 1.1.

[352] Source: material synthesized by the compiler derived from the *Worcester Chronicle* on the year 1016; Osbern, *Vita Dunstani*; Ælred, *Vita S. Edwardi*; data on the death of King Edmund, cf. William of Malmesbury, *Gesta Regum* i. 217–8; also, local tradition associated with embroideries of Queen Emma.

After he had been elevated to the supremacy of the royal throne, ldly, with reliance on God's help, into battle against the army of on the hill called Ashingdon. He played the part of an energetic ..... and good commander; he would have crushed all of them together, had it not been for the schemings of the treacherous Ealdorman Eadric. And there was a massacre in that place of almost the whole array of the nobility of the English, who never received a more wounding blow in war than there.

Eadnoth, Bishop of Lincoln, formerly the superior of Ramsey, and Abbot Wulfsige were killed, having come together to make supplication to God for the soldiers as they waged war. The monks of Ely who, in accordance with the custom of the Church, had gone up to Ashingdon with relics, were laid low, too, and the relics of the bountiful virgin Wendreth which they had taken with them were taken away and have never to this day been restored to the church. For the story goes that at that time they were removed by [King] Cnut himself and given a new resting-place in Canterbury. And, not long afterwards, King Edmund, returning to London, was killed by the treachery of the Eadric mentioned earlier, pierced by an iron skewer in his private parts while he was taking his seat in a privy, and he was buried with his grandfather Edgar at Glastonbury, while his sons and brothers reckoned no part of the kingdom worth anything; instead, Cnut was raised to the throne by the whole people of England. [And thus,] within two years, there ruled three kings of England, so that there would come about fulfilment of what Dunstan said to Æthelred in the Lord's words.

The same King Cnut received in marriage Æthelred's queen, Ælgifu, alternatively named Emma, and in the same way that she had adorned the church of Ely with honours and gifts in the other king's time, she similarly, under this present one, made it her aim to augment its grandeur. She also made a remarkable {pall of}[353] *purpura*, bordered all around with orphrey, and decorated over all its parts with gold and precious gems, with wonderful artistry, in a sort of chequer design,[354] and gave it as an offering there, with the result that no other is to be found in the territory of the English of such artistry and value. For the work seems to be superior to its raw material. And she also made the offering to our other saints of a silk covering for each, even if of lesser costliness, embroidered with gold and gems, which are kept in our house to this day. She also made altar-hangings: an outstanding large pall, green in colour with gold spangles, so that, fronting the altar during a feast-day, it would appear quite high up,[355] and, above, fine linen of a brilliant

---

[353] Supplying, perhaps, conjecturally (p. 149.6, ed. Blake): *Insignem quoque <pallam> purpur<e>am . . .* or *<e> purpura <palla>m*, cf. *LE* iii. 50 (p. 294.9ff., ed. Blake).

[354] Lat. *auro et gemmis pretiosis mirifico opere velud tabulatis.*

[355] Lat. *magnam pallam viridi coloris insignem cum laminis aureis ut in faciem altaris per diem sollemnem celsius appareret.*

blood-red colour, one-foot wide, the length of the altar, reaching to its horns and right to the ground, with orphrey, provides a spectacle of very precious beauty.

80. About the passing away of Abbot Ælfsige, who was succeeded by Leofwine, and he by Leofric, both consecrated, in the period that followed, by Bishop Ælfwine of Elmham.[356]

Subsequently Ælfsige, the aforementioned abbot of the church of Ely, adorned with the grace of sanctity, died in the observance of the commandments of God, following the acquisition of much glory and many church-properties. He completed his days, moreover, at a good old age and was buried in a tomb next to his predecessor, the first abbot of the church. Well then, he died in the time of King Æthelred, by whom he had been appointed abbot, and having reached the fullness of his age, left the place devoid of a shepherd. Oscytel, alternatively named Leofwine, replaced him as his successor, but took charge for only a short time, as death overtook him. In fact, we find no mention of him in our written records, with the exception only that in an English chronicle[357] one reads that, after being deposed by his men, he went on a journey to Rome, with Æthelnoth, Archbishop of Canterbury, who was going to collect the pallium,[358] and there, in the sight of Pope Benedict, he cleared himself by compurgation of the charges brought against him, and thus succeeded in being accepted back into the favour of his men. After Leofwine, Prior Leofric was raised to the abbacy, the two abbots succeeding at different dates. Hence it came about that Ælfwine, Bishop of Elmham, blessed these two abbots, on the instructions of King Cnut and, equally, at the request of the whole monastery.

81. About Easter, Fambridge and Terling.[359]

In the days of Abbot Leofric, during the reign of Cnut, there was a woman called Godgifu, the widow of an earl, who after her husband's death distributed her goods among churches, †so that they might be sharers <of her

[356] Source: synthesis by the compiler of local traditions commemorating Abbot Ælfsige and his successors; specific reference to *Anglo-Saxon Chronicle*. Date: according to the *Chronicon*, Abbot Ælfsige died in 1019, but according to *LE* in the reign of King Æthelred, i.e. before 1016. Abbot Leofwine is said to have ruled the monastery for three years, and Abbot Leofric to have died in his seventh year of office.

[357] *Anglo-Saxon Chronicle* (versions E and F) on the year 1022.

[358] A circular band of white woollen material with two hanging strips and marked with six dark purple crosses, conferred by the Pope on archbishops as a sign of their office.

[359] Source: monastic archives – grant of the Lady Godgifu, in English; cf. Miller, *Abbey and Bishopric of Ely*, p. 22, n. 1; Hart, *Essex Charters*, no. 44.

goods> in <commendation>[360] of her meritst. She was a regular keeper of vigils of prayers to Æthelthryth, betrothed of the Lord Jesus, and thanks to the beauty of the monastery and the devoutness of the brothers, became fired[361] with the greatest love towards them. In consequence, from her own lawful entitlement, she gave several country estates, <small>[362] but outstanding ones, to the blessed virgin and those serving God in that place – and confirmed the gift in her will, in English. Their names are given here: Easter, Fambridge and Terling.[363]

82. A privilege of King Cnut about the exchanging of the vills of Cheveley and Ditton.[364]

In the name of Christ, the Saviour of the World, who reigns for ever, by whose deployment all the distinctions and powers belonging to every dignity and princedom are ordered, who is by right the Prince and Ruler over everything, by virtue of being the Creator of all, I, Cnut, King of the English-born race, prompted by love of it and of Ælfwine the venerable Bishop of the East, and Abbot Leofric of the monastery of Ely, and spurred on by the requests of their brothers, and with the healing of my soul in view, have made an exchange at the house of the abbot of this same monastery, namely Leofric, giving to them in reciprocal exchange the vill which is called by the proper name of Ditton, with all things which lawfully pertain to it, its length and width being as established under my power, and also receiving for it a woodland vill named Cheveley, with all things which belong to it, consisting in meadows, pastures, woods, and in any enterprises whatsoever. This exchange has been made in the 1022nd year of the Lord's incarnation, the fifth year of the indiction, there being fifteen epacts and seven concurrents; on the day of the feast of St Æthelthryth, queen and virgin, who with her sisters, namely Wihtburh and Seaxburh, and the daughter of Seaxburh, Eormenhild, is, by virtue of her holy merits, patroness and ruler over that monastery. If anyone with evil devising machinates to alter this our agreed exchange from what is the will of the servants of God residing in that monastery, let his portion be with the Devil, taking a share of all his punishments for evermore; nor let there ever in perpetuity come about for

---

[360] Reading conjecturally at p. 150.8, ed. Blake e.g.: *ut ad meritorum suorum <commendationem bonorum suorum> participes forent apud Deum.*

[361] Reading at p. 150.10, ed. Blake, with BG: *accenditur.*

[362] Reading conjecturally at p. 150.10, ed. Blake e.g.: *aliqua rura <parva> sed precipua.*

[363] All in Essex. See also *LE* ii. 96. The association of Easter with Godgifu is remembered in the place-name Good Easter. Margaret Fox (pers. comm.) informs me that there are remains of a former residence of the Bishops of Ely at Terling.

[364] Source: monastic archives, cf. cartularies CDM. Date: 1022.

him that change of circumstances whereby he may hope for any j͕
himself in this age or in the future.

83. About Barking.[365]

It further remains to report how Godgifu, the Lord's faithful follower, sent
greetings in writing to Bishop Ælfric and Leofric, Abbot of Ely, and what she
wished to disclose concerning her salvation. <. . . >[366] This, furthermore, is
the manner in which she gave utterance: 'O my lords, unhappy woman that I
am: I may have attended to the salvation of my soul less than prudently,
never mind how much less, and the time of my death is at hand: even so,
since it is still open to me to take action, I make known to your blessed selves
what action I stipulate and grant should be done in respect of my property, in
relation to my lady, the most holy virgin Æthelthryth in Ely. It is this: I
present to that place in perpetuity the land at Barking[367] which lawfully
belongs to me by virtue of inheritance from my parents, so that there may
continually be remembrance of me among them.'

84. Who it was by whom Abbot Leofsige of Ely was consecrated[368] and what good deeds he performed there, and that at the behest of King Cnut an annual levy of food-rent for the church is instituted.[369]

King Cnut, moreover, on having come to power, was fired with the devotion
of the kings who had preceded him, with regard to the most blessed
Æthelthryth and the servants of the holy place, and also with regard to
Leofsige, the pastor of the church who had succeeded Leofric and had for a
long time been without consecration. He gave instructions that he be
summoned to his presence at Woolwich and consecrated by Æthelnoth,
Archbishop of Canterbury.

Making exacting demands not for his own, but the Lord's, glory, Leofsige
strove with the greatest energy to promote the place, and not to receive
anyone as a monk in the community except men distinguished in learning
and of particularly good birth,[370] by whose generosity the church might

---

[365] Source: monastic archives – will of Godgifu, probably the same lady referred to in *LE* ii.
81, in the form of a letter. Date 1022 X 1029.

[366] At p. 151.13, ed. Blake, *quoque* seems problematic, if a lacuna is not presupposed.

[367] In Suffolk, see also *LE* ii. 74 for another holding there.

[368] Date: 1029 (see Blake, Appendix D, p. 411).

[369] Source: local text commemorating Abbot Leofsige as successor to Leofric, so probably a
chronicle of the abbots in succession; it includes detailed documentation about a food-rent
system and allusions to the *Rule* of St Benedict.

[370] Lat. *electos in scientia et preclaros genere*.

become rich to a higher degree, so that the brothers henceforth might have food and clothing in greater abundance than had been customary. In the case, indeed, of those who asked to be admitted to association with them on the strength of moveable property, everything that they offered was to be distributed piecemeal[371] to the company of monks, and they were each to receive portions from the offering: gold or silver set beside everyone's loaves in the refectory, and thus, by a fair agreement, a communal allocation was made for whatever there was a need. Thus, the place expanded externally by the accumulation of estates, and internally was adorned with beauty of vesture. What Abbot Leofsige prohibited most of all was the practice whereby no one of those from within the monastery was allowed to perform administrative tasks in the place, but rather people from outside:[372] he said that one should beware of outsiders, wanting the community-members to be protected, as our Lord in the Gospel wished His disciples to be protected, from 'the leaven of the Pharisees'.[373]

He contributed, also, fine ornaments for the beauty of the house of God, amongst which was a very fine alb with amice, with a *superale*[374] and maniple embroidered with gold and stones, and a red chasuble, spread to the rear with flowers above and below in wonderful workmanship, and in the front it is protected by a kind of panel with jewels and gold,[375] the workmanship of which we are inadequate to describe. He also made gold and silver vessels for the Lord's service, which afterwards were sold off in the turmoil brought about by the Normans.

The father to whom we are referring kept watch insistently over the Lord's flock, pleading with them and rebuking them, 'mixing times with times'[376] in gentleness, always striving particularly after that principle of the blessed Benedict, 'to be more loved than feared'.[377] With the consent and approval of the king himself, he also instituted a system of designating sources of food-rent[378] which would be sufficient throughout the year for the

---

[371] Reading conjecturally: *frustatim* for *frustratim* (p. 152.12, ed. Blake).

[372] The Latin here, which at first sight seems to mean something quite different, has been interpreted in the light of what is known of the compiler's attitudes, e.g. from his account of the abbacy of Simeon.

[373] Matthew 16.6; Mark 8.15; Luke 12.1.

[374] Following E, which has in the margin: *cum stola*, 'with a stole.'

[375] Lat. *velud quodam tabulatu gemmis et auro ante munitur.*

[376] Benedict, *Regula*, chapter 2, 'On the kind of man an abbot should be.'

[377] Again, Benedict, *Regula*, chapter 64.

[378] Lat. *firma*. There is no modern English term exactly equivalent to this word, which can mean either 'farm' or 'rent', and here either 'provisioning (in kind or cash)' or 'an estate supplying such provisioning'. The system is clearly that each of a number of the monastery's estates is assigned the duty of supplying provisions for specified weeks or days in the year.

supplying of food for the church, and, for preference, sources of food-rent[379] chosen from among the villages and lands which, by their more than usually abundant sweetness and exceptionally rich turf, are recognized as productive of crops. Their names are listed here: first of all, Shelford paid a food-rent of two weeks; Stapleford, of one; Littlebury, of two; Thriplow, of two; Hauxton, of one; Newton, of one; Melbourn, of two; Gransden, of two; Toft, of one, and Cottenham, of one, and Willingham, of one; Ditton, of two, [and] Horningsea, of two; Stetchworth, of two; Balsham, of two; Hadstock, of four days; Swaffham, of three days; Spaldwick of two weeks; Somersham of two; Bluntisham of one, and Colne, of one; Hartest, of one; Drinkstone, of one; Rattlesden, of two; Hitcham, of two; Barking, of two; Nedging, of one; Wetheringsett, of one; Bridgham, of two; Pulham, of two; Thorpe and Dereham, of two; Northwold, of two; Feltwell, of two; but Marham was to convey a food-rent to the church of Norfolk, and for the sustenance of people arriving at, and leaving, the monastery. And if these estates contributed less than their stated assignment at their specified times, the Isle would supply the deficit, having been designated for this purpose.[380]

85. With what difficulty King Cnut arrived at Ely for its festival and, hearing the monks from afar, composed a song.[381]

So then, on one occasion, this same King Cnut was making his way to Ely by boat, accompanied by Emma, his queen, and the nobles of the kingdom, desiring to celebrate solemnly there, in accordance with custom, the Purification of St Mary, starting from which date the abbots of Ely are accustomed to hold, in their turn, their position of service in the royal court. When they were approaching the land, the king rose up in the middle of his men and directed the boatmen to make for the little port[382] at full speed, and then ordered them to pull the boat forward more slowly as it came in. He <raised>[383] his eyes towards the church which stood out at a distance,

---

[379] Lat. *firma*, again.

[380] See R. Lennard, *Rural England 1086–1135* (Oxford 1959), pp. 118ff.

[381] Source: local tradition, unattested elsewhere.

[382] Lat. *ad portum pusillum*. 'Port' rather than 'harbour',if we are to envisage arrangements like the later medieval wharfs excavated by the Great Ouse at Ely in 2000: a set of parallel inlets, the width of a barge, at right-angles to the river-front. It seems implied by Cnut's poem, as well as the interpretation here, that it was possible to row considerably nearer to the monastery than Turbotsey, the landing-stage used for Wihtburh's translation, and maybe the cut had already been made by the early eleventh century which now brings the River Great Ouse to the edge of Ely. But it would be unsafe to rely on such an inference from a poem.

[383] Reading conjecturally at p. 153.21, ed. Blake: *ipse oculos in altum <elevat> contra ecclesiam, que haut prope eminet.*

situated as it was at the top of a rocky eminence;[384] he heard the sound of sweet music echoing on all sides, and, with ears alert, began to drink in the melody more fully the closer he approached. For he realized that it was the monks singing psalms in the monastery and chanting clearly the Divine Hours.[385] He urged the others who were present in the boats to come round about him and sing, joining him in jubilation. Expressing with his own mouth his joyfulness of heart, he composed aloud a song in English the beginning of which runs as follows:

> Merie sungen ðe muneches binnen Ely
> ða Cnut ching reu ðer by.
> Roweþ cnites noer the lant
> and here we þes muneches sæng.[386]

> The monks in Ely sweetly sang
> When nigh rowed Cnut the King.
> Knights, row closer to the land
> And let's hear these monks sing!

This is how it sounds in Latin:

Dulce cantaverunt monachi in Ely, dum Canutus rex navigaret prope ibi. Nunc, milites, navigate propius ad terram et simul audiamus monacorum armoniam.

This and the remaining parts that follow are up to this day sung publicly by choirs and remembered in proverbs.

The king, while tossing this around {in his mind}, did not rest from singing piously and decorously in concert with the venerable confraternity, until he reached land. And when, greeted fittingly by the brothers, he was led in procession into the church – as is customary treatment for a member of the royal house or a particularly exalted personage – he thereupon confirmed

---

[384] Since Cnut's time there has been a lot of infilling of the valley to the south and west of the present cathedral. Eighteenth-century prints showing the cathedral's south-western ramparts still convey the impression that its site is a cliff-top.

[385] A fantasy! Even now, with the river navigable perhaps much closer to the monastery site than in Cnut's day and certainly no further away, it is never possible to hear singing in the cathedral from the riverside, even when there are massed choirs and an organ at full blast. One might surmise, rather, that the grain of truth behind this poem's narrative was that the monks processed down to the waterside, singing, to greet their king.

[386] See C. W. Stubbs, *Historical Memorials of Ely Cathedral*, pp. 49–52 for comments by W. W. Skeat on the language of the poem.

by his charter and authority, in perpetual stability, the possessions granted to the church by the kings of the English preceding him. And upon the high altar, where the body of Æthelthryth, the holy virgin and betrothed of Christ, rests in her tomb, facing the church before everyone, he solemnly decreed that the rights of the place were free in perpetuity.

Now then, it happened on several occasions that the king was unable to come to this festival because of the excessive frost and ice in the locality, the marshes and meres being frozen all around. But the king was not in such circumstances swayed from the zeal of his goodness. Although he had been groaning deeply and full of anxiety, he trusted in the Lord God and took it into his head, at a time when a severe frost was continuing unabated, to travel all the way to Ely over the mere from Soham in a wagon upon the ice. But he declared that he would complete, and not defer, the difficult journey more confidently and less fearfully, if someone would go ahead of him. Well, it chanced that standing by in the crowd [on that occasion] was a certain large and rugged man from the Isle, Brihtmær surnamed *Budde* on account of his bulk, and he promised to go ahead of the king. Without delay the king followed behind in the wagon at a fast pace, while everybody marvelled that he should have attempted such a great act of daring. When he arrived at Ely he joyfully celebrated the festival there according to custom. For, in accordance with what is set forth in the Book of Wisdom – 'Love is strong as death,'[387] and 'Love is the keeping of laws'[388] – the glorious king relied only upon the love and devotion of the virgin of Christ, Æthelthryth, and in him there was fulfilled the utterance of the Lord: 'All things are possible to a believer.'[389] Indeed, to the glory of the blessed virgin, the king was accustomed to recount that it had [so] come about[390] and been granted to him by the Lord that a large and rugged countryman had perceived not the slightest hindrance anywhere along the way, so that he himself also, an able-bodied man of ordinary stature, had been permitted to follow after, unswervingly and without fear. And moreover the king,[391] being generous-minded and munificent, and wishing to reward the man's effort, made a grant whereby he, together with his land-holding, became entitled to perpetual freedom. Hence, the sons of his sons right to this day have remained [free on the strength of a grant of this description and] in enjoyment of exemptions.[392]

---

[387] Song of Songs 8.6.

[388] Wisdom of Solomon 6.18.

[389] Mark 9.22.

[390] Following the text of F, as in Blake.

[391] Following E (p. 154.27, ed. Blake).

[392] Lat. [*liberi ex istius modi donatione et*] *quieti.*

86. That Bishop Ælfwine placed monks at *Bedericesworthe* {Bury St Edmunds} for the first time, and afterwards, having relinquished his bishopric and returned to us, chose to have his burial place here.[393]

Ælfwine, that holy confessor of the Lord, attaining the high position of bishop by the meritoriousness of his life and the probity of his morals, as we have mentioned before, succeeded in obtaining consent from King Cnut, that, in accordance with his petition, the estate of Wood Ditton, mentioned earlier, be exchanged for Cheveley, and that, with respect to the latter place, he be confirmed in perpetual right of ownership. [He also, by the decree of the king himself, for the first time brought a contingent of monks to *Bedericesworthe*. He established there some monks from his own church of Ely, but others from Holm; and] he supplied them with subsidies [in abundance,[394] with Earl Thorkell providing assistance, and, in addition,] himself, for his own part, supplying the place with a collection of a great many goods and ornaments. [He made a grant assigning it to eternal liberty] and he appointed in authority over them as father and abbot, a humble, modest, gentle and pious man, named Uvi. As for the priests who used to live there without subjection to a rule: he either raised them up to the highest level of the religious life in that same monastery,[395] or transferred them, provided with other possessions, into other monasteries. And after having conferred many benefits upon holy places, he finally resigned from the bishopric which he held and returned to contemplative peace in the monastery at Ely, where he remained to the end of his life. And him, too, we translated with honour among the rest from his former burial place during the time of Bishop Nigel.

87. How or, specifically, when and by whom, the body of Wulfstan, confessor of the Lord, was translated.[396]

So then, many ages later, in the reign of Stephen, the glorious and most

---

[393] Source: lost *History of Seven Illustrious Men,* with a borrowing from an expanded version of the *Worcester Chronicle* (OMT, vol. ii, p. 350), on the year 1020. Dates of Ælfwine's episcopate, see Blake, p. 144, n. 7; p. 155, n. 5.

[394] The square brackets enclose a portion of text given in F: in E the original reading has been partly erased.

[395] That is, the status of monks.

[396] Source: the opening of lost *History of Seven Illustrious Men.* For bibliography on Wulfstan, an extremely distinguished Archbishop of York, some of whose writings are extant, see: Dorothy Betherum, *The Homilies of Wulfstan* (Oxford 1957); Keynes, *Anglo-Saxon England: A Bibliographical Handbook* (2001), pp. 44, 121. Dates: Wulfstan died in 1023, having first been a bishop in 996.

pious King of the English, relics of venerable men, thanks to whose gifts our monastery increased in prosperity, and thanks to whose <examples>[397] our community advanced in holy religion, were translated from their old coffins to the northern part of our church, under the supervision of Prior Alexander. These coffins, buried long ago deep down, and none the less eventually discovered with unambiguous marks of identification, received – each of them – separate burial places with inscriptions bearing the names of the men.[398]

First of these in order is the excellent man Wulfstan, even though – as an inevitable consequence of the ordering of our narration – we have referred to some of the others above. An excellent man, he became powerful on the basis of good morals. First monk, then abbot, he finally succeeded the blessed Oswald, Archbishop of York, to become the third holder of the pontifical see. All his practices and acts, indeed, were in the service of religion; and he lacked neither nobility of birth nor this World's honour. For Byrhtheah, the son of his sister, was Bishop of Worcester, too, and he had many other kinsmen who were men of good breeding, and he was considered by everyone to be worthy of honour as much for his birth as for his holiness.

Concerning him, the marvellous fact was related that it was through cutting of his mother's womb that he had been brought into the light of this World, and that he was reared at the teats of a cow through the diligence of his kinsfolk.

And he was in his prime during the times of Æthelred, Edmund and Cnut, Kings of the English, by each of whom equally he was loved as a brother, equally, too, honoured like a father, and was frequently called upon in furtherance of the great affairs of the kingdom, as being the most learned of counsellors – someone in whom the very wisdom of God used to speak, as it were, in a spiritual temple. On account of his outstanding merit, King Cnut, in his time, conferred on him the following honour: he invited Wulfstan to dedicate the church built by himself, Cnut, and Earl Thorkell on Ashingdon hill, and in their presence he, together with many other bishops, dedicated it in a glorious and honorific manner.

Finally, what kind of a man Wulfstan always was in the sight of God became manifestly evident in the period around the end of his life. For it happened that at a certain time he visited this church [at Ely][399] for the

[397] Reading conjecturally at p. 155.20, ed. Blake: *quorum beneficiis locus noster adcrevit et quorum <exemplis> cetus noster in sancta religione profecit.*

[398] The relics of these worthies were again translated in the reign of Edward III to the north wall of the choir, and yet again in 1769 to their present position, in Bishop West's chapel, where they are still commemorated together, with Archbishop Wulfstan in first place.

[399] 'At Ely': an explanatory addition in F.

purpose of prayer, and the brothers of the monastery met him in procession with great reverence, as was fitting. And when he had just been conducted into the church, and was standing at the head of the procession, as is customary for a bishop, leaning on his pastoral staff, suddenly the staff sank into the ground almost up to its middle. Having been spiritually forewarned by this sign, he predicted to the many listeners, in a prophetic utterance of David, that his resting-place was to be in that place, thus: 'This is my resting-place throughout all ages: here will I dwell.'[400] In consequence, too, he loved this place fervently as long as he lived, made it rich with ornaments and confirmed many charters of ours with his signature, foremost among the foremost.

After a while, indeed, when the day of his summoning was near, when he was already beginning to experience dissolution, he gave instructions that his body be brought here from York, and he obtained a place of burial in the old church at the spot where his crosier had been driven in. At his tomb there often occurred miracles. These happened in the old church: even so, one finds, as a result, men alive to this day who were cured there of foul diseases.[401] Subsequently, after the building of the new church which now exists the brothers decided to remove him from the former place and view his body within the tomb. They found his body, indeed, decayed away, but his chasuble and pallium fixed with little gilded pins,[402] along with a stole and maniple, and thus it was a miracle that, given such a long time had elapsed, it had been possible for those things to last, partially at least, while subjected to the decay of the body. Moved, accordingly, from the place of his first burial-place on account of the needs of the new work, which was then under construction, he was buried for the time being outside the church, next to the chancel, in the cemetery of the brothers, awaiting the time when, on completion of the same work, he might be translated, as he deserved, into a better position. Finally, after many years, we brought this to completion, with God's consent, under the worthy father Bishop Nigel, assigning him first place in a row of other men, whose identity a future narrative will clarify.

And Wulfstan died at a great age, and was placed before his ancestors in the 1023rd year from the incarnation of the Lord, on Monday, 28th May. God be universally blessed.

---

[400] Psalm 131.14 Vulgate = 132.14 RSV, where, in line with the Hebrew, the punctuation followed here differs from that in p. 156.24, ed. Blake.

[401] The reference here can hardly be to the date of the compilation of the *Liber Eliensis*: rather to the date of its source-text, or even of a source of the source-text.

[402] One of these at least is extant: see illustration in J. Maddison, *Ely Cathedral: Design and Meaning* (Ely 2000), p. 9.

88. About Balsham and Wetheringsett and Stetchworth.[403]

There is a fertile vill, extensive in its pastures and fields, called Balsham, which belonged to the woman Leofflæd, the wife of Oswi and daughter of Byrhtnoth styled Ealdorman, people whom we have mentioned above.[404] Following the example of Martha, this Leofflæd was a woman intent on constant ministering: she used to clothe the naked, feed the wretched, honour the Church with all her soul and bestow benefactions on the servants of God, wherever she was able. And, towards the end of her life, she addressed a letter to King Cnut, the contents of which are as follows:

'To you, most beloved Lord and my most worthy Lady, the Queen, I express in every way my gratitude that you have been willing to act benevolently towards me, your servant, and have permitted me, in as much as my husband was taken from me, to dispose of my property as I wished. Now, therefore, I make clear in this little book that I grant, after my day is over, the vill of Balsham, with all that belongs to it, to God and St Peter and the holy virgin Æthelthryth, for the sake of the soul of my husband and for my children, whether alive or dead. Further, I allow my two daughters Ælfwyn and Ælswith {recte Æthelswith} to hold Stetchworth as long as they live, and after their days they are to let it pass freely to the holy place of Ely. To my other daughter, namely Leofwaru, I grant the vill of Wetheringsett, on this condition, that she remain in chastity or accept a lawful husband, lest she and our progeny be disgraced by the taint of fornication. By your favour, lord King, I, your servant, am making arrangements for the assigning of these and other properties, after my day, to churches as well as to my family, and may they stay confirmed in perpetuity. May none except you – perish the thought! – take them away or diminish them, and may anyone who tries to remove anything from them have the curse of our Lord Jesus Christ, and with Judas the traitor hear the evil tiding: "Go, accursed ones, into the eternal fire which is prepared for the Devil and his angels!" ' These things are recorded in a document written out in triplicate. There is one at Ely, another is in the king's treasury and Leofflæd possesses the third. When she had died, her body was brought to us and buried in the cemetery of the brothers. Not long after she was buried, the aforementioned Æthelswith, her daughter, scorned alliance with a husband and, surrendering herself to the church along with the estate of Stetchworth, made the profession that she would remain there for ever. She was given Coveney, a place close to the monastery, where in

---

[403] Source: monastic archives – wills of Leofflaed, daughter of Ealdorman Byrhtnoth and wife of Oswi, and of her sister, Leofwaru, wife of Lustwine.

[404] See especially *LE* ii. 67.

great seclusion she used to devote her time to gold-embroidery and tapestry-weaving, in company with young girls,[405] and, at her own expense, she made with her own hands a white chasuble, being very expert at this sort of craft. And her sister Leofwaru, an extremely well-dowered wife to Lustwine, a very noble husband, after some time added to the possessions of the church the land at Wetheringsett and many other properties, of which we will include mention in what follows concerning the gift of her husband.

89. About Ditton and *Burch* and Knapwell and the other properties which are named in that writ.[406]

Seeing that we have spoken of many people, it would not be right to pass on without mention of this friend of ours, Lustwine, to whom Leofwaru, the woman mentioned above, was joined in marriage: we very much owe it to him to mention him among the others. Both these people were devoted to God, drawn to the love of this place by the miraculous powers of our lady saints and the religious devotion of the brothers. They made an agreement with them – about membership of the fraternity and about the burial of their bodies – accompanied by an extremely lavish bequest of properties. Both of them were secure in the hope of good things to come, both intent on the devoted observance of holy religion. But, more particularly, it was towards us that they had decided to direct their goodwill, and from their inheritance, as their charter shows, they granted to our church as a perpetual right, the properties which are duly being included here.[407] For they gave to God and St Æthelthryth, for the expiation of their souls, Ditton – not the wooded one[408] – and Knapwell, with the exception of half a hide; also a tunic of red *purpura* bordered all round the hem and from the shoulders with orphrey, and they added the following specific properties: Little *Burch*[409] and Weston and Kedington and Pentlow, Wimbish, Yardley, Hanningfield and Ashdon, with their appurtenances. These grants too were made and recorded in writing in the book of their will before a large gathering of the common people and of their own kindred.[410]

---

[405] Lat. *puellulis* (diminutive) suggests that she was keeping a school.

[406] Source: monastic archives – will of Lustwine and Leofwaru. Chapter-title as in F.

[407] Reading, with O, *inseruntur* for *inferuntur*.

[408] That is, Fen Ditton as distinct from Wood Ditton, though the latter is specified in E's version of the chapter-heading.

[409] Identified by Keynes and Kennedy as Burrough Green, Cambridgeshire.

[410] One might have expected here an account of the death of Cnut, as a preliminary to the next piece of narrative, but we do not find one in either E or F. The omission was later to be rectified in ms. O.

90. In what a nefarious way Prince Alfred, the brother of the glorious king Edward, was betrayed.[411]

About the same time, the innocent princes, Alfred and Edward, sons of Æthelred, formerly King of the English, came from Normandy, where for a long time they had been staying with their uncle Richard, to have a talk with their mother, who was spending some time in Winchester. They had crossed the Channel in a few ships, having brought many Norman knights with them. Some powerful men were indignant at this and deeply disinclined to tolerate it: unjust though it was, they were much more in favour of their brother Harold than of them. This was the case particularly, so they say, with Earl Godwine.

Version of E

Godwine, in fact, detained Alfred, when the latter was going in haste to London for a talk with King Harold, at the king's command, and placed him under close guard. But as for his companions: some of these he drove asunder, some he put in fetters and afterwards blinded, some he tortured by scalping, and mutilated by the cutting off of hands and feet; he gave orders also for many of them to be sold, and he put an end to six hundred men by various pitiable deaths at Guildford. However, it is believed that the souls of those whose bodies were so cruelly murdered in the fields, for no fault of their own, now rejoice with the saints in Paradise.

On hearing about this, Queen {Emma, also known as} Ælgifu sent her son Edward, who remained with her, back to Normandy with the greatest haste. Then, at the command of Godwine and certain others, Prince Alfred was brought to the Isle of Ely, most firmly chained up. But as the boat reached land, his eyes were most bloodily gouged out, in the boat, and thus he was handed over to the monks to be kept under guard. After living there for a little while, he passed away from this light, and his body enjoys due honour in the south *porticus* in the western part of the church, whereas, indeed, his soul enjoys paradisiacal loveliness. In that place wonderful and beautiful visions of lights and of works of power[412] have often occurred.

Version of F (as printed in Blake's edition)

Godwine, in fact, detained Alfred, when the latter was going in haste to

---

[411] Sources: E follows the *Worcester Chronicle* on the years 1035–36; whereas F revises the account in E by substituting material from William of Poitiers, *Gesta Guillelmi*, chapter 3. Date of the death of Prince Alfred: 5th February, 1036.

[412] Lat. *visiones luminum et virtutum.*

London for a talk with King Harold, at the king's command.[413] [Trapping him by a nefarious trick, he betrayed him by a most evil action. For Alfred went to meet Godwine of his own accord, as if with honorific intent; he kindly promised him his service, giving him kisses and his right hand as a guarantee. Moreover, he shared a table with him in friendly fashion and also shared his plans. But in the middle of the following night, Godwine tied his hands behind his back, when he was unarmed and drowsy with sleep. Once he had been overwhelmed by this mode of delightful behaviour, Godwine dispatched him to King Harold[414] in London, and some of his retinue similarly bound. As for the rest, he sent some to the dungeons, separated from one other by a pitiful wrenching apart, and foully murdered the others, cutting out their innards in a horrific manner.

Harold rejoiced at the sight of Alfred in chains. He gave orders that his best retainers should be beheaded in his presence and that Alfred himself should have his eyes put out, then be carried on horseback, dishonoured by being naked, to the Isle of Ely, with his feet bound beneath the horse, so that there he should be tormented by exile and deprivation. The impious man took delight in the fact that his enemy's life was more painful than death. At the same time he was aiming to scare off Edward completely by his brother's calamities.

Thus was destroyed a most handsome young man, one with the highest reputation for goodness, the son of a king and a descendant of kings. And he could not survive for long, given that, when his eyes were gouged out by the knife, its point damaged his brain.] But as for his companions [as we have said]: some of these he drove asunder, some he put in fetters and afterwards blinded, some he tortured by scalping, and mutilated by the cutting off of hands and feet; he gave orders also for many of them to be sold, and he put an end to six hundred men by various pitiable deaths at Guildford. However, it is believed that the souls of those whose bodies were so cruelly murdered in the fields for no fault of their own, now rejoice with the saints in Paradise.

On hearing about this, Queen {Emma, also known as} Ælgifu sent her son Edward, who remainded with her, back to Normandy with the greatest haste. And thus Alfred was brought to Ely and handed over to the monks to be kept under guard. After living there for a little while afterwards, he departed this life, and his body enjoys due honour in the south aisle in the western part of the church, whereas, indeed, his soul enjoys paradisiacal loveliness. In that place wonderful and beautiful visions of lights and of works of power have often occurred.

---

[413] The passage in square brackets contains the material from William of Poitiers.
[414] Harold I, second son of Cnut, who immediately after his father's death shared the kingdom with Harthacnut.

91. How Edward became king, and with what devotion he endeavoured to repay the benefits conferred on him in his infancy by the church.[415]

Not long afterwards, the aforementioned Edward came to England from Normandy, where he had been in exile for many years, and was received with honour by his brother King Harthacnut, who had succeeded his brother Harold, surnamed *Harefoh*,[416] in succession to whom he was himself raised up to be king, at London.

And now that he was raised to the kingship, he certainly did not forget the benefits which he had enjoyed as a boy in Ely, for he made it his endeavour to present it with suitable rewards by way of repayment. For he had been taken there in his cradle by his father, the king, and his mother, the queen, and had been presented as an offering on the holy altar, wrapped in a cloth embroidered in the orbiculate style with small roundels of a pale green colour,[417] which is still shown there and, according to the account of the older men of the church who were eye-witnesses and party to it,[418] he received his upbringing there in the monastery for a long time with the boys, and learnt in their company the psalms and hymns of the Lord. And his generosity showered itself upon the church of Ely beyond the munificence of all preceding kings, presenting it with all the gifts which are contained in the privilege set out below.

92. His charter on all the properties that the church owns.[419]

Edward, by the grace of God king of the English, to all Christ's faithful people: eternal greeting in the Lord. Although God, the King and Lord of all, lacking in nothing, possesses everything, He brings it about by the ineffable love with which He has loved mankind that, from the created things which He generously provides for human use, He Himself graciously receives some as if they were gifts, in order thereby to render those who worship Him more devoted to the aim of serving Him, so that, after a little while, He may permit them to reign with Him in perpetual liberty. Our fathers of old, fired by this aim of serving Him, made it their endeavour first of all to lay down their

---

[415] Sources: first paragraph: *Worcester Chronicle* on the years 1041–42; second paragraph: local text apparently of eleventh-century date; tradition associated with an embroidered wrap preserved in the minster. Date of the accession of King Edward: 1042.

[416] So ms. E, whereas F has *harefah*.

[417] Lat. *palla involutus orbiculata brevibus circulis non plene viridi coloris*. Interpretation involves guess-work, but see *Novum Glossarium Mediae Latinitatis* svv. *orbiculare, orbiculus*.

[418] This detail about the upbringing of Edward is not attested anywhere else. See F. Barlow, *Edward the Confessor* (second edition, Newhaven and London 1997), pp. 28ff.

[419] Source: monastic archives, cf. cartularies CDGM. Date: 1042 X 1057, but 'hardly . . . authentic in its present form'. See Blake, Appendix D, pp. 417f.

possessions before the Lord, afterwards receiving heavenly things in exchange for the things of this World, everlasting things in exchange for things temporal. Following diligently in their footsteps, Edgar, my grandfather and predecessor in sceptre-wielding power, bringing their exemplary precedents to more complete fulfilment, restored the monastery of Ely – others too, but that one in particular to a higher degree than the rest – and in restoring it, enriched it, and in enriching it, gave it immunity with liberty of every kind, having been advised and assisted by St Æthelwold's assiduous urging, and his generous augmentation of its estates. This was confirmed in a privilege, with St Dunstan and all the foremost leaders of the realm eagerly uniting in approval. Æthelred my father, too, in the time of his government, conferred certain estates on the same place, and confirmed its earlier liberty with a privilege, granted by himself and his kin. I, Edward, by the grace of God their admittedly unworthy successor, although it is as one far from their equal that I see displayed in them devout piety towards the church of God and the practical application of religious devotion, I by no means presume to infringe their venerable statutes: rather, to the best of my ability, I desire to defend them strongly and, in every possible way, to augment them.

Hence, I additionally make subject to the aforesaid monastery the vill named Lakenheath in firm and hereditary possession, so that, in a way, I may join their community and may increase in greatness by the help of the saints, who, amid much praise of their merits, repose there. With regard to the liberty restored, as we have said, by these same {monks}, possessed in earlier times by the virgin queen herself, by virtue of her most holy mode of dwelling there, sanctified by her possession of it and made venerable by the sanctification – it is my decision that this liberty remain inviolate and be forwarded in every way, and I proclaim to people of the present time and of the future that it is permanently established by the testimony of this privilege and the agreement of those loyal to me. We will set forth in a full listing, therefore, the sum total of the properties which are attached to that place in this our time, specifically subject to it, even, by legal custom.[420] In the county of Cambridge: the Isle itself with its two hundreds and all appendages; outside the Isle: Swaffham, Horningsea, Ditton, Hauxton, Newton, Stapleford, Shelford, Thriplow, Melbourn, Armingford, Gransden, Stetchworth, Balsham, Fulbourn, Teversham, Westley, Trumpington, Wratting, Snailwell, Ditton, Hardwick, Milton, Impington, Cottenham, Willingham; and every fourth coin of public funds in the county of Cambridge, and other[421] lands in the town {of Cambridge} itself. In the county of Suffolk: Hartest, Glemsford, Hitcham, Rattlesden, Drinkstone,

---

[420] Following the mss. reading, without *quali*, at p. 161.30, ed. Blake.

[421] So E: *alie*, F has *alique*, 'some'.

Nedging, Barking, Barham, Wetheringsett, Livermere, Occold, five-and-a-half hundreds at Wicklow, Sudbourne, Melton, Kingston, Hoo, Stoke, Debenham, Brightwell, Woodbridge, Brandon. In the county of Norfolk: Feltwell, Bridgham, Methwold, Croxton, Weeting, Mundford, Bergh, Westfield, Fincham, Northwold, Walpole with its appendages, Marham, Dereham, Thorpe, Pulham. In the county of Essex: Hadstock, Littlebury, Stretley, the two Rodings, Rattlesden, Amberden, Broxted, Easter, Fambridge, Terling. In the county of Hertford:[422] Hadstock, Hatfield, Kelshall. In the county of Huntingdon: Spaldwick with its appendages, Somersham, Colne, Bluntisham.

We grant to that monastery these properties and their[423] appendages, whether greater or smaller – and, over and above them, all possessions added, or to be added, by anyone whomsoever, where their ownership rests on the testimony of good men – with all *sake* and *soke*, without any exception in respect of secular or ecclesiastical jurisdiction. We declare them granted and settled, in the same liberty with which the saints glorified the aforesaid monastery, so that neither bishop nor earl nor the collector of any taxation should presume without the permission or invitation of the abbot and brothers in any way to enter into or to disturb in any respect the property of the lady saint. And let it be within their discretion, as it has always been, for them to be ordained or their possessions consecrated, by whichsoever bishop they happen to choose.

It is, indeed, by an appropriate dispensation that the lady saint enjoys this liberty: a queen who, deserting a king and a kingdom and the glittering World, took possession of the Isle as her marriage-portion, where she served Christ, her betrothed, with the utmost chastity, as is shown by the fresh state of her flesh in the tomb, along with the fact that her clothing is undecayed. She received any bishop she wished, but St Wilfrid, Archbishop of York, was a particularly close friend to her, and he it was who consecrated her, along with her community of virgins. When, moreover, at a much later date – the service of God being in almost complete decline – Edgar restored the monastery, settling a congregation of monks there over whom he appointed abbots, whom St Æthelwold and St Dunstan and St Oswald ordained, furthering their interest, so long as they lived, as if they were their men. After these, they used to attach to themselves with a chain of love the best available men,[424] some of whom they had lodging with them in the monastery.

Consequently, whereas I had not been the institutor of these customs, I prefer to be a witness and a faithful conservator rather than a faithless and

[422] Interpreting *Hereford* at p. 162.15, ed. Blake as 'Hertford'.

[423] Reading with CDM at p. 162.16, ed. Blake: *horum*.

[424] Here the vague reference appears to be to the bishops called upon by the monks of Ely.

detestable overturner, and I call upon God, the most exalted Preserver,[425] to this end: that any one who shall break these established customs and the heritage of our saints may, unless he repents, subsequently incur the displeasure of the saints and of the Almighty, clothing himself, as it were, with a curse, while he emulates the disgrace of Judas.

How solicitous the benevolence of the pious king was in its generosity is attested by the following privilege of the Apostolic Father, included under the same seal as its inseparable companion: it confirms the king's munificence with the authority of Peter. For the king, a most pious man, wished to have ratification of his enactment from the place from which the foundation of the whole church proceeded, and by way of an oracular prophecy of its future permanence, to affix no other seal than that of Peter. Therefore, to the end that faith may conquer infidelity, and truth conquer falsehood, and so that lawful ownership may reject all calumny from henceforth, Pope Victor with his name and authority concurs with the grant in accordance with the law, betokening that the grant which he is confirming is ever-victorious.

93. A privilege of Pope Victor about the liberty of the place and all things that appertain to it.[426]

Victor, Bishop, servant of the servants of God, to Edward, King of the English, his most beloved son, and to all the chief people of the kingdom: greeting and apostolic blessing. In response to your pious petition, we summarily renew the privilege written down in ancient times by apostolic authority and that of the Roman Church, and ratified very frequently in the witness of many people, on the subject of the monastery of Ely, which glorious fathers of Holy Church founded with pious love and with generous hand. We confirm it, moreover, in perpetual stability – no, rather, we proclaim it to have been confirmed. We command, therefore, and enjoin, by apostolic right, that the church be free and also all things which are contained there or appertain to it, or which shall be added to it, in respect to: daughter-houses, lands, fields, pastures, marshes, woods, game-preserves, waters, fisheries, liberties, services, dues, tithes, rent, payments of head-penny, legal rights {of administering ordeals and compurgation procedures},[427]

---

[425] Reading with CDEM (p. 163.2, ed. Blake): *servatorem* – an allusion back to *conservator*.

[426] Source: monastic archives, cf. cartularies CDGM; see Blake Appendix D, p. 418, for a suspicion that the privilege may have been expanded to defend the monastery against the aspirations of bishops; discussion also in W. Holtzmann, *Papsturkunden in England*, i. 104; ii. 77. Ostensible date: 1055 X 1057; see Blake, p. 418.

[427] Interpretation of *legibus* (p. 163.25, ed. Blake).

customary rights, rights of hearing pleas, punishments and reparations, whether ecclesiastical or secular, and absolutely all the things which can be recalled, on the strength of written deeds or wills belonging to the monastery, or the testimony of good people, as having been conferred or granted to the saints in that monastery by kings or by any one of the faithful. The aim of this confirmation is that no one may presume to withdraw, diminish or abolish anything from the items referred to, on the ground of any expedient circumstance, judicial decision or exercise of power, nor may a bishop or official of any rank meddle in its affairs. Rather, if anyone, incited by a spirit of ill-will, wishes to infringe the liberty of that place and to despise our privilege or reject it, let him be condemned by God and all his saints and let him be excommunicated by us, as far as is possible, and separated from the company of all faithful people, unless he regains his senses.

94. How Wulfric became abbot.[428]

It was surely in the days just referred to that the aforesaid Abbot Leofsige, after having done much to the advantage of his church, met his death, and was buried next to his fathers in the church of the holy virgin Æthelthryth. When he was dead, King Edward appointed at Winchester a kinsman of his own, Wulfric, as abbot to the aforementioned community, and had him consecrated there by Stigand, Archbishop of Canterbury, in the third year of his reign, in fact, in the 1045th year from the incarnation of the Lord, and confirmed him in his place by the testimony of this document in the vernacular language.

95. The stability of the place confirmed by the king.[429]

Ædward cyning gret ealle mine biscopes 7 mine eorlas 7 mine scirgerevan 7 ealle mine þegenas on þam sciran þer þa lande to liggað into Hely freondlice, 7 ic kyþe eow þat ic habbe geunnen Wulfrice þat abbodice in Hely on eallan þingan, binnan burgan 7 butan, tol 7 team infangenþeof, fihtwite 7 fyrdwite, hamsocne and gryþbryce, sitte his mann þer he sitte, wyrce þat he wyrce, 7 nelle ic geþavian þæt ænig man <him> of handa ateo nan þæra þinge þæs <þe> ic him geunnen hæbbe. God eow gehælde.

---

[428] Source: local tradition on the succession of abbots. Date of the accession of Wulfric: possibly 1044 or 1045, but see Blake, Appendix D, p. 412, on the possibility of a later dating, and also the question of when he died.

[429] Source: monastic archives, cf. cartularies CDG. Ostensible date: 1044 X 1066, i.e. in the abbacy of Wulfric. The text is given as in Blake's edition, not as in E.

95a. Again, on the same matter.

I reckoned this letter ought to be translated into Latin and, that I should incorporate it into the history:

Ædwardus rex Anglorum episcopis, baronibus et vicecomitibus et omnibus fidelibus in quorum comitatu abbatia de Ely terras habet salutes. Notum sit vobis quod donavi Wlfrico abbatiam de Ely cum omnibus rebus ad eam pertinentibus, infra burgum ex extra, tol et team et infanganþeof, fihtwite et ferdwite, hamsochne et greðbrece et omnes alias forisfacturas que emendabiles sunt in terra sua super homines suos, et nolo ut aliquis subtrahat ex his omnibus que illic concessi. Deus vos conservet.

I, Edward, King of the English, to his bishops, barons,[430] and sheriffs and all his loyal men in whose county the Abbey of Ely has lands: greetings. Be it known to you that I have given to the Abbey of Ely to Wulfric with all things pertaining to it, within the fortified town and without, with *toll* and with *team* and with *infangentheof, fihtwite* and *fyrdwite, hamsocne* and *grithbryce*[431] and {jurisdiction over} other offences emendable {by money-payments}[432] in his own land upon his own people, and I do not wish that anyone should take away anything from all these things which I have granted to that place.[433] May God preserve you.

96. That the church of Ely granted the vill of Easter to a certain person to hold temporarily.[434]

The matter of the well-known vill of Easter, now called by another name, Pleshey, ought not to be passed over. Rather <one needs>[435] to bring it into the open how pitifully and unjustly, according to the ancient documents of the place, it was stolen from the church of St Æthelthryth.

---

[430] Lat. *baronibus;* OE: *eorlas.*

[431] These terms are explained in the Introduction, under 'Old English Legal Terminology'.

[432] Lat. *omnes alias forisfacturas que emendabiles sunt:* a standard formula paralleled in later charters. But there seems to be no equivalent in the OE text as given.

[433] Perhaps read at p. 165.7, ed. Blake: *que illi* (not *illic*) *concessi.*

[434] Source: local tradition relating to an English document conceding the vill of Easter to Æsgar the Staller; or maybe extrapolations from such a document by the compiler of *LE.* Date: abbacy of Wulfric, 1044 X 1066.

[435] Here (p. 165.9–11, ed. Blake) the Latin loses its way: the translation presumes that what was intended was something like: *praetereundum non est, sed <necesse est>* . . . *in palam producere.*

BOOK II

A certain Æsgar, the Staller,[436] – he is called *dux* in Latin[437] – forced entry into that estate. In forcing entry he took possession of it; in taking possession, he began to misappropriate it as though it were his own, and henceforth improperly became the possessor of something to which, by right, he would have no entitlement. But the abbot, the aforesaid Wulfric, and the brothers of the place, kept asking for it back, assiduously, albeit in vain; in view of their having achieved nothing through a direct approach to him, they went to the pious King Edward, complaining about their enemy's unlawful act of usurpation and imploring him for his support. But Æsgar, raised as he was to eminence by his wealth and position of honour, feared neither God nor man, and, in no way complying with the royal orders, imitated the one who said, 'I will place my seat to the North' and 'will be like the Most High.'[438] But just as that individual fell from Heaven to Hell, so this one, through his pride and misconduct, was inevitably to fall into scandal and disgrace, when the Normans, by the judgement of God, very quickly gained possession of England in war, and soon he was to be thrust, with a number of others, into the dungeon of a prison, bound with iron, right until the day of his death.

The brothers, moreover, once they had recognized that his mind was not being swayed in their favour by dint either of entreaties or of promises, proceeded to strike him with the javelin of excommunication, and on no day would they refrain from passing this sentence on him. For quite a long time he treated this as of little account, despite the fact that he was great and powerful in the kingdom, as the king's constable. But now that he had been excluded from the church and from the company of the faithful, he was in the end reluctantly forced to come to contrition, having become by now detestable in everyone's sight. To be specific: following the lead of his heart's envy and avarice, he misappropriated the gifts of the faithful, which they had assigned to God with a ready will for their own redemption and that of their families. He managed them, moreover, as it pleased him, but with the church continually claiming its property and, in accusation of him, publicly exhibiting the will of the person who gave it[439] and the charter of the king set down in writing above. As a result, he was subjected to much reproof and put under arrest, too, by the king. Returning to his senses, he made a bid to obtain, at last, by entreaty, what he had not hesitated to seize with his law-breaking hand. In recognition of this, they actually then acceded to his

---

[436] That is, a retainer of the king. See Blake's note *ad loc.*

[437] The term indicates the high nobility of an 'ealdorman' or a 'duke'.

[438] Isaiah 14.13–14 .

[439] The Lady Godgifu, see *LE* ii. 81.

entreaties, being 'children of God'[440] who kept 'peace with all,'[441] and they yielded it to him, although this was to their disadvantage, upon his swearing that, after his lifetime, possession would return to the church free from all disturbance of the peace on the part of his kin.

This, in fact, was done and stipulated in a written document in the English language and we are bringing this, like the others, into {historical} sequence, translated from the English, and this is its text:

Abbot Wulfric and the community of the church of Ely have, therefore, come to an agreement with Æsgar the Staller, that the same Æsgar may hold and possess the estate of Easter with the blessing of God in his lifetime and with their permission, and after his day it is to return to the church, freely, with all its contents.

The aforesaid King Edward and the queen, with the nobles of the kingdom, are, in point of fact, witnesses to this grant, just as a written account of what happened up to this time relates.[442]

97. How Abbot Wulfric granted certain properties of the church to his brother, without the knowledge of the community; and about his death.[443]

After that, the abbot at first watched his step honourably, and he had zealously sought to aggrandize the monastery with possessions. For he had a meeting with a certain earl called Ælfgar[444] and bought from him, for twenty-five marks of gold, the estate of Barham and had this confirmed in a charter of the king which he had acquired, with the seal already affixed.[445] And although he had carried out this transaction advantageous for his church, he refused to behave intelligently so as to do well to the end: instead he went out of his wits, through becoming involved in worldly concerns in pursuit of human glory. Because of this, he slid downhill into ignominy and opprobrium. For he had a brother, Guthmund by name, to whom he had arranged to join in marriage the daughter of a very powerful man. But because Guthmund, although noble, certainly did not hold the lordship of

[440] 1 John 3.1–2.

[441] Hebrews 12.14.

[442] Lat. *sicut hactenus geste rei scriptum perhibet.*

[443] Source: local tradition on the succession of abbots.

[444] Not Ælfgar the Staller, but Ælfgar, son of Earl Leofric of Mercia, himself Earl of East Anglia (1051–52 and 1053–57) and then of Mercia (1057–62). Information from Blake *ad loc.*

[445] Lat. *in presignata regis carta, quam adquisierat.*

forty hides of land, he could not be counted, at that time, among the foremost nobles,[446] and the girl rejected him. He returned to the abbot, extremely shame-faced as a result of this, lamenting the misfortune brought upon him, and made a most earnest plea that, on the strength of their relationship as brothers, he should entrust to him some estates of the church, so as not to be frustrated of the union of matrimony which he desired, especially in view of the consideration of honour. The abbot indeed, loving his brother in too worldly a manner,[447] leased to him, not with legal entitlement or written witness but merely as a loan, the estates listed below, namely: part of Marham, with the court of the village, Livermere, Nacton, Occold, Benstead and Garboldisham, and he did this secretly, so that it would not become known to the monks. He did not foresee or anticipate how much of a crime and danger it is to make accessible to the hands of laymen, even for a moment, sacred properties and goods given as offerings to the Lord, and so to be obliged, to retrieve it without a dispute, upon completion of a marriage-ceremony.

The deed did not remain hidden from the monks for long: as was proper, they assailed him disrespectfully with reproaches and rebukes for having committed such a breach of rectitude. He, indeed, became all the more fearful of what he had done† because he had let it come to light <and he>†[448] retreated to the place called Occold, bewailing, in the presence of all, the fact that he had perpetrated a sin, or rather a criminal offence, against God and his soul, in contravention of the professed object of the order to which he belonged, in taking away possessions from the holy monastery which were the payment of the pious for the redemption of their souls. Remaining there for some considerable time, he in the mean time declined into feebleness, because of the turmoil and disquiet of his soul. However, he had expectation of the remedy of salvation, and at a time when he believed he was recovering, he died and was carried to Ely for burial. For, indeed, he considered it a salutary thing to die in that place, so that through his death it might become a well-known fact that the church, having negligently and unfittingly approved a theft, was obliged to plead for the return of what was stolen.

After Wulfric's death, his brother, the aforesaid Guthmund, certainly did not relinquish the estates: rather, an agreement was made with Wulfric's successor, Abbot Thurstan, that he, Guthmund, might hold them for his

---

[446] According to the Latin (p.167.6, ed. Blake): Guthmund is *nobilis*, but not numbered among the *proceres*.

[447] Lat. *nimium carnaliter*.

[448] Reading conjecturally at p. 167.18, ed. Blake (with transposition of *quod exposuerat* and a supplement): *Ipse multomagis factum expavit quod exposuerat <et> ad unum secessit locum Acolt vocitatum.*

lifetime. But when, very soon afterwards, the Normans gained possession of the kingdom, one of their knights, Hugh de Montfort, took possession of these same lands and to this day has withheld them from the church.[449]

98. How Archbishop Stigand held the position of Abbot of Ely; and the grand scale of his gift of ornaments to that place.[450]

After the passing away of Abbot Wulfric, it was actually the Archbishop of Canterbury, Stigand, who took for himself the position of Abbot of Ely, and a great number of other abbacies and bishoprics too, and by courtesy of both of his masters, namely, King Edward and King Harold, he kept them, bereft of pastors of their own, under his own control as long as he liked, and assigned them to persons of his own choosing. For he had taken under his own control the abbacies of Winchester, Glastonbury, St Alban's and St Augustine's, and Ely – before Abbot Thurstan – and he was holding on to them as if they were his own. It was also at the archbishop's prompting that Harold, who at that time was wielding the sceptre of the realm,[451] caused Thurstan himself to be consecrated by this same Stigand. And indeed, even though an abbot had been appointed to Ely, Stigand was taking charge of the litigation of the church. Moreover,[452] he kept his hold over some of its best properties, as the *Book of Lands* reports in detail,[453] to the very great cost of the place.

However, he bestowed gifts in abundance upon religious communities, and particularly upon those which he is known to have kept in his own control. Certainly at Ely he contributed greater and lesser vessels of gold and silver for the liturgy of the holy altar, which were broken up and dispersed[454] in the surrender to the great King William. He had also made there a great cross plated all over with silver with a life-sized image of our Lord Jesus Christ and, next to it, images of Mary, the holy Mother of God, and of St John the Evangelist, of similar workmanship, made with bronze. These, and very many other items, Bishop Nigel at a later date took away and broke up. In addition, Stigand made an alb and a cantor's cope and a chasuble of priceless workmanship and costliness, than which none in the kingdom is reckoned

---

[449] Hugh de Montfort died c. 1092.

[450] Source: local tradition on the succession of abbots. Date: see Blake, p. 412: 'either the vacancy', in which Stigand administered the abbey, 'was very short or the *Chronicon* ignored it in giving Wulfric a term of twenty-two years'.

[451] Adopting an emendation from O: *sceptrum regni* for *regnum sceptri* (p. 168.9, ed. Blake).

[452] Reading conjecturally at p. 168.11: *sed <et > quasdam illius optimas possessiones* . . .

[453] The reference is to the *Inquisitio Eliensis*, appended to the E text of *LE*.

[454] Reading with E: *distracta* (p. 168.15, ed. Blake).

richer or more valuable. This was subsequently removed by the aforesaid king, and has to this day been impossible to retrieve.

99. About Bishop Osmund.[455]

Now we have to speak of Bishop Osmund, who some time ago received translation with honour amongst the men referred to above.[456] On his arrival in England from the region of Sweden where he had been bishop, he attached himself for a while to King Edward and followed his court around, enjoying the king's great favour. He was, moreover, a very aged man and worthy of honour, loved, for reverence of him, by all the foremost men of the kingdom. So, it was while he was involved in the royal court that he was delighted by a report about the religious life of Ely and decided to visit the monastery itself, wishing to spend the remaining part of his life there, if the goodwill of the brothers should accord with his desire. Arriving there, he was induced by the pleasantness of the monastery and the devotion of the brothers to stay. Received into full fraternity, at the brothers' request he used to carry out all the functions of a bishop in their house. For all bishops retiring here kept for themselves a single privilege: that now that they had relinquished the care of their bishoprics, they were to exercise no office but that of a bishop. And this Bishop Osmund, a most pious man, stayed resident at this church from the times of Abbot Wulfric, who had received him, right up to the times of Abbot Thurstan. When, under Thurstan, he passed away, he left to us the episcopal ornaments granted to him for his lifetime, and finally he rests in peace, after translation by us from his old burial-place.[457]

100. About the death of King Edward; and that, after him, Harold became king, and was the person who appointed Thurstan as abbot in Ely.[458]

The peaceable King Edward, glory of the English people, busy though he was with secular concerns, had nevertheless for the most part cast aside honours

---

[455] Source: lost *History of Seven Illustrious Men.*

[456] Presumably 'above' in the compiler's source-text.

[457] Blake, p. 168, n. 5, contrasts the unfavourable report on Bishop Osmund by Adam of Bremen. But note that Adam's hostility has been sceptically criticized by historians of Sweden. See P. H. Sawyer, *Kings and Vikings: Scandinavia and Europe* A. D. 700–1100 (London 1982), who favours a suggestion that Osmund's doctrine, deemed unauthoritative by Adam, was in fact Byzantine; that he had been consecrated in the territory of Kiev, and that the Swedish king, like Jaroslav of Kiev, had been attempting to create a 'national' church. In December, 2004, the current Bishop of Skara visited Osmund's tomb in Ely.

[458] Source: extended quotations from *Worcester Chronicle* on the year 1066, including Bury St Edmunds interpolation (Darlington and McGurk, OMT, vol. ii, p. 648); local material on Abbot Thurstan. Dates of Thurstan's abbacy (see Blake, p. 412): 1066–72.

– harmful things – and was a fervent pursuer of theological studies. Hence the King of Kings revealed many mysteries to him and informed him of a number of things concerning the future, as we have learnt from the accounts of people advanced in age.[459] In the mean time, while he was leading a life entirely dedicated to God in true innocence, he met his death at London and, the following day, was buried in royal fashion. He was lamented most bitterly with no lack of weeping by all who were present. When he had been placed in the tomb, the under-king Harold, son of Earl Godwine, whom the king had chosen before his decease as successor to the kingdom, was elected by the foremost men of all England to the supremacy of kingship, and, the same day, was honourably consecrated as king by Ealdred, Archbishop of York. And soon, having received the kingship, he appointed Thurstan to be abbot in Ely, as Wulfric, the father-superior of this same monastery, had died recently, and Thurstan was a man of proven virtue and abstinence, sufficiently educated within the monastery from boyhood, in English and Latin.

101. That King Harold, a year later, was killed by William, Duke of the Normans, who acquired the right of kingship by war.[460]

King Harold, therefore, as soon as he had taken charge of the government of the kingdom, began to abolish unjust laws and lay down just ones, to become the patron of churches and monasteries, to cultivate and at the same time to venerate bishops, abbots, monks and clerics, to present himself in relation to all good people as devout, humble and affable, to hold malefactors in abomination and to exert himself strenuously by land and sea in the defence of his country. However, it was for a limited time and with little joy and gladness that he held power: he lost his kingdom together with his life.

In the mean time, a message came to him that William, Count of the Norman people, had arrived with an innumerable host of slingers, archers and foot-soldiers, and had beached his fleet at the place which is called Pevensey. In consequence, the king immediately moved his own army towards London in great haste and, although it was not yet the core of his army that he was assembling, he none the less did not fear to confront the enemy as quickly as he possibly could, and joined a pitched battle with them. Indeed, from the third hour of daylight right until the dusk of night-fall, King Harold resisted his enemies with the utmost bravery and so valiantly and strenuously defended himself by his fighting that it scarcely proved possible for him to be killed by the enemy's expeditionary force. But, after large numbers of men from both sides had hurtled to their deaths, he himself

---

[459] The *Worcester Chronicle* is being followed here.

[460] Source: extended quotations from *Worcester Chronicle* on the year 1066, with editorial comment from the compiler or his source, on William's place in the history of England.

fell – alas! – at dusk, and with him the more noble of the men of all England.

Subsequently, the victorious Count William was consecrated with honour by Ealdred, the Archbishop of York mentioned earlier, on the very feast-day of the Lord's Nativity, at Westminster, promising on oath beforehand, as this same archbishop demanded of him, in front of the altar of St Peter the Apostle, in the presence of clergy and people, that he was willing to defend the holy churches of God and those in charge of them, and also to rule the whole people subject to him with justice and with royal prudence; to institute and uphold an upright legal-system, and utterly to forbid pillaging-raids and unjust trials. And this man was the first of the Normans to rule in England – of those, I mean, who were Norman on both sides of their family, and brought up in Normandy. That this came about, in fact, by God's providence, rather than by a sudden turn of events or by an accidental mischance, the sequence of events in itself makes clear.

And now, what am I to say about England? What am I to say to future generations? Woe to you, England, you who in former times were sanctified by your angelic progeny, but are now utterly distraught with groans for your sins! You lost your native king and in war, with great shedding of your people's blood, became subject to a foreigner. Your sons were miserably slain within your bounds, and your councillors and leaders were overwhelmed, or put to death or deprived of their inheritance!

Now, about the battle itself, Frenchmen who were present still testify that, although success fluctuated between the two sides, so great, even so, was the slaughter from the rout of the Normans that the victory which they won was, truly and without doubt, to be ascribed to nothing other than a miracle of God who, by punishing through it a crime[461] of perjury on Harold's part, showed that He was not a God whose desire is for iniquity.

And so, William having become king, I shall not neglect to say – profitless though it may be – what he did to the leaders of the English who were able to survive this very great battle. For what benefit would it bring if I were to say that not one of them in the whole realm was permitted to enjoy his former power, but that all were driven into a woeful state of poverty or deprived of their inheritance and exiled from their homeland, or made the object of men's scorn by the gouging out of their eyes or the amputation of other parts of the body or, indeed, being tortured most wretchedly and then deprived of life? Likewise, I reckon it to no good purpose to speak of what was done to lesser folk, not only by William but by his followers, given that we know that this is difficult to speak of and perhaps, because of its monstrous cruelty, beyond belief.

Well then, since it was King William's wish that there should be observance in England of the practices and laws customarily adhered to by his

---

[461] Adopting Blake's emendation, *scelus* for *celus*, at p. 171.17.

forefathers and by himself in Normandy, he appointed throughout the whole land bishops, abbots and other leaders from among the sort of persons in whom it would be considered disgraceful if they did not in all respects, setting aside any other consideration, obey his laws; disgraceful, too, if any one of them, by virtue of any power whatsoever belonging to this World's honour, dared to raise up his head against him. For everyone knew the origins and identities of the appointees, and to what end they had been appointed. Everything, therefore – both in God's domain and that of mankind – looked to the king for approval.

In particular, he caused the monasteries of all England to be thoroughly searched and gave orders that the money which the wealthier men of England had deposited in them, because of his harshness and pillaging, should be removed and transferred to his treasury. And, at a council which was held, Stigand, Archbishop of Canterbury was demoted, and similarly Stigand's brother, Æthelmær, Bishop of the East Angles, was deposed at Winchester. Some abbots were demoted there, too, as the king was taking pains to ensure that as many as possible of the English should be deprived of their office, so that he could substitute for them persons of his own race, ostensibly for the consolidation of his newly-acquired kingdom. To this end he also deprived of their honours, and kept committed to prison until the end of their life, a number of bishops and of abbots, too, with no obvious justification, these being men whom no councils or secular laws condemned. With great speed and with ferocious resolve, he unrelentingly kept laying waste to the country everywhere, kept slaughtering people and doing many wrongs, prompted merely, as we have said, by suspicion of his new kingdom.

102. That, in fear of the new king, the nobles of the country fled to Ely and, having been defended for a long time by the strength of its position, rebelled against him, with the result that the king, moved by great indignation, ordered all the properties of the church to be seized.[462]

However, Earl Edwin[463] and Earl Morcar,[464] because King William wanted to

---

[462] Sources: quotations from the *Worcester Chronicle* on the year 1071 (OMT, vol. iii, ed. P. McGurk, 1998); the remainder is apparently a local source, no longer extant, whose author drew heavily on the Vulgate text of 1 and 2 Maccabees. The compiler had access (see *LE* ii. 107 fin.) to a work on the deeds of Hereward by one Brother Richard, presumably of Ely and evidently deceased. Some phrases are certainly paralleled in the extant *Gesta Herwardi*, but the relation of *LE* to this work is not that of direct copying. Dating: the *LE* is not trustworthy for the chronology of the siege of Ely. See Blake's notes on the conflation of materials originally referring to different years.

[463] Earl of Mercia from 1057, in succession to his father, Ælfgar, who had also been Earl of East Anglia.

[464] Earl Edwin's younger brother, created Earl of Northumbria following a Northumbrian

put them in prison, escaped by stealth from his court and for some time rebelled against him on the Isle of Ely. But when they saw that their enterprise had not turned out a success, Edwin decided to approach Malcolm, King of the Scots, but, while actually on his way, he succumbed to an ambush and was killed by his own men.[465]

Morcar and the Bishop of Durham, Æthelwine, and Siward surnamed *Barn* and Hereward, a most energetic man, along with many others, once again made for the Isle of Ely by boat. But, on hearing of this, the king with his boatmen blocked all means of exit for them on the eastern side of the Isle, and gave orders that a causeway two miles long be built on its western side.[466] However, when the above-mentioned men saw that they had been blockaded in this way, they raised a siege-work of peat-blocks in resistance to the strategems of the king's army, and fought for many days. And when the king learnt that Hereward, that most brave warrior, was there, and mighty men with him, he gathered an exceedingly large force to fight against them and plotted evil against the holy place and thought of destroying it, because that place was by its intrinsic nature very well fortified, centrally situated in the country, and incapable of being stormed. For it repeatedly caused the kingdom wearisome trouble and now it was bringing many insidious strategems against the new king, because those who were fleeing from evils were added to their number and came to serve as reinforcements to them.[467]

Hereward became leader and commander-in-chief to these men and he said to them: 'Now, brothers, be zealous for the liberty of your country and give your souls for the heritage bequeathed to you[468] by your fathers, since we have been made trash and an object of contempt in the sight of all neighbouring kingdoms and regions, and it is better for us to die in war than look upon the evil afflictions of our race and our saints.' And the king moved his camp towards the Isle near to the River Ouse, having in his company a large number of cavalrymen and footsoldiers, and blockaded their escape-routes on all sides, with the aim of subjugating them to his rule. And

---

revolt against Tostig, brother of Harold.

[465] This paragraph is from the Worcester Chronicle, apart from the words translated as 'on the Isle of Ely'. It contradicts all the subsequent *LE* narrative of the siege of Ely, in which it is supposed that Edwin stayed there till the end, when he was taken captive.

[466] Note the specification that this causeway was in the west: hence in the vicinity of Aldreth rather than Stuntney.

[467] For bibliography on the English resistance to the Normans see S. D. Keynes, *Anglo-Saxon England* (third edition), pp. 167f.; P. Rex, *The English Resistance* (Stroud 2004) and *Hereward: the Last Englishman* (Stroud 2005).

[468] 'For the heritage bequeathed to you by your fathers': Lat. *pro testamento patrum*, from 1 Maccabees 2.50.

it came to pass that, when the men on the Isle had lifted up their eyes at break of day – behold! – innumerable troops were carrying a heap of wood and sand in sacks, with the aim of making the bed of the swirling river fordable, and capturing the siege-work. And the Isle was besieged in the 1069th year from the incarnation of the Lord, in the third year of the reign of this same King William. And Hereward with a few men went out to obstruct them, and they were overwhelmed by him. The others fled in order to escape.

But Hereward himself returned to Ely with his men, taking with them many spoils, and his name became known to all and people talked about his battles all around the kingdom. The king, on hearing those tales, angrily ordered brave and strong men to gather together from villages and cities with a view to taking them by storm. And Hereward sent men out to spy on the army, and they reported back to him, saying that an exceedingly numerous force had gathered from all over the kingdom to take them captive and kill them without mercy. And the men who had been with him took fright and kept crying out to him, 'How shall we few be able to fight continually against an unconquered multitude?' At this Hereward rose up and, confronting them head-on, fell upon them: some he struck down, others he dispatched to death in the water, and thus, that day, he rescued his men from fear and on the Isle people rejoiced, blessing the Lord who did great things in Israel and gave those men victory. And for a few days they kept quiet.

After this, the king's chief court-officials came to him and said, 'Let us make peace with these men, for the place which we are besieging has been fortified and we are not having success against them. It is for the sake of the heritage bequeathed to them by their fathers[469] that they have been making these attacks on us.' And what was said seemed good in the sight of the king and the chief nobles. He sent someone to them to make peace and they received him and they {Hereward's men} swore an oath to them {the Normans} and ceased pillaging. However, they {the people of the Isle} did not entrust themselves to them {the Norman nobles}, knowing their ferocity and their intolerable despotism, and neither did they fail to maintain their watch over the approach-routes.

The nobles, in fact, broke the treaty and made void the pledge which they had made to them, and they would gouge out the eyes of anyone they could capture, and cut off his hands and feet. Moreover, Æthelwine, Bishop of Durham, who was one of the besieged, was taken prisoner by the king's men on his way to that place, and the king sent him into custody at Westminster where, exceedingly heart-sick, he departed this life. However, the people of Ely, on hearing this, groaned deeply and at the same time

---

[469] Lat. *testamenta patrum.*

decided on a plan. They called back Hereward to assist them, placing great confidence in his militia.[470] He came in haste and not reluctantly, having gathered from everywhere kinsmen and freemen whom the king had condemned to be exiled and disinherited, and their company was strengthened in opposition to their enemies. Carrying out pillaging-raids and depredations far and wide, a hundred men at a time, or more than that, being often killed by them, they kept returning to where they came from in the Isle, as a result of which a number of people confidently placed themselves under their protection, along with their wealth. But they would not admit anyone into their company unless they previously pledged their loyalty[471] by swearing an oath upon the corpse of the most holy virgin Æthelthryth [to act with them] in purpose of mind and strength of body,[472] because they knew most certainly, not without discernment, that these people could play false. For instance: at that time the king, for urgent reasons, ceased his assault and concentrated his effort on putting his kingdom's affairs in order. Given that from every direction barbarians from the neighbouring kingdoms, that is, from Scotland and Ireland, from Wales and Denmark, were making incursions by land and sea, he was not able to offer resistance to all equally. However, having been incited beyond all measure to anger, he distributed to his knights all the goods and estates of the church which were situated outside the Isle. This was on the advice of William, Bishop of Hereford, and other councillors of his, about whom the Psalmist says, 'Those who please men have been put to confusion.'[473]

103. That Archbishop Stigand, fleeing from before the King, came to Ely and how the relics of St Alban were conveyed there.[474]

Meanwhile, the oft-mentioned Archbishop Stigand was on the move, fleeing from place to place and hiding, and there was no place in which he could conceal himself or his possessions safely. Eventually he made his way across

---

[470] Lat. *in ipsius tirocinio valde subnixi.* For the translation 'militia', see du Cange, s.v. *tirocinium.*

[471] The vague syntax of 'anyone ... they ...' corresponds to the Latin.

[472] The words translated as 'to act with them' are found in F but not E; the words 'purpose of mind and strength of body' paraphrase the simpler Latin: *animis et viribus.*

[473] Psalm 52.6 Vulgate; from which Psalm 53.6 RSV diverges.

[474] Sources. The last sentence contains a quotation from the *Worcester Chronicle* on the year 1067. Otherwise the sources are presumably local Ely traditions. The one about Archbishop Stigand's visit to Ely is discussed by Blake, p. 425; the one about Abbot Ecgfrid, which does not conform to traditions from St Albans about the relics of that abbey's patron saint, in Blake's Introduction, pp. xxxviif.

to Ely with the whole contents of his treasury. And, realizing that serious trouble was threatening him, he secretly instructed Ecgfrith, whom he had previously appointed Abbot of St Albans, to come quickly to the Isle of Ely with the treasures of his church and with the relics of that saint, and to wait there until the outcome of his trial was known, when he should either stay there henceforth or return home, according to the way things turned out.

And Abbot Ecgfrith faithfully expedited the task laid upon him, taking with him two monks, *Semannus* and *Ælricus,* and made his way to the Isle and abbey of Ely with all the items referred to above. And in a certain church which was then small, in the name of Christ,[475] he placed the bier of the holy corpse. There it remained for nearly half a year. Finally – in view of the fact that Stigand had been deposed from the archbishopric and Lanfranc appointed in his place, and at St Alban's church likewise, Abbot Paul had been installed – Ecgfrith himself, by now utterly without hope of recovering his abbacy and seething with enormous grief and anger, began to devise a scheme whereby at least he could inflict everlasting punishment upon the monastery unjustly taken from him, by depriving it of that heavenly treasure. For his preference was to keep so sublime a token of his entitlement with him rather than to lose it entirely. After much mental deliberation, therefore, he finally came to an agreement with Thurstan, the Abbot of Ely mentioned earlier, that the holy corpse should be translated ceremoniously, at a gathering of the people, ostensibly as an honorific gesture, from that little church into the larger one, to a position next to the body of the blessed Æthelthryth, and that afterwards, at an opportune time, ostensibly without his knowledge, it should be removed secretly by his colleagues and placed in the perpetual guardianship of the people of Ely and that he, Ecgfrith, should be received into the full status of brotherhood. Rejoicing at this, Abbot Thurstan therefore gave orders that a day in high celebration of the translation of St Alban be announced to the whole people. After a numerous congregation had gathered, and [[parties of people]] had come thronging in [[from all around]], this translation was carried out with all ecclesiastical [[rejoicing]].[476]

After these matters had been transacted in this way, the king went in haste to Normandy, taking with him the archbishop and many others of the foremost men of the kingdom, whom he kept in custody to the end of their life.

---

[475] Puzzling word-order in the Latin: *et in quadam, que tunc parva erat, in nomine Christi, ecclesia feretrum sancti corporis collocavit* (p. 176.25f., ed. Blake).

[476] Additions in double square brackets by a second hand in F (p. 177.7, ed. Blake).

BOOK II

104. That King William caused a full account of the whole of England to be written; that he imposed intolerable taxation upon the English; and about the enormous severity of a famine such as never was from the beginning; and that the king's fellow-countrymen were slaughtered at the river through the trickery of Hereward.[477]

Now, King William had completed the pieces of business, and put in good order all the affairs on account of which he had crossed the sea, assembling, in the course of his travels, a large force of warriors from all around. This done, he did not bide his time before returning to England. In fact, he sent word ahead, instructing the mayors and constables of the provinces to keep their fortifications strongly guarded against assault and trickery on the part of Hereward and the men who were holding out on the Isle, and to prevent them from making expeditions outside it.

Moreover, on his arrival, he imposed an unbearable tax upon the English and, that same year, gave instructions that a full account of the whole of England be written down: how much land each of his barons possessed, how many knights holding lands in fee, how many carts, how many villagers, how many animals – no, how much live-stock – each possessed in the whole of his kingdom, from the greatest to the smallest, and how much revenue each property could render. And the land was subjected to harassment, with many calamities following as a consequence.

And there came upon every living soul fear and tribulation such as there has not been from the beginning. All creation, on that day, was overwhelmed by grief. Calamity was afoot among men, plague among animals, destruction and famine on the land. For, indeed, King William kept on laying waste of Northumbria, along with other provinces of England, and slaughtering people; he spared no age-group.[478] And thus, while the Normans were all the time directing their energies towards their savagery, the famine which ensued became so overpowering that people ate the meat of horses, dogs and cats, and human flesh.

The king, it is certain, always had it in mind to destroy the men who had shut themselves up in Ely, and to plunder the monastery, yet he could not. Hence, in a state of great fury, he put his army ashore[479] a second time,

---

[477] Sources. After a link-passage discussed by Blake, p. 177, n. 3 (paragraph 1 of the translation), paragraphs 2 and 3 quote from, or paraphrase, the *Worcester Chronicle* on the years 1067–69. Paragraphs 4 and 5 and the subsequent chapters, *LE* ii. 105–7, were derived from Richard of Ely, *De Gestis Herewardi*, and have parallels in the extant *Gesta Herwardi incliti exulis et militis.*

[478] Text as in E, without [[*precepit*]]; infinitives are construed as 'historic'.

[479] The verb used – *applico* – usually refers to landing from a boat, but here a causeway is definitely the route by which the army reaches dry land, or something of the sort.

near Aldreth,[480] where the waters of the Isle are less than usually wide, across a causeway which he had made ready some time previously.[481] However, the width of the waters from that place extends a distance of four furlongs. He therefore ordered all sorts of wood and ballast to be thrown into the river: many trees and good-sized logs; when these were intertwined, he caused the skins of flayed sheep to be thrown on top of them, with the fleece turned inwards[482] and filled with sand, so that the load and weight of those walking on top would be more easily borne. This done, the whole horde passed over that causeway at high speed, thirsting for the gold which they falsely[483] believed to have been hidden on the Isle, but they all perished together, miserably drowned in the deep, along with the causeway, which soon became entirely useless to them. And as evidence of [this] fact, we quite often see weaponry dragged out of those very depths. And miraculously, from such a great horde, only one was able to escape, and he with difficulty. He was a friend to the king and a loyal knight. Straight away, he was brought to Hereward and, with the warriors looking on, made a successful plea to him that he should not be deprived of life. And he was not only saved but honourably received by him. Hereward asked his name and learnt that he was called Deda.

The king, thinking back over this, groaned from deep grief of heart, and he retreated with the small remaining band of soldiers to Brampton,[484] all hope abandoned of taking the Isle by storm in future.[485] But he did not remove his guards from that place either, so as to allow them any easy route out for the wreaking of havoc.

---

[480] The identification of *Alrehethe* with Aldreth poses difficulties because of the likely width of the waters between Aldreth and dry land in the eleventh century; see Blake, Introd. lvii. However, Reaney, *Place-names of Cambridgeshire and the Isle of Ely*, unequivocally identifies *Alrehethe* with Aldreth. Maybe there was some natural dry land or an artificial embankment, sufficient for the army to gather on, by the Old West River, which interrupts the present Aldreth causeway at a point perhaps little more than 'four furlongs' away from the eleventh-century fortifications on the Isle.

[481] Reading with EO: *pridem* 'some time before', rather than *pridie* 'the previous day', as in F (p. 178.7, ed. Blake).

[482] Reading conjecturally (p. 178.11, ed. Blake): *versa pelle* for *versi pelle*.

[483] The compiler has made no effort to reconcile his sources on this point!

[484] That *Brandune* in the narratives relating to the Norman blockade means Brampton, in former Huntingdonshire, a royal manor, rather than Brandon, Suffolk, seems the inevitable conclusion to be drawn from the narrative in chapter 106, where Hereward makes his escape from *Brandune* through woodland at Somersham.

[485] Lat. *omni spe deposita ultra insulam debellare*.

105. With what a great tribute of praise a knight set free by Hereward extolled the magnificence of the place before the presence of the king.[486]

The knight, therefore, having been conveyed to the Isle, enjoyed a lavish outpouring of luxuries there no less than at a royal court. Moreover, although he stayed there for a considerable time, after requesting, and being given, their permission, he made arrangements to return to his master, the king; but, before this, he gave an assurance, accompanied by an oath, that he would not make a report about them other than in accordance with what he saw or had discovered. And, on his arrival, he was stared at by everyone with amazement and called upon to reveal, in the king's presence, the state of affairs on the Isle. They rejoiced, one and all, at having received back, safe and sound, their comrade-in-arms, for whom they were grievously lamenting as one who had been sucked down to the bottom of the swirling water of the mere along with countless others. And it was specifically at that time that the king held a council with the foremost men of the kingdom, as to how to defeat the rebels or come to an amicable agreement with them. Deda himself, to be sure, was silently ascertaining what response each of them was giving on this subject; and finally he opened his lips as follows:

'If my lord the King orders it, I, your servant, commend to you what I have learnt and found out amongst those people whom you imagine to be blockaded within the Isle.

'They make expeditions every day for whatever purpose they desire, and will not be in the least afraid to encounter confrontation with a large force. There are a great many troops of soldiers there, sound both in morale and in strength. Their leader [[is]] Hereward, a man in the prime of life and one who has in all respects been most energetic in warfare ever since his youth; among free men, he is by no means of low rank where nobility or riches are concerned. With him there are men ranking very high in the country's nobility, Earl Edwin,[487] Morcar and Tosti, and two great leaders,[488] Ordgar and Thurcytel, who are very distinguished men. In addition to these, there is a band of robust young men, some of them from the district, others from elsewhere, firmly resolved to fight for the defence and liberty of their

---

[486] Source: Deda's report is paralleled in the extant *Gesta Herwardi* and presumably was derived from Richard of Ely, *De Gestis Herewardi*. The *LE* version of the siege-narrative differs from the extant *Gesta Herwardi* in being concerned to stress the respectability of the monastics, and to suppress any hint that there were monks actively involved in the resistance fighting.

[487] For the rest of the narrative of the siege of Ely it is consistently asserted that Earl Edwin was alive and one of the leaders of the resistance, in spite of the report in chapter 102 (p. 173.6, ed. Blake), taken from the *Worcester Chronicle*, that he had been killed by his own men on his way to Scotland.

[488] Lat. *proceres*.

country, preferring, should the contingency arise, to meet their death rather than be subject to strangers. At the hands of these men, all the king's friends and liegemen who have engaged in sword-fights with them have perished; and they are continuing ceaselessly to perpetrate slaughter and pillaging all around in the kingdom. And so long as we do not make peace with them, we are suffering failures every day and shortages are causing hardship, especially a lack of bread to eat. And how shall we escape their hands?

'The monastery, as the lord king's majesty knows, is, thanks to the providence of God, inherently well-defended by natural means, and made the more secure by strong fortifications; it is magnificent in its riches, glorious in its relics; it flourishes and has flourished under the tutelage of Christ, thanks to the presence and beneficent acts of blessed women, namely Æthelthryth, Wihtburh, Seaxburh and Eormenhild, on whose assistance it confidently relies. And the provost and ruler of this place is called Thurstan; he exercises the office of abbot and is a man worthy of the highest veneration. The community of monks in that place[489] is living in accordance with a rule, and he is not only teaching them by sound precepts to attain to the beatitude of the life of Heaven, but is inviting them to do so by his example of holy living. Moreover, he is descended from an excellent family of the English in the vill called Witchford, which is the capital of the two hundreds of the Isle. Having become a monk in the monastery [[there]],[490] he has from infancy to this day maintained a commendable style of life. However there is a single respect with regard to which he departs inharmoniously from what is good: the fact that he has indignantly refused to accept it as right that anyone from our race should be put in charge of him. Being, as a consequence of this, very discountenanced and fearful with regard to the king and the kingdom, he is governing [[and]] controlling on his own initiative the men whom he has with him.'

And, because he kept extolling them for a considerable time in magnificent fashion, Earl William de Warenne, whose brother Hereward slew †some time before,†[491] flared up with weighty indignation, and alleged that he had been enveigled by a bribe and was lying. The others, delighted by his tales, encouraged him to continue with what he had begun, and to disclose in the king's presence whether they were afraid or lacking in provisions. And he said:

---

[489] Reading conjecturally *illic* for *illuc* (p. 180.12, ed. Blake).

[490] E has simply: *in monasterio monacus factus* . . . (p. 180.12, ed. Blake).

[491] The mss here have *perindie*, 'the day after tomorrow', which cannot be right, given that the parallel passage in the *Gesta Herwardi* has 'dudum'. Perhaps we should read *pridem* 'previously' or maybe *previe*, also sometimes used with this meaning in MedLat, had been the term used in Richard's account.

212

'They are not worrying,[492] on the Isle, about our blockade: the ploughman is not failing to put his hand to the plough, neither is the huntsman there abandoning his traps, nor is the bird-catcher taking a rest from snaring birds. Rather, they think they are being safely guarded by a militia of their own men. And what more am I to say? If you wish to hear what I have learnt and seen, I will recount it all to you. The Isle is, in its interior, amply provided with rich resources. It is full of all sorts of crops, and superior to the other parts of England in its very rich soil. It is also very pleasant as a consequence of the loveliness of its fields and pastures, well-known for the hunting of wild animals, a productive breeding-ground for farm-animals and beasts of burden. †Yet again,†[493] it is equally praiseworthy for its woodlands and vineyards, enclosed[494] by large meres and wide marshlands, as if by a strong wall.

'Upon the Isle there is an abundance of domesticated animals and a host of wild ones:[495] stags, little roe-deer, goats and hares, in woodland glades and alongside the marshes just mentioned. In addition there is an ample supply of otters, weasels, stoats and polecats,[496] which are now, as winter weighs down, caught in traps, snares and every sort of ingenious device.

'But what am I to say about the variety of leaping[497] and swimming fish which exist there in shoals? At weirs placed in the windings of those waters,[498] innumerable eels are netted, large wolf-fish and pike, perch, roach, burbot and lampreys which we call water-snakes. It is, indeed, recorded by a number of people that salmon and likewise the royal fish, sturgeon, are occasionally caught.[499]

'About the birds that dwell there and nearby, yet again,[500] we will make a report – unless this is regarded as tedious – just as we have about the other things: there are countless geese, fig-birds,[501] coots, divers, cormorants,

---

[492] *Sollicito*: 'I am anxious', a MedLat usage attested elsewhere.

[493] Reading conjecturally at p. 180.26, ed. Blake: *n<amque> eque* . . . Cf. p. 181.5. for *namque*.

[494] *Obsita* must be intended to represent the past participle of *obsero* in the sense 'shut in'.

[495] This passage has been translated with detailed reference to J. E. Marr and A. E. Shipley, *Handbook to the Natural History of Cambridgeshire* (Cambridge 1904), in which the chapter on fish (pp. 108–9) sets out very similar data. The zoological observations are not derived from the *Gesta Herwardi*, where there is only brief reference to the natural resources of the Isle.

[496] Lat. *putesiarum*, cf. French *putois*, 'polecat'.

[497] Lat. *volantium*, literally: 'flying'.

[498] Reading with EO: *aquarum illarum*.

[499] Translating as if the reading at p. 181.5 were *capi memorantur*.

[500] Interpreting *namque* as introducing a new subject of secondary importance.

[501] Lat. *ficedule*, 'fig-peckers', may mean any 'small birds', considered as delicacies, or more specifically 'chiff-chaffs', which have the alternative name of 'fig-birds'.

herons and as for ducks, of which there is a very great abundance: in winter-time or when birds are changing their plumage, I have seen them caught in hundreds and three-hundreds, more or less. Sometimes the custom is for them to be caught in traps and nets and with bird-lime.[502]

'Well then, it is generally agreed that the Isle is seven miles long and four miles wide. And all the time that I stayed there, I used to dine every day with the monks in their refectory, plenteously enough, in the manner of the English. A knight always took refreshment with a monk at luncheon and dinner and, next to each one, shields and lances hung, attached to the wall, and, in the middle of the house, over their seats, there were placed close at hand, cuirasses, helmets and other suitable pieces of armour, from the head down, so that, should the need arise, they would be able very rapidly to carry out the chance requirements of war. But at the highest table, the aged abbot, that most devout man, reclined[503] with the three earls previously mentioned and those two most distinguished men, Hereward and Thurcytel, along with him, one on his right and the other on his left. And the choir of monks there, living in accordance with their rule under the discipline of St Benedict, nearly all the time sing praises together so sweetly that you would think the songs were resonating to the Lord in vocal sounds of every variety.[504]

'It would be a long task to give, in addition, a full account of the glory and dignity of the monastery , and the multiplicity of the estates which are recognized as belonging to that monastery, and which have been declared as such[505] not by some person of insignificant standing, but, freely and without claim, by the authority and stability of apostolic fathers, kings, archbishops, bishops and monastics, to the end that neither bishop nor earl nor the collector of any tax may presume to insinuate [[himself]] into the property of the lady saint, whether outside or inside {the Isle}, or disturb it in any way. This is asserted by many writs, without any exception, whether in secular or ecclesiastical law, <nor>[506] is anyone to take anything away from it, lest he incur the curse of almighty God and all the saints.

'In declaring this to you, however, my lord King, my object is not that you should desist from vanquishing these men.[507] May you indeed with all

---

[502] Bird-netting is still remembered (Cynthia Woodbridge, pers. comm.) as having been practised in the Isle in the mid-twentieth century.

[503] Lat. *recumbebat*.

[504] Not in the extant *Gesta Herwardi*. Lat. *Chorus autem monachorum illic . . . ferme omni tempore tam dulciter laudes concinit ut omnigenis vocibus odas Domino reboare putares* (p. 181.18ff., ed. Blake). Lat. *vox* can mean 'note' as well as 'voice'.

[505] At p. 181.24, ed. Blake, *sunt* needs to be supplied or understood with *conclamate*.

[506] At p. 181.27, ed. Blake, *nec* seems required before *quicquam*.

[507] Reading with E: *non ut eos debellare desistas*, after which strong punctuation is required before *utinam* (p. 181.29, ed. Blake). The text of F, printed by Blake, adds *statuas vel*, so that

speed make them subject to your jurisdiction, or else admit them to your love as people in harmony with your sovereignty.'

106. How Hereward, disguising himself as a potter, gained information that evil was being devised against him.[508]

And Deda had scarcely completed his speech when one of the men whom the king had earlier stationed at the ditch of Reach stood up and said, 'Do these reports strike you as baseless, or like delirious ravings? Surely not. [[For]] yesterday, I saw some men who had come out of the Isle in military garb, just seven of them, tall in stature, unrivalled in courage, and, though they had seen us, they passed us by, and did not break off from their undertaking, not being at all terror-stricken. They turned off to a little village near by, called Burwell, set fire to it and burnt it down. As we outnumbered them, we did not tolerate their audacity: we attempted to prevent their return and to take them captive. But those men, observing that there was an ambush, made their way forwards slowly towards the ditch which I have mentioned, coming right up to us, [[and]] – something I have never before seen in the whole expanse of the lands of Gaul from men so few in number – they put their trust, so I believe, in God's power alone, attacked our wedge-formation, and so we, on both sides, came up against one another at lance-point. And we fought them for a long time. In the end, all our men fell, and I alone escaped with difficulty to bring this news to you.'[509]

But on hearing these reports, the king, as if deeply wounded, flew into a rage and said, 'Now, my most valiant men and sharers in the plight of my kingdom, what were we to have done about this? We are not having success against these men, and we are not anticipating their stratagems.' For he had it in mind to make peace with them. But those standing next to him – the plunderers of those men's possessions and goods – dissuaded him from this course of action. Their fear was that, if they were received into a treaty of friendship, the estates and rents of properties would undoubtedly return to those men's control, as was merited. For this reason they stirred up his mind into a furious rage against them, saying, 'If you let them go unpunished any longer – these men who are attacking your kingdom, devising trickery against our lord, and are neither humbly repentant, praying tearfully for a sense of piety, nor of their own accord, in the proper manner, with the humility of suppliants, pleading indulgence for their offence[510] from the Majesty of your Highness – some of them, insolent and encouraged by the

---

the meaning becomes: 'not that you should decide to vanquish them or desist from doing so'.

[508] Source: probably Richard of Ely, *De Gestis Herewardi*; parallels in extant *Gesta Herwardi*.

[509] 'I alone . . .': a recurrent phrase in Job 1.15–19.

[510] Reading at p. 182.21, ed. Blake: *offensus* (gen. sing.) for *offensos*.

precedent of this piece of audacity, will not be afraid to make mock of your Excellency.'

And while they were thus conferring about these matters, a knight called Ivo, surnamed Taillebois, said in his indignation, 'I have known for a long time a little old woman who, if she were here, would solely by her art destroy the strength of those people and their garrison on the Isle and reduce any men – no matter whom – to a state of terror, and, if the king should be in agreement, she should be fetched with all speed.' Those present praised this idea and urged forcefully that it was not something to be resisted, but rather to be positively welcomed, and that a reward of a great many gifts should be given, if anyone by ingenious machination, or by any means whatsoever, should bring about the defeat of the lord king's enemies. And the king, shaking his head, hesitated, uncertain what he was to do. Finally, yielding mentally to their efforts at persuasion, he gave orders that the old woman just mentioned should be brought in secret, so that the action would not be taken openly.

Arguments such as these were being bandied around but, for the time being, they were unknown to Hereward and the men who were with him. However, they realized that evil was being prepared against them. As a result, at a council called at the same time, they made a plan to send out one of their number on reconnaissance outside the Isle. And, as they failed to find anyone suitable for this task, Hereward himself took it on, and hastened forth on his way, although the others for a long time were reluctant that he should take such a task upon himself and stood in his way, saying that it was on him alone – after God – that all hope of their salvation rested. Hereward, unsurprisingly, did not accede to their pleas but, mounting his mare,[511] which was called 'Swallow'[512] because of her speed, and had an amazing capacity for enduring strenuous exertion, he put himself in the way of danger for the common protection of his people, his object being that through him all the others might be liberated, or that he himself might confront danger on behalf of all.

And when he had made his way out of the Isle a short distance, a potter coming from the opposite direction, carrying pots, encountered him. Taking these pots from him,[513] Hereward lifted them on his shoulders, pretending to be a potter, clad in the man's pale yellow[514] garment. And thus, with his hair and beard cut short, he made his way to Brampton, where the king had been planning tactical moves against the Isle.

---

[511] Reading with E at p. 183.12, ed. Blake: *ascensa* for *accensa*.

[512] Lat. *Arundo*. But the name is '*Hyrundo* (in English)' in the *Gesta Herwardi*.

[513] Punctuating at p. 183.15: *quas suscipiens ab eo, tulit eas in umeris suis* . . .

[514] 'Pale yellow': Lat. *lurida* : in the *Gesta Herwardi* (p. 385) the garment is *lubrica* (meaning: 'greasy'), and Hereward has put on this disguise before meeting the potter.

BOOK II

On his arrival there, he received lodging in the home of a little woman: lodging there at the same time was the aged witch who had been brought there with a view to the destruction of the Isle. For a large part of the night, Hereward heard her mumbling something to herself: for she had counted on his being a rustic and unacquainted with her mode of speaking,[515] and she paid very little attention to him. In the middle of the night she arose, and went apart to the springs from which streams flowed down on the eastward side [of that same] house. Hereward followed her secretly as she went out, and caught her making an attempt at her spells. For he heard her asking for answers of some sort from the watchman in charge of the springs, not someone known to her; the watchman wanted to kill her, but the questions – inaudible – which she was asking, caused him to postpone his attempt at this.

And when morning dawned, Hereward with all haste picked up the pots and left that place. At the king's court he began to cry out, in the manner of potters on their wanderings from one place to another:

'Pots! Pots! Good pots and jars!
These are all earthen vessels and all first class!'

Then he was led by the king's servants into the kitchen, in order for them to buy pots. Present there, among other people, was an official who came from nearby, and he declared that he had never seen anyone more like Hereward in facial appearance than this particular[516] rustic and poverty-stricken individual. As a result of this remark, there came running from all sides retainers and grooms, wanting to see the mighty hero Hereward or someone resembling him, and inside the court, among the young knights and great lords here, this talk came to people's notice. And, though they looked at him very closely, they did not believe that such an ugly rustic was going to be the worthy Hereward and kept saying that it was not he. Hereward kept standing still, like an idiot, and answered none of the questions which were put to him in French, though he understood it perfectly well. They asked [him] whether he had ever seen, or become acquainted with, the unspeakable man. In the end he gave them an answer in English, as follows: 'I wish that man of Belial[517] were here now – my enemy in all things. I would take vengeance on him, good and proper! You see, he stole a cow from me, and four sheep, and because of this I have been forced to beg wretchedly, and have become caught up in such hardship that – with great shame and hard work – I am scarcely

---

[515] According to the *Gesta Herwardi* (*loc. cit.*) the language she was speaking was *lingua Romana*.

[516] Assuming that *isti*, if not a mistake, is conceived of as equivalent to *isto* (ablative of comparison).

[517] For this word for 'good-for-nothing', cf. e.g. 2 Samuel 16.7.

making a poor living out of this pack-horse and pottery.'[518]

And as they were exchanging these words, there appeared someone who had been sent from the king's presence, and he ordered them to hurry up with the royal food and, as a consequence, they kept quiet for a while about the things said previously. And it was not long before the cooks and gluttons,[519] eating and drinking, became completely drunk and, looking at Hereward, formed the opinion that he was stupid. Seizing him and arranging his pots round about, they kept pushing him forward, blindfolded, so that he would break them. Then, as he lay stretched out, pummelling them with his fists,[520] they began cruelly picking out hairs from his chin and, in the course of this sort of foolery, were about to shave the crown of his head. But the matter did not turn out as they hoped: they were to pay the penalty without delay. As Hereward, struggling against this, too, did not submit to them straight away, one of them, seizing a stake from the fire-place, belaboured him around the head, but he in return, parrying the blow, pressed it down upon his assailant, as a result of which the man collapsed unconscious. Seeing this, all his colleagues made an attack on him with pitch-forks and three-pronged glaives. Hereward defended himself manfully against them: one of them was thrown down to his death and many were wounded by him as well. He was taken captive, dragged away and shut up in the guard-house. And, while he was being held in the guard-house, someone holding shackles in one hand threatened to chain him up, while in the other hand he was holding a sword. Hereward snatched this sword from his hand, thrusting it forward, and swiftly killed the man with his own weapon and wounded others too.

And thus he fled and escaped through the hedge, found his horse again and mounted it. A crowd of young men tried to catch up with him as he fled, but Hereward was quicker than they and plunged into Somersham wood and, by night, as the Moon was rising, he found his way to the Isle. And he gave orders for there to be armed men at suitable positions all around, in case perhaps something evil might suddenly happen at the instigation of their enemies.

When the king, returning home,[521] learnt of this, he expressed

---

[518] This reply, though not all the detail leading up to it, is found in the *Gesta Herwardi*, p. 386.

[519] Lat. *ganeones* where the *Gesta Herwardi* text has *garciones*, 'boys'.

[520] *tundendo . . . reluctando* (p. 184.18ff., ed. Blake). In view of *quoque* and the context in general, it must be Hereward who is resisting in both cases, though the grammar would more naturally suggest that the actions of his assailants are being referred to. Cf. the loose use in modern Italian of forms derived from the Latin gerund. The account of the fight in *Gesta Herwardi* is briefer but no clearer, owing to use of the nominative absolute.

[521] The *Gesta Herwardi*, which presents a fuller version of the last stage of the escapade, explains (p. 387) that he had gone hunting.

admiration for the courage of the most invincible Hereward, giving most earnest instructions that, if he were ever captured, he ought to be kept unharmed.

107. How Hereward, cautiously on the attack, subverted and set fire to the siege-works of the king; and about a conspiracy of a great many people against their lord, the king.[522]

Now the king, at that time, had given instructions for absolutely all boats to be gathered together and for them with their boatmen to make a rendezvous with him at *Cotingelade*[523] on his arrival, so that they could transport in the direction of Aldreth a pile of wood and stone which had been collected there. For a second time, he was trying – though in vain – to see if it were possible to cross to the island by an unusual route. Fishermen hurried there from all around with boats, ready to carry out the king's command. Amongst them, Hereward arrived in a very small skiff, supposedly in an effort to hasten forward with extreme efficiency the work imposed on the others. But the Sun did not set, that day, before he made a secret approach and set fire to the whole heap. Soon, he took off the fishing-clothes in which he had been clad, and put on battle-armour; he urged his followers to act manfully and, at a given signal, he approached the massed ranks of the enemy with strong young men, and filled the camp with extreme fear and confusion. Throwing fire-brands, he also set light to the wooden towers which had been erected against them and, following the success of their actions they praised merciful God in their native language. For a hundred men were routed from terror of one man, and a thousand of the enemy, from confrontation with ten of that man's followers. Some on horses which they had seized, some on foot, some along roadways, most off the beaten track, rushed from there headlong into the marsh. Hereward and his men, familiar as they were with their own district, while eagerly pursuing them, smote[524] their guilty backs, and thus, that day, triumph came happily running, thanks to their rapid action.

Also, the witch referred to previously had been stationed in a very high place, above everyone else, so that she might more freely devote herself to

---

explains (p. 387) that he had gone hunting.

[522] Sources: probably Richard of Ely, *De gestis Herewardi*, given that there are parallels in the extant *Gesta Herwardi*; for events outside the Isle of Ely, various general histories; there are parallels in Orderic Vitalis, *Hist. Eccl.* ii, on the year 1069 and William of Poitiers, *Gesta Guillelmi*; but some material is unaccounted for in extant sources.

[523] Cf. modern 'Cottenham Lode'. Cottenham church is visible in the distance from modern Aldreth, across the plain which, when flooded, formed the mere known as *Cotingelade*.

[524] Lat. *cedunt*, equivalent here to *caedunt*, cf. a phrase of William of Poitiers, p. 202, eds. Davis and Chibnall (in the narrative of the Battle of Hastings): *cedentes rea terga*.

her incantations. Smitten by fear as if by a whirlwind, she fell from on high. And thus, she who had come for the infliction of death upon other people, herself perished first, dead from a broken neck.

The blazing of the fire, too, as the wind arose from an unfavourable direction, spread into the reed-swamp to the apparent extent of nearly two furlongs. This monstrosity of horrible appearance, running riot there, absolutely terrified the ranks of the Normans, and the noise of burning from it, audible all around, as the branches of willow crackled, had driven them nearly mad.

The king, viewing this from a high place, sank into measureless grief and, reduced to semi-consciousness, was brought to his tent in the hands of his attendants. He retreated to Cambridge Castle, gnashing his teeth and threatening to inflict the monastery[525] of Ely with a permanent loss of revenue. For he had now put aside hope[526] of any longer taking it by storm. And, having received into his presence all those of his men who had taken possession of the estates of St Æthelthryth, he gave his sanction that they were to be held as their inheritance in perpetuity, forbidding anyone from henceforth to render any payment from them, except if summoned by himself. This very soon became known at the monastery on the Isle, with the result that, extremely distressed, they called upon God and the blessed Æthelthryth in supplication for help towards confronting such a serious crisis.

It is in brief only that I am recounting the magnificent deeds of Hereward. My choice is to write about them in the medium of plain prose, so that future readers will understand the very splendid events with perfect clarity.

Now, the king gave instructions to his troops as necessity advised: they were to blockade the area near by, as if it were an easy matter for them to be able to entice those men out to fight a pitched battle or to intercept them when they had gone out and about pillaging. He was himself summoned to other business, namely to hasten to Normandy for a conference with Philip, King of the Franks. He made enquiries first, however, by means of envoys, as to whether he might be able to force a way through the approaches to the Isle by enticement of the monks.

Meanwhile, Hereward and the greater nobles of England, so far as they were able, were acting in concert in their assertion of power, making of entreaties and payment of money, and they won the Scots over to assist them. Quickly the Welsh joined with them: they were seeking an alliance against the Normans. In addition, the Danes favoured their cause and

---

[525] Lat. *locum*, lit. 'the place', here as in many contexts with reference to the monastery.

[526] At p. 186.13, ed. Blake one must either understand or supply conjecturally *spem* with *deposuerat*.

wanted to help them, with the objective of triumphing over the Normans.

But the matter turned out very differently – since[527] we shall be reporting what actually happened: that those people were without a doubt to be overthrown by the forces of the Norman commander. And he was to punish most of them mightily by imprisonment, exile and[528] dire chastisement. Only those who had retreated back within the Isle were escaping, whereas cities and fortresses everywhere were compliantly obeying him. But our King William, second to none among rulers where courage was concerned, was to deal their excessive boldness a severe blow, accompanied by no little slaughter, and to drive forth those men, like others of the region who were refusing to give their allegiance.

Meanwhile, a storm of bellicosity raged through England. Certainly most people did not have the confidence to rise up in arms openly but, in region after region, they engaged in armed conflicts and conspiracies, to see whether by means of any deceptions they might perhaps succeed in doing damage. Specifically, the people of Anjou, the Bretons and the people of Maine, in furtherance of a resolute conspiracy, refused military service, insistently complaining that they could not obey a master who was for ever making excessively immoderate demands. The loyalty of the Normans, too, had become so shaky and unstable that, along with troops they had mustered and their blood-relations, they declared war against their natural ruler at the instigation of Earl Ralph de Waher.[529] And so they were moved out of contumelious defiance to a joint conspiracy, having enlisted for this the support of the distinguished and mighty man Hereward, and other very powerful Englishmen, namely, Edwin, Morcar, Æthelwine,[530] Waltheof, Siward and Edgar,[531] whose persistent endeavours made their country turbulent with seditious uprisings.

It was with this in view that Hereward, having committed the island to safe custody, set out at that time on an expedition against the people of [East][532] Anglia. A strong force of young men accompanied him, and

---

[527] The translation here is rather tidier than the original. After Lat. *quoniam*, 'since', the sentence seems to lose its way. The future tenses in the Latin of what follows are translated in the English as futures looked at from the past, 'were to have . . .' etc. , just as the presents are taken to be 'historic' and thus equivalent to past tenses.

[528] This translation follows the reading of EO, without F's addition of *alios*.

[529] The great rebellion of Ralph de Waher took place in 1075, later than the siege of Ely. See Blake's note *ad loc.* on difficulties presented by the *LE* narrative.

[530] Despite Blake's doubts, the person referred to here is surely the Bishop of Durham mentioned in connection with Morcar, Earl of Northumbria, in chapter 102.

[531] Edgar Ætheling, the pretender, son of Edward Ætheling, son of Edmund Ironside.

[532] E reads *Anglos* where F has *Estanglos*, but Blake notes (with reference to p. 188.7) an erasure in E after *versus* and thus just before *Anglos*.

wherever they went forth in arms, no one presumed to counter them with resistance. In their confidence, they transported from there abundant booty, reckoning that no power whatsoever could harm them.[533]

By way of explanation: we are excerpting these facts from a number of *Histories* and at the same time combining them, albeit in summary fashion – recording brief and tiny extracts taken from numerous, large-scale sources. Our objective in this is that excessive prolixity should not be the outcome, and that things which are beyond belief should not be related, even if they are true. They are to be found, however, more fully recounted in a book about the deeds of Hereward himself, written some time ago by Richard of blessed memory, a venerable man and a most learned brother of ours.

108. With what violence the monastery of Eynesbury was taken from the church of Ely.[534]

Well then, in the midst of these flare-ups of stormy commotion, every wayfarer plundered what was rightfully and duly the property of God's virgin Æthelthryth, and reckoned it the gain of piety. All those in the chief positions of power rejoiced and clapped their hands in applause, and multiplied the frequency with which harm was inflicted upon her estates. One of them was the famous Gilbert de Clare,[535] a man highly renowned for his descent and his worldly distinction, but hostile in all respects, with his whole soul and strength, to St Æthelthryth, the lady of the church of Ely. Stealing from her the monastery of Eynesbury, he had the presumption to claim it for himself, and forced our men by violent means to depart from it. Some [[of them]], indeed, he was unable to drive out from the place, emaciated though they were from continual starvation and long burdened by harassment. However, he ordered that they be dragged out, and sent them across the sea to Bec to be consigned to perpetual custody, thinking in this way to tame their pertinacity at long last. And so, our own monks having been expelled and banned from that place, he brought monks from Bec and placed them instead of our men, illogically and illegally, at Eynesbury. And right to this day, though this ought not to be so, they have remained wilfully in possession of it, and we are engaged frustratingly in a legal dispute about the troublesome problem of this outrage.

---

[533] Reading conjecturally (after Orderic Vitalis, *Hist. Eccl.* ii. 196, p. 232, ed. Chibnall): *minime sibi vim ullam nocere posse arbitantes* (instead of *noscere*).

[534] Source: perhaps independent expansion by the compiler of themes found also at the end of *LE* ii. 29.

[535] See Blake, pp. 188–9, n. 3: 'The *LE* consistently uses the name Gilbert de Clare, where Richard Fitz Gilbert, the founder of the house of Clare, must be meant.'

109. That the monks of Ely made an approach to the king's clemency; and about the atrociousness of the journey of his army and horses.[536]

The monks of Ely, therefore, aware of the evil things going on in the kingdom, became deeply grieved both that a general take-over was happening where the resources of churches were concerned, and that the encroachment was being brought about by a foreign nation. Mindful of the magnificence of the temple of the Lord and of the holy place, they were frightened by the thought that such a crisis was threatening them: weeping with unanimous emotion, they kept on calling for help from Heaven and for the protection of their eternal advocate, Christ's beloved betrothed Æthelthryth. And, with the Divine Clemency as inspiration, they finally entered upon a salutary plan: they resolved to send envoys to the king to beg for his mercy and peace.

For famine had become intense, as we have said above,[537] throughout the whole region, and as for the innumerable thousands of the bellicose company in that place: even the grain-reserves of Egypt would not suffice for need on such a scale. The remains of food-supplies in the monastery had now been exhausted, the reason being that it was now the seventh year[538] from the time when people had revolted against the new king. It had not been possible for any amount of corn to provide sufficient supplies for long. For it was impermissible for the order of monks to feed on stolen, or forcibly requisitioned, property.

And, summoning to their presence the captains who were guarding the city and the exit-routes by water, <they made threats>[539] that they would drive them out from there, and that, if they rejected their plans, they would be handed over to the Norman troops. Soon, terror-stricken by these words, they became bitterly indignant at the extremely grave course of action which had been initiated. They had no hope whatsoever for a happy outcome from it: considering the fighting of battles easy, if compared with these evils. A severe famine was pressing down on them; extreme fear was causing them anguish inwardly, and they did not dare to go out to collect consignments of booty, unless in a strong force, fearing the swords of the Normans above all

---

[536] Sources: unidentified materials, unparalleled in the *Gesta Herwardi*, some of which were claimed to be based on the recollections of the Norman invaders themselves. Two sentences only in the first six paragraphs of translation are noted by Blake as reminiscent of phrases used, with reference to other campaigns, by Orderic Vitalis. There are a number of further borrowings from this author in the last two paragraphs.

[537] Cf. chapter 104, rather than the report of Deda in 105.

[538] An exaggeration, if we accept 1071 as the date of the surrender of Ely. Cf. the seven years mentioned in 1 Maccabees 6.53.

[539] Supplying conjecturally at p. 189.22, ed. Blake e.g.: <*minati sunt*> after *muniunt*.

other danger.

And the monks hastened on their way and sought out the king respectfully at the famous town of Warwick with the necessary supplication, commending themselves and all their possessions to his clemency. And so Thurstan, Abbot of Ely, with his monks, stood in the presence of the great King William, begging and beseeching him by the mercy of God to avert the anger of his outraged feelings from them and from their city, promising faithful obedience in all things from henceforth. And, with an entourage of great nobles standing round about, the abbot had regard for what was best, saying that his Majesty had tolerance at a level above himself, because the right of kingship had been granted to him by God. However, he put it to him that even if he {the king} were to treat them fittingly, he could only achieve the end of his labours without dubiety, and obtain entry to the Isle with all speed if, for God's sake and for the salvation of his soul, he were to bring about the restoration of the estates and goods seized from the monastery by his men. And the king made a promise. These proposals were heard and made known in the midst of the barons, and they rejoiced. God gave the abbot grace in the sight of the king and the king gave instructions to Earl William de Warenne and the venerable Gilbert de Clare to be guarantors of the promise. The abbot, in fact, in accordance with his wishes, conferred with the king himself, in the necessary way, about gathering together the estates of the church. And afterwards, < . . . >[540] returning to his own domains, first instructing the king about a means of making a counter-offensive, instructing him also not to be afraid, even though he had been so often repulsed by the people up in arms against him.[541] For these people, the abbot explained, were without his own guidance and support and, as a consequence, he was aware that their morale was very quickly collapsing.

Then, indeed, the king, better able to see ahead, went on an expedition around remote parts of the kingdom, fortifying suitable places, so that from them he could thwart the forays[542] of the rebels, and more easily tame their stubborn resistance <. . .>[543] None the less, startled though he was by this news, he rejoiced with unaccustomed joy: he was triumphant as if already made secure by victory. And having gathered together, to the best of his capability, a force of infantry and cavalry, he promised his followers honours and gifts and he made it his plan to move towards the place where he knew most of the enemy were to be found, namely Ely. He made haste; he prepared

---

[540] A main verb seems lacking here after *remeans* (p. 190.15, ed. Blake).

[541] 'People up in arms against him': Lat. *ab inimica gente*. The remainder of the sentence suggests that *gens* here means, as often in MedLat, a relatively small 'band of men', rather than a 'nation', though national interests were, of course, at stake.

[542] Plural as in E and Orderic Vitalis.

[543] Marking a lacuna at p. 190.20, ed. Blake, after *posset*. Probably a change from one source-text to another has been inadequately coped with.

siege-engines. The place, as has already often been said, was extremely well fortified. Day by day, he laboured in preparation for taking it by storm. For indeed, in days gone by, even the ingenious valour of Cnut did not avail to storm this fortress.

It deterred many to be advancing in armour across marshy ground which would hardly support the footsteps of a man or of any animal. And you could see that it posed threats, easily targeted as it was by an arrow-shot from afar: collapsing like chaos into a whirlpool of solid matter into which, when loosened by the slightest rain, flow <waters>[544] in streams and rivers, disguised all the time by the hazardous beds of flag-iris which, in general, marshy ground encourages to grow. It can be conjectured on the basis of these considerations how treacherous the beds of these waters are,[545] like headlong descents to the Abyss. Indeed, when touched by the slightest fine weather, <the mud>[546] splits open in wide, deep cracks. In addition to these adverse conditions, the knights were often assailed by very heavy rain, with hail mixed in from time to time. Exhausted over and over again, as a result, and close to abandoning everything, these men who had suffered hardships became aware that on this journey[547] there remained hardships greater still. The facts which we are recounting were learnt by us from the faithful recollection of the men who had endured them.[548]

Well then, the narrowings and windings of the causeway were hindrances to sight and speech. Each man in his anxiety for his own safety, scarcely gave a thought to his lord or his friend. Already, the Bretons and others had deserted because of the enormity of the operation: they wished to go back to their native land, but an order from the king prohibiting this had kept them from taking to their boats. Returning to acceptance of his orders voluntarily and with pleas of supplication, they followed in the rear. They were forced by shame to keep going since they saw the king himself nimbly going ahead. Moreover horses killed in the marshes sometimes served the function of a bridge. The king – who truly had the determination that Julius

---

[544] Reading conjecturally (p. 190.28, ed. Blake): *ac brevissimo imbre resolutum rivis et amnibus influunt <aque que> iugiter periculosis gladioletis sunt velate, que solum palustre fovere solent.*

[545] No actual word for waters in the Latin, merely *earum* 'of them' (feminine plural: hence *aquarum* is a likely word to be understood).

[546] Supplying conjecturally (p. 191.1, ed. Blake) e.g.: *Tactum vero serenitate aliquantula <lutum> fissuris aperitur amplis atque profundis.* Conceivably, the need to supplement could be avoided by assuming that *solum palustre* is to be understood as the subject.

[547] Reading with E **as well as** F at p. 191.3, ed. Blake: *in hoc itinere* (cf. the phrasing of Orderic Vitalis, *Hist. Eccl.* ii. 198 compared by Blake *ad loc.*)

[548] The compiler of *LE* is presumably here quoting word for word from a document based on reminiscences of members of the first Norman garrison at Ely.

Caesar, a most exceptional commander, is reckoned to have conjured up in a dire emergency of this kind – did not deem it right to detain his men at this juncture by large amounts of exhortation or by new promises, as if they were cowardly or lacking in stamina. He nevertheless answered their queries in a few words: if they were obedient to his command, it would be to their advantage for the remainder of their undertakings; if, on the other hand, they were to desert, he was going on – to a place where matters of urgency were summoning him – and he was not afraid of being hindered by their departure from carrying through to the end, without slackness, the undertakings which had been initiated. He, for his part, proposed to overcome the greatest possible difficulties for the sake of securing tranquillity for the kingdom.[549] Finally, he led the army unharmed right the way across, to a position nearer than anyone's expectation anticipated to the waters of Ely.[550]

110. How, with the departure of Hereward from the Isle, the king finally made his entry.[551]

Now, at that time the two brothers Edwin and Morcar, who were never in greater enjoyment of favour and honour at the court of Edward than in that of our free king, William,[552] on learning that he was now on his way to Ely to take it by storm, unexpectedly deserted him, with a view to avenging their nation. They took council together, no less than if their leader and general Hereward were present, and were prepared to put up resistance. At the same

---

[549] The rare construction used here – a genitive gerundive expressing purpose – indicates, as does the reference to Julius Caesar, that the unidentified source here was an imitator of classical historiography. *Equidem* (normally meaning 'I, for my part') suggests that William's address may have been originally presented in direct speech.

[550] The route taken by William is unclear. If any reliance can be placed on Matthew Paris, *Chronica Maiora,* on the year 1071, King William's operations prior to the capture of the Isle were more complex than the *LE* account suggests, and included the erection of a castle at Wisbech, and long causeways.

[551] Source: an unindentified pro-Norman historian, unaware, apparently, of the story of Thurstan's negotiation with King William and his betrayal of the secret path to the Isle. Paragraph 1 of this translation takes us back to the situation on the Isle, in Hereward's absence, just before the arrival of the king's troops. Paragraph 2 harks back to the king's previous two attempts to break into the Isle by means of a causeway in the vicinity of *Alrehethe.* Paragraphs 3ff., after a summary account of another crossing of the fen (another version of the 'secret path' tradition?), seem to take the narrative on from where it left off in chapter 109: with an assault by siege engines across a river. Paragraphs 4 and 5 are dense with parallels with the narrative of the march to Chester (year 1070) in Orderic Vitalis and with William of Poitiers' narrative of the battle of Hastings; see Blake's notes.

[552] Lat. *in liberi regis nostri Willelmi.*

time, people who up till then had remained somewhat covertly in arms were now ashamed not to follow their friends and neighbours. They went out every day in boats and along narrow tracks, slaughtered Englishmen and Frenchmen indiscriminately, seized horses and arms throughout the neighbourhood and were continually piling up a vast quantity of goods found in the monastery, as spoils of war.[553] For indeed, they were fortified by optimism. They knew that about eight thousand soldiers of their own people who were in exile among the Danes were to return, accompanied by Danes, in the near future, and they knew that the place itself was the most convenient hide-out in all England for rebels. Moreover, they had no fear that it could be assailed successfully by anyone.

The Normans, indeed, had already crossed the lake called *Cotingelade,* but neither side was of the opinion that those strong defences could be stormed. However, the king declared that the thing should be attempted, and that the work of good men who were endeavouring to put an end to such a multitude of evils, should not be treated as worthless. He exacted exemplary punishments so that would-be perpetrators of rebellion would be frightened. And for the first time, he then took possession of the rivers with an armed fleet, so that access to the coastal regions would not be available. For a second time, on the other hand, he gave instructions for the marshland to be bridged with pontoons, and the king himself stipulated in advance in what way and from <what> material they were to be constructed. And his own sweated effort was all the time involved. Assailants descending on them from the Isle killed a number of men and demolished part of the siege-work: this caused his burning aggression, and equally that of the knights, to flare up even more.

Apart from the marsh-lands, numerous standing waters and fast-flowing streams formed a barrier, and the king himself was not ashamed, in order to give courage to the fearful, to lead the way through some river by which he was submerged almost to the top of his helmet. He came eventually into the neighbourhood of the Isle, to a marsh of horrific appearance, of infinite depth, festering all around to the depths of its hollow bed. The enemy troops on the bank opposite, having assembled[554] peat-blocks as a means of defending themselves, prepared to bar their crossing with stones and missiles. The Normans were greatly discountenanced[555] by the double obstacle. The king, pressing his undertakings on to their conclusion, had little boats transported there through the fen, by an amazing feat of engineering, and simultaneously, at the cost of huge effort, he caused siege-

---

[553] Interpreting *praedis* as a predicative dative.

[554] Reading at p. 192.22, ed. Blake with E: *congestis* in place of *coniestis.*

[555] Reading with E: *perturbantur.*

engines to be erected, with which to bombard their opponents. The unstable ground shook, threatening everyone supported by it with drowning. The thousand French knights, in body-armour and helmets, who had gone across towards those men, joined battle; three thousand of the pirates and greater numbers of English militia, collected from the midlands, apart from the common people of the Isle.[556] Then, as the Normans kept up the assault with catapult-engines, using all sorts of projectiles, the wretched men gave way and were routed in flight. Hastening to pursue them, the king led the army very swiftly across a weak and shaky bridge, constructed on top of little boats with poles and wicker hurdles.[557] However, when they had crossed, there still remained for them a difficult struggle out of pools of water: they scarcely made it, in the end, to solid ground through pit-falls and eddies of mud.

Then a resounding cry of victory drove the enemy with high speed from the Isle. The Normans, flaring up and surrounding some thousands, in a moment destroyed them, so that few escaped, and they with difficulty. Quite apart from the wounding blow, a considerable part of the enemy lost heart at the sight of this amazing and terrible warrior. For he went into action – something[558] which should be immortalized in praise – with the legion whose commander he was, attacking and striking down with great boldness.

It is not within our capability, nor is it our intention to promise, to narrate all that man's courageous deeds. Someone with the utmost mastery of the resources of speech who had gained his knowledge of that war with his own eyes would have difficulty in describing consecutively all its individual incidents. The writer of the *Thebaid* or of the *Aeneid*[559] – the authors who in those books sing great songs about great events in the poetic manner – would, on the basis of this king's actions, compose a work equally great and more well-deserved, by relating true facts in song.[560] Certainly, if they were to discourse in condescending verses on a level proportionate with the greatness of his dignity, they would cause him, by the beauty of their writing, to be given a place amongst the immortals.[561] Our plain prose, on the other hand, has merely been offering extracts in brief, presenting a lapidary record[562] of a battle of this most invincible ruler, in which he so valiantly won the victory.

---

[556] In the Latin both these military contingents are apparently enumerated in the nominative case, as the subject of *oppugnabant*.

[557] Reading conjecturally at p. 192.31, ed. Blake: *cratibus* for *crateribus*.

[558] Reading at p. 193.3, ed. Blake: *quod* (not *quid*) *eternandum est laude* . . .

[559] The classical Roman epic poets Statius and Virgil.

[560] Cf. William of Poitiers, *Gesta Guillelmi*, pp. 110ff., eds. Davis and Chibnall.

[561] Lat. *inter divos*.

[562] Here, 'presenting a lapidary record' is a rendering of Lat. *titulando*.

111. How cruelly the king took vengeance on his enemies for the injury done to him; and that the monks secured a firm treaty with him, giving him considerable amounts of money, to pay which in full, everything outstanding by way of gold and silver was removed from the church.[563]

The king, therefore, on entering the Isle, went around the crooked fen-paths on a most difficult march, and surrounded the enemy host by an ambush in a place which was terrible beyond all the difficulties which he had previously overcome. The armed men were led out: first the leaders, then a considerable number of men who were prominent because of their reputation or some mark of distinction. He sentenced some to imprisonment, some to the loss of eyes, hands or feet; he released unpunished the mass of the common people. And the plentiful goods found there compensated many times over for the horses that had been killed and all inconveniences of this sort. Edwin was taken captive and, with him, countless men of great standing and power; they were arraigned and chained up with the utmost security. The army lamented the escape of Morcar, and the king's friends were heated with indignation at the flouting of the surrender. Morcar himself, and a few men, with difficulty, escaped.[564]

And it was not long before the king, approaching the monastery, gave instructions to a large force to guard the doors and entrances of the church, his aim being that, when he went there to pray, there should be no means of access for the monks to seek him out or come to meet him in the appropriate supplicatory guise with crosses and the relics of the saints.[565] Supposing that the opportunity were not denied them, the consequence would be that he, having been received with respectfulness of this sort, would be obliged, in terms of justice, to be placated, and leave unpunished the injury resulting from their offence. On his arrival at the monastery, eventually, standing a long way from the holy body of the virgin, he threw a gold mark on to the altar, not daring to approach closer: he was afraid of having judgement passed on him by God for the evils which his men perpetrated in the place.

And, having allocated a site for a fortress within the monks' precincts, he both made arrangements for people from the shires of Cambridge, Huntingdon and Bedford to carry out the building-work, and committed it to the charge of knights of his choosing whom he had brought across from Gaul. Having similarly garrisoned the fortress of Aldreth with men from

---

[563] Source: local tradition with no parallels identified, except for the rhetoric in the second half of English paragraph 6, which is based on William of Poitiers, *Gesta Guillelmi* on the rebellion of William of Arques.

[564] Blake notes (p. 193, n. 5) how this record conflicts with that of other historians.

[565] Here the Latin becomes confusing, though the sense can be worked out with reasonable certainty if Stewart's *ne* for *nec* is accepted.

Gaul who were loyal to him, he returned by the route by which he had come in. Such was the upheaval that day that there was no celebration of the mass in the place. The day in question was 27th October.

Meanwhile, after the king's departure, the entrances of the church were barred, and Gilbert de Clare, who has been mentioned earlier, came in to view the domestic buildings of the monks, and, going round all of them, he came to the refectory. The monks were eating a meal and he spoke to them as follows: 'O wretched and deluded men! Surely it would not be impermissible to take your luncheon at a different moment, while the king is visiting you and is standing in the church?' At these words, they all left the tables and ran to the church, but they did not find the king.

As a result, they became greatly alarmed and, being devoid of hope except in the Lord God, they pleaded with this same Gilbert de Clare to ensure, through his mediation, that they might obtain a stable peace, because the king, in view of their injurious actions, had rescinded the pact made with them, his intention being to pile evil upon evil. Gilbert, taking the task upon himself, had a meeting with the king on the subject at issue, and with difficulty fulfilled his undertaking, though with the stipulation that the monks should meet him in person and mollify his anger by entreaty or payment of money, in whatever way they could. And, after being admitted to the king's presence at Witchford where he was staying at that time, they were with difficulty received back into favour, thanks to Gilbert and other men of influence, on their promising him a sum of money, namely seven hundred silver marks. The monks then, in fact, took whatever precious articles there were in the church: crosses, altars, reliquaries, gospel-books, chalices, patens, lavers, stoups, straws, bowls, and gold and silver dishes, in order to pay in full the specified sum of money.

And they had been required to pay out the money in question to the king's servants at Cambridge on a stated day, but a drachm {one-eighth of an ounce} had been fraudulently abstracted by a trick on the part of the moneyers, so it was found, on being put in the balance, to be of an incorrect weight. When the king learnt of this, he became extremely angry, and denied them all hope of respite and peace in future. For, in spite of the fact that he had gained entrance and been relieved of distress, an extraordinarily bitter fury enflamed[566] him: he was going to exact retribution for what belonged to him, as if it had been criminally supplied in short measure. There arose great misery all around. Upheavals, depredations and robberies raged, threatening devastation. There remained no place for peace or security.

Subsequently, the monks, utterly immobilized by the pain inflicted and now renewed, finally entered into a new agreement with him: they promised

---

[566] Reading conjecturally at p. 194.30f. Blake: *furie accendunt*, cf. William of Poitiers, *Gesta Guillelmi*, p. 54, eds. Davis and Chibnall: *furiae incendunt*.

to add t ee hundred marks to the previous seven hundred, that is, to supply a thousand, in order to gain possession of his favour, along with the liberty of the plac and the restoration of its estates. To this end, everything remaining in the c urch that was made of gold and silver, to cap it all, the image of St Mary w th her child, seated on a throne, of marvellous workmanship, which Abbot lfsige had made of gold and silver, was broken up. Similarly, the images f the holy virgins were despoiled of much ornament of gold and silver, s that the sum of money could be paid. But, in spite of this, they had no confidence about the hoped-for settlement.

112. Ab ut the passing away of Abbot Thurstan.[567]

The dis nguished abbot, Thurstan, who had been in charge of the monastery, was a an adorned with the glory of learning and goodness, a fearer and lover of God. During the time when he was storm-tossed among the fierce whirlwi ds of warfare and the crises of insurrection, he was not deflected from th work which it was his good resolve to undertake. For he was a complet despiser of worldly things, and willingly took upon himself the deepest basements and tribulations. If it had been permissible to stand in the way of ivine predestination and the unanimous prayer of the brothers, he would not have sought a great and onerous position.[568] Yet, encumbered though he was by such a burden, he used to range round the heavens with his mind already disengaged.

Certainly, he was smitten by enormous grief on seeing that the resources of the holy church were being eroded. As a consequence he began insistently to state his case against the despoilers of his properties, his aim being that, once they had been chastised and made to withdraw, as being guilty of a crime, he might be reconciled with them. There were those who were stubborn and inclined to fight back, and were unwilling to come to their senses after a public warning. Instead, by exercise of their power, they laid claim to God's sanctuary as an inheritance for themselves. These he did not hesitate to smite with the lance-blow of an anathema. He laid down, moreover, that not only they, but all of their progeny, yet to be born, who would continue appropriating the properties of the monastery by similar thievery, were liable to the condemnation of an everlasting curse. He also decreed that prayers were to be made against them for evermore in the course of the sacrosanct mysteries of the mass: the psalm, 'Ad te levavi', the 'Pater Noster' and the prayer, 'Ecclesie tue, quaesimus, Domine, preces placatus

---

[567] Source: local commemoration of Abbot Thurstan. Date: 'Thurstan must have died before 1076' – the date given in this chapter – 'as his successor Theodwin attended the London council of 1075.' So Blake, p. 195.

[568] In the Latin, this sentence is cast as an unfulfilled condition in the (historic) present.

intende.[569] That this has redounded to their destruction from generation to generation no one today doubts.

And Abbot Thurstan completed his days at a ripe old age and was laid beside his fathers in the 1076th year from the incarnation of the Lord, and in the eleventh year from his taking up of his position, during the reign of the oft-mentioned William. The same king had it in mind to depose this abbot, having summoned him to a council: he wished to substitute in his place a certain monk Gemesciens;[570] on the other hand he had experience of Thurstan's wisdom and outstanding conduct. Even though he did not remove him from his position, moreover, he continually harassed him with injurious actions of the utmost severity.

113. How the king appointed as Abbot of Ely Theodwine, who would have been unwilling to take on the position, had not the king restored to the place everything that had been taken away, and who, having arrived there, was after a short while taken from this World's light without a blessing of his appointment, and left the position vacated by himself to a distinguished and prudent man, Godfrey.[571]

So it was that the king, having very soon learnt of the aforesaid abbot's death, sent to Ely and gave orders that all the best items among the ornaments and miscellaneous chattels which he had heard of as existing there, should be taken away and put in his treasure-house; similarly, a great weight of silver and gold which had been found close to the monastery in a place called Wentworth,[572] with which the brothers had it in mind to replace the altar-vessels that had been broken up, and to repair the monastery's losses. Also the outstanding vestment which Archbishop Stigand, in his capacity as a bestower of benefactions, had provided for the glory of the house of God, than which there is said to be found none richer in any kingdom on Earth: the king took this away from St Æthelthryth and placed it amongst his treasures at Winchester, so that, as a result, right to this day the church is without it. Then he summoned to his presence the monk Theodwine Gemesciens, someone sufficiently well known to the courts of Normandy – the man whom he had long thought of putting in charge of Ely – and he appointed him, this time, to the task of governing the monastery.

This abbot, on his own initiative, before he entered upon his abbacy, recalled to it all the property consisting of gold, silver and jewels which,

---

[569] Psalm 24 Vulgate = 25 RSV, the Lord's Prayer and a prayer beginning, 'Hearken peaceably, O Lord, we pray, unto the prayers of thy church, . . .' Alistair McGregor (pers. comm. 2.12.2000) compares *Corpus Orationum*, no. 2404; Bruylants, *Les oraisons du Missel Romain*, no. 517.

[570] A monk of Jumièges also known as Theodwine; see *LE* ii. 113.

[571] Source: local tradition on the succession of abbots.

[572] But cf. *LE* iii. 50, p. 289.26ff., ed. Blake.

before his preferment, the king had removed from it: for he utterly refused to take on the abbacy unless the king would command the return of all that he had ordered to be removed. And so, with the stolen goods of the church restored, Theodwine took up the abbacy of Ely: he was to bring it great profit, but to live for all too short a time. And when he had taken up his position, he caused a very remarkable snow-white cope to be made available, not only that but also a *tabula*[573] made of gold and silver, of marvellous workmanship, in the middle of which was a throne with an image of the Lord and round about images of silver completely gilded, and on each side bands ornamented with precious stones. It was reckoned to be worth an exceptional price, above the wealth of the realm of England.[574] Bishop Nigel later broke it up – and everything of value from the church. And the aforesaid abbot would have done things of greater worth, were it not that the time which immediately followed brought about his departure from life. For after two-and-a-half years, in which he had lived honourably and beneficially, he died, without consecration as abbot, leaving the monk Godfrey, who had been his particularly close colleague, as his deputy, so to speak, in his place. [After the death of Theodwine, the king's officials immediately arrived and hauled out into the open the contents of the treasury of the shrine of the Lord and the blessed Æthelthryth, and at the king's behest listed them in full, distinguishing the individual items, one by one, as the following chapter sets forth.][575]

114. What items from the treasury of the church there were found to be after the death of Abbot Theodwine.[576]

These are the items which Eudo the steward and William de Belfou and *Angerus*[577] found in the church of St Æthelthryth according to a document of the Abbot of St Edmunds, witnessed by Ralph Taillebois, Picot, Hardwin de Scalers and *Eiraldus:*

  19 chalices with patens, and 4 without patens.
  12 gospel-books and the covers of 2 gospel-books.

---

[573] That is, a panel-shaped work of art. We learn from *LE* iii. 50 that it was, in the early twelfth century, if not before, set up in front of the altar in the shrine of St Æthelthryth.

[574] At p. 196.16, ed. Blake, we perhaps need to emend as follows <*que*> *super divitias regionis Anglie precipui* (genitive of value) *estimabatur . . .*

[575] In E, this last sentence is differently placed and chapters 114–17 are not in the same order as in F or in Blake's edition. E adds here the words which form the last two sentences of chapter 115 in F.

[576] Source: document from the archives at Bury St Edmunds. Date: 1075; with a later addition of perhaps 1081.

[577] The surname 'Angier' or 'Ainger' survives in the Isle of Ely to this day.

19 large crosses and 8 small, and 9 amulets.

8 chasubles: one of them embroidered; another, white with orphrey; another red likewise, another of *purpura*; likewise, another, red with orphrey in front and all around, with two flowers;[578] likewise one of blood-red *purpura* with orphrey in front and all around, with a number of flowers; another red, from which Abbot Theodwine took the orphrey which was on its front; another, from which he took a flower; another ready for use.

8 albs: 1 is of silk with orphrey and with an amice; 6 are with amices and with orphrey; 1 without an amice; 3 amices with orphrey.

3 dalmatics with orphrey and 2 without orphrey.

3 tunicles with orphrey and 4 without gold.[579]

15 stoles with maniples with gold.

2 pendant-strips with gold.

44 albs with the same number of amices with gold.

43 pendulous cloaks.[580]

5 palls with gold and 5 without gold, which are placed over the saints.

6 altar-palls with gold with 5 coverings.

33 copes: 4 of them with gold, others without gold.

3 *taiselli*[581] for use with copes.

14 chasubles with gold; 18 without gold.

6 sets of priests' vestments and 7 of deacons' vestments.

2 stoles with silver embroidery and 6 maniples with silver embroidery.

4 tapestries.[582]

3 altars with silver.

13 reliquaries with silver and gold.

3 silver thuribles.

2 silver candle-sticks.

3 silver straws.[583]

30 hangings.

20 woollen back-hangings.

50 bench-covers.

---

[578] Lat. *floribus*.

[579] Here, and in a number of subsequent references to vestments, the document as recorded in EF makes simple reference to 'gold' (*aurum*), whereas G refers to orphrey (*aurifrisum*).

[580] Lat. *pallia pendentia*.

[581] Janet Mayo, *A History of Ecclesiastical Dress* (London 1984), p. 39, suggests that 'tassels' were 'probably ornamental plates or buttons sewn on to the orphrey, to which were attached the bands or morses that held the cope together in front'. In Norman French, *tassel* could mean 'clasp', as well as 'tassel', 'fringe'.

[582] Lat. *tapeta*.

[583] Used for the administration of communion wine. See Migne, *PL* clxvi, col. 1427A.

7 pastoral staves; Robert, Abbot *de Cruce* had the seventh.[584]

2 tapestries for altars: two *capitalia*[585] and 4 *arcones*[586] and 6 borders of hangings.

2 caskets with silver.

1 embroidered maniple.

The items that follow were not in the aforesaid document.

This is a supplement witnessed by the monks themselves, at the time subsequent to which Godfrey took the abbey into his charge.

2 silver chalices with patens and one gold one with a paten.

5 copes, 2 with orphrey in front and all around; 2 without gold, 1 with a fringe; 2 fringes; 2 stoles with maniples with gold.

2 dalmatics.

1 tunicle.

1 alb with an amice and with orphrey.

[115. About the death of Abbot Theodwine; and that he left Godfrey as custodian in his place.[587]

The aforesaid Abbot Theodwine had, in fact, lived in Ely only briefly but – as we have already established – very beneficially, when he departed from the concerns of mankind, and left Godfrey, a monk of this same monastery and a man in all respects loyal to himself, as his proxy. This Godfrey, with the permission of the king and the protection of the monks of this same church, remained its faithful custodian for nearly seven years, devoting himself to its interests no less than if he were abbot. And around the date of his own departure, on which he was to be translated to the abbacy of the church of Malmesbury, he grieved that <the church>, seeing itself as it did surrounded by wolves, <had been> harassed not a little as a result of the absence of a shepherd.[588] He did, none the less, on his own initiative, successfully lay

---

[584] The reading of E: *vii baculos*, is accepted here.

[585] 'Head-pieces' of some kind.

[586] 'Curved pieces' of some kind. The mysterious word *arcones* seems to derive from OF *arçon*, a diminutive of the word for 'bow'. For a range of possible meanings, see OED s.v. 'bow'.

[587] Source: local tradition on the succession of abbots. N.B. This chapter does not occur in this form in E. See above on the different endings of chapter 113 in E and F. Date of Theodwine's death: 1075 or 1076; Godfrey's custodianship lasted till 1081, when he became Abbot of Malmesbury. On the dating and status of the document, see Blake, pp. 412f., 426; also now D. Bates, *The Acta of William I*, no. 116.

[588] Reading conjecturally at p. 197.26ff., ed. Blake, e.g.: *Et ipse circa discessus sui terminum, quo ad Malmesberiensis ecclesie regimen erat transferendus, <ecclesiam> non modicum ex pastoris absentia vexatam <es>se doluit, que lupis undique circumdatam se vidit.*

claim to the liberty of the church of Ely as set forth in writing below. But soon he caused it great sorrow by his departure.][589]

116. In the sight of which prominent men the possessions of the church were ratified.[590]

In the year from the incarnation of the Lord 1080, in the 11th {recte 3rd} year of the indiction, there being 26 epacts, on the second day of April, there was a consultation[591] concerning the abbey of Ely. This abbey, having been for fourteen years deprived of the protection of King William and stifled by unjust exaction of taxes on the part of his servants, was afraid, under this oppression, of being utterly extinguished. But, in the time when the monk Godfrey was custodian of the properties of the lady saint, the king at last, prompted by awareness of the mercy of God, gave instructions to prominent men assembled by the Bishop of Bayeux to discuss these matters, an examining court of the three nearest counties having been assembled at Kentford.

At this debate many people were frequently present, of whom we have recorded in writing below a number who brought an end to the dispute by their reliable affirmation of the official decision. Four abbots – Baldwin of Bury St Edmunds, Wulfwold of Chertsey, Wulfcytel of Crowland, Ælfwold of Holm – with their men, French and English; the king's envoys – Richard, son of Earl Gilbert, Haimo the steward, Tihel de Helion[592] – sheriffs similarly with their men: Picot, Eustace, Ralph and Walter, as representative for sheriffs Roger and Robert;[593] Hardwin, Wido, Wimer, Wihumer, Odo, Godric, Norman, Colsuein, Godwine, and also very many proven French and English knights from the counties of Essex, Hertford,[594] Huntingdon and Bedford.

---

[589] On Godfrey's character and his work at Malmesbury see William of Malmesbury, *Gesta Pontificum*, v. 271.

[590] Source: up to 'charters' in the last paragraph of the translation, local document in the form of the minutes of a meeting, in an elaborate prose style with rhyming effects; at the end, a transition passage presumably added by the compiler. Date: ostensibly, 2nd April, 1080, but the date is distrusted by Blake, p. 426 and Bates, no. 118, who see this chapter as conflating the findings of several enquiries in the period 1075/6 X 1081/2.

[591] Eng. 'consultation': Lat. *discussio*.

[592] See W. Page, G. Proby, H. E. Norris, *Victoria History of the County of Huntingdon* (London 1926) for the identification of this adventurer's home as Helléan near Ploermel in Brittany.

[593] The counties thus represented by sheriffs and their deputies were Cambridgeshire, Huntingdonshire, Essex, Suffolk and Norfolk.

[594] As in *LE* ii. 92, *Hereford*, *Herford* refers to Hertford (p. 198.17, ed. Blake).

Thus: the venerable immunity of this Liberty[595] is constituted in accordance with the absolute integrity of the way in which the sainted queen held her possessions from the outset and is confirmed by the privileges of King Edgar and King Æthelred [[and]] King Edward, in view of the fact that these possessions were restored by the effort of holy men, and most of all by that of Æthelwold, and amply exempted by their financing of it from all power of secular authorities; and a curse of damnation has been set down in writing, and acclaimed by general assent, upon people who malignantly make efforts to contravene it.

The provident and benevolent assiduity of the king has provided safeguards to ensure that no claim should be able to disturb this most valid consultative investigation and most circumspect ordinance, corroborating it with instructions, confirming it with edicts, augmenting it with benefactions, and defending it with charters, one of which the sequence of events demands should be set out in writing below, as it is pertinent to our present subject-matter.

117. Charter of the king about the liberty and dignity of the monastery.[596]

William, King of the English, to all his faithful people and to the sheriffs in whose shires the abbey of Ely has lands: greeting. I direct that the abbey is to have all its customary rights, namely *sake* and *soke*, *toll* and *team* and *infangentheof*, *hamsocne* and *grithbryce*, *fihtwite* and *fyrdwite*, within the borough and outside, and all other emendable forfeitures on its own land with respect to its own people. It is, I say, to have these customary rights just as it had them on the day when King Edward lived and died, in accordance with the investigations extending through several shires conducted at my command at Kentford before my tenants-in-chief: Geoffrey, Bishop of Coutances, and Abbot Baldwin, and Abbot Æthelsige and Abbot Wulfwold and Ivo de Taillebois and Peter de Valognes and Picot the sheriff and Tihel de Helion and Hugh de Hosdeng and Goscelin of Norwich and a number of others. Witness: Roger Bigod.

These transactions in the times of the monk Godfrey brought about for the church of Ely a considerable consolidation of its position. By what sequence of events this man Godfrey attained to the position of ruling over Ely we have briefly related.[597]

---

[595] 'Liberty': 'a district within the limits of a county, but exempt from the jurisdiction of the sheriff, and having a separate commission of the peace.' So OED.

[596] Source: monastic archives, cf. cartularies CDGM, British Library, MS Add. 9822, fo. 15v; concluding comments by the compiler. Date: Blake's dating, 1080 X 87, is discussed by Bates, no. 122.

[597] Here in E there follows a chapter-heading introducing what Blake, in line with F, prints

118. That King William moved Godfrey to Malmesbury from Ely and there appointed in place of him Simeon, who, contrary to custom and the dignity of the place and the instruction of the king himself, received consecration from the Bishop of Lincoln, without the knowledge of the sons of the church.[598]

Now, after Godfrey had been translated to the abbacy of Malmesbury, Simeon, the venerable prior of the church of Winchester, the brother of Walkelin, the bishop of that same church,[599] was sent, at King William's command, to be abbot of the church of Ely. Considerations recommending Simeon's person at the time in question were his venerable old age, his cleanness of living, his benevolence of mind and the frequency of his almsgiving – and his goodness endeavoured to exceed in its grand scale his reputation, which had reached the ears of many people.

So, having taken up his position of office, Abbot Simeon augmented his past endeavours by new works, specifically: raising up the church of Ely on a new foundation and concurrently building, with total commitment of effort, the rest of the monastic buildings,[600] his object being that the outward achievement should bear witness to the mood within,[601] and that it should not be vice but virtue which would be present in abundance as the accompaniment of wealth, and that whatever earthly substance the hand of the Almighty had conferred upon him should not now be the raw material of degenerate idleness but of spiritual activity.

Also, despite the fact that he was presenting a pious spectacle of himself to people living near and far off, and his concentration was fervently being directed to one particular end – that the territory and the religious life of Ely should flourish again in his times – he became exceedingly[602] anxious, in the first years of his tenure as superior, about his consecration as abbot. He was, however, for some considerable time prevented from attaining to this, the main reason being that Remigius, Bishop of Lincoln, considered, contrary to law, that the consecration was his right, whereas what King Edward laid

---

as chapter 139. The chapter-heading has been erased except its initial *quod*, 'that', but presumably was equivalent to entry in the index which runs: 'That the aforesaid abbot Godfrey caused a written account to be made of what else he had found in the treasure-stores.'

[598] Source: local commemoration of Godfrey's successor, Abbot Simeon; a brief succession list of earlier abbots of Ely is included. Date: 1081 or 1082, see Blake, p. 413.

[599] Bishop of Winchester 1070–95.

[600] Lat. *novo scilicet ecclesiam Eliensem suscitans fundamento reliquasque officinas toto annisu coedificans.*

[601] Lat. *ut interiorem affectum exterior testaretur effectus.*

[602] Reading conjecturally at p. 201.1, ed. Blake: *nimis* for *minus.*

down, and Pope Victor confirmed, was that the abbots of Ely might receive their ordination from whichever bishop they preferred, without the obedience that belongs to subordinate status – a liberty of which previous abbots up until his days took advantage. The scheme of this work seems to demand that at this point the order of their succession be written below.

Well then: St Dunstan of Canterbury and St Æthelwold, Bishop of Winchester, who bought the aforesaid monastery from King Edgar in exchange for some land of theirs and no small amount of gold, blessed the first abbot, Byrhtnoth by name, on the orders of that same king. After Byrhtnoth's death, at the orders of King Æthelred, the aforesaid Æthelwold appointed another man, named Ælfsige, in his place, and conducted the consecration himself. At the same time, indeed, there was a certain monk Ælfwine, who had progressed in virtues to the point that he was chosen by the same King Æthelred to take charge of the bishopric of Thetford,[603] but who was, however, a life-long friend to the aforesaid monastery. It was for this reason that it came about that he blessed two abbots there, Leofwine and Leofric, as they succeeded at different times, and this on the orders of King Cnut. After Leofric, Cnut appointed Leofsige as abbot, and gave instructions that he be consecrated at Woolwich by Æthelnoth, Archbishop of Canterbury. After Leofsige's death, King Edward instated Wulfric as abbot in the same place, whom he had appointed at Winchester, and there he had him blessed by Stigand, twice[604] Archbishop of the city of Canterbury. After Wulfric's death, before King William had conquered England, King Harold gave orders that Thurstan should be raised to the rank of abbot by Stigand.

Bishop Remigius, acting in defiance of this custom and liberty, made it his endeavour, in the case of Simeon, to usurp the right of blessing the abbot of Ely, and stirred up serious conflicts between himself and the abbot in question on this account. And each of them for a long time held fast to his contention, and defiance of this sort disturbed the peace on both sides, though the letters of King William instructed that the ancient discretionary power[605] with regard to the ordination of an abbot was to be preserved. However, Simeon was compelled by the insistence of his brother, Bishop Walkelin, to receive consecration from Remigius. For his brother, seeing that he was encumbered by extreme old age and fearing that he would die without consecration, with difficulty persuaded him in the end, by prolonged urging, to give his agreement to this, so that he would be consecrated, no matter how, by Remigius – setting aside the discretionary power of past generations

---

[603] Strictly speaking: the bishopric of Elmham.

[604] Problematic: see Blake's note *ad loc.*

[605] 'Discretionary power': Lat. *auctoritas.*

he custom of his church. However, with respect to this ordination he firm to the proviso that the bishop should not lay claim to this right against the next abbot as a settled issue, but that his remaining successors should have complete liberty to contest it, a liberty just as free as it ever was for anyone before him.

The monks of Ely, therefore, on hearing that their abbot was returning with his right violated, shut the doors on him, closed the gates, did not receive him as a father, as a brother, as a †welcome†[606] guest, but repulsed him as an enemy. And his overthrow would have been complete, had it not been that, thanks to the mediation of his brother, Bishop Walkelin, the firm stand of the brothers broke down into love of him and changed to acceptance of him as father, on account of his religious devotion, the improvement of the monastery, and the visible evidence of his labours.[607] And so, having gained acceptance, Abbot Simeon presided over the brothers and the monastery in a beneficial and honourable manner, expending all his effort on the building-up, numerical enlargement, material resources and religious devotion of the brotherhood and monastery. And now, through the increase of his virtues, he attained the grace of the heavenly Lord to such an extent that He showed that he was pleasing to Him by means of divine revelation.

119. How William, Earl of Warenne, after his death, was damned in respect to his soul.[608]

The fact is this: Earl William of Warenne [at this time] stole certain vills from the brothers of Ely by violent means. As a result, after having been frequently castigated by the abbot and not induced to mend his ways, he ended his days in a miserable death. This was happening a very long way from the Isle of Ely and the abbot had lain down for the night, at rest in the dormitory, meditating on heavenly things, when he suddenly heard the soul of the earl, who had been carried off by demons,[609] crying out with a distinct and recognizable voice: 'Lord, have mercy! Lord, have mercy!' And immediately, in a chapter-meeting the next day, he told all the brothers what he had heard, and that the earl in question had died. And, to be sure, he had not yet heard other reports of this. But following the elapse of the third or fourth day afterwards, the earl's wife, sending a hundred shillings to the church of Ely for his soul, conveyed the news that the hour of his death had been the very

---

[606] Reading conjecturally at p. 202.8, ed. Blake, e.g.: *non salut<ar>em ut hospitem* . . .

[607] Lat. *operum evidentia*, this might specifically be interpreted as 'the visible evidence of his building works'. Throughout subsequent chapters, *opus* frequently means 'building work'.

[608] Source: miracle narrative, included in B *(Book of Miracles)*.

[609] Reading at p. 202.20, ed. Blake, with BE: *a demonibus portatam*.

one which the abbot had indicated. But neither the abbot nor any one of the brothers deigned or dared to accept his hundred shillings, not considering it safe to keep the money of one who was damned.

For the rest, what liberties, dignities and possessions the abbot in question acquired for his church, what claims he quashed through legitimate argument and royal favour, what powers he succeeded in winning, how often he vindicated the liberty of Ely in public debate, can be understood with the greatest ease from the royal charters which the church possesses.[610]

120. A charter of the king about the giving back of the church's properties by their usurpers.[611]

William, King of the English, to Archbishop Lanfranc and Roger {recte Robert}, Count of Mortain, and Geoffrey, Bishop of Coutances: greeting. I command and instruct you to cause to be assembled for a second time all the shires which were present at the meeting concerning the lands of the church of Ely held before my wife came, most recently, to Normandy. Together with them let there also be those of my barons who shall be able, as is appropriate, to attend, and who attended the aforesaid meeting, and who hold lands of the same church. When they have been gathered together, let there be chosen a number of those Englishmen who know how the lands of the aforesaid church lay on the day when King Edward died, and let them bear witness there on oath as to what they have said on that subject. When this has been done, let the lands be restored to the church which were in its demesne on the day of King Edward's death, exceptions being made of the ones which people †shall claim†[612] that I have given them. Submit those, indeed, to me under seal, in writing, indicating which they are and who holds them. People, on the other hand, who hold thegnlands,[613] which they undoubtedly ought to hold from the church, are to make an agreement with the abbot as best they can, and, if they refuse, the lands are to revert to the church. Let this happen too in the case of people who hold *soke* and *sake*. Finally, give instructions that the people who are to construct the bridge[614] of Ely are those

---

[610] The text of E is followed here. F adds at the end: *que adhuc in eadem continentur ecclesia*, 'which are still kept within the same church'.

[611] Source: monastic archives; document perhaps identifiable with Ely, Dean and Chapter, charter no 1, which Blake reports to be 'legible only in parts'; copies also in cartularies CDGM. Date: 1080 X 1087 (Blake); 1081/2 X 1083, before 18th July (Bates, no. 120).

[612] Reading with D: *clamabunt* rather than *clamabant* EF 'used to claim'.

[613] On tenure by thegns in the eleventh century, see Harmer, *Anglo-Saxon Writs*, pp. 52f.: 'Thegns were persons of high rank, some under the immediate lordship of the king, some under the lordship of other persons.'

[614] Lat. *pontem de Ely*; the term *pons*, 'bridge' could equally be translated as 'causeway'. An

who have up to this time, at my behest and according to my specification, been customarily engaged in its construction.

121. Again, another instruction about the same matter.[615]

William, King of the English, to Bishop Geoffrey and Robert, Count of Mortain: greeting. Cause to come together all those who hold lands of the church of Ely on the basis of supplying their landlords with food, and my will is that the church should hold them just as it used to hold them on the day on which King Edward lived and died. And if anyone should say that on this basis he holds anything as a gift from me, send word to me of the extent of the land and how it is that he is claiming it and I, according to what I hear, will either give him lands back in exchange, or take some other action. Bring it about also that Abbot Simeon shall hold all customary rights which pertain to the abbey of Ely, as his predecessor held them in the time of King Edward. Bring it about also that the abbot is put in possession of those thegnlands which belonged to the abbey on the day when King Edward died, if those who hold them refuse to come to an agreement with him. And summon to this meeting of yours: William of Warenne and Richard the son of Earl Gilbert and Hugh de Montfort and Geoffrey de Mandeville and Ralph de Belfou and Hervey de Bourges and Hardwin de Scalers, and others whom the abbot shall name to you.

122. Another charter of the king about the giving back of the church's properties.[616]

William, King of the English, to Archbishop Lanfranc and Geoffrey, Bishop of Coutances: greeting. Cause the Abbot of Ely to be put in possession again of the following lands which the following people hold: Hugh de Montfort, a manor called Barcham; Richard, son of Earl Gilbert, Broxted; Picot the sheriff, Impington; Hugh de Berners, three hides; Bishop Remigius, one hide; the Bishop of Bayeux, two hides; Frodo, brother of the abbot,[617] one manor; the two carpenters, one hide and three virgates, providing that the abbot can demonstrate that the aforesaid lands[618] are from the demesne of his church, and providing that the aforesaid men are unable to demonstrate that they

---

area adjacent to the Stuntney causeway is still known locally as 'Bridge Fen'.

[615] Source: monastic archives; copies also in cartularies CDFM. Date: 1082 X 1087 (Blake); perhaps late 1082, earlier 1083 (Bates, no. 119).

[616] Source: monastic archives; copies also in cartularies CDG. Date: 1082 X 1087 (Blake); 1081/2 X 1086, but perhaps 1070 X 1086 (Bates, no. 121).

[617] Not Abbot Simeon, but Baldwin, Abbot of Bury.

[618] Reading, with E, at p. 205.4, ed. Blake: *terras* for *terres*.

had held these lands as a gift from me. Bring it about also that the aforesaid abbot has *sake* and *soke* and other customary rights, as his predecessor had them on the day on which King Edward lived and died.

123. A charter of the King about the five hundreds in Suffolk.[619]

William, King of the English, to Archbishop Lanfranc, Geoffrey, Bishop of Coutances and Robert Count of Mortain: greeting. Cause Abbot Simeon to have his *sake* and *soke* just as his predecessor did in the time of King Edward – specifically, with reference to the five hundreds of Suffolk – and have it from all men who hold lands in those hundreds. See that the aforesaid abbot does not injuriously bring about the destruction of anything, and see to it that he holds all his properties with great honour.

124. The king's order prohibiting the Bishop of Lincoln or the secular judiciary from suing for customary rights within the Isle.[620]

William, King of the English, to Archbishop Lanfranc and Bishop Geoffrey and Robert, Count of Mortain: greeting. Prohibit Bishop Remigius from suing for new customary rights within the Isle of Ely. For I do not wish that he should hold anything there except what his predecessor held in the time of King Edward, that is, on the day on which that specific king died. And if Bishop Remigius wishes to sue in respect of this issue, let him sue in respect of it just as he would have done in the time of King Edward, and let this suit be held in your presence. Let Abbot Simeon be exempt with respect to the garrisoning of Norwich, but let him cause his own fortress in that place[621] to be consolidated and guarded. Cause the plea to be stayed concerning the lands which William de Eu and Ralph Fitz Waleran and Robert Gernon are claiming. If they refuse to go to law on that matter on the same terms on which they would have previously gone to law in the time of King Edward and in accordance with the way in which the abbey at that time held its customary rights, I desire that you should bring it about that they hold them entirely in such a manner as the abbot, through his charters and through his witnesses, may be able to establish as correct.

---

[619] Source: monastic archives; copies also in cartularies CDG. Date: 1082 X 1087 (Blake); 1081/2 X 1087, possibly 1081/2 X 1083 (Bates, no. 124).

[620] Source: monastic archives; copies also in cartularies CDG. Date: 1082 X 1087 (Blake); 1081/2 X 1087, perhaps 1081/2 X 83 (Bates, no. 123).

[621] See below, chapter 126, for a further reference to this fortress of the Abbots of Ely in Norwich.

125. That King William gave instructions that the Abbot of Ely be blessed by an archbishop according to the ancient usage of the Church; and that he gave orders that the place's lesser and greater properties be listed in full.[622]

William, King of the English, to Archbishop Lanfranc: greeting. I wish you to look at the charters of the Abbot of Ely and, if they say that the abbot of the place in question ought to be given his blessing wheresoever the king of that land instructs, I command that you yourself are to bless him. Additionally, see to it that those who have been accustomed to constructing the bridge of Ely construct it with no making of excuses. Enquire through the Bishop of Coutances and through Bishop Walkelin and through others who have caused the lands of St Æthelthryth to be recorded in writing and attested to on oath: how they were attested to on oath, and who attested to them on oath, and who heard the oath, and which lands they are, and how large they are, and how many, and what they are called and which people hold them – these matters to be taken note of with precision and written down. See to it that I quickly know the truth of the matter through your brief and that an envoy of the abbot comes with it.

126. An instruction of the king that the original customary rights arising from the liberty of the former church be preserved undiminished.[623]

William, King of the English, to Archbishop Lanfranc and Geoffrey, Bishop of Coutances and Count Robert. I command you to bring it about that the Abbot of Ely without delay has his blessing and his lands and all customary rights, as I have frequently instructed you by means of my writs. And, whatever he has acquired through suit of law concerning his demesne, let no one grant anything from it to anyone, except by my permission; and do for him what is right at the bench of pleas,[624] preventing anyone from cutting down his woodlands. Let him have his own fortified place in Norwich and let his men be there when the need arises and let him hold all his possessions with honour. Witness: Roger *de Lureio*.

---

[622] Source: monastic archives; copies also in cartularies CDG. Date: 1082 X 1087 (Blake); 1081/2 X 1087, probably 1085 X 1087 (Bates, no. 127).

[623] Source: monastic archives; copies also in cartularies CDG. Date: 1082 X 1087 (Blake); 1081/2 X 1087 (Bates, no. 125).

[624] Or 'customary place for meetings': Lat. *sede placitorum*. *Sedes* is a 'sitting-place' or any fixed venue for particular events. *Placitum* is the standard term for 'meeting' in *LE*, but was also commonly used in the more specialized sense 'plea', and indeed the English term 'plea' derives from it.

127. That the king was keen to discover by detailed enquiry how firmly based the foundation of the place is.[625]

William, King of the English, to Archbishop Lanfranc and Geoffrey: greeting. I desire that the consecration of the Abbot of Ely, which Bishop Remigius claims, may remain unsettled until I learn, by means of your letters, if Remigius has demonstrated, or will be able to demonstrate, that his predecessors had consecrated abbots of Ely.[626] Let what pertains to Christianity be done in that abbey and, as for the customary rights in respect of which Remigius is laying claim to wine, let him have them, if he can demonstrate that his predecessors had them in the time of King Edward. Let the mill of Cambridge which Picot has constructed be demolished, if it is being a nuisance to the other mill. Let the abbot be put into possession of the demesne lands of St Æthelthryth as I have instructed on another occasion. People who hold other lands, or *soke* or *sake*, should make their recognizance to the abbot, and hold their lands by service, or else surrender them.

[[**128. A charter of the King about *Estona*.**[627]

William, King of England, to Bishop W. and Bishop S. and to Chaplain R. and to his justices and to Walter, Sheriff of Gloucester and to all his faithful people, French and English: greeting. You are to know that I have granted to Bishop Hervey that land which Harscoit Musard gave to him, with my permission, namely *Estona*,[628] and I am willing that he should hold it honourably. Witnesses: W., Chancellor, and Urse de Abetot, on the Isle of Wight.]]

129. About a certain brother who had gone out of his mind but was cured by the merits of St Æthelthryth.[629]

The purpose, brothers, for which Christ the Lord so frequently brings about

---

[625] Source: monastic archives; copies also in cartularies CDG. Date: 1082 X 1087 (Blake); 1081/2 X 1087, perhaps 1085 X 1087 (Bates, no. 126).

[626] Or 'the abbots of Ely': the Latin, *abbates de Ely*, could be interpreted either way.

[627] Source: this charter, though printed by Blake as chapter 128, is not in E or the main text of F; nor is it included in the Ely cartularies. It appears in the margin of F added in a later hand, identified by Blake as probably that of O. Dated by Blake to 1096 X 1098. Though belonging to the reign of William the Conqueror, it does not fit in with the sequence of charters illustrating Simeon's abbacy. Rather, it concerns Bishop Hervey of Bangor, who was to become the first Bishop of Ely in 1109.

[628] Probably Aston Somerville, Gloucestershire.

[629] Source: miracle narrative also included in B *(Book of Miracles)*.

through His saints evidences of his activities is so that the faith of hearers may increase as the outcome of what they hear, and so that ardent love may loosen devout lips for the praises of God. Hence, at the present time, it is incumbent upon us, whose life and tongue Christ has charged with His service, either to bring His deeds to the notice of many people by means of our studious endeavour, or most decidedly to bring reproach upon our knowledge in His sight. So then, in order that we may make our memory commendable before God, let us relate what He has deigned to bring to pass amongst us who are involved in the church of Ely.

When Abbot Simeon of blessed memory was presiding over us, our community and monastic house certainly made no little progress both in moral well-being and in wall-building.[630] For the place had been seriously destabilized by repeated changing of personnel and by the king's delegates and, if there had been any cooling of ardour for strict observance of the rule – because of the violent action on the part of worldly powers and the absence of an abbot in control – that holy man, once he had taken up his office as pastor, brought about its reform with devoted solicitude. And, being a good shepherd, he found among us a good flock, and to this shepherd's voice the flock, as soon as quiet was restored, hastened to listen. And since there was a breathing forth of reciprocal affection towards the shepherd on the part of his most lowly flock, and the sacred order was being brought into flower once more amidst these gardeners, the hand of the Lord did not fail to support such a high degree of alacrity: rather, He came to greet those most happy workers with the applause of miraculous feats. For, while the place was advancing internally and externally by a two-fold process of building, and the effort of the father and his sons was exerting itself to the utmost in the work of Martha and Mary, miracles began to happen among the citizens of Heaven, some of whom Father Simeon had brought from the church of Winchester and others of whom he had found in that of Ely.

As a result, our ancient Enemy, seeing that concord between the brothers had conspired against him, and that the weaponry of spiritual merits confronting him was increasing day by day, began to attack the walls of morality with manifold ingenuity and, not finding with ease a means of gaining entrance, finally committed the following act of malice against the militia of Christ.

A certain youth called Edwin was standing for Compline in the presence of the abbot and the others, in silent thought at first. The Devil persuaded him to leave the choir before the hour of that office was completed. And, straight away, to everyone's astonishment, he seized him cruelly, subverting his whole mind into raging madness, so much so that he would have struck

---

[630] Lat.: *moribus et muris.*

his master, Siward, who was in pursuit of him, with a board[631] which he had picked up, if the man's foresighted energy had not interposed greater strength to obstruct him.

And there was one of the monks from Winchester there, Godric by name, a man of great holiness and, on account of his reverence, brought to Ely by the abbot to be an exemplar of the religious life for the monks of Ely. God frequently opened this man's spiritual eyes and had made him renowned for many revelations. Nor was it necessary to look for a guarantor, other than his manner of life, to vouch for things he said, as everyone knew that he considered a lying tongue like an enemy. Well then, this man, as he related afterwards, saw someone black, like a boy, holding firmly on to the youth's cowl and dragging him forcibly after him, and the outcome of the incident proved that it was a spirit who had been damned.

Without delay, when the service was over, the abbot and the community, as they went out to the first entrance of the cloister, saw the demoniac youth raving against everyone, making wild threats, flailing around with abuse,[632] and trying to hurt some of the men who were constraining him within their arms, by kicking with his feet and biting with his teeth. And the abbot, summoning with his nod some of the older and sounder men, broke the night's silence by a brief talk with them, saying: 'We know no one who may better come to his aid than that lady whose servant he is: once presented to her he will, so we believe, recover rapid sanity. Go then, and taking him along under close custody, spend a vigil close to the tomb of this lady of ours, diligently; pray for help.'

The brothers, together with their brother, took refuge, so to speak, with their mother, and kept vigil almost the whole night awaiting God's mercy. From the outset the young man – no, the demon within the young man – finding the presence of the holy body unendurable, for some time behaved in a most horrible way, now shouting out, now tearing his tunic with his teeth, and causing not a little trouble to those whose watchfulness was restraining him from evil actions. And thus he spent the night till the approach of day until, thanks to those famous[633] merits of the virgin saint, he fell asleep for a little while, recovered his reason and, shortly afterwards, ejected his tormentor through his foul orifices.

For after his sleep, the young man, coming to his senses, gave word to his guards that he was now feeling well and had completely recovered in all

---

[631] Lat. *tabula*, which might be any flat wooden object from a plank to a panel-picture, or even a liturgical percussive board.

[632] Reading at p. 209.9, ed. Blake: *conviciis insultantem*, cf. **B** (*Book of Miracles*) : **convitiis**.

[633] Translating the text as in p. 209.20, ed. Blake: *meritis sancte illis virginis*; but perhaps read *illius* for *illis*.

other respects, except that the internal looseness of his stomach was torturing him, and was in need of evacuation in a privy. After being taken, therefore, to the necessary place, he experienced as great an efflux as if all his bowels were being poured out and, after the raving of his mind, such a stink of the stomach was ejected that the air throughout all the nearest domestic buildings was scarcely bearable, as the polluted exhalation spread itself through every nook and cranny, and scarcely anyone escaped its vapour. And this uncleanliness was no less extreme than the former madness, but rather, both attacks turned out equal, one to the other: one horrible because of his going out of his mind, the other astonishing, because of the effluvium of his stomach, as if that most evil spirit was either totally being changed into excrement or, on being ejected, was taking the latrines themselves with him.

However, the servant of the Lord, on being freed by the hand of the lady, was astounded at their recounting such things about himself, being seemingly unaware of what he had been doing. He provided, by the example of his case, an object-lesson of how great was the awesomeness of the holy community, coming into[634] whose presence the insidious Temptor was afraid to enter the brother, whereas, on finding him outside, wolf had thus attacked sheep. We would have written this down while the brother was alive, were there not a fear that the evil Waylayer would be given a pretext for tempting him, and would reckon that something which deserved to be reported as good news from Heaven was redounding to his own discredit.

So, this outcome marks the end of the course of this narration, the import of which is that the power of Æthelthryth should be held in honour in the memory of the sane, and that common prayer should be regularly observed with the greatest devotion and that no monk should go wandering off outside the monastery at the statutory hours. For everywhere the Adversary meets us, at the ready, and if he should discover a poor little sheep wandering outside the proper limits, he attacks violently, rejoicing mightily in the losses of the church, whose warfare is as terrible to him as an encamped army in battle-array.[635]

130. About two dumb men.[636]

After this miracle there followed another which, once heard, is bound to bring about a delightful outpouring of the gifts of God upon well-wishing minds. One of the miracles was made manifest in a different manner from the other, but with equal glory. There were two men, dumb from birth, who

---

[634] For 'coming into' the Latin has simply *in* +acc.

[635] Song of Songs 6.3 Vulgate: *terribilis ut castrorum acies ordinata.*

[636] Source: miracle narrative also included in B (*Book of Miracles*).

lacked human speech: one was called Ulf, the other Ælred. They could not demonstrate functionally the notions of the intellect which were conceived by them, as they had the harmony of their voice obstructed, and possessed their rationality not in the functioning of the voice but in nature alone. For, as regards the definition which dialectic makes concerning such people: fitness for reasoning – that fitness whereby, according to dialectic, 'any man is fit for speaking, even if the ability to speak has never been present in him'[637] – was present in these men as an isolated entity. Therefore, in order that 'ability' might be added to 'fitness', both of the men in question, at different times certainly, but in a similar frame of mind, approached the body of St Æthelthryth, making their prayers for the gift of speech by means of emotions rather than voices. Nor did the betrothed of the Lord fail to respond to such great devotion but, to the glory of Christ and her own glory, she restored full fluency to Ulf, but, in the case of Ælred, it was her wish that a human educative process should succeed, and just as boys starting from syllables are taught the whole art of rhetoric,[638] similarly the aforesaid man, having been taught human words by a gradual process, subsequently gave utterance to complete thoughts.

In the case of both men, therefore, the extent of the power of our lady saint was demonstrated, and so was her will, through the fact of her doing in the case of one what she could have done in the case of both. She intimated, in the case of the second man, how much she loved her servants, whose assistance she elected to use in collaboration, so to speak, with herself, for the carrying out of the miracle. For she would have been capable with the greatest ease of restoring the same state to both men in the same way, if she had not assigned to one of them this particular route consisting of taking advice. In this she followed the Saviour God Himself who, though capable of having cured the eyes of a blind man by speech alone, preferred, by a mysterious dispensation, to restore them to the light by means of mud and spittle.[639] Many other things, too, come about in this manner: what they impute to our lady Æthelthryth, with respect to the character of her action, is not powerlessness, but a similar dispensation.

---

[637] Unidentified quotation. 'That rationality has something to do with language; that one can be rational but silent; or noisy in the way of a parrot, but irrational; that one can be the sort of being that does so-and-so, even if one is oneself unable to do that: these are all commonplaces, not tied to any one school': so Nicholas Denyer (pers. comm. 2.1.02). For a seventeenth-century view of the problems at issue, with references to classical sources, see A. Deusingius, trans. G. Sibscota, *The deaf and dumb man's discourse* (London 1670; facsimile reprint: *English Linguistics* viii, Menston 1967).

[638] Lat. *ut pueri sillabis ad plenam dictionem instruuntur.*

[639] John 9.6.

131. About Picot the sheriff, who brought many discomfitures upon this church.[640]

While narrating the glories of the Lord and His mighty works and the miracles which He has performed in respect to St Æthelthryth, we have become a marvel in our own sight, daring as we do to venture with insipid diction into subject-matter of such grandeur, most worthy of rhetorical declamation or the voice of angels. But there is consolation for us in this matter: the simplicity of the apostles, who were appointed to preach the faith of Christ and the salvation of the World, while orators and philosophers were spurned. To their magisterial authority all learning is made subject, lest in verbal sapience the cross of Christ should be made vain. Hence the faithful listener is to expect here facts rather than words, and he is to venerate and revere with his whole mind the sublime occurrence which will be narrated in simple style. And while there are many pieces of evidence which might restrain the aspirations of any powerful men, whoever they might be, from invading rashly the lands of the saints, it is, however,[641] particularly in this man's unexpected and unheard-of death, that there is a clear object-lesson to be learnt: in what a salutary manner belongings are returned, by no matter whom, to their possessors; also that, in contentment with what is one's own, one should not transgress the ancient boundaries which one's fathers laid down.

Well then, the county of Cambridge had fallen by chance to the lot of Picot, a Norman by race, a Gaetulian[642] by temperament. A starving lion, a footloose wolf, a deceitful fox, a muddy swine, an impudent dog – in the end he obtained the food which he had long hankered after and, as if the whole county was one carcass, he claimed it all for himself, took possession of the whole of it and, like an insatiable monster bent on transferring the whole of it to his belly, did not allow any one to be a sharer of his portion – not God, not an angel, none of the saints, not – and this is what I am leading up to – the most holy and famous Æthelthryth, who up till then had owned a great many properties – lands or vills – in that same county, by the gift and grant of prominent people of former times.

He was approached several times by a number of people, saying that it was not in his best interests to mutilate the portion of the virgin and to diminish her liberty, to send forth his scythe into the harvest of another; that he should be content with what was his own, mindful of Æsop's dog and the popular proverb, for fear that, 'while thirsting for all,' he should 'lose all'. In reply to them he said: 'Who is that Æthelthryth whose lands you say I have

---

[640] Source: miracle narrative also included in B (Book of Miracles).

[641] Reading with E and B at p. 210.35, ed. Blake: tamen.

[642] The Gaetuli were a people of north-western Africa.

usurped? I know nothing of Æthelthryth and I will not let her lands go'.

Dost thou hear these things, O Lord, and keep silence?[643] How long, O God, shall an enemy send forth reproaches? It is not to us, O Lord, not to us, but to Thee that an 'enemy hath sent forth reproaches' and a 'foolish' man 'hath assailed Thy name. Have regard to Thy covenant' and 'be not forgetful of the voices of thine enemies'[644] who have said, 'Let us take possession of the sanctuary of the Lord as an inheritance.'[645] For he hath said in his heart,[646] 'God hath forgotten. He hath turned away His face, so as not to see to the end.'[647] Dost Thou hear these things, O Lord, and keepest silence? Rise up, then, Lord, and shatter the arm of the sinner and the Evil One!

'The sin of that man shall be sought and not found.'[648] Hearken, ye islands, and hearken, ye peoples far off, what the Lord of all the World, her betrothed, did for the lady ruler of the Isle of Ely! 'That man's sin shall be sought,' he says,[649] 'and not found.' 'Sought' by whom? By Him to whose sight nothing is hidden. By whom is it not to be found? By no one of mankind certainly, since today it is not known where he has gone, why he has fled or how he has perished: whether he has gone down to the Abyss alive, with Dathan and Abiron,[650] or has entirely gone to destruction, having changed into a beast, in company with Nebuchadnessar,[651] or has perished in some other unspecified manner, doomed to everlasting damnation. Glory be to Him who has given victory over the enemy.

132. About Gervase, who was extremely hostile to the people of St Æthelthryth, and used to torment them.[652]

Now, that man – the most vile man in the populace – who thought to destroy the inheritance of the Lord, was removed from our midst, as we have previously explained, 'like the dust which the wind blows forth from the face

---

[643] Here the rhetoric moves into a yet more high-flown register, drawing extensively on the Old Testament. There follow several allusions to Psalm 73.18–23 Vulgate = 74.18–23 RSV.

[644] The last three allusions are to Psalm 73 Vulgate = 74 RSV, vv. 18, 20,23.

[645] Psalm 82.13 Vulgate = 83.12 RSV.

[646] Psalm 52.1 Vulgate = 53.1 RSV; also Psalm 9.34/10.13 Vulgate = 10.13 RSV.

[647] Psalm 9.32/10.11 Vulgate = 10.11 RSV

[648] Psalm 9.36/10.15 Vulgate = 10.15 RSV.

[649] *Inquid* (p. 211.23, ed. Blake) introduces, in imitation of classical rhetoric, an objection by an imagined adversary.

[650] Ecclesiasticus 45.22.

[651] Daniel 4.28.

[652] Source: miracle narrative also in B *(Book of Miracles)*.

of the Earth'.[653] He was imitating none but him who fell [when cast forth] from Heaven, with all his abominable confraternity, headlong into Hell.[654]

For, indeed, he had followers, who were the administrators of a perverse taxation, the enactors of trickery. But God 'hath scattered the proud in the imagination of their heart.'[655] One from among them, Gervase by name, full of evil, ignorant of good, a perpetrator of anger, a deviser of crime, confused holy with unholy.[656] To him, as being one who was more loyal than the rest, his master, the aforesaid Picot, had entrusted the business of the whole shire on behalf of his evil self.

This man was extremely hostile to St Æthelthryth's people and, as if he had undertaken a special campaign against her, assailed the whole of her property with oppression, whenever he could. So everyone who was for whatever reason oppressed by him, confronted him with the name of the lady saint, with the aim that he might act with greater restraint: he would put one in fetters, pronounce condemnation on another, keep calling another to court, keep on afflicting another with cruelty. The abbot, indeed, finding the daily complaints of his people hard to bear, gave instructions to the community to chant seven psalms close to the tomb of the holy virgin, to obtain mercy from her.

Little time elapsed before the abbot himself was summoned to court and the date and place for the enactment of the proceedings was fixed. The brothers therefore were urged to pray and then the abbot set out on his journey. He was already on his way when he heard that his belligerent prosecutor had ended his life with a miserable death. The order of events whereby this thing came about was as follows.

On the night preceding the day on which the abbot was to come there, St Æthelthryth appeared in the form of an abbess with a pastoral staff, along with her two sisters, and stood before him, just like an angry woman, and reviled him in a terrifying manner as follows: 'Are you the man who has been so often harassing my people – the people whose patroness I am – holding me in contempt? And have you not yet desisted from disturbing the peace of my church? What you shall have, then, as your reward is this: that others shall learn through you not to harass the household of Christ.' And she lifted the staff which she was carrying and implanted its point heavily in the region of his heart, as if to pierce him through. Then her sisters, St Wihtburh and St Seaxburh, [[who had come along with her,]] wounded him with the hard points of their staves. Gervase, to be sure, with his terrible groaning and horrible screaming, disturbed the whole of his household as

---

[653] Psalm 1.4. Latin text repunctuated, without a comma after *ventus* (p. 212.3, ed. Blake).

[654] Cf. Isaiah 14.12.

[655] Luke 1.51, from the *Magnificat*.

[656] Unidentified hexameter line.

they lay round about him: in the hearing of them all he said, 'Lady, have mercy! Lady, have mercy!' On hearing this, the servants came running and enquired the reason for his distress. There was a noise round about Gervase as he lay there and he said to them, 'Do you not see St Æthelthryth going away? How she pierced my chest with the sharp end of her staff, while her saintly sisters did likewise? And look, a second time she is returning to impale me, and now I shall die, since finally she has impaled me.' And with these words he breathed his last.

Now that this outcome had been arrived at, people went to meet the abbot; the matter was recounted, the abbot returned, and the report spread through the whole of the country. The lady saint became feared among all those who lived nearby, and for a long time none of the nobles, judges, administrators or men who had any power, dared to commit any outrage[ous theft] with respect to the property of Ely, because the holy virgin protected her possessions everywhere in manful fashion. And it is apparent in her case, how wonderful, with respect to His saints, is God, who lives and reigns for ever and ever. AMEN.

133. That the Lord God, placated by the prayers of the holy virgin Æthelthryth, averted His indignation and anger from this place.[657]

We are urged by the words of the prophets to sing the mercies of the Lord for evermore and hence, so that we may not be adjudged ungrateful for the benefactions of God, it is entirely fitting always to praise and glorify Him who brings to pass death and life, who casts down and raises up. And in the case of the subject-matter of which we are giving a summary account, albeit not in a very learned way, let us extol without ceasing His indignation and His graciousness, His judgement and His truth.

Now, a pious tradition of the faithful records the action which we are recounting as having happened in the time of Simeon, whom we have mentioned previously. This abbot was reviled with abuse by the monks on the ground that, as we have related above, he received consecration, as he ought not to have done, from the Bishop of Lincoln, this being contrary to the custom of the place. Anger had been disguised, though not stilled, but in the mean time,[658] despite the fact that he had found in that monastery a pious and good flock dedicated to theological studies, he reckoned he would have achieved nothing unless he were to hand over the place's positions of authority to outsiders brought from elsewhere. And although there was no logical reason why this should be done, he obtained royal permission for it. Empowered by the king's authority, he brought monks, ten in number, from

---

[657] Source: miracle narrative also included in B *(Book of Miracles)*.

[658] Two elements in the Latin sentence are transposed here for the sake of clarity.

Winchester, into whose control, so he reckoned, he put all positions of office, whether concerned with internal or with external administration. As the result of this, the church to this day, enduring its tribulations with heavy resentment, aches with sorrow, as is made clear from what follows.

But one of them, Godric by name, characterized by religious devotion and a pious disposition, was like a star shining amid clouds. In view of his reverent attitude he was entrusted with taking care of the church, and he was unique in directing his effort in all things towards the will of God, not towards savagery and domination, as is the custom of outsiders. He was inspired solely by the things which are of Christ; he was entirely devoted at night to vigils without ceasing and by day to psalms and meditation. One night, at an hour later than the brothers' customary vigils, he was wearying his aged limbs by withholding them for a very long time from the rest which is the due of the flesh, when, right amidst the sighing of his heart and the manifold petitions of his devout prayers,[659] his strength failed him, and, though sitting rather than lying down, he fell asleep. Whether it was in his sleep that he was shown such a vision, or whether it was outside the functioning of his mind – either way, he saw himself being snatched up suddenly into Heaven. In truth, what we are relating ought not to be a matter of doubt to any of the faithful: it is as if the brother who had seen it were still alive and telling of it.

So then, the venerable man saw things which were delightful in the extreme and worthy of remembrance, being full of all joy: namely, the mercies which the Lord has brought to pass and displayed to us. But it customarily happens among men that there are things, many and great, which, †although†[660] they are serious, are <treated>[661] with scant caution and reckoned as not in need of correction. It is revealed by clear factual evidence – even sometimes from Heaven, with what precision of scrutiny they are examined before the eyes of the Judge who dwells within us, because, as is evidenced by the matter under consideration, they were not at all unimportant, but caused deep displeasure. But, with regard to our sins: while vengeance is what the Judge's balanced assessment[662] is provoked by them to demand, the goodness of this same Judge converts the strictness of His severity into the gentleness of leniency. Pope Gregory of blessed memory makes this point, saying: 'The mercy of the Redeemer has changed the

---

[659] Here I translate as if the reading at p. 213.28, ed. Blake were: *crebra orationum devotarum precamina.*

[660] Reading conjecturally at p. 213.35, ed. Blake: *quam<vis> gravia sint.*

[661] Reading conjecturally, *loc. cit.*, e.g.: *minus caute <tractentur> et non corrigenda estimentur.*

[662] Reading with B (*Book of Miracles*) at p. 214.1, ed. Blake: *equitas iudicis* (rather than *iudicii*).

severity of the law into gentleness.'[663] But let us hear, now, how the thing was.

That man, in some <way> or other,[664] stood, as it seemed to him, in the highest Heaven before the judgement-seat of the glory and majesty of God, near to which there stood a queen, of star-like brightness, who was, however, groaning and in anguish, totally immersed in a flood of prayers for her servants and children: she was trying, with supplication, to win over the mercy of the Thunderer.[665] Straight away, then, he saw some personage in the distance holding a bow, stretched with an arrow, in his hand: someone sent by the Lord against the church, to deal it a piercing wound. Then the Lord, in his mercy, was moved by the prayer of his beloved virgin, and gave orders that the person whom He had previously directed to take vengeance should now be recalled. And immediately, after being recalled by those standing nearby, he set aside his weapon from killing.

As a result of seeing these things, Godric was severely shaken in his sleep, and woke up. Recalling to mind the sequence of events in the vision, he reflected inwardly on it with groaning, and came to understand that the person he could see had been sent [across] to no other place but here – Ely[666] – to wreak destruction. He believed, indeed, that he was under an obligation to make tearful entreaties to God about this matter, so that He who mercifully spared Nineveh would [now] not deny us pardon for our sin.

At that same time, a number of men from the monastery were being snatched away into the sleep of death; some were becoming seriously ill;[667] a large part of the brotherhood was languishing in the infirmary, already close to death though feebleness of body. As a result, a great fear arose in everyone, as each saw before him a colleague either dead or dying, and, if anyone was [in danger of] perishing in this same calamity, he hastened to cleanse his conscience and to wipe away the rust of sin by the making of confession, one to another. And it came about, while they were all vigilantly intent on freeing <themselves> in readiness for salvation,[668] that the brother previously mentioned, as usual, set about †putting himself directly at God's

---

[663] Gregory the Great, XL Homiliae in Evangelia, ii. 33, 1597, Migne PL lxxvi, col. 1243.

[664] Reading conjecturally at p. 214.5, ed. Blake: *quoque <modo>*.

[665] Cf. Bede's poem on St Æthelthryth, cited in LE i. 33, for the identification of the Christian God with Jupiter, the wielder of the thunderbolt.

[666] Here, at p. 214.14, ed. Blake, I have translated the reading of BE *huc*, together with the clarificatory gloss in F: *ad Ely*.

[667] Here, at p. 214.16, ed. Blake, I translate *invalescebant* – the reading of B as well as EO – as 'became ill', a non-classical but well-attested MedLat usage. MedLat. F's *ingemiscebant* must have been a conjecture by someone who doubted its correctness.

[668] Here, at p. 214.22, ed. Blake, I translate as if the reading were *dum sic <se> expedire cuncti circa salutem vigilanter intenderent* . . .

disposal†[669] with sorrow and weeping, for the sake of the brothers' salvation and for the protection of the monastery, until such time as they should obtain grace from God and the aid of the blessed Æthelthryth. And while he was standing tirelessly the following night, maintaining constant vigil, he finally won the reward of seeing during sleep things such as are to be related. So it was that the Lord, once more, gave him a further revelation of His mighty works.

And he looked and – behold! – as he raised up his eyes, round about the high altar where the bodies of the blessed virgins lay concealed, there arose from their tombs human forms of female appearance, clothed in the habit of nuns, wielding crosiers in their hands. These he reckoned for certain to be our saintly ladies, Æthelthryth, Wihtburh, Seaxburh and Eormenhild. They proceeded from there through the choir to the cloister and thus came right to the infirmary. Walking slowly behind them, he perceived that they stayed there for three or four hours. Indeed, she who is our sole solace and hope after God and His Mother, that lady and advocate of ours – for ever manifesting a devout compassion from the depths of her inward being, just like a mother towards her sons – approached each man's bed, on her way around the house, touched the head on the pillow most gently with her hand, and removed by wiping with the edge of her cloak or the sleeve of her tunic, whatever dust or noxious dirt she pressed down upon. As the ladies were returning by the same route, Godric prepared, fearful though he was, to confront them, being dazzled by the brightness of their facial appearance, it was with difficulty that he eventually dared to step forward and humbly asked them to say who they were, or what <they meant>[670] by going around the monastic buildings while everyone was struggling in danger of death. One of the ladies, whom he recognized well enough from his previous night's vision, walking ahead of the others, approached him, as if masking her appearance, and began to speak to him with these words: 'I whom you see [am] Æthelthryth, the mistress of this place, [and I] am spoken of as the lady who constantly intercedes for your sins before God; I am she whom you earned the privilege of contemplating, in the middle of last night, amidst the choruses of the blessed, pleading with the majesty of God; and now in this time of mortal disaster I have been on a visit to the infirmary with my beloved sisters so that together we may bring these men assistance for their recovery.' After she had said this, he woke up with a jolt, and the heavenly vision disappeared.

And behold, it came to pass that all the men who had been sick from

---

[669] Reading conjecturally at p. 214.24, ed. Blake: *apud Deum se prorsus addiceret* . . . (cf. *afficeret* B).

[670] Reading conjecturally at p. 215.5, ed. Blake, e.g.: *et quenam essent vel quid tunc <intenderent> officinas girando cunctis in discrimine mortis laborantibus, ut edicant, suppliciter rogat.*

different diseases suddenly recovered, and, thanks to the merit of St Æthelthryth, health called back to life all those whose sickness was deathlike. And when morning came, the abbot – and the few men who had narrowly escaped that disaster – rising at daybreak, hastened to the infirmary, where sick men in peril used to face the hazard of death. But now he caught sight of them all walking through the *atrium*,[671] glorifying God for their health and fitness! And there were men whose breathing, of late, had been totally unreliable, in whom a state of recovery was now immediately brought about that was better than their previous state, with no lessening of strength! Then, marvelling at everything that had happened, they remembered the report which had been told them about the brother who had related his vision.

There was something further that happened, and one must marvel greatly at this latter miracle. To explain: the abbot and brothers most earnestly wished that the outcome of the matter be set down in writing, as a guaranteed record of a chastisement, for the attention of posterity. Among them, at that time, there was a certain monk called Goscelin, a most eloquent man: all around England he brought about a transformation of the lives, miracles and deeds of the saints, male and female, by setting them forth in histories, and in liturgical sequences.[672] Now, at the time when that other man, Godric, by the will of God, penetrated the mysteries of Heaven, the eye of his heart being opened wide – at the same moment and hour this man Goscelin, not allowing himself the sleep of idleness, was, by chance, devoting his attention to the sequence of St Æthelthryth, the beginning of which is: '*Christo regi sit gloria . . .*' {'Glory be to Christ the King.'} Also included in it is another verse: '*Astat a dextris regina, interventrix alta. Hinc dat terris miracula.*' {'There stands on the right a queen, an exalted intermediary. From here she bestows miracles upon the lands.'} By the fact that he composed this sequence in this way, with God's will as his inspiration, while still unaware of what had happened, he became, figuratively speaking, the recipient of a miracle. And when he presented the composition in public, they all expressed thanks to God and to St Æthelthryth, and decreed that the sequence should henceforth be sung in memory of that act of veneration.

In this happening, one observes three noteworthy things: first, that our God and Lord should not be provoked some day by our wrongdoings and consequently be compelled to exact punishment; secondly, that we are not to

---

[671] Lat. *atrium*: presumably, some kind of forecourt, lobby or entrance hall. Remarkably, Ely in the twenty-first century has a 'health and fitness' centre called 'the Atrium Club', named without awareness of its eleventh-century predecessor; rather with the '*atria*' of the heart, and the concept of 'openings', in mind. (Kathy Bradney, pers. comm. 12.2.01.)

[672] Eng. 'in histories and in liturgical sequences': Lat. *in istoriis, in prosis*. The extent of Goscelin's contribution to Ely hagiography is assessed in Rosalind Love's *Goscelin of Saint-Bertin and the Lives of the Female Saints of Ely* (Oxford 2004).

let our hope in His mercy flag either in good times or in bad; thirdly, that we should glorify Him who, when He wills, gives inspiration to whomever He wills, and to the extent that He wills. To Him be glory throughout all ages. AMEN.

134. That King William harassed the church severely a second time; and about his decease and where he lies buried.[673]

At that[674] time, to be sure, the whole of Scotland, with all its troops of warriors, was endeavouring to revolt against our King William and to oust [him] by force. Intrepid as he was, he hastened to confront them with a naval and cavalry force †and reduced them to submission, as a preliminary to driving them forth, for he had triumphed, now that their head had been cut off, being by now superior to them in strength.†[675] In the midst of this, Malcolm, King of Scots, on meeting him, became his man.

Now, King William had given orders to both the abbots and the bishops of all England that their obligations regarding military provision should be fulfilled, [and] he laid down that, from then on, garrisons for the kings of England were to be paid for, as a perpetual legal requirement, out of their resources, with a view to military campaigning, and that no one, even if supported by the utmost amount of authority, should presume to raise an objection to this decree. This decree has worn down the Church of the English, founded though it was in the glory of freedom and,[676] from that time, it has not ceased to harass the Church to an intolerable extent, as if it were capable of extinguishing it.

And when notification of requirements of this sort was brought to the Abbot of Ely, he was most deeply aggrieved on account of the extremely long process whereby the energy of his house had been sapped. Sorrowfully, he entered into consultation with the brothers as to what should be done. His aims were these: they should console him, like good sons, in this difficult situation of hardship, huge in scale though it was, and they should safeguard

---

[673] Sources: some material in first paragraph from the Worcester Chronicle on the year 1072, and in last paragraph from the same chronicle on the year 1087. Otherwise, the source is presumably a local narrative about Abbot Simeon, with allusion also to the *Book of Lands*, meaning the *Inquisitio Eliensis*.

[674] Reading with EO: *tunc*.

[675] The text of the obelized passage (p. 216.11f., ed. Blake) is exceptionally difficult because of unaccountable changes of tense; the translator can do no more than guess an approximation to the intended meaning. I render here as though *reddidit* were the reading in place of *reddet*. But difficulties remain: there is no agreement of number in the clause *fortiores . . . triumphaverat*. The *Worcester Chronicle* is one of the sources being used in this passage, but it appears that some other material is being clumsily conflated with it.

[676] Reading conjecturally at p. 216.18, ed. Blake: *et inde . . . non cessat*.

the peace of the monastery by intense supplication before the piety of their holy mother Æthelthryth; nor should they cease to speak out openly – something which they judged most advantageous. At the consultation, the abbot received the advice to approach without delay the king's majesty; he should remind the king of the extent of the liberty with which the place had been endowed, when received [from him], dedicated to eternal quietude as it was on the authority of kings and popes; reminding him, too, that it was neither proper nor expedient to oppress it now with intolerable and unprecedented exactions: rather, that an affront to the bountiful virgin was something to be feared above all peril, since there has been no potentate or king, ever since the Lord removed her from the body, who, after posing a threat to her monastery, with respect either to its dignity or to its resources, has not speedily died a despicable death. He had become sufficiently aware of this, too, where his own men were concerned, but, for the sake of God and the salvation of his soul, caught up as he was, more especially, in troublesome involvement in other matters †<he had kept silence in order to>⁶⁷⁷ avoid becoming constricted by criminal proceedings against him on a charge of this magnitude. But if the king <should> grant in due season <that>, contrary to what happened on his taking over of his new kingdom†⁶⁷⁸ he would not now weigh the monastery down with the yoke of perpetual slavery, he {the abbot} would promise numerous prayers before the Lord and, in addition, a subvention of money, in accordance with his request.

But the king spurned his prayers and donations, and did not cease to eradicate statutes in an evil manner: instead, meaning to add further weight to the yoke, he instructed the abbot to keep under the king's orders a garrison of forty knights for the Isle. Saddened as the result of this, the abbot, on his return, hired knights – retainers of his own, however, and men of good birth, who were loyal to him – and equipped some more with armour. Moreover, in accordance with the king's command, he maintained, as a matter of custom, the previously stipulated military contingent within the congregation's hall,⁶⁷⁹ receiving its victuals and wages daily from the hand of the cellarer – a measure which could have distressed the monastery to an intolerable degree, beyond all limits.

In fact, as a result, the abbot, not of his own volition, and not from favouring the rich or from fondness towards relatives, permitted usurpers, such as Picot the sheriff, Hardwin de Scalers, Roger Bigod, Hervey de

---

⁶⁷⁷ A lacuna is marked here (p. 217.6, ed. Blake) and a supplement suggested, e.g.: *aliorum potius correptus incomoditate, <tacuisse se ut> tanti criminis reatu constringi vitaret*, as a rather desperate expedient to account for the imperfect subjunctive, *vitaret*.

⁶⁷⁸ Reading conjecturally (p. 217.7, ed. Blake): *Quod si maturius praestaret ut . . .* What follows: †*non ut in translatione nunc novi regnit*. . . is a very puzzling muddle. The whole obelized passage is exceptionally hard to construe.

⁶⁷⁹ Lat. *aula*.

Bourges, and others, to hold in fee certain lands of St Æthelthryth, as the *Book of Lands* reveals,[680] but none of them on terms of complete lordship.[681] This was to enable him to comply with the king's behest every time he went campaigning, and to ensure that the church would be permanently spared exhaustion, and would survive.

And, not long after these happenings, the need arose for the king to make haste to Normandy. Then, on arrival in France with his army he set fire to the town of Mantes and all the churches in it – and two recluses. But not long afterwards, just as he was on his way back, an intestinal pain gripped him and he realized that the day of his death was imminent, and it was on that same day that he died. To be precise, it was for twenty years and six months that he held sway over the English, and he was buried at Caen. His successor was his son William.

135. That, when Abbot Simeon was failing in strength, a certain retainer of his took possession of the estate of Witcham, and some other people, of other properties of the church.[682]

Well then, William, surnamed Rufus, had been received as successor to the throne after his father, but soon, as a result of these circumstances, enormous dissension arose between the leading men of the kingdom: one section of the nobility – though a very small one – was in favour of the king, but the other side was in favour of his brother Robert, in this following the advice of Bishops Geoffrey of Coutances, William of Durham and Odo of Bayeux, whose desire was to hand him – [the king] – over alive to his brother Robert or deprive him of his kingdom by assassination.

The king, therefore, observing that great danger was threatening him, [now] demanded from the churches, using violent means, the obligatory service which his father had imposed. And now that the kingdom had been [for a second time] stirred up by insurrection,[683] the Church of the English people was everywhere weighed down by innumerable incumbrances. On the Abbey of Ely, in point of fact, †<he imposed a demand for >†[684] four-score knights, that is to say, he now compelled forty knights from those whom his father had stipulated should be kept on the Isle as a garrison, to be made

---

[680] That is, the *Inquisitio Eliensis*.

[681] Lat. *nullam vero penitus de dominio*.

[682] Source: local narrative commemorating Abbot Simeon.

[683] Reading with E (at p. 218.9, ed. Blake): *regno seditione commoto*: words in square brackets translate supplementary material from F, which has *regno in seditionem nunc iterum commoto*, 'now that the kingdom had now for a second time been stirred up to sedition'.

[684] At least a main verb, e.g. *iniunxit*, needs to be supplied here (p. 218.11, ed. Blake).

ready, as a matter of obligation, for campaigning on his own behalf.[685] Abbot Simeon, on realizing this, let forth groans of unspeakable deepness, calling upon God as Judge with respect to the things which they had done to him. For now, although he had scarcely completed seven years as abbot, he had grown old †<and the heaviest> possible†[686] incumbrances were multiplying all around the place, and deprived of strength as he was, he had become incapable of going out and about to look after his interests.

At that time, certain wicked individuals, fearing neither God nor men, did not shrink from invading properties of St Æthelthryth which had twice previously been upheld on oath by the authority of the great king William, first when Thurstan was in charge of the affairs of the church, and once again under Simeon, on the instructions of the same king. And, although he was enduring sorrowfully every day the tearing apart of his properties, Simeon, debilitated though he was [from old age] by no means ceased from [works] on which a beginning had been made: for he completed the domestic buildings[687] of the brothers in a suitable fashion, now laying new foundations for the church which, after the elapse of a great many *lustra*[688] remained incomplete[689] because of concerns which put hindrances in the way, but most of all because the superiors[690] of the place exercised their charge somewhat inefficiently. But the abbot, having become from that time onward extremely incapacitated, started walking around the buildings with difficulty, supported by a stick, and very soon collapsed into bed: for seven years on end there was nothing he could look forward to except feebleness for the rest of his life. For this reason, internally, 'the things that are God's'[691] had begun to cool down, and external affairs, as the consequence of serious upheavals, were threatening ruin. Indeed, subordinates of the abbot and others in whom he used to confide, now that their leadership was enfeebled, returned to their own place, and he was left alone, languishing and wasting

---

[685] The supposition seems to be that a further forty would be required to maintain the garrison.

[686] Reading conjecturally (p. 218.14f., ed. Blake): *Iam enim senerat, cum vix in abbatia septem complesset annos <gravissimaque> queque incommoda circa locum pullulabant . . .*

[687] Lat. *fratrum officinas* (p. 218.22, ed. Blake).

[688] *Lustra* were five-year periods.

[689] Lat. *nova nunc iaciens fundamenta ecclesie, que post plurima lustra, impedientibus curis sed potius loci superioribus curam segnius adhibentibus imperfecta remansit.* The word *ecclesie*, here translated as a dative for clarity's sake, might also be thought of as genitive; but the general meaning would be unchanged. The concluding singular verb shows that what is being represented as incomplete is the church, not the foundations.

[690] Like the reference to 'very many five-year periods' (*plurima lustra*), this plural suggests that the plan to enlarge the minster-church went back well before Simeon's time.

[691] Cf. Matthew. 22.21.

away, and rare was the man who remained steadfastly with him until the end.

Well now, one of the former sort was William, known as *Peregrinus*[692] because of his innate cunning. He was someone whom the abbot had previously raised up from a very lowly position, to bring him the lawsuits of villagers from the outside world. He was an expert in many sorts of cunning deployment of words: he used to further the interests of some people, while obstructing those of others. However, on observing that his master was treated by everyone as burdensome and contemptible, he himself likewise forgot the kindnesses done to him and treated everything concerned with Abbot Simeon as of little account, and took possession for himself of a certain piece of countryside in Witcham from the church's lawful property. It was the Lord's devout worshipper Osmund and his son Agamund who, when hastening to the war in Scotland mentioned above, had given this land to God and the bountiful virgin Æthelthryth as an everlasting source of revenue and, so that no one should alienate it from the possession and provisioning of the monks, the abbot anathematized this very same thing in the presence of a large gathering of the people.

Other people, too, stole several properties, and their descendants right up to this day assert that they hold them as a gift from Abbot Simeon, reckoning it all joy to heap up riches from the stolen property of the church. In the end, however, the abbot thought out a means of thwarting the arrogance of his men, in view of the fact that they did not respond to him when he called them, hating the sight of him in his old age. He summoned justices of the kingdom for a meeting with him, so that they might, in his stead, protect the property of the lady saint against her enemies.

And soon they came in and conducted an investigation in the treasury, assailed many people with contumely, sparing no one – old man, widow, minor or pauper – from money-payments. Then a good-for-nothing man, Ælfwine, surnamed *Retheresgut*, that is, 'cow's paunch', came forward and accused his neighbours of secret dealings, and the Isle was afflicted with great oppression. Ælfwine also asserted himself by contriving trickery against the brothers of this church; what is more, he kept making false allegations against the provost, Dom Thurstan, a man deserving of everyone's praises for his honourable character. And he so roused up Ranulf Flambard[693] against him that he made a demand for the communal wealth over which he, {Provost Thurstan}, was keeping guard. Breaking into the treasure-chest of the church by violent means, he removed from it much money, and very

---

[692] 'Traveller abroad', 'foreigner', 'pilgrim', cf. *LE* iii. 52 (p. 297.11, ed. Blake) for another adverse comment on the character of *peregrini*.

[693] See Blake's note, p. 219, n. 4, for bibliography on this man, later Bishop of Durham.

BOOK II

fine vestments which the aforementioned lover of the Truth[694] had collected
for the service of the altar and the glory of the Lord's temple. At this, the
heart of the abbot became exceedingly fearful, being unable, moreover, to put
right the wrong-doings, because the iniquitous plunderer, in the insolence of
his actions, was now invoking the favour of the young successor-king, as
much as he had invoked that of his father, whose chaplain he was. He
instigated – and refrained from instigating – all things as it pleased him. He
did, however, make an agreement that the following provisions should be
made for the victualling of the monks.

**136. That a certain Ranulf, at the command of the king, instituted an
allowance for the monks, but a meagre one.[695]**

These are the provisions which this same man Ranulf and Abbot Simeon, by
order of King William, decreed should be granted every year for the
supplying of the brothers' needs.

For their clothing: seventy pounds.

For their kitchen: sixty pounds and two hundred pigs for fattening and
the pigs which are fed in the courtyard, and all the cheese and butter apart
from that which is in the food-rent of the provosts,[696] and each week seven
trays[697] of corn and ten trays of malt.

For the lighting of the monastery: the present church with the graveyard
of the town; everything pertaining to St Botulf,[698] with the festival.

And if there should be wine sufficient in quantity,[699] they shall always
have an allowance at the Twelve Readings,[700] and also on Saturday; or
otherwise, a half-measure of mead.

137. How Abbot Simeon cast off human mortality.[701]

And so, hard pressed as he was by these difficulties, the abbot eventually,

---

[694] Lat. *ille amator veritatis*: presumably the reference is to Abbot Simeon.

[695] Source: monastic archives, cf. cartularies CDG. Date: probably 1086–87, though see Blake
p. 220, n. 1.

[696] Lat. *in firma prepositorum*.

[697] Lat. *treias*; a 'tray' was a standard measure equivalent to one-fifth of a quarter.

[698] There was a reliquary at Ely reputedly holding this saint's skull and larger bones (*LE* ii.
138); but see also iii. 90f., on Hadstock.

[699] Outdoor viticulture in Ely is often hampered by cool and cloudy weather in summer.

[700] The 'Twelve Readings' belonged to the vigils of Holy Saturday and the four Ember
Saturdays. (Alistair Macgregor, pers. comm. 16.11.01, citing the *Gregorian Sacramentary*.)

[701] Sources: local commemoration of Abbot Simeon, quotation from an elegiac poem on the same
subject. Date of Simeon's death: 21st November, 1093.

263

with groans of lamentation, voiced his feelings to the monks – that he was answerable before God for his sins and that he had failed them grievously – and he pleaded piteously with them not to despise their father, enfeebled as he was because of old age, and close to death. For:

> Wearied by fullness of years, old age having weighed down upon him,
> Vainly, alas, many times, called he for other men's help.

In fact, although where his many virtues were concerned, he was a force for good, and outstanding in his religious devotion, he is none the less considered to have transgressed seriously in three respects, as the result of ingenuousness, so we believe, not on purpose: in the first place, with respect to his consecration as abbot, undertaken, as it ought not to have been, by the Bishop of Lincoln; in the second place, because, contrary to the custom of the whole Church, he brought along outsiders who, like visitors who were not to stay permanently, did a great deal of damage to the monastery with respect to its relics, ornaments and the ceding of estates; in the third place, because he allowed officials of the king to conduct legal proceedings on the Isle. Nor was he so overwhelmed with grief and insistent in his groaning as to drive the outsiders out of the place or its domestic buildings. Instead, right up until his death, they arranged all its affairs at will, inside, now, as well as outside.

And now Abbot Simeon, full of days, in the course of his hundredth year, passed away, full of virtues, upon St Edmund's Day. He passed away to the Lord of Hosts, to the ranks of the saints, to the kingdom of the heavens, departing from the realm of vices, the dwelling-place of sins, the day of evils. And he left the place where he had held office desolate and sorrowful for seven years after his death, deprived as it was of his own presence and that of other abbots. And we have no doubt but that this man, who held Christ the Lord enfolded in a spiritual embrace, is given a welcome as one fulfilling the role which belonged to that former aged and saintly Simeon, the servant of the Lord who also cradled Christ in his arms,[702] and that as a result he is linked in his reward with one to whom he was linked by his name, and being sharers of a one and the same desire, one and the same meritoriousness will make them companions. For both similarly had a yearning to see Christ; both to be discharged from service and to be with Christ; both yearned to cry out, 'Now lettest thou Thy servant depart in peace';[703] the desire of both, therefore, was fulfilled; each of them knocked and it was opened unto him;

---

[702] Cf. Luke 2.28f. We have here an exercise in *syncrisis*, 'comparison', between two individuals, a recognized literary form inherited from classical rhetoric. For another, see *LE* iii. 93.

[703] Luke 2.29.

each of them found what he sought; received what he asked for.[704] The former Simeon did so once in the body, though symbolically: both of them, in actuality, subsequent to bodily life, not within the changefulness of temporality but in eternity.[705] May their souls, now that they see the goodnesses of the Lord in the land of the living, pray for us who still live in the land of the dying.

To be precise, Abbot Simeon died in the 1093rd year {from the incarnation}, when he had ruled over the community for fourteen years.

138. [The depredations which monks from elsewhere inflicted upon the church of Ely.[706]

But, what evils came to pass once Simeon had been removed from our midst? Or, more specifically, what were the sins that his own men committed? This we make clear, our objective being that it should be 'known among the nations'[707] for evermore. To be sure, the seven monks who still remained from the men whom Simeon had transferred to Ely were grief-stricken by the abbot's death, extremely troubled and utterly shaken; trembling seized them. For they had come to expect that it would no longer be safe for them to remain there; nor was their own exertion capable of keeping the upper hand for a moment; nor, from now on, was everything being done on the basis of, or with regard to, their behest. They now prepared to return to Winchester with all speed.

However, they were afraid to return unprotected and empty-handed, for fear of being accused of ignominious conduct. Hence, fired by pangs of envy, and simultaneously on fire with the heat of covetousness, they attempted to demolish and ruin everything with the greatest avidity, in a monastery where they had never been by any means useful, or, at the most, only in small matters. They therefore put forward specious words, advanced cunning arguments, piled trick upon trick, and put much effort into these endeavours, as if they constituted justice.

Now that the abbot's body had been placed in the church, they made out that it was both their wish and their obligation to pray for him as very much their bounden duty. And, by means of head-nodding and, insolently, with hand-signals, they compelled the local monks, just as they were attending to the exequies of their pastor and abbot, to leave the church and go to eat a

---

[704] Cf. Matthew 7.7f.; Luke 11.9f.

[705] Reading at p. 221.18 (with E): *non temporum mutatione, sed eternitate.*

[706] Source: local text commemorating ev nts following Simeon's abbacy; also included in B (*Book of Miracles*).

[707] Psalm 78.10 Vulgate = 79.10 RSV.

meal. Meanwhile, after immediately locking the entrances, they hid themselves away inside, leapt like madmen upon all the goods and the highest-quality articles, seized and took possession of them for themselves, specifically: the most richly decorated vestments, garments made of silk, and a very valuable and famous hanging, than which none could be valued. or found anywhere round about, that was more precious, for all its decoration[708] seemed covered with gold. What is more, they also hid and kept with them phylacteries with the relics of many saints, irreverently extracted from shrines, and, to top it all, the head of the blessed confessor Botulph and his larger bones, the casket having been violently broken open. And thus, when they had removed these and everything they could lay their hands on, and had provided themselves with a great deal of silver and gold in replenished bags, they wasted no time before departing.

And the deed was done. For on the fourth day, indeed, they succeeded in coming apace to Guildford, full of joy, like men rejoicing, after the defeat of their enemies, at how much plunder there was and at their being victorious. In that place they were received at a guest-house and spent a considerable time in banqueting and drunkenness, with a great fire lit in their midst. The flames suddenly burst forth and the whole house started to catch light. When the revellers noticed this, they escaped outdoors, incapable of doing anything to rescue the doomed house, and leaving all their things inside. By the judgement of God, in vengeance for their trickery, the goods were completely swallowed up in the flames, so that[709] they might not bring to Winchester even a single thing from the great collection of spoils which, in their wickedness, being the unfaithful servants and enemies that they were, they had stolen from the Lord and the most blessed virgin Æthelthryth; instead, the goods were consumed by fire and reduced to ashes.

And when the deed done on their journey or, to put it another way, what had befallen them, was reported and brought to light among their people at the monastery, all alike were reduced to a state of shock and then deep groaning; they took action to assail with reproofs and chastisements the perpetrators of this deed and the outrage of their abominable transgression, and they certainly did not omit to castigate with examination under torture the audacity of their wrongful presumption. This account is well known there and amongst our community's aged members to this day,[710] and they have related it to us in a credible account, so that posterity may learn that loss of goods always comes about where there is administration by outsiders.]

---

[708] Lat. *paratura*.

[709] Reading conjecturally at p. 222.25, ed Blake: *ne* (instead of *nec*) *secum Wintonie ex multa copia spoliarum vel prorsus aliquid deferrent* . . .

[710] The date of the source-document rather than that of the *Liber Eliensis*.

139. [What manner of things Ranulf found in the treasure-chests of St Æthelthryth.]⁷¹¹

*(This chapter exists in two versions and in ms. E is placed after ii. 117, as part of the account of Godfrey's provostship.)*⁷¹²

Version of E

Title erased except for initial *Quod* = 'That . . .' or 'What . . .'⁷¹³

Introduction:
<. . . .> and how, on his personal initiative, the estates belonging to the jurisdiction of St Æthelthryth were recorded fully in writing and defined by the sworn testimony of reliable men, just as he took care to list the ornaments of the treasure-chests, something which we have reckoned ought to be written down here among the rest. The listing of objects was as follows.

Version of F (placed after ii. 138, so that the inventory is assigned to the end of Simeon's abbacy).

Title: [What manner of things Ranulf found in the treasure-chests of St Æthelthryth.]

Introduction:
[Furthermore, the listing of the things which Ranulf found in the treasure-chests of St Æthelthryth after the time of Abbot Simeon, in accordance with

---

⁷¹¹ Source: monastic archives; Blake cites no copies in cartularies. This chapter occurs in different contexts and with different initial material in E and F, the latter correcting the former. Hence the variant chapter-headings and introductions are set out in tabular form, before the inventory which they introduce.

⁷¹² The inventory cannot possibly have belonged to the provostship of Godfrey because of the reference in it to Simeon's abbacy as apparently in the past. Hence the repositioning of the chapter in F after the account of Simeon's death.

⁷¹³ In the table of contents of E there occur two headings which Blake cites as possibly once attached to the inventory recorded here:

Title 1 (listed after our chapter 117): **That the aforesaid Abbot Godfrey caused what he had found in the treasure-chests of the church to be listed in writing.** (The mistaken use of the term 'abbot' with reference to Godfrey, suggests that this heading, if by the compiler, belongs to an early draft of his work. It looks like a variant title for our chapter 114.)

Title 2 (listed after our chapter 113): **That he on his own initiative obtained permission from the king to cause the possessions of the whole abbey to be attested on oath and he declared them to be restored.** (The word translated as 'possessions', Lat. *possessiones*, normally refers in *LE* to lands; cf. the title of our chapter 116.)

the assessment of the whole community, namely seventy-two monks, in whose presence all these articles were exhibited and described {was as follows.}][714]

27 crosses, small and large, and 6 images, from 3 of which a certain amount of silver has been stolen – all the crosses, however, ornamented with gold and silver, and the images similarly.

12 reliquaries, either large or small, with gold and silver applied to them, and 8 unadorned.

14 gospel books, large or small, ornamented with gold and silver.

3 altars, adorned with gold and silver.

2 altar-*tabule*,[715] adorned with gold and silver.

4 frontals, 2 large and 2 small, adorned with gold and silver.

2 thuribles, adorned with gold and silver.

8 phylacteries, 3 adorned and 5 unadorned.

27 chalices, large or small, of which 1 is solid gold and another, solid silver, and the others, completely made of gold and silver; 4 of them lack patens.

3 silver straws, adorned with gold.

3 silver cruets, of which one is gilded.

3 thuribles: 1 is all of silver without gold; another of silver, gilded; a third one of bronze, gilded; and all their chains are of silver.

2 silver candle-holders, adorned with gold, and 4 of bronze adorned with gold.

1 small silver ewer, adorned with gold, and a laver of solid silver.

20 *infulae*, but 6 are ornamented with gold and jewels and 3 are well adorned with orphrey and the others, adorned in one way or another; in addition, indeed, to these, there are 24 *casulae* without ornament.[716]

46 copes, of which 8 are well adorned with orphrey and jewels; the rest are in some way or other adorned with gold thread-work; 2 of them were completed in the time of Abbot Simeon.

102 albs and the same number of amices: of these albs, 2 are finely edged with pall-cloth above and gold thread-work below; and 9 others adorned with pall-cloth below and gold thread-work above; and 44 are adorned around the neck with orphrey, the rest are not adorned, and nor are their amices.

There are 2 girdles: 1 wholly of gold thread-work; the other of pall-cloth, its hanging parts being finely ornamented with gold thread-work.

32 stoles with the same number of maniples: 21 of these stoles are

---

[714] The F version gives nothing equivalent to E's *huius modi erat*, but the sentence is incomplete without something of the sort, and there has been some scribal oversight.

[715] Not altar-tables: these were apparently frontals consisting of board overlaid with precious metals, cf. *LE* ii. 113; iii. 50.

[716] *Infulae* and *casulae* are usually regarded as alternative words for the same thing: chasubles.

adorned with gold and 4 adorned with silver; the others without either.

There are 6 maniples without stoles, of which 1 is finely worked with gold and the others with silver.

15 dalmatics: 5 with gold thread-work applied to them.

9 tunicles: 4 with gold thread-work applied to them.

15 altar-palls, large or small: of these 8 are adorned with gold, 7 unornamented.

23 cloths of which 3 are adorned with gold-embroidered pall-cloth, and 2 adorned with gold-embroidered linen; and 17 are of linen, adorned with pall-cloth.

4 tapestries.

33 woollen back-hangings.

51 bench-covers.

41 curtains.

1 canopy.

And 6 iron and bronze candle-sticks.

1 sprinkler; and 6 staves which are carried at festivals, ornamented with gold and silver.

3 pairs of lavers[717] for the service of the church.

And 23 short of 300 books; of these 19 are missals and 8, lectionaries; and 2, benedictionaries; 22, psalters; and 7, breviaries; and 19, books of antiphons; and 12, books of graduals.

140. How the abbacy was given to Richard, a monk of Bec.[718]

In that period there were some people who were obedient to the will of the king rather than to justice. Ranulf {Flambard}, mentioned above, was one of these. In contravention of ecclesiastical law and the level of his rank – for he was a priest – he received from the king, as his property, first abbacies and then bishoprics, whose fathers {in God} had recently departed this life, and from these sources paid to him no small sum of money every year, particularly at the expense of the abbacy of Ely, which he held for a number of years. For his manipulativeness and cunning were so extreme, and increased in a short while to such an extent, that the king appointed him justiciar[719] and the exactor of the whole kingdom's taxes. Having received such

---

[717] Reading with E at p. 224.6, ed. Blake: *pelvium*.

[718] Sources: *Worcester Chronicle* on the year 1100, including material from Bury St Edmunds interpolations (Bodleian Library: MS Bodley 297) edited in OMT, vol. iii, ed. P. McGurk, p. 317; this material is combined with a local record of the succession of abbots, continuing from previous chapter, which supplied the information that Ranulf Flambard held the abbacy of Ely for some years. Dates of Richard's abbacy: 1100–07 (deposed: 1102, reinstated: ?1103).

[719] Lat. *placitator*.

enormous power, he everywhere, throughout England, mulcted a number of the richer and more comfortably endowed monasteries by the removal of goods and lands, and oppressed the poorer ones ceaselessly with heavy and unjust taxation and, both before his tenure of bishoprics and in the course of it, he harrassed the greater and lesser monasteries alike in many ways, and this continued until the death of this same king. For on the day when this same king died – violently slain – Ranulf held in his control the archbishopric of Canterbury and the bishoprics of Winchester and Salisbury. And William Rufus, the king in question, reigned thirteen years, barring thirty-eight days.

His younger brother, Henry, succeeded him and straight away, on Sunday, 5th August, was consecrated king at Westminster by Maurice, Bishop of London; but it was by Thomas of York that he was crowned. On the day of his consecration he set at liberty the Holy Church of God, which in his brother's time had been sold and used as a source of revenue,[720] and he did away with all the bad practices and unjust exactions by which the kingdom of England was being unjustly oppressed. He established stable peace throughout his kingdom and commanded that it be kept. He brought back into use the laws of King Edward and made them common to all again, with all the amendments by means of which his father had corrected them. But, as for the forests which the last-mentioned king established and controlled, he kept these under his own control. And on the very day of his consecration he gave the abbacy of St Edmund to Robert the son of Hugh, Earl of Chester, and that of Ely to Richard, son of Richard, son of Earl Gilbert.[721]

141. That Abbot Richard refused to accept a blessing from the Bishop of Lincoln, and made it his endeavour to convert the abbacy into a bishopric.[722]

The good character of Dom Richard, Abbot of Ely, in point of fact, calls for an explanation and so, because of this, we present one, at the forefront of our discourse, by adding an account of his ancestral lineage: that he was the son of parents who were both high-born, namely Richard, son of Earl Gilbert and the well-respected Rohais.[723] Though both his parents were of royal descent,

---

[720] Lat. *ad firmam posita.*

[721] see Blake, pp. 188–9, n. 3; p. 190, n. 1, on Abbot Richard's father and grandfather. Confusingly, it appears that it is his father, and not his grandfather, who is consistently referred to in *LE* as Gilbert de Clare.

[722] Source: if not the compiler's independent writing, a local text commemorating Abbot Richard, presumably the encomiastic work on the abbot specifically referred to in this chapter (p. 225.28f., ed. Blake).

[723] That is, he was the son the man confusingly referred to in *LE* ii. 108, 111, as Gilbert de Clare, in actuality Richard de Clare, son of Gilbert de Brionne. The abbot's mother, Rohaise,

the fact is that they dedicated their illustrious offspring to the King of Kings to spend his life as a monk in the monastery of Bec.

Straight away, while he was still a boy, pleasantness of manners began to commend his pursuance of the life assigned to him, and, while progressing up the ladder of virtues with wonderful fervour, he was educating his well-bred mind with an ever higher aim in view. The result was that his demeanour at that age was already admirable and worthy of imitation as much by the old as by the young. And so, having by his exceptional behaviour already shown signs auguring the splendours of his future rank, he measured out the space of thirty years under the discipline of the house. He had also already obtained public recognition to the extent that he ascended from the ladder of moral improvement to the ladder of office-holding: specifically, he was called to the position of being ruler over the church of Ely, on the instigation of God and the recommendation of King Henry, and to the applause of the clergy and people.

On attaining to this rank, he redoubled his aspirations in every meritorious activity of the intellect. In a reciprocal fashion that was pleasing, he made his manner of life more illustrious by his learning, and his learning more illustrious by his manner of life, and he balanced within himself, in more or less perfect equilibrium, the theologian and the philosopher. In fact, he used to emulate the morality of the ancient fathers with regard to what secular knowledge contained that was disreputable or honourable,[724] in some instances pruning it away, in others, retaining it. But because there exists a book specifically about him, in which his praise is set forth in writing at considerable length, let my pen concur with other pens which approach the same topic, and now let the sequel be spoken of, and let what is said be believed: that hostile ill-will, obviously, was the inevitable accompaniment of such great claims to fame.

For, in the first place, Robert, Bishop of Lincoln, launched an attack, saying that it was his right to consecrate him as abbot, arguing that Richard's predecessor, Simeon, had given obedience to his own predecessor, Remigius. But Richard, protesting that, in Simeon's case, the blessing of Bishop Remigius had been given under duress and improperly, kept himself back from consecration by him, on the basis of the legal status of his church and with the backing of much authority. His fear was that it would be a curse, and not a blessing, that he would incur, if he were to allow himself to be blessed in contravention of his lawful right. And so the consecration in question was suspended and there was never to be, thereafter, a consecration of an abbot of Ely, either conducted by a bishop of Lincoln or by anyone else at all. And, to

---

was the daughter of Walter Giffard, and the manor of Eynesbury is reported to have been in her hands in 1086 (see *LE* ii.109 with Blake's note, pp. 188–9, n. 3.

[724] Adopting at p. 225.27, ed. Blake, the original reading of E: *honestum*.

allude to the outcome of the matter and note its cause: perhaps, in the postponement of this consecration, the monastery destined to be converted into the seat of a bishop was auguring its advancement to higher status. Endowed as it was with ancient liberty, and about to be endowed with new, it was prevented from having any part of its lawful position violated.

Now that reference to these matters has been interposed by way of digression, let the story be taken up from where we digressed, and let it be said that there had been a fatherly attitude in Abbot Richard which served his whole flock rather than domineered over it. He added lustre to the place and to the fraternity with rich ornaments and useful individuals, and he accommodated[725] himself to the ways of everyone with marvellous generosity. And if, as commonly happens, such a high degree of generosity would give place to severity in response to a combination of accidental circumstances, he quickly tempered it with the humility of Christ, and did not allow headstrongness to hold sway over himself: instead he controlled all impermissible ardour by means of powerful reason.

And now his steadfastness, deserving as it was of a martyr's crown, began to be worn down by frequent provocation as, after the conflict with the bishop, anger on the part of the king also confronted him, keeping up the attack until he was deposed, as we will relate in the chronologically appropriate place.

142. How King Henry, at the instigation of men of ill-will, expelled Richard from the abbacy; and Richard himself went on a journey to Rome.[726]

The sole factor that brought about his deposition was, for certain, the ill-will of evil men. What caused their hatred to flare up against him was his nobility of mind and birth, which was receiving advancement in honour and becoming pre-eminent in power. The sheer number of his kinsfolk and the abundance of his riches provoked passionate awe[727] in everyone, and constituted a source of fear to those for whom it could not be a source of love. To sum up: when he attended the king's court, he was second to the king alone in the singular way in which he was feared, protected as he was on all sides by a crowd of kinsfolk: that his family consisted of the Richards and Giffards was a fact which the whole of England knew – and felt.

For the Richards and the Giffards, two families, that is, coming from places in close proximity, had made their lineage noble by their reputation for

---

[725] Reading with E: *conformans* (p. 226.14, ed. Blake).
[726] Source: local commemoration of Abbot Richard, as in chapter 141. For information about the Richard and Giffard families, see Blake, p. 226, n. 3. On the deposing of the abbot, and other evidence about the upshot of his visit to Rome, see Blake, Appendix D, p. 413.
[727] Lat. *violentam . . . reverentiam.*

valour and the sheer number of their progeny and, wherever a meeting of nobles took place, their procession was supported by a huge entourage which was terrifying. Moreover, it was no longer safe, in their presence, for anyone at all from among the magnates to compete with them over the reception of guests or the conduct of lawsuits, since frequent killings were carried out at court by their hands and on many occasions they had struck terror into the king's majesty.

As a consequence, Abbot Richard, endowed as he was with great eloquence and noble descent, had incurred the king's hatred, both on the ground that he came to attendances at court with too much pomp, and because he was accused of being contemptuous of the king himself, in his refusal to obey his orders in the way that the other nobles were seen to obey them. In fact it was out of rigorous observance of justice rather than the swollen-headedness of pride that he was not abiding by certain commands of the king: with discerning prudence, he was rendering 'unto Caesar the things that are Caesar's, and unto God the things that are God's.'[728] For, being a man of liberal outlook, he knew that the king was human,[729] and possessed nothing more than other mortals, except that he was given precedence over them by a certain dignity of office. On this reasoning, Abbot Richard was unwilling to bend his will to the king's every behest, or act like 'a reed shaken in the wind',[730] but rather he raised the shield of the Faith as defence against every gale, and, with his foundations not built on sand, but on rock,[731] he was like a second, doubly inspired[732] Elisha.

As a result, therefore, the king's rage flared up against him, and took as a pretext for deposing him the fact that he was not yielding to his – the king's – will in all respects, in that he had such confidence in his nobility of birth that he ejected from his house a jester of his who was insulting him shamefully.[733] And so, now that he had been deposed, the clergy became supporters to the king, zealous devotion to God declined, and fear of the secular authorities[734] became oppressive everywhere: it was impossible to

---

[728] Matthew, 22.21; Mark 12.17; Luke 20.25.

[729] Cf. e.g. Ambrose of Milan, *Epistle* 51.

[730] Matthew 11.7; Luke 7.24.

[731] Cf. Matthew 7.25f.

[732] Cf. 2 Kings (= 4 Kings Vulgate) 2.9.

[733] The Latin (p. 227.17, ed. Blake) does not make it unambiguous whose jester (Lat. *mymus*) was insulting whom, given that classical practice regarding the difference between *suus* and *eius* is not always rigorously observed in MedLat. It seems, however, that the jester belonged to a party other than the owner of the house, and that the latter was also the party subjected to abuse. As Richard must be the person who was deemed presumptuous on the strength of his noble birth, the jester presumably belonged to the king, and the house to the abbot.

[734] Eng.: 'Secular authorities . . . their reputation': paraphrase of Lat. *saeculi . . . cuius famam*.

assail their reputation in ways that were fitting; no one could attack their manner of life, or upbraid them for their character. The work of the church, because of this, went into abeyance for a while: but it was not dismissed from service. The king might indeed think that the abbot's spiritual sons[735] were being disempowered by the abbot's deposition, but glory undiminished was beginning to make their position all the more exalted: sometimes, fear of this glory of theirs had a constraining effect on the majority of the nobles and on the king himself. So it was that, after being deposed, Richard began, in a way which was not disadvantageous to himself, to make a public complaint that he had suffered violence, and that an injustice had been done to him. He started making appeals to Rome and, against the king's will, when he was ordered to return his crosier, kept it, and returned it instead to the church of Ely as one who was going to return, having the brothers' permission to do so. The reason why God's secret dispensation brought this about was to ensure that his good character should become known in that most exalted see, and that he should return in all the greater glory, with authority from Rome.

143. That Richard, coming back from Rome, was reinstated in his post and built the new work[736] of the church begun by his predecessor.[737]

And thus the abbot, having been greatly vexed by the king, journeyed to Rome and, in the presence of the venerable Pope Paschal, who was at that time presiding over the Church of Rome, explained the cause of the difficulty constraining him. Having been favourably received by the Pope and treated with great respect, he obtained what he had petitioned for, was given protection against the ill-will and evil-doing of enemies by means of privileges bearing apostolic authority, was taken back into the grace and favour of the king, and restored to the monastery at Ely. This was with great rejoicing on the part both of the receivers and of him who was received.

The abbot had discovered amidst his difficulties that the blessed Æthelthryth was most merciful, and he was far from neglectful of the building-work which he had begun. Rather, in order to advance the building all the more energetically to its completion, he directed his whole attention specifically towards it, so as to be free for this work alone and, as long as he lived, he built the church begun by his predecessor with as fitting an appearance, and on as fitting a scale, as possible. The result has been that, if Fame is not ill-disposed and, mendacious as she is, does not detract from the truth of its worth and true entitlement, this church seems, by a certain

---

[735] Eng.: 'spiritual sons': Lat. simply: *progeniem.*

[736] Lat. *novum opus ecclesie . . . edificavit.*

[737] Source: local commemoration of Abbot Richard, as for the two preceding chapters.

judiciousness of its compositional design[738] and the superiority and grace of its fine-wrought craftsmanship, worthy to be preferred [deservedly] by beholders above all the churches in the same kingdom, whether constructed in past ages or built anew in our own time.

144. About the second translation of the body of the holy virgin, which the same abbot brought about.[739]

Out of deep yearning, consequently, he desired and purposed to translate the body of the most holy virgin [Æthelthryth], within his own lifetime, from the old church into the new – from a church of moderate size into a larger and more beautiful one. In this he was mindful of the fact that Joseph had translated the body of his father from Egypt into the land of Canaan, so that it might receive greater reverence.[740] His purpose was that so bright a lamp and shining light should not 'hide under a bushel' but rather should be, as it were, 'set upon a lamp-stand' and should become clearly visible and shine forth to the advantage of all,[741] in the presence of witnesses and amid the thronging of multitudes. He fixed a day, namely the sixteenth day {inclusive} before the Kalends of October {recte November}, so that her first translation is celebrated at the same time as the new one.[742] And so, being a man of great and liberal disposition, he issued an invitation first and foremost, with the reverence which he owed and which befitted him, to Anselm, Metropolitan of Canterbury, a venerable and deeply religious man, with the aim of strengthening this solemn ceremony with his solemn and, most of all, his pontifical authority, inviting him to deign to show forth his presence in company with as many of his assistants as he might wish from those of his retinue whom he might consider particularly devout. Invitations also went to as many men as possible of pontifical dignity and honour, and to abbots and religious monastics and other ecclesiastical persons equal to highest pontiffs in merits, if not in dignity, and worthy of comparison with them, not to say preference over them. There were invited by him also nobles and magnates of the kingdom, to attend this most joyful festivity, and so that they themselves might rejoice in the rejoicings of others. Moreover, while some

[738] Here 'compositional design': Lat. *compositionis*.
[739] Source: local material, chiefly from *Vita S. Withburge* CT, chapters 16–18, 21, ed. R. Love; also allusion to Bede and others on the translation of Æthelthryth, and Ælfhelm's *Exhortatio* (= *LE* i. 43–9). A separate booklet *De secunda translatione*, comprising our chapters 144–8, is included in ms. B between books i and ii of *LE*, and this may be a copy of the compiler's source-text, though Blake (Introd. pp. xxxvif.) argues that it could have been copied from *LE*.
[740] Cf. Genesis 50.1–14.
[741] Cf. Matthew 5.15; Mark 4.21; Luke 11.33.
[742] The date, in modern terms, was 17th October, cf. *LE* i. 28.

were prevented from coming by previous private or public engagements or difficult circumstances, others, destined by Divine Providence and well suited for the bringing of this matter – so remarkable for its nature and its grandeur – to its conclusion, and most of all, those people who had close personal connections, came thronging together with great devotion. Among them were Herbert, Bishop of Norwich, a praiseworthy man; Ealdwine of Ramsey; Richard, Abbot of St Albans; Gunter of Thorney; Wido, Abbot of Pershore; Nicholas, Archdeacon of Lincoln; Geoffrey, Treasurer of Winchester and innumerable other men of great honour and authority.[743] In due order, therefore, in an ordered procession, they reverently approached the tomb of the holy and worshipful virgin Æthelthryth, made of Parian marble, pure white, as befitted her virgin whiteness.

Long ago, her most blessed sister, Queen Seaxburh, finding her perfectly preserved corpse sixteen years afterwards, reburied it, milk-white and undefiled, with body and clothes intact, in this tomb, which had been prepared by the aid of the angels and provided by Divine Grace for those seeking it, amid shouts of wonderment and blessings that raised the sound of praises to Heaven. Hence it now accrued to her greater glory that no one presumed to open her tomb or to look into it.

For once, when the pagans invaded this place, one of them made a hole in it as the result of a blow, and was soon deprived of his eyes and his life. Afterwards, an incautious priest, a sort of president of the minster, pushed a piece of twig into that hole and twisted it into a fold of cloth, pulled out part of the garment and with extreme madness cut it off – when suddenly, the hand of her who lay within pulled it back to herself, in vigilant indignation! Furthermore, the assailant proceeded to insert a candle fixed to a rod: the candle, falling on the sacred corpse, burnt out completely and did no damage to anything – but the presumptuous man perished, along with all his household. These matters having been additionally given fuller consideration in connection with the miracles of this same saint,[744] let us return to the narrative.

Finally, with enormous devotion, they lifted the sacrosanct body of the virgin and[745] brought it into the church with praises and canticles. And so the royal lady Æthelthryth, without having been tampered with or looked

---

[743] Blake notes, p. 229, n. 1: 'In the *Vita S. Withburge* this list comes later and enumerates those who inspected Wihtburh's body.'

[744] The grammar here is very unclassical, involving a nominative absolute.

[745] Here, the following expansion, intended to replace the simple 'and', is found in the margin of E: 'carrying it from the old church away from the place to which the most blessed Seaxburh had translated her and where she had buried her, where also the venerable father Æthelwold afterwards, on restoring and rebuilding the ruined church, left her as he found her, most certainly untouched, unmoved and uninspected, not hiding beneath the earth but prominently placed above it; from there they now . . .'

upon, was transferred into a new shrine, full worthy of the praise of the singers, and placed behind the original altar in the prepared bridal chamber. Finally, as was fitting, a sermon was preached to the congregation on the subject of this exceptionally important ceremony, and in the context of it, by[746] the venerable Bishop Herbert, a most eloquent man. With regard to the life and death and miracles of the blessed virgin and the wonderful incorruption of her sacred body, he urged the congregation on to a sign of the supreme joy and happiness that was brought about in the tents of the righteous:[747] you would rarely see anyone in all that congregation – huge though it was – who either wished or was able to restrain himself from tears, being awash with the grace of Heaven.

But of the many things which happened at the translation of the most holy virgin Queen Æthelthryth, we report for everlasting recollection one thing alone, something which countless of the faithful who are still alive, and our fathers who were eye-witnesses and were present, have related to us. The fact of their relating it, and their authoritative standing in life, and the honourable character of their morals, has taught us that no one should have doubts about its having actually happened. It is this. On that occasion there was a repetition of the miracles which one reads as having happened at the discovery of the body of the blessed martyr Stephen.[748] For there came about thunder-claps, storm-gusts[749] and lightning-bolts[750] of such a kind that almost all the windows of the church were shattered by jagged lightning-strikes, and frequent flashes fell down on to the pavement near the holy corpses. And it was a miraculous thing that the fire fell without the effect natural to it amidst wood and straw; and other flammable materials changed their quality, so that whatever of this sort fell into the church was harmless. This great miracle, worked by that saintly woman, happened thus, according to the opinion of some, so that she might show, by means of the terror from Heaven, that she was displeased at being so handled in public, and yet was doing nothing to harm the church[751] in this indignation of hers, with the consequence that it would escape no one's notice that the stars of Heaven were obedient to her behest. There was scarcely anyone present, therefore, whose inward thoughts were not declaring that these things, whose horror he was on the one hand afraid to behold and, on the other, glad to escape, were portents of some great occurrence.

---

[746] Reading: *a* (instead of *et*) *venerabili episcopo Herberto.*

[747] Cf. Proverbs 14.11.

[748] Cf. *Epistula Luciani*, Migne, *PL* xli, cols. 807–18.

[749] Reading with BEO: *tempestates* (p. 230.9, ed. Blake).

[750] Cf. Revelation 8.5.

[751] Reading conjecturally: *ecclesiae* for *et* (p. 230.15, ed. Blake); cf. comparable confusion below, p. 230.31 (with Blake's note *d*).

Archbishop Anselm, too, situated though he was far away in Kent, on seeing the Heaven riven with such tumult, said, 'I know that our brother Richard, the Abbot of Ely, has today translated his lady saints and treated them irreverently, and I have no doubt but that this stormy weather is a sign of ill omen.' Nor was his opinion mistaken, because few of those who were present at the time, and had seen St Wihtburh face to face, survived the whole year. For this reason, most beloved brethren, you who with righteousness and holiness call to mind, not momentarily but continually, the memory of a virgin of such importance, within sight of the presence of her holy body, must pray and most earnestly make supplication that He who caused the water to flow in abundance from the rock, when Moses struck it, for a thirsty people,[752] may †for ever†[753] deign to sprinkle both you and us with the dew of grace. To whom be praise, honour and glory throughout all ages.

145. How he found the other lady saints and how he translated them.[754]

And so, when the virgin Æthelthryth had been placed in the position, so to speak, of doyenne, opposite the high altar, Richard, as the leader of that remarkably large congregation, made known to the senior representatives of the church[755] that now for the second time, on the same day on which the first translation of the blessed virgin Æthelthryth had taken place with St Seaxburh presiding, there should take place the translation also of all the saintly women reposing in that place. And they opened[756] the tombs of the mother and daughter, which St Æthelwold had sealed with lead on both sides, that is, the tombs of the saintly Queen Seaxburh and the praiseworthy and celebrated Eormenhild, with their many privileges of precedence. They found their earthly remains to have decomposed in the manner customary for the human condition, and to have paid their tribute to the Earth, their mother. Now, he found the body of holy Seaxburh in silk and clean muslin – bones and dust placed separately – and both parts in individual boxes made of wood within a stone memorial, as blessed Æthelwold had left her. They repositioned her to the east towards the feet of St Æthelthryth. On the other hand he found the relics of the most holy Eormenhild in an unadorned pavement-tomb, without covering, buried there in this way by St Æthelwold.

---

[752] See Numbers 20.11.

[753] Reading conjecturally – but without conviction – at p. 230.26, ed. Blake: *perpetue* for *per vos sue*.

[754] Source: local, cf. *Vita S. Wihtburge* CT 22, ed. Love. According to Blake, Æthelwold's translation of Seaxburh and Eormenhild is not recorded anywhere else.

[755] Reading, with BEO, *ecclesie* as opposed to *et* (p. 230.31, ed. Blake).

[756] Lit. 'opening', present participle.

Collecting these too in a perfectly clean cloth, and enfolding the dust separately, he replaced them in their former coffin to the south and to the right of St Æthelthryth with not dissimilar care, and he resealed each mausoleum again with lead.

146. That before the solemn enactment of this translation, with a view to the enlargement of the building, he moved the sepulchres of Seaxburh and Eormenhild from their former position where the blessed Æthelwold had placed them, similarly moving the sarcophagus of the bountiful Wihtburh, but careless servants accidentally broke it.[757]

In point of fact, they had moved the famous burial-casket of Wihtburh from its place and positioned it elsewhere in the church four years before[758] the translation of the holy virgins. The fact is that the construction of the church in progress was unavoidably necessitating this, and it could not remain any longer on this side.[759] And because the memorial-sarcophagus was being removed down a descending series of steps and the careless servants were unfit for this task, the lower stone, on which the distinguished virgin was reposing, was broken – at which juncture there appeared a large crack in the sarcophagus! But I believe that it did not do so improvidentially, but so that the power of the Lord should show forth the merits of the holy virgin and should mend the break in the casket by a new miracle.

They moved the excellent queen, blessed Eormenhild, similarly, as the matter of the church's enlargement was an invitation to an exceptional undertaking. In the tower, to be sure, Æthelthryth, queen and famous virgin, was resplendent, entombed on the south side at her own altar, and her glorious sister, Seaxburh, shone forth in solemn grandeur, buried to the north in the same place. These two olive trees of the celestial mercy remained[760] in their place – these olive trees which pour forth the richness of a liquid full of grace for the kindling[761] of the enlightenment of minds, and very frequently remove outward blindness from sluggish hearts. They stood still, I say, these two columns of the house of God, two pearls of the supernal King, totally unmoved until that time of which God had foreknowledge, when He conveyed by inspiration to the faithful His will concerning the need to translate their bodies.

---

[757] Source: local, cf. *Vita S. Withburge* CT 19, ed. Love, but not principally from this source.

[758] That is, in 1102.

[759] Lat. *citra*, 'on this side', presumably in relation to the place where the writer was working or expected his work to be read.

[760] 'Remained': *perseverant* here (p. 231.30, ed. Blake); and likewise *infundunt, remanent, inspirat,* have to be taken as historic presents.

[761] Reading with E: *accendendam* (p. 231.31, ed. Blake).

147. That the abbot prepared a new sarcophagus, but its size was more or less than that of the form of Wihtburh's body; and that he opened to view her sacred body and replaced it in the old sarcophagus, which had been restored by divine agency.[762]

For the glorious Wihtburh, too, the aforesaid ruler of the court of Ely, Richard, had prepared a new sarcophagus to the exact dimensions of the old one, which had been broken long before, so that the incorrupt virgin, when placed in the new sarcophagus, might have an incorrupt lodging-place. But Heavenly Providence rendered this piece of planning vain by means of a new and unusual miracle. For when the new coffin which was to receive the holy body was standing ready, with a rod the length of the previous measurement placed by it, it turned out to be shorter by one foot! Whoever tried to repeat the measurement of them both found it to be no longer: always the new coffin was shorter than the old by the amount aforesaid. They were all dumbfounded in astonishment and ecstasy, seeing their plan for the shrine being frustrated by the dimensions of a body which was too long. Meanwhile, when the cover of the gaping coffin was removed, greater marvels struck terror into everyone. Specifically, the virginal corpse – which was assumed long since to have decomposed, after so many centuries, though a clear report based on early experience spoke in her defence – was seen to be whole, in respect both to bodily parts and to clothes, just as it was originally buried. Even the wooden casing whereby it was conveyed to Ely was preserved undamaged, apart from the fact that the iron nails were rusted away.

Meanwhile, some people thought that it was the undisturbed dust of a decayed body, presenting only the appearance of wholeness, but the truth that its solidity had lasted to the present day became evident from touching. For a certain elderly man called Warner, from the apostolic flock of Westminster, one of several people who had gathered there, approached with a marvellous audacity of faith, touched the virginal limbs all over and, on the strength of this investigation, reverentially lifted up the flexible joints of her hands and arms. By his exclamations at the wonderful works of God he brought a number of respected people to come and look. However, no one's irreverence approached with eyes the beauty hidden by snow-white coverings. A face with rosy cheeks is shining for the Lord, animated with the breath of life! Breasts upstanding are flourishing in the springtime of their integrity! Unmarried limbs are flowering in paradisiacal loveliness!

Bishop Herbert, whom we have mentioned earlier, a most learned man, came from Thetford, fearfully made an inspection and blessed the Lord – glorious as He is in respect to His saints. In addition, several other men of

---

[762] Source: *Vita S. Withburge* CT 19f., 22, 24, ed. Love; 'chronicles of England.' Text of the chapter-heading as in E.

conspicuous honour were present, whom we have mentioned above, and saw with their eyes these miracles of God. But let the fastidious feelings of listeners pardon these pieces of evidence which we have recounted as arguments in support of belief! At length, indeed, the distinguished Bishop Herbert gave an account of these joyful things – so wonderful and so new – to a packed congregation, and enflamed everyone to the praises of God and the pouring out of thanks. Nay, rather – things which might seem incredible to those not present – such enormous grace issuing from the dew of Heaven came to prevail in this place that more or less everyone was awash with rivers of weeping.

But, amid this exultation, all were worried as to what they should do, given that the old coffin seemed injurious to the dignity of the virgin because of the breakage, whereas the new had ceased to be something one could recommend, having been reduced in size by divine agency. In the end, the pious and helpful lady, {Wihtburh}, dismissed these hesitations and proved by means of a glorious miracle that she did not wish to change from her earlier resting-place. For that fissure, through which one could thrust a knife or reed right to the other side, was suddenly restored to solid wholeness, in such a way that, from then onwards, no trace of the break was visible there. At this point, too, everyone's questioning was brought to an end; for they knew that, thanks to such an obvious sign, the virgin did not wish to be transferred from the corpse-bed of her old memorial. Therefore, after the cover had been put on and the sarcophagus carefully closed, they carried her with the gladdest jubilation across to her blessed sister, from the old monastery into the new, and placed her most agreeably at her side, facing the east.

Concerning the incorruption of the most holy virgin Wihtburh, this, by way of explanation, is how the report runs in the chronicles of England. In the year of the Lord 798, the body of St Wihtburh was found without decay after about 55 years, at Dereham. If one adds 202 years to 798, the total of 1,000 years is reached; the 106 other years which have followed these make together 354 years from the falling asleep of blessed Wihtburh herself up until the day in our time on which she was shown as in bodily incorruption.[763] Likewise, too, as has been said, people lovingly associate with her Seaxburh, her blessed sister, and this same lady's most holy daughter Eormenhild – meritorious ladies brought into association with the extremely meritorious – in which position they both singly and together make privileged intercession on behalf of supplicants for the benefactions of Heaven.

---

[763] The calculator (so also in *Vita S. Withburge* CT 24) has forgotten to count in the first 55 or so years.

148. In what year that translation came about, and with how much feeling Abbot Richard endeavoured to venerate the bountiful virgin Wihtburh.[764]

In a beautiful mystery, therefore, the Lord, lighting these four lamps, brought them into His nuptial church.[765] So that they may symbolize people entering from the four corners of the World, they are the followers, in number and merit, of those four-winged animals in Heaven which have been assigned each separately to the four corners of the Earth, and which fly to the heavenly regions with conjoint wing-feathers of loving-kindness, living the life of angels as they thunder forth proclamations of Christ one to another. Emulating, as well, the four rivers flowing from the one fountain of Paradise, Christ, these ladies used to irrigate the life of single-mindedness by the quadripartite teaching of the Gospels, and they do not cease to refresh with their waters those who thirstily seek divine remedies. These are, I say, four women-servants of the Gospels and four nurselings of the virtues; four women-percussionists[766] of the fourfold cross of Christ,[767] striking forth with four-fold notes the heavenly tetrachord;[768] they are the four faces of the earth taking pity as they do on arriving strangers; and, following the Marys of the Gospels, they are fragrant anointers of Christ, whose name is an ointment poured out, the scent of which is fragrant above all sweetness.

---

[764] Source: *Vita S. Withburge* CT 23f., ed. Love.

[765] Lat. *Dominus . . . nuptiali intulit ecclesie sue.*

[766] Lat. *timpanistrie*, an extremely rare word of classical origin, meaning female performers on e.g. drums, timbrels, tambourines, tambours.

[767] The imagery suggests a cross-shaped instrument consisting of four differently tuned wooden planks: a version of the *semantron*, a wooden percussion-instrument still used in Orthodox monasteries to summon the monks to worship. According to a well-travelled informant, Archimandrite Maximos Lavriotes (pers. comm. 28.12.99), hand-held *semantra* today are 'usually cross-shaped'. In the eleventh century, Archbishop Lanfranc in his *Constitutions* (*Decreta Lanfranci Monachis Cantuariensibus Transmissa*, ed. & trans. D. Knowles, London 1951) had called for the use of this same board-and-mallet device (*tabulae cum malleolis*, p. 34) in English monasteries for a number of purposes, e.g. to signal the end of a chapter meeting, also, most notably, in place of bells 'from the *Gloria* of Maundy Thursday till that on Holy Saturday' (p. 33).

[768] Lat. *timpanizantes quaternis vocibus diatessaron celeste*. The date of the *Liber Eliensis* is too early for there to be a probable reference in *quaternis vocibus* to four-part vocal counterpoint, and the use of *timpanizantes* would be strange for any music but percussion – though the percussion instrument might be pitched. *Vox* may mean 'note' as well as 'voice'. *Diatesseron*: in theological contexts, the word used for Tatian's *Harmony of the Gospels*, and this meaning must surely have been in our author's mind along with his knowledge of musical theory, in which it is the term used for the interval of a fourth or, as in the *Introductio musicae* of the thirteenth century theorist, John of Garland (*Script. Mus.* i, 1864 ed., p. 164), a tetrachord, 'the conjunction of 4 notes and the arrangement of two tones with the addition on one semitone'.

And this foursome of the Lord[769] was translated in the 1106th year of the incarnate Word-born One,[770] on the ame day on which the blessed Æthelthryth was translated long before, y an arrangement which was certainly most appropriate, its purpose bein that there should be – and this has happened – a single feast-day for all of them, who had one faith, one spirit and one love.

So, from that day onwards, the lord Abbot began to venerate St Wihtburh with particular devotion in view of her incorruption, and would have made her a silver tomb, if he had been able to live longer. For, in fact, other occupations in various ways kept him back from this undertaking, and particularly the fact that he was endeavouring to frustrate the claims of the bishops of Lincoln, by changing the monastery of Ely into an episcopal see. To be specific, he first of all brought this matter secretly before the king and, on obtaining his favour, dispatched envoys that same year on this business to the Apostolic Father. Finally, Abbot Richard laid the bodies of the saints together in the places where they are now seen to rest,[771] and afterwards he won such favour from the king that he was reckoned his chief councillor among the nobles of the kingdom.

Hence he negotiated with him and, by a just settlement made in the king's presence, wrested from the Bishop of Durham, Ranulf Flambard, the vill of Hadham, which that bishop had violently stole from the church[772] through the agency of London clerics, as the following charter of the king proves.

149. That this same abbot established a title to Hadham.[773]

Henry, King of the English, to Maurice, Bishop of London, and Hugh de Buckland, Sheriff of Hertfordshire, and to all his faithful people, both clergy and laity: greeting. Know that Richard, Abbot of Ely, has in my court at Romsey, in the presence of me and my barons, established a title to the episcopal manor of Hadham against Ranulf of Durham, for the demesne of St Peter and God's blessed virgin Æthelthryth of Ely, and of the monastic brothers serving God there. I wish, therefore, and instruct that the Abbey of

---

[769] Lat. *quadrige dominice*. In classical Latin, *quadrigae* is standard for a team of four horses.

[770] Lat. verbigene, gen. of *verbigena*, a term used of Christ by Prudentius in *Cathemerina* 3.1; 11.17.

[771] Ms. O and a thirteenth- or fourteenth-century marginal note in E, give the following updated version: 'Accordingly in the places in which the aforesaid abbot laid the bodies of the saints together, they rested until Hugh de Northwold, the eighth Bishop of Ely, moved the said foursome into the new presbytery constructed by him from its foundations – without inspection of the bodies of the holy virgins Æthelthryth and Wihtburh.'

[772] Lat. *ecclesie*: dative, a classical construction with *aufero*.

[773] Source: monastic archives, cf. Dean and Chapter, charter no. 2 and cartulary G. Date: 1105.

Ely should have and hold in its demesne that aforesaid manor of Hadham, peacefully and without claim, from now on and for evermore, the witnesses being specified in writing below: Ralph, Bishop of Lincoln, William Giffard, Bishop of Winchester, and John, Bishop of Bath, Ralph, Bishop of Chichester, and many others whom it would be a long task to list.

150. How, when Abbot Richard was dying, he saw the blessed Wihtburh standing close to him.[774]

The venerable Abbot Richard became bed-ridden and now that he was about to be summoned to render account for his talent,[775] he ordered that the community of brothers should gather in his presence and, on receiving, after a confession of the utmost purity, the departing traveller's food of life, he saw, standing close by, the most holy Wihtburh, the virgin most dear to him. With eyes all of a sudden fixed on her, he addressed the men standing around him with a loud cry: 'Make way!', he said. 'Make way, brothers! See! My lady Wihtburh is coming! See! She is standing here! What? Do you not see her? Do you not notice that she is standing here? O lady,' he said. 'Have mercy on me!' And, on giving up the ghost shortly afterwards, he left the place bereaved, plunged his sons into the deepest grief, and commended his body to the World and his soul to God. As a consequence, the whole day in that place was spent in lamentations and prayers, and when the next day came, he was buried in the monastery with the honour befitting him, magnificent man that he was. And the envoys who had gone to Rome left off their negotiations on hearing of the death of their lord.

But we are by no means capable of going through the particular details, and so come to the end of the text of the second book. In our estimation there are a few things, out of the many, which will be of signal importance for posterity's understanding. And may you who read or hear these things grant the solace of your prayers, so that the Lord may deign to send us help from Heaven and may command that the well-spring of intelligence be allowed to gush forth freely upon the slowness of our sense-perception, giving strength to everyone's weakness.

Here ends the second book about the history of the Isle of Ely, comprising an account of the times of the abbots and monks in Ely until the change of the abbacy into a bishopric.

---

[774] Source: local commemoration of Abbot Richard, cf. chapters 141–3. Date of Richard's death: 1107.

[775] Cf. Matthew 25.14–30.

BOOK III

Here begins the prologue of the third book on the same subject, reporting the times of the bishops and the things which befell them.

The subject now to be treated is how the bishopric of Ely began. From the time when the minster first began to have monks up until the ninth year of King Henry, it had the following successive abbots: Byrhtnoth, Ælfsige, Leofwine, Leofric, Leofsige, Wulfric, Thurstan, Theodwine, Simeon and Richard. The last-mentioned abbot, refusing to tolerate the oppression of his house, rebutted the claims of challengers with righteous oratory, and manfully wrested his domains from his enemies, supported by the authority of kings and apostolic fathers, giving a clear account of his church,[1] to the effect that, right from the time the first monastery was built there by St Augustine, Apostle of the English, presumably through the mediation of King Æthelberht, and later, under the most blessed Æthelthryth and the holy women who succeeded her, and [now] too, in the time of the abbots, it had been freely constituted, encumbered by nobody's yoke of subjection; rather they used to call upon whichever archbishop or bishop they happened to choose or like, to carry out their consecrations. Conversely, Abbot Richard made it known that the Bishop of Lincoln had no legal right as a consequence of this, and ought not to demand it; and he asserted its liberty on the basis of several pieces of documentary evidence.

But since Ely was perceived as bordering upon his diocese, the Bishop of Lincoln reckoned it <to be his own>,[2] but wrongly, and was now machinating to make it subject to himself, by assiduous litigation. As a consequence of this, though not until he had suffered many instances of disrespectful maltreatment, the leader of the flock, the lord Abbot Richard,[3] prudently formed a plan to exalt the status of the monastery itself and to thwart utterly the chicanery of men of ill-will; and he secured from the king, secretly, the right to change it into an episcopal see. But it was not Richard himself but the man who succeeded him, who carried out this measure, as the following chapters explain more fully.

One more point: the written content of this book comprises the time of two bishops, specifically: Hervey, the first bishop – so we have ascertained –

---

[1] Here (p. 237.10, ed. Blake) one expects the accusative and infinitive construction of indirect discourse to follow from *ostendens*, but this does not happen.

[2] Reading conjecturally at p. 237.17, ed. Blake: *arbitratur illam <suam esse> sed falso, sibi assiduis nunc molitur actionibus subicere* . . .

[3] So E. F's reading means 'the leader of the Lord's flock, Abbot Richard'.

of the place in question, though on the basis of consecration performed elsewhere, and Nigel, its second bishop, but the first to have been consecrated there.

Here ends the prologue.

Here begin the chapter-headings.

1. How, after the death of Abbot Richard, Hervey, Bishop of Bangor, having been driven out of his see, was directed by King Henry to go to Ely, to exercise his episcopal charge from there. This man, by speaking to them in flattering terms and talking them round, won over the brothers' hearts in favour of him, his plan being to change the church from an abbey to a cathedral and for them to receive him as bishop, and without the knowledge of the monks, he was despatched to Rome by the king to have this confirmed.

2. That Bishop Hervey received from the lord Pope a mandate to Henry, King of England, about raising the abbacy of Ely to the status of a bishopric, and about instating him there as bishop.

3. With how much honour Hervey was received by the lord Pope is abundantly evident from the Pope's own mandate addressed to King Henry.

4. A mandate of the lord Pope to the archbishop and bishops of England concerning the setting up of a bishopric in Ely.

5. That the bishopric in Ely is established on apostolic authority.

6. A charter of King Henry as to how he changed the abbacy of Ely into a bishopric.

7. A charter of the king about the whole liberty of the church.

8. A charter of the king to the effect that the monks of Ely should have a fair share of the properties of the abbey.

9. How manfully Bishop Hervey rescued his church of Ely and its properties from unlawful oppression.

10. A charter of King Henry about a comprehensive conferment upon the church of its estates.

11. Another charter of the king against the usurpers of estates and goods of St Æthelthryth.

12. A charter of the king about exemption from the guarding of the town of Norwich, and about freedom from a state of burdensome servitude as a consequence of which the church of Ely was struggling miserably.

13. Another charter of King Henry against those who by their power were withholding the church's properties and services due to it.

14. [Another mandate of the king about the liberty of the five hundreds.][4]

15. A charter of the king about a concession with regard to the knights who used to be demanded compulsorily from the church of Ely.

16. Again, a charter of the king about a remittance of money which used to be unjustly exacted from the church.

17. That Bishop Hervey, by his own effort, gained possession of the house of Chatteris, and annexed it to the church of Ely with perpetual right of possession.

18. A charter of King Henry about the grant incorporating the Abbey of Chatteris, with all things pertaining to it, into {the Isle of} Ely.

19. Another charter of the king, which he granted to St Æthelthryth in Ely, about the relaxation of a requirement for money from the church of Chatteris.

20. A charter of King Henry about the release of the vill of Hadham from a claim.

21. A charter of the king to the effect that the monks and church of St Æthelthryth in Ely are to be exempt from the imposition of tolls everywhere throughout England.

22. Again, another charter about the same matter.

23. Charter of the king about the liberty of the hundreds of St Æthelthryth.

---

[4] Chapter-heading not in E. The whole chapter is a marginal addition at the corresponding place in the text. It refers to the five-and-a-half hundreds of Wicklow, Suffolk.

24. Another charter of the king to the effect that St Æthelthryth should everywhere have free jurisdiction over her people.

25. That Bishop Hervey separated the victualling of the monks from the affairs of the bishopric, instituting an allowance for them, but a meagre and wholly insufficient one, in conflict with his oath that he would maintain the church, that is, the monastery, and the affairs of the whole place, without upheaval.

26. A charter of Bishop Hervey concerning the details of the arrangements which he instituted for the victualling of the monks.

27. Praise of the author concerning the miracles of St Æthelthryth which happened in the times of Bishop Hervey.

28. That the tower at the entrance of the church of St Æthelthryth was saved from fire resulting from a stroke of lightning.

29. About a crippled man cured at the shrine of the blessed Æthelthryth.

30. About a man with dropsy who earned the gift of health at the shrine of the blessed Æthelthryth.

31. About a crippled woman cured at the shrine of the blessed Æthelthryth.

32. [That a causeway was made through the fen to the shrine of St Æthelthryth as the result of a revelation.]⁵

33. Concerning Byrhtstan who, after having been put in fetters, was set free by the blessed Æthelthryth.

34. How someone was freed from a pain in the head by putting the chains of St Æthelthryth against his cheek.

35. About Ralph the schoolmaster, who was freed from a swelling of the throat by invocation of the name of St Æthelthryth.

36. That someone deprived of all bodily functions was restored to his former state of health.

---

⁵ This chapter-heading and the chapter itself are marginal additions in E; the chapter is in the text of F.

37. In what a malignant way action was taken against the church of St Æthelthryth.

38. How a certain notable handed himself over to St Æthelthryth for service as a monk.

39. How hard Bishop Hervey worked to free his church of Ely from people who were treating it injuriously.

40. A charter of King Henry to the effect that the people of St Æthelthryth should be exempt from the jurisdiction of shire and hundred.

41. How Hervey, the first Bishop of Ely, reached his life's end.

42. That the blessed Æthelthryth appeared to a certain sick man, promising him restoration of health.

43. How St Æthelthryth was seen praying in a certain church, holding a psalter in one hand, and in the other a lighted candle.

44. How, with the king's consent, Nigel was elected as bishop, and by whom he was consecrated.

45. With what honour Bishop Nigel was received by the community of monks in Ely and by the people who came to meet him.

46. How, after the decease of King Henry, his nephew became king; and that he had made it his intention to venerate the Church in England with all his might.

47. That certain malignant individuals on the bishop's side devised deceptions upon the monks.

48. That the lord Bishop Nigel gave instructions that the properties of the blessed Æthelthryth be listed in full; and which ones he reclaimed for the church on his own initiative.

49. A charter of King Stephen about the whole liberty of the church of St Æthelthryth.

50. How the bishop gave orders that the goods of the church contained within it should be listed in full; and the identity and number of the articles which he found there.

51. With what violence the bishop stole the monks' properties from them and entrusted them to Master Ranulf their enemy, afflicting them cruelly; they themselves, however, waited in acceptance of the scourge of the Lord, in the expectation of release.

52. How Ranulf, overtaken by an evil impulse, lured accomplices to join him with a view to subversive action against his country, but took flight on being detected, thanks to St Æthelthryth, as complicit in an act of treason.

53. That the bishop, terror-stricken as the result of the judgement of God and St Æthelthryth, gave the monks their properties back, being sorrowful at having behaved badly towards them.

54. A charter of the bishop about the things which he altered for the benefit of the monks.

55. A privilege of the lord Pope containing reference to the properties of the whole bishopric, confirming them in perpetuity.

56. Another privilege of the lord Pope about the provisions which Bishop Nigel established for the monks, small though they were.

57. The miracle of how a blind woman was given sight at the shrine of St Æthelthryth.

58. About a certain man who did not wish to hold the feast of St Æthelthryth.

59. How a sick man was cured by the tunicle of St Æthelthryth.

60. About a girl blinded in the right eye who was given sight beneath the body of the blessed Æthelthryth.

61. About a certain monk of ours, mortally sick but cured by St Æthelthryth.

62. How sedition arose in the land, and that, in fear of the king, Bishop Nigel departed from Ely.

63. A charter of King Stephen to the effect that the monks of Ely might hold their properties in peace.

64. That King Stephen handed over the Isle of Ely to be garrisoned, and how Bishop Nigel remained in exile.

65. A mandate of the lord Pope to the Bishop of Winchester, at that time Legate of England, concerning the restoration of Bishop Nigel to his see.

66. Another mandate of the lord Pope to King Stephen about restoring Bishop Nigel to his see.

67. A mandate of the lord Pope to Bishop Nigel, which kindly assents to his petitions.

68. Again, a mandate of the lord Pope to the archbishop and bishops of England about restoring Nigel to his place.

69. That supporters of the bishop, entering Ely secretly, were overwhelmed by Geoffrey, a military commander on the king's side.

70. An instruction of King Stephen to the effect that the monks of Ely are to hold their possessions freely and in peace.

71. <Again, an instruction of the king concerning the fact that he had given orders that the monks be given back rents which were their due.>[6]

72. How King Stephen was betrayed by his own men, and that the lady Empress gained control of nearly the whole country.

73. How Bishop Nigel, with the help of the lady Empress, regained his see.

74. How King Stephen was rescued from captivity.

75. A charter of King Stephen about his having taken Bishop Nigel back again in peace.

76. An instruction of King Stephen to the effect that the monks of Ely should have the food-rents due to them from their lands.

77. How Bishop Nigel was summoned to Rome.

78. What belongings of his church Bishop Nigel lost, and which ones, on a second occasion, he took from it, when he went on his journey to Rome.

79. What sort of mandate it was, addressed to the archbishop and the bishops of England, that Bishop Nigel obtained from the lord Pope.

---

[6] Supplied by Blake from the text where the chapter occurs.

80. What mandate the lord Pope gave to the chapter of Ely through Bishop Nigel.

81. A mandate of the lord Pope to King Stephen in favour of Nigel, Bishop of Ely.

82. That Bishop Nigel once again incurred the king's displeasure, and what sort of trouble there was in England.

83. A mandate of the lord Pope to the Archbishop of England in favour of Bishop Nigel.

84. Another mandate of the lord Pope to the Archbishop of Rouen and the bishops of Normandy in favour of Nigel, Bishop of Ely.

85. A privilege of the lord Pope which Bishop Nigel acquired on the subject of the properties of the monks of Ely – small as they were – which he had established for them.

86. That Bishop Nigel had incurred the king's displeasure a second time; and how he was reconciled to him.

87. A charter of King Stephen about his granting of peace to Bishop Nigel.

88. Another charter of the king; that he gave instructions that the properties of the monks should be in peace.

89. That the bishop took goods of the church, contained within it, to pay money promised to the king.

90. A charter of the bishop about how he returned the vill of Hadstock to the monks.

91. On the same matter: a charter of Archbishop Theobald.

92. Who the men were who gave surety for the bishop with regard to the money taken from the church; and how miserably events turned out for them.

93. How pleasant a vision was made manifest concerning the blessed Æthelthryth.

BOOK III

109. An instruction of the lord Pope to the effect that the monks of Ely are to receive back their property and hold it freely.

110. A mandate of the lord Pope to the chapter of Ely to the effect that they are at liberty to take possession of their property of Stetchworth.

111. A charter of the Bishop of Hereford concerning the property returned to the monks of Ely.

112. Again, a charter of the same bishop; on what kind of terms he ejected the usurpers from the estate of the monks of Ely.

113. A charter of Archbishop Theobald about the estate returned to the monks of Ely.

114. A charter of King Stephen, to the effect that the monks of Ely are at liberty to have possession of their vill of Stetchworth.

115. That someone obligated by debt to the monks of Ely incurred a charge of perjury.

116. How mercifully God acted with regard to a certain sick man cured through the merits of St Æthelthryth at her spring.

117. Another miracle about the spring of St Æthelthryth.

118. Again, a miracle about the same spring.

119. With what severity the Lord avenged the injuries inflicted on his beloved virgin Æthelthryth.

120. Once more, how God wreaked vengeance on the enemies of the blessed Æthelthryth.

121. About a priest who did not wish to celebrate the feasts of our lady saints.

122. About the pall of St Æthelthryth: in what a merciful way it was restored to the church of Ely.

123. That Bishop Nigel was suspended by the Pope for the dispersal of the goods of St Æthelthryth.

124. Mandate of the lord Pope to the chapter of Ely about this same man.

125. Likewise to the archbishop, about this same man, on the subject of the recall of the goods of St Æthelthryth to the monastery of Ely.

126. Exhortatory letter of the Archbishop of Canterbury about the recall of the goods dispersed from the church of St Æthelthryth.

127. Another instruction of the lord Pope to the archbishop and bishops of England about the recall of goods to the church of Ely.

128. Again, a mandate of the Pope to the King of England about constraining the malefactors who had harmed the church of Ely.

129. That Bishop Nigel, on the instruction of the Pope, swore to restore the goods of his church, and thus earned release from suspension.

130. A miracle concerning a certain boy-monk healed by St Æthelthryth.

131. About a demoniac rescued by the blessed Æthelthryth.

132. About sailors in peril on the sea saved by St Æthelthryth.

133. [[A mandate of Bishop Nigel for the estate of Bawdsey.]][7]

134. A charter of Bishop Nigel to the effect that the monks of Ely should hold their churches freely and in peace.

135. Another charter of the bishop to the effect that none of his successors should harass the monks of Ely with respect to their holdings.

136. Again, another charter of the bishop, concerning the estate of *Ærnethern*.

137. How Bishop Nigel became ill, and about his demise.

138. With what severity God avenged the injuries done to His virgin Æthelthryth, and how Robert the chamberlain gave Denny to St Æthelthryth.

139. A charter of Robert the chamberlain to the effect that he gave Denny to St Æthelthryth.

---

[7] This chapter-heading is lacking from EF and is supplied from O. The chapter itself is a marginal addition in E.

140. A charter of the Count of Brittany about the same matter.

141. A charter of Aubrey Picot about how the monks of Ely bought his part of Denny.

142. A charter of Bishop Nigel about the same matter, to the effect that his monks are to hold Denny freely and in peace.

143. The passion of the most holy Thomas the martyr, Archbishop of Canterbury.[8]

---

[8] There follow here in E, with no change of hand, further headings which may be translated as follows: 'A listing of the lands of the church of St Æthelthryth as an extension of the volume; a *Life of St Seaxburh*, a *Life of St Eormenhild*, a *Life of St Eorcongota the virgin*, a *Life of St Wærburh the virgin*, a *Life of St Æthelburh the virgin*, a *Life of the bountiful virgin Wihtburh.*'

BOOK III

**Here begins the Third Book in the *History of the Isle of Ely*,
comprising the times of two bishops,
fully reporting what action, more or less beneficial, they took.**

1. How, after the death of Abbot Richard, Hervey, Bishop of Bangor, having been driven out of his see, was directed by King Henry to go to Ely, to exercise his episcopal charge from there. This man, by speaking to them in flattering terms and talking them round, won over the brothers' hearts in favour of him, his plan being to change the church from an abbey to a cathedral and for them to receive him as bishop, and without the knowledge of these same monks, he was despatched to Rome by the king to have this confirmed.[9]

To resume: after the death of Abbot Richard, Hervey, Bishop of Bangor, who had been ejected by force from his episcopal see, was sent by the king to the monastery of Ely to be provided there temporarily with support from the church's resources until the king had more fully made up his mind what to do with regard to him.

Now, Bangor is a monastery in Wales, filled, as Bede reports, with so many occupants that, if it were divided into seven parts, each division would contain no fewer than three hundred men. When Hervey was exercising his episcopacy in this place, he began to treat a rebellious people with extreme rigour, observing in their behaviour wickedness so great that no one could readily tolerate it. The upshot was that, because they did not maintain any reverence for fear of their bishop, he twice wielded a sharp sword with the aim of subduing them: curbing them now with a frequently repeated anathema, now by means of a large force of his kinsfolk and other men. The rebellion of the people was on no smaller a scale: they began to attack him with such recklessness that they murdered his brother, intending to punish Hervey in a similar fashion, if they could lay hands on him. The bishop became terrified by the misfortune assailing him: most of his kin had been killed or severely wounded; he saw that people were seeking to take his own life and that he did not have adequate defenders, so he fled to the protection of the King of England, achieving the exile expedient for him. And, as he was a bishop well-known at that time and devout, the king, warmly welcoming his arrival, decided that he should be sent to the church of Ely and subsequently receive his episcopal charge from there.

In point of fact, when he arrived there, thanks to his graciousness, his demeanour and his marvellous wisdom, he formed bonds of affection with

---

[9] Source: local text commemorating Bishop Hervey as successor to Abbot Richard. Wildly anachronistic allusion to Bede, *Hist* Eccl. ii. 2, on the monastery of Bangor; the details describe refer to the era of St Augustine's mission.

almost all the monks, so that, had it been possible, they would have adopted him as their bishop. Seeing this affection surrounding him,[10] he began gradually, in various efforts at talking them round, to set before them the monastery's best interests, to make appeals to the brothers' feelings, and to promise many things that would be agreeable, supposing they should be willing to raise the standing of the abbacy to that of a bishopric; and he promised them his assistance towards the fulfilment of this object, provided only that they would grant him their assent. And once they had been won over by him – an easy matter – he approached the king.

The king granted his requests. He invited Robert, Bishop of Lincoln, for a talk, his intention being that, because the monastery in question appeared to be in his diocese, the change which he had in mind should not take place without this bishop's leave. The object was that his diocese should not suffer an injustice, as it would if, without consultation with its bishop, another bishopric were introduced in rivalry with him. In addition, the future bishopric needed to have a diocese of some sort, and he requested that this should be apportioned to him by the church of Lincoln, under canon law and with fair compensation. Accordingly, the manor of Spaldwick was granted to the church of Lincoln as a perpetual right in exchange for the bishop's taking charge of Cambridgeshire. And, after this secret negotiation between the king and Bishop Robert had been concluded – entirely without consultation with the monks, sons of the church though they were, and without their knowledge – Bishop Hervey was sent off to Rome with letters from the king, to have this proposed arrangement confirmed. On arrival there, he obtained what he was requesting, bringing back from the Apostolic Father writs of the kind that he wished for regarding his case, addressed to the king and the archbishop and the other bishops of his province. To write out the text of these below is neither an otiose nor an onerous task.

2. That Bishop Hervey received from the lord Pope a mandate to Henry, King of England, about raising the abbacy of Ely to the status of a bishopric, and about instating him there as bishop.[11]

Paschal, Bishop, servant of the servants of Christ, to his beloved son in Christ, Henry, the glorious King of the English, greeting and apostolic blessing. We give thanks to almighty God that he has established such a king in our times as you, who are governing an earthly kingdom wisely to the honour of God, and holding before your mind's eyes a concern for the eternal King. Specifically, you have asked us by your letters that a new bishopric

---

[10] Reading conjecturally (p. 245.27, ed. Blake): *quam circa se affectionem aspiciens* . . .

[11] Source: monastic archives, cf. cartularies CDG. Date: 21st November, 1108.

should be instated on apostolic authority in the place called Ely because, you have said, the bishopric of Lincoln is of such great extent that one bishop is by no means sufficient to carry out fully the tasks which belong to the episcopal office. With respect to this, we both praise the devoutness of your desire and grant assent to the arrangement, providing, however, that it be established in a well-known place, lest the name of bishop – perish the thought – be devalued. For the purpose for which a bishop is instated is both to teach the people of God by his speaking and to instruct it by his manner of life and to render account to God, the true Shepherd, of the gains of souls committed to him. With regard also to the other matters about which you have asked: although some things in them seem irregular, we are, however, by no means able to oppose your will. Beside, your glorious self knows that the lord Bishop Hervey, whose manner of life and considerable learning commend him, has been expelled from his see by excessive ferocity and harassment on the part of barbarians, and has been driven into flight by a great massacre of his retainers and brothers. In order that this man may have the power to yield, by his learning, the fruit which does not perish and to present, by his life, a good example to the people of God, we desire and request that, if anywhere in your land a vacant church has called upon him, he be instated there on apostolic authority, lest a man who presents[12] evidences of the life of Heaven in his learning and morals, be inactive in fruitless[13] silence for a long time. May almighty God guard you and your progeny by the prayers of His apostles and grant you, after an earthly kingdom, that of Heaven. Given: 21st November.

The Pope also sent another letter to the same king, of which this is the text.

3. With how much honour Bishop Hervey was received by the lord Pope is abundantly evident from the Pope's own mandate addressed to King Henry.[14]

Paschal, Bishop, servant of the servants of God to his beloved son Henry, the glorious King of England, greeting and apostolic blessing. We have received the letters of your very sweet loving-kindness towards us, displaying as they do the sweetness of your affectionate self towards the blessed Peter and towards us who serve him. With respect to these, we have amply rejoiced in the fact that we recognize in the heart of an earthly king the love of the heavenly Father, and, therefore, the more certainly we find that you are

---

[12] Reading with E (p. 247.2, cf. 248.5, ed. Blake): *qui vite celestis documenta in scientia et moribus portat. . .*

[13] Reading with E (p. 247.1, cf. 248.5f., ed. Blake): *ne infructuoso diu silentio torpeat. . .*

[14] Source: monastic archives, cf. cartularies CDG. Date: 21st November, 1108.

making requests which are pleasing to the heavenly King, the more gladly and readily we grant assent to your requests. Moreover, as regards the matter which your affectionate self took care to intimate to us in secret, we have undertaken to exert as much effort as we have been able. In general also, in whichever matters we have been able to make enquiries, for the honour of God and for the enhancement and exaltation of your glory, we have gladly been making them. In addition, concerning that exchange about which your loving self has asked us through our brothers Bishop Hervey and Peter the chamberlain, if it would be possible for it to be brought about for the benefit of the church as you have commanded, we grant assent to your requests. We commend solicitously to your glorious self the same brother, Bishop Hervey, whom we know to be beloved by you.

From this it is evident that this man's sagacity was worthy of praise: with the king's favour he also earned the good will of the Apostolic Father and brought here the authority of Rome for his preferment. Now that he had been put in a strong position by numerous writs – by numerous testimonies, so to speak – the letters set out here commended him to the archbishop also.

4. A mandate of the lord Pope to the archbishop and bishops of England concerning the setting up of a bishopric in Ely.[15]

Paschal, Bishop, servant of the servants of God to his venerable brother Anselm, Archbishop of Canterbury, greeting and apostolic blessing. Your fraternal self knows that, as is generally considered to be the case, on apostolic authority, every bishop appointed by men is being placed for the sake of men amidst the affairs which relate to God. Your brother, this Hervey of yours, a man whose life and learning commend him, has not been able to fulfil the episcopal office in the church in which he was instated, owing to the savagery of barbarians, which they have cruelly brought to bear on his brothers and other Christian people. Therefore, so that the office enjoined upon him may not remain fruitless, we are issuing a mandate to your loving self, asking you to provide for him with particular attentiveness, and, if any vacant church amongst you shall have called upon him, to instate him in it on the authority of the Apostolic See, to the end that he may have the power to serve God there and to fulfil, with God's generous aid, the office of a bishop, so that a man who presents evidences of the life of Heaven in his learning and morals may not be inactive for a long time in fruitless silence; in the mean time, moreover, you are to consider him commended in all respects. For here with us he has shown himself keen on furthering your interests in a satisfactorily energetic and loyal manner. May the power of God long keep

---

[15] Source: monastic archives, cf. cartularies CDG. Date: 21st November, 1108.

your fraternal self in safety. Given: 21st November.

With the assistance of the grace of God, this wise man performed effective service when in the environs of Rome: by receiving a prerogative of honour from the hands of Peter, the very head of Christendom, he was attached to the church of Ely by means of three letters and one charter – as it were, with a three-ply rope and an anchor. The meaning implicit in this is that both a Trinity and a Unity are to be preached by a servant of God, or that, if a quadernity is to be noted in the 'three' and the 'one', it is his solidly based position that is signified by a solidly based number. Let us see in what the fourth item consists.

5. That the bishopric in Ely is established on apostolic authority.[16]

Paschal, Bishop, servant of the servants of God to his venerable brother Anselm, Archbishop of Canterbury and his other fellow-bishops of that province: greeting and apostolic blessing. That, in relation to the other kingdoms of the World around it, the kingdom of the English has a particular tendency towards love of the Apostolic See and obedience to it, is a fact which the writs of the Apostolic See and the drift of the annals of England make plain. This fact, unsurprisingly, provides a powerful incentive for solicitous endeavour on our part to foster the churches of that kingdom with particularly intimate attentiveness and to watch over its arrangements with all the greater care. And so, we understand from the letters of our son, the king, and from your own letters that the bishopric of Lincoln is so large and extensive that one bishop can by no means suffice for the carrying out of the function which belongs to the episcopal office. In view of this, the same best-beloved son of ours and most Christian king of the English, Henry, is requesting from us, at the desire of the Bishop of Lincoln, that in one part of his bishopric a new bishopric be established with the consent of the Apostolic See, specifically in the place which is called Ely. We have gladly granted assent to his requests, because they seemed of a religious character, and we grant permission for the establishing of a bishopric in the aforementioned place on apostolic authority, making it statutory that the episcopal see established in the aforesaid place shall continue to exist for all time henceforth, and shall possess in perpetuity the diocese which your fraternal self – together with your aforesaid brother, the Bishop of Lincoln – and the king's foresight, shall have assigned to the said bishopric. Further, regarding the monastery in which the episcopal see is instated, the customary practice of English monasteries in which bishops are instated shall be observed. May those who abide by this arrangement enjoy the blessing of almighty God and

---

[16] Source: monastic archives, cf. cartularies CDGM. Date: 21st November, 1108.

His apostles for evermore. AMEN.

On receipt of these letters concerning his confirmation in office, Hervey made haste to England with the apostolic blessing, made his way to the king and archbishop, showed them the letters, obtained their assent, and in the following year brought the whole business to its consummation, namely in the 1108th {*recte* 1109th} year of the incarnation of our Lord, in the tenth year of the pontificate of the lord Pope Paschal II. In that year, too, King Henry changed the abbacy of Ely into an episcopal see and put the same Hervey, Bishop of Bangor, in charge of the same church, giving him confirmation in the following charters.

6. A charter of King Henry as to how he changed the abbacy of Ely into a bishopric.[17]

In the name of the holy and Undivided Trinity, the Father and the Son and the Holy Spirit. In the 1108th {*recte* 1109th}[18] year of the Lord's incarnation, in the <. . . > year of the indiction, in fact, in the tenth year of the lord Pope Paschal II, and likewise also in the tenth year of my reign, I, Henry – by the providence of the Divine Clemency, King of the English and Duke of the Normans, son of the great King William, who legitimately succeeded King Edward to the kingdom by right of inheritance, {issue the following decree}. The harvest of the church in my reign is plenteous and, moreover, the tillers of the soil are few, and for that reason struggling with the harvest, and in this harvest, the church of Lincoln is fertile with a large lay population. Therefore, on the basis of authorization and consultation with the aforesaid Pope Paschal, and with the consent and, likewise, at the entreaty of Robert, Bishop of Lincoln, who was at that time the person presiding over the aforesaid church, and of all his chapter with him, with the approval of Lord Anselm of blessed memory,[19] Archbishop of Canterbury, and of Thomas the Second, the venerable Archbishop of York, and all the bishops and abbots of all England, and in addition, all the dukes, earls and foremost men of my kingdom – I establish and confirm in perpetuity as an episcopal see – free and without indebtedness, as are the rest of the bishoprics of my realm – the monastery of Ely in which, up until my times, abbots had been in charge, and with it Cambridgeshire – in so far, that is, as it used to belong to the jurisdiction of the church of Lincoln – along with its two abbeys, Thorney and Chatteris. And in exchange for the relinquishing of jurisdiction and all episcopal customary rights pertaining to the aforesaid church of Lincoln, on

---

[17] Source: monastic archives, cf. British Library, Harley Charters, 43. C. 11; cartularies CDG. Date: 17th October, 1109; at Nottingham.

[18] Here the cartularies preserve the correct date where the *LE* mss. are in error.

[19] The archbishop had died on 21st April, 1109.

the advice, and with the assent, of Pope Paschal, I hand over to the aforesaid church of Lincoln and to Robert, the bishop of the same see and his successors, from the benefices of the same monastery, the vill called Spaldwick with its appendages, which is situated in the territory of Huntingdon, with all the customary rights which belong to the aforesaid vill, to be possessed with perpetual legality, as freely and peaceably as ever the monastery of Ely held it. In the first instance, there was consideration of this business in London, at Westminster, during the feast of Pentecost in the presence of Archbishop Anselm of happy memory and of all the bishops and abbots and nobles of my kingdom, and the common assent of all of them was favourably achieved. But it was after the death of the aforesaid pontiff Anselm, on the authority of the lord Pope Paschal, as has already been stated above, that it was concluded and finalized, through the mercy of God, at a council held at Nottingham Castle on the day of the translation of the blessed Æthelthryth, virgin of the same see. Given: 17th October.

7. A charter of the king about the whole liberty of the church.[20]

Henry, King of the English to his archbishops and bishops and abbots and earls and barons and sheriffs and officers and to all his faithful people, French and English, of all England: greeting. You are to know that I have granted to Bishop Hervey the bishopric of Ely with all the lands and possessions belonging to the same bishopric, and I will and enjoin that the aforesaid church of Ely may have honourably and freely and peaceably all its customary rights inside the town and outside, in respect to land, water, marshes, open country and woodland, namely: *soke* and *sake*, and *toll* and *team*, *infangentheof* and *hamsocne* and *grithbryce* and *fihtwite* and *fyrdwite*, and offences emendable {by money-payments}[21] – as it best held them on the day on which King Edward lived and died, and as the matter was determined in the time of my father at Kentford in the presence of my father's barons, Bishop Walkelin, Geoffrey, Bishop of Coutances, Baldwin, Abbot of Saint Edmund's, Ivo de Taillebois and Peter de Valognes, and the witness of several shires. And may you know that I am not the giver of a warrant for anyone to stake a claim in respect to these aforesaid customary rights. Witnesses: Ranulf the chancellor, Gilbert de Aquila and Haimo the steward and William de Abbenais and Payn Peverel and William Peverel of Dover. At Castle Holdgate in Shropshire.

---

[20] Source: monastic archives, cf. British Library, Cotton Charters, X 8; cartularies CDGM. Date: 1109 X 1116; at Castle Holdgate, Shropshire.

[21] 'Offences emendable {by money-payments}': Lat. *forisfacturas emendabiles*.

8. A charter of the king to the effect that the monks of Ely should have a fair share of the properties of the abbey.[22]

Henry, King of the English, to his archbishops, bishops, abbots, earls, sheriffs and officials and to all his faithful people, French and English, of the whole of England: greeting. You are to know that I wish and grant and give instructions that the monks of the church of Ely are to have from their abbey a just apportionment and fair share in accordance with custom and ecclesiastical law, in respect to all things, namely lands, estate-holdings, positions of honour and goods, which have been donated and granted to them as their own, for their use and sustenance, through the generosity of faithful people, seeing that the abbey itself has been solemnly, and in its entirety, changed into a bishopric. And I do not wish that they should suffer any trouble or increased deprivation as a result of this: rather let their share and the property of the abbey as a whole be divided one from the other with fair-mindedness and, after having been enquired into carefully through the sworn testimony of good and faithful men from the honour of St Æthelthryth, they are to be assigned in writing and are to remain permanently allocated from henceforth in freedom and calm, for the provision of their livelihood and necessities, and no one is to presume to harass them over these matters. Witness: Ranulf the chancellor, [and] Gilbert de Aquila, and Haimo the steward and William de Albini [and] Payn Peverel. At Castle Holdgate in Shropshire.

9. How manfully Bishop Hervey rescued his church of Ely and its properties from unlawful oppression.[23]

So, confirmed as he was in his position as bishop, Hervey made every effort to ensure the increase of the resources of his church and, energetically and with all his might did away with the various encumbrances by which he found the church was fettered. For there were a number of individuals holding properties of the bishopric by force, whose power was increasing, partly as a result of money given to the king, partly through the wealth of their relatives. Against the will of the bishop they had for some considerable time been holding the fortification of the bridge, and certain official positions of the bishopric relating to external affairs, and they had repeatedly kept harassing the bishop himself with a number of feuds. The bishop, indignant at their hostility, finally contrived to extirpate it by a sensible plan: he reckoned it a miserable thing that his neck was in subjection to so many lay-people. In addition, there were some dues owed by law to the king relating to

[22] Source: monastic archives, cf. cartularies GM. Date: 1109 X 1116; at Castle Holdgate.
[23] Source: local tradition commemorating Bishop Hervey, if not, entirely or in part, inference by the compiler himself from the charters set out in chapters 10–16.

the garrison at Norwich, consisting of twenty-five shillings and five pence and one half-penny, for the purpose of the Norwich night-watch: these were burdensome to him, and he considered that the heavy contributions owed to that same castle were a nuisance.[24] Also, some men had invaded the lands of the bishopric by forcible usurpation, not deigning either to respond to the bishop or to perform service. In the first place, therefore, he endeavoured in every way that he could to win over the king's feelings in favour of himself, and such great things did he achieve in relation to the king by the abundance, amenability and insistence of his gifts, his friends, and his entreaties, that he cast off from his neck the guard duty at Norwich, extremely onerous as it had been to himself and his men, and commuted it, by means of a grant in perpetuity, into a duty {to maintain the guard} of his own castle.[25] Meanwhile, in addition, the men who had usurped control over the island in contravention of his lordship were ejected, and the contributions and customs and the wages of the watch of Norwich Castle were remitted, and the people who had refused to acknowledge church lands as held from him, were made subject to his lordship or else completely driven out. He also obtained from the king remission for himself of forty pounds of those hundred pounds which the aforesaid church used to give as scutage, and he released himself and his men from the payment of twenty shillings, in lieu of guard-service, which was demanded from his land. And, concerning all these matters, he acquired charters of perpetual liberty specific to each – treating of each matter as a single item, and these are written out in full here.

10. A charter of King Henry about a comprehensive conferment on the church of its estates [all at once].[26]

Henry, King of the English, to all the barons and all people, French and English, who hold lands from the bishopric of Ely: greeting. I wish and instruct and grant that the church of Ely and Bishop Hervey should have in their domain all those lands, together with people and customary rights, which Abbot Simeon was holding on the day on which he lived and died, unless they can demonstrate that at that time they held them rightfully by the permission of the King of England, and by the permission of Abbot Simeon and the community of the church of Ely. Witness: Robert, Count de Meulan and Gilbert de Aquila.

---

[24] Reading with EO: *gravesque operationes eidem castello debitas molestas habebat.*

[25] Cf. Miller, *Abbey and Bishopric of Ely*, pp. 157–8.

[26] Reading with the chapter-heading lists of E and F (p. 238.20, ed. Blake): *Carta regis Henrici de colligendo possessiones suas ad ecclesiam.* Source: monastic archives, cf. cartularies CDGM. Date: 1109 X 1133.

11. Another charter of the king against the usurpers of estates and goods of St Æthelthryth.[27]

Henry, King of the English, to the archbishops, bishops, abbots, earls, sheriffs and all faithful people of the whole of England: greeting. I wish and instruct that all those people who hold those lands which the Bishop of Ely claims, which my charter of Winchester testifies as having been sworn to as belonging to the fee of the church of Ely in the time of my father, and of which verbal notification has been set before my judiciary: let them acknowledge the lordship of the Bishop of Ely and let them subsequently perform service to him, such as I shall deem fit, according to the value of the lands. Witness: Geoffrey the chancellor and Geoffrey de Glinton and Payn Fitz John. At St Pierre-sur-Dive.

12. A charter of the king about exemption from the guarding of the town of Norwich, and about freedom from a state of burdensome servitude as a consequence of which the church of Ely was struggling miserably.[28]

Henry, King of the English, to the archbishops, bishops, abbots, earls, barons, sheriffs and all faithful people of the whole of England: greeting. You are to know that I have declared Bishop Hervey of Ely and all bishops of Ely succeeding him exempt now and for evermore from the provision of a guard of knights which they used to cause to exist in my castle of Norwich, and from those twenty-five shillings and five pence and a half-penny which they used to give every year from their allowance for my night-watch of that castle, and I declare him exempt from all their services, all customary procedures, all actions and all matters, which used to be brought about for the aforesaid castle at the expense of the bishopric of Ely. And I grant that the same Bishop Hervey and all the successors of that bishop may from henceforth have their own guard on the Isle of Ely performed by their own knights and all the services which they in former times used to perform in the previously named castle, as well and as fully as they used to be performed, to their fullest extent, in the castle. And I am making this exemption and grant, complete and unshaken, to Bishop Hervey and all bishops succeeding him, for the salvation of my soul and those of my father and mother, and for the forgiveness of my sins. Witness: Roger, Bishop of Salisbury and Alexander, Bishop of Lincoln, and Oinus, Bishop of Evreux, and Geoffrey the chancellor, and Robert, Earl of Gloucester, William, Earl of Warenne and William de Albini and Brian Fitz Count, and Hugh Bigod and

---

[27] Source: monastic archives, cf. cartularies CDGM; Brit. Mus. MS Add. 9822, fo. 73v. Date: Sept. 1127–July 1129; at Saint-Pierre-sur-Dive.

[28] Source: monastic archives, cf. Ely, Dean and Chapter, charter no. 3; cartularies CDGM. Date: 1123 X 1130; at Windsor.

Miles of Gloucester and Geoffrey de Glinton and William de Albini, *Brito,*
and William de Pont de l'Arche. At Windsor.

13. Another charter of King Henry against those who by their power were withholding the church's properties and services due to it.[29]

Henry, King of the English, to the archbishops, bishops, abbots, earls, barons,
sheriffs and all his faithful people of all England, French and English:
greeting. You are to know that I wish, grant and instruct that all those barons
and under-tenants who hold those lands which my charter of Winchester
about my treasury declares to have been sworn to in the time of my father as
belonging to the fee of the church of Ely, are to make acknowledgement of its
lordship and are, in consequence of this, to hold them as tenants of the
aforesaid church and the Bishop of Ely from henceforth and for evermore,
performing knight-service to the church, in accord with their tenure, and on
the understanding that services are statutory in respect to these same lands
and with the stipulation that the barons and under-tenants holding these
same lands are to be exempt, with respect to me and their other lords, of as
much service as they shall have been obliged to perform for the bishop and
the aforesaid church in statutory knight-service. And I wish and instruct that
the bishop and the church are to hold them well and honourably, in peace
and quiet, with *sake* and *soke* and *toll* and *team* and *infangentheof* and with
all their other customary rights and exemptions, as well and as quietly and
honourably as ever they hold another fee of theirs with these rights. And
those land-holders are from henceforth to perform their service in respect to
the aforesaid lands to the bishop, where the bishop performs other service of
his own in respect to his church. Witness: Roger, Bishop of Salisbury and
Geoffrey the chancellor and Robert de Sigillo and William de Tancarville and
William de Albini, the butler, and Ralph Basset and Geoffrey de Glinton. At
Eling, on my way through.

14. Another mandate of King Henry concerning the liberty of the five hundreds.[30]

Henry, King of England to Bishop Herbert[31] and Ralph de Belfou[32] and

---

[29] Source: monastic archives, cf. Ely, Dean and Chapter, charter no. 6; cartularies CDGM.
Date: perhaps 1127; at Eling.

[30] In E this charter is found added in the bottom margin. Source: monastic archives, cf. Ely,
Dean and Chapter, charter no. 4b (fragmentary); cartularies GM. Date: 1109 X 1115; at Castle
Holdgate.

[31] Bishop of Norwich, 1091–1119.

[32] Sheriff of Norfolk.

Ralph Passelewe[33] and all his faithful people from Suffolk, French and English: greeting. I am giving instructions that the episcopal see of Ely and Hervey, the bishop of that same place, may hold and possess in a good, quiet and honourable manner all customary rights belonging to the bishopric,[34] namely *sake* and *soke* and *toll* and *team* and *infangentheof* and *hamsocne* and *grithbryce* and <*fihtwite* and>[35] *fyrdwite* and all other rights of exacting penalties in the five-and-a-half hundreds of Wicklow, in as good a manner as this very church of Ely held them on the same day on which King Edward lived and died, and as was determined in the time of my father at Kentford, in the witness of several shires and in the presence of barons of my father, specifically, in the presence of Geoffrey, Bishop of Coutances and Walkelin, Bishop of Winchester and Baldwin, Abbot of St Edmund's and Peter de Valognes and very many others. And you are to know that I am not the giver of a warrant for anyone to have these rights – either concerning *soke* or concerning *sake* or concerning any other customary right – in the aforesaid hundreds, unless with the permission of the Bishop of Ely. Witness: Ranulf the chancellor and Gilbert de Aquila and Haimo the steward. At Castle Holdgate in Shropshire.

15. A charter of the king about a concession with regard to the knights who used to be demanded compulsorily from the church of Ely.[36]

Henry, King of the English to the archbishops, bishops, abbots, earls, barons, sheriffs and all his faithful people of the whole of England, French and English: greeting. You are to know that I have conceded outright to the church of St Æthelthryth at Ely, for the love of God and for the soul of my father and that of my mother and for the redemption of my sins, and at the request of Hervey, the bishop of this same church, forty pounds of those hundred pounds which the aforesaid church used to give in respect of scutage [when scutage was current throughout my land of England],[37] so that the church from now on for evermore shall only give, in respect of it, sixty pounds, at future times when scutage has been levied throughout the land, and thus the aforesaid church is to be quit for evermore of obligations concerning the aforesaid forty pounds. Witness: Roger, Bishop of Salisbury, Geoffrey, my chancellor, and Robert de Sigillo and William of Tancarville and William de Albini, the butler, and Ralph Basset and Geoffrey de Glinton and William de Pont de l'Arche. At Eling, on my way through.

---

[33] Justice in Norfolk.

[34] Here the Latin has simply: *omnes consuetudines suas*.

[35] The fuller version is attested in cartulary M, and is in line with the standard formulation.

[36] Source: monastic archives, cf. cartularies CDGM. Date: perhaps 1127; at Eling.

[37] An addition in F.

16. Again, a charter of the king about a remittance of money which used to be unjustly exacted from the church.[38]

Henry, King of the English, to the archbishops, bishops, abbots, earls, sheriffs, barons and all his faithful people of all England: greeting. You are to know that, from henceforth to eternity, for the benefit of God and St Æthelthryth and the church of Ely and Bishop Hervey and his successors, I have renounced claim to the forty shillings which used to be asked for from their land in respect of payment for a guard and in respect of his men. And I forbid that they should be demanded or given from henceforth, and that anything be taken on this account from its property or that of its men. And I make this concession for the salvation of my soul and the stability of my kingdom and for the souls of my father and mother and of my wife, Queen Matilda, and of William, my son, and of my predecessors and successors. Witness: John, Bishop of Lisieux and Robert de Sigillo and William de Tancarville and William de Albini and Geoffrey de Glinton and Payn Fitz John. At Argentan.

17. That Bishop Hervey by his own effort gained possession of the house[39] of Chatteris, and annexed it to the church of Ely with perpetual right of possession.[40]

On a different subject: Chatteris is a dwelling-place of nuns in the environs of the Isle of Ely, where[41] the monastic community, nominally established as an abbey, was hard pressed by the greatest difficulties, so long as it existed under royal control. Hervey, a man of great discernment, saw that the place was close to destruction and that the poor handmaidens of God were greatly distressed and completely unable to live in the place without better patronage. Guided by a sense of paternal duty, he therefore brought to bear the solicitude he felt as a bishop to bring about the emancipation of the household of Christ. Moreover, with wonderful efficiency, he procured the king's favour as the means of carrying out his desire. And, having taken this very great burden upon himself, he applied himself to the matter, his aim being to annex that house to the church of Ely with the right of perpetual ownership, and to hold from henceforth the principal power of appointing mothers and installing nuns there. At all events, the merciful hand of the

---

[38] Source: monastic archives, cf. Ely, Dean and Chapter, charter no. 4; cartularies CDGM. Date: perhaps 1129; at Argentan.

[39] Lat. *locus*.

[40] Source: local text commemorating Bishop Hervey, if not simply the compiler's inferences from the charters in chapters 18 and 19. The chapter was subsequently copied into the *Cronica fundationis monasterii seu abbatie de Chateriz*, Brit. Mus. MS Cotton, Julius A.i, fos. 75v. ff.; for which see now: *The Cartulary of Chatteris Abbey*, ed. Claire Breay (Woodbridge 1999).

[41] Reading with AE: *ubi*.

Lord brought it about that their father in matters of the soul should also be their father in material matters, and that, in all the emergencies with which a band of women had insufficient means to cope, they might, as daughters, have recourse to a father, and find appropriate assistance. Let no one, therefore, think that so great a bishop, abundantly endowed as he was with earthly resources in multiplicity, had in this affair acted in furtherance of any sinister intention: his motive in this enterprise was not earthly self-interest, but concern that the handmaidens of the Lord should not be taking thought for the morrow.[42] And how firmly he staked his claim to that house, for himself and his successors, and under what advantageous terms that house yielded itself to him, is testified by the following two charters, which the king's generosity granted to the church of Ely. And they are of this kind.

18. A charter of King Henry concerning the grant incorporating the Abbey of Chatteris, with all[43] things pertaining to it,[44] into the Isle of Ely.[45]

Henry, King of the English, to the archbishops, bishops, abbots, earls, sheriffs, barons and all the faithful people of the whole of England: greeting. You are to know that I have given and granted to God and the church of Ely and to Bishop Hervey, for mercy's sake, the Abbey of Chatteris, with its lands and properties and all things belonging to the same abbey. And I wish and instruct firmly that he shall hold it in peace and quietly and honourably with *sake* and *soke* and *toll* and *team* and *infanganetheof* and all customary rights and liberties, as well and as quietly and honourably as he holds his other lands belonging to the bishopric of Ely. Witnesses: Geoffrey the chancellor, William de Albini the butler, Geoffrey de Glinton, Payn Fitz John. At Saint Pierre-sur-Dive.

19. Another charter of the king, which he granted to St Æthelthryth in Ely, about the relaxation of a requirement for money from the church of Chatteris.[46]

Henry, King of England, to the archbishops, bishops, abbots, earls, barons, sheriffs and all his faithful people of all England, French and English:

---

[42] Cf. Matthew 6.34.

[43] Following the reading of E.

[44] Source: monastic archives, cf. cartularies CDGM; also copied into the Chatteris cartulary. Date: September, 1127 X July, 1129; at Saint-Pierre-sur-Dive.

[45] Lat. *de concessione abbatie de Chaterihs in Ely*. See *LE* i pr. S for the perception that Chatteris belonged to the Isle.

[46] Source: monastic archives, cf. Ely, Dean and Chapter, charter no. 5; cartularies CVGM; also copied into Chatteris cartulary. Date: perhaps 1127; at Eling.

greeting. You are to know that I have remitted for the benefit of the church of St Mary of Chatteris – which I have granted and given for mercy's sake to the church of Ely, for the love of God and the soul of my father and that of my mother and for the forgiveness of my sins and at the request of Hervey, first bishop of that same church – six shillings and seven pence of guard-money, which the aforesaid church of Chatteris used customarily to pay every year, so that from henceforth it is to be for evermore exempt from this in peace and quiet. Witness: Roger, Bishop of Salisbury and Geoffrey the chancellor and Robert de Sigillo and William de Tancarville and William de Albini, the butler, and Ralph Basset and Geoffrey de Glinton and William de Pont de l'Arche. At Eling, on my way through.

20. A charter of King Henry about the release of the vill of Hadham from a claim.[47]

Henry, King of the English, to Richard, Bishop of London and Hugh de Buckland and all his barons and all his faithful people of Hertfordshire, French and English: greeting. You are to know that I have given back to the Lord God and to St Peter and St Æthelthryth the virgin and to Hervey, Bishop of Ely, the manor of Hadham, in peace and quietude from now and for evermore, in accordance with how best the Abbey of Ely held it in the time of my father and in the time of King Edward, with *soke* and *sake* and *toll* and *team* and *infanganetheof,* inside and outside the town, this being a manor which Ranulf, Bishop of Durham, used to hold unlawfully. Witness: William, Bishop of Winchester and Roger, Bishop of Salisbury, and Robert, Bishop of Lincoln and William, Bishop of Exeter, and Robert, Bishop of Chester, and John, Bishop of Bath, and Ralph, Bishop of Rochester, and Ranulf the chancellor and Earl Roger de Mellent and Gilbert de Aquila and William de Albini and Hugh the steward and Nigel de Albini and Hasculf *de S. Jacobo* and Alan *filius Fialdi,*[48] and *Hanalus de Bitun.*[49] At Windsor. At Pentecost in the year in which the King's daughter was given in marriage to the Emperor.

21. A charter of the king to the effect that the monks and church of St Æthelthryth in Ely are to be exempt from the imposition of tolls everywhere throughout England.[50]

Henry, King of England, to his sheriffs and officers of England: greeting. I give

---

[47] Source: monastic archives, cf. cartularies GM. Date: 1110; at Windsor.

[48] So EG; *filius Flaldi* F, *Fladaldi* M.

[49] *Halanad' de Bidon* F.

[50] Source: monastic archives, cf. cartularies GM. This charter seems to date before Hervey's episcopate; see Blake's note. Date: 1103 X August, 1106; at Sawtrey.

instructions that, wherever the monks of Ely shall have been able to find timber and lead and iron and stone for sale, and other things of which there is need for the building of the church, they are to be exempt of all payment of toll and customs duty. Witness: Roger Bigod. At Sawtrey.

22. Again, another charter about the same matter.[51]

Henry, King of the English, to all his sheriffs and officers of all England: greeting. I give instructions that, wherever the monks of Ely shall have been able to find timber and lead and iron and stone for purchase, and other things of which there is need for the building of the church of Ely, they are to be exempt from payment of toll and all ferry-money and customs duty in exactly the same way as I instructed through my other writ, and no one is to do them injury on account of this or insult as a result of it, on pain of my penalty. Witness: the chancellor. At Sawtrey {*recte* Ditton}.

23. Charter of the king about the liberty of the hundreds of St Æthelthryth.[52]

Henry, King of England, to all barons who hold land in the hundreds of the Bishop of Ely: greeting. I instruct you to come to the bishop's meeting of the hundreds in accordance with the summons of the bishop's servants, with as good and full attendance as you and your people used best to come, from the time of my father and brother and latterly in my own time, and in the way that you are obliged to come, so that the church's holding of pleas and maintenance of the right may not be stayed because of the penury of those administering justice. And do for the bishop also, latterly, whatever you were accustomed to do for his predecessors. Witness: the chancellor. At Eling.

24. Another charter of the king to the effect that St Æthelthryth should everywhere have free jurisdiction over her people.[53]

Henry, King of England, to all sheriffs in whose shires Bishop Hervey has land: greeting. I do not wish men from the bishopric to engage in litigation, concerning suits with respect to which they have lodged pleas, in any place other than where they were accustomed to plead cases in the time of King Edward and in the time of my father and brother. Witness: the chancellor. At

---

[51] Source: monastic archives, cf. Ely, Dean and Chapter, charter no. 5B; cartulary G. Date: 1103 X August, 1106; at Sawtrey according to *LE*, but at Ditton according to Ely, Dean and Chapter, charter no. 5b.

[52] Source: monastic archives, cf. cartulary G. Date: perhaps 1127; at Eling.

[53] Source: monastic archives, cf. cartulary G. Date: 1109 X 1131; at *Cliva*.

King's Cliffe.

In fact, the bishop obtained many grants of protection from the king set out in the testimonies of written documents, and these are deposited among the treasures of the church for the safeguarding of the house.

25. That Bishop Hervey separated the victualling of the monks from the affairs of the bishopric, instituting an allowance for them, but a meagre and wholly insufficient one, in conflict with his oath that he would maintain the church, that is, the monastery, and the affairs of the whole place, without upheaval.[54]

Well then, in the diocese of Ely there is Thorney, a community of monks, and Chatteris, one of nuns, and Barnwell, one of canons regular. Bishop Hervey presided in honourable fashion over these three sorts of people living under a rule; he gave instruction in high moral standards to this diversity of orders, devoting such attention to all that you would think he had been attending to a single one.

It was also he who first separated the victualling of the Ely monks from the affairs of the bishopric – in a very constricting manner, however, bringing about the pain of perpetual expense and dissension. For he assigned to them, instead of many extensive and high-quality lands, some barren scraps of them, and scarcely any of those with fertile soil. These were insufficient to provide food for themselves and the guests who kept arriving. One reads in the *Gesta Pontificum Anglie* {*Deeds of the Bishops of England*}[55] that, although the bishopric of Ely is valued at the sum of £1,800, sustenance for what should be the monastery's proper complement – namely seventy-two monks and as many servants – is by no means provided, rather, it is for a much smaller number, namely, ninety, that provision is made, and that in the most meagre way. All the revenues allocated by God's dispensation to their use and enrichment had been disbursed and set aside for the bishops.[56]

For now that he perceived that he was protected by the king, the bishop began to contrive to bring about their diminution in all respects, although they themselves never gave their consent in writing or in anyone's witness. Nevertheless, they kept quiet, groaning under their breath, so that they should not be seen to be in dispute with the king and should not, by their

---

[54] Source: local text commemorating Bishop Hervey, that is, if the chapter does not consist entirely of speculative inferences by the compiler from the charter cited in *LE* iii. 26, together with another, not actually transcribed in *LE* (Dean and Chapter, charter no. 51), in which a more restricted allocation of resources is made for the monks. Specific reference is made to William of Malmesbury, *Gesta Pontificum*, iv .183.

[55] William of Malmesbury gives the figures: £1,400 to the bishop; scarcely £300 to the monks.

[56] Reading conjecturally at p. 261.20, ed. Blake: *episcopis*.

resistance, bring reproach, so to speak, upon their glorious reputation – should not be seen, that is, engaging in litigation while subject to a bishop – given, especially, that Archbishop Anselm of blessed memory neither gave his approval, nor bore witness in writing, to the changing of the place into a bishopric. And since the bishop was unwilling to heed the advice that the affairs of the place should continue as they had up till now, and at the same time without upheaval, the monastics of the group of neighbouring churches met together, observing that famous precept of Solomon: 'Do everything by consultation, and you will not be sorry after the deed,'[57] and they earnestly requested the safeguarding of these matters by means of prayer. But since the times were bad, they nevertheless accepted with reluctance what was offered, even though against their will – except that they always kept requesting larger amounts, until such time as a fair allocation for their needs should be granted, in accordance with the ordinances of canon law. It was particularly considered a priority that the income of an archdeaconry should never be subtracted from their share, where changes were being specifically made concerning their table-provision.

As a result, Bishop Hervey promised to improve and augment everything, to pay attention to customary practices, put small things in order and confirm the arrangements made, then to take measures for supplying the needs of the others, as each one's case demanded, out of consideration for their close relationship. The amount of love that is owed to this father may be appreciated from the charter written out below.

26. A charter of Bishop Hervey about the details of things which he laid down with respect to the victualling of the monks.[58]

Hervey, by the grace of God first Bishop of the church of Ely, to all children of the Church, both present and future: greeting. When, by God's ordinance, the religious community of Ely was to be committed to my rule and had been altered to the rank of an episcopal see, its title of 'coenobitic monastery'[59] having been abolished, with the authorization of the lord Pope Paschal and with the consent of our ruler Henry and the council of his nobles, I made the

---

[57] Ecclesiasticus 32.24 Vulgate, cf. 32.19 New English Bible.

[58] Source: monastic archives, cf. cartularies CDGM; Brit. Mus. MSS. Add. 9822, fo. 65; Egerton 3047, fo. 36. Ostensible date: 1109 X 1131. N.B. There is extant another charter of Bishop Hervey (Ely, Dean and Chapter, charter no. 51, printed in Miller, *The Abbey and Bishopric of Ely*, pp. 282–3) presenting a settlement less generous to the monks; but the compiler of *LE* did not chose to record it. The authenticity of the charter set out in *LE* is therefore disputed. Blake, Introd. p. l (= 50 in Roman numerals), after discussion, eventually accepts it as a genuine, later replacement of the less generous settlement. Nicholas Karn (pers. comm. 24.6.02) means to consider, in his forthcoming *Episcopal Acta* volume, whether it is a forgery, deriving its wording from Bishop Nigel's settlement, as recorded in *LE* iii. 54, 56, 85.

[59] Lat. *coenobium*.

decision to separate the monks' needs from the affairs of the bishopric. For the needs of the monks were previously catered for communally by means of all the wherewithal of the monastery in question. But I, fearing the fomenting of dissension on some such ground, if the arrangement remained thus in future, have organized the affairs of the monks separately from the affairs of the bishopric, and, for their needs, with their immediate agreement, I have allowed them to possess separately the properties listed below, and I grant that these properties should remain for evermore, just as they have been granted and apportioned, unless some more generous arrangement regarding the monks be made by my successors. These[60], therefore, are the names of the lands.[61]

Within the Isle: Sutton, Witcham, Witchford, Wentworth, Turbutsey, Whittlesey, Stuntney, with twenty-three thousand eels which lie near that manor,[62] and all revenues and offerings belonging to the altars of the mother church, for supporting the needs of the same church. And the church of St Mary of Ely with its lands and tithes and all things pertaining to the church itself. And specifically all the tithe of my Barton. And one dairy-farm in *Biela*.[63] And Stretham, subject to the following division: that two parts should be for the purposes of the guest-house, but the third for the needs of the monks. Also four weys of cheese in respect to Dernford. And six weys of salt in respect to Terrington. And certainly also timber in Somersham and in Bluntisham, as best they had it in the time of my predecessors. And upon the river-bank of Bluntisham a messuage with five acres of land where timber may be collected and with eight acres of meadow, where the oxen for dragging the timber may graze. Also their vineyard in Ely, just as they possessed it before I came to my bishopric. And six fishermen, along with their dwellings, to fish in the waters where they customarily did.

Outside the Isle, in Cambridgeshire: Hauxton, Newton, Shelford, Melbourn, Meldreth, Swaffham. And twelve skeps of corn and malt which the heirs of Hardwin de Scalers owe. In Suffolk: Barham, Winston, Stoke, Melton, Bawdsea, Sudbourne, Brightwell with *Rixemera*; also the soke of five-and-a-half hundreds,[64] Lakenheath, Undley, *Sceppeia* and *Fotesdorp*[65] are at the monks' command. And thirty thousand herrings from Dunwich. And I grant to them all their own servants in all their ministrations, so that

---

[60] At p. 262.17, ed. Blake, for *he* read *hec*; cf. p. 300.9.

[61] See maps in Miller, *Abbey and Bishopric of Ely*, following pp. 76 and 220.

[62] In *LE* iii. 54 (Bishop Nigel's charter) the eels of Stuntney are described more fully as: 'twenty three thousand eels which are caught in the marshes and waters which lie near that manor.' This is one argument for the inauthenticity of the charter-text in iii. 23.

[63] Identified with Beald Farm, near Ely, by Reaney, *Place names of Cambridgeshire and the Isle of Ely*, pp. 223f.

[64] Repunctuating at p. 263.8, ed. Blake, with comma rather than full stop after *dimidii*.

[65] Described as in Norfolk in *LE* iii. 54.

they may possess them freely with all their messuages. I permit moreover that they may have, and freely possess, all the gifts which have been given to the same monks before the time of my episcopate, or in my time, or shall be given in the future, whether consisting in lands or in churches or in tithes or in fisheries or in cash, or in any revenue whatsoever which any of the faithful may have bestowed upon them up to now or shall in time to come bestow upon them. Moreover I grant to them all the things written above and, in addition, their own court with all the liberties and customs which are observed in the lands which are in my jurisdiction, with absolutely nothing excepted, so that none of my successors may interfere in any respect whatsoever with their affairs, with the exception that he is to protect and maintain them with all their possessions faithfully and unceasingly. But if anyone, motivated by a spirit of ill-will, should wish to infringe, despise or reject this our grant and donation, let him be condemned by God and by all His saints, and let him be excommunicated by us in as far as this is allowed, and cut off from the company of all the faithful. Let it be done! Let it be done! AMEN.

27. Praise of the author concerning the miracles of St Æthelthryth which happened in the times of Bishop Hervey.[66]

The purpose, brothers, for which Christ the Lord so frequently brings about, through His saints, evidences of His activities, is so that the faith of hearers may increase as the outcome of what they hear, and so that ardent love may loosen devout lips for the praises of God. Hence, at the present time, it is incumbent upon us, whose life and tongue Christ has charged with His service, either to bring His deeds to the notice of many people by means of our studious endeavour, or most decidedly to bring reproach upon our knowledge in His sight. So then, in order that we may make our memory commendable before God, let us relate the things which He has deigned to bring to pass amongst us who are involved in the church of Ely, in the times of Hervey, our first bishop, to the glory and praise of his holy virgin Æthelthryth.

28. That the tower at the entrance of the church of St Æthelthryth was saved from fire resulting from a stroke of lightning.[67]

So then, in the 1111th year of the Lord's incarnation, on 20th April, the day in

---

[66] Source: material introductory to the miracle narrative recorded in *LE* ii. 129 and paralleled in B *(Book of Miracles)*. In the present case, specific reference to Hervey's episcopate has been added by the compiler.
[67] Source: miracle narrative also found in B *(Book of Miracles)*.

question being the sixth of the lunar month, in the 432nd year from the translation of the bountiful virgin Æthelthryth, but the fourth from the beginning of the bishopric, after a Monday night had already begun, there were great thunderclaps and horrendous lightning flashes right up till midnight, and the tower of St Peter, which is situated at the entrance of the church of Ely,[68] was in the night set on fire by being struck by lightning at its highest point, but with the help of God's mercy and with the support of the merits of the saints, it was miraculously saved from the fire. I say that it was miraculously saved because it is never normal for fire ignited by lightning to have been quenched by water. And moreover, neither the raging fire nor the red-hot iron they were holding with bare hands, nor the lead falling in molten drops on their heads and backs, did any harm to the men who had climbed up on ladders, in the midst of the blaze, to save the tower. Some of them even held burning pieces of charcoal in their hands and were not burnt.

This fire is to be contrasted with the Babylonian fire which produced destructive forces out of the kindling laid beneath it, after having been ignited with flimsy sticks in the natural manner. This more recent fire, on the other hand, which had fallen from the firmament itself, was entirely burning out the forces of its nature in its horrible crackling noise and powerful conflagration. Violent though it was in the lightning-strike, the thunderbolt and the blaze, emitting as it did bursts of light, causing as it did timbers to burn and shake, and metals to melt, it did not harm human beings. Now, that other fire – one of lesser power to the extent that things which are from Heaven are not the same as earthly things – that fire, which for long stretches of time scarcely began to burn up dry timbers and spared a mere three men, provided evidence of the power of God by means of a great miracle, but the people in respect to whom it was made manifest were few in number. Moreover, this more recent fire, in spite of the collapse of beams, became controllable: whereas it spared neither iron nor the stones themselves and whereas the burning heat was by now not imaginary but very real, it acted upon flimsy timbers and weak bodies in the opposite way, in each of the two cases withdrawing whatever it was that might cause harm. Please, then, may all successive future ages join in celebrating the divine miracle and the power of God in both of the two cases: for it was the power of God that provided the means of escape from approximately comparable harm both for the beams in the tower and for the three men in the furnace.

---

[68] *Ecclesia*, the term translated as 'church' here, does not necessarily mean the abbey church as distinct from the monastery as a whole. So the reference is not necessarily to a tower on the site of the present west tower (the Norman work of which is thought to be of a somewhat later date), though it quite possibly could be. The *Winchester Annals* on the year 1111 declare: 'In the same year there came about a very powerful storm and terrible thunder, as the result of which a tower of the church of Ely fell, and the church caught fire.'

29. About a crippled man cured at the shrine of the blessed Æthelthryth.[69]

The treasure-house of miracles open to us confers riches from its abundance upon an impoverished sensibility, and hence it is not so much the case that we speak of it, as that it speaks in us. Although, as a consequence of its abundance, it makes any sensibility, however great, inadequate to bring it to public knowledge in its entirety, [nevertheless] it has left available to us the following expedient: we may speak of great things even though we ourselves are small, and in the particulars of which we shall have spoken, we may show forth feeling rather than cleverness.

So then, a certain Wihtgar supplies to us the following narration. With one foot bent back to his kidneys in a very bad curvature, he used to present a very sorry spectacle. Being aware that the merciful lady was very capable of being won over by prayer in every case of need, and had granted to many the successful outcome of her intercession, at the urgent prompting of his illness and at the invitation of his hope, in the end he approached the holy tomb of the lady saint, poured out sighs of supplication, sought aid and found a remedy. For the lady whose help he was invoking had pity, and immediately the ligature of his leg was unloosed,[70] his muscles relaxed, his foot was straightened out and made strong for firm walking. The church echoed with the sound of people rejoicing. The praise of God was proclaimed by all. St Æthelthryth became the subject of preaching. Report spread afar. Crowds of sick people were brought and mighty works of healing were performed, which to a large extent have escaped our memory, because of their very numerousness, and because of the shortage of writers or else their negligence. But there are a few exceptions, and of these we are going to give a truthful narration.

30. About a man with dropsy who earned the gift of health at the shrine of the blessed Æthelthryth.[71]

We observed one Baldwin swollen by the disease of dropsy, whose belly protruded like a wine-skin, and one of whose calves, along with the whole leg from the groin at the top as far as the sole of the foot, was swelling up like a thigh-boot. After having been long and wretchedly afflicted by this plight, he began imploring the help of God and St Æthelthryth. And the dutiful care of the lady saint did not withhold for any length of time the good health that

---

[69] Source: miracle narrative, not paralleled in B (*Book of Miracles*).

[70] Reading at p. 265.3, ed. Blake: *statim solutum est cruris vinculum* (expanding **from E: solut'**).

[71] Source: miracle narrative, not paralleled in B (*Book of Miracles*).

he longed for: rather, the effecting of a cure followed upon the volition of the suppliant, in that miraculously the skin around his shin-bone split, as if surgically incised, and so much pus flowed out that it was as if there were nothing but liquid in his body. And so, when he had been relieved of that burden, he henceforth obtained a complete recovery, giving thanks to the heavenly Physician and bearing the marks of a heavenly cure.

31. About a crippled woman cured at the shrine of the blessed Æthelthryth.[72]

Ralph, son of Colsuein, a monk of ours, while he was still tarrying in the secular World, had at his home at Soham, a serving-woman who was rendered totally disabled by heels bent back towards her buttocks and one hand immovably fixed under the armpit on her other side. On one feast-day of St Æthelthryth, she had herself transported in a cart with her candle, and because the crowd of people kept her not only from approaching the altar but even from entering the church, she invoked the aid of the holy virgin when she was at the entrance. Without delay, before the eyes of all, that whole crippling distortion melted away. The soles of her feet became firm and she made for the holy tomb with unhampered gait, carrying a light, and she caused the lips of one and all to fall open and proclaim God in a tumult of shouting. And so it was that there was multifarious celebration of that feast: as a result, monks sang together; as a result, congregations joined in acclamations, everyone joining together simultaneously in rejoicing and everyone together praising God. As for the woman who had been cured, she took the veil, made a promise of perpetual chastity, and every Saturday sought out the holy corpse, walking barefoot from the district of Soham. These events occurred in the times of Bishop Hervey – the one concerning the man with dropsy as well as the one concerning the woman.

32. That a causeway was made through the fen to the shrine of St Æthelthryth as the result of a revelation.[73]

Here is another thing which ought not to be concealed in silence. The proof of it is the fact that many people report it and it is well known.

Well then, in the time of Bishop Hervey, St Edmund appeared in a vision to a farmer from the vill of Exning, and spoke to him in the following words, chivvying him into action by saying: 'Good man, attend carefully to what I am saying. Fulfil the commands given you without fail, and, on

---

[72] Source: miracle narrative, not paralleled in B (*Book of Miracles*).

[73] This chapter is a marginal addition in E. Source: miracle narrative also found in B (*Book of Miracles*).

rising, go with all haste to the Bishop of Ely. And you are to say in my name that he should provide me with a causeway by which I may go to visit my lady, the most blessed Æthelthryth.' And soon, in Ely, just as he was commanded, the man hurried to the bishop and reported to him the command which he had received. The bishop, on hearing such remarkable news, wept for joy and put the question to several people as to whether he might by any chance be capable of fulfilling the command. And, as no one was coming forward to undertake the venture, a certain monk of that very church, called John, a man of the utmost simplicity of nature, speech and appearance, came and presented himself to the bishop, saying that he was willing and, with God's help, able, to carry out this work. And in fact, subsequently, on the orders of the bishop himself, he began to measure out a route from the land of Soham and cut a swathe of reeds to make a causeway; he also arched over river-beds with little bridges, and in this way that man, beloved of God as he was, in a short space of time was successful, and brought the work envisaged by Heaven to its conclusion. He constructed a causeway right into Ely through trackless expanses of marshland, while everyone marvelled and blessed God.

33. About Byrhtstan who, after having been put in fetters, was set free by the blessed Æthelthryth.[74]

While we are still dwelling on the subject of the praiseworthiness of the most blessed virgin Æthelthryth, we wish to refer to something which has been brought about recently: it is something worthy of report, sweet to those who hear it – and deservedly so; advantageous to those who keep it in remembrance, perhaps of future benefit to those as yet unaware of it.

In the time of Henry, King of the English, Duke of the Normans, in the sixteenth year of his reign in England, and in the tenth year of his tenure of the earldom[75] of Normandy, there was in the province of the church of Ely a man in the vill which is called Chatteris, Byrhtstan by name. He was born, as is the customary lot of mankind, amidst the eddies and adversities of the World, and it was amidst these also that he was brought up, in the customary way, with the nurture appropriate to boyhood and adolescence, until he reached adulthood. He then began to be ensnared more and more in the shameful entanglements of the World to such an extent that, as a result of

---

[74] Source: the first of a group of four miracle narratives found in CCCC 393 (which probably antedates *LE* ms. E), as well as in B *(Book of Miracles)*. Blake reports (p. 266, n. 3): 'A slightly different version of this miracle appears in Orderic Vitalis . . . where it is said to have been written up by Abbot Warin of Saint Evroult at Bishop Hervey's request.' See Orderic Vitalis, *Hist. Eccl.* iii. 122–33, translated in OMT ed. M. Chibnall, vol. vi, pp. 347–61.

[75] Lat. *comitatus*, cf. *comes Wilhelmus* in *LE* ii. 101 (p. 170.18, ed. Blake) from the *Worcester Chronicle*.

unfortunate involvements in usury, <neither>[76] gains nor any means of support whatsoever from any other sources, were forthcoming to provide him with a livelihood. His life was for a very long time spent in these shameful circumstances, and in this time he fell into such great bodily sickness that eventually he seemed to be very close to death. And after he had been immobilized for some while by so very unbearable an illness, he was inspired by the grace of God – as the outcome proved – and promised faithfully to surrender himself, in the monastic life, to the holy virgin Æthelthryth, in her monastery, for as much as remained of the rest of his life. Without delay, moreover, collecting together and bringing with him all his belongings, he most devoutly approached the monastery of the virgin, wishing to fulfil his promise, it being the lord Bishop Hervey who was exercising pastoral care of the place at the time. He begged for mercy from the monks, handing over himself and his belongings, for their enrichment.

But alas! That evil one, through whose ill-will Adam fell from Paradise, will never cease to direct his ill-will towards Adam's descendants until the last one who is to come. But God, who mercifully and sweetly arranges all things, always, omnipotent as He is, makes good things out of evil, and better things out of good. So, the news that the aforesaid Byrhtstan was desirous of adopting the religious life was heard by many people, and subsequently a certain minister of King Henry – and a servant, specifically, of the Devil – Robert, by name, and surnamed *Malarteis,* acted in pursuance of the teaching of his master, who always tells lies and is a deceiver. He arrived and issued a prohibition at the king's behest forbidding Byrhtstan from adopting the religious life, saying that he was a thief and that he had in his possession, in consequence of theft, money belonging to the king; that he was concealing this fact, and that he was requesting admittance to the monastic life with no other salvation in mind than that of escaping justice and the penalty for this crime. Need I say more? He was eventually sent to trial, guarantors of surety being provided, with Ralph Basset sitting in judgement, and with all the people of the province assembled at Huntingdon, as is the custom in England. The aforementioned Lord Hervey, Bishop of Ely, was present, with the Abbots Reginald of Ramsey and Robert of Thorney, and many monks and clerics. And, to cut a long story short, Byrhtstan, the accused, was brought before the court and the charges falsely laid against him were renewed. He denied the actions which had not happened: he was unable to confess what he had not done. He was charged by the other side with lying;[77] he was

---

[76] Reading at p. 266.25f., ed. Blake: *ut ex usuris infelicibus <nec> acquisita nec omnino aliunde victui suo alimenta provenirent.* In the version of Orderic there is no reference to illness or poverty: Brihtstan is simply represented as a money-lender.

[77] Reading with change of word-division at p. 267.18, ed. Blake: *de mendatio (= mendacio) arguitur.*

derided and abusively[78] treated. Certainly, a great many false allegations were undeservedly brought against him and then they passed a prejudiced judgement upon him, like that upon Susanna: he was to be handed over, with all his property, for the enlargement of the king's wealth. Then, under guard, he was bound and taken to London, where he was thrust into a dark dungeon, and there he was firmly and shamefully confined with iron chains of sufficient weight, and for a considerable time he was hard pressed by the daily torments of hunger and cold.

And, as his circumstances were of so miserable a character, such was his pressing need that he kept praying, as far as his ability and knowledge allowed, for the help of God. But because he had no confidence in obtaining this by his own merits – which he believed to be slight or, to be more truthful, non-existent – he began calling incessantly, with a tearful heart and what voice he could command, upon St Benedict, to whose precepts, as had been said, he had vowed to submit himself, and also upon the holy virgin Æthelthryth, in whose monastery he had envisaged doing so. So it was that being, for one thing, oppressed and constrained by iron, and for another, tormented with cold, and for yet another, exhausted by hunger, he endured for five whole months a wretched life, grieving in the darkness. Without doubt he would have preferred to die rather than to live [so] unhappily. And seeing that absolutely no human aid was available, he did not cease to call upon St Benedict and St Æthelthryth with continual groanings, sighs, sobs and sometimes tears, as he ruminated in his heart or with his lips. Need I say more? One night, when throughout the city the bells signalling the praises of nocturns were being rung[79] and he, in his dungeon, along with the rest of his hardships, had been starving without any food for three days on end and was, by now, almost unconscious and despairing utterly of bodily recovery, he kept repeating, with a plaintive voice, the names of the saints previously mentioned. But God, in His clemency and mercy, who is for evermore the unfailing fount of all goodness, who despises no one in circumstances of need, and chooses no one for his power or riches, at last showed the petitioner His mercy – mercy which had been sufficiently yearned for, and which had been delayed for a purpose: that of making the yearning greater, and ensuring that, once mercy was obtained, all the more delight in it would result.

For there in his presence, as he cried out, were St Benedict and St Æthelthryth with her sister Seaxburh! But, being terrified by the unaccustomed light which went before the saints in advance of them, he covered his eyes with his hand. As the saints arrived along accompanied by

---

[78] Reading at p. 267.18, ed. Blake, with AB and CCCC 393: *conviciis.*

[79] Lat. *cum signa . . . ad nocturnas laudes pulsarentur.* Note that here (p. 267.35, ed. Blake) as also later in this chapter at p. 269.9, the reference could be to the striking of *semantra* as much as to the ringing of bells.

this same light, St Æthelthryth addressed him as follows: 'Byrhtstan, why are you so repeatedly assailing us with tears? Why are you disturbing us with such great cries?' He, for his part, weakened from lack of food, on hearing himself called by name, was rendered seemingly witless and filled with joy at the magnitude of the miracle: as a result, he became completely incapable of making a reply. Then the lady saint said, in addition: 'I am Æthelthryth whom you have been so frequently invoking. This saint here with me is Benedict, under whose way of life you have vowed to serve God, and from whom you have many times over asked for help. Do you want to be set free?' On hearing this utterance his spirit revived and he said, as if waking from sleep: 'My lady, were it by any means possible for me to live, I would want to get out of this execrable dungeon. But now I see myself so afflicted by diverse constrictions that, having lost all my bodily strength, I have no hope any longer of escaping.' In reply, the lady saint said, 'What you are saying does not accord with what logicality demands. No. I want you to be returned to life, and then, as you proposed, to be my servant for the whole remainder of your life.' Then the holy virgin turned to St Benedict. 'Come on,' she said, 'Dom Benedict. Do what was ordered by the Lord!' At these words, the venerable man, Benedict, approaching the man bound in fetters, inserted a finger in the iron ring between two fetters and, drawing it forward with what appeared to be slight effort, dragged those fetters, now broken at God's command, away from the feet of the man in chains, who felt nothing! But when he had removed those fetters from him, he threw them from out of his hand as if in indignation, and hit the largest joist of the floor above with such force that the soldiers who were lying on the upper floor woke up in terror at the sound of such a loud impact.

Afraid that the prisoners had escaped, they speedily came running together to the dungeon with torches ablaze. And, finding that the entrances were completely undamaged and secured, they entered, using keys. But, seeing that man whom they had sent to be fettered set loose, they marvelled all the more. And they asked questions about the loud noise they had heard – for instance, who had made it and had set the man in fetters loose as well – and another man, chained up with him in the dungeon, replied to them, while he himself said nothing. 'I do not know', he said, 'who the persons were who came into the dungeon accompanied by a very bright light and spoke a great deal with this companion of mine. But as for what they said or did, ask the man best acquainted with the facts.' And, turning to Byrhtstan, they said, 'Tell us what you heard or saw.' And Byrhtstan, said: 'St Benedict was here with St Æthelthryth and her sister Seaxburh, and they took the fetters from my feet. But if you do not believe me, believe the evidence of your eyes.'

And on seeing the miracle, they had no doubts about it, and, when morning came, they reported it to Queen Matilda, who happened to be in that same city at the time. She immediately sent one of the chaplains of the court, called Ralph, to the dungeon, to enquire whether the reports were true or not. On arriving and seeing how the fetters had been broken, and also hearing, through his companion, about the three persons who had entered the dungeon accompanied by light, about the words which they had spoken, about the sound which they had made, and observing that these had undoubtedly come about by divine agency, he began to weep copiously. And, turning to Byrhtstan, he said: 'Brother, I am a servant of St Benedict and St Æthelthryth: speak with me in love of them.' And he replied, 'If you are the servant of the saints to whom you refer, your arrival is welcome. Be assured that the things which you see or hear of as having been brought about with regard to me, are true and not the outcome of sorcery.' And Ralph embraced him and, amid joy and weeping, brought him to the presence of the queen and of many nobles of the land who were in attendance.

Meanwhile, the report flew through the whole city of London, faster than any bird, and reached the ears of more or less all the citizens. Then, all around, the citizens lifted a shout to Heaven. Irrespective of sex and age they all, with one accord, blessed the Lord and ran to the court, to which they had heard he had been led. A great number of people[80] shed profuse tears of joy. The rest who saw or heard, marvelled.[81] The queen, indeed, filled with joy at the unusual character of this exceptionally great miracle, ordered the bells throughout all the monasteries of the city to be rung and the praises of God to be sung in every community of a religious order of the Church. And while Byrhtstan was visiting as many as possible of the churches of the city, rendering devout thanks to God from his overwhelming joy, a great crowd was following him and going ahead of him through the streets, and everyone was eager to see, as it were, a new man. Moreover, when he had arrived at the church of the blessed Peter which is called Westminster, Gilbert, the abbot of the place in question, a man learned in liberal and theological letters, led a procession with all the monks outside the monastery to meet him. For he said: 'If it is our duty that the relics of some dead person should be welcomed in a church with festal pomp, let us, as an even greater duty, receive with honour living relics, namely, this man. For, whereas in the case of a dead person, we who are still set in the midst of a fragile life are in doubt as to where his spirit may be: concerning this man, on the other hand, we are well aware that in our presence he has been visited and set free by God, who does nothing contrary to justice.'

After these matters had thus been brought to their conclusion, the queen hoped to have possession of these same fetters at her bidding, but

---

[80] Adopting with Blake (p. 269.7) the reading of F, *quamplurimi*.

[81] Or, following A, CCCC 393: 'the rest marvelled at what they saw or heard'.

Byrhtstan was totally unwilling to be separated from them before taking them to the monastery of the virgin and queen St Æthelthryth, by whose intervention he knew that he had been rescued from chains. And so the queen, once she had heard his reasoning, did him no violence, but ordered that he be honourably conveyed to the aforementioned place. As he[82] went out of the city, young men and old were astonished by him, virgins and widows were amazed, crowds beyond number of both sexes looked on, giving thanks to almighty God. And equally, when he arrived at the monastery referred to, the bishop and all the brothers came forth to meet him in procession, joining in the praises of God and their lady intermediary, St Æthelthryth. There, he carried out his resolve in adopting the monastic life. And they placed the fetters by which he was shackled in the same church, suspended in front of the altar as a memorial of this most important miracle, as a public spectacle, in praise of our Lord Jesus Christ, to whom be honour and glory throughout all ages. AMEN.

34. How someone was freed from a pain in the head by putting the chains of St Æthelthryth against his cheek.[83]

One should not pass over in silence, in view of its importance, yet another miracle which was brought about in the aforementioned church through the merits of the same glorious virgin, who by the integrity of her mind and body was pleasing to the Bridegroom of virgins.

Now, it came about that a brother – according to the flesh – of a certain provost of this same monastery was tormented by God with a serious and intolerable toothache, so that neither the refreshment of food nor the taking of sleep could benefit him. And so, beset by the distress of that torment, he was nearly driven mad by the extreme inflammation, and began to dip his jaw, from which the agony originated, frequently into water, so that the horror of this raging pain might be mitigated and a little rest obtained for a moment. But although, thanks to this endeavour, he was finding the discomfort less hard to bear, he still could not arrive at a cure by this means. Having vainly made these and other efforts at obtaining restoration of health, he made his way to a street in Ely and asked a blacksmith who dwelt there and was skilled in the practice of this kind of art, to extract the tooth for him. Seizing the instruments suitable for this operation, he took hold of the tooth, the source of the pain, but the instrument in question sprang back, broken! Furiously angry, therefore, because the instrument had broken and all effort at remedy had proved vain, he threw the iron tool from his hands to the ground. He instructed the patient to go outside while he made

---

[82] Reading with B, and CCCC 393 at p. 269.25, ed. Blake: *exeunte.*

[83] Source: miracle narrative, included in CCCC 393 as well as in B *(Book of Miracles).*

adjustments to the iron tool which would extract the source of his pain from the root. The patient, going out, hesitated in anxiety as to what he was to do, and where he should turn. Finally, he was struck by a salutary plan: he took himself off in the direction of God's medicine of merciful compassion, knowing, and faithfully trusting, that he could be saved from all discomfort of sickness, if he would deign to be present there.

Well then, he recalled to mind the way in which the blessed Æthelthryth, shortly before, had released a certain prisoner from fetters: the way in which, through her glorious merits, the beneficent power of God had broken these same fetters; how full of pity and how powerful she had been in this business. He made his way, walking quickly, to her church. Full of devotion, he planted kisses upon the fetters hanging before the altar in reverence of her, not once but over and over again, and with all his might asked that the pity and power of the holy virgin be demonstrated to him in the distress and urgent need arising from his extreme pain. In that place there came about a fulfilment and demonstration of what the true and highest Truth had preached for the strengthening of the minds of the faithful: 'Ask and ye shall receive! Knock and it shall be opened unto you!'[84] For the door of divine mercy was opened for this man when he knocked, as the outcome of the matter in what followed made clear. Eventually, when he had thoroughly kissed, over and over again, with enormous devotion, the fetters in which the power of God and the merit of the glorious virgin was made manifest, he moved the ring which was between the fetters against his jaw, then touched the tooth with it and – something marvellous to relate – after the touching, such an abundance of sweat came flooding from his body that you would <not>[85] doubt that he had been very generously douched with water! What observation is one to make about this fact, except that simultaneously, along with the sweat, the discomfort of the pain also left him, through the merits and intercessions of the blessed Æthelthryth? The man, to be sure, giving thanks to God and the glorious virgin – to God, as the enactor and the virgin as the supplicant – returned, with good health and joy, to his own home, spreading the report all around of the good things done with regard to him by the pity of God.

35. About Ralph the schoolmaster, who was freed from a swelling of the throat by invocation of the name of St Æthelthryth.[86]

Ralph, a miserable sinner, also known as the *Monitor* of the school of

---

[84] Matthew 7.7; Luke 11.9.

[85] Translating as if the reading at p. 270.31, ed. Blake, were: <*non*> or <*haud*> *dubitares*.

[86] Source: autobiographical miracle narrative by Ralph of Dunwich, also included in CCCC 393 and in B (*Book of Miracles*). It includes allusions to the Book of Tobit, the *Actus Theophili*, Gregory the Great, *Dialogues*, and to a phrase from Greek theology.

Dunwich, to his kind masters and brothers, the performers of daily service to the virtuous virgin and most puissant lady saint, Æthelthryth: the eternal joy of true salvation.

While I owe very many thanksgivings to Christ, the virgin Son of a virgin Mother, for His very many benefactions, and at the same time to the holy virgin Æthelthryth, see, in your hands is what, for me, is especially marvellous to contemplate, outstandingly a source of joy, and particularly recent. I have considered it the most important thing to obey your command with humility and not to go astray in any respect from the straight line of truth – to the best capability of my memory – in my testifying to all that is holy.

The well-known Avenger of crimes – powerful in that He does not lack[87] a Discloser, whose insight finds a way through all dark, remote and secret matters, whatever they may be, penetrating also the hidden recesses of our hearts with the most keen perception – <seeks out> in the place of my abode, round about me and within me, all habituation to evil and dishabituation to good – if I may express my thoughts with brevity of language but amplitude of feeling.[88] For what does a pretence to good qualities, or the concealment of bad, achieve, since good fruit does not result from either? And again: what do good works achieve, that are done for worldly gain or worldly glory, when the prophet forbids virgins, violated in their thinking, to trust in the words of falsehood, while over and over again representing proudly as the temple of God what is, in fact, the bawdy-house of Hell? Therefore, He who is believed by the Greeks[89] {to oversee all things} †PANTEFORAN†[90] and by us to be OMNIUM CONSPECTOR {the Observer of all}, looking down upon the rebellion of my little self and casting me down from the support of his right hand, left me suddenly powerless, in such a way that I should clearly feel it, as if I were all of a sudden handed over to the jurisdiction of a tyrant. For I who, just now, used to be healthy in all parts of my body, who just now had been exerting my strength menacingly against my brothers, who just now had been walking with chest held high,

---

[87] One might have expected *qui* rather than *quo non eget indice vindex* (p. 271.6f., ed. Blake).

[88] This extremely difficult sentence begins, in the Latin, with what appear to be two lines of hexameter verse, from which the author slides into prose. At p. 271.7, after *vindex*, I have notionally replaced Blake's full stop with a comma, and e.g. after *penetrans* (p. 271.8) have supplied e.g. <*petit*>, as the sentence otherwise has no main verb.

[89] The poetic form is used: *ab Argolicis* = 'by the Argives'.

[90] At p. 271.15, ed. Blake, the *LE* manuscripts have PANTEFORAN, which might be interpreted as equivalent to Greek ΠΑΝΤ ΕΦΟΡΑΝ, 'to oversee all things'. Indeed, from the CCCC 393 and *Book of Miracles* it appears that Ralph must originally have used Greek letters. The reading in CCCC 393 is plainly ΠΑΝΘΕΦΩΡΑΝ, to which is added the interlinear transliteration *panteforan*. The Greek spelling is problematic and one would expect a substantival form to balance the Latin *conspector*, rather than an infinitive.

who just now was insolently breathing menaces against those nearest to me <. . . >[91]. †But at this point there was a new deal of the right hand of the Most High.†[92] Immediately, I became ill in all parts of my body; in my illness, I felt a very great weakness coming upon me; in my weakness, I fell right to the ground; when falling, I almost stopped breathing.

The disease[93] which people commonly call 'felon'[94] invaded my poor throat with its dire poison; having invaded it, it puffed it out generally, in such a way that the lethal swelling in question spread in all directions – to right and left, in shoulder, back and chest – and it projected over them like a bag: from a human chin there hung, as it were, the dewlaps of a bull. Furthermore: the strength contained in the poison was sufficiently indicated externally by a discoloration of the skin. And while, externally, that plague was swelling up to an exceedingly horrible extent, it was swelling internally as well in a dangerous way. Alas! What an accumulation of misery constricted my wind-pipes, the passages of my throat, and the thoroughfares of my neck, and left no way through for either voice or food. What pitiful things to remember! That poison of the worst kind crept into my tongue, caused the tongue to swell up so as to fill the palate-cavity and to force my jaws to gape open in a pitiful manner. My mouth, ears, eyes, nostrils, hands and feet were deserted by their functions and lay prostrate, as if buried.[95] My shins, thighs, kidneys, flanks, stomach, innards, all individually were severely tormented by their own particular aches. Was urine of a blood-red colour, and searingly hot, not an avowal of intestinal pain? The following was a vision of mine, which came in the night but not while my eyes were closed or I was sleeping: a long rope was tied at one end to my wretched tongue and at the other end was being pulled up high.

I played this game of chance for four days. Nicholas, one of my brothers – the one I had summoned and most longed to see – visited me. Other people visited me too. But, finding me without voice, without sight, without hearing, without any sensory perception, without movement of the limbs, they went away without being recognized by me, as I learnt from them when they disclosed it later on. And while my flesh was being oppressed by ills of this magnitude, as if by death, my mind none the less was, itself, at all events, alive, and sensitive to the discomforts of my body. It was in a state of anguish; it kept on being ferociously accused by its conscience; it kept making promises to God of repentance and the making of amends, if such a great flagellation

[91] Assuming a lacuna at p. 271.19, ed. Blake, after *spirabam*.

[92] Lat. *sed hec mutatio dextere excelsi*. Perhaps we should read *hic* ('here', 'at this point') for *hec*.

[93] Reading at p. 271.21, ed. Blake: *morbus*, not *morbum*.

[94] Lat. *fello*.

[95] The Latin of the last part of this sentence scans as a hexameter.

should be a matter of holy chastisement, and not yet of rightful damnation.

So, grieving though I was, inwardly, as much about the fact that I had offended God as about my suffering, mute though I was and unable to use my tongue, I none the less drew breath and with heartfelt sighing prayed, by the power of the Holy Cross, about my restoration to health, to the Lord who rose from the dead victorious on the third day, whose voice the dead hear. I also prayed to the Mother of the Lord in her immense power, by her share in the suffering of the death of the Lord, the Lady whose soul a sword pierced – the Lady who rescued Archdeacon Theophilus from the very claws of the Devil by the retrieval of his written pact.[96] I prayed also to the Archangel Michael, along with the rest of the angels: for, as leader of the heavenly host, provost of Paradise and victor over the dragon, he comes to the aid of the people of God. The Baptist, who plucks up and breaks down, builds and plants, preparing the way of the Lord, received prayers from me; also the Prince of the Apostles with the rest of the apostles, against whom the gates of Hell do not prevail; †<not only they> but <also,>†[97] along with the first martyr, and our precious lord King Edward and the rest of the martyrs, the blessed Blaise, martyr and Bishop of the city of Sebaste, to whom the power has been conferred by the Lord of curing all manner of throat-ailments. The power of Martin, the father of Tours, along with the other confessors, was invoked by my groanings – he who is an equal of the apostles and the distinguished resurrector of three dead men. Nor, along with the rest of the virgins, did I fail to call upon her who was forgiven many sins, whom He greatly loved, thanks to whose tearful prayers another man who was four days gone, came back to life.[98]

In this way and that, I sought for consolers, and they were not liberators: my suffering, you see, was weighing down on me increasingly, presumably because, having offended the Lord, I had equally offended them all. Meanwhile, deprived of all hope and racked by the greatest possible amount of pain, I would not have had a refuge . . . when the saving thought came to my mind, even in my stupidity, of the most elegant mercifulness of St Æthelthryth who, in a recent miracle, had already brought light to the

---

[96] The reference is to a work entitled the *Actus* (or *Historia* or *Poenitentia*) *Theophili*, translated from the seventh-century Greek by Paul, a deacon of Naples, in the late ninth century, which 'recounts the story of Theophilus . . . archdeacon of Adana in Cilicia, who humbly declines a bishopric but is then consumed by envy of the new bishop. He signs away his soul to the Devil, but later repents and prays to the Virgin Mary, who regains from the Devil the charter that Theophilus has signed in his own blood.' Information from http: www.wmich.edu/medieval/research/saslc/volone/the.htm

[97] Reading conjecturally, at p. 272.15, ed. Blake, in line with an idiom frequent in *LE*: *sed <et> cum protomartire et pretioso domino nostro Ædmundo rege et ceteris martiribus beatus . . . Blasius . . .*

[98] For the identification here of Mary of Bethany (cf. John 11.1ff.) with other women in the Gospels, including Mary Magdalene, see F. L. Cross, *Oxford Dictionary of the Christian Church*, article on 'Mary Magdalene'.

nocturnal shadows of a dungeon, had with mercy and power set loose the feet of a chained-up prisoner, had broken the iron fetters as easily as if they were wax, and let him depart to her holy burial-place, unchained, free and giving thanks with joy and honour.

As I was ardently and confidently repeating my request for St Æthelthryth's merciful, swift and miraculous aid, my lady ally[99] – to whom I had allied myself through a priest, as Tobias allied himself to Sarah through an archangel[100] – likewise promised my service to this merciful saviouress, St Æthelthryth, to whom she had previously vowed herself when rescued by her holy merits from the brink of death. I made my vow by means of my mind only; she, by means of both mind and lips: we both vowed the same thing. May God be universally praised, and God's friend, the mighty St Æthelthryth, by whose merits the Lord had mercy on me. For after the prayers and vows, my wretched tongue began to be split apart near the front, to the right: poisonous filth flowed down from it. And now, through that fissure of my tongue, the venom, as if through the aperture of a fountain, was channelled off, flowing in all directions – that venom which, as you will recall I have already said, had caused general swelling of the tongue itself, the gullet, the throat and the neck. There spread in abundance through my slack lips that most filthy of all salivations. I shudder to admit, and you perhaps may shudder to hear, how, since my weary jaws were unable to spew out that viperous slime which had accumulated in the whole palate-cavity – slime of the greatest possible foulness – other people's fingers ejected it, squeezed my extended tongue, scraped it and washed it. It is in just this way that the guts of cattle are treated[101] by butchers. But that is not all: when a number of days had passed – after the plague had at last[102] been expelled, and my senses had been recovered, my body had recovered little by little and my heart had recovered gradually – now that my hope of rising to my feet and walking should have been made a reality – see! – here was double trouble: my hope was made vain. For I had a shin bent back wretchedly towards the thigh, the muscles of my knee[103] having become contracted. Many days saw the continuation of my lameness. Wretched as I was, ungrateful and faithless, I manifested the state of my heart in my bodily lameness. Once again I made new vows, new prayers, as follows: 'O most powerful lady, St Æthelthryth, thou who hadst mercy upon a man four days gone: bring it about, and bring it about for one who is lame, that I may be able to go to the holy threshold of thy house of prayer to give thanks, and to the other thresholds of the saints,

[99] Lat. *socia mea*. His wife is meant, but the language used of her is eccentric.

[100] See Tobit 6.9ff.

[101] Reading with BE and CCCC 393: *tractantur*.

[102] Reading conjecturally: *tandem* for *tamen* (p. 273.4, ed. Blake).

[103] Reading conjecturally (after *poblitis* in E): *poplitis* (p. 273.7, ed. Blake).

those across the sea as much as those on this side of the sea. May their sanctity aid me to bring this to pass!' Let renewed praises be offered to the most holy lady, in view of the renewal of her benefactions! Rejoicing, therefore, that my health was being returned to me: I set out to Ely, as was fitting.

But now, near the village of Kentford, the lofty building of the holy house was already presenting itself to view, and it was no secret either to the shadows of my ignorance – dark as night though they were – by whose power it was that my health was restored when – see! – high up in the clouds, which were my travelling-companions, the shining face of the Full Moon appeared. To one side and the other there were lights sprinkled around, imitating, if not its beauty of magnitude, at any rate its brightness. Furthermore, this manifestation shone out above the place of the holy burial-place of our blessed lady and her saintly lady companions, the time being about the first hour of daylight on the 21st July, when it was not yet the date of the Full Moon's appearance, but approximately that of the {New Moon's} conjunction, as the Sun was leaving the third Moon {of the lunar month} in the Nabatean regions,[104] the Moon being calculated without any intercalated days.[105] That shining light, moreover, appeared in all its brilliance 'to me most recently of all, as to one born out of due time',[106] my companions being astounded and pointing it out: it was not a grander spectacle in my eyes than also in theirs. For not even did Benedict's vision[107] become wholly clear in his beholding of it – if it is permissible to utilize an analogical scaling-down whereby that which concerned the whole universe is applied to a few heavenly bodies, and that which concerned saintly masters, applied to blameworthy servants. But I was thoroughly amazed, as a man is where unusual things are concerned, and in consideration of the fact that the heavenly bodies shed their light upon unworthy beings, I gave all the more profuse thanks for such a great sign of beneficence.

Exhausted though I was by the abnormal exertion of the journey, sometimes staggering along with blistered feet, sometimes supported by the

---

[104] A poetical way of expressing 'the East'.

[105] Lat. *cum iam non esset terminus pleni lunii, sed fere synodi, nabateis in partibus sole relinquente lunam tertiam, nullis epactis regulatam.* The whole interpretation here is speculative, but it seems that Ralph wished to stress that the phenomenon which he saw was not actually a Full Moon. It manifested itself, in fact, close to the beginning of the 'synodic' month (the month from New Moon to New Moon). Intercalated days would have meant that what was nominally a New Moon was not in fact completely new. Ely is to the North-West of Kentford, so Ralph would have had the rising Sun behind him when he saw his vision.

[106] See 1 Corinthians 15.8.

[107] See Gregory the Great, *Dialogues*, 2. 35, for St Benedict's vision of 'the whole universe gathered, as it were, under one sun-beam'. There is still extant an eleventh-century manuscript of Gregory's *Dialogues* which is believed to have come from Ely; see Meadows and Ramsay, eds., *A History of Ely Cathedral*, p. 157.

arms of my companions or a stick, I nevertheless came all the way to Ely that same day. But as soon as I reached the holy Isle, the Isle, that is, which the presence of the holy virgin ladies sanctifies, it was with firm footsteps – with all parts of my body revived, as if I had suffered no tiredness or hurt – and without the support either of my companions or of my stick – as if I were transformed out of myself into another person – that I approached the monastery, soaked the holy threshold with tears – less than I should have done – lying prostrate on the ground, and presented myself to my most precious saviouress, St Æthelthryth, as her servant by right for evermore, with thanksgiving. But, because to give thanks is to render pleasing service, it remains – O most beloved brothers, who on seeing that I had given my surrender to your lady have adopted me as a brother – that you take brotherly care of me by aiding me with your prayers, so that she who is to receive perfect thanks – she who restored my bodily members to health – may also give me back a healthy mind. May He grant this, to whom, with His saints, belong salvation, honour and dominion, for ever and ever. AMEN.

36. That someone deprived of all bodily functions was restored to his former state of health.[108]

It would also be unbecoming to conceal in silence the fact that the ineffable mercy of God restored a certain knight to health through the blessed Æthelthryth. This man, who lived not far from the monastery of St Edmund's, on his own estate, in the vill which is called Barningham, fell ill for causes of which perhaps even he was unaware. As the trouble gradually became worse, he took to his bed. His physicians were unable to cure him: no, they despaired of him, and so he was abandoned by them. Not to speak of other afflictions affecting the different parts of his body, he entirely lost his sight, hearing and the power of speech. Now that his wife and his household of children <and>[109] servants had seen him afflicted by this illness, so unusual and generally unheard of, they had long forgone every type of joy; then, as a consequence of their excessive unhappiness, they came to hate – not happiness, I am not saying that – but the memory of him, and they assumed a lugubrious demeanour, so to speak, not so much in body as in mind. While he was in the grip of this kind of sickness or – to speak more correctly – in this kind of death, for fifteen days and as many nights, without any sign of improvement, all that time an onlooker would have thought that he was someone from the homes of the Egyptians when they lost their first-born,[110] except that here there was more wailing and mourning. To be

[108] Source: miracle narrative, included in CCCC 393 as well as in B (*Book of Miracles*).
[109] Reading conjecturally at p. 275.11, ed. Blake: *pignerum servorum<que> familia*.
[110] Exodus 11.1ff.

precise, he was mourned by all his neighbours; for they loved him. But all his family and friends had more hope of the burial of their anxieties than of his recovery. Some were wondering at the magnitude of his illness; others were making entreaty for the invalid's restoration to health: all in their compassion with the struggling patient were grieved at his slipping away.

However, the Lord, who is wisely provident in all His dealings, arranged matters kindly, out of pity for him. For, one night, the most holy virgin Æthelthryth appeared in St Edmund's town to a certain married woman, when she was neither fully awake nor completely asleep. While she was hesitating in doubt as to whether she was asleep, she was all at once woken up, and then said that she was awake. The virgin said to her: 'Tomorrow, after the Sun is once more to be seen over the fields, and you take a walk through the market-place, perhaps to conclude some pieces of business, you will hear some people commiserating with one another about a man named Leofmær, who is in the grip of a serious illness, in Barningham. When you have heard their laments, and have made enquiries as to who he is and what illness it is by which he is gravely afflicted, you are to say to them: 'Go. Make candle-wick, and with it encircle the truckle-bed on which he is lying, that is, from his head along his right side as far as his feet, then from his feet along his left side as far as his head, and afterwards cover the wick with wax and make a candle. He, for his part, is to take that candle, in person, if he is well enough, to the Isle of Ely to the church of the virgin Æthelthryth, or send it by means of some faithful messenger to the end that, through her prayers, he may recover from this illness.' And as the woman was pondering who it might be who was talking with her about this matter unknown to her – and at night – the virgin, not wishing to leave her to her own thoughts, in uncertainty, answered her saying: 'I am Æthelthryth, who repose in Ely, and you are to do faithfully what I tell you, having no doubts about the things which I am saying.' With these words, she disappeared.

And when morning came, the woman, not forgetting the secrets which had been revealed to her by divine agency, rose with all speed. And wanting to test whether the things she had heard were true, she made her way to the market-place, perhaps for other matters of business, but especially for the sake of Leofmær. For a little while, she walked around, looking at the goods for sale, with ears wide open to the voices of different people, waiting to discover whether she would hear anything of the matters referred to earlier. And while she was doing so, she heard some people with whom she was little enough acquainted, speaking to one another as follows: 'Alas! Alas! Leofmær, our friend, is dying.'

Going up to them inquisitively, she said: 'What are these things which you are discussing with one another? And why is it that you are showing signs on your faces of such great sadness?' As she seemed someone who would feel sorry for them, they carefully related in sequence the things which had befallen the oft-mentioned Leofmær. They indicated the manner and time of his illness, asking her, if she had any knowledge pertinent to the matter, to make plain what she would usefully advise. And she, as if taught by a good schoolmaster, said: 'When I had laid my limbs to rest after my day's work,[111] at a late hour, as is usual among working people, the noble virgin Æthelthryth appeared to me when I was not completely asleep and told me, one after another, the things which you are talking about, adding something which has just been proved true: that, when I came to the market-place today, I would find you having a conversation about this matter.' And the woman added: 'Go as fast as you can to the house of the sick man, make a wick, encircle his bed with it, and making a candle, send it to the church of the aforesaid virgin by his, or someone else's, hands, so that, through her prayers, God may look favourably upon him and he may enjoy better health. I am giving you this information not on my own account but at the behest of the blessed virgin.'

And they, on the one hand knowing the extreme distress of the sick man, and on the other, hearing the command of the virgin conveyed, at God's instigation, through the woman, returned to the home of the bedridden man without delay, with a view to carrying out, albeit doubtfully, the command they had received. Need I say more? The man of whom we are speaking was lying down, having lost the free movement of all his limbs, deprived of the functioning of his eyes, tongue and ears, too. On their arrival, the men of whom we have been speaking, eager to carry out what they had been commanded to do, made haste to make a candle-wick, and bound the little bed with it, all around.

What I am about to say is marvellous to relate, a stupendous fact and a thing impossible to believe from hearing of it, had I not learnt the story from people who were present and were eye-witnesses. The fact is that the men who were desirous of the recovery of the sick man had not yet totally encircled the truckle-bed, even though they were making sufficient haste, when – behold! – the man who was deprived of sight opened his eyes and looked at them, and he who previously was unable to speak, asked what they were doing by moving in a circle around his bed. And they, thunder-struck with amazement and joy, as if raised from the dead, remained silent for a long time, standing in what seemed like ecstasy, as if they had borrowed Leofmær's loss of speech from him. But when they had returned to their wits – for they had been out of them – their tongues were no longer in the least capable of describing how much wonderment they were experiencing, as the joy which they were feeling was greater! For, although they wanted to begin to produce words, you would hear them not speaking, but making sounds of jubilation, wishing to speak but not being able to. However, as Leofmær, who

---

[111] Reading at p. 275.14, ed. Blake, with B E as well as F: *diurnum*.

had arrived from I know not where, was insistent and kept asking what they were doing, they eventually explained by relating, in sequence, the appearance in a vision of the virgin Æthelthryth, and her command, and also what the woman to whom she had appeared had told them, and the fact that it was in order to carry out this instruction that they were now making a ring around the bed and were intending to make a candle in honour of St Æthelthryth, using the girdling-string.

Leofmær, hearing of these things and giving the most hearty thanks of which he was capable, with a mind full of devotion, to God and to the holy virgin, his lady helper, said: 'God, who took away an illness from King Hezekiah,[112] lengthening his life so that he could devote time to penitence, has restored me to health by his mercy and the prayers of his handmaiden. Therefore, make the candle quickly, because I want to run fast to the church of the virgin Æthelthryth.' When the candle had been made, the man rose from his bed, the health of all parts of his body having been restored, and made his way, with joy and gladness, to the church of the holy virgin, carrying[113] the candle with him. On arrival there, he placed the candle on the altar and, with no small amount of praying and, with tears flowing abundantly all the while, he gained a respite for a short space of time, and dedicated himself, with a pure heart, as a servant of the blessed virgin Æthelthryth, recounting to all who wished to hear, the things which had befallen him.

37. In what a malignant way action was taken against the church of St Æthelthryth.[114]

In order that we may disclose in sequence the events which are of relevance to our story-line,[115] it is worthwhile recalling to mind some themes which have long been left untreated. Well then, when, by the Lord's dispensation, Ely was being promoted from an abbacy to the dignity of a bishopric, the Archdeacon of Cambridgeshire of the time, called Nicholas, gave back, by the hands of the sacrist and precentor, for the use of the monks, all income from his tenure of the archdeaconry, just as it had been diverted to him from their provisioning-fund, with the sole exception of an allowance sufficient for his needs. Subsequently, after prejudicial treatment of him by the bishop, he made an appeal to Rome. While he was hastening there, he succumbed to a sudden illness, and died on his journey.

---

[112] Cf. 2 Kings = 4 Kings Vulgate, chapter 20.

[113] Reading at p. 276.5, ed. Blake, with BE: *portans*, not *partans*.

[114] Source: local text commemorating the times of Bishop Hervey.

[115] Repunctuating, at p. 276.16, ed. Blake, as follows: *Ut que in seriem nostre congruunt actioni pandamus . . .*

However, the bishop, on hearing this, obtained a mandate from King Henry, which was conveyed all of a sudden to the monks of Ely, as seemingly from him. It contained the following instruction: that they should promptly accept his steward, William *Brito*,[116] a kinsman of the bishop, as archdeacon. They, while not presuming to put up resistance to the orders, nevertheless admitted him to the archidiaconal office on the following conditions: that he would, like his predecessor, faithfully disburse the annual sum, and would never make a habit of laying his hands on it for his own purposes, whether internal or external, and especially not with respect to anything within the Isle. Rather, the rights of the monastery would stand firm, as of old, with its liberty now more enhanced than diminished as a consequence of its being a bishopric, founded as it has been in freedom and peace on the firm foundation of kings and apostolic fathers. William *Brito* promised straight away to keep everything untouched, but soon, after having been admitted to office, he broke the agreement on the strength of the power and favour of the bishop, his kinsman. He turned to trickery, abnegated what was lawful, kept back completely what was owed to the monks, muddled together in confusion what was holy and what was unholy.

From that time on, alas, alas, the holy monastery of Ely fell from the rank of a good place. Right up till now, sighing amidst her[117] hardships, she has been keeping a mournful silence; everyone treats her with contempt, inflicts losses, treacherously dupes her, seizes her goods, and there is no one who acts as judge: 'among her dear ones there is no one to console her.'[118] But surely the Lord will not everlastingly 'cut off his mercy for ever'[119] so as not to be 'well pleased with those who fear Him and and those who put their trust in His mercy'?[120] Surely, as a result, He will wreak vengeance upon his enemies and bring retribution upon those who hate Him?

38. How a certain notable handed himself over to St Æthelthryth for service as a monk.[121]

There was at that time a good man, Harscoit, surnamed Musard, a tax-official, who was greatly honoured in the household of his master, the king,

---

[116] 'The Breton'.

[117] The change of gender is strange, but we have moved into the thought-world of the Book of Lamentations; (the Isle of) Ely rather than the monastery would be thought of as feminine.

[118] Lamentations 1.2.

[119] Psalm 76.9 Vulgate = 77.9 RSV.

[120] Psalm 146.11 Vulgate = 147.11 RSV.

[121] Source: local commemoration of Harscoit Musard. Contrast *LE* ii. 128: a charter according to which *Estona* had been given to Hervey by William I, before he became Bishop of Ely, the property having previously passed from Harscoit Musard to the king.

praiseworthy for his probity, deserving of being compared with – if not reckoned superior to – the nobility. He had knights beneath him, but did not in the least adhere to the vices in which men of this kind customarily become involved, namely inflated pride or ostentatious arrogance: instead, he was entirely dedicated to honour and freedom. He was not in the habit of harassing anyone; he did no one an injury; he exercised his authority only in affairs of a salutary kind. He had doubtless heard that the story of the blessed Æthelthryth was being very thoroughly publicized, everywhere this side of the boundaries of the king's domains, with advertisement of her merits: he made haste in the direction of holy Ely, hoping that remedies for his sins could be obtained through the redoubtable prayers of the lady saints there. He was received with respectful deference there and was also delighted by the devoutness of the brothers, but soon he was seized by a brief bodily illness. He sensed that his death was imminent, and, on the assumption that he was about to pass on from this life, did not defer the task of acquiring protection for himself by the necessary acts of penitence and almsgiving. For he summoned the brothers, together with the prior of the church; he explained that he wished to become one of their company, praying and beseeching them, for the love of their lady advocate, Æthelthryth, to receive him into the monastic life, and, so that they would not be slow to grant assent, he promised to surrender, along with himself, the manor of *Estune*. In fact, on being received and made a monk, he assigned his gift to the church under his own seal, before the eyes of the clergy and knights. In addition, Robert, the son of this same Harscoit, was present, and he declared the gift of his father a lawful possession for the church of Ely in perpetuity, free from claim by himself and his heirs. And the church held this estate, too, for a long time, freely, and the brothers used to assign all its revenues to charitable purposes until Bishop Hervey, of whom we have spoken earlier, took ownership of it from the monastery and assigned it to a certain kinsman of his. As a consequence of this, the monastery has been completely deprived of it, right up until today.

39. How hard Bishop Hervey worked to free his church of Ely from people who were treating it injuriously.[122]

To resume: it will not be easy to recount misery on the scale which England endured in those days because of the king's taxes. They spared no level or rank of society, they spared none of the saints, male or female, they spared no church, and as a consequence there arose weeping and wailing everywhere among the populace of the realm. No bishop, no abbot, no high-ranking

---

[122] Source: local text commemorating Bishop Hervey, if not entirely the compiler's inference from his general knowledge and the charter cited in the following chapter.

authority whatsoever, was capable of putting up resistance. On the contrary: whoever might present evidence that he had a right, based on ancient legal provision, to hold his possessions freely and without disturbance, would be assailed by calumnies, put under pressure, subjected to injustices and – rich and poor alike – afflicted by constraints. On observing this, Bishop Hervey, a very shrewd man, sighed very deeply and was terrified by the continuance of the loss of revenue and state of crisis, specifically, the fact that the people of St Æthelthryth were every day being harassed, subjected to injurious treatment and despoiled of their goods. He could not contemplate without the deepest sadness of heart the fact that the possessions of the lady saint were being subjected to unbearable harassment. And, fired by a father's sense of duty, he directed every effort towards the liberation of Christ's paupers, and, setting out promptly on a journey, did not hesitate to weary his aged limbs overseas and, with amazing efficiency, swayed the king's favour in the direction towards which his own yearnings tended, and made such a heavy-weight onslaught on the business which he had undertaken that he was able to restore the monastery and the affairs of the church, and energetically got rid of various encumbrances which oppressed the church and caused it grief. And, at a stroke, by means of the following writ of the king, he rescued and protected himself and his people from the assaults and harassment of the wicked, from whichever direction they came.

40. A charter of King Henry to the effect that the people of St Æthelthryth should be exempt from the jurisdiction of shire and hundred.[123]

Henry, King of the English to the archbishops, bishops, abbots, earls, sheriffs, barons and all his faithful people of all England, French and English: greeting. Know that I have made a concession and decreed an exemption for Bishop Hervey of Ely and all his successors as bishops of the church of St Æthelthryth of Ely, to the effect that no one in his domain is to render suit or engage in proceedings at the courts of their shire or hundred: rather the bishop is to hold all rights of forfeiture over his people freely and peaceably, now and in perpetuity, as best he had it on the day on which King Edward lived and died, and I give orders that nothing is to be required of that place or given by it from henceforth, nor is anything to be taken, on this account, from the bishop's, or his people's, property. I grant this, moreover, for the salvation of my soul and the stability of my kingdom and for the souls of my father and my mother and of my predecessors and successors. Witness: John, Bishop of Lisieux, Robert de Sigillo and William de Tancarville and William de Albini and Geoffrey de Glinton and John Fitz John. At Argentan.

---

[123] Source: monastic archives, cf. cartulary G. The charter cited in chapter 16 was likewise issued at Argentan, with some of the same witnesses.

41. How Hervey, the first Bishop of Ely, reached his life's end.[124]

And so, after these happenings, Hervey, the first Bishop of Ely, with the sense that his life's end was imminent, declined into weakness, from excessive old age, and accepted with unassuming patience that the hand of the Lord was weighing down upon him. Being a man of shrewd understanding, he wished, furthermore, to do all things with forethought, so that he would not repent of his action afterwards. He was aware, indeed, therefore, that life is short and material existence destructible and, being afraid to face an enquiry into his stewardship,[125] he made it his plan to use his Lord's money to make friends for himself who would receive him into everlasting tabernacles. And for the carrying out of this purpose, no one seemed to him more suitable than Gilbert, that celebrated man who was universally extolled by national fame in every branch of learning.[126] Hervey was, moreover, connected with him by a close blood-relationship. Family attachment and affection prompted him, as a consequence, to consult with Gilbert about this matter, and his extremely urgent need in itself made his speedy arrival essential. Having received his invitation, the man finally came flying to him in haste, and now, in the secrecy of confession, discussed the good of the soul, the salvation of the mind, the question of how one should live, the correction of wilfulness. You would see there, gushing forth from two abysses, rivers now of tears, now of learned discourse, as 'abyss called[127] upon abyss' to bewail the human condition or crave supernal quietude, in no other mode of expression than in 'the voice of the cataracts' of God.[128] Hence their 'heart broke forth into a good word',[129] and they practised what they preached. And so their talking together reached the following conclusion: that Bishop Hervey ought to divest himself of the World altogether, disdaining the anxiety of temporal existence, and, as a monk, dedicate the remainder of his time to heavenly living. Subsequently, there were prayers on both sides, lamentation on the part of both, and a parting, one from another, and now, after Gilbert's departure, Lord Hervey was preparing himself to become a monk when, lo and behold, because of events which supervened, he was compelled to defer the matter for so long that in the end he was overtaken by

---

[124] Source: local text commemorating Bishop Hervey.

[125] Reading, with alteration from Blake's word-division: *timens in villicationis sue quaestionem incidere* (cf. Luke 16.2–9 Vulgate).

[126] Gilbert 'the Universal', Bishop of London (1128–34).

[127] Reading conjecturally at p. 279.12, ed. Blake: *cum . . . abyssus invocare<t> abyssum . . .*

[128] Allusions to Psalm 41.8 Vulgate (= 42.7 RSV): *abyssus ad abyssum invocat in voce cataractarum tuarum.*

[129] Allusion to Psalm 44.1 Vulgate (= 45.1 RSV): *Eructavit cor meum verbum bonum.*

death and expired. The brothers mourned for their father, the flock grieved for their shepherd, and all commended him to God. And, so that no one may be in doubt about his manner of passing:[130] he departed from this World frequently shriven and fortified by the heavenly wayfarer's food, on 30th August, and on the last day of the month was laid to rest, buried in the church.[131]

But to enumerate one by one the misfortunes which followed the death of our father in God would be a long task: for straight away the hand of the king flung entanglements around the land-holdings of the church, and placed cruel masters over us. While subjected to their power, all we monks of Ely, in our private and public prayers, insistently made it our aim to obtain a competent and honest pastor.[132]

42. That the blessed Æthelthryth appeared to a certain sick man, promising him restoration of health.[133]

The marvellous renown of St Æthelthryth, which emanated from the most exalted well-spring of sanctity, flowed forth in many streams to many provinces and, by virtue of her Isle, made the whole island of England illustrious. For[134] this Isle of Ely, by providing a lodging place for the holy body, brought to bear upon all parts of England its very distinguished reputation for continual mighty acts, and this reputation, having reached even foreign parts, attracted many people every day from distant places to come in order to venerate her. Among them was a certain knight, Robert de Alta Ripa, a man suitably endowed with worldly goods and, because of his reputation for probity, reckoned a great man in the district of Arundel. The way in which he gave proof of the power of our lady saint was as follows. By the judgement of God he was smitten by a serious sickness, and his whole standing[135] underwent such a change upon his falling sick that, because of

---

[130] Reading at p. 297.21, ed. Blake: *transitus* (as suggested by Blake).

[131] O adds at this point: 'before the cross in the year of our Lord 1131, and the 32nd year of the reign of King Henry I. He presided over the church of Ely for 22 years, barring 6 weeks, 5 days. In the third year afterwards Nigel, the chancellor of the said king, the nephew of Roger, Bishop of Salisbury, succeeded him.'

[132] Here follows in O: 'On the ornaments which he gave to his church, and on the priors there were at Ely in his time. The aforesaid Bishop Hervey gave to the church of Ely one alb of silk, with a decoration of best orphrey; it was sewn round in a circle with a collar. Likewise, one maniple, one chasuble which is called "Flowery Passover" (i.e. "Palm Sunday"); two large tapestries and one pastoral stave with the upper part gilded. Also: in his time there were two priors in Ely, namely Vincent and Henry.'

[133] Source: miracle narrative, also included in B (*Book of Miracles*).

[134] Reading with E: *enim.*

[135] Reading conjecturally at p. 280.10, ed. Blake: *status. . .* for *stratus*; for a confusion between *statum* and *stratum*, cf. p.313.3.

the length of his illness, he was turned into an object of disgust and contempt in the sight of all his people: it was a rare person who could endure the trouble caused by him. So it was that, with only the memory of him surviving, he came to be nothing but a prostrate corpse, and now nothing else was awaited but the only thing that remained: the consummation of his death. Finally, however, a woman persuaded him to make a candle-vow to our house: she told him about the mighty powers of the saint, saying that he could easily obtain health through her mercy.

So then, three days had elapsed after the departure of the woman and he began to complain deeply to himself, both because he was neither dying nor recovering, and because his household was so disdainful of him. Then he dissolved into tears and said, 'O most holy virgin Æthelthryth, if the things told of thee are true, cause me to feel thine aid, and from henceforth I will order my life's estate in a better way, and will devotedly seek out thy portals in honour of thee.' And the house in which he was lying was built of stone, and had wide windows a long way from the ground. And as that man, pondering on what would save him, was keeping silence, tired as he was after praying, suddenly a person who had the appearance of a girl, entered through a window, resplendent in the snowy whiteness of her garments. Her sudden entry and unusual beauty had perturbed the man's senses not a little, prompting silent, doubtful thoughts as to the means whereby she had reached him from outside without a ladder and noise. But, without delay, the virgin spoke to the man and said to him, caught up as he was in a multiplicity of thoughts: 'I am that Æthelthryth whose help you think will be advantageous to you, and your thinking on this subject will not prove unfounded. No, you will soon obtain what you are requesting. So do not any longer countenance doubtful thoughts about me. Rather, in the knowledge that what is being said to you is true, amend your way of life as you have proposed and, in the first place, seek out my church in Ely with a candle and then make haste to travel to St James in Galicia and, on your return from there, consider wisely what you are to do from henceforth.'

With these words, the virgin disappeared and he, immediately feeling himself cured of all illness, summoned his servants with a mighty shout, and in a perfectly strong voice, asked for his boots and made it known that he wanted to go to church. His servants, thinking that he was mad, did not dare to approach nearer but, standing a long way off, said, 'Sign your breast, master, with the sign of the cross of Christ, so you may be freed forthwith from this madness! For what need do you have of boots – you who have been ill for such a long time? See! Your boots have been put away elsewhere, because we gave up hope of your making use of them. Even so, if we were sure that it had been mercifully brought about that you were capable of using boots, you would have what you are asking for with all speed. For your sudden release makes your utterance seem insane, were it not that your sober gesturing seems to promise some incredible hope, underlying some kind of fear.' And he answered them: 'Do not reckon the mercy of God a madness, but bring quickly what I am asking for, and hold your peace until I have returned from church and I tell you what I have seen.' So the boots were brought. He went to pray, reported his vision to the priest, confessed his sins, received his penance, returned home, recounted what he had promised. Those who heard rejoiced: his friends came running. They all praised God and St Æthelthryth. Then preparations were made for a departure in fine style, and he hastened on his journey to this church of Ely with such alacrity that it was a rare servant of his who could keep up with his speed as he made his way there. And, on arriving eventually at this very place, he was led, after his prayers, into chapter, and in the presence of us all related the sequence of events, received membership of the brotherhood, and went away rejoicing, to complete the rest of his undertakings. That very well-known man did these things, which were very well-known in his own district, to the praise and glory of almighty God, with whom St Æthelthryth dwells in the palace of Heaven, and may she protect us in the duration of this life and by her holy solace may life in Heaven be ours throughout all ages, for ever and ever. AMEN.

43. How St Æthelthryth was seen praying in a certain church, holding a psalter in one hand, and in the other a lighted candle.[136]

Greetings to the noble fathers of the most excellent senate of the church of Ely from Osbert, a native of the municipality of Clare and a fellow-senator of their capitol.

The splendour of the blessed and glorious virgin Æthelthryth which sends lightning-flashes through diverse parts of the World by means of diverse mighty works and signs, is presenting you with a new joy of spiritual celebration and is enlarging the glorious celebration of her, manifest as it has become to the World.

There is a matter worthy of public and precious report, which the Prior of the church of Daventry, Dom Osbert, has related to me. He is a man of authority and graciousness, whose life of outstanding virtue is conspicuously prominent in the house of the Lord, and whose religious observance is an

[136] Source: a letter of Osbert of Clare, Prior of Westminster, to the monks of Ely, containing a miracle narrative recounted to him by Osbert, Prior of Daventry. The chapter is paralleled in B (Book of Miracles). Edition (from a different manuscript source, BL, Cotton Vitellius A xvii): E. W. Wilkinson, ed. Osbert of Clare, Letters (Oxford 1929), pp. 116–19, 219–20. There is an account of Osbert's connection with Ely in the Introduction to this work.

exemplary instance of faithful aspiration to the things that are of Heaven. For he has been a Cluniac monk since early days and at first shone as a canon in the church of the plain of Bromholm, within the confines of which there came about a high point of history which ought to be kept in remembrance at your communal gatherings. Furthermore, for a long time as the distributor of alms in the holy virgin Milburh's sober congregation of clerics, he used to succour the multitude with the left-overs of their seniors, of whom some, in their piety, survive as witnesses to this story. For, there came into their company in the course of their travels people to whom the Lord deigned to show forth from the supernal regions the glory of the blessed virgin.

In ancient times there was fabricated in the province of the Mercians a wooden church, which was said to have been constructed long ago by the blessed Anna, King of the East Angles. He was the father, according to the flesh, of the glorious virgin Æthelthryth, and he founded the aforesaid church while on a cross-country journey. For he had left the boundaries of his kingdom out of desire for the company of some dear ones, his aim being to make a very intimate visit because of the sweet affection that comes of kinship, and thus to bring satisfaction to the West Country for some while by his presence. But on his return, he constructed this edifice, one overflowing, in later times, with celestial marvels. Situated on the border between the Britons and the English, it took its name from the blessed virgin Æthelthryth. And indeed the church is still, today, named as hers, and she is invoked in it by faithful people, to the honour of God.[137]

Well, when the family of a certain knight, namely Herbert de Fourches, was staying in lodgings throughout these country districts thus being obliged to wend its way from one knight's residence to another, a certain respectable woman[138] who used to educate his children wished to go in to pray. But she could not prevail upon any of her comrades to be willing to go to the house of prayer with her and make bullock-sacrifices of holy devotion to the Lord on the altar of the mind. She herself, finally, touched by the grace of the Holy Spirit and longing to bring her own yearning to fulfilment, went in with the aim of sacrificing herself as a whole offering.

After having slipped inside the entrance, the woman soon stopped in her tracks. For, on the one hand, a portentous fear had deeply shaken her and, on the other, a celestial vision was giving her strength. For she beheld before the altar a triumphant virgin intent on prayer. Her appearance was so charming and her beauty was so comely that it cannot be described in human

---

[137] Wilkinson, *op. cit.* 219, identifies the church as that of Hyssington, on the border of Shropshire and Montgomeryshire, the only known early dedication to St Æthelthryth which fits the description.

[138] 'Respectable woman' = Lat. *matrona*.

language. With one hand she was holding out a psalter and in the other she was carrying a lighted candle. In this manner, with these accoutrements, the virgin was devoting herself to holy thoughts, when the woman approached nearer to her and diligently made enquiry with regard to her name. 'Who are you, glorious lady?', said she. 'What sort of person are you and where are you from, to be gleaming with such brightness? I see your face to be so charming and distinguished! Tell me your famous name, for the sake of Christ!' [139] The resplendent virgin gave a reply and was not slow to soothe her with affable sweetness: 'Since you are concerned to remind me of the love of God and are asking, through Him, to be informed of my name: people call me by the name of Æthelthryth, the holy virgin, whose integrity of maidenhood is united with the heavenly Bridegroom. But you are not to be eager to reveal to anyone what God has deigned to show to you.' With these words, the high-born heroine[140] stopped speaking, and the woman prayed as long as she wished. The virgin was praying in the sanctuary, keeping vigil before the altar: the woman was praying prostrated on the pavement outside the choir. But no matter whether it was a pavement or the ground, she was devotedly ministering to herself the mystery of prayer. As long as the woman was in the church, she could see the celestial personage: indeed, when she went out, she left her inside.

And returning to her companions, who were making preparations for travel, she urged them to proceed without delay on the rest of their journey. But, having mounted horses and promptly given rein to them, they suddenly heard, coming out of the church, strains of heavenly music resounding in the air and the sound of a sublime melody being solemnly sung by angelic voices. 'What is this that we have been hearing?', they said. 'What is this most sweet sound, which we are not accustomed to drinking in with our ears? Some delightful kind of heavenly harmony is being compounded, which perhaps God has deemed fitting to reveal to our minds.' Then the woman who was governess of the knight's children said, 'Oh, you pitiable and unfortunate people! Oh, how irreligious and lazy you are! Through your carelessness and inertia you have not been able to behold the miracles of the Lord which, through His grace, it was possible to see in the little church not long ago. For I saw within it the blessed Æthelthryth, a famous virgin, radiant with beams of celestial light of ineffable beauty. Having looked upon her psalter and lighted candle, I am thankful for having been honoured by the glory of such a vision. And the pipes of heavenly organs are resonating in a manner corresponding to the oft-repeated

---

[139] Here I follow Wilkinson's edition of the Cotton ms. which prints *quae*, rather than the erroneous *quem*, after *nomen tuum* (p. 282.22, ed. Blake).

[140] Here, as elsewhere in the *LE*, *heros* is used as equivalent to *herois*.

frequency of the miracles with which, through Him, she customarily abounds.'

They were immediately saddened and downcast beyond all measure, and made up their minds to return to the aforesaid church, to see whether perhaps they might look upon the glorious face of the blessed virgin. But though they ran hot-foot to the church, they did not win the reward of an oracle of the celestial shrine, or the privilege of drinking in the sweetness of the angels of heaven.[141] Thus, the object of their desire was totally denied them, and they did not win the reward of seeing the glory of God inside, or of partaking any more in the angelic hymnody. Once more, giving rein to their horses, they hastened on their way and, when they had gone on a little distance further from the church, they straight away heard, on their way, the celestial melody. For the second time, they returned, just as they had done previously, and the nearer was their approach to the church, the greater was the diminution that they experienced of the heavenly music-making. And they turned back, frustrated of the object of their desire, and after they had gone on for a little while, they were for the third time solaced by the heavenly sweetness and they marvelled on hearing the delightfulness of the voice of angels. And returning, they hastened to the place where the melody was resounding in the air and, though they were hoping for a fuller concord of musical sounds, they found the district devoid of the ambrosial sweetness. To be sure, on realizing that God had been cruelly vexed by their sin, they humbly lamented their hardness of heart, for in their wretchedness they had offended against the Divine Mercy.

And what more is there to say? They had spent the whole day fruitlessly, almost until it was fully dark, and, as they kept going back and forth, they kept losing the celestial harmony of the organs, and the long-desired light did not shine upon them. They proceeded therefore in the direction in which their journey was beckoning them to take lodging, and they proclaimed the miraculous favour before God of the merits of the holy virgin Æthelthryth. The venerable Osbert, Prior of the church of Daventry, at that time still distributing alms to the poor of St Milburh the virgin, learnt this – truthfully reported – from the lips of the people to whom God partly gave and partly denied permission to hear this sound. Their tears and long-drawn-out sighs summoned from the bottom of the depths of their hearts, vouched for the reliability of their testimony. For the distinguished man did not distrust the good faith of these people, to whom the cell of Christ's poverty had often provided refreshment before, and he had no doubts but that the report was truthful.

---

[141] Taking *aditi* as the equivalent of *adyti* (p. 283.7, ed. Blake).

44. How, with the king's consent, Nigel was elected as bishop, and by whom he was consecrated.[142]

To resume: the beloved and renowned metropolis of Ely for a long time grieved and languished, bereft of her protection and all the time deprived of consolation; she lamented the death of her blessed father Hervey like a mother bewailing her children and, in accordance with her custom, in vigils and in stints of fasting she kept on imploring God in continual prayers to come to the aid of the tears of her fatherless children, praying that He should see fit to provide a suitable bishop for His house. And, by the dispensation of Divine Providence, the pleading of the monks of Ely began to be given a hearing at the court of King Henry; for the time was then approaching when he was obliged to cross the Channel in festive state. Eventually, the king granted the petitioners' request, but on condition that they should elect and accept none other than one Nigel, a cleric, his treasurer, whose honourable conduct gave lustre to the whole court, whose power controlled it, whose generosity exalted it; a man whom the king himself honoured, the clergy loved and the whole of England vaunted. Now it came about that, while the king was still in this country, both at his command and with his favour, Nigel was appointed bishop on 28th May at *Burna*[143] and then, at Lambeth, adjacent to London, he was consecrated by William, Archbishop of Canterbury, on 1st October.[144] And, coming to his episcopal see, he was received with great glory, enthroned and took command in manly fashion. Furthermore, in case anyone should wrongly think that the joy at his reception was restricted to a single group and only moderate: all the street through which he was to pass was arrayed with hangings, tapestries and decorated seats, with monastics, canons and clerics standing nearby in processional order and pastoral leaders of various ranks standing round about him. I omit a great many things which are more fully related in the little historical works of our brother Richard, a most studious man of letters and someone of the greatest eloquence.[145]

---

[142] Source here and for chapter 45: local text commemorating Bishop Nigel. This text was almost certainly the work by the monk Richard II of Ely referred to at the end of the chapter as treating the subject of Nigel's consecration more fully. Richard receives further mention in *LE* iii. 45, 96, 97, 99, 101. The compiler evidently abbreviated Richard's work, but felt free to make additions to it – flattering references to the author, for example.

[143] Perhaps Bishopsbourne, Kent.

[144] According to AO: 29th September. O specifies that the year was 1133.

[145] Note the evidence here that Richard was an admired colleague of the compiler of *LE*, and so not identifiable with him.

45. With what honour Bishop Nigel was received by the community of monks in Ely and by the people who came to meet him.

And on the stated day, and with everything made ready, the lord Bishop Nigel came to his see in Ely and was honourably received by his monastic children in magnificence and glory. A crowd, which had assembled for that festal day from 'every nation which is beneath Heaven',[146] went forth to meet him. Moreover,[147] given that, in those days, an abundance of all manner of delightful things was continually flowing in, you would have thought that all the elements were smiling together specifically upon him on his arrival, and were now doing their service to their new master. The next day, indeed, he came into a chapter-meeting and delivered words of exhortation to the brothers; he subtly added pieces of advice of a consolatory kind; he urged them to uphold with equanimity the professed objective[148] of their order, in accordance with the institution of the holy father Benedict; he devoutly pledged that he wished to love them above all people; he professed that he wished to guard the possessions of the lady saint, to gather together things which had been dispersed and, once they had been gathered together, to keep them untouched. This, in fact, he would have done energetically, perhaps, if the words of a priest could have been 'reckoned' in any way[149] as equal to 'a quivering of a scale pan'.[150]

I would, to be sure, write of these things more expansively, but since they are found in full in the little works of the venerable father Richard mentioned earlier, we move on, in haste, to other matters.

For at that time it was becoming incumbent upon the bishop, because of urgent affairs of the kingdom, to go to London, and involve himself in them in all haste, because he was the custodian of the treasury of the king and of the state. As a consequence, against his will admittedly, but because he was anxiously concerned about these affairs, he entrusted care of the entire bishopric to a man named Ranulf. Meanwhile, Henry, King of the English, who had recently crossed the Channel, died in Normandy,[151] having held the kingdom for a period of thirty-six {recte thirty-five} years and four months. His body, however, was brought to England and buried at Reading. His successor was his sister's son, Stephen.

---

[146] Cf. Deuteronomy 4.19.

[147] Repunctuating without a comma between *sed* and *et*, p. 284.17, ed. Blake.

[148] Reading with E at p. 284.21, ed. Blake: *propositum* (not *prepositum*) *sui ordinis secundum institutionem sancti patris Benedicti equanimiter ferre commonuit* . . .

[149] Reading conjecturally at p. 284.25, ed. Blake: *ullatenus* for *nullatenus*.

[150] Cf. Isaiah 40.15.

[151] Date: 1135.

46. How, after the decease of King Henry, his nephew became king; and that he had made it his intention to venerate the Church in England with all his might.[152]

Now we will recount how King Stephen came to the throne. It was as follows. While King Henry was mortally ill, his potentates gathered around him, that is to say, a throng of powerful and noble men, awaiting the departure of their lord amid groaning and sorrow, and they began more and more to enquire what arrangements he was making concerning himself or about the handling of the kingdom's affairs. Bringing his life's work, in this way, to its consummation, he disclosed to them what he had been most beneficially pondering, or what he had judged to be most beneficial. 'You!', he said. 'Great men and wise! I present to you as king my comrade-in-arms Stephen, an earl of mine, my most beloved kinsman, noble in his valour, but exceedingly devout in his trust in God; I lay down that you should accept him in place of me and by right of inheritance, and I solemnly affirm that this is, in all respects, how things are.' No sooner had this happened when the king breathed his last.

The earl, for his part, taking the task upon himself, collected a strong contingent of soldiers from all around and made haste to England. He made his way to London and, because he had been well known and a generous, honest and much-loved earl and an energetic warrior, and was descended from the royal line, they accepted him as King of England – the chief nobles and the people of the city having been enticed by money and promises, and the clergy being afraid that he might throw the country into upheaval, if repulsed. But what helped him most of all to achieve this, in accordance with the instructions of his uncle, the king, was the oath of Hugh Bigod, which he swore with his hand on the Gospels before clergy and people, that he had been in the king's presence when he was dying and had heard him granting the kingdom to his nephew Stephen, and that he had set out in haste to England in order to bear witness to this. In recognition of this oath, Roger, Bishop of Salisbury, on whose 'yea' or 'nay' all the business of the kingdom used to hang, accepted him and so did the rest of the prelates,[153] and, on 19th December, he was consecrated king in London, at Westminster, by William, Archbishop of Canterbury, with none of the earls present, however, except Henry, the son of David, King of Scots.

---

[152] Source: not identified by Blake, so perhaps still the work on the episcopate of Nigel by Richard II of Ely or the compiler's free composition; some words (on the new king's lawgiving) from *Worcester Chronicle* on the year 1066, already used in *LE* ii. 101. The information on Reading is recorded in *Annales Radingenses*, ed. F. Liebermann, in *Ungedruckte Anglo-Normannische Geschichtsquellen*, p. 11; *Flores Historiarum*, ed. H. R. Luard, ii. 58.

[153] 'Prelates': Lat. *primates*. The word *primates* could mean 'nobles' in general, but the absence of earls from the coronation is strange if it bears this sense here.

And straight away, on having become king, he made it his plan to destroy unjust laws, to establish just ones and to observe the ancient customs of the country; to venerate the Church of God with all his might; to respect, and simultaneously to protect, bishops, abbots, monks and clerics; he undertook to present himself to all good people as pious, humble and affable, and to regard evil-doers with absolute abhorrence. Indeed, how much good came about with regard to the standing and stability of the Church as a result of his initiatives, is something we do not neglect to notice, in view of his generosity: it is something which deserves to be recalled. For he endeavoured to uphold and allow the liberty of the Church, sworn to at his consecration: namely, in the case of every office-holder, free election from among his own community: a well-founded practice which is remembered as having begun in the case of Edward, elected by the community of Reading.

47. That certain malignant individuals on the bishop's side devised deceptions upon the monks.[154]

Then, indeed, as the church of Ely was conducting itself honourably under an honourable pastoral leader, it was impossible that it should escape the ill-will of the Devil: inevitable, rather, that, amid the rest of the misfortunes of the kingdom, which were already proliferating all around them, they should have a share of the trouble. For a cruel false denunciation was being prepared by some envious and malicious individuals, who wanted to make free with the property of the monks, demoting the monks from their position of power.

The cleric Ranulf, already mentioned, was among the entourage and liegemen of the same bishop of Ely. He was an apostate and ex-monk, who had earlier left the practice, order and habit of monastic religion, which he had taken upon himself at Glastonbury, and returned, body and heart alike, to 'Egypt'[155] – 'as a dog returns to its vomit'.[156] Eventually, having been made, as he had desired, custodian of everything pertaining to the bishopric, he now did not consider himself to be subject to a lord or to be his lord's

---

[154] Source: the material in *LE* iii. 47 and 51–3 on the conspiracy of Ranulf, characterized by sustained imitation of Sallust, *Conspiracy of Catiline*, is set out as a single chapter in B *(Book of Miracles)*,starting with the prefatory matter placed at the opening of *LE* iii. 52. Presumably Brother Richard II of Ely would have covered the events in his treatment of Bishop Nigel. The exact relation of the 'conspiracy' chapters in *LE* to his text cannot now be determined. The parallel in the *Book of Miracles* does not mean that they could ultimately not be derived from Richard's work; cf, e.g., the case of *LE* iii. 119 and 120, where material from *LibÆ* is also paralleled in B *(Book of Miracles)*. But at the beginning of *LE* iii. 52 the wording suggests that he was copying from a miracle book.
[155] For allegorical use of the term 'Egypt', see Revelation 11.8.
[156] Proverbs 26.11.

deputy: rather he had raised himself up as equal to his lord in all respects and now even above him. What he endeavoured to do was not to gather together what was scattered but to dissipate what had been gathered.

Ranulf himself was, if not in name, at any rate on the proven evidence of fact, a Catiline of our time. Of rustic and ignoble birth, he was from infancy, and during infancy itself, inclined to all manner of vices. On attaining a more advanced age, he was the more inclined to wrong-doing. And in the period when he was carrying out single-handedly the task entrusted to him of administering the bishop's affairs, this slippery individual, being of capricious and inconstant temperament, would – in his inefficiency – make a start on everything, but bring to completion nothing that was not malpractice. Disdaining the company of honourable people, he had round about him, as it were, massed ranks of criminal elements in battle order. And, with the object of depriving the wretched monks of Ely by usurpation, of their rightful command over land-proprietorships and estate-holdings, he very frequently misled the bishop by ill-intentioned whisperings, and, though he was prevented from this by the mercy of God, his aim was to bring to an end the religious life and the monks who had been long settled in that place at the instigation of holy fathers. He was confident that he had to a large extent obtained the bishop's backing for this, and had entirely gained his consent. So it came about that the monks could not talk peaceably with him about anything, since from that time, and thereafter, he kept mustering up indignation and anger against them.

48. That the lord Bishop Nigel gave instructions that the properties of the blessed Æthelthryth be listed in full; and which ones he reclaimed for the church on his own initiative.[157]

Moreover, the lord Bishop had given the instruction in his earliest days that all the property of the church should be recorded in writing by the hand of the aforementioned Ranulf, so that he should have knowledge of what it possessed or received in the way of lordship, rent and knight-service. This was with the aim that no right belonging to him and misappropriated should become anyone else's property, but that rather he should make rigorous enquiry of every person, of whatever social standing that person might be, monastic or secular, so that he might receive and possess what belonged to him according to the decrees of our forebears and the statutory provisions of councils. Be that as it may, in furtherance of the completion of this task, he received the properties which are listed here by the judicial decision of both of two kings, in the first place, that of the old king, namely Henry of blessed

---

[157] Sources: see on chapter 46. There is reference to a *Book of Lands* penned by the ex-monk Ranulf at Bishop Nigel's behest.

memory,[158] and likewise that of the new, present one, the gentle Stephen, <who>[159] in all cases tendered his authorization.

Within the Isle, in point of fact: Coveney and Mepal, and outside: Stetchworth, Wratting, *Strede*, and the Rodings, Thriplow, Impington, Pampisford, Marham, Cottenham, Snailwell, Gransden, Terrington, Darmsden, *Thaderege*, Kingston.

The bishop also, by use of his power, wrested these and other estates from the usurpers of the properties of St Æthelthryth and at Wandlebury, with Ralph Basset and Aubrey de Vere presiding as judges, in the presence of nine hundreds and, on the authority both of the old king and, as we have said, likewise now that of the present king, they were given judicial assent and agreed by general acclamation, on the instruction of the church. We present this king's charter in order to give written evidence of the endowment.

49. A charter of King Stephen about the whole liberty of the church of St Æthelthryth.[160]

Stephen, King of the English and Duke of the Normans to the archbishops, bishops, abbots, earls, barons, sheriffs, officials and all his faithful people of all England, French and English: greeting. You are to know that I have granted to the church of Ely all lands and possessions belonging to it and I wish and instruct that this same church of Ely should hold honourably and freely and peaceably all its customary rights within the borough and outside, in respect to land and water and marshes and open country and woodland, namely [both] *sake* and *soke* and *toll* and *team* and *infangentheof* and *hamsocne* and *grythbrige* and *fihtwite* and *fyrdwite* and all other offences emendable {by money-payments}, as best it possessed them on the day on which King Edward lived and died, and as was determined in the time of my grandfather, William the Great, at Kentford in the presence of his barons, Bishop Walkelin and Geoffrey, Bishop of Coutances and Baldwin, Abbot of St Edmund's and Ivo de Taillebois and Peter de Valognes and in the witness of several shires. And you are to know that I am not the giver of a warrant that anyone should lay claim to these aforesaid customary rights. Witness: Philip the chancellor, William de Ypres, William Martel. At Cambridge.

---

[158] The expression of this sentence is very convoluted and this translation assumes repunctuation of the text as follows: *utriusque regis, veteris scilicet bone memorie Henrici ipsius maxime iudicio et iusticia que hic inferuntur recepit possessiones, sicut novi* . . . The gist is clear, but there may be unidentifiable textual corruption.

[159] Reading conjecturally at p. 287.24, ed. Blake: *sicut novi nunc regis Stephani mansueti <qui> auctoritatem in omnibus protendit.*

[160] Source: monastic archives, cf. cartularies GM. Date: late 1139 X 1140; at Cambridge.

50. How the bishop gave orders that the goods of the church contained within it should be listed in full; and the identity and number of the articles which he found there.[161]

We have recorded above the identity and the size of the estates which the bishop claimed back for the church: now we must not omit to mention what he found inside it, from out of the treasury. Well then, after the festive celebration of a great day was over and the throng which had assembled had eventually been given their dismissal by him – specifically, on the fifth day of January – he caused the whole treasury of the church of St Æthelthryth in Ely to be inspected, consisting of gold and silver, palls and books and all manner of ornaments belonging to the same church, with the following men present and bearing witness: Prior William; Henry, a former prior; Denys; Benedict; Byrhtmaer; Robert of Drinkstone; Adam; William, the nephew of Denys; Peter, the son of Geoffrey the constable; Herbert; and Ralph the sacrist and Ælfstan the subsacrist, and Ælfric the succentor. These were the men who displayed all the goods listed in writing below. Also witnesses were the following clergy: Archdeacon William; Ranulf of Salisbury; Richard of St Paul; Alexander, a cleric, and Hubert, a cleric, and Henry of Ely, a layman.

In that place there is[162] a shrine in which is enclosed a marble receptacle containing the virginal corpse of St Æthelthryth, facing her own altar, the most excellent lady being in just the same state, totally undamaged, totally incorrupt, in which she went to rest in the tomb – something brought about for her by the hands of angels at the command of God, so we believe, just as Bede, the most learned of Englishmen, relates in the *History* of his nation. The side of this shrine which faces the altar is, in point of fact, of silver with images in high relief, well plated with gold. Around the 'Christ in Majesty'[163] are seven stones between beryls and crystals and two onyx stones and two alamandine stones and twenty-six pearls, and in the crown of this 'Christ in Majesty' is one amethyst and two cornelians and six pearls and eight glassy stones. And in the four corners there are four large crystals. And in the surround: nine crystals. And on the southern horn of this side there is a golden necklace studded with one topaz and three emeralds and three sardian stones. In the diadem of the upper image there are seven precious stones and eleven pearls. There is a boss bearing a cross made of copper, well-gilded, with twelve crystals. On the left-hand side of this shrine the whole wall is of silver, well gilded, with sixteen images in high relief, with ninety-

---

[161] Source: monastic archives – an inventory dated 5th January, 1134, interpolated subsequently (after 1143) by the compiler, or someone previous to him, to take account of losses to the minster's treasures during the episcopate of Nigel. The opening remarks are probably imaginative inferences by the compiler from the date of the document.

[162] The formula '*ibi est*', here translated as 'In that place there is . . .', will in the case of most subsequent occurrences simply be translated as: 'There is . . .'

[163] The Latin term used is simply: *maiestas*.

four large crystals and a hundred and forty-nine tiny, crystalline and glassy stones. The eastern side of this shrine is of silver with gilding all over, with images in high relief. There are two crystalline lions with thirty-two crystals and three glassy stones and eight pieces of enamel-work and seven smallish jewelled ornaments. There is a 'Christ in Majesty' which belongs to the frontal of the altar. On the southern side there are sixteen images of silver without gilding and the lower border is of silver-gilt. On this side there are twenty-six crystals. There is another boss made of copper bearing a copper cross, well gilded, with twelve crystals.

There is a *tabula* in front of the altar of silver, well plated with gold, with images in high relief which Abbot Theodwine made[164] with the money which had been found at Wentworth in the time of the beloved lord Abbot Thurstan.[165] On this, there are around the 'Christ in Majesty': two calcedonies and ten stones between crystals and beryls, and three pieces of enamel-work and forty-two pearls, and there are missing ten pieces of enamel-work and three stones and five pearls. And to the right of the 'Christ in Majesty' there are twelve, and to the left, similarly, twelve stones between crystals and beryls. And, in the circuit of the two chariots[166] of the Sun and Moon, there are eight stones between beryls and crystals, and there are missing eight stones and there are missing sixteen pearls. And around the 'Christ in Majesty' there are four images of angels made of ivory, and in the outermost border of this *tabula*, made of silver without gilding, there are missing twenty-eight stones and in the inner, gilded, border there are missing twenty-four stones.

This *tabula*, also, Bishop Nigel, later destroyed, and the shrine of St Æthelthryth, at the instigation of evil, peace-hating people, and removed and broke up all the gold and silver which was upon them.[167]

To the north of this tomb, assuredly, to the left of the most excellent virgin Queen Æthelthryth, the virgin Wihtburh, her sister, shines forth in festal splendour in vernal freshness of her whole body, having been <translated> to that place from the region <of Norfolk and> buried <there>.[168] To the east, assuredly, that is, at the feet of that same doyenne Æthelthryth, there is laid the blessèd Seaxburh, another sister of hers, and

---

[164] 'Made' = Lat. *fecit*. Here and in a number of other instances, the actual meaning may have been: 'caused to be made'. The literal translation, 'made', is used, however, throughout this inventory, because it emerges that donors might, sometimes at least, also be makers, and evidence comes to light that monks at Ely participated in vestment-making.

[165] Cf. *LE* ii. 113.

[166] Taking literally the Latin: *et in circuitu ii curruum solis et lune* . . . (p. 289.31, ed. Blake). Or perhaps *curruum* is to be taken as equivalent to, or a mistake for, *cursuum*, 'courses'.

[167] Cf. *LE* iii. 89.

[168] Reading conjecturally at p. 290.7, ed. Blake, e.g.: *soror eius Withburga virgo toto vernans corpore illuc e regione < Nortfolche translata et illic> sepulta sollempniter refulget.*

there the merits of her mighty powers do not cease to flourish. To the south, assuredly, to the right of Æthelthryth, the betrothed of Christ, there rests Eormenhild, a sweet friend of God, whose health-bringing tomb speaks of the many signs of her mighty powers.

Above the great altar, on a beam placed high up, facing the church, there is made of woodwork, beautifully carpentered and painted, an effigy, as it were, of the atonement, where a large cross with the Crucified, of silver, and images likewise of the blessed Mary and St John, stand together, towards the altar, with gilding in places. It was Archbishop Stigand who made these for the magnificent adornment of the temple of the Lord, but Bishop Nigel removed them, and many other things, of which we will include full mention in their proper context.[169]

There are seven reliquaries of silver-gilt all around, and two reliquaries three-quarters silver, and two very small reliquaries, one plated all around with silver and the other three-quarters silver-plated, and these are full of the relics of saints, apostles, martyrs, confessors and virgins. But the brothers of the church later removed gold and silver from seven of these, at the onset of a time of famine and, so far, they have not been restored to their original state.

There is a box made of silver for the eucharistic host, studded with stones, hanging by a gilded copper chain. There are two phylacteries carved from ivory.

There is a cross which King Edgar gave as an offering to St Æthelthryth in witness of his donations, completely of gold on its front side, and with three golden images and with precious stones, and silver-gilt all over on the other sides. But the foot of this cross is three-quarters of silver with gilding in places. And there are five crosses with images of ivory, of silver on all sides with gilding in places, of which four are with precious stones. And nine other crosses, larger and smaller. Five of these are with images of ivory, of silver all around, gilded in places; of which four are with precious stones. On one of them there are two lions made of crystal. Guthmund the sacrist made two of these crosses; it was Ælfwaru, a wealthy lady, who adorned two others lavishly with gold and silver;[170] and Provost Leo gave the other cross, of silver all over, gilded in places, with relics of St Vedast and St Amandus inside the images.[171] And Bishop Nigel afterwards broke up the three last-mentioned crosses. Also there are three crosses of silver gilded all over[172] in front and on both sides, of which two were brought there with the body of

---

[169] Cf. *LE* ii. 98; iii. 89.

[170] Cf. *LE* ii. 61.

[171] Cf. *LE* ii. 54.

[172] Lat. *per locum.*

Ealdorman Byrthnoth.[173] And two crosses of silver, gilded, for processions: it was Archbishop Wulfstan who gave one, Bishop Æthelstan the other.

There is a text of the four Gospels which King Edgar gave to St Æthelthryth[174] with the above-mentioned golden cross, in confirmation of the liberties of the church. This gospel-book has, along with a 'Christ in Majesty' and four angels and twelve apostles, its whole surface-area gilded with precious stones and enamels. The other side of this gospel-book is of silver with images of virgins. There is another gospel-book, which Abbot Richard made, of silver-gilt, with 'Christ Crucified' and two cast-metal images, and its whole ground is of silver, well gilded, with stones <and>[175] enamels. There is a third gospel-book, which Abbot Ælfsige made, completely silver-plated on one side and well gilded, with a 'Christ Crucified' and cast-metal images with carved stones all over. There is a fourth gospel-book, silver-coated and well gilded on one side, with a little 'Christ Crucified' of ivory with stones, which the monk Tosti made. There is a fifth gospel-book, which the sacrist Guthmund made, silver-covered on one side, with a 'Christ in Majesty' of ivory, seated upon a throne, with crystals. There is a sixth gospel-book, which Abbot Ælfsige made, covered with silver, with a 'Christ Crucified' and images of cast metal, gilded. There is a seventh gospel-book, covered with silver, with a little 'Christ Crucified' and with two cast-metal angels, well gilded,[176] which the same abbot made. There is an eighth gospel-book, covered with silver with a 'Christ Crucified' and images of ivory, well gilded. There is a ninth gospel-book, ornamented by a *tarsellus* with stones and innumerable pearls, which has been removed by theft. There is a tenth gospel-book, covered with silver, with images of St Æthelthryth, completely gilded, which the cantor Ælfric made. There is an eleventh gospel-book, covered with silver, partly gilded, with a 'Christ Crucified' and flat images with an engraved border around, which Abbot Ælfsige made. There is a twelfth gospel-book, covered with silver, with a small 'Christ Crucified', gilded in places, on a flat ground. There is a thirteenth gospel-book with a golden cross without images, covered with silver round about, with golden borders. There is a fourteenth gospel-book, small, covered with silver, with a 'Christ Crucified' and images in relief, gilded throughout, one of Abbot Ælfsige's artefacts – which the bishop lost at Wareham.[177] There is a fifteenth gospel-book with a throne of enamel-work, well provided with gilding on one side and with silver on the other, which Siward of Maldon, a comrade of Hereward, gave to St Æthelthryth. There are, in addition, two other, very

---

[173] Cf. *LE* ii. 62.

[174] Cf. *LE* ii. 4.

[175] Reading conjecturally at p. 291.4–5, ed. Blake: *cum lapidibus <et> esmaltis.*

[176] Reading at p. 291.14, ed. Blake: *deauratis.* (E: **deaurat'**).

[177] Cf. *LE* iii. 78.

small, gospel-books covered with silver.

There is a chalice all of gold, assessed at[178] four marks and seven ounces,[179] which the monk Wulfstan made – but which Bishop Nigel later took away. And there is a large chalice of silver, well decorated, with handles, and well gilded, with a paten, of twenty-two marks and two ounces, which Wulfwine, provost of this church, made. And a large chalice of silver, well decorated and gilded, with enamels, assessed at seven marks and five ounces. And a chalice, completely gilded, assessed at three marks of silver. And there are eleven chalices of silver, partially gilded, with one paten without a chalice, assessed at twenty-one marks of silver. And the bishop has one chalice, totally gilded, in his chapel, assessed at twenty-three shillings – which he lost at Wareham – and one chalice in his chapel at Downham, partially gilded, assessed at twenty-one shillings. And there is a large golden chalice, assessed at seven marks and one ounce, which Sithric, the provost of happy memory made – but it is missing because of trickery perpetrated by Goscelin, surnamed 'of Ely'.

And there is a tower-pyx of silver, of rounded shape with three legs, well decorated, assessed at twenty-three marks of silver, which Edith, the daughter of King Æthelstan gave to this church, on which was written, 'Edith had ordered that this excellent vessel be made for herself, and she offered it to St Æthelthryth as a gift.' And at the top of this tower-pyx, a cross of silver with the Crucified, well decorated and gilded, assessed at five ounces and twelve pennyweights – which Bishop Nigel took away.[180] And a tower-pyx of silver of square shape made of wood within, well decorated and gilded, assessed at four marks and five ounces. At the top of this tower is a cross, conveying a double representation of the cross, in which there are visibly enclosed fragments from the wood of the Lord's cross,[181] and from the tomb of the Lord and from the tomb of St Mary and from Mount Calvary, and from the crib of the Lord and from the birthplace of the Lord, and from Gethsemane, all these items placed within in such a way that they can be seen; this cross, indeed, was thrown into a fire, and we learn from people of former times that it could not be burnt. And one flagon[182] of silver with a handle, well decorated and gilded, assessed at one mark and five ounces. And a flagon of silver for wine, partially gilded, assessed at five-and-a-half ounces. And the bishop has two flagons of silver in his chapel, one totally

---

[178] 'Assessed at': where this expression is used in the translation of this inventory, the Latin simply has genitives to express the assessment of value or weight.

[179] The measures in this inventory seem to accord with the Troy-weight system whereby 1 mark = 8 ounces (two-thirds of a 12-ounce pound); 1 ounce = 20 pennyweights.

[180] Cf. LE iii. 89.

[181] Lit. simply 'the wood of the Lord'.

[182] Lat. caneta, following the reading of E.

gilded and the other without gilding, worth fifteen shillings. And the bishop has an incense-box of silver with a silver spoon, assessed at three marks. The bishop also has two candle-sticks of silver, engraved, without gilding, assessed at twelve marks – which later the bishop took away.

There is one thurible of silver with decoration and gilding, with a pan of iron placed inside, assessed at ten marks and one ounce and eight pennyweights, which Abbot Thurstan made. And another thurible of silver, decorated and gilded, with a pan of iron, assessed at eight marks, which the sacrist Guthmund made. And a third thurible of copper, gilded, with a silver chain and a silver top. And a thurible of silver with a pan of iron, assessed at three marks. And the bishop has one thurible of silver, well decorated and gilded, of five marks, which Wulfstan made – and this the bishop lost at Wareham.

There is one ewer of silver-gilt, assessed at five marks and five ounces, which Abbot Thurstan made. And two basins of silver assessed at four-and-a half marks – which the bishop broke up.

There is one frontal, well decorated with gold and silver, which the venerable Queen Emma decorated in honour of St Æthelthryth – but the 'Majesty of the Throne' is missing. And one decorated with onyx-work [and] silver. And three staves with silver grips, well decorated and gilded, which Abbot Ælfsige of happy memory made. And two staves with crystal grips, which Ralph the sacrist made. And two staves with ivory grips, decorated with silver. And one staff with an ivory grip, without decoration. And two crosiers entirely of ivory. And two other crosiers. And four are with the bishop. And one chrismatory, decorated with silver. And two large candle-sticks fashioned of copper and gilded. And two reliquaries covered all over with bone, and several very small reliquaries, adorned with gold and silver, filled with relics of the saints. There is one gold ring with a sapphire, assessed at one ounce and three pennyweights of gold, which Bishop Hervey presented, but later a certain sacrist stole it, motivated by a desire to exert power. There are two boots of samite and sandals of leather, and a mitre, and four pairs[183] of gloves.

There is one red chasuble well-embroidered, which was Abbot Leofsige's.[184] And one chasuble of *purpura*, well-embroidered, which Bishop Æscwig presented. And one chasuble well-embroidered all over, made of the cloak of King Edgar. And one chasuble of *purpura* well-embroidered, which the brothers of the church bought from Ælfbold, a burgess of Thetford. There

---

[183] Reading at p. 293.2, ed. Blake, *paria* for *pallia*.

[184] In the subsequent parts of this inventory, frequent use is made in the Latin of the possessive genitive to credit particular vestments to particular individuals. In the translation, this idiom has, where possible, been rendered simply by adding an apostrophe + 's' to the names. But simple 'possession' is not always what is being expressed: monastics, theoretically at least, could possess nothing; in some cases the names are those of donors, in others, those of makers, or even sellers.

is one red chasuble, well decorated, which the Lady Githa, the wife of Earl Godwine, mother of Queen Edith, the wife of the glorious King Edward, presented. There is one white chasuble, well-embroidered, which the Lady Æthelswith made.[185] And one good, black chasuble, which Bishop Nigel gave. And twenty-one chasubles with slight decoration, of which one was Bishop Osmund's, and one, Archbishop Wulfstan's and one, Bishop Æthelstan's. And twenty-six chasubles without decoration.

And there are nine precious stoles with their maniples: one was Leofsige's; one, Ælfbold's; one, Provost Thurstan's; one, Theodwine's; one, Bishop Osmund's; and two pairs were Abbot Ælfsige's. And fourteen stoles with their maniples, with slight decoration: one was Eadfrith's; one, Bishop Æscwig's; one, Abbot Thurstan's; one, the monk Tosti's. And fifteen stoles with their maniples, of slight value. And five maniples without stoles: three excellent ones were St Æthelwold's and one, Bishop Hervey's.

And two well-decorated belts: one, made of the girdle of King Edgar and one, Ælfbold's.

And four albs of silk, excellently decorated with orphrey: one was Abbot Leofsige's; one, Provost Sihtric's; one, Ælfbold's; one, Provost Thurstan's. And two linen albs, excellently[186] decorated: one was Abbot Ælfsige's, one Abbot Richard's. And eleven albs lightly decorated at their lower edge with orphrey: one, from the boots of King Edgar; two, from the cloth in which the body of St Æthelthryth had been wrapped; one was Abbot Wulfric's; two, Abbot Simeon's; five, St Æthelwold's. And sixty-four albs decorated with pall-cloth: twenty-four were St Æthelwold's; four, the cantor Ælfric's; four, Prior Thembert's; two, those of the orphrey-embroideress *Liveva*; four, those of Godwine, a burgess of this town; and four, those of Wulfwine, a baker. And there are a hundred and ten albs without decoration at the lower edge.

And five super-humerals, that is, amices <. . . >:[187] one was that of Abbot Leofsige, of blessèd memory; one, Provost Sihtric's; and one, Ælfbold's; one, the sacrist Guthmund's; one, Provost Thurstan's. And ninety-four super-humerals decorated with orphrey: twenty-four, of unornamented orphrey, were St Æthelwold's; thirty with stones and ornamentation: eight being Abbot Ælfsige's; eight, Provost Thurstan's; four, Provost Sihtric's; four, the sacrist Ralph's.

And one cope of black *purpura*, well decorated and star-spangled all over, which Wulfstan at first, and later Guthmund, worked upon, but Ralph completed. And one other cope of black *purpura*, decorated with orphrey all over with golden roundels and flowers, which Prior Thembert once made;

---

[185] Cf. *LE* ii. 88.

[186] Reading with E: *optime.*

[187] It is strange that it is not explained what distinguished these amices from the others, and probably a description of their decoration is lost.

and he brought to pass many good works for us with respect to ornaments and buildings .

And four copes: one of pall-cloth spangled with stars arranged in a circle, well decorated, which Provost Thurstan of worshipful memory made, and another of sinople-green cloth, well decorated, was Abbot Richard's. And a third[188] of black *purpura*, Provost Sithric's. And a fourth,[189] of white *purpura* with flowers in a circle, well decorated, was Abbot Theodwine's. And one old cope of St Æthelwold, moderately well decorated. And eleven copes moderately well decorated: four were Provost Thurstan's; two, Abbot Richard's; two Wulfstan's; one, the monk Tosti's. And fourteen copes with slight decoration: two were St Æthelwold's; two, Abbot Richard's; three, Provost Thurstan's; one, Archbishop Stigand's; one, Queen Matilda's; one, the Bishop of Salisbury's; one, the monk Ingelmær's; one, Abbot Leofsige's; two, Abbot Thurstan's. And there are twenty-nine copes without decoration: twelve were St Æthelwold's; two, Abbot Thurstan's; two, Prior Thembert's; two, Abbot Ælfsige's.

There are two precious dalmatics: one, Bishop Ælfwine's, the other, the Lady Æthelswith's. And eleven dalmatics of little value: one, of white pall-cloth, is that of St Æthelthryth, which she possessed in life, or with which her body was wrapped after her death; four are St Æthelwold's; others were given by other people of whom we have no record. And there are there fourteen tunicles of little value: seven were St Æthelwold's; others, donated by various people.

There are seven palls with orphrey: one of *purpura*, excellently decorated all around with orphrey and stones, which Queen Emma gave to St Æthelthryth, who also made a pall of *purpura* for each of our saints, and bestowed them on the separate altars for the beautification of the church. And there are six large palls. And sixty-two small palls:[190] twenty-six were St Æthelwold's; others, from outside, were given by various people.[191] And there are thirty-four good, woollen, back-hangings: sixteen were St Æthelwold's and two large ones, those of Leofwine son of Æthulf, and two were the sacrist Ralph's; two, the Lady Ælfwaru's; four, Queen Emma's and two, those of Ingrith, the orphrey-embroideress. And three back-hangings of scant value, which were St Æthelwold's. And three large tapestries: one, Abbot Richard's; two, Bishop Hervey's. And two small and worn-out tapestries of St Æthelwold; two, of Leofwine, son of Æthelwulf. And fifty-four bench-covers, twenty-four being St Æthelwold's. And thirty-four curtains, nine being St Æthelwold's. And two cushions of silken cloth. And nine

---

[188] Reading conjecturally : 'iii.' in place of simply 'iii' at p. 293.35, ed. Blake.

[189] Likewise reading conjecturally 'iiii.' at p. 293.36, ed. Blake.

[190] Or 'cloaks'. Cf. the *pallia pendentia* mentioned in ii. 115.

[191] Reading, with a supplement to E at p. 294.12, ed. Blake: *alia de exteriori <a> diversis data sunt.*

pillows of silken cloth, three being St Æthelwold's. And six silken napkins for the making of offerings, three being St Æthelwold's. And twenty-seven cloths of particularly fine-spun silk and twenty-four linen napkins for altars, and a good number of other linen cloths.

And in the outer tower[192] there are nine bells, four large and five medium-sized: six, St Æthelwold's; two, Ælfbold's. And in the tower of the church there are four medium-sized bells and six smaller ones. In that place there are extremely precious fetters which St Æthelthryth broke, hanging before the altar.

Bishop Nigel found these and many other things in the church; and also in the cupboard a number of books, which would cause great annoyance[193] to the reader, if he were to be kept in suspense by the giving of an account of them.

51. With what violence the bishop stole the monks' properties from them and entrusted them to Master Ranulf their enemy, afflicting them cruelly; they themselves, however, waited in acceptance of the scourge of the Lord, in the expectation of release.[194]

Meanwhile, urgent matters of state were arising, which were making the bishop continually anxious. They kept forcing him to stay outside the monastery for long periods, so that, after many days, he scarcely came home, and many crowds followed him. Now, he had arranged a banquet for his entourage, like a king's banquet, and they 'sat down to eat and drink and rose up to play games.'[195] Amongst them, there were bad men banqueting with him, mixed with the good, pseudo-supporters,[196] so to speak, and they kept continually confronting their lord himself with whisperings and falsehoods, studiously endeavouring to stir him up into anger and hatred against the

---

[192] So E: *in exteriori turri* at p. 294.21, ed. Blake, but F replaces *exteriori* with *interiori*: 'the inner tower', perhaps in recognition of a factual error, perhaps because of an actual change of position of the bells. The upper parts of the present west tower are to be dated later than Bishop Nigel's time. See J. Maddison, *Ely Cathedral: Design and Meaning*, pp. 37ff. on the contribution of Nigel's successor Bishop Geoffrey Ridel to its building. See *LE* ii. 146 for a reference to a 'tower' which was the earlier resting place of St Æthelthryth and St Seaxburh, and iii. 28 for the 'tower of St Peter' at the entrance of the *'ecclesia* of St Æthelthryth', struck by lightning in 1111, but not destroyed.

[193] This translation presupposes repunctuation at p. 294.25, ed. Blake, thus: *sed et in armario numerum librorum, valde qui lectorem fastidiret si narrando suspenderetur.* Alternatively one might surmise that the adjective *magnum* was inadvertently omitted before *valde*.

[194] Source for *LE* iii. 51–3: see above on chapter 47.

[195] 1 Corinthians 10.7.

[196] Lat. *speudo, ut ita dicam, collaterales* (p. 294.34, ed. Blake), cf. the formulation *pseudoapostoli* in 2 Corinthians 11.13.

innocent monks. At all events, they certainly contrived a malicious plot against them, inwardly thinking wrong thoughts. They strove to make out that the lord Bishop had no need of the monks in anything, and that it was not obligatory for them to stand by him, as sons of the church, in his altar-ministry or at the dedication of churches. Not only this but they would say that it was not at all obligatory for them to be present at the pleading of lawsuits or in pursuance of the legal rights of the monastery, though in actual fact the legal rights of the church, the greatest and the smallest, rightly and canonically, depend upon, and have reference to, the agreement of those men with their spiritual father. For, most particularly, it is in accordance with laws and decrees that any individual is permitted to hold a position of standing on behalf of the state,[197] and the law of nature grants to everyone what is his, and in no way ought a bishop's decision, either at a dedication or at a synod, stand without the presence of the sons of his own church, as it is a proven fact, on the strength of the twenty-second chapter of the Council of Carthage,[198] that: 'the decision of a bishop shall be invalid unless it is confirmed by the consent and presence of his clerics',[199] and, in fact, not by just any clerics, but by those who are from the bosom of his own see, whether they are monks, or canons, or scholars, that is, secular clerics. For all who are in holy orders are generally considered to be covered by this name of 'clerics'. Moreover, by custom, the monks of Ely are recognized as having, in relation to their bishop, by due custom, both a higher status and greater rights of access, than do other monasteries under a bishop.[200] This is because they were certainly[201] not brought into being and constituted by the bishop: rather it is a proven fact that, on the contrary, the bishop was brought into being and constituted by them. The notion that it happened otherwise does not concur with what is remembered.

Nevertheless, the bishop was stirred to a state of extreme agitation for fear that there might be 'tumult' arising 'amongst the people'.[202] He had already made it his aim that the monks should be utterly excluded from his judicial sphere. And so, spurred on by continual malign utterances on the part of Ranulf, he entrusted the monk's affairs to him – without even discussing their present circumstances, as he reckoned them not worthy of a hearing – he slanderously accused them, in Ranulf's presence, of criminal activities.

At that time, the venerable monk William was exercising the office of

---

[197] Lat. *stare pro re publica*.

[198] The fourth council, dated 398.

[199] See Pseudo-Isidore, *Decretalium Collectio*, Migne, *PL* cxxx, col. 345, no. xxiii.

[200] Lat. *ceteris locis episcopalibus*.

[201] Reading with F: *profecto* (p. 295.18, ed. Blake).

[202] Matthew 26.5; Mark 14.2.

Prior of the church of Ely. The bishop had installed him in the first year of his episcopate. This prior had stood the test in his leadership of the church and in his manner of life as a monk: within the monastery and in its external affairs, he had been demonstrably useful and faithful to his lord and to his brothers. As a consequence, that pernicious man Ranulf, fearing that Prior William, being a man of this sort, had the edge over him in his lord's favour, deprived him, by a maleficent trick, of his control over external business, and assumed the position of a tyrant in relation to the business of the brothers, neither fearing God nor honouring the lady saints to whose obedient service those brothers had pledged themselves.

So, now that the prior and monks had been debarred from the power that belonged to them, this man, in person, immediately brought about a variety of hardships: he ejected rightful office-holders and put in new ones – men who would not be like servants in their ministrations, but rather would engage in trickery; he made changes to responsibilities, abolished sources of support, decreased victuals, withheld revenues; he prohibited external travelling: he blocked every path by ramparts, and hedges and guardposts, so that the monks might not go out to make a public plea about the violence inflicted upon them. And so, seeing themselves imprisoned in this way, they bore the scourge of the Lord patiently, in expectation of mercy, approaching with prayers and stints of fasting the bodies of the lady saints in whose protection they were putting their trust. And it was the eve of St Leonard the Confessor[203] when this affliction had come upon them.

Thus, too, that whole year went by and, while the monks suffered extreme neediness, that Ranulf – who was to suffer the great wrath of God in the following year – kept acting with increasing insolence with regard to their affairs. And the hand of the Lord was already preparing to provide a remedy for the monks of Ely when they had been wretchedly afflicted for two years: thus it would be that divine vengeance would make a pre-emptive strike against that evil tyrant whom no sentiment of pity had caused to crack. The chapter which follows will explain the way in which this happened.

52. How Ranulf, overtaken by an evil impulse, lured accomplices to join him with a view to subversive action against his country, but, on being detected, thanks to St Æthelthryth, as complicit in an act of treason, took flight.[204]

It is our aim that the operation of God's strength and power should be praised in all things everywhere and that it may be glorified in all its ways – these

---

[203] 6th November. 'The year is 1135, as the discovery of the conspiracy precisely two years later (*infra*, chapter 52) was one of the reasons for Stephen's return from Normandy in Advent, 1137 (Orderic Vitalis, *Hist. Eccl.* v.91).' So Blake, p. 296, n. 1.

[204] Source: see above on chapter 47.

in all things everywhere and that it may be glorified in all its ways – these being mercy and truth – as much in its granting of forgiveness as in its inflicting of punishment. To this end, we have thought it right to include mention in this little work, among the miracles of the blessed virgin Æthelthryth,[205] of a deed which was brought to pass in the district of Ely, for the future benefit of prosperity, on the reasoning that it was a great and astounding miracle. In it, undoubtedly, it is made most plainly evident how fair the balance of justice is whereby God is accustomed to ordain vengeance against the impenitent as much as pardon for the penitent.

To continue: the aforesaid Ranulf – impious and unbelieving as he was, and secretly a heretic with regard to most of the sacraments and tenets of the Church, even though he had not been publicly convicted – 'set his face against Heaven'[206] and prohibited the celebration of saints' feast-days which deserve to be reverenced, in contravention both of the service of piety and the duty of humanity. At the same time, cruel and inhuman man that he was, anticipating in his own time, by his malice, the times of the Antichrist, he often denied burial to the dead, and granted it to no one if he did not receive money for it.[207]

By a just judgement of God, there had flowed into him the bilge-water of all the vices, and so the result was as follows. A brother of Ranulf's, not dissimilar to him, had wrongful relations with a certain concubine, with a pretence of legitimacy and in the public view – preferring her to other women in accordance with the precedent of Herod, who had seduced the wife of his brother Philip[208] – and, despite the fact of the concubine's effrontery towards him, Ranulf did not rebuke this sin and unchastity on the part of his brother, for all its magnitude. And Ranulf himself, accustomed as he was to living in idleness, magnificently and comfortably, not on his own wealth, but on that of other people, exceeded the limit, through not knowing any limit: he set his heart on uncertainties in place of certainties, on war instead of peace. For such was his character that laziness had taken over his mind, lust had made it empty, pride had invaded it and other people's food had bloated it. Set though he was amid such an abundance of possessions – directed towards his own needs, as afterwards emerged – it was in an ill-advised and improvident way, in relation to everyone, that he dealt with all the things which he was grudgingly denying to those who were faithful servants to the bishop. It was in accordance with his deserts, therefore, that, having become committed to a bad idea, he began swollen-headedly to rise further and further above himself, day by day, to place his seat, as it were, facing the

---

[205] Note this indication that the compiler was drawing on a miracle book here rather than direct from, for example, Brother Richard's *History*.

[206] Psalm 72 Vulgate = 73.9 RSV.

[207] Lit.: 'if he did not sell it'.

[208] Cf. Mark 6.17.

North Wind, together with the notorious prime instigator of his ruin,[209] and to conspire with his henchmen, aspiring to obtain, by whatever means, the kingship of the English people. Evil thinking had taken over his mind and it was as the result of his obstinacy of heart that he brought upon himself the first judgement of his condemnation, as the result of which an unexampled blindness brought his public disgrace to everyone's notice. Blinded, therefore, as he was, because of the judgement of God, he summoned two of his close associates, of whom one, somewhat prophetically, was known as Henry *Peregrinus* with allusion to his fidelity,[210] and the other was called Ralph *Burgundio* in accord with the meaning of this name, since members of the Allobrogian tribe are disloyal.[211]

And the traitor himself revealed to them the nature and scope of the undertaking which he had in mind.[212] Addressing them at considerable length, he instilled it into their minds how much glory, renown and dignity they could easily obtain. Henry and Ralph applauded the enterprise in all its magnitude and promised him confederate forces for all his undertakings, and in secrecy they won over all the worst men to his detestable plan. Then, every man who had destroyed his patrimony, or who had plundered someone else's inheritance, or had blown up a huge bubble of debt, or had been convicted in a court of law, or was a defendant who had escaped justice, latched on to them as their closest and most intimate comrade. And they reckoned no one worthy of their friendship, if he were not besmirched by some stain of criminality or an evil reputation.

Eventually, they had a meeting together in Stretham church, and abominable oaths were sworn, on this account and on that, against their native land and in favour of the death of everyone of French birth. Both clergy and laity in large numbers were enticed in by entreaties and hired for money. Then Ranulf had arms of various kinds, fearsome to behold, made in the vill of Stretham, with the object, if it had been allowed, of bringing what he had wickedly conceived to its even more wicked fulfilment. And now that his counsel regarding this had been shared frequently with his accomplices and with his council convened without the spirit of counsel, he turned from a fool into a madman, and began sharing out the kingdom, appointing the future king, distributing bishoprics and earldoms at will. Though an enemy

---

[209] Lat. *cum illo primo ruine sue auctore*: presumably the Devil.

[210] Cf. *LE* ii. 135 for disparaging use of the term *peregrinus*, 'traveller', 'pilgrim'.

[211] Cf. Horace, *Epode* 16.6, according to which the Allobroges were 'disloyal in revolution'. The Allobroges, a tribe of south-eastern Gaul in Roman antiquity, whose territory was later to become part of the medieval kingdom of Burgundy, were responsible for informing on Catiline to Cicero, consul at the time of his conspiracy. They were thus disloyal to Catiline, though not to the Roman establishment. Ralph *Burgundio* was to fulfil a similar role in relation to Ranulf's conspiracy.

[212] At p. 297.13, ed. Blake, strong punctuation is assumed after *Allobroges*.

of liberty and peace, he took to promulgating laws as if for liberty and peace, and to promise things which he neither possessed nor could have to any extent possessed, in order, in this way, to drive them to folly. He cited precedent from the histories of ancient times: how few in number had been the men who so often had taken possession of the whole of the Roman state and had thoroughly disrupted it; how great had been the massacres which they had perpetrated, and often it had been a few men from out of an enormous multitude who had triumphed!

Some of them coerced by intimidation, some drawn by love, some seduced out of simple-mindedness, some the victims of ambition, declared themselves prepared to go to the death or the dungeon for love of him and in favour of him. Ranulf, on the other hand, in his desire for glory, derived from the support of his flatterers confidence for carrying out his undertaking, massive though it was. He would make empty boasts, as if he were already seated on the throne of the kingdom. And, every day, he would go in pomp through the town and the Isle of Ely, and would frequently arraign, load with obligations and rob of money those whom he despised or whom he despaired of having as allies in his conspiracy, and he would afflict them with many acts of harassment. And so the hateful murderer, the detestable betrayer of his country – who was heaping up wealth for himself at the expense of other people, and was welcoming comrades from among men of the worst possible character – intended to kill, together with the forces of his retinue, the lord whose grace and favour he so long misused, the lord who raised him, in his want, from the dust, and set him upright when he was lying in the dung, and caused him to sit with princes, the lord who often drank wine beside him at table from a gold and silver cup. Like a second Judas he was preparing, in his cruelty, to present to him a drink of deadly poison!

But the grace of God opposed so evil a plan on the part of this man. Consequently, he fell into a pit of his own making, and eventually a divinely ordered dispensation uncovered the purpose of his wickedness and cast him down from the hope of his vanity. And, so that it may be evident with what rational deliberation God makes all His provisions: it was on the Eve of St Leonard, the same date on which two years previously Ranulf had set himself up over the affairs of the monks, that the most heinous treason began to be brought to light. For a concealed horror about the enormity of an undertaking of such magnitude had gained possession of him: he was insufficiently confident about the loyalty of his men, and did not reckon that such a massive undertaking could be kept secret among so many accomplices; nor did he envisage that the time suitable for such ventures had yet arrived. Because of this, he decided, for his own part, to take flight, taking with him what things he could, and abandoned the whole affair to his supporters. One of them, Ralph *Burgundio,* on learning this, suddenly came rushing into the monastery and fled to the body of St Æthelthryth. He did so out of fear that someone else might anticipate him in uncovering the crime and, at the same time, on the reasoning that, through this disclosure, he might win the favour of the lord Bishop and immunity from bodily punishment. He was acting not in the fervour of penitence but in the stench of his guilt. And, without delay, the report was conveyed to the ears of the bishop. He was astonished, he came running, he gave the case a hearing, he was reduced to stupefaction. And such news could not, from then on, be concealed, because it had now come to entail the safety of the entire populace. And so the monks, freed from a cruel tyrant by the merits of their lady, St Æthelthryth, and the advocacy of their patroness, exulted in a great dance of joy and extolled with praises God and his bountiful virgin.

Now that finally the 'counsel of Ahithophel'[213] had been disclosed and, by God's agency, reduced to folly, Ranulf escaped, taking flight and, by divine revelation, the accomplices of his conspiracy were captured and convicted. Some of the laymen were hanged on the gallows: the clerics suffered condemnation to perpetual exile. Oh, how marvellous are the acts of vengeance which God brings about through the merit of the blessed Æthelthryth! The man whom, a moment before, they had all venerated as a master and feared as a tyrant, now that his conscience was shaking with terror, dwelt as 'a wanderer and exile on the earth', like a second Cain[214] after his act of fratricide, doomed as he was not to die once but to suffer the seven punishments of Cain, so that whoever came upon him seemed his slayer and he died a death without dying. For his punishment, so to speak, kept coming to life again.

53. That the bishop, terror-stricken as the result of the judgement of God and St Æthelthryth, gave the monks their properties back, being sorrowful at having behaved badly towards them.[215]

The bishop, returning at last to his senses, was terror-stricken by these massive calamities, in view of the fact that he had stretched forth his hand against the monks, his own flock, contrary to their deserts. Understanding that they were innocent and repenting of the fact that he had been cruelly enraged against them, he restored to the prior and community command over their properties, but by no means in full: he kept back for himself some properties of the church[216] which he wanted, and very good ones they were.

---

[213] 2 Kings Vulgate = 2 Samuel RSV, 17.14.

[214] Cf. Genesis 4.14–16.

[215] Source: the account of Ranulf's conspiracy narrated in chapters 47 and 51–3 and paralleled in B (*Book of Miracles*) concludes here; there follows a transition by the compiler, introducing the charter and privilege set out in chapters 54 and 55.

[216] Reading at p. 299.12, ed. Blake, with E: *rebus ecclesie.*

Moreover, despoiler that he was, he ought long to have ceased from his despoiling, and to have corrected his former transgression by a complete amendment of ways, and to have cut himself off from all transgression for the future. In fact, however, he became forgetful of the divine vengeance inflicted upon his supporters and of his own escape from danger and of the unjust distress which had been caused to the flock subject to him. He made a plan to change their holdings for the better and amplify them – so he asserted. But the monks put up opposition, and certainly did not agree with his cutting away and diminishing of properties, and the bishop utterly refused to make a concession or grant concerning the estates and the goods of the place in accordance with the statutes of the church or lawful decrees or with a fair division or just apportionment. Certainly, the cruelty which, unjustly and without due cause, he had exercised against the wretched monks had become common knowledge all around. Fearing that the losses occasioned by his savagery would be made public, he prepared to appoint delegates, and found men from his most intimate circle to act in this capacity: the objective of this was to bring about confirmation by a Roman privilege of the customary holdings of the monks, amplified, according to what he had said, by a grant of his own. In fact, Bishop Nigel's aim was to bring report of himself to the Romans, to propagate a reputation and to gain favour.

And the envoys had taken with them, on the instruction of the bishop, a charter of his to obtain confirmation of the things in it which had been changed by the bishop without the monks' consent, and which were very scanty in relation to their needs. This charter, because it is earlier than the privilege, will be set down first, and the privilege in second place.

54. A charter of the bishop concerning the things which he altered for the benefit of the monks.[217]

Nigel, by the grace of God, consecrated first bishop of the church of Ely,[218] to all children of the Church, both present and future: greeting. When, by the ordinance of divine grace, I had entered into the ruling of the church of Ely and had found the affairs of the church to be badly transacted in many respects, especially the things provided for and set apart from the affairs of the bishopric, which had been instituted, inadequately, for the needs of the monks, I decided immediately to enstate for the monks a more satisfactory arrangement of their affairs. Consequently, having entered into consultation

---

[217] Source: monastic archives, cf. British Library, Harley Charters, 43. H. 5, cartularies CDGM and other copies cited by Blake. Date 1133 X 1139. Cf *LE* iii. 26, which Nicholas Karn believes to be a forged derivative from the text presented in iii. 54. Confirmations by two popes of Bishop Nigel's charter are set out in iii. 56 and 85.

[218] Lat. *Elyensis ecclesie primus consecratus episcopus* . . .

with my friends, I have made the arrangements for them which are set down in writing below – as much in respect to their ownerships of the lands and the churches attached to the same lands as in all other matters which pertain to their work – and I grant that these arrangements remain thus for evermore. These, therefore, are the names of the lands.

Within the Isle: Sutton, Witcham, Witchford, Wentworth, Turbutsey, Whittlesey, Stuntney, with twenty-three thousand eels which are caught in the marshes and waters which lie near that manor, and all revenues and offerings belonging to the altars of the mother church, for supporting the needs of the same church. And the church of St Mary of Ely with its lands and tithes and all things pertaining to this church itself. And, specifically, all the tithe of my Barton. And a dairy farm in Dernford. And in *Biela*. And seven weys of salt in respect to Terrington. And also, certainly, timber in Somersham and in Bluntisham, as best they had it in the time of my predecessors. And upon the river-bank of Bluntisham a messuage of land with five acres of land, where timber may be collected, and with eight acres of meadow, where the oxen for dragging the timber may graze. Also their vineyard in Ely, just as they possessed it before I came to my bishopric. And six fishermen, along with their dwellings, to fish in the waters where they customarily did.

Outside the Isle, in Cambridgeshire: Melbourn, Meldreth, Hauxton, Newton, Wratting, Stetchworth, Swaffham. And twelve skeps of corn and malt which the heirs of Hardwin de Scalers owe. And Stapleford. In Suffolk: Bergham,[219] Stoke, Melton, Sudbourne, Kingston; *soke* and *sake* with all royal customs in five-and-a-half hundreds. Twenty shillings in respect to *Rescemere*. Lakenheath, Undley, *Scepeia*. In Norfolk, *Fotestorp* at the command of the monks. And thirty thousand herrings from Dunwich. And I grant to them all their own servants in all their ministrations, so that they may possess them freely with all their messuages. I permit moreover that they may have and freely possess all the gifts which have been given to the same monks before the time of my episcopate, or in my time, or shall be given in the future, whether consisting in lands, or in churches, or in tithes or in fisheries, or in cash, or in any revenue whatsoever, which any of the faithful may have bestowed upon them up to now or shall in time to come bestow upon them. Moreover I grant to them all the things written above and, in addition, their own court with all the liberties and customs which are observed in the lands which are in my jurisdiction, excepting absolutely nothing, so that none of my successors may allow himself to become involved in any respect whatsoever in their affairs, with the exception that he is faithfully and unceasingly to protect and in every way maintain them along with all their possessions. But if anyone, motivated by a spirit of ill-

---

[219] The parallel passage in *LE* iii. 26 has 'Winston'.

will, should wish to infringe, despise or reject this our grant and donation, let him be condemned by God and by all His saints, and let him be excommunicated by us in as far as this is allowed, and cut off from the company of all the faithful, unless he returns to his senses. Let it be done! Let it be done! AMEN.

55. A privilege of the lord Pope containing reference to the properties of the whole bishopric, confirming them in perpetuity.[220]

Innocent, Bishop, servant of the servants of God, to his venerable brother Nigel, Bishop of Ely, and his successors to be appointed to that prelacy for evermore. The request of a pious will ought always to be fulfilled by subsequent enactment of it, so that sincerity of devotion may laudably shine forth and the expedient action may unequivocally gain reinforcement. In thankful regard for this consideration,[221] venerable brother Bishop Nigel, we assent with clemency to your petitions and, by the text of the present privilege, we safeguard the church of Ely, over which you are recognized to be in charge beneath God's authority, by decreeing that whatever estates and whatever goods this same church canonically possesses at present or shall in future be able to acquire by the grant of popes, by the generosity of kings and princes, by the giving of offerings by believers, or by other lawful means, are to remain on a firm footing and untouched by you and your successors. Among these, we have deemed it right that the following should be specifically referred to, with mention of particular names: the abbey of the nuns of Chatteris, which we solemnly decree to possess its customary and long-possessed liberty, together, of course, with all its appurtenances: daughter-houses, estates, arable lands, pastures, marshes, woods, game-preserves, waters, fisheries, services, tithes, dues, rents, head-penny payments, legal entitlements, customary rights, rights of hearing pleas, rights of inflicting correction, rights of imposing fines, whether ecclesiastical or secular, and, in addition, writs or wills or other things belonging to it. No one of mankind, therefore, is to be permitted rashly to disturb the aforementioned church of Ely or to take away its possessions, or, moreover, to usurp or hold on to possessions taken away, diminish them, or by any means whatsoever exhaust them, by acts of harassment. But all things belonging to the people for whose governance and support they were granted, are to be kept untouched, to the furtherance of their purposes. Your part in this, therefore, is so to exert yourself in furtherance of the restoration of this same church, so to work more and more, with all your strength, for

---

[220] Source: monastic archives, cf. cartularies CDGM; copied also in the Chatteris cartulary; date: 5th December, 1138; printed also in W. Holtzmann ed. *Papsturkunden in England*, ii, no. 17.

[221] Reading with E: *gratia* a t p. 301.24, ed. Blake.

the recovery of those properties which have been removed or usurped, that the Lord almighty may be honoured by your actions, and the church may obtain longed-for assuagements of its losses. Indeed, if any person, whether churchman or lay, should rashly attempt to contravene knowingly the text of this our enactment, if, after having been warned a second or third time, that person does not make amends for his guilt by a suitable penalty, he is to be deprived of his dignified position of power and honour and is to recognize that he is guilty, by the judgement of God, of the wickedness which has been perpetrated, and he is to be alienated from the most sacred body and blood of the Redeemer, Jesus Christ, our Lord and God, and is to be subject to strict vengeance at the Last Judgement. The peace of the Lord Jesus Christ be upon all those who uphold the rights of that place, so that they may receive the fruit of good action and, before the Final Judge, may discover the rewards of eternal peace. AMEN. AMEN. AMEN.[222]

56. Another privilege of the lord Pope about the provisions which Bishop Nigel established for the monks, small though they were.[223]

Innocent, Bishop, servant of the servants of God, to his venerable brother Nigel, Bishop of Ely, and to his successors to be appointed canonically in his place for evermore. Installed as we are, by God's dispensation, upon the high vantage-point of the Apostolic See, it befits us to love and honour our brothers situated near and far away, and to uphold their jurisdiction with respect to the churches entrusted to them by God. Consequently, venerable brother Bishop Nigel, we have deemed it right to assent to your requests with fraternal good-will, and we honour the church of Ely, over which, with the Lord's authority, you are presiding, with a privilege of the Apostolic See, decreeing that, whatever estates and whatever goods you justly and lawfully possess, or which – God being propitious – this same church shall be able to obtain in future, by the generosity of kings or princes, by the giving of offerings by believers, or by other lawful means, may remain established for you and for your successors, without infringement. Among these, we have deemed it right to make mention by name of the following.

Specifically, whatever things King Henry of distinguished memory out of his devotion granted and conceded to this same church: specifically, relaxation of the requirement for the knight-service of the bishopric of Ely, which used to be customarily performed at Norwich Castle; also the remission of the requirement for twenty-five shillings and five pence and

---

[222] In the copies in CDM there follow words meaning: 'On the nones (5th) of December, in the second year of the indiction, in the year of the Lord's incarnation 1139, but in the ninth year of the pontificate of the lord Pope Innocent II.'

[223] Source: monastic archives, cf. cartularies CDGM; copied also in the Chatteris cartulary. Date: 27th April, 1139.

one half-penny, which used to be given annually for the guard of the castle; in addition, the relaxation of the requirement for all the service and works which the retainers[224] of the church of Ely used to perform in the aforesaid castle; also remission of the requirement for forty pounds of scutage, these concessions being in accordance with what is known to have been laid down by the same king and confirmed in writing.

Moreover, we confirm that the abbey of Chatteris, with all its appurtenances, belongs no less to the church of Ely, with the specification, however, that the nuns who are there, or[225] shall have been there previously, are to live under a rule in accordance with the ordinances of St Benedict.[226] And also we give instructions that the remission of ward-penny in respect to the lands of the said church and the church of Chatteris and no less the restitutions of lands, liberties and dignities made by the illustrious man King Stephen, are to be kept firm and undisrupted for you for evermore. In a similar way, too, we confirm for the said church the possessions, liberties and dignities conferred by other kings of the English and leaders of your church and confirmed by our predecessor, Pope Victor of good memory, for you and your successors, and through your mediation. Furthermore, whatever goods you have conferred upon the monks of this particular church with a view to the maintenance of religious devotion and the furtherance of hospitality, we sanction that these shall remain for them without diminution, with the stipulation, however, that it shall not be allowed to you or your successors, or to the monks referred to, either to take away or to assign to a military function any of the holdings of the monks, or any of those which you have reserved for the purposes of the bishopric. No, rather you are to have free capability to recover those things which have been seized and to keep those things which have been recovered within the jurisdiction <and control of the church.> And we forbid in every possible way <the monks themselves> to grant <their lands for anyone> to hold <by right of inheritance.>[227]

The names, in point of fact, of the lands and estates which you have granted to these same monks are these. Within the Isle: Sutton, Witcham, Witchford, Wentworth, Turbutsey, Whittlesey, Stuntney, with twenty-three thousand eels which are caught in the marshes and waters which lie near that manor and all revenues and offerings belonging to the altars of the mother church, for supporting the needs of the same church. And the church

---

[224] Lat. *homines.*

[225] Reading with CDM: *aut* for *ut* at p. 303.18, ed. Blake, cf. p. 331.1.

[226] Punctuating with a full stop after *vivant* (p. 303.19, ed. Blake) cf. punctuation marked in E.

[227] Angle brackets here mark material which, though missing in the *LE* transcripts, is found in other copies of the charter. Supply at p. 303.30, ed. Blake: *ditione tue* (rather than *tua*) *ecclesie*; cf. p. 331.12.

of St Mary of Ely with its lands and tithes and all its appurtenances. And specifically all the tithe of your Barton and a dairy farm at Dernford and one at *Biela*.[228] And seven weys of salt in Terrington. And also timber, certainly, in Somersham,[229] as best they had it in the time of my predecessors. And upon the river-bank of Bluntisham a messuage of land with five acres, where timber may be collected and with eight acres of meadow, where the oxen for dragging the timber may graze. Also their vineyard in Ely, just as they possessed it before you were bishop. And six fishermen, along with their dwellings, to fish in the waters where they customarily did.

Outside the Isle: Melbourn, Meldreth, Hauxton, Newton, Wratting, Stetchworth, Swaffham, Stapleford, Barham, Stoke, Melton,[230] Sudbourne, Kingston; *sake* and *soke* with all royal customs in the five-and-a-half hundreds. Twenty shillings in respect to *Rescemere*. Lakenheath, Undley, *Scepeia*, *Fotestorp* at the command of the monks. And thirty thousand herrings from Dunwich. And twelve skeps of corn and malt which the heirs of Hardwin de Scalers owe. And I grant to them all their own servants in respect to all their ministrations, so that the monks may possess them freely with all their messuages,[231] while the following liberty, in addition, has been indulgently granted and confirmed by you for the benefit of these monks: that not only the aforesaid items which have been conferred upon them by your devotion or by the giving of offerings by any believers, whoever they may have been, but also, equally, items to be conferred upon them in future on reasonable terms, are to remain freely available for their sustenance and freed from all specification of conditions. We decree, therefore, that leave is not to be granted to anyone whomsoever to disrupt the aforesaid church rashly or to seize its holdings or hold on to them after seizure, diminish them or exhaust them by any acts of harassment. Rather, all the holdings of the monks which shall have been granted for their government and sustenance are to be kept whole, for the furtherance of all their various purposes. Therefore, if any person, ecclesiastical or lay, in time to come, shall have attempted knowingly to contravene the text of this our agreement, if, after a second and third warning, he has not made amends by appropriate satisfaction, he is to suffer the downfall of his honour and power and is to be alienated from the most sacred body and blood of our God and Lord Jesus Christ, and he is to be subjected to strict vengeance at the Last Judgement and is to be struck down by the sentence of excommunication. The peace of our Lord Jesus Christ be to all who keep to their legal rights with regard to this same place, so that they may both receive the fruit of good action and, before

---

[228] Here the parallel passage in *LE* iii. 54 adds: 'Also four weys of cheese in respect to Dernford'.

[229] The parallel passage in *LE* iii. 54 adds here: 'and in Bluntisham'.

[230] Here the parallel passage in *LE* iii. 26 adds: '*Baldreseia*'.

[231] Repunctuating with a comma after *possideant* at p. 304.18, ed. Blake.

the strict Judge, acquire the rewards of everlasting peace. AMEN. AMEN. AMEN.[232]

57. The miracle of how a blind woman was given sight at the shrine of St Æthelthryth.[233]

At the time when our lord Bishop Nigel was still alive, a certain woman from Cottenham suffered blindness for four years. Coming to the feast of St Æthelthryth, she kept vigil all night through till dawn. At break of day, therefore, she began to concentrate with increased attentiveness on her praying and, after a little while she cried out thankfully that she had recovered her sight to some small extent. And gradually her disability turned into ability and, now that darkness had been driven out, the most brilliant light made its entrance. In order that this should be proved to the people standing by,[234] half-pennies were thrown to her, and farthing-pieces of different mintings, the embossed designs of which she would distinguish between with complete certainty, while they all looked on. It was recognized that she had indubitably recovered her powers of sight. And so, after solemn chants of thanksgiving, which the clergy and people sang in acclamation, the woman who had come with someone to guide her found her way back to where she belonged without a guide!

58. About a certain man who did not wish to hold the feast of St Æthelthryth.[235]

The narrations which we are giving are very few in number, and the listener is not to expect that all[236] the achievements of this lady saint can be held in our memory or collected together by our eloquence. For we, burdened as we are by such abundant material, would by now have given up, like the weak and feeble, under the weight of what we had taken upon ourselves, had not the piety of the holy virgin been pouring out her moderating grace upon our endeavours. Hence, in subsequent, as in past, narratives, we need the good will of the reader, in order that we may be capable of weaving an additional web of discourse appropriate for the narratives which lie immediately ahead.

---

[232] Here the copies in CDM continue with subscriptions meaning: 'Given at the Lateran by the hand of Aimericus, Cardinal-Deacon and Chancellor of the Holy Roman Church, on 27th April, in the second year of the indiction, in the year of the incarnation of the Lord 1139, but in the tenth year of the pontificate of Pope Innocent II.'

[233] Source: miracle narrative written after the death of Bishop Nigel in 1169, also included in B (Book of Miracles).

[234] Reading conjecturally at p. 305.9, ed. Blake: *adstantibus* for *abstantibus*.

[235] Source: miracle narrative also included in B (Book of Miracles).

[236] Reading with E: *omnia* for *omnis* (p. 305.15, ed. Blake).

For there comes to mind report of a delightful miracle of the kind to delight pious ears with glorious exultation.

Well now, a certain priest gave instructions that the feast of St Æthelthryth should be solemnly observed. One of his parishioners, contemptuous of this instruction, <in no way>[237] undertook to make any contribution to the effort. Divine vengeance did not hesitate to punish his guilt: on the contrary, detestable misfortune followed upon his detestable audacity. For downfall, quick to precipitate downfall, served to cause him an unexpected and headlong fall through a hedge: colliding with this hedge at high speed, he was pierced between the ribs by a very sharp stake. He extracted himself from the hedge by violent shaking and, because the stake broke off, he went away severely wounded, carrying around with him a piece of the stake inside his body.

As a result, his pain increased day by day and now, though the scar had closed over, he began to putrefy internally. Imagine! Not knowing what was inside himself, he summoned physicians and though a succession of them came, he was more harmed than helped. And thus he spent a whole year in the greatest wretchedness until, on the return of the feast of the holy virgin, he was persuaded by his people to be brought to the tomb of the lady saint whom he had offended, on the surmise that perhaps what she had so long before conceived might even then come to fruition. And so he was transported there and, all night and day, he asked for mercy and did not obtain it and then, already reduced to despair, he made ready to return home. And when, on his way, a pleasant piece of level ground lay before him, the man in his distress began to look back at this church in piety with tears in his eyes and in a few words poured out this prayer: 'O most blessed lady, if thou wouldest be willing to show forth the generosity of thy mighty power in regard to my wretched self, I would observe thy feast every year with the greatest devotion. Forgive me, therefore, for the sin which I committed against thee. Let what I have endured be sufficient for thee as retribution, and have mercy on me.' Having said this, he immediately felt a certain miraculous itching in the region of the wound and he began to scratch there for such a long time that the skin was broken and the piece of stick leapt out of his body with much putrefying matter. And so, rejoicing and full of amazement that the cause of his suffering had been cast out, he immediately went back to the church, gave thanks to the lady saint, reported the happening, and afterwards returned to his own district, carrying with him the piece of wood as evidence of a very great miracle, to advance the proclamation of the glory of God and St Æthelthryth.

---

[237] Reading conjecturally at p. 305.22f., ed. Blake: *Cuius precepti quidam parrochianorum* (so E) *suorum contemptor existens, <nullo modo> quippiam operis suscepit agendum.*

59. How a sick man was cured by the tunicle of St Æthelthryth.[238]

Let us not suppose that the virgin has worked miracles of healing only in the place of her repose: she deigns mercifully to be with those who invoke her, wherever they are. So that her holiness may become more widely known, mighty works productive of joy have been brought to pass even as a result of her garments. For we have a certain old dalmatic, which she herself made, or in which her corpse had been wrapped, or which had been her tunic when she was still living as a queen, in secular raiment. And so, certain traces of her sanctity followed it around, as if it were complicit in the extreme greatness of her dignity, and it brought a cure to many sick people upon its simply being touched. As a result it was almost entirely cut up into pieces,[239] as believers kept asking for a piece of it. Let us relate one of its remarkable achievements: our brother Byrhtmær, on entering the house of one William, surnamed *Flandrensis*,[240] had with him this same tunicle, along with other relics, the reason being that he was in charge of the bridge and used to call for contributions of the faithful by preaching. And in that house there was a boy still lying in his cradle, the son of his host, sick and almost dying. By now he could not move, and looked very like a corpse, and so he was causing his father and mother not a little grief. When that brother of ours drew near, therefore, he gave orders that the child's body should be wrapped in the famous tunic and, before he had said the Lord's Prayer over him a third time, the boy drew towards himself first one foot and then the other; after that he moved the whole of himself, rose up, ate food and, on the third day, recovered the completest health. And so these and similar happenings spread the fame of the lady saint far and wide.

60. About a girl blinded in the right eye who was given sight beneath the body of the blessed Æthelthryth.[241]

In the second year of the consecration of our lord and father Nigel, the venerable pontiff of the holy church of Ely, on 6th June, at the hour of the day when dusk was falling, a very celebrated miracle at the tomb of the blessed virgin Æthelthryth became well enough known. For there was a maiden[242] with a beautiful face and of noble birth, outstanding in moral

---

[238] Source: miracle narrative, also included in B (*Book of Miracles*); note the transitional material with which it begins, showing that already, before the compilation of *LE*, it belonged to a collection.

[239] Reading at p. 306.26, ed. Blake, with E: *frustatim* not *frustratim*.

[240] I.e. 'of Flanders', 'Fleming'.

[241] Source: miracle narrative, also included in B (*Book of Miracles*), based on reminiscences by Reinburgis of Cirencester, other members of her family and members of the Ely community.

[242] The word translated here as maiden is *virgo*, 'virgin', a term frequently applied also to St

character, according to the reports of people acquainted with her, and praiseworthy for her honourable conduct. But she had sight in the left eye only, the right eye having been utterly taken away. At a vigil of the holy virgin, she earned the privilege of receiving her sight and to drink in the colours of things with both her eyes. How this came about by holy revelation, a public record, based on a true narrative, will make clear.

It was from the province of Mercia that the aforesaid girl came forth in splendour, born of distinguished parents in the ancient city of Cirencester. Bereft of her father before she was grown up, she moved, in company with her mother, to the territory of the West Saxons. There her mother, having as her lot a second marriage, contracted an alliance with a certain distinguished man by the name of Ranulf, in the famous vill of Wallingford, a man who deserves to be welcomed with open arms by faithful men, being of famous memory for his benefactions, and who, because he was somewhat corpulent, received the surname of *Grossus* on account of his fatness. Second to none among wealthy men, he brought up the girl as his daughter, to shine in the honour of chastity and to aspire to rich returns for her moral character and charms.[243]

One night, when she went to bed, she was thoroughly terrified by a vision and began to fall seriously ill. For there appeared to her a splendid lady warrior,[244] with a vivid complexion and eyes striking to look upon, the strength of whose inexhaustible vigour the girl sensed. Taking her stand nearby in the girl's bedroom, she struck her, semi-conscious as she was, piercingly in the face, so that a very copious surge of blood leapt forth from her nostrils and, stained with its flooding the clothes touched by it. But notwithstanding[245] the fact that she struck the right side of the half-awake girl with a great effort, in a state of great frenzy and with fire in her fearsome eyes, she went away in a reverent manner, without speaking to her at any juncture. And on being roused from her sleep and equally from her dream, the maiden soon became feverish with a very serious sickness and the whole household was deeply shaken by her ill health. On coming nearer, they understood the vision which had been recounted, adducing a parallel for its imagery in the sanguineousness[246] of her true state. And, given that there is

Æthelthryth. It is merely for the sake of clarity that it has seemed desirable to use different terms to designate the virgin girl who is the recipient of the miracle and the lady saint herself.

[243] Reading conjecturally at p. 307.15, ed. Blake: *et ad opulentos reditus morum venustatumque suspirare.*

[244] Lat. *virago*, cf. the description of St Seaxburh in *LE* i. 35 (p. 51.7, ed. Blake) as *pretiosa virago*, 'a precious lady-warrior'.

[245] Reading with mss.: *atqui . . .* (p. 307.18, ed. Blake).

[246] Lat. *in sanguine veritatis conicientes ymaginem* (p. 307.24, ed. Blake). The language derives from the physiological theory of the 'four complexions', of which one is the 'sanguine',

a saying by Solomon, 'Rod and correction will bring about wisdom, but a child who is left to his own desiring will confound his mother,'[247] God perhaps saw fit to educate her by flagellation of this sort, so that after these happenings[248] she would not be subject to a threat to her virginity. Accordingly, bodily losses were inflicted on the virgin in this way as a means of preserving her humility. The day following the night in question was {a Friday}, the sixth day of the week, the day on which Christ engaged in conflict with Zabulus[249] on behalf of the World. Additional evidence came of illness so serious <that>, had she possessed sufficient property to divide, she would have made her will in haste.[250] The maiden was ill for a whole week, until {Thursday}, the day which pagan custom has designated by the name of Jove.[251] In the course of this, while her spirit was almost failing, she diligently sought after ministers of the church. After having made her confession and received in faith the sacraments of the Lord from between their hands, she quickly fell completely silent.

Once again, when <the maiden was asleep>[252] that same night of the following week, the night which precedes {Friday}, the day on which man was created,[253] there stood by <her> a noble personage clothed in white garments, to be specific: a woman of imperious authority. 'Hey, Reinburgis!', said she. 'Are you awake or asleep?' And as the girl, speechless, did not produce the intonations of any response but lay facing the wall, as if resolved upon death, the aforementioned heroine renewed her approach and for a second time addressed her by her own name. 'Reinburgis, why do you not give any response? There is no emperor's daughter in the World, no child of a ruling consul, who does not readily take heed of an utterance of mine and respond carefully to my questions!' The virgin heard all of this, but could not reply. Then the woman spoke a third time: 'Wake up, Reinburgis! Wake up! For I see that you are suffering under the weight of an amazing state of stupor!' And turning round, the distinguished heroine after a little while said to herself: 'I am waiting too long! Too long! I am wasting too much time in speaking.' And, producing a flower which she extracted from her bosom,

---

in which blood predominates over the other three 'humours'.

[247] Proverbs 29.15.

[248] Reading conjecturally at p. 307.27, ed. Blake: *post hec.*

[249] On the name Zabulus, here, and elsewhere, clearly applied to the Devil, see R. Martínez Ortega, 'La voz zabulus en los textos de las cancellerias medievales': http://www.anmal.uma.es/anmal/numero6/Ortega.htm

[250] Reading conjecturally at p. 307.30, ed. Blake (transposing *ut*): *Tante infirmitatis accessit testimonium, ut, si sibi suppeteret unde divideret, sub celeritate faceret testamentum.*

[251] Lat. *dies Jovis.*

[252] Reading conjecturally at p. 307.35 – 308.1, ed. Blake e.g.: *Cum nocte iterum eadem que sequitur, que lucem, qua creatus est homo, precedit, <virgo dormiret,> adest persona . . .*

[253] Cf. Genesis 2.2, 7.

she very quickly inserted it in the girl's mouth. Her voice and speech were restored to her immediately, and yet she was not roused from sleep. And the woman said: 'O Reinburgis, do you recognize the face of the person exchanging words with you? Do you know who I am, where I have come from, and why? Are you able to feel <with what>[254] healing I am restoring this ailing flesh which is weighing down on you all around?' Replying to her, the damsel said: 'I do feel it, lady! I do feel it, and through your intervention, by the grace of God, I am regaining my health.' Then the noblewoman – a notable heroine and †equally† praiseworthy too – said, 'It is according to justice that you are obtaining a cure through me, by whose right hand it is that you are enduring a body weighed down with heaviness. It is from my blows that your cheeks are pallid, yellow with wasting sickness and your side is livid and wracked with pain. As a consequence of this, my mistress, the distinguished virgin and queen, Æthelthryth, has sent me: she could not endure your mother's tears any longer, and has sent you an antidote for curing you. This remedy has been sent by her from Heaven's vault on high as a cure for you, with me as intermediary. And she commands your continuous attendance on her, disrupted though it is to be, forthwith, by dangerous turns of event.'

Her mother, from the first day of her illness, had been continually knocking on the door of the clemency of the most holy virgin Æthelthryth, and by prayers and tears, in a solitary effort, it was this saint alone, above all others, whom she had swayed to an outpouring of pity. 'I give thanks', said the damsel, 'because there is nothing left of my bodily malady.' Her sufferings went away; her strength returned, and the languor which had overtaken her body departed. 'You will still suffer a heavy and cumbersome burden, and you are not, as you suppose, recovering completely. But be daughterly for a moment and bear up, and you will be totally cured of this same lethargy.' And she moved her hand gently to the girl's side and, painlessly breaking it open, twisted her hand around inside, up to the elbow, and gently touched her heart with the tip of her fingers. Then the young maiden said, 'There is no danger, O lady warrior. See, madam, I am fit and well, with all my illness now driven out.' The other said in reply: 'It is a serious illness that is being cut away from you, and perfect health is not yet restored.' The woman withdrew her right hand once more, and again thrust it in, to give the girl relief. And she went through a procedure similar to the previous one, and reckoned it a second repetition. 'Now, madam,' said Reinburgis, 'I am completely well: entirely restored to health.' And the woman said, 'That cure of yours will be at hand when a third treatment has been added.' For the rest, she carried out again what she had done twice previously, in the name of the

[254] Reading conjecturally at p. 308.14f., ed. Blake: *An sentire vales <qua> medela restituam hanc, quam circumfers, carnem egrotam?*

Holy Trinity, and removed her hand from the girl's heart and inner organs. And she besmeared with an ointment the side which she had been excising, and restored the anointed area to its original health. She urged her very insistently, a second time, to present herself at the tomb of the blessed virgin and not to interpose delays in carrying out the journey.

The maiden favoured the warrior-woman with, instead of a vow, as much as was at her command. 'I am ready,' she professed, 'to carry out your instruction and present myself at the holy house of the blessed queen.' 'Go!' said the personage, a third time. 'Do not delay! Do not neglect the orders given to you! Remember how great the excellence is that is pre-eminently manifest in the queen, whose goodness has restored[255] you to health and, when you come to her, will make you perfectly well. The maiden, giving her word eagerly, added that she would certainly not of her own volition fail to carry out what she had promised, providing only that a companion would be available who would help her. 'What sort of protection is it, maiden,' she asked, 'that you are asking for by way of assistance?' She answered: 'I am a powerless girl, bereft of the solace of a father, subject to the authority of my mother, and without her agreement, I am not allowed to be subject to another person's plan.'

There was someone, silent and attentive, avidly taking in the words of Reinburgis as she made her replies, but he had not been able to hear the voice of the person addressing her or see her appearance: the younger brother of the maiden, sitting with her by her bed, compassionately accompanying her in her decline, amidst her calamities and misfortune.

Well then, it was by no means fallaciously that the girl's soul[256] dreamt what was an image of truth. For, without delay, the enactment of a celestial judgement caused this envisaging to move forward to the performance of mighty works. However, the woman, presenting an authoritative mien, addressed the maiden. She was displaying an expression more than usually severe, and the words she used were of this kind: 'I present you with orders!', she said. 'I address you with cajoling and dire warnings! I argue on the basis of the serious troubles by which you are being overthrown! The queen has commanded: let her commands be fulfilled! The most holy virgin Æthelthryth: she it is who is my mistress! It is her warning which is now being given, even though it is expressed by the voice of another person. Now, because you are presenting an excuse, raising a mistaken objection and not speedily making your way to visit the lady whose copious favour has anticipated your needs,[257] you shall recognize what kind of mighty power and merit are hers, by this sign branded upon you! And you shall not quickly

---

[255] Reading at p. 309.1, ed. Blake, with BE: *restituit.*

[256] Lat: *animus.*

[257] 'Anticipated your need' = Lat. *prevenit.*

unlearn the lesson of your habituation to it: it is something which, once experienced, you shall know from your senses to be a reality.' The virago rebuked her with bitter words; upbraided her with a menacing expression on her face and, all the time displaying <a choleric temper>[258] – something which she did not find difficult – she put the maiden on her guard by her obvious anger. And seizing the eyelashes above which protruded her right eyebrow, she dragged it over the eye's pupil and added, by way of a threat, words of this kind: 'Because you are disregarding salutary warnings and evading by subterfuge the combining of beneficial medical treatments with a crooked lack of faith,[259] your right eye shall be twisted awry and shall lack the ability to look upon the activities of mankind. And you shall not recover the privilege of your former sight until you attend upon God's [holy] virgin Æthelthryth.' Notice in advance having thus been given of these things, the female warrior disappeared.

When the maiden, on awakening <. . . >,[260] she shed continuous tears: tears, the companions of a sense of shame; tears that vouched for the truth of the vision. And it was impossible that she could be tormented more by pain than by her shame. But this happening has to be declared a compassionate act of grace, not a random throw of fortune's dice. Although, for the praise and glory of God, it took away from the girl the light that is visible, it preserved intact the liberty of her rationality.[261] Thus, while she was wave-tossed in the brine of misfortune, she made use of a philosopher's tools, as if she were on dry land. Reason palliated her blindness; discernment combined trust with good hope. The consequence was that she did not fall away from the good that belongs to the virtues, and nor did desperation exhaust her. The maiden concealed the severe inconvenience of her dim-sighted eye for eight days, as honourably as she was able.

With the falling of dusk, the fifth day of the week {Thursday}, came to its close, and the sixth day began with the onset of night; her comrades[262] were settling down to sleep and she herself was lying down in her bedroom, ready to take her rest. At this juncture, then, the virago[263] who had come for a second time, came for a third, and called out to the girl, addressing her by

---

[258] Reading conjecturally at p. 309.19, ed. Blake: *dumque rem exhibet haud sibi difficilem, <coleram>, ex ostensa reddit iracundia cautiorem.*

[259] Repunctuating at p. 309.22, ed. Blake: *'salutares admonitiones quoniam negligis, et medicamentorum compositiones utilium quia subterfugis obliqua fide, dexter obliquabitur oculus, ut obtutu careat in humanis rebus.'*

[260] Postulating a lacuna after *evigilans* (p. 309.25, ed. Blake).

[261] Lat. *animus.*

[262] The word used is *contubernales*, normally a military term: 'tent-companions'.

[263] At p. 309.35, ed. Blake, it may be that *ergo* is a mistake for *virago*, or we may have to assume she is the antecedent of *que*.

name: 'Reinburgis', she said. 'See! I have returned again †to you in person,†[264] being worried about you.' At these words, the girl moved near a party-wall, and ushered the imperious woman to a sitting-place.

Suddenly, someone of no great stature, someone more disposed to feminine dress than to femininity,[265] with a scowl on her face, laid down a truculent edict, replete with bitter sentiments and full of threats: 'What!', she said. 'You detestable young thing! That you should have dared such an enormity! That you should have so often disregarded a command of my mistress, that has been intimated to you! How is it that, without a sign of contrition on your brow, you have not been ashamed to delay an action that so great a queen has ordered you to perform? How is it that, in the stupidity of your mind, you have fallen headlong into such insanity that you are being prevaricatory in breach of a decree specifically directed at you? Why has the inertia of your evil mentality been tardy about fulfilling what the blessed virgin Æthelthryth has instructed you to do? As the result, moreover, of your failing of inconstancy and remarkable levity, you have run away from being balanced by the discriminating power of your reason. Because of this, you will experience the proofs of your lack of discernment. I shall carry out, therefore, a just punishment, on the orders of my mistress. You shall come to the ruin resulting from the indignation you have caused, so that it may correspond with your merits!'

Then the warrior-woman who had arrived first said: 'Hey there! Handmaid and message-carrier as you are of such a great virgin, put mercy before justice and defer the flagellation entailed in such a great act of vengeance! Withdraw the rod, so that she may perceive that her sentence is unchanged!'

'I cannot make the postponement for which you are pleading,' said the other. 'And I dare not abandon the action which you are asking to be remitted. The incorruptible virgin gave orders for the punishment of negligence[266] on account of a transgression, so that after this you might take notice of a sentence of stringent severity and its cause.'

On hearing this, the imperious personage groaned and interceded on the girl's behalf, a second and a third time. Her pleading was in vain and without effect, and the woman of shorter stature could not be prevailed upon by these entreaties, powerful though they were, to have mercy. Enacting retribution for the girl's guilt, she immediately lifted her up by the hair and, seizing an iron nail of amazing length, which she had previously kept hidden in her possession, she thrust it cruelly into her head, between eye and

---

[264] It seems something is missing before *personam* at p. 309.36, ed. Blake.

[265] Lat. *femineo sexui femineum preferens habitum*.

[266] The Latin as it stands lacks any personal pronoun to specify who has been given the instruction. Perhaps, at p. 310.11, ed. Blake, *puniri* should be read, rather than *punire*, with the meaning, 'that negligence be punished . . .'

brain, and pierced her with intolerable pain. 'I have carried out the command enjoined upon me, obeying the will of my empress!' She said these words and disappeared.

Then the other, praiseworthy, heroine very quickly let a drop of a healing liquid fall upon the iron nail, removed the whole instrument of torture from her head and as it was being pulled out it sprang back a long way from her neck. And Reinburgis, rescued once more from disaster, was saved by the heavenly medicament. All the matter before you, radiant with the lightning-flash that characterizes mighty works,[267] has the recommendation of God-sent evidence.

The lady healer had made her approach in a soothing manner and with gentle words, and it was with the greatest authoritativeness that this imperious personage called out to the girl: 'Now then, it is an extremely remarkable thing which I have been appointed to foretell to you, having already engaged in a struggle with you many times about your progress and restoration to health.[268] You ought to have offered gladly what is being forcibly twisted out of you by torture: to give your veneration freely, instead of being afraid. The command from the blessed Æthelthryth is that you should delay no longer: rather, that you should go to visit her as quickly as you can. And you shall not have an experience of her as being the artificer of your salvation unless it is the case that good raw material in you gives her assistance. Visit that place which we inhabit, together with our mistress, and give glory to, by the presence of our bodies. When you arrive there, you are to light a candle and then to go gently to sleep in sweet slumber between the sarcophagus of the glorious virgin and queen and the tomb placed in seemly manner to the north of it,[269] and when you awaken from sleep you will receive the sight of which you have been deprived for so many days.

'I forbid you to drink any spirituous liquor until you present yourself at the place of which frequent mention has been made. It was great concern for you on my part that brought about the emptying of a yesterday's cup of water <placed>[270] at the entrance of your bedroom as a means of causing death. If you had swallowed the draught which you had taken to your lips, and your gullet had not vomited out what it had swallowed, the poison in the deadly vessel in which it was secreted would have been the gateway to your everlasting ruination. I punched you, too, with my fist between your shoulder-blades, and freed you from this manner of death.

---

[267] Lat. *virtutum fulgore radians.*

[268] Tentatively repunctuating at p. 310.24ff., ed. Blake: '*Praeclara namque res est, cuius tibi facta sum prenuntia, sepius iam tecum de tuo profectu et sospitate luctata. Hilariter debueras prestitisse . . .*'

[269] That is, the tomb of Wihtburh: see *LE* iii. 50 (p. 290.5ff., ed. Blake).

[270] Reading conjecturally at p. 310.35, ed. Blake, e.g.: *hesternum aque poculum <positum> ad hostium thalami quodam mortis offendiculo . . .*

'So, do the thing which is best and salutory for you: insist on going speedily to the virgin whose command, made on so many occasions, you have heard. Let the image of your vision remain firmly impressed upon you, so that the memory of the joyful reality may not recede. Let {Friday}, the day that bears the name of a lady in armour,[271] by no means have you stay until evening in this part of the country, if you are concerned to obtain the promised restoration of your health. No, if you procrastinate, not leaving the town, and the flame of devotion does not turn into a blaze, because there is a lack of the more vehement sort of love in you, the impetus in this flame will grow cool and you will not, on the strength of it, arrive at your longed-for salvation. But there is something which it is yet more seriously incumbent upon you to hear: unexpected death will seize you with a pernicious embrace and, having grasped you, will tear you out of this body.' With these words, the visual image of the apparition disappeared and Reinburgis woke up and arose from sleep.

She recounted the revelation to her mother and begged her very insistently that she should quickly expedite her journey. All that she had seen rapidly became common knowledge. Her step-father and her mother brought about the fulfilment of her desires. In addition, there arrived, unexpectedly, and singled out for the purpose of her vow, a brother of the girl by her mother's first marriage, who had been away from the district for a long time. He defrayed the costs and made rapid departure possible: starting from the day which had been specified to Reinburgis, a journey was entered upon in all haste to the Isle of Ely. Something which is worthy of wide publicity is that what the girl endured happened just before the dawning of the day on which she made haste on her beneficial journey in the direction of St Æthelthryth.

The faith in her breast was fervent and correspondingly there came to her body the capacity for swiftness which belongs to complete health – with the sole exception that her right eye was incapable of opening. Moreover, sleep never crept up on her on this journey: rather, wakefulness all the while tired her long-exercised eyes.

She arrived eventually at the tomb of the most sainted virgin and, around the time of the evening rites, she stood by for holy pernoctation. Later, when the maiden was lying down to the north of it, with her lamp lit, as she had been commanded, it came about that she fell gently to sleep on the pavement. A little while before, she had fearfully made known to the senior monks of the church what had happened to her and the blindness of her eye, which was oppressing her. And this was a punishment weighing heavily down upon her, inflicted by a hand from on high, which was a source of

---

[271] Lat. *dies armate trahens vocabulum* = Friday (OE *frigedæg*), named after the goddess Frig.

shame to her, since ignoble blood did not stain her birth and, where her family was concerned, shortage of wealth did not cast a shadow over the nominal possession of nobility.

The high-born damsel had, therefore, evidently taken a little rest, and it had been beneath the tomb of St Æthelthryth, most sainted virgin and distinguished queen, that she had laid down the nape of her neck, when something unexpected happened: all of a sudden, blood came out of her right nostril and thus compelled her to rouse herself instantly from her sleep. With the sleeve of the muslin garment in which she was clothed, she staunched the flowing surges of blood, to prevent the noxious overflow from reaching the pavement. And, crying out in a very high-pitched voice with the greatest devotion, she said, 'Thank you, most splendid virgin, venerable and glorious queen, for the fact that I can see the things of the temporal World – so I think – which hitherto had been closed to my instrument of sight!' And putting down by the enclosure-wall the wax candle which she was holding in her hand, she closed her left eye with her left hand and, with her right hand, made some sign to her right eye, resolving, by this means, to test with greater certainty to what extent the outcome of the holy revelation was capable of proof.[272] The faithful who were present were stupified: about an hour earlier they had seen her eye's star clouded and swollen, and now they looked upon it shining and relieved of all deformity! A cry of the saints rose to the stars; the voice of the people danced in celebration with infinite joy. The news did not cease to go out to the church <. . . those>[273] whom love of the queen and virgin had gathered together there from different parts of the kingdom to the praise and glory of God.

The maiden, all aglow and beautiful, was taken to stand before the holy table of Christ, now subtly transformed by the animation of her countenance and the prettiness of her face. She told everybody who wanted to know what it was that, by the grace of God, had been brought about in respect to her, and she clearly unfolded the successive stages of the matter recounted above, as we have set them out in our connected narrative.

And so, good Jesus, with regard to these and thine other miracles, 'We praise thee as God' and 'we acknowledge Thee as Lord' of Heaven and Earth, for Thou so glorifiest far and wide the merits of Thy blessed betrothed and most chaste virgin, Æthelthryth, that they are seen as full of grace by all who look upon them or hear report of them. And the precentor of the church solemnly began the hymn to which we have alluded above,[274] at which the

---

[272] Repunctuating as follows at p. 311.29ff., ed. Blake: *Suppositoque, quem manu tenebat, ad maceriam cereo, sinistra sinistrum clausit oculum et dextra dextro quoddam ostendit signum, per hoc instituens experiri certius quam probabilis esset sacre revelationis effectus.*

[273] It seems that at p. 311.35, ed. Blake, some words are missing before *quos*, for which there is no antecedent.

[274] The canticle beginning with *Te Deum laudamus* . . .

whole congregation, with spiritual joy and tears, readily took up the theme of the mighty works of God. And it is suitable that everyone should know for sure that, just as it was in the evening that re<ve>lations[275] were made to her on the last three {Thursdays, those} days which took their name {dies Iovis} from the name of Jove, similarly it was at this time – the hour of Vespers – that she merited to attain to the consummation of her health.

She poured out in profusion copious tears, prayed insistently at the tomb of the consecrated virgin, and, on being granted leave, returned to where she belonged, bringing great joy to her people by the Heaven-sent restoration of her good health. In place of that girl with her impaired sight there emerged one who found, in that lady, the free gift of a very great cure.

Furthermore: perhaps the holy virgin of Christ and celebrated queen, Æthelthryth, has in our time shown forth other things to us in secret but, in the course of the modern era,[276] she has never manifested so ceremonious a miracle in such a bright light.

61. About a certain monk of ours, mortally sick but cured by St Æthelthryth.[277]

While God brings to pass through the merits of His saints remarkable feats, in numbers past counting and of high distinction, wheresoever one turns in the climes of the World, there are a number which, because of the carelessness of modern writers, are not committed to the page of record at all for repeated telling. Objections to this carelessness are raised in particular by those assigned to the task of exercising the science of letters. For fear that I might be accused, therefore, of such an offence, by people emulous of me, I have considered it right to expound for the benefit of all, to the best of my ability and to the praise and glory of the blessed Æthelthryth, a certain miracle which happened, thanks to her merits, at a recent date, to me personally, Thomas by name.

Well then, by the dispensation of the grace of God whereby He scourges every son of His whom He loves, I was tormented by the severe constraint of an unbearable illness. For, continually seething with the burning heat of high

---

[275] Reading conjecturally at p. 312.1, ed. Blake: re<ve>lationes.

[276] Lat. in serie moderni temporis.

[277] Source: autobiographical narrative by the monk Thomas, also included in B (Book of Miracles). As Blake argues, pp. xlvif., it is on stylistic grounds not plausible that this writer should be identified with the compiler of LE. The manner is flowery, as is characteristic of the materials collected in the Book of Miracles, but shows perhaps a certain lack of control which sets it apart from that of the earlier miracle narratives in book iii, which read like masterpieces of the short-story form. The description of St Æthelthryth as matrona and virago is unusual, and seems to hark back to the Reinburgis narrative (LE iii. 60). It should not be presumed that early ascriptions of the LE to Thomas, e.g. in Wharton's edition of the Chronicon, have any other basis than false inference from this passage.

fevers, I was rendered destitute of the vigour of my whole body's powers. On the one hand, the whip-lashes of all manner of sufferings were goading me, and on the other, the groans of my sorrows were scarcely allowing me to breathe: such being the case, I had almost been consigned[278] to the jaws of death, with my own jaws very often agape.[279]

What need for many words? Wretched and anxious, I kept on[280] with this thankless life, trailing behind me bouts of weariness, stabs of pain, torments, sorrows. So, finding myself at death's very door, exhausted by my outlay of anguish and suffering, I was beginning to despair altogether of a remedy to restore my life. The brothers gathered around: they grew fearful of a death. They lamented over me in my weakness, suffering as I was from a variety of ills. So, as my sickness became more intense and all my bodily sensibility was growing languid, it was with the greatest difficulty that, as if suffocated, I could form a very few words. And since I had no confidence in my recovery, I cleansed myself correspondingly with particular care by the cleansing of a sincere confession, receiving the food of the departing wayfarer with a contrite heart, so that I might become[281] the more free from care after my passing from this life. Then I made earnest entreaty that the things which are to be shown to a dying man be shown to me. But the brothers deferred this to the next day, warming me with the consoling thought of recovery. I acquiesced in their sound advice, not lacking faith in God's free gift.

He who does not spurn those who believe in Him, those who have hope in Him, who brings comfort again to the wretched and takes thought for them – He heard the brothers. For, though I was almost destitute of the breath of life, I firmly placed my whole hope in the Lord, the compassion of whose copiously flowing pity guards the desolate with its protection. This being, then, the sole refuge of man,[282] I had recourse to the advocacy of the blessed virgin Æthelthryth, whose help I implored, tearfully. My plea, made in pure devotion, was for the remedy that she should petition the Highest Physician on my behalf, to the end that He might restore me, in joy, to my former health. Lamenting and sighing with innumerable groans, I addressed her with sobbing words of the following kind: 'O Æthelthryth, our own special lady, blossoming in the privilege of thine incorruption of body, offering the benefits of thy generosity to all who seek thee with the trust of deep-felt devotion: hear me, a most miserable sinner, weighed down as I am unmanageably by a burden of lethargy, fleeing humbly to thine aid, calling

---

[278] Translating as 'consigned to' the reading of the LE mss: *addictus*; but B (*Book of Miracles*) has *adductus*, 'led to'.

[279] Reading conjecturally at p. 312.23, ed. Blake: *oscitans* for *ocitans*.

[280] Reading conjecturally, ibid.: *actito* for *accito*.

[281] Reading at p. 312.31, ed. Blake: *fierem*.

[282] Taking *Hoc . . . refugium* (p. 313.4, ed. Blake) to be a nominative absolute.

upon thee in particular for solace. Extend to me the health-bringing aid of healing, so that the anguish of my sores may be relieved: I am fatigued by them to the point of being weary of life, preferring to die rather than to endure this suffering any longer. Do not leave me desolate, most clement mother, but deign to visit me in thy clemency, rescuing me from this lamentable death, only half-alive though I am, so that, thanks to thy copiously flowing piety, I may have the strength to recover from this vale of sorrow and misery. For thou art, after God and His glorious Mother, my sole patroness, my only advocate and lady. My hope, firm and continual, relies upon thee: <wherefore>, let what I am earnestly requesting by no means lack the effective outcome of prayer.†[283] Behold, I place thee as intermediary between me and God, to see if, by thine intervention, He may grant me a space of time for living in which[284] I will make amends for a mis-spent life.'

No sooner said than done. When a cycle of eight days had rolled by from the time when I had begun to lie sick in the infirmary, I was caught up in an ecstasy at the last glimmer of the light of day, and seemed to be present at the gathering of some procession, where the sweet-sounding harmoniousness of singing was resonating, with hymns alternating with vocal jubilation. In fact, overjoyed at the harmoniousness of this singing, I straight away sensed that the propitious saving graces of Æthelthryth, our blessed lady advocate, were at hand. So when the procession of that company was over, a mass began, with festive ceremoniousness. I listened to it carefully, with my heart's attention undefiled. In addition, in the midst of the proclamation of the gospel-message leading up to the consecration of the body of the Lord, I caught sight of an altar of Parian marble resplendent with shining jewels and gold. After the celebration of mass, I looked again at my little bed and saw a matronly woman,[285] most beautiful in appearance, wearing the habit of a nun. With the utmost care she wiped filth from my bed-clothes[286] with her sleeve, removing bits of dirt and contaminating specks of dust, turning over the sheets and coverlet. After the cleansing of my bed, the virago just mentioned disappeared. I recognized her to be, most certainly, the blessed virgin Æthelthryth, since it was she upon whom I most insistently called as my benefactress.

Meanwhile, I had been roused from sleep. When awake, I was very

---

[283] Reading conjecturally at p. 313.18, ed. Blake, e.g.: *In te constat mea spes firma et continua: qu<ar>e <quod> subnixe efflagito nullatenus careat efficacia.*

[284] Reading with E: *si tuo interventu* . . . and interpreting as if the reading were *quo* . . . as distinct from *quod* . . . *vitam* . . . *emendabo* at p. 313.20, ed. Blake.

[285] 'Matronly woman' = Lat. *matrona*, which normally implies the married state and is thus a surprising word to use of the virgin Æthelthryth. But the same term has been used to describe Reinburgis' principal visitant in chapter 60.

[286] Reading with E: *stratum* for *statum*, p. 313.31, ed. Blake; cf. p. 280.10 for another confusion between *status* and *stratus*.

astonished at where I had been. I called some brothers who were present near at hand, and gave them an orderly account of the vision which had befallen me. On hearing news of this character, they gave thanks to God and to my lady liberator,[287] in gratitude for my joy; they firmly asserted that I was safe, and burst forth into the following utterance, saying: 'Blessed be Thou in thy marvellous works, O God, Thou who mercifully, at the prompting and prayers of the blessed Æthelthryth, art not refusing to help Thy servants who put their trust in Thee!' For, from that hour onward, I began to recover day by day, and to fulfil my vows to almighty God and to the holy virgin who, for her own sake, gave me the riches of the light of this World. Let nobody, then, be lacking in the faith to believe this miracle, in disparagement of the lady saint, seeing that I have taken it upon myself to include on this page the above item about myself, with the aim that God should be magnified in regard to His glorious virgin. Let us, then, praise the Lord, marvellous in His works, venerating with a dance of joy this lady, His virgin betrothed, a fit subject, in view of her miracles and mighty powers, for preaching throughout the World. Let us, I say, manifest towards her the glory of devout veneration, so that she may have an eternal reminder of us with her in Heaven. May the Lamb, the Bridegroom of virgins, grant this to us. To Him be praise, honour and imperial power throughout all ages, for ever and ever. AMEN.

62. How sedition arose in the land, and that, in fear of the king, Bishop Nigel departed from Ely.[288]

And in the fifth year of the episcopate of Bishop Nigel, that is, the fourth of the reign of King Stephen, and also much earlier, in places all over England and Normandy, there were pillaging raids and killings and by this time evil-doings had become endemic in the land, with brigands on the prowl and barons breaking faith with their lord the king and making preparations to rebel against him while, all around, things were falling apart into dissension. For he did not find 'faith in the land',[289] and thus came about the fulfilment of a prophecy which had long before been made about him by a certain wise man: 'Piety will bring upon its possessor harm from the impious.'[290] Indeed, although a rich king, pious and gentle, he was strong in body and is approved as having been the bravest of the men of his time 'above all the men of the

[287] Reading at p. 313.38, ed. Blake: *liberatr<ic>ique.*

[288] Source: according to Blake (p. 314, n. 1), 'The account, which follows, of events in the period 1138–40 is independent of other known sources'. Probably the compiler has returned to following local narrative of the episcopate of Nigel, last used in chapter 53, whose author seems to be identifiable as Richard of Ely (cf. chapters 44, 96).

[289] Cf. Matthew 8.10; Luke 7.9.

[290] 'Prophecy of Merlin', from Orderic Vitalis, *Hist. Eccl.* iii. 12, on the year 1128.

East'.[291] But let us return to the main threads of our history.

So then, it was Baldwin de Redvers who brought about the first beginning of this bad business in England, and afterwards, Bishop Nigel, at the instigation of evil men, against the strenuously expressed advice of the monks, had positioned at Ely a very strong fortress against the king, built of stone and cement, which, thanks to the holy power of Æthelthryth, kept collapsing. Consequently, he constructed by the river, near the siege-engines, a fortress made of wood; he surrounded it with a rampart; equally he restored Aldreth and placed it under guard. On learning of this, some men who were powerful in the land, had talks with the bishop and consolidated a pact with him to keep the place very strongly fortified, with his help, against the king. On hearing of this, the king sent an army to storm the island, but they struggled for a long time in efforts which were unavailing. Going down to their assistance, the king put in at Aldreth. There he collected boats together and, placing wicker hurdles on top of them, made the shallow water[292] passable for knights on horseback. And as soon as they realized that the king was there, thousands upon thousands of his enemies threw away their armour and, fleeing before his face, terrified, hid themselves all over the marshland, amidst the sedge and in bolt-holes,[293] although, if a few of them had put up resistance to the king along with his men, they would easily have laid them low. But the bishop, with only three associates, had departed previously, by night, to the lady Empress, who at that time was staying at Gloucester; he made a quick get-away and thus escaped unharmed.

The monks, however, terrified by this, were vehement in their lamentations. They were aware that the issue was an immensely contentious one and a source of continual expense for the church. They had, for certain, prostrated themselves in supplication, pleading many a time with the bishop, for fear of God, for reverence of the saintly lady virgins and for the honour of his rank, to desist from rash presumption and the scheming of evil men, to give due obedience to the king, and to plead for indulgence for his past action. However, the bishop utterly refused to agree to this. Consequently, the king ordered that all his possessions be seized and put under his own control. †Then the monks, in their wretchedness, making their excuses before him, both <asserted forcibly> that <they> were not at all accomplices in the bishop's plan or in the action he had taken,†[294] and made a plea that he should not punish the offence by taking means of livelihood away from

---

[291] Allusion to Job 1.3.

[292] The wording could suggest that there was a landing place on slightly raised ground by the Old West River near Aldreth, but shallow water between there and the mainland of the Isle.

[293] Lat. *in feno et speluncis . . .*

[294] Reading conjecturally at p. 315.8, ed. Blake, e.g.: *et minime conscios <se asseverant> esse consilii vel commissi episcopi et, ne offensam vindicet in eis . . . miserabiliter efflagitant.*

them or by inflicting a financial penalty upon the monastery. The king, benign and pious as he was at heart, not only granted that they be unharmed but, at peace with them, put all their holdings on a stable foundation by means of the following charter, and let them go.

63. A charter of King Stephen to the effect that the monks of Ely might hold their properties in peace.[295]

Stephen, King of the English and Duke of the Normans, to all the earls and barons and sheriffs and justices and officials of all places in which the monks of Ely have holdings and to all his faithful people of all England, French and English: greeting. Know that I grant to the monks of Ely all their goods and holdings, wherever they hold them, as free and exempt from claim, as honorably and freely, as at best they ever held them in the time of any king or bishop, with all customary rights for which the charters of the church give confirmation and testimony. And I give instructions that, if anyone receives anything from their properties, violently or unjustly, let it be returned or, if the recipient refuses to make restitution, you are to put him under surety, and I am to have my right with respect to recompense for such an offence, and the monk's belongings are to be restored to them. Witness: Philip the chancellor and the Earl of Warenne and William Martel. At Cambridge.

64. That King Stephen handed over the Isle of Ely to be garrisoned, and how Bishop Nigel remained in exile.[296]

King Stephen, after his arrival in Ely, forced the bishop's knights to leave the castle of Aldreth, handed it over to his own men to guard, and received into his own control the affairs of the entire bishopric, both with regard to internal matters and external ones; in fact, he deprived the bishop of all his goods and deposed him; having deposed him, he left him stripped bare. As a result, at Gloucester, the place to which he had retreated, the bishop utterly lacked provision for his needs on the scale to which he was accustomed, and so his supporters who had fled to him began to be encumbered by penury. Moreover, in the crisis of his exile, the bishop himself was inconsolable and prayer was made continually for him to God by his sons, the monks. And, having finally initiated a plan, he sent envoys to Rome to the High Pontiff, to give notice of the difficulties weighing down upon his church and to make plain his own state of deprivation. These were Alexander, a monk, and later prior, of our church, a man of good religious demeanour, learned and

[295] Source: monastic archives, cf. Ely, Dean and Chapter, charter no. 7; cartularies GM. Date: winter 1139/40; at Cambridge.
[296] Source: local tradition.

eloquent in the Latin, French and English languages, and others, present with him, who were men renowned for their knowledge and distinction. And, transacting their business most energetically, they received from his Excellency, the Dignitary of Rome,[297] letters to the archbishop and bishops of England and the Archbishop of Rouen – letters which the reader will understand to be pertinent also to our history.

65. A mandate of the lord Pope to the Bishop of Winchester, at that time Legate of England, concerning the restoration of Bishop Nigel to his see.[298]

Innocent, Bishop, servant of the servants of God, to his venerable brothers, Henry of Winchester, Legate of the Apostolic See and also to the archbishops and bishops established throughout England: greeting and apostolic blessing. On the testimony of Holy Scripture, we have learnt that 'a threefold cord is not easily broken'[299] and that, if two have been joined together with the glue of loving kindness, they will be able mutually to cherish each other and to provide opportune help to one another in the face of threats confronting them. For indeed, in this way, not only is the benefit of loving kindness amicably maintained between brothers but the malice of wicked men is kept under control, too, by suitable punishments. With this in view, we issue a mandate, in the form of a request, and by means of this mandate, instruct your fraternal selves to uphold steadfastly the sentence which Nigel, Bishop of Ely, passes against those who are unjustly, and with violence, alienating the properties of his church, and cause it likewise to be steadfastly upheld throughout your dioceses, in the knowledge that measures which the discernment of this same brother of ours shall have brought to bear upon usurpers of this kind have been upheld by our good will, on the basis of the Lord's authority. Given at the Lateran, 29th April.

66. Another mandate of the lord Pope to King Stephen about restoring Bishop Nigel to his see.[300]

Innocent, Bishop, servant of the servants of God to his most beloved son in Christ, Stephen, the illustrious King of the English people: greeting and apostolic blessing. If almighty God, the King of Kings and Lord of Lords, did

---

[297] Lat. *ab excellentia Romane dignitatis* . . .

[298] Source: monastic archives, cf. cartularies CDG. Date: 29th April, 1139; at the Lateran. See Blake, p. 316, n. 2 for arguments that the compiler has mistaken the historical context for this charter and the others dated '29th April'.

[299] Ecclesiastes 3.12. What follows also alludes less precisely to Ecclesiastes 3.9–12.

[300] Source: monastic archives, cf. cartularies CDG; document printed in Holtzmann, *Papsturkunden in England*, ii, no. 23; date: 29th April, 1139; at the Lateran.

not spare His own Son for the liberty of Holy Church, it is fitting that we who are called His members[301] should follow closely in His footsteps and should strive with all our might to preserve and increase that same liberty. We therefore issue a mandate to Your Serenity, asking that you permit the church of Ely to retain in their entirety the dignities and liberties granted to that same church both by kings of long ago and by King Henry of distinguished memory and by you yourself – dignities and liberties established in writing and confirmed by a privilege of Pope Victor, our predecessor of holy memory, and that you provide counsel and aid to our venerable brother Nigel, the bishop of that same place, in respect to the recovery of his properties, unjustly taken from his church. Nor are you to allow the church itself to endure anything prejudicial to its rights on account of the fact that it is now a long time since it lost the goods belonging to it. Given at the Lateran, 29th April.

67. A mandate of the lord Pope to Bishop Nigel, which kindly assents to his petitions.[302]

Innocent, Bishop, servant of the servants of God, to his venerable brother, Nigel, Bishop of Ely: greeting and apostolic blessing. We have received kindly the messengers – conscientious men, to be sure – despatched to the Apostolic See by your fraternal self and we rejoice in the devotion and love which you bear towards the Holy Roman Church. Since we have received information that you are engaged in many items of business, we release your fraternal self and Robert, Abbot of Thorney, on whose behalf you have made supplication, from presenting yourselves at the Council. It behoves you therefore, beloved brother in the Lord, to venerate the blessed Peter and the Holy Roman Mother Church with your innermost heart and with sincerity, so that you may be found deserving to receive from the Apostolic See the greatest favour and honorific regard. For we love, and wish to honour, your person with true love in Christ. Given at the Lateran, 29th April.

68. Again, a mandate of the lord Pope to the archbishop and bishops of England about restoring Nigel to his place.[303]

Innocent, Bishop, servant of the servants of God to his venerable brothers

---

[301] Reading at p. 317.13, ed. Blake: *membra* for *menbra*.

[302] Source: monastic archives, cf. cartularies CDG; document printed in Holtzmann, *Papsturkunden in England*, ii, no. 24. Date: 29th April, 1139; at the Lateran.

[303] Source: monastic archives, cf. cartularies CDG. G records a version of the letter addressed to the Archbishop of Rouen. This letter, unlike those recorded in chapters 65–7, does refer to the events recounted in chapter 64. Date: 5th October, 1140; at Trastevere.

Theobald, Archbishop of Canterbury, and his suffragan bishops: greeting and apostolic blessing. Just as the human body is kept safe because the members in the frame of the body cherish and have affection for one another, so in the Church of God, similarly if, at a time when wicked men have been making some disturbance at the instigation of the Devil, archbishops, bishops and other ecclesiastical persons have been firmly based in the solidarity of unitedness, they cure things which are unhealthy, prune things which need pruning and bring corrupt and errant people to the way of righteousness and truth. Further to this, we have received information that our venerable brother Nigel, Bishop of Ely, has been expelled from his see unjustifiably and unreasonably, and despoiled of things belonging to him, and therefore we issue a mandate to your fraternal self and, in issuing the mandate, give instructions that, putting aside all luke-warmness, you are to provide him with aid and counsel for the recovery of his see and of the goods belonging to him that have been taken away. If anyone hinders him or presumes to hold on to the goods that have been taken away, or his revenues: proclaim the sentence of excommunication against him. As for clerics or monastics or lay-people of the diocese of Ely who have been rebellious against him and have not obeyed his mandates as those of their own bishop: enchain them with the constraint of an anathema, until they give satisfaction. Given at Trastevere, 5th October.

69. That supporters of the bishop, entering Ely secretly, were overwhelmed by Geoffrey, a military commander on the king's side.[304]

However, two years had not yet elapsed since these happenings when, behold, when they were saying, 'Peace and security!' [305] for a second time, suddenly a calamity overcame them when they were off their guard. For an energetic man at arms, Earl Geoffrey de Mandeville, with Earl Gilbert as his ally, was dispatched by King Stephen to Ely with a troop of soldiers. The object was that he should expel, or cut down with the sword, supporters of the bishop who had secretly fled there.

Arriving in haste, Earl Geoffrey put the enemy's common soldiery to flight but ordered that the knights be held captive. And he led them all the way to Ely, putting them on horseback with their feet tied beneath their horses, in the public gaze. And despite the fact that the monks came to meet them with crosses and reliquaries on the reasoning that, in this way, if in no other, they would assuage the fury of the tyrant, it was only grudgingly that in the end he deigned to receive them into his favour. Indeed, he hurled this affair at them as a criminal charge, raging and threatening their death and the laying waste of the holy place, and with cruel indignation he reopened a

---

[304] Source: local tradition; cf. Blake, p. 319, n. 1.

[305] Cf. 1 Thessalonians 5.3.

wound already recently inflicted, completely cutting off their livelihood and estates.

In fact, it was under compulsion, as the result of this, that they approached King Stephen who, receiving them with devotion, not only consoled them with kind talk but dispatched the following mandate to the earl on their behalf, and restored all their properties in their entirety.

70. An instruction of King Stephen to the effect that the monks of Ely are to hold their possessions freely and in peace.[306]

Stephen, King of the English people, to Geoffrey de Mandeville: greeting. I give you instructions that you are so completely to bring it about for the Prior and monks of Ely that they hold all their lands and men and all customary rights as well, and peacefully, and honorifically, and fully, in all matters, as they held them on the day on which King Henry was alive and dead and the day on which Bishop Nigel departed from Ely, that in this way they lose nothing for lack of justice. Witness: Turgis d'Avranches. At *Hereford*.

71. Again, an instruction of the king concerning the fact that he had given orders that the monks be given back rents which were their due.[307]

Stephen, King of the English people, to Geoffrey de Mandeville: greeting. I give you instructions that you are to distrain Hugh de Scalers and Stephen de Scalers until they render again to the monks the food-rent which they owe to them, as best, and as fully, as they used to do before I captured the Isle of Ely, and you are to take such serious action with regard to this matter, that I shall not hear a complaint about this arising on account of a lack of full justice. Witness: Turgis d'Avranches. At Bury St Edmunds.

72. How King Stephen was betrayed by his own men, and that the lady Empress gained control of nearly the whole country.[308]

It is generally agreed that the saying of the Lord of which we read in the Gospel, 'Every kingdom divided against itself shall be laid waste', most

---

[306] Source: monastic archives; cf. cartulary G, in which it follows the charter quoted in *LE* iii. 63; date: 1140; at *Hereford*, probably meaning Hertford.

[307] Source: monastic archives, cf. cartularies GM. This letter is written in the margin of E and incorporated in the main text of F. Date: 1140; at Bury St Edmunds.

[308] Source: the generalizations translated in the last four sentences of the first paragraph are from the *Worcester Chronicle* on the year 1136, but otherwise the source is not extant, and may have been Richard of Ely's account of the episcopate of Nigel. See Blake, p. 320, n. 4, for places where the *LE* narrative diverges from other sources for the national history of the period.

certainly came to fulfilment, at that time, in the case of England. Certainly the Queen of Lands was now being reduced to stupidity and ignominy and was not being ruled by the people by whom it ought to be ruled, but was, instead, oppressed by injustice and multifarious savagery. The powerful brought force to bear upon the powerless. Everyone despoiled someone else, terrorized with threats the individual engaged in gainful employment. Anyone who resisted was put to death. The wealthy magnates of the realm consulted only their own interests and those of their kin; they fortified castles and towns for their friends, and manned them with troops of soldiers.

Their lord, the benign and pious King Stephen, was, in thought and deed, an exceptional man: they harassed him by stirring up war; they provoked him to armed combat with the intention of putting an end to him, if they could, when off his guard, or at least of entrapping him by tricks and deceptions, so as to deprive him, eventually, guiltless though he was, of his honour and the kingdom. And it was done. For later, when the king asked Ranulf, Earl of Chester, to hand back Lincoln Castle, which he had handed over to him to guard, he refused[309] to give it back to him. Instead, taking with him to that place a very large contingent of earls and barons, he prepared to wage war. Specifically, he took Robert, Earl of Gloucester, whose daughter he, Ranulf, had married, Baldwin de Rivers, King Morgan of Wales,[310] and Brian Fitz Count with a contingent of his own men, and very many others, the intention being to enter battle with the king without delay. Finally, the two sides confronted each other and, entering the fray of battle, fought furiously for a long time. But those on the king's side who were of higher ranks and in positions of leadership, despite the fact that they had victory fully within their grasp, turned tail, intending flight. The king was left alone, with scarcely two or three comrades, in the middle of a wedge-formation of warriors; and his adversaries, aware that the king had thus been deprived of his knights, soon surrounded him and, like alien tribesmen[311] attacking Samson, tried to lay him low. Wickedly, they rushed in attack against their lord with swords and cudgels.[312] In their minds and in their fighting they were cruelly savage. Forgetful of their loyalty and their oath, they did not hold back, being prepared to slay the Lord's anointed. So it came about that these men, having abandoned their loyalty were proved traitors and detestable for ever more. And they fought and fought, from morning to evening, against the king in his isolation and against Baldwin Fitz Gilbert

---

[309] Deleting *et* before *ipse* (p. 321.1, ed. Blake).

[310] Reading with E at p. 321.4, ed. Blake: *regem* (not *regum*) *Morgarum Waloniae*.

[311] At p. 321.10, ed. Blake, *allophili* is a loan-word representing a Greek term for 'people of alien tribes' used in the Septuagint's Book of Judges to designate Samson's opponents, the Philistines.

[312] A reminder here of the arrest of Jesus: Matthew 26.47, 55; Luke 22.52.

and Richard Fitz Urse, illustrious men loyally keeping up the struggle of the resistance to them along with their lord, and against those few who had stayed with them. Almost all day long, that is, on 2nd February, the whole army, comprised of the huge throng of infantry and cavalry referred to above, were thirsting solely for the king's blood or his downfall. However, the king, behaving in a manly and steadfast way, in actual peril of death, held out, invincible, amid the thickest showers of weaponry and clashing swords: like a lion mauling his prey he struck his enemy all around, to the right and to the left, with dishonouring blows, and scattered them. As a result, his adversaries, groaning, finally raised a shout and, frenzied in their onslaught, threw a †mass of cloaks†[313] over him and rushed headlong upon him to the end that, by this method if no other, they would hold him, overwhelmed or suffocated – this man whom they could not conquer by any sort of fighting.

And what more is there to report? The king was captured, dragged off, made mock of in many ways; pummelled with fists, bound very tightly with thongs, and brought before Robert, Earl of Gloucester, a kinsman of his. On seeing him, the earl became, amazingly, both grief-stricken and joyful, and did not allow himself to be separated from him before he had been brought all the way to the neighbourhood of[314] Bristol and put on show to the Empress Matilda, who was travelling down[315] to that place. But she gave orders when he was brought before her that he should be bound in fetters and put under close guard, and soon afterwards she had gained control over the most powerful men of [more or less] the whole of England. And also, with her assistance, Nigel, Bishop of Ely, who had been spending his exile at her court, received back once more his position and the things which had been taken away from him.

73. How Bishop Nigel, with the help of the lady Empress, regained his see.[316]

The bishop, therefore, much longed-for by all, returned at last to his see in Ely after various struggles and loss of weight due to lack of food, and before the completion of two years in the difficult circumstances of his exile. He was

---

[313] Lat. † copiam vestiam† (p. 321.22f.) is here interpreted as if the reading were copiam vestium.

[314] Taking ad (p. 321.32, ed. Blake) to mean 'towards' rather than 'to', following classical usage with town names.

[315] Reading with E: deiebat, presumably to be interpreted as from deeo. Blake asserts, on the basis of the Worcester Chronicle and William of Malmesbury, that 'Stephen was taken to the Empress at Gloucester and afterwards moved to Bristol'; it could be that the E version of LE here records a detail glossed over by other sources: that she had already gone some way along her route before the king was brought to her.

[316] Source: not extant; almost certainly Brother Richard's work on the episcopate of Nigel.

received most honourably, with due devotion, with concerted singing by the monks and a welcome from the common people who went out to meet him. And, supported by the assistance of the lady Empress, he took over control of the entire bishopric, together with the fortress of Aldreth, from Geoffrey de Mandeville and Earl Gilbert, who had invaded the Isle on the king's behalf, and he went around every day taking beneficial action in respect to the needs of the place, concentrating his attention diligently upon the task of his ministry. He also treated the monks now as close friends and beloved sons and he consulted them as a matter of course and he involved them in all his undertakings. He made a particular point of showing himself favourable and benevolent towards them. He planned to correct wrongs and increase benefactions, and this he would doubtless have done, if the wickedness of his men had not prevented this from happening. The men in question were Goscelin of Ely, Ralph the steward and Alexander the butler, and at their instigation he was coerced into plundering goods inside the monastery and putting estates of the church up for sale.[317]

Meanwhile, increasing evils all around in the kingdom were threatening ruin, the affairs of the kingdom seemed to be changing in a deep-seated way: strong-men, trusting in their fortresses, would invade the properties of churches and lay them waste, and, leaving aside their game-preserves,[318] would become hunters [of men] within city-walls. What was more, each on his own property[319] altered, and within his own borders devalued and adulterated, coinage and bronze and the standard rate of commercial exchange,[320] and stamped on coins whichever image he chose, an exception to this being the drachma of Ely, which was kept untouched <and> is recorded to have been, thanks to the bishop, of choice silver and of its publicly declared weight.[321]

74. How King Stephen was rescued from captivity.[322]

However, circumstances changed and suddenly the cry went up that King Stephen, by God's grace and pity, had been set free and had left prison

---

[317] F adds *nonnullis*: 'to several people'.

[318] Adopting the reading of E, without the addition of F: *homines*.

[319] Lat. *apud se*.

[320] Lat. *numisma . . . et es et formam commercii*.

[321] Reading, with a conjectural supplement, at p. 322.16ff., ed. Blake: *quod integrum servebatur <et> ex argento electo ac pondere publico per episcopum extitisse memoratur.*

[322] Source: probably Richard of Ely on the episcopate of Nigel; the reference forward to the charter quoted in the next chapter (*LE* iii. 70) might either be due to the compiler or to Richard, who is seen from the history of the Stetchworth case (*LE* iii. 96–114) to have been an assembler of documentary sources.

through the efforts of his queen, Matilda[323] – who, like a second Queen of Sheba,[324] was at that time outstanding in her wisdom and prudence – and of her brother, Henry, Bishop of Winchester, at that time Legate of the Roman See, of William, Earl of Warenne, William, Earl of Arundel, Geoffrey de Mandeville, Earl Gilbert and of other powerful aides, who had laboured insistently, with all their might for the specific purpose of extricating their lord †< . . .> of the men referred to above†[325] from the yoke of captivity. And after being brought out, he subdued a great many of the rebels and took many spoils from the men who had fled from him, and gained control over the cities. And the hand of his enemies was weakened.

On hearing this, Bishop Nigel became extremely frightened and, convinced that he would nowhere be safe in an encounter with him, now bewailed what had begun as a pleasing venture. Finally, after taking council with his men, he sent envoys to the king, carefully made a plea for 'the things that are of peace',[326] and what he requested in piety, he earnt the privilege of receiving through kindness, as the following charter intimates.

75. A charter of King Stephen about his having taken Bishop Nigel back again in peace.[327]

Stephen, King of the English, to his justices, sheriffs, barons, officials and all his faithful people in whose areas of jurisdiction Bishop Nigel holds land: greeting. I give instructions that Nigel, Bishop of Ely, is to hold and to possess all his lands and men and all his belongings <and>[328] all the liberties of his church of St Æthelthryth, as well and as peaceably and freely and quietly and honorably, as he best and most freely ever held them, since he has peace with me and has made an agreement with me. And I forbid anyone to do injury or insult to him or his belongings over this matter. Witness: the Earl de Warenne and William Martel.

---

[323] A marginal note in EF, included in the text of O, identifies her as 'daughter of Eustace, Count of Boulogne'.

[324] See 1 Kings (= 3 Kings Vulgate) 10.1ff.

[325] Reading conjecturally at p. 323.3, ed. Blake: *quatinus* < . . .> *virorum memoratorum de iugo captivitatis eruerent.*

[326] Romans 14.19.

[327] Source: monastic archives, cf. cartulary G; this charter is introduced by the previous chapter, and may have been integrated in the narrative source already, before the compiler of *LE* set to work. Date: perhaps 1142. Compare the charter-text given below in *LE* iii. 87, identical except for the mention of Ipswich as the place of issue.

[328] Supplying at p. 323.14, ed. Blake <*et*> after *honorifice*, from the parallel text in *LE* iii. 87. The text of cartulary G has 'his own liberties and those of his church of St Æthelthryth'.

76. An instruction of King Stephen to the effect that the monks of Ely should have the food-rents due to them from their lands.[329]

Stephen, King of the English people, to Hugh de Scalers and to his nephew Stephen. I give you instructions that you are either[330] quickly to give back to the monks of Ely their food-rent, as well and fully as you used to do before I captured the Isle of Ely, or give back to them their fief which you are holding. And unless you do so, Aubrey de Vere is to distrain you until you do. Witness: Robert de Oilli. At Oxford.

77. How Bishop Nigel was summoned to Rome.[331]

And King Stephen sat on the throne of his kingdom, and 'the land was silent in his purview'.[332] And, on his arrival at London, which is the capital of England, peacemakers met him, receiving him with great honour. There, in a united council of clergy and laity, comprising bishops and abbots, monks and clerics, and a crowd of lay-people beyond number, under the presidency of the Legate of the Roman See, the lord King's brother Henry, Bishop of Winchester, and Theobald, whom he had recently made Archbishop of Canterbury,[333] he discussed with them the state of the kingdom and instructed them to proclaim the sentence of the church's severity upon the enemies of peace and the country. And while they were discussing matters with one another, a certain priest named Vitalis made a complaint in the presence of everyone that the lord Bishop of Ely had expelled him from his church without formal judicial procedure. The legate took a favourable view of him on all counts and wished to support him. As the result of his machinating, some men of great authority and prudence rose up, at the ready, against the lord Bishop Nigel: Zolinus, Prior of Eye, a monk of honourable demeanour and reputation, and another man, namely Robert, Prior of Oxford, a man of outstanding nobility and eloquence. They summoned him to appear before the presence of the lord Pope, accusing him of a great many sinister things, above all of having stirred up sedition in the kingdom and wasted the goods of his church on soldiers. And, assailing him with invective, they cast other reproaches upon him.

---

[329] Source: monastic archives, cf. cartulary G. Date: late 1139 X 1140. Blake comments: 'This writ should precede chapter 71, where Geoffrey de Mandeville is ordered to apply the constraint threatened here.'

[330] Text as in E, with *vel* after *precipio vobis quod . . .*

[331] Source (chapters 77–8): once more, probably the account of Nigel's episcopate by Richard of Ely.

[332] Cf. 1 Maccabees 1.3.

[333] Lat. *Cantie* = strictly: 'of Kent'.

78. What belongings of his church Bishop Nigel lost, and which ones, on a second occasion, he took from it, when he went on his journey to Rome.[334]

After these transactions had been completed thus, they all returned as quickly as possible to their own domains, in a state of fear, reckoning it unfortunate and wrong that the kingdom had been quickly thrown into upheaval in this way, and the whole of it placed in jeopardy, so that there came to be no safety anywhere.[335] But the Bishop of Ely decided to seek out the assistance of the lady Empress for the business which presented him with such an immediate threat, and to consult with people on his own side. While he was on his way to do this, the king's men were roaming all around and in control of positions. More or less all of them had been on the alert against Bishop Nigel, in case they could do him some evil mischief. By chance it was at Wareham that, coming upon him, they made their attack and robbed him mercilessly of his possessions. With their filthy hands they seized his horses and clothing and, in addition, very fine chapel-equipment, which the bishop had brought with him from the church, to be precise: an alb extremely well decorated with pall-cloth very beautifully covered with gold, which St Æthelwold gave to the church, and two albs with decorations of pall-cloth, and two stoles with maniples, one of which – exceedingly beautiful – was the gift of Abbot Ælfsige, and two tunicles and two dalmatics; and the two copes of Abbot Ælfsige,[336] and a green chasuble which the Lady Ælfwaru gave, finely worked in gold with a border; a thurible with a cover of silver-gilt with silver chains, which Abbot Ælfsige gave, and two silver cruets; a silver chalice well gilded, a gospel-book, of gold with relics;[337] one privilege-document, for which the church later expended fifty-two marks; one altar-pall. And when they had taken all these things, they returned to their garrison.[338]

But, none the less, the bishop who was the object of their search, with the help of God, escaped unharmed. In answer to prayer, he obtained from the lady Empress what he had requested, and then he made his way quickly to Ely, his intention being to start out on his journey to Rome straight away, despite the fact that, during it, he would find it extremely difficult to

---

[334] Source: see on chapter 77.

[335] Reading at p. 324.26, ed. Blake: *securum* (conjecturally, instead of *secure*) and *fieret* (as in E).

[336] Cf. *LE* iii. 50, p. 294.3–4, ed. Blake

[337] The fourteenth *gospel-book* listed in iii. 50, p. 291.20ff., ed. Blake.

[338] Wareham Castle, near the bridge over the River Frome, was much contested between Stephen and Matilda. See William of Malmesbury, *Historia Novella*, ed. K. R. Potter (1955), 75f.; Terence Davis, *Wareham: Gateway to Purbeck* (second edition, Wincanton 1997), pp. 17–20.

withstand ambushes, and robberies by his enemies, anywhere along his circuitous route. Because of this, as no amount of his personal resources would be sufficient for him to carry through the effort of such a long journey, he gathered to a meeting, in deep secrecy, the men whom he considered particularly[339] close friends, namely: Goscelin surnamed 'of Ely', William of *Laventona*, the cleric Hubert, William surnamed *Monachus*,[340] Henry *Peregrinus*,[341] Ralph Fitz Olaf, Alexander the steward. These were the men of whose services, by 'the counsel of Ahithophel',[342] he generally made use, to the repeated detriment of the church. His object was to make known to them openly what it was most expedient for them to understand concerning the crisis arising from this latest misfortune. They, moreover, unhesitatingly obliged him by giving him the advice that he should appropriate items from the treasures of the church but that, in order to prevent uproar or mutiny among the monks, he should give back to them the vill of Hadstock, to which they had long laid claim, and confirm this by means of a charter, and permanently set his seal upon it.

And when he put this proposition to the monks, pleading with them, they finally accepted the offer – with groaning and tears, not of their own free will but under duress – on condition that, once the estate had been restored to them and <the charter> granted along with it, he would completely reinstate within three months of his return, whatever he had removed.[343] A record of these needs to be made, and this we are not neglecting to provide. They were, to be specific: a gold chalice of five marks of gold from the shrine of St Æthelthryth, then[344] thirty-six marks of silver, and two images, assessed at two marks of silver, and two basins of silver weighing six marks, two candle-sticks weighing sixteen marks.

After this, having been amply supplied with his costs, he set out on a journey – one involving much painful expenditure of effort – with Rome as his destination, and there, before the presence of the lord Pope, the Supreme Pontiff Lucius, he not only refuted his enemies' complaints against him by legitimate reasoning, but absolved himself of the charges brought against him and, by a unanimous verdict, deservedly obtained acquittal in respect of the vexatious allegations of the wicked. In this he was supported and assisted

[339] Reading at p. 325.15, ed. Blake: *admodum* for *ad modum*.

[340] *Monachus*: 'Monk'.

[341] *Peregrinus*: 'Pilgrim'.

[342] Cf. 2 Samuel 17.7.

[343] Reading conjecturally at p. 326.2f., ed. Blake: *ut reddita possessione et iugiter concessa <carta> infra tres menses reditus sui in integrum reformaret quicquid extulerit.*

[344] Lat. *tunc*: two interpretations are possible: either 'at that time', with the implication that the then exchange-rate was 36 marks of silver to 5 marks of gold; or 'in addition', in line with a rare, but classical, use of *tunc* in enumerations.

in many ways by the efforts of Archbishop Theobald, as the writs appended below intimate.

79. What sort of mandate it was, addressed to the archbishop and the bishops of England, that Bishop Nigel obtained from the lord Pope.[345]

Lucius, Bishop, servant of the servants of God, to his venerable brothers Theobald, Archbishop of Canterbury, and to the bishops in office throughout England: greeting and apostolic blessing. Our venerable brother Nigel, Bishop of Ely, coming to the Apostolic See, has complained to us that, particularly in the period after his expulsion from his bishopric, goods and estates of the church of Ely have been stolen and taken over and are being held unlawfully by certain wicked individuals resident in your dioceses. Some people, also, rob vills and the people belonging to them in the name of protection-money,[346] and oppress them with unlawful activities and exactions. Accordingly, since prelates ought to give one another mutual comfort, and constrain usurpers of ecclesiastical property with the punishment due to them, we command you by these present writings, to warn earnestly those residents in your dioceses about whom you have received complaints from this same brother of ours, that they are to restore in their entirety those things which have been stolen, and to desist completely from the harassment of the estates and liegemen of the church of Ely. If they have failed, through contempt, to carry out your admonition within two months of it, you are to exercise canonical justice concerning the individuals themselves and their lands. For, if they wish to pretend that they have committed sacrilege of this kind at the command, or with the permission, of the king or of princes, this excuse is to have no validity where they are concerned. For where power orders what ought not to be done, it is to be treated with contempt. For one ought to obey God more than men. In accordance with the authority of the sacraments,[347] we also enjoin, equally, that you are absolutely not to receive back those whom the same bishop has canonically excommunicated, nor to presume to grant them communion or give them absolution. As for you, brother Archbishop, in the event that bishops shall have appeared negligent in the carrying out of justice, you are to compel them to enact canonical justice, in accordance with the inherent purpose of your office. Given at the Lateran, 24th May.

---

[345] Source: monastic archives, cf. cartularies CDGM.

[346] Lat. *tenseriae*.

[347] Interpreting *sacrorum* at p. 327.4 (ed. Blake) as equivalent to *sacramentorum*. The same formula occurs in chapter 84, below.

80. What mandate the lord Pope gave to the chapter of Ely through Bishop Nigel.[348]

Lucius, Bishop, servant of the servants of God, to his beloved sons Robert, Abbot of Thorney, and the chapter of Ely: greeting and apostolic benediction. We wish it to be known to you that the verdict upon the case of the priest Vitalis, specifically, <his prosecution for>[349] simony, held at the synod of Ely, has been discussed and re-examined in our presence. Recognizing that it is reasonable, we have confirmed it on the authority of the Apostolic See and we decree that it remains ratified. Given at the Lateran, 24th May.

81. A mandate of the lord Pope to King Stephen in favour of Nigel, Bishop of Ely.[350]

Lucius, Bishop, servant of the servants of God to Stephen, King of the English: greeting and apostolic blessing. Our venerable brother Nigel, Bishop of Ely, despite having been defamed by certain charges in our presence, was not, however, convicted, and neither did he admit to them by confession. Consequently, in sending him back to his own see with our favour, we command your noble self to love him for reverence of the blessed Peter and of us, and not to inflict injustice or harassment upon him or his church, nor to allow it to be inflicted by others. In addition, if any items are taken from him by your men after he has made his journey to us, you are to cause them to be restored in their entirety. Given at the Lateran, 24th June.

82. That Bishop Nigel once again incurred the king's displeasure, and what sort of trouble there was in England.[351]

However, the bishop prolonged his stay for quite a long time and, in the mean time, his house was daily caused hardship by innumerable constraints. In addition, the king's men, in league with one another, were devising stratagems against the holy place of Ely. As the men guarding the Isle were not numerous enough to fight back against them, they gave admittance to Earl Geoffrey {de Mandeville}, at that time an enemy of the king, who was harassing the country with arson and sedition, and they also put the castle of Ely and that of Aldreth under his control, for the sake of strengthening their

---

[348] Source: monastic archives, cf. cartularies CDG. Date: 24th May, 1144; at the Lateran.

[349] Adopting the correction *simonie* (for the manuscript reading *simonia*), printed in Holtzmann, *Papsturkunden in England,* ii, no. 39.

[350] Source: monastic archives, cf. cartularies CDG Date: 24th May, 1144; at the Lateran.

[351] Source: resumption of (Richard of Ely's?) narrative of the episcopate of Nigel, cf. chapters 77–8.

defences. This man, completely taken over by madness, occupied the noble monastery of Ramsey. The company of monks was put to flight, and then he put in a garrison; and likewise at Benwick, at the very crossing-point of the waters. From there he retreated peacefully through Ely to Fordham, which he usurped for himself, in defiance of his enemies, securing it with a strong band of knights. As a consequence, King Stephen was mightily incensed to anger. He supposed that all these actions were the result of machinating by Bishop Nigel and, immediately, in vindication of his feelings of hatred, he ordered that the estates of the church everywhere be usurped by his men.

And, as a consequence, now that the monks' supplies from their estates had been cut off, they were extremely hard pressed, within their church, particularly from lack of food to eat. So it was that, deprived of their allowances of victuals, groaning and filled with anxiety, they appropriated the treasures which, small though they were, remained in the place, specifically, they appropriated the silver which they found, and the gold, from eight reliquaries, which have not been restored at all since then. For famine had come to weigh down upon the whole region and 'the sick cornland' had been 'denying' all 'food'.[352] For twenty or thirty miles there was no ox, no ploughman, to be found tilling the smallest piece of land. One could scarcely buy the tiniest measure {of corn} for two hundred pence, and so great was the human disaster that followed from the scarcity of bread that, throughout the lanes and streets, people lay dead in hundreds and thousands, swollen like {wine-}skins, and their corpses were left unburied for the wild beasts and birds.

For there had been no such time of tribulation for a very long time past, in all the kingdoms of the earth. All the powerful men round about, wreaking widespread devastation, were hiring knights on the strength of stolen property, burning down vills and tormenting people by leading them captive for long distances; they would bind the pious in fetters and the noble in iron manacles. And so an insane frenzy raged on. Wickedness rejoiced, undefeated. They spared no one of either sex, or of any age. They inflicted a thousand kinds of death in order to extract money from people in trouble. There was a dreadful clamour from people wailing. Everywhere the grief of mourners was a shuddering presence. And it is generally agreed that there was fulfilment of what is proclaimed through the gospel: 'Men shall seek to die and death shall flee from them.'[353] However, amid these grievous events and amid the crises caused by the great number of scandalous happenings, the Church of God stayed afloat and flourished most gloriously. These things became well enough known to the bishop, far away though he was during his stay in Rome. And now, provided as he was with gifts from on high by the

---

[352] Cf. Virgil, *Aeneid*, iii. 142.
[353] Revelation 9.6.

favour of the lord Pope, and put in a strong position at last against the machinations of his oppressors by the following documents, he returned home rejoicing.

83. A mandate of the lord Pope to the Archbishop of England in favour of Bishop Nigel.[354]

Lucius, Bishop, servant of the servants of God, to his venerable brother Theobald, Archbishop of Canterbury: greeting and apostolic blessing. Our venerable brother Nigel, Bishop of Ely, has intimated to us through his letters that, while he was on his visit to the thresholds of the apostles and to us in person, Earl Geoffrey de Mandeville forcibly usurped the Isle of Ely, the site of his episcopal see, and took possession of certain fortresses upon it. Moreover, while these estates within {the Isle} are being occupied by this particular earl, King Stephen has usurped all the outlying estates of this same church and has wilfully shared them out, in an illicit manner. Consequently, through these present writings, we issue you with a mandate that, taking with you other bishops whom you know to be suitable for this task, you are to issue a serious admonition both to the king himself and to the earl, on behalf of ourselves, that they are to restore in their entirety the Isle, the estates and the other items which have been alienated, and repair the losses which have been inflicted. If, on the other hand, they prove contemptuous, after consultation with your fellow-bishops in the province, you are so to curb them by ecclesiastical censure, that they restore the things which they have usurped or stolen and in a fitting way make satisfaction for their very great sacrilege.

84. Another mandate of the lord Pope to the Archbishop of Rouen and the bishops of Normandy in favour of Nigel, Bishop of Ely.[355]

Lucius, Bishop, servant of the servants of God, to his venerable brothers Hugh, Archbishop of Rouen and the bishops in office throughout Normandy: greeting and apostolic blessing. Our venerable brother Nigel, Bishop of Ely, coming to the Apostolic See, has complained to us that goods and possessions of the church of Ely have been stolen and usurped by certain wicked people originating from your dioceses, especially in the period when he was in exile from his bishopric, and that they are being held by them contrary to justice. Certain individuals are also despoiling vills and their inhabitants in the name of protection-money and are exerting oppression through unlawful activities and exactions. Therefore, because prelates ought

[354] Source: monastic archives, cf. cartularies CDG. Date: Summer, 1144.
[355] Source: monastic archives, cf. cartularies CDG. Date: 24th May, 1144; at the Lateran.

to comfort one another mutually and curb usurpers of ecclesiastical properties with due punishment, by these present letters addressed to you, we issue a mandate that you are to warn earnestly the men who originate from your dioceses to restore in their entirety the stolen properties and desist altogether from harassment of the possessions and men of the church of Ely. But if they contemptuously refuse to carry this out in the two months following your warning, you are to enact canonical justice upon the men themselves and their land. For if they should wish to put forward the pretext that they have committed sacrilege of this sort on the command or with the permission of the king or of princes, this excuse is to avail them nothing. For, where a power orders an action which ought not to be done, it is to be disregarded. For one ought to obey God more than men.[356] In accordance with the authority of the sacraments,[357] we no less give you the injunction that you are not under any circumstances to receive back people whom the said bishop has canonically excommunicated, nor give communion to them, nor presume to give them absolution. But as for you, brother Archbishop, if the bishops appear negligent in the enactment of justice, you are to compel them to enact canonical justice, in line with the inherent purpose of your office. Given at the Lateran, 24th May.

85. A privilege of the lord Pope which Bishop Nigel acquired on the subject of the properties of the monks of Ely – small as they were – which he had established for them.[358]

Lucius, Bishop, servant of the servants of God, to his venerable brother Nigel, Bishop of Ely and to those who shall be canonically appointed in place of him as his successors for evermore. By virtue of the apostolic office entrusted to us by God, it is fitting that we should further the interests of our brothers with fatherly foresightedness, both those who live nearby and those in places far away, and fitting, too, that, for the benefit of the churches in which they are recognized to be doing battle on the Lord's behalf, we should protect their interests in law, so that just as, by God's ordinance, we are called by the name of 'father',[359] we may no less be proved fatherly in what we do.

[356] Cf. Acts of the Apostles 5.29.

[357] The same phrase, at p. 330.4, ed. Blake, as in chapter 79: *iuxta sacrorum . . . auctoritatem.*

[358] Source: monastic archives, cf, cartularies CDGM; Chatteris cartulary. On the relation of this charter with that set out in *LE* iii. 56, probably a forgery, see the initial note on that chapter. In addition to the monastic properties listed in the charter attributed to Bishop Hervey's time, we find mention here of: Little Thetford (on the Isle of Ely) and land at Isleham and Henny Hill (both in Cambridgeshire), and in London. Date: 24th May, 1144; at the Lateran.

[359] The plural 'fathers' is used in the Latin, in conformity with the use by the Pope of the 'royal' plural.

Hence, venerable brother Bishop Nigel, assenting to your just desires with paternal benevolence, we receive under the protection of the blessed Peter and of ourselves, the church of Ely, over which you preside, by God's authority, and we strengthen it by the privilege of the present writ, making it statutory that whatever estates and whatever goods you justly and religiously at present possess, or which, by God's favour, this same church shall be able to obtain in future, by the generosity of kings or princes, by the giving of offerings by believers, or by other lawful means, may remain established for you and for your successors, without infringement. Among these, we have deemed it right to make mention by name of the following: specifically, whatever grants and concessions King Henry of distinguished memory, out of his devotion, made to this same church: that is to say, relaxation of the requirement for the knight-service of the bishopric of Ely, which used to be customarily performed at Norwich Castle; also the remission of the requirement for twenty-five shillings and five pence and one half-penny, which used to be given annually for the guard of the castle; in addition, the relaxation of the requirement for all the service and works which the men of the church of Ely used to perform in the aforesaid castle; also remission of the requirement for forty pounds of scutage, these concessions being in accordance with what is known to have been laid down by the same king and confirmed in writing.

No less than this, moreover, we confirm that the abbey of Chatteris, with all its appurtenances, belongs to the church of Ely, with the specification, however, that the nuns who are there or who shall have been previously there, are to live under a rule in accordance with the ordinances of St Benedict, as they have done previously, and we confirm remission of ward-penny in respect to all the lands of the said church of Ely and the church of Chatteris. And also we order that the restitutions of lands, liberties and dignities made by the illustrious man, King Stephen, are to be kept firm and undisrupted for you for evermore. In a similar way, too, we confirm for the said church the possessions, liberties and dignities conferred by other kings of the English and leaders of your church and confirmed by our predecessor, Pope Victor of good memory, for you and your successors and through you. Furthermore, whatever goods you have conferred upon the monks of this particular church with a view to the maintenance of religious devotion and to the furtherance of hospitality, we sanction that these shall remain for them without diminution, with the stipulation, however, that it shall not be allowed for you or your successors, or, furthermore, for the monks referred to, either to take away or to assign to a military function any of the holdings of the monks, or, furthermore, any of those which you have reserved for the purposes of the bishopric. No, rather, you are to have free capability to recover those things which have been seized and to keep those things which have been recovered within the jurisdiction and control of your church.

Moreover, we absolutely forbid the monks themselves to grant their lands for anyone to hold by right of inheritance.

The names, in actual fact, of the lands and estates which you have granted to these same monks consisting both in vills and in the churches of these vills and in all manner of appurtenances belonging to them, are these. Within the Isle: Sutton, Witcham, Witchford, Little Thetford, Wentworth, Turbutsey, Whittlesey, Stuntney, with twenty-three thousand eels which are caught in the marshes and waters which lie near that manor; and all revenues and offerings belonging to the altars of the mother church, for supporting the needs of the same church. The church of St Mary of Ely with its lands and tithes and all its appurtenances. And specifically all the tithe of your Barton and whatever you used to possess at Isleham and Henny Hill and at *Biela*. Seven weys of salt in respect to Terrington. And also timber, certainly, in Somersham and in Bluntisham, as best they had it in the time of your predecessors. And upon the river-bank of Bluntisham a messuage of land with five acres, where timber may be collected, and with eight acres of meadow, where the oxen for dragging the timber may graze. Also their vineyard in Ely, just as they possessed it before you were bishop. And six fishermen, along with their dwellings, to fish in the waters in which they customarily did.

Outside the Isle: Melbourn, Meldreth, Hauxton, Newton, Wratting, Stetchworth, Swaffham, Stapleford, Barham, Stoke, Melton, Sudbourne, Kingston; *sake* and *soke* with all royal customs in the five-and-a-half hundreds. Twenty shillings in respect to *Rescemere*, Lakenheath, Undley, *Scepeia*, *Fotestorp* at the command of the monks. And thirty thousand herrings from Dunwich. And twelve skeps of corn and malt from the heirs of Hardwin de Scalers. And all their own servants in respect to all their ministrations, so that the monks may possess them freely with all their messuages, while the following liberty, in addition, has been indulgently granted and confirmed by you for the benefit of these monks: that not only the aforesaid items which have been conferred upon them by your devotion, or by the giving of offerings by any believers, whoever they may have been, but also, equally, items to be conferred upon them in future on reasonable terms are – in accordance with the confirmation given by my predecessors, namely the aforementioned Victor and Innocent of happy memory, pontiffs of Rome, and the grant and writs of kings – to remain freely available for their sustenance and freed from all specification of conditions. We also confirm for the aforesaid monks, by a similar sanction, the lands which they hold in London. We also add that, in accordance with the stipulation of the holy Council of Calcedon concerning absentee bishops,[360] the goods of that

---

[360] Council of Calcedon (date: 451), canon xxiv.

same church are not to be seized by anyone whomsoever, but are to be preserved for the purpose of the church and with no diminution of the power of the person who exercises his stewardship after him.[361] We decree, therefore, that it is not to be allowed for anyone whomsoever to disrupt the aforesaid church rashly, or to seize its holdings, or to hold on to them after seizure, diminish them or exhaust them by any acts of harassment. Rather, all the holdings of the monks which shall have been granted for their government and sustenance are to be kept whole, for the furtherance of all their various kinds of customary practices – providing that in everything the authority of the Apostolic See is upheld. Therefore, if any person, ecclesiastical or lay, in time to come shall have attempted knowingly to contravene rashly the text of this our agreement, if after a second and third warning he has not made amends by appropriate satisfaction, he is to be deprived of his position of honour and power, he is to know that he is[362] by divine judgement guilty of the evil which he has perpetrated, and is to be alienated from the most sacred body and blood of the Redeemer, our God and Lord Jesus Christ, and is to be subjected to strict vengeance at the Last Judgement. And the peace of our Lord Jesus Christ be to all who keep to their legal rights with regard to this same monastery, so that they may both receive the fruit of good action and, before the strict Judge, acquire the rewards of everlasting peace. AMEN.

86. That Bishop Nigel had incurred the king's displeasure a second time; and how he was reconciled to him.[363]

Given additional protection by these charters, Bishop Nigel returned to Ely from Rome. It was in trepidation that he took up residence there, and he did not dare to go out of the place without being escorted by a great number of knights and attendants. To explain: during the period when he was on his prolonged stay abroad, Geoffrey, the earl mentioned above, perished at the hands of the king's army. And thus, by the judgement of God, a ravager of the country was taken away, and, as a consequence, the power of the warriors who, together with him, had used a heavy hand to wreak the destruction of poor unfortunates, suffered a major collapse. For they realized that the Lord Christ was giving the king in his faithfulness triumph over his enemies and was mightily shattering his adversaries. At this, the heart of his enemies took fright and people who had previously been fighting against the king became friends, promising faith and obedience in all things. As a consequence Bishop Nigel, also, was utterly terror-stricken: he was in fear of King Stephen, who

---

[361] Lat. *successoris sui ichonomi potestate illibata serventur*. Here the spelling *ichonomus* is a variant on *economus*, from the Greek for a 'manager of a household', 'steward'.

[362] The feminine form *ream* is used for 'a culpable person', because *persona* is a feminine noun.

[363] Source: (Richard of Ely's?) narrative of the episcopate of Nigel (continued).

was at that time very seriously offended, for the following reasons: he, Bishop Nigel, was, so it was alleged, inciting the country's insurrectionists against the king, welcoming them and generally assisting them; he had utterly failed to keep the pact which he had quite often entered upon with him, and had taken away by stealth the hostage given by him for the keeping of the pact. The king had, in fact, at that time, given instructions to his men for the goods of the bishop everywhere to be seized, something which they were preparing to carry out without delay. They went on the rampage, seized all the properties and claimed them for themselves.

The bishop, as if smitten by a deep wound, groaned at being responsible for such a crisis; he kept pleading for the mercy of God and the help of the blessed Æthelthryth with piteous and insistent cries. His plea was that she who never ceases mercifully to come to the aid of her people in every tribulation, should, for the love of her Lord Jesus Christ, now deign to be present with him in the critical moment of his present adversity. And indeed, he had the sense that what he was with devout emotion praying for was speedily brought to fulfilment through the merit of the holy virgin.[364] For although for a long time no one dared bring word from him to the king, it chanced that there had arrived to visit the bishop a certain very eloquent cleric, of an outstandingly noble family, honoured and greatly loved by the king, his name being Richard de Punchardon. This man undertook the business for the bishop, brought it to the king, and energetically carried out the undertaking delegated to him: to come without fear and without hesitancy into the king's presence, and to settle whatever pact or agreement he could with him. And it was done. Moreover, on the appointed day, after he had been led by his kinsfolk and the nobles of the kingdom before the king at the royal town of Ipswich, he succeeded in the end, with difficulty, thanks to the supplication of many people, in obtaining an agreement – or a favour – from him, conditional, however, on the handover of a sum of money, namely three hundred marks of silver and, in addition, upon his giving as a hostage for a second time his own son, an adolescent whom he was bringing up in the monastery,[365] on whose behalf and at whose hands the church was harmed by serious and repeated discomfitures. Once the agreement was confirmed, therefore, by a pledge of fidelity and the swearing of an oath, the bishop withdrew, receiving from the king the following guarantee of peace and concord.

---

[364] Repunctuating at p. 333.7f., ed. Blake as follows: *Et quidem sensit sibi celeri effectu esse collatum quod devoto affectu exorabat, per sancte virginis meritum.*

[365] Richard Fitz Nigel (or Fitz Neal), later to be Archdeacon of Ely and, subsequently, Bishop of London.

87. A charter of King Stephen about his granting of peace to Bishop Nigel.[366]

Stephen, King of the English, to his justices, sheriffs, barons, officials and all his faithful people in whose ares of jurisdiction Bishop Nigel has land: greeting. I give instructions that Nigel, Bishop of Ely, is to hold and to possess all his lands and men and all his belongings, and all the liberties of his church of St Æthelthryth, as well and as peaceably and freely and quietly and honourably, as he best, and most freely, ever held them, since he has peace from me, and has made an agreement with me. And I forbid anyone to do injury or insult to him or to his belongings over this matter. Witness: the Earl of Warenne and William Martel. At Ipswich.

88. Another charter of the king; that he gave instructions that the properties of the monks should be in peace.[367]

Stephen, King of the English, to his archbishops, bishops, abbots, justices, earls, sheriffs and all his officials and faithful people, French and English, of the whole of England: greeting. You are to know that I have given back and conceded to the monks of St Æthelthryth of Ely all their lands and holdings as well and fully as ever they held them on the day on which Bishop Nigel last set out to go to Rome. In view of this, I wish and instruct that they are to hold them as well, and peaceably, and freely, and quietly, and honourably, with all their appurtenances, as they have ever held them. Witnesses: Earl Gilbert and Robert de Vere, and Turgis d'Avranches and John, son of Robert. At Bury St Edmunds.

89. That the bishop took goods of the church, contained within it, to pay money promised to the king.[368]

So, the king was pressing for what had been promised and was hoped for, and no amount of the bishop's own resources provided him with enough. He assembled cunning arguments, calculating that, by dint of talking the monks round, he would be less liable to a charge of malpractice, if he were to steal from the church what remained there. Moreover, he summoned the chief officials of his household, the intermediaries through whom he was known

---

[366] Source: monastic archives, cf. cartulary G. Date: Blake suggests 1144 or 1145. However, note that, apart from the fact that Ipswich is named as the place of issue, and minute textual variants, this charter is identical with that given in *LE* iii. 75 (dated to perhaps 1142), even having the same witnesses.

[367] Source: monastic archives, cf. Ely, Dean and Chapter, charter no. 8; cartularies GM. Date: late 1144 or 1145; at Bury St Edmunds.

[368] Source: resumption of (Richard of Ely's?) narrative of the episcopate of Nigel.

to commit abuses with respect to many, serious matters, namely: Goscelin with the surname 'of Ely', William of *Laventuna*, the cleric Alexander, Ralph the steward and others whom we shall not refrain from mentioning in the present chapter. He advised these men to approach the monks with smooth cajolery, to try to win their minds over, to soften them into agreement by means of any entreaty or promise, the object being that permission would at least be given to take just two hundred marks of silver from the ornaments of the church.

On hearing this, the monks were exceedingly saddened; they gave thought to the fact that the house of God would need to be despoiled of all its beauty within; they unanimously gave him their refusal. But the bishop, in his urgent need, was for ever insistent in his pleading, making pledges, promising on oath that within a year he would certainly restore everything for the better. In addition, in a piteous plea to them, he asserted that he would grant them the vill of Hadstock, with its appendages, for their purposes for evermore, and he produced givers of surety who were to affirm this on oath. And so he continued with his pleading until he received as a gift what he had been asking for.

He therefore took from the shrine of St Æthelthryth seventy-four marks of silver and from its front twenty-five marks – for he had taken the other side of the shrine, that is, the right-hand side, previously – and, from the *tabula* before the altar, sixty-four marks of silver and two marks and three-and-a-half ounces of gold; from the two images of the blessed Mary and St John, towards the altar, fifty-seven marks of silver and two-and-a-half marks of gold. He took two candle-sticks – eighteen marks; a large tower-pyx of silver which it was our custom to carry on feast-days – seventeen marks and two ounces of gold. He took three crosses – twenty-five marks of silver and two marks, one-and-a-half ounces of gold; and a chalice of three marks of silver. All these items were of fine workmanship and Bishop Nigel took them from the church, with these men giving surety on the understanding that, if ever he should be discommoded by any adverse mischance to such an extent that he could not replace the treasure, they would give recompense on his behalf from their private property and to restore what the church had lost; in the presence of the brothers standing together in agreement, they made a pledge and swore an oath that this matter was to be kept under the control of Prior Thembert. The surety-givers were, specifically: Archdeacon William, for sixty marks; Goscelin of Ely, forty marks; the physician Ernulf, for ten marks; the cleric Peter, for ten marks; the cleric Alexander, for twenty marks; the chaplain Gilbert, for ten marks; Albert *Anglicus*, for ten marks; Henry *Peregrinus* for fifteen marks; the cleric Hubert for five marks; William of Shelford for twenty marks: total, two hundred marks. To be precise: the above-mentioned men, as we have said previously, promised that they would give this recompense – though they had never given any part of the sum; the bishop too swore an affidavit with his hand upon the high altar that he would abide by this, and he confirmed by the following charter {that} the manor of Hadstock {was assigned} to the furtherance of works pertaining to the church for the purposes of the monks, for evermore.

90. A charter of the bishop about how he returned the vill of Hadstock to the monks.[369]

Nigel, by the grace of God Bishop of the church of Ely, to all his clergy, barons, officials, retainers and friends, French and English, of the whole honour of St Æthelthryth and to all children of Holy Church: greeting and blessing. Since it is particularly important, among other works of faith, to honour one's mother, the Church, with devoted acts of service and give it ample means by benefactions of various sorts, the following honourable duty falls most of all upon us who bear the burden and honour of pastoral rule: that, with the precedent of the Tabernacle of the Law and the ancient Temple, we should beautify it with precious ornaments consisting of gold and silver, of jewels, of vestments and vessels, and supply items necessary for the purposes of the servants of God. For this reason, I, Nigel, Bishop of Ely, to the end that I may have some share in the company of saintly pastors, desire to give increase and amplification, by gifts and persons and possessions and buildings and other benefactions of different kinds, to the community of monks, serving God in the church of Ely, which has been committed by divine agency to my charge. And therefore I relinquish to them, with complete liberty, and settle upon them, the manor of Hadstock, with the church which is there, as being a former possession of theirs and their own property, with all its appurtenances, specifically, with respect to all its rights of jurisdiction, liberties and customary rights, woodland, open ground, arable land, tithes, revenues, fisheries, marshes and all other things, belonging both to this particular manor and to this same church, on a firm and stable legal basis from now on and for evermore, peculiarly and specifically for the purpose of carrying out works concerned with the shrine of St Æthelthryth and the altar.[370] And I wish and instruct and by my present charter confirm, that the same monks of ours are to hold without infraction this same manor, with the aforesaid church along with all the items mentioned above, for the purpose of the aforesaid works, as well, and peaceably, and freely, and quietly, and honorifically, as the way in which they held them with the greatest freedom and honour in the time of the predecessors of mine, the abbots of the church of Ely whom you mention, namely: Ælfsige, Leofsige, Wulfric,

---

[369] Source: monastic archives, cf. cartularies DGM. Date: late 1144 or 1145.

[370] Lat. *ad facienda opera feretri sancte Æðeldreðe et altaris.*

Thurstan, Theodwine and Simeon. These same monks of ours, indeed, on our instruction and advice and decree, have made provision that, because that place had been consecrated to the religious life of former times under the blessed Abbot Botulf, who reposes there,[371] it should be maintained henceforth at a higher level of religious devotion, for the honour of God and of His saint, and that the former religious life – which had gone to ruin through the negligence of the people in possession of it – should be to some measure restored in that place. Therefore, let anyone who shall have observed this confirmation, made by our authority, receive the blessing of almighty God and of all the saints. But whoever shall be a violator, unless he quickly recovers his senses and gives suitable satisfaction, let him be allotted eternal damnation with the Devil and his angels and, in accordance with the utterance of the apostle Paul, let him be 'anathema maranatha'[372] throughout all ages, for ever and ever. AMEN. With the following witnesses: Robert, Abbot of Thorney; Prior Thembert; Archdeacon William; Goscelin [of Ely], cleric; Peter, cleric; Alexander, cleric; William *Monachus* of Shelford; Ralph the chamberlain, and many others.

91. On the same matter: a charter of Archbishop Theobald.[373]

Theobald, by the grace of God, Archbishop of Canterbury and Primate of all England, to his venerable brother Nigel, Bishop of Ely: greeting and paternal benediction. The majesty of ecclesiastical governance has inherent in it a concern which belongs especially to it: that of rejoicing in the pious endeavours of brothers everywhere and of strengthening them, by means of its stable authority, against all attacks. Consequently, venerable brother Bishop Nigel, we embrace with pleasure and venerate, as is fitting, the benevolent generosity on your part, by means of which you are endeavouring to increase the resources of the church of Ely which has been committed by divine agency to your charge, to strengthen it, with persons, estates, ornaments and other necessary benefactions, for perpetual divine service, and to bring commendation to your memory before God throughout all ages. We lay down, therefore, and confirm by our authority the ratification and inviolateness of your most devout gift whereby you have restored for all eternity to the monks of Ely the manor of Hadstock, as being a former possession together with the church of the blessed Botulf established in that same place and all the rights of jurisdiction there which the charter of this your grant includes, specifically and statedly for carrying out works

---

[371] On relics of St Botulf see also *LE* ii. 138.

[372] 1 Corinthians 16.22, imperfectly understood.

[373] Source: monastic archives, see Ely, Dean and Chapter, charter no. 83; cartularies DGM; also printed in Saltman, *Theobald, Archbishop of Canterbury*, pp. 319–20; no. 98.

concerning the altar and shrine of St Æthelthryth. And as for the former religious life which you have determined to restore in part in the aforesaid church of the sainted Abbot Botulf, who reposes there, we too, by our inviolable decree, determine that it be restored. Any of your successors, therefore, or any other person whosoever, who keeps this confirmation of ours inviolate, is to become a sharer in God's blessing and ours. But if anyone should presume to violate it, whoever that person might be, whether ecclesiastical or lay, let him be subject to eternal anathema, regardless of his rank or power, unless he swiftly mends his ways. AMEN.

92. Who the men were who gave surety for the bishop with regard to the money taken from the church; and how miserably events turned out for them.[374]

And now, to be sure, while our pen is in our hands, we proceed to the conclusion of our account of what has to be recorded about the men referred to above, so that our work may not waver, through weariness, from its initial aim.

Now, these givers of surety for the funds of the church were constant companions of the bishop, for ever giving him the advice – during his ruination of the monastery's goods – to seize for himself, from the monastery, all the best items and those of particular importance;[375] to diminish and steal things which were necessities for the monks, their aim being that, in this way, if no other, they might compel them[376] to relinquish the monastery and their belongings to them, a course of action which they knew to be pleasing to their lord himself. For Bishop Nigel did not recall for a moment the kindnesses and love which, in their compassion for their father in his times of need, the monks had bestowed upon him. Instead, even in the midst of all these events, his madness was not deflected: rather, his hand was still stretched forth to cause havoc, and he transferred all the customary rights of the church into his own jurisdiction. Now that it had been utterly emptied of its sacred vessels, he wanted it to be the habitation not of divine worship but of his henchmen. He was continually in a rage against the monks, and hostile to them, with the result that it was unclear that he was waging war against men more than against God.

---

[374] Source: resumption of (Richard of Ely's?) narrative of the episcopate of Nigel. This chapter includes a list of charges against the bishop, and an appeal to his conscience, which read as if originally intended for use in legal proceedings.

[375] The text here (p. 338.15, ed. Blake) is confusing: as there are too many words for 'and', the translation presumes deletion of *et* before *optima*.

[376] Again there is a problem of redundance (p. 338.16, ed. Blake): I am translating as if there were no second *vel* after *compellerent*.

So it was that he took the remains of the ornaments of the temple of the Lord – that temple once crowned, but now languishing and fallen prostrate to the ground in misery – and deposited them with the Bishop of Lincoln as security, namely: the chasuble of King Edgar of blessed memory, and his girdle, an alb with an amice of the monk Thurstan, a provost of this same church, and his stole; these would have been lost straight away, at one stroke, if the monks had not very quickly come to his rescue, at his request, with thirty-nine marks. Having with difficulty raised these thirty-nine marks, stinting themselves of food and clothing, they gave them to him, by the hand of the prior of that time, but the bishop, on receiving them, spent them on purposes of his own. On a second occasion, a date was specified to the monks as a deadline for them either to make a settlement, there and then, or thereafter be deprived. Once more, the church, by the hands of the †sacrist, William,†[377] made a gift of sixty-seven marks of silver. Again, for objects which the bishop had earlier placed at pawn in London, specifically with the cleric Nicholas – a large chalice and a silver tower-pyx from which the relics enclosed in it were stolen at that time – the church now paid redemption-money of fifty-seven marks and six shillings and eight pence. Again, he gave someone from Thetford five marks for a little golden gospel-book and for a silver handle;[378] and, in addition to these things, he took from the sacristy in one year twenty-four marks and six shillings. Previously, indeed, he had similarly handed over to the Jews at Cambridge, in exchange for money, the cross mentioned above,[379] and the gospel-book[380] which the glorious King Edgar, to whom frequent reference has been made, had donated in that place as a sign of its liberty and munificent endowment and, so that they would not be deprived of this most important guarantee of their entitlement to protection, the monks gave two hundred marks by the hand of Prior William. In addition, Bishop Nigel for three years spent the offerings and revenues – all that had come to the altar of St Æthelthryth – on his falconers and hunters. But, on hearing or reading these things, he is not to suppose that we have been talking about great things from among small: no, rather, they are a few, small things from among many, great ones, spoken of so that he may have pity on his ransacked and mangled church, may be moved to compassion thus, if in no other way, and so, by ceasing his continual harassment of the servants of the Lord in that place, may lose the habit of doing them injury. For the Lord, too, 'will bring about retribution upon His

---

[377] The sacrist of the time is named, later in the chapter, as Ralph; William was the prior's name.

[378] Lat. *ansa* = a 'handle', or anything on which one takes a grip. Here, perhaps a spare part for a wine-flagon, cf. *LE.* iii. 50 (p. 292.12–16 ed. Blake), following the readings of E.

[379] Cf. *LE* iii. 50 (p. 290.24, ed. Blake).

[380] Also mentioned in *LE* iii. 50 (p. 290.37f., ed. Blake).

enemies' and one day 'will be propitious to the land of His people'.[381]

Let us continue, however, following the sequential order of our promised narrative, albeit reluctantly. For as for what he did in lands and villages, with respect to revenues and estates: the crying out of the common people spreads the report of it, and the excessive scale of his insolence makes it visible from afar.

The clerics mentioned above were undoubtedly instigators and guilty perpetrators, of things of this kind. Goscelin, specifically, was uppermost in offering advice, versatile in his ingenuity, foremost in trickery, second to none in rascality. This man in his earliest days trapped Bishop Hervey by his cunning and enticed him to side with him, in accordance with his wishes. He even brought a prosecution before King Henry against his own master who had fed him, Thurstan, a provost and monk of this same church, and had him ejected from his office, and he was not afraid to become, through these fraudulent means, his successor in it. And whereas he ought in rights to have paid back to the monastery all the goods he had, he did the reverse: gave back evil instead of good, and brought about the loss of the gold chalice of the monk Wulfwine, assessed at four-and-a-half marks;[382] in addition he took as his colleague someone very like him in all his cunning deceitfulness, Osbert, surnamed 'of Wattisham'. Both of them, as if one of them were Diocletian and the other Maximian, were enemies of God and St Æthelthryth: they unrelentingly used to pilfer her goods, diminish them, usurp them and took it upon themselves to harm her with the wound of an inestimable loss. This undertaking they cruelly carried out in many ways.

And, in fact, Goscelin, the commanding officer in this war, had the presumption to break into the tomb of the virgin Æthelthryth by night in a foolhardy piece of bravado. In line with the text where one reads: 'all violent plundering' comes about 'with tumult',[383] he, too, was entirely carried away by fury when he made his audacious attack. He was the first[384] to lay his hand on it; he cast forth gold, silver, precious stones and all the decorations, tearing them away with axe and blade;[385] with reproofs he implored the men destined to commit the crime, to carry out without delay the orders of the lord Bishop. He did not know – poor wretch – that he would suddenly, in the future, pay very heavy penalties, imposed by God in vengeance for the holy virgin Æthelthryth. For he was unexpectedly assailed by {gout}, the severe pain of the feet which physicians call, in Greek, *podagra*. He was completely

---

[381] Deuteronomy 32.43.

[382] Cf. *LE* iii. 50, p. 291.25ff., 34ff. and Blake's note. There is confusion as to which of three chalices was lost because of Goscelin.

[383] Cf. Isaiah 9.5.

[384] Taking *prius* at p. 340.8, ed. Blake as equivalent to, if not a mistake for, *primus* (cf. *secundus* in line 21 below).

[385] Taking *acia* (p. 340.9, ed. Blake) to be a mistake for *acie*.

deprived of the capacity to walk. Moreover, suffering though he did for a long time from inflammation as a result of the misfortune so described, it was with impatience that he bore his punishment from Heaven and he was still unwilling to understand in order to act well. Nor did he repent of the error of his bad behaviour in having spent the time of his priesthood in luxurious living, and having dissipated the whole income of his official position in arrogance and malpractice. The result was that he ended his life in poverty and tribulation. Moreover, none of those who were his accomplices in his outrage were at all conscience-stricken. Hence 'the memory of them has' now 'perished with the sound' of them.[386] I shall recount this fully in appropriate contexts.

Another member of the council of the ill-intentioned was, to be sure, William of Shelford, mentioned above, Goscelin's colleague in everything. At the ready for criminal action, he went ahead fearlessly with mattocks, mallets, smiths' tools; he, in person, was the second to lay hands on the shrine; he took the bronze from it, but soon was most bitterly sorry for his deed. For although he was a very rich man and lacked for nothing, as the result of a misfortune he became reduced to such poverty that he did not even have the necessities of life. And now that all his resources had been used up, he did not know what to do or where to turn. Eventually, after much prolonged pleading with the monks in Ely, he with difficulty succeeded in being received into the monastic brotherhood, where, constant in grief and tears, in vigils and prayers, he bewailed his guilt: he spent the remaining period of his life in true repentance. Again, Prior Thembert and Ralph the sacrist, who ought to have given protection like a wall to the house of Israel, agreed to the evil scheme. Beguiled by favour and the gratitude of mankind, they were obedient to the bishop in the desires of his mind, although one ought to obey God rather than man. And, man-pleasers though they were, they were put to confusion, because God spurned them, as the miraculous sequel demonstrated. All of a sudden, they simultaneously felt the vengeance of God, the just Judge, and the punishment of their guilt, and they were assailed by a troublous infliction of ills and pain, that is: they became infirm and there was no one to help them.[387] The first-mentioned of these two men, smitten by an incurable paralysing disease, was deprived of almost all movement of his limbs and the use of his tongue; as for the other, he was injured by a mortal wound: †this face began[388] to swell because of the excessive torment of the pain, which[389] had turned his whole jaw into

---

[386] Reading with Psalm 9.7 Vulgate after Septuagint (= 9.6 RSV): *cum sonitu*, for *LE* mss.: *consonitu*.

[387] Cf. Ecclesiasticus 51.10 Vulgate = 51.7 NEB.

[388] So F, correcting E, at p. 340.35, ed. Blake.

[389] Reading *que* for *quem* (p. 340.36, ed. Blake).

bloody pus,[390] and had spread the gravity of the affliction into the wound.†
And thus they groaned continually in their sufferings and sickness rendered
both of them useless. As no physicians' expertise availed these men, they
were fatally tormented for a long time and ended their lives with a pitiful
demise, God and St Æthelthryth wreaking vengeance upon them. For, in
hostility towards the lady, they replaced good with evil and love with hatred.
Whereas she nurtured them and raised them up, they, for their part, full of
contempt, treated her with scorn.

93. How pleasant a vision was made manifest concerning the blessed Æthelthryth.[391]

Many things relevant to this history are coming to light which even the
greatest of poets would have extreme difficulty in handling, while an
inexpert person with an ill-informed tongue is not at all capable of coming to
grips with them. However, trusting in the Lord God, who 'makes the tongues
of infants eloquent'[392] and opened the mouth of a dumb animal,[393] I believe
I shall share in the resurrection with my [most beneficent] mistress
Æthelthryth. This lady, I declare, will always be, after God and His most pious
Mother, a refuge for me and a remedy for sorrow – she who brought me up
and led me to this day of light and had mercy on me as I sighed deeply over
sins and crimes because of which I deserved her anger and the darkness of
exile. For her glory I have set up this little book, like a new testament, as an
advertisement and record of her mighty works, like a lamp,[394] I have raised it
up on high from beneath a bushel,[395] and I have gathered together to form a
single entity things written about her in various scattered places. Moreover, I
have done this not at the dictates of my own intellectual inclination, but with
the inspiration and assistance of God's glory.

I do not say these things to exalt my own voice or <because>[396] I
consider myself to be something.[397] 'My strength failed me, and the light of

---

[390] Reading at p. 340.36–7, ed. Blake, with altered word-division: *in saniem.*

[391] Source: preface to a 'little book', forming part of a 'history', evidently already begun, and
relating to St Æthelthryth, followed by a miracle narrative. Preface and narrative together
are also included in B *(Book of Miracles)*. The narrative includes a rhetorical comparison
(syncrisis) in the classical manner between two pupils of a 'rhetorician'.

[392] See Wisdom of Solomon 10.21.

[393] Numbers 22.28ff., on Balaam's ass.

[394] Translating as if the text were: *ut lucernam exaltavi de sub modio in altum . . .* (p. 341.15,
ed. Blake).

[395] Cf. Matthew 5.15 and parallels.

[396] Reading conjecturally at p. 34.11, ed. Blake: *aut <quod> me aliquid existimem.*

[397] Cf. Galatians 6.3.

my eyes – it also went from me.'[398] And all day my words pursue me, in that every day it is said to me, 'Where is your God? Where is your hope?[399] Or your Æthelthryth, whom you have proclaimed to be continually bringing you aid? In what respects has she helped you before or does she help you now? You praise her and cherish her, love her and venerate her; you attempt to commend her in your heart and with your mouth, as well as in the titles of your written works. "Sing well; keep revisiting song, so there may be recollection"[400] of her. We, however, do not accept your writings or sayings, we despise them, we cast them off.' But even as we recount these things, we shrink back, impotent, from the purpose of our journey. Now we request the favour of the reader that his reverential eye may grant its attention to the matters set out below.

Well then, at a time when the populace of England was in a state of anarchy, divided into two factions, one against the other, and was in furious turmoil accompanied by devastation, arson and slaughter, nobles were being expelled from their manors, and the inhabitants of the land, afflicted by many disasters, were being driven to their deaths, as they fled through country-estates and fortresses. A few barely saved themselves by hiding in churches. So it came about that, along with innumerable others, a rhetorician named Julian, 'as his foot had not found rest',[401] landed at Ely while Lord Nigel was exercising the office of bishop.

He was a man admirable for his learning, second to none in the grammarian's art,[402] deserving to be rated more highly than some of the Latins; he was extremely eloquent in his advancing of points for disputation and in his offering of reasoned explanations; he had the greatest facility in every field of knowledge. His wisdom was swiftly acknowledged, and he was received with great reverence. So it was that he had first taught grammar overseas, and the so-called 'liberal' arts; also philosophy and rhetoric in his own city, London, the capital of England,[403] and, in the course of time, theology, as the monks discovered that his discourses and utterances, adorned as they were with rhetorical figures, were distinguished by a sophisticated charm. And, in fact, he used always to speak in the context of conversations with an intimate circle, and as a consequence of these, in a most seemly way, he prompted several to move on to the Scriptures.[404]

---

[398] Psalm 37.11 Vulgate = 38.10 RSV.

[399] Cf. Tobias 2.16 Vulgate.

[400] Cf. Isaiah 23.16.

[401] Cf. Deuteronomy 28.65.

[402] 'The grammarian's art': Lat. *grammatica*, which included the study of literature and elementary composition in addition to 'grammar' as we understand the term.

[403] Lat. *in sua civitate Lundonia capite Anglie.*

[404] The seven liberal arts – *trivium*: grammar, logic, rhetoric, and *quadrivium*: geometry, arithmetic, astronomy and music – were considered preparatory to the study of the Scriptures.

But the junior monks – may God see fit to forgive him for this[405] – he compelled to study. In an especially thorough and diligent way he endeavoured to educate two more than the others. He encouraged them in the direction of honourable pursuits, and admonished them to shun depravities and avoid the defilements of the World; he insistently gave them a thorough training in the best things he knew, as if they were his sons; his desire was to lead their souls to the Lord by his exhortations. I am not, however, including mention of their names, because I have as witnesses of their manner of life everyone who knows the monastery of Ely. Both of them had been accepted in the monastery from boyhood as lay-brothers.

The one who was younger in age was the first to take up the monastic life, but he was of an arrogant, proud and vain mentality, and neither the strictness of the rule nor the rigour of the discipline could at all tame him, and as he grew older in years, he increased correspondingly in vice. Having despised the fear of God and reverence for the holy life of religion, he was completely brought low; although he was 'in honour', specifically, in the citadel of forgiveness, 'he did not have understanding; he was compared to foolish cattle and was made like them'.[406] He always delighted in brawls,[407] and was prone to hatred, a trouble-maker, irascible, and insolent in speech; he sought out discord and sowed disputes among the brothers, distressing the whole congregation so much that he was scarcely tolerable in anyone's view. And he had dragged his life through every malpractice, so that he was considered extremely notorious for his shameful acts when, one day, his conscience was smitten, by the mercy of God, and he finally turned to repentance. He attempted to wash away the filth of his earlier crimes by fountains of tears, and <did> not even <dare> to raise his eyes to Heaven[408] or invoke the name of the Lord, but spent the time in nothing but groans, as if buried alive, and now, somehow, kept giving forth a moaning and groaning of the heart. Thus, conscience-stricken through the grace of God, he now gained a grip on the hope of salvation, of which he had earlier despaired, and although he had wasted his time in neglectfulness, he nevertheless loved the virgin of God, Æthelthryth, with all his mind, and fired to devotion to her by his ardour, he produced by his own effort a little book about her life and mighty powers.

---

[405] Cf. the attitude of Ralph the schoolmaster, when his sickness drove him to repentance (*LE* iii. 35). He is a possible author of the main miracle collection used in *LE* iii; and may perhaps be identifiable with the sacrist Ralph, who, after having received a wound, died of a throat ailment similar to that described in iii 35 (*LE* iii. 92).

[406] Quotation from Psalm 48.13 Vulgate.

[407] Reading at p. 342.19, ed. Blake: *iurgiis,* not *virgiis.*

[408] Reading conjecturally at p. 342.24f., ed. Blake: *et nec quidem levare oculos ad celum neque nomen Domini invocare <audens>,* . . . The combination *et ne(c) quidem* is not classical, and maybe the *et* should be deleted accordingly.

The second monk, senior to the other in age, but a later entrant to the monastic life, having been received in the monastery at the same time as him,[409] was, by contrast, humble-minded and placid-looking.[410] He was extremely well-versed in Holy Scripture, and thanks to a gift divinely conferred on him, he gained a command of great knowledge about many things which the other monk did not know, and had acquired the habit of providing edifying instruction. Young though he was in age, he was nevertheless mature in his behaviour: exercising strict self-control upon himself under the rule of holy living, he led a life of due attention to simplicity and prayer. He followed in all respects the life which he had learned that the venerable Æthelthryth had led. And in view of the fact that he had grown in fear of the Lord so that the unbelievable austerity of his life was praised even by outsiders, he was chosen there for the ministry of the priesthood. After his ordination, it was shown to him in a revelation that his death was not far off. And, lo and behold, he did meet his end, overcome by a fever.

However, not long after his burial, he appeared to the negligent colleague just referred to, as if in a certain place in the monastery, in the *porticus* of the blessed Paul. As this colleague of his, in his vision, remained pensive and dumbstruck for a long time about him, wondering whether he had died, he soothed him by the placid expression on his face, as he was a man of extreme simplicity and innocence, and answered his question with alacrity: 'You are not to be afraid, thinking I am dead! I am alive and extremely happy.' The brother pondered this, and realizing that what he had seen was in no way a spectre, without any fear of the dead man, took him by the hand and, with a friendly gesture, made him sit down beside him. What I have to report is wonderful, and exceedingly joyful news for the present weakened condition of mankind, and, secret though the happenings were, the pity of God has not wished that they should be hidden from us. Further to these words, he said additional things of a similar kind; for what he said was, 'I was in Heaven before the sight of the Divine Majesty, where I also beheld the most holy virgin Æthelthryth, holding a book in her hand, kneeling as a supplicant in the presence of God Most High. What is more, I saw her giving thanks with her lips for the oft-mentioned brother – she referred to him by name – who produced the book in question, as a testament of her glory and as her everlasting memorial.' With these words, the apparition disappeared.

Be assured, the brother who had seen this[411] is reliable, and we trust his

---

[409] Punctuating with a full stop after *conversatus* (p. 342.31, ed. Blake).

[410] Reading conjecturally at p. 342.31, ed. Blake: *vultu placidus* (for *placitus* at p. 342.31, cf p. 343.4: *placido*).

[411] Reading conjecturally at p. 343.15, ed. Blake: *hoc* for *hic*.

BOOK III

words. He committed it to writing, and I acquired what he had written belatedly, only just in time, and hastened to set it down on this page, so that all might think back upon, and appreciate, our venerable lady advocate, Æthelthryth, knowing with what great loving-kindness and sweetness she embraces and fosters those who love her and devotedly take part in her ministry. Blessed be God, who chose himself such a handmaiden, so that we may exult and rejoice in her, and 'find satisfaction at the teats of her consolation'.[412] AMEN.

94. About St *Ælgetus*, the farm-bailiff of St Æthelthryth.[413]

Nor will I be silent about this event which is reported as having happened by the testimony of a great many people. There was a man living in the village of Gretton. He was noted in that neighbourhood not for the abundance of his wealth but for his faith and goodness. For he gained the daily livelihood of his little household by manual labour, going out to his work at daybreak, and he remained thus at his labours until nightfall. In the sweat of his brow he fed upon his own bread, so that, whereas his body was thin from lack of food, his mind, not luxuriating in pleasures, was more ready to meditate upon celestial things. One day, when he was resting on his bed, while he was neither totally overwhelmed by sleep nor quite awake, he saw in a dream a man standing before him clad in shining raiment, who roused him by shaking him gently with his hand, and urged him to wake up, saying: 'Rise in haste and at daybreak, as fast as you can, make no delay in hastening to Bury St Edmunds. Enquire there diligently for Dom Ording, the abbot of that place, and, when you have been summoned to him, issue the following instructions. Saluting him in the name of the Lord, you are to say to him that he is to come from hence, in a state of readiness, to the church of this town and, in such and such a place in its cemetery which is indicated and marked out <he is to search for>[414] the most blessed man *Ælgetus*, at one time the farm-bailiff of the venerable Queen Æthelthryth' – of whom <we have made mention>[415] above, specifically, in the first book published about the mighty

---

[412] Cf. Isaiah 66.10–11.

[413] Source: miracle narrative, also included in B *(Book of Miracles)*. Explicit reference is made to a previous 'first' book on the mighty acts of St Æthelthryth (*de virtutibus ipsius virginis*) in which *Ælgetus* was mentioned. The reference could be to the first book of *LE*, where there is *Ælgetus* there in chapter 23, or else it might be taken to refer to the first book in a miracle collection. In the latter case it would make sense to interpret the prefatory material in *LE* iii. 93 as having originally introduced the second book of the same collection.

[414] Supplying conjecturally at p. 343.35, ed. Blake: *et tali in loco eiusdem cimiterii ostenso et designato <petat> virum beatissimum Æilgetum . . .*

[415] Supplying conjecturally at p. 343.37, ed. Blake, e.g.: *cuius supra <recordati sumus> in primo videlicet libro . . .*

423

works of the virgin herself. 'When the abbot finds this man, up till now unrecognized by men, buried beneath the turf, he is to exhume him and entomb him where he may be held in veneration.'

And on waking from his sleep he turned over in his mind the vision which he had seen. He arose and hastened to Bury St Edmunds. There, he was led into the presence of the abbot, and explained the matter in an ordered fashion, in accordance with the command he had received in his sleep. The abbot, hearing this, glorified the Lord for the fact that He had willed to make manifest His saint through his own agency and in his times. And he would have carried out without delay the command given to him by God, but, owing to troubles confronting him as the result of some misfortunes, he decided to delay the matter for the while, with the consequence that, prevented and hindered by much anxiety, he did absolutely nothing subsequently to carry out the undertaking.

95. An instruction of the lord Pope to Nigel, Bishop of Ely, concerning the recall of properties to the church of St Æthelthryth.[416]

Eugenius, Bishop, servant of the servants of God, to his venerable brother Bishop Nigel and his beloved sons, the Prior and Chapter of the church of Ely: greeting and apostolic blessing. The authority of holy canon law has established that no bishop or abbot may alienate ecclesiastical properties or transfer them into the power of princes or of other persons and, if the deed has been done, it is to be considered void. Therefore, following closely in the footsteps of our predecessors and of other holy fathers, we recall as void, alienations of estates of the church of Ely made by the said Abbot Richard, by Bishop Hervey and by you, brother Bishop. By these present letters addressed to you,[417] we command you to make an effort, as a prudent shepherd and a diligent guardian, to recover the estates of your church which have been alienated unreasonably by the aforementioned persons, and you, my beloved sons, Prior and monks, are manfully to assist your bishop to do this. Moreover, if any layman in future has been holding these same estates by violent means <and has refused, after being warned by you, brother bishop, to come to his senses>, you are to coerce him, on our authority, by a censure in accordance with canon law, and we will consider what you canonically advance against him to be ratified by the Lord's authority. Given at the Lateran, 17th March.

---

[416] Source: monastic archives, cf. cartularies CD. Date: 17th March, 1150 or 1153; see discussion in Holtzmann, *Papsturkunden in England,* ii, no. 63 and Blake, p. 344, n. 1. The text in angle brackets is omitted by the *Liber Eliensis* mss. but found in the cartularies.

[417] Following the reading of CDEO: *tibi scripta.*

96. That a certain man appropriated the vill of Stetchworth for himself by fraud.[418]

So, as time went on, the Enemy of the human race stirred up a storm against the holy city of Ely. For he never ceases to pour out upon it the poison of his malice and to drive it, by the javelins of wickedness, off-track towards a revival of the hazards of the temptations, and he attempts to eject it from the citadel of the love of God. He does so with the objective that Christ's people may always have something against which to wage war, in accordance with the saying of the apostle that 'all who desire to live a godly life in Christ are to suffer persecution',[419] and so will not be able to elevate their mind inwardly, since even the slightest adverse circumstances in outward life all the time cause them weariness.

And, in point of fact, there was sent to them an adversary from near at hand, someone who used to take food with them at their table, a cleric called Henry, the son of a former archdeacon of the district of Cambridge, who, however, had now been deposed. This Henry was an irreligious man, a plotter of crime. He troubled the monks of Ely in many ways; he imposed very heavy pressures upon them and harassed them for a long time with slanders, and finally was not afraid to seize their goods. He built up malice on the basis of iniquity by the treacherous machination of a venomous heart. He made a pit and fell into it.[420] To be specific, he assembled arguments for proving a falsehood and forged the seal which is the lord Pope's *bulla*, and with it stamped a number of spurious documents so that he could write 'how', 'when', 'what', 'to whom', or 'against whom', according to whatever, from time to time, suited his purposes. But he was arrested, brought before the bishop to stand trial, accused, found guilty of the charge, held, bound, consigned to prison; but afterwards he was rescued by Archbishop Theobald. And soon, freed as he was from unlawful oppression and from the atrociousness of the dungeon, he brought a false charge against Bishop Nigel. With the Pope's consent, he summoned him to give answer promptly[421] about the allegations which he was audaciously making against him in the presence of everyone. For the archbishop and Hilary of Chichester had been

---

[418] Source: resumption of narrative on the episcopacy of Nigel. It seems a near-certainty, on the basis of chapter 45 and the uniform character of much of the prose-narrative since then, that *LE* iii, with the exception of materials from miracle-collections and documents from the archives, had a single narrative source for the episcopacy of Nigel, and that its author was the monk Richard, who is said in this chapter also to have compiled a separate *historia* of the Stetchworth case.

[419] Cf. 2 Timothy 3.12; perhaps read *patientur* ('shall suffer') in line with the Vulgate.

[420] Cf. Psalm 7.15.

[421] Reading conjecturally at p. 345.17, ed. Blake: *prompte* for *prope*.

presence of everyone. For the archbishop and Hilary of Chichester had been giving him assistance. They had helped to bring about all these actions on the reasoning that Bishop Nigel had brought about sedition in the kingdom by his repeated adulation of the insurrectionists, and, having been seduced by the faction-fighting of tricksters, seized the goods of his church, frittered them away, dispersed and put up for sale the estates of the place, despite the fact that his orders prohibited this. It was as a result of this that they were not only opposing him but also actively preparing means of attack and he, moreover, was still not at all confident of the king's friendship.

Hard pressed as he was, in this way, by difficulties on all sides, Bishop Nigel hoped to be able to evade yet greater dangers. On the advice and instruction of the aforementioned bishops and without consulting with the monks, he instated the cleric Henry, the enemy mentioned above, in the estate of Stetchworth, which he was asking for, his aim being to escape from this man's disgraceful action to establish his claim. This was against his vows and the authority of privileges and the statutory provisions of canon law. In connection with this, the monk Richard, the author of this work, committed to writing this history as well.[422] Undertaking the case and its business on behalf of the church, he alone of all men put up a resistance, and, through the name of the Lord, in the power of the Holy Spirit and all the saints, prevented the consensus of wicked men from winning the day, and called for the matter to be decided by the arbitration of the lord Pope, as the following letter intimates.

---

[422] Lat. *Ad hoc monacus Ricardus auctor huius operis et hanc hystoriam stilo commendavit.* For discussion, see Blake, p. 345 n. 6. It is implausible that we have here self-identification by the compiler, who always writes of Richard as an esteemed colleague (see *LE* iii. 44, 45, 101). But, in my view, the words in *LE* iii. 96 translated as 'this work' have to refer to a literary work: they cannot possibly refer to Richard's 'work' in pleading the brothers' cause in Rome, for there has as yet been no mention of this undertaking, and Bishop Nigel is the only person whose activities have been referred to in the immediately preceding passage. Possibly, *auctor huius operis* might mean 'instigator', rather than 'author' in the modern sense, of the *Liber Eliensis* project; though see *LE* i. 32 (title): *Oratio auctoris ad dominam suam . . . Ædeldredam*; iii. 27 (title): *Laus auctoris de miraculis sancte Æðelðrede que contigerunt temporibus Hervei episcopi.* On the other hand, 'this work', as D. J. Stewart, *Liber Eliensis* (1848), p. vi, argued, perhaps need not mean the *Liber Eliensis*: rather, the words might refer to the work by Brother Richard on the episcopate of Nigel which – there is reason to believe – was the source for this chapter as of many previous others, and then their implication would be that the historian of Nigel's times also wrote a separate 'history' of the Stetchworth case. The words referring to *Ricardus* could either be Richard's own (in the tradition of Julius Caesar's use of the third person in autobiographical narrative) or an interpolation by the compiler of *LE*. In the former case, we might surmise that Richard incorporated in his main history – and introduced with the words recorded in *LE* iii. 96 – an excursus containing what had originally been a separate collection of materials on the Stetchworth case. In the latter case, one would have to suppose that the compiler meant by *hoc opus*, 'the work before me' rather than 'the work which I am engaged in'.

BOOK III

97. A letter of the church of Ely to the lord Pope about the great oppression which had been inflicted upon it.[423]

To the lord and most blessed Supreme Pontiff Eugenius, the humble community of monks of the church of Ely gives greeting and the support of prayers with true obedience. May your blessed fatherly self know that continual and miserable exhaustion of our church, at first through usurpations of our estates and later by devastations by fire of our houses and our corn, compels us finally to place a complaint in the ears of your Holiness about a certain Henry, who was accused, also, on these charges in the presence of our bishop and with witnesses, and could not clear himself. To explain: once, this man, coming from your Majesty with letters, was not afraid to usurp for himself unlawfully an estate which had been in the possession of our church for two hundred years: Stetchworth, to be specific; and he did so for no other reason than for a military purpose and for secular uses, supported by we know not what mendacious documents,[424] ones which had absolutely not been heard of nor seen by us ever, except in as much as we have gathered from letters of yours that he presented the land and goods taken by himself to your Excellency for inspection by means of letters of confirmation which, even afterwards, we did not know had been forged, †due to the fact that,†[425] on returning once more from your Paternal Presence, he reported back by referring to letters of your Majesty. All these things, however, were similarly based on trickery and he conceived dolour[426] in the same way as he had previously given birth to iniquity through the letters of confirmation, on the pretence that he had received them from Bishop Hervey and Prior Vincent and the community of the church. All of this is falsehood. And on the basis of these mendacious and invalid documents he is asking,[427] similarly, for an inheritance in the sanctuary of God – he who was the son of our archdeacon, born in adultery after his father was made archdeacon – and he is asking for the restoration of land

---

[423] Source: monastic archives, cf. cartulary G; probably, like the subsequent documents, this one was included in Richard's *Historia* of the Stetchworth case. The letter itself was certainly not written by Brother Richard, who is referred to by the letter-writer in the third person. The Latin both here and in chapter 103, a letter where Prior Alexander is specifically named as the chief sender, contains some rather odd expressions. Did the prior, a noted linguist (*LE* iii. 65), write it? Probably not. The letter in chapter 103 contains a third-person reference to 'the lord Prior' and names the cantor Salomon and one Brother Robert as responsible for it. Date: 25th April X December, 1150.
[424] The adjective *emendicatus* is used with the intended sense *ementitus*, 'forged', a rather strange usage, which however is paralleled in some reputable medieval authors.
[425] Reading conjecturally: *per quod* (cf. French *parce que*) for *per quos* at p. 346.15, ed. Blake.
[426] Lat. *concepit dolorem*: word-play harking back to previous use of *dolus* (trickery); for the imagery cf. also Isaiah 59.4 Vulgate: *conceperunt laborem et pepererunt iniquitatem*.
[427] An odd piece of Latin: *interrogat* is not normally used for 'request'.

427

concerning which he has never been instated, as all the clergy of our region and laymen with legal knowledge join in testifying. And moreover, he claims the right of possession for himself against the decrees of holy fathers and against the privileges of our church, specifically those of the blessed Victor, Paschal, Innocent and Lucius,[428] pontiffs of the Holy Roman See, and of other bishops, and also privileges of kings of England, from the time of Edgar and in the times of a great many kings of that land, on the basis of an ancient right, and he claims it despite the fact that the Church of God has possessed it inviolately up until the present day, the aforesaid estate having been acquired thanks to the holy Archbishop Dunstan and the holy Bishop Æthelwold from the aforesaid glorious King Edgar, and specifically constituted for the victualling of the monks of the church.[429] Moreover the ancient customs of the lands and the new ordinances concerning the revenues of these same lands of the church,[430] set down as they have been in writing, join in testifying to these facts. On the basis of these false claims, to be sure, the hand of many people, seeking their own interests rather than those of Jesus Christ, has long weighed down on us in no light way.

To explain: in connection with this, we went to the lord Archbishop in search of help and justice, held meetings with him, and – not just once or twice, but often, on being summoned by him seemingly for this purpose – we even went on out-of-the-way journeys, not near by, but in very remote parts of England, and finally we came to Harrow,[431] a vill, that is, of the lord Archbishop. And there, on Rogation Day,[432] not without pressing need, we summoned that cleric Henry, the enemy of our church, before your presence, with a view to the ultimate help afforded by your mercy, on *Letare Ierusalem* Sunday {the fourth Sunday in Lent}, to make answer on charges of unlawful appropriation of an ancient possession of theirs and false pretences, our intermediary being Dom Richard, a monk of ours, a man of upright life and honourable demeanour, a monk since childhood. For we are now incurring many losses, not knowing by what favour that enemy of our church has been protected in the sight of the courtiers of our lord Archbishop; for he had already extorted many things from us, which were speciously represented as losses of his own, while we always made objections and denials, because no one from amongst us has ever taken or received or usurped anything from his property or from him.

---

[428] See *LE* ii. 93; iii. 5, 56, 85.

[429] Edgar's privilege *LE* ii. 5 provides for future acquisitions in aid of the monks' food and clothing, but, according to ii. 66–7, Stetchworth was not acquired until after Edgar's death.

[430] See *LE* iii. 26, 54.

[431] Lat. *Heres*; see Blake's note *ad loc.*

[432] 25th April, the Major Rogation Day; see entries on the Rogation Days in the *Catholic Encyclopedia* and Cross, *Oxford Dictionary of the Christian Church*. Expert correspondents assure me that Blake was wrong to date Rogation Day, 1150, to 8th May.

Meanwhile, the lord Archbishop came into our province, to the house of St Edmund, where Henry was questioned, on these matters and at our behest, by many persons of religion. This was so that, at least in that province in which his estate and the property at issue is situated, the archbishop would become aware of the truth from Henry's neighbours and fellow-provincials. And we were still asking for the letters authorizing our summons, even though we painstakingly asked for them within the five-day limit, and what we were requesting in these was no favour except the simple power[433] and means of making the summons, because we heard that our adversary had already received his letters authorizing the appeal[434] and letters of commendation. And when, in fact, he had been diligently sought out with a request concerning this matter, we finally obtained what we wanted for Henry and ourselves on a stated day, on the aforementioned estate, in the presence of neighbours and fellow-provincials, judges being given to us, in addition, on behalf of the archbishop: the lord Bishop of Norwich and the Abbot of St Edmund's, both of them being in the neighbourhood of his lands and themselves neighbours of the people of the aforesaid vill. Many came there from the diocese of Norwich and many from the diocese of Ely, and people from the neighbourhood were summoned, and they came to examine the truth of the matter regarding the claim contested between the church of Ely and the aforementioned Henry, concerning the vill of Stetchworth. And indeed, on the joint testimony of these people – and {this was} because they were raised and reared in this same vill and in its neighbourhood over a long time-span – they united in testifying that he never had any legal right in respect to it or had in any way, lawfully or unlawfully, gained possession of it, as can be ascertained from the letters of the lord Bishop of Norwich and the Abbot of St Edmund's conveyed to your fatherly self and the archbishop. This Henry therefore, protected by the letters and support of his people, with we know not what dispensation and favour from the archbishop – but may God see it and judge it – went ahead before the day of our summons. May the Lord preserve your Holiness for us.

98. A letter of the Bishop of Norwich to the lord Pope on behalf of the church of Ely.[435]

To the most holy lord and father Eugenius, the Supreme Pontiff, William, unworthy priest of the church of Norwich sends greeting and unfeignedness

---

[433] Reading with E: *virtutem* (p. 347.19, ed. Blake).

[434] Lat. *apostolos* (p. 347.20), a recognized technical term for such letters.

[435] Source: Stetchworth archive, collected by Brother Richard, cf. cartulary G; document printed in Holtzmann, *Papsturkunden in England*, ii, no. 62. Date: 25th April X December, 1150; see Blake, Appendix C.

of obedience. In view of the fact that we know that mercy and justice thrive in the Apostolic See and we see it to be a gathering-place frequented[436] by everyone thirsting for justice, as it were, at the bowels of maternal devotion, we supplicate your Excellency on bended knees with respect to the intolerable wearing-down of the church of Ely: may justice come its way, so that its innocence may not be put at risk. We have briefly mentioned this in advance to your paternal self, because a troublesome business has arisen against the interests of this same church – a church of fine devotion and honourable demeanour – concerning an ancient and time-honoured property-holding, confirmed as belonging to that church by papal privileges and firmly assigned to the purposes of those serving God in that place. And since the facts about this matter which have come to our notice ought not to be hidden from your Holiness, we inform your Excellency that, at the command of the Archbishop of Canterbury, the Abbot of St Edmund's and I were appointed judges to enquire into the dispute between the said church of Ely and a certain cleric Henry, in a certain manor of that church in respect to which the cleric in question claimed legal entitlement. There, on the testimony of a great number of respectable persons, monks as well as clerics and also lay people, we learnt that the aforementioned cleric had never at any time possessed the said land or had any legal right: rather, what they said with one voice was that he had perpetrated this false claim of his on the strength of misappropriated seals, and had based his pretences on forged letters. Commending to your paternal self the honourable and religious character of the conveyor of these present letters, the monk Richard, we beg on his behalf that you give him a full hearing on the business of his church as may seem pleasing to your Holiness, because in our sight and in his church he has been well-recommended for a long time and is someone on whose words we are not doubtful about placing reliance. May your Holiness fare well.

99. On the same matter, a letter of the archbishop to the lord Pope on behalf of the church of Ely.[437]

To his most loving lord and father by the grace of God, the Supreme Pontiff Eugenius: Theobald, minister of the church of Canterbury sends greeting and all obedience along with the highest devotion. We have carried out with due veneration the command of your Holiness with respect to the case contested between Henry and the men of Ely and we have endeavoured to the best of our abilities to bring it to pass. Consequently, we and our venerable brother Hilary, Bishop of Chichester, summoned both parties before our presence with respect to this case and heard it. When we had done so, Richard, a monk

---

[436] Reading conjecturally at p. 348.6, ed. Blake: *frequentari* for *frequentare*.

[437] Source: Stetchworth archive, cf. cartulary G; document printed in Holtzmann, *Papsturkunden in England*, ii, no. 67. Date, in Blake's view: 25th April X December, 1150.

of Ely, summoned him to a hearing before you, concerning the forgery which he engaged in concerning you, and the unlawful appropriation of an ancient and long-standing property-holding of theirs, confirmed by the privileges of apostolic fathers as assigned to the purposes of the monks of that church. But now, referring the hearing of the case in all respects and by all means to your Majesty, in view of what came to our attention concerning these matters, we leave it to you. May your Holiness fare well for all eternity.

100. The lord Pope's reply to the archbishop providing for protection of the church of Ely.[438]

Eugenius, Bishop, servant of the servants of God, to his venerable brothers, Theobald, Archbishop of Canterbury and Legate of the Apostolic See and Hilary, Bishop of Chichester: greeting. From an inspection of the letters which your brotherly selves have despatched[439] to us, we have understood that Joseph wished to prosecute Henry in your presence on a charge of forgery. We have also taken carefully into consideration, in respect to these same letters, the fact that you did not in the least acknowledge the witnesses whom Joseph produced with a view to securing his conviction, because of their lack of worth, and the fact that you adjudged Henry <cleared by> compurgation on this charge.[440] And since these and other things which are contained in these letters removed †<. . . >†[441] from his undertaking, he summoned the prosecutor himself to our presence. So, after both parties had been presented for our inspection, we heard the case carefully from both points of view and recognized clearly that Joseph could not proceed with the prosecution in question. Therefore, because we do not wish this same Henry to be importuned by Joseph, we are sending him back to you, so that you may accept his compurgation and release him in all respects from the impeachment of this same Joseph, and cause the charters to be restored to him which were taken away from him because of the charge brought against him. Indeed, after a short while, when you have summoned both parties to your presence and carefully heard the arguments on this side and on that, and have sufficiently examined them, you are to bring to an end the dispute which exists between Henry and the brothers of Ely concerning the estate of Stetchworth, which they have claimed to pertain to their own use and food-

---

[438] Source: Stetchworth archive, cf. cartulary G; document printed in Holtzmann, *Papsturkunden in England*, ii, no. 64. Date: 22nd December, 1150; at Ferentino.

[439] Adopting the emendation *destinavit* for *estimavit*, found first in ms. O.

[440] Reading conjecturally at p. 349.17, ed. Blake for *purgationem: purgatum* or *purgatione <quietu>m.*

[441] Taking the second *que* in p. 349.18, ed. Blake to be corrupt and in need of conjectural replacement.

supply. You are to bring it to an end, with no appeal allowed, by a termination according with canon law, and by the direction of the Lord. In addition, we issue a mandate to your discerning self, that you are to send Archdeacon William, who is recognized to be the instigator of the dispute, to our presence. Given at Ferentino, 22nd December.

101. How prudently and consistently our brother Richard exerted himself in Rome concerning the hardships of the monastery.[442]

It is indeed the case that the Brother Richard referred to, someone worthy of all veneration, has performed good and faithful service in all his duties. Wise steward that he is, he has distributed the communal wealth in a fitting and discerning manner, as he has known it to be expedient for each person, in accordance with the need of the particular individuals; as a result he is the recipient of favour and gratitude. Moreover,[443] when he was at the Roman curia, he had so vigilantly set about his task that, as a result of his obvious virtue and pleasantly phrased speech, he deservedly succeeded, more than the others had, in gaining access to the Supreme Pontiff's presence and means of engaging him in conversation. As a result, in a state of great joy, he had a talk with him about the needs and discomfitures of his church and, by his complaints, he made it clear,[444] particularly, that dignities and liberties had fallen and slipped away from the monastery through the detestable voraciousness of greedy and envious people, resulting in the fact that they were engaging in trickery against its servants. They wished to bring to naught the beauty of the eternal liberty of the temple of God. In addition, the Archdeacon of Cambridge kept on inflicting hardships over and over again, and unlawfully received customary dues with respect to churches of the Isle which are recognized[445] as having belonged, from ancient times, to the mother church. Furthermore,[446] his complaint about these matters, and his claim, were acknowledged by the Supreme Pontiff of the Roman See and then he returned, encouraged in his opposition to the audacity of wicked men by this authorization of the lord Pope himself. Moreover, on the strength of this exceedingly mighty protection, he demonstrated at a well-attended synod in London that his church of Ely ought to receive back what

---

[442] Source: eulogistic comments about Brother Richard, presumably by the compiler of *LE*, introduce material from the latter's Stetchworth *historia*, which may be followed *verbatim* in the chapters that follow, a collection of documentary sources relating to the Stetchworth case.

[443] Reading with E: *sed et,* a form of conjunction much favoured by the compiler of *LE*.

[444] Translating as if the text read: *cum eo contulit sermonem et conquerendo ostendit,* with transposition of *et* from after *contulit* (p. 350.13, ed. Blake).

[445] Reading *noscuntur* (p. 350.18, ed. Blake, cf. line 29).

[446] The text is translated as if the reading were *sed et,* not just *sed* at p. 350.18, ed. Blake.

were its rightful belongings, this being the final decision of the Apostolic Father's instruction and judgement.

102. Once again, an instruction of the lord Pope to the effect that the monks of Ely should have possession of the churches of the Isle in peace.[447]

Eugenius, servant of the servants of God to his venerable brother Theobald, Archbishop of Canterbury and Legate of the Apostolic See: greeting and apostolic blessing. The conveyor of these present writings, Richard, a monk of Ely, has come to our presence and complained that William, Archdeacon of Cambridge, has unlawfully received customary dues from the churches of the Isle which are recognized as belonging to the mother church, and is inflicting hardships and also extorting money in respect to holy chrism, and is also appropriating and withholding from these same monks of Ely their churches of Hauxton and Newton. Hence, issuing a mandate, we give instructions that you bring it about for the monks in question that their churches be restored to them in their entirety, and that they have possession of them untroubled by that man's oppression, because it is our wish for every individual that what belongs to him should be held by him. Moreover, if he is found to have received anything for holy chrism, he is to be judged guilty of simony. Given at Ferentino, 22nd December.

103. On the same matter, a letter of the community of the church of Ely sent to the lord Pope.[448]

To their venerable Lord, Eugenius the Supreme Pontiff, Prior Alexander and the entire community of the church of Ely: all manner of submission with the highest devotion. We know well from recollection that it has reached the ears of your Holiness by whatsoever fluctuations of unjust litigation our church has now for a long time been vexed. And since we are aware from our endurance of heavy sufferings that, owing to obstruction by Satan, these things have not yet reached your ear[449] – yet daily we are more and more overwhelmed. Therefore, Reverend Father and Lord, in whose presence the examination of truth flourishes and to whom the evident existence of falsehood is deservedly repellent, we once more pour out – through these

---

[447] Source: Stetchworth archive, cf. cartulary G. Date: 22nd December, 1150; at Ferentino.

[448] Source: Stetchworth archive, cf. cartulary G. On stylistic grounds, it seems certain that it was written by the same Latinist as the letter in chapter 97. Prior Alexander is named as the sender, along with the whole community, in the opening greetings, but 'our cantor, Salomon' and one Brother Robert are named as intermediaries responsible for conveying their brothers' complaints. Date: Lent, 1151 X June, 1152.

[449] Reading conjecturally at p. 351.11, ed. Blake: *aurem* for *auram*, though the error might be authorial. The whole sentence is bafflingly constructed.

our brothers, our cantor, Salomon, and Robert, honourable men, satisfactorily useful to our church – our miserable and truly lamentable complaint about the fraudulent[450] business whereby Henry, an archdeacon's son, is ceaselessly harassing our church in contravention of justice. For who can tolerate the goading of such a wicked and such an unjust act of persecution? Our lord and bishop, a venerable man, who has been accustomed to provide us with assistance in the aforementioned case with his ingrained goodness, is notwithstanding unable to support us sufficiently by his hand alone, since he scarcely has the breath to heave a sigh, so many are the obstacles in his way, and of such injustice. What need for many words? If we are not to obtain compassion by swift, effective action on the part of your Holiness, truly, the religious community of our church, struggling as it is with a scarcity of household goods, will inevitably have to be dispersed. However, the case of the aforementioned Henry is weak and feeble, and from the outset up until now has involved falsity. That it is the generally agreed view of the English Church[451] that, at the foundation of the church of Ely, established in honour of the blessed Peter, the venerable King of the English, Edgar, gave the manor of Stetchworth to this same church for the particular purposes of the monks, is a fact questioned by none of our people.[452] Moreover, that this grant was corroborated and confirmed by privileges of Roman pontiffs – Victor, Paschal, Innocent and Lucius of good memory – is transparently established even by our adversary. This same man, under extremely strong compulsion from the goad of wickedness, rendered the aforementioned guarantee of the security[453] of the holy men void. Trusting in his own authority, without judicial consultation, he drove away a monk of our church from that place by armed force, and stole this same vill from us by violence. Now, indeed, having no confidence in the truth of his case, he is looking for many diversions,[454] his aim being not to reply to us, in accord with the tenor of the letters of your Holiness, in the presence of the judges appointed, about the rightful ownership of this same manor. For he is demanding from us, on sworn surety, moveable and immoveable stock which he falsely claims to have lost through our doing, advancing perjuries by the same people who, not long before, in the presence of the venerable man William, Bishop of Norwich and our lord Bishop,

---

[450] Here (p. 351.14, ed. Blake) *dolosa (fraudulent)* may be a mistake for *dolorosa* (sad).

[451] Reading with EG: *Anglice ecclesie.*

[452] The reading at p. 351.28, ed. Blake, is *nostrarum* = 'of our women', which would have surprised the Pope! Presumably the intended reading was a masculine form, *nostrorum*, or *nostratium.*

[453] 'Guarantee of . . . security': Lat. *cautio.*

[454] Lat. *divortia*: 'forks in the road'.

Nigel of Ely and the greatest possible number of abbots and before a multitude of clerics and laity present there, gave their oaths that Henry never had, or ought to have, any right to the manor of Stetchworth. For the rest, the restoration of charters which is being demanded of us seems to have nothing to do with us, since the lord Prior and the monk Richard, who were the only men from among us who had been involved in the case previously, confirmed on oath at a well-attended synod, that nothing by way of evil trickery had taken place regarding the charters which Henry claims to have been genuine but lost by him. But now, in view of the fact that we know that mercy and justice thrive in the Apostolic See, we supplicate your Excellency on bended knees with respect to this intolerable wearing-down of our church, to the end that justice[455] may come its way so that its innocence may not be put at risk. May the Lord Almighty preserve your Holiness.

104. An instruction of the lord Pope to the Bishop of Hereford for the aid of the church of Ely.[456]

Eugenius, Bishop, servant of the servants of God, to Gilbert, Bishop of Hereford: greeting and apostolic blessing. More or less the whole of England knows, because of the atrociousness of the wrongs committed, of the case which has already long been the subject of vexed litigation between the monks of Ely and Henry, and we do not believe it has failed to come to your notice. Further to this: after the restitution of the vill of Stetchworth to this said Henry, which was made in the presence of our venerable brothers Theobald, Archbishop of Canterbury, Legate of the Apostolic See and Hilary, Bishop of Chichester, the aforesaid monks, in fact, summoned the same Henry to an audience with us in respect to forgery of our letters. Both parties, in fact, came to us, and at that time, since the monks of Ely were quite incapable of proceeding with their prosecution of him, this Henry made a complaint to us against them that, after he had set off in haste on his way to us, he was robbed of his belongings in that same vill by retainers of these very monks. In view of this, we referred the case to our aforesaid brother, the Archbishop of Canterbury, for trial. But when the issue of restitution was being discussed and Henry had prepared himself to prove that robbery had been perpetrated against himself by retainers of the monks, the monks once more summoned the same Henry to an audience with us, saying that they were victims of oppression. Finally, on their return to our presence, because of the fact that neither party had come prepared, the case could not be brought

---

[455] Deleting *in* before *iustitia* at p. 352.18, ed. Blake, in view of the parallel formulation at p. 348.7.

[456] Source: Stetchworth archive, cf. cartularies CDG. Date: 15th June, 1152; at Segni.

to its required conclusion in our presence. Putting our trust in the integrity of your honour, therefore, we have deemed it fitting to refer the case to your scrutiny and for it to be terminated with a suitable conclusion, and through these present writings we command you, when both parties have been summoned before your presence at a suitable place and time, to bring about the complete restoration to the oft-mentioned Henry of whatever he may by lawful means be able to prove to have been stolen from him by retainers of the same monks, or by others at their instigation, after the restitution to himself of the aforementioned vill had been brought about. When this has been done, if the monks of Ely should wish to bring an action on the issue of ownership, you are to hear it carefully and, with justice as intermediary, define it. Given at Segni, 15th June.

105. Another instruction of the lord Pope to the effect that the monks of Ely should hold peaceably the churches of their lands.[457]

Eugenius, Bishop, servant of the servants of God, to his venerable brother Theobald, Archbishop of Canterbury and Legate of the Apostolic See: greeting and apostolic blessing. At times when people whose attention is directed to divine services under the observance of a rule of life have rights belonging to them unlawfully stolen from them, it is incumbent upon us to take all the more care that they should recover what is their right at least by judicial intervention, in as much as they are not very capable of expending effort on disputes, given that their proposed aim in life impedes this. We have recently received a complaint, on behalf of our sons, the Prior and monks of the church of Ely, that William the Archdeacon holds, in despite of the monks, the churches of Hauxton and Newton, Philip de *Meisi*, the church of Melbourn and the cleric Wulfweard, the church of Lakenheath – churches which had been assigned for the victualling of these same monks; that Nicholas, a chaplain, has received the church of Wentworth and Joseph, a priest, the chapel of Stuntney, without the acquiescence of the monks and are having the presumption to keep charge of them, though these churches had been designated[458] for the lighting of the aforesaid monastery. Since, therefore, the presumptuous action which is being taken against the Church of God,[459] in contravention of canonical sanctions and the rule of law, needs

---

[457] Source: monastic archives, cf. cartularies CDG. The charters in this and the next two chapters do not relate specifically to the Stetchworth case, but presumably were included in Brother Richard's dossier. Date: 5th February, 1152; at Segni.

[458] The translation assumes an accidental mistake in the document at p. 354.4, ed. Blake: *deputatas*, rather than *deputata*, would be more grammatical.

[459] Again, carelessness in the writing of the document has resulted in an error in all mss. at p. 354.6, where Blake prints a conjecture: *presumitur*.

to be called to a halt by the vigorous enactment of justice, we issue a mandate to your fraternal self, by these present writings, that you are to summon to your presence all the people referred to, along with some of the aforementioned brothers, and then with diligence hear and examine the cases at issue, and in this way arrive at a decision[460] about them, by common consent or judicial verdict, so that the monks to whom we have been repeatedly referring may thus recover their rights by your endeavour and not be obliged thereafter to make a complaint for lack of justice. Given at Segni, 5th February.

106. A charter of Archbishop Theobald on the churches of the monks of Ely.[461]

Theobald, by the grace of God, Archbishop of Canterbury, Primate of the English and Legate of the Apostolic See, to all children of Holy Church: greeting. The case which was contested between the monks of Ely and Archdeacon William of *Laventuna*, concerning the churches of Hauxton and Newton, has been settled by means of judicial proceedings in accordance with the settlement to which the charter of the monks bears witness, and we deem it ratified and confirm it, saving the monks' annual rent which the said archdeacon is to pay to them every year, namely ten shillings *per annum*. The cases of the other churches, too – specifically the church of Melbourn, held by Philip *de Maisi*, who is to pay them five shillings annually, and those of Lakenheath and Undley, in respect of which Wulfweard is to pay five shillings annually – we have settled by common consent on the terms that the aforesaid men are to keep their holdings for their lifetime in the name of the monks, and that after their deaths they are to return to serving the purposes of the monks. Exceptions are made of a third *garba* of Lakenheath and two *garbae* of Undley, which the monks keep in their possession. Also, from the chapel of Stuntney, Joseph is to pay each year twelve shillings at the four quarter-days. After the demise of this particular man Joseph, the aforesaid chapel is to return to providing the lighting of the church of Ely. For indeed, the matter was determined along similar lines before our time. We ratify and confirm the agreement made between the monks themselves and Nicholas, Chaplain of Wentworth, exactly as the charter of our brother, Nigel, Bishop of Ely, attests to its having been made. Witnesses: Thomas *de Lund'* and Philip the chancellor and William de Vere and Peter the scribe. Farewell. At Teynham.

---

[460] Reading at p. 354.10, ed. Blake, with CD: *decidas*.

[461] Source: monastic archives, cf. cartularies DGM; printed in Saltman, *Theobald, Archbishop of Canterbury*, pp. 321–2, no. 100. Date: Teynham, 1152.

107. Again, a charter of the same archbishop to the effect that the monks of Ely are rightfully to hold the churches of the Isle.[462]

Theobald, by the grace of God, Archbishop of Canterbury and Legate of the Apostolic See and Primate of the English, to his venerable brother, Nigel, Bishop of Ely and all faithful people: greeting. <In respect to>[463] the case which used to be disputed between the men of Ely and William, Archdeacon of Cambridge – by a change of name 'of Ely' – on the matter of the archdeaconry: on the basis of mandates from the lord Pope Eugenius and the intervening transaction, the same William shall hold and shall have customs from the churches of the Isle which are recognized as pertaining to the mother church, and shall possess them in the name of the monks, paying them an annual ten-shilling rent, and he shall do this likewise in respect to the churches of Hauxton and Newton, tendering an annual sum to them, and after his death all these things are to revert to the purposes of the monks. For, concerning his other churches, received in accordance with canon law, †these were <the decisions and judgements made before>†, and this is the decision and judgement we make now, with our authorization.[464] Farewell.

108. A letter of Gilbert, Bishop of Hereford, to the lord Pope, occasioned by excessive oppression of the church of Ely.

To his venerable father and lord, the Supreme Pontiff Eugenius, Brother Gilbert, minister of the church of Hereford gives the love of a pious well-wisher and the dutifulness of a humbly obedient servant. With respect to the case delegated to us by your Munificence, concerning Henry and the monks of Ely, we report, Father, to your Highness in this present writing on the proceedings conducted in our presence. Acknowledgement of your letters was given in a statement presented by the monks, but by them alone; there was none at all from Henry. We then summoned the parties, following the procedure set out in your mandate, designating, so we hoped, a convenient place, Warwick, and 23rd September as the date. They presented themselves there on that precise day but, as we were unable to attend, being prevented by an emergency, we fixed upon 25th September, at St Albans, clearly a place easy of access for them, but remote from us. When we had taken our seat there, on that exact day, to give them a hearing, Henry said that he had been put under pressure by our two urgent summonses, and for this reason had

---

[462] Source: monastic archives, cf. cartulary G; Saltman, *Theobald, Archbishop of Canterbury,* pp. 323, no. 101. Date: 22nd December, 1150 X early 1152.

[463] Reading at p. 355.12, ed. Blake : *<In> causa* . . . (cf. p. 355.25).

[464] The Latin is elliptical: at least a phrase meaning 'were adjudged lawful', or the like, seems to be required after *canonice susceptis* (p. 355.19, ed. Blake).

arrived not at all ready to plead. Consequently, so that there should not be a protracted dispute about place and time in addition to the business, we yielded to the will of the two parties, and because we specified Northampton as the place,[465] and {25th November}, the octave of the feast of blessed Martin, was requested by both parties as the date, we now took our seat on that exact day in the specified place, and when the parties themselves had presented themselves, we proceeded with the hearing of the case in the following manner.

Your letters were read out in their presence, including as they do in their mandate the following order: that we 'are to cause to be restored to Henry in its entirety whatever he may by lawful means be able to prove to have been stolen from him by retainers of the same monks or by others at their instigation, after the restitution to himself of this vill' – the one at issue – 'had been brought about'. After these words had been read through, the case set out by Henry was as follows: 'Whereas I could legitimately ask for three hundred pounds of silver, what, in fact, I am asking to be restored to me on the authority of this mandate – so as to conduct myself with greater moderation – is two hundred pounds, because I am ready to prove on the testimony of these twenty witnesses that this was the amount stolen from me after the restitution.' The twenty witnesses produced did, in fact, assert that a loss of this amount had been inflicted on him, as will be stated in what follows. In response to these claims the monks said: 'The restitution which marks the beginning of the period from which restoration of stolen goods to you is pending, was made to you at the hand of the lord Bishop of Ely on the quarter-day around the time of the feast of St Pancratius {12th May}, two years and a few months ago. The property-holding at issue is one with few resources, so that you yourself, in the presence of the lord Pope, represented it as worth – at an excessively high valuation – one hundred shillings. Hence, the brief time-span and the meagreness of the estate make it plain that you are being unjust, and that your petition is <unjust>.'[466]

Henry in response said: 'A restitution was indeed made to me at the time of which you speak by the hand of the lord Bishop of Ely, but in addition, long before this, namely in the middle of Lent, the vill in question was restored to me on the authority of the lord Archbishop of Canterbury and the lord Bishop of Chichester. Hence, I am petitioning for the restoration of things taken from me not only after the latest restitution but after the first.' When, in fact, we enquired of Henry the extent of the loss he incurred in the intervening period, he valued the loss in the intervening period at fifty pounds, the witnesses agreeing with this. Following this up, the monks said: 'The lord Pope in his letter refers expressly only to the restitution which was

---

[465] Reading conjecturally at p. 356.9, ed. Blake: *quia loc<um> statui<mus> Norðhamtunam.*

[466] Adopting Blake's supplement at p. 356.24.

made to you "in the presence of" the lord Archbishop of Canterbury and the lord Bishop of Chichester, not to a restitution, if there were any, made "by" them; and †<it is clear>†[467] that the restoration referred to is the one which the lord Bishop of Ely made to you in their presence. On the authority of this rescript, you are not right in petitioning for any goods to be restored to you except those stolen from you after this restitution.'

Henry in response said: 'Granted that the lord Pope in his letter, when appointing a judge in the preamble, refers to a specific restitution, he does not, however, specify any particular one when he goes on to attach his mandate. Hence, because the concluding part of the mandate does not make an exception of any restitution, it is giving instructions that the goods stolen after the restitution about which I am speaking should also be restored to me. Again, by the same right that the lord Pope was able and obliged to give instructions that the goods stolen from me after this latest restitution be returned to me, similarly he was able and obliged to give instructions that those stolen from me after the restitution about which I am speaking be returned to me. It follows that, if my petition for them is ruled out, that is undoubtedly to depart a long way from the verdict of the lord Pope.' The monks in response said: 'Given that the lord Pope makes his meaning clear in the prologue, the same express meaning is to be expected where the conclusion of the mandate is concerned, in view of the continuity of the letter in a unitary format. For authority holds[468] that a word once set down, even if it is not repeated in a discourse, is frequently none the less taken as understood in subsequent utterances. Hence, since the preceding explicit utterance is to be linked with the subsequent mandate as well, your petition for fifty pounds, already referred to, is negated.'

The monks were insisting, therefore, that we should make a pronouncement in favour of them where this point was concerned; then there was the consideration that defendants are more deserving of favour than prosecutors, and then again, a church which they said was being caused serious hardship by the petition for such a large sum, was deserving of favour. In spite of these considerations, however, we paid attention to Henry's complaints and indulged them by conceding the instruction for restitution. Moreover, because something which has been granted as an indulgence in favour of someone ought not to be twisted around again so as to harm him, we did not in any way limit the stipulation of your agreement and also allowed, on the authority of your writ, his petition for the aforementioned fifty pounds, if he could prove that they had been stolen from him, and that this was after the restitution made to him.

In response to this, the monks said: 'Hitherto, Henry, we have succeeded

---

[467] Reading conjecturally after *exprimit* at p. 357.2, ed. Blake, e.g.: <et li>que<t> quia . . .

[468] Lat. *auctoritas habet.*

in fending off your petition for fifty pounds, because we state plainly that the restitution of which you speak never took place.' But since Henry produced twenty witnesses in order †to clinch the matter†,[469] a hearing was given to them. All, one after the other, gave their testimony in the following manner, not adding or taking away or changing anything: 'I testify that, after the restitution of the vill of Stetchworth made to my lord, Henry, in the middle of Lent, two years, and several months of this year, ago, that vill has suffered depreciation of two hundred pounds through the contrivance and action of the monks of Ely and their retainers.' But when we enquired how they knew that the restitution had been made to Henry in mid-Lent, they answered: 'We certainly do not know if he was given restitution by the archbishop, or by any judge, but one thing we do know is that, at that time, he entered into the vill in question and easily persuaded us that he had been given restitution by the lord Archbishop of Canterbury and the lord Bishop of Chichester.'

The monks in reply said: 'We reject all your witnesses, Henry. In the first place, because they have presented themselves as witnesses of a certain restitution made to you and now, a moment later, have confessed that they are completely ignorant whether the restitution was ever made to you. In the second place, because, although they are not slaves, even so they are of the social standing which is closest to slavery, namely, that of tenants in villeinage,[470] who can be sold and granted with the land, and are to such an extent in subjection to you that they can be compelled by the power that you command over them to do whatever may have been your desire. In the third place, on the ground of the quality of their words and testimony: for such is their uniformity that they do not differ by a syllable and hence they are seen to be standing up to give testimony instructed and suborned, rather than conscious of the truth. In the fourth place: though they are witnesses for you of a loss that has been inflicted, and what has been stolen from you is not coined money, they make no division of the loss into a list of specific items so that one would be given to understand that they had a certain knowledge of the matter at issue. In the fifth place: on the reasoning that, although they assert that the loss was inflicted on you by us and our retainers, they do not, however, specify any of our retainers by their names or by any definite clues to their identity. If they were to specify them, we would prove their innocence where these charges are concerned. Indeed, we are prepared to prove that Godard, the only person whom they name, was, at the time of the inflicting of the loss, in no way subject to us.'

Henry's reply to these points was: 'It is not to the point to reject my witnesses on the strength of these objections since, even though they do not

---

[469] An attempt to render the reading of G: *invectionem*, which E changes to *eivictionem* (p. 357.26, ed. Blake).

[470] Perhaps we should read, at p. 357.40, ed. Blake, not *asscripta* but *asscripte* (agreeing with *conditionis*) or *asscripti scilicet glebe* . . .

make a division of the loss into specific items or identify by name those responsible for the loss, they are plainly "giving evidence" in accordance with the procedure specified in the letter of the lord Pope.' But, noticing that his witnesses were extremely hesitant about the restitution about which we were most particularly enquiring, Henry promised that, if a date were granted him, he would prove the point on which they were giving inadequate evidence – the matter of the lord Archbishop of Canterbury and the lord Bishop of Chichester. Consequently, to avoid a situation where truth might be at the mercy of obscurity, and a hasty verdict might overturn the just entitlement of Henry, if it in any sense existed, we named a date for him: {9th December}, the octave of the blessed Andrew, at London, a date on which there was to be a meeting of the lord Legate and his suffragans, for the monks were enduring serious hardship. This very day, taking our seat in London and inviting the lord Bishop of London to join us, we made ourselves available and, because Henry was presenting none of the individuals whom he had promised,[471] we made enquiries of the lord Legate, through the lord Bishop of London and other persons, to find out what he acknowledged about the oft-mentioned restitution. While he was not without recollection of the business transacted in his presence, he answered that he had never made the restitution to Henry of which he was speaking. Therefore, as Henry failed on this point, we absolved the monks of the oft-mentioned petition for fifty pounds which, from Henry's statements and reasoning, we discovered not to have been stolen after a restitution made to Henry. In fact, as the monks were demanding that a verdict be pronounced for them about the petition for the rest, that is, for one hundred pounds, we assisted the council of the wise[472] to pronounce our decision. Henry, not waiting for our verdict, made a summons to a hearing before you, naming 1st August. But the monks, expecting to be involved in protracted proceedings, called for a hearing before you at a date near *Quasimodo geniti*, {Low Sunday}, and placed upon us the burden of what they had enjoined.[473] May almighty God in Christ preserve for long ages your safety, long to benefit His Church, beloved father.

109. An instruction of the lord Pope to the effect that the monks of Ely are to receive back their property and hold it freely.[474]

Anastasius, Bishop, servant of the servants of God, to his venerable brothers Theobald, Archbishop of Canterbury and Legate of the Apostolic See and

---

[471] Following Blake's conjecture (p. 358.22): *promiserat* for *premiserat*.

[472] Lat. *sapientum consilio*.

[473] Reading conjecturally at p. 358.32, ed. Blake: *iniuncta nobis imposuere*.

[474] Source: Stetchworth archive, cf. cartulary G; document printed in Holtzmann, *Papsturkunden in England*, ii, no. 80. Date: 28th September, 1153.

Gilbert, Bishop of Hereford: greeting and apostolic blessing. We are obliged, as a consequence of the apostolic office laid upon us by God, to concern ourselves with the upkeep of churches and to provide attentively for the peace of the brothers who by the gift <of the faithful>,[475] exercise their soldiery within them. It is because of this that we have entrusted to your discerning judgement, for investigation and settlement by you, a long-contested dispute about a certain manor between the monks of Ely and the cleric Henry. Certainly our predecessor, Pope Eugenius of holy memory, entrusted the settlement of this very same case to you, our brother Gilbert, Bishop of Hereford. Because it could not be brought to an end in your presence by a suitable final verdict, owing to the interposition of an appeal, the aforesaid case was once more recalled for examination by the Apostolic See. And we have decided, in view of the fact that the aforesaid Henry in his prevarication – as is apparent from the nature of the timing of his appeal and from what followed – evaded your judgement by appealing, and did not in any way pursue his appeal, we have made the decision, on the basis of the shared consensus of our brothers – to preclude the possibility that leave to appeal might perhaps still appear to be available to him – that the monks of Ely are to be brought into possession of the manor about which there has been a long-contested dispute between them. We confirm your verdict absolving the church of Ely from the petition for the fifty pounds which the said Henry was claiming back from it, and we absolve the same church both from the petition for charters and from the petition for the hundred pounds which the same Henry was likewise claiming back from it. By means of the present writings, therefore, we issue a mandate to your fraternal selves that, on the authority of the Apostolic See, you are to bring the oft-mentioned monks into possession of the manor of Stetchworth, with the following conditions: that,[476] if the aforesaid Henry, should come within a year and put a guarantee of attendance and obedience into your hands, and if, after a lawful summons and the granting of a necessary stay of proceedings, the parties should be called into one another's presence, he is to enter into a court-case, and stay until its final verdict, and hear the verdict and, once it has been heard, obey it without the option of an appeal. It is to be permissible for him to recover in this way, in accordance with standard legal procedure, the aforementioned 'possession' of the manor, or the detainment of it, which he used to have previously, on the following condition: that, until the case in question is finalized, it is to be by no means permissible for him to usurp properties of this same manor or alienate them by any means. If by any

---

[475] Reading conjecturally at p. 359.3, ed. Blake e.g.: *et quieti fratrum in eis < fidelium> dono militantium.*

[476] In the text at p. 359.21f., ed. Blake, either *ut* or *quod* seems redundant, but deletion is not an option, because the same redundancy occurs in the parallel passage in the next chapter, p. 360.32f.

chance he should not wish[477] to do this, you are to restore the aforesaid manor to the oft-mentioned monks, with all right of appeal removed, to be their possession in perpetuity on the authority of the Apostolic See. Furthermore, as it is our wish to uphold the statutes of our predecessor Pope Eugenius of holy memory, if it should come about that the aforesaid Henry should be successful in this same lawsuit, then after Henry's death, the church of Ely is to have the oft-mentioned manor, in accordance with the decision of this same predecessor of ours, and, moreover, you are to cause this decision to be firmly upheld.

110. A mandate of the lord Pope to the chapter of Ely to the effect that they are at liberty to take possession of their property of Stetchworth.[478]

Anastasius, Bishop, servant of the servants of God, to his beloved sons the Prior and Brothers of the Monastery of Ely: greeting and apostolic blessing. Since we have undertaken the care of the Universal Church – responsibilities being conferred by God as it pleases Him – whenever any disagreement arises against any one of the churches, it is right that we should investigate it with the utmost diligence, so that they may not, through our neglect, incur any loss of their legal entitlement, nor be obliged to be exhausted by long prolongations of quarrelling brought about by deviousness on the part of the opposing party.[479] It is for this reason that – desiring as we do to bring about a suitable conclusion of the case which is known to have been in contention between you and the cleric Henry for a very long time, not without great weariness on the part of both sides – in the first place, we are confirming by an apostolic judgement[480] the verdict which is known to have been promulgated by our venerable brother, the Bishop of Hereford – who[481] undertook to try the case in accordance with the mandate of Eugenius, our predecessor of holy memory – concerning the fifty pounds which Henry was claiming back from you, and we sanction, in accordance with his verdict, that your church should remain permanently absolved from his claim regarding this. Secondly, it has been taken into account that[482] when, after the allegations of both parties had been sufficiently listened to and investigated,

---

[477] Reading with E: *noluerit* (p. 359.28, ed. Blake).

[478] Source: Stetchworth archive, cf. cartulary G; document printed in Holtzmann, *Papsturkunden in Enland*, ii, no. 79. Date: 28th September, 1153; at the Lateran.

[479] Adopting Holtzmann's conjecture, *partis* for *pacis*.

[480] Deleting *sed* at p. 360.13, ed. Blake, after Holtzmann.

[481] Reading, with Holtzman, *qui* for *quod* at p. 360.12, ed. Blake.

[482] 'It has been taken into account that . . .': Lat. simply: *quoniam*. The very long sentence, p. 360.15–28, ed. Blake, has been split up and slightly recast in this translation for the sake of clarity.

the aforementioned bishop was ready to promulgate his verdict with respect to the remaining hundred pounds, the oft-mentioned Henry made an appeal to the Apostolic See, with a view to escape rather than to legal proceedings, but, whereas you came on the pre-arranged date for this appeal, he himself did not come, and did not offer any excuse whatsoever. So, as it pertains to our office to put an end to the subterfuges of contending litigants, in the light of the full investigation conducted by us into the allegations of this same Henry about these same {hundred} pounds, on the basis of the written statements of the above-mentioned brother of ours, to whose scrutiny and examination they were subjected, and, in view of our finding that Henry utterly failed to provide proof concerning this matter and produced suspect witnesses, we absolve your church of his claim for one hundred and fifty pounds, and we judge that it remains from henceforth free and absolved with respect to these {hundred and fifty} pounds. And this is also our decision regarding the charters which the oft-mentioned Henry said ought to be restored to him by you, specifically: that he should engage no more in legal proceedings about their retrieval. In addition, since the aforesaid Henry has long been wearying your church with his subterfuges, and has in no way followed up his appeal, we have decided, in order to preclude the possibility that leave to appeal might seem to remain[483] any longer available to him, that you are to be put into possession of the manor of Stetchworth, with the proviso, however, that, if he should wish to enter into legal proceedings within the year, with a guarantee of his attendance and obedience[484] put into the hands of the designated judges, he is obliged to stay subject to their judgement until a verdict has finally been promulgated; <. . . >[485] he may rejoice in the restoration of the estate, but with the condition still imposed that, should he be unwilling to stay until the final judgement and hear it without making an appeal, he is to lose that same estate and have no opportunity any longer of retrieving it. Given at the Lateran, 28th September.

111. A charter of the Bishop of Hereford concerning the property returned to the monks of Ely.[486]

Brother Gilbert, minister of the church of Hereford, to all children of Holy Mother Church, beloved as you are to him in the Lord: the joys of peace and salvation. We have undertaken to make known to your discerning selves, by

---

[483] Taking *servare* at p. 360.31, ed. Blake to be an error for *servari* (cf. p. 359.13).

[484] Lat. *cautio*: that a 'guarantee of attendance and obedience to the court' is meant is shown by p. 361.16, ed. Blake.

[485] Marking a lacuna at p. 360.34, ed. Blake, after *debeat*. A clause seems lacking which would have expressed the notion, 'and then, if he should be successful in his appeal . . .'

[486] Source: Stetchworth archive, cf. cartularies GM. Date: after expiry of the deadline in September, 1154.

this present writ, the settlement of the case which has long been in contention between the monks of Ely and a cleric named Henry over the manor of Stetchworth, and which, after a while. was brought to an end by Pope Anastasius of good memory. Our object is to root out forthwith the outgrowths of an old lawsuit by means of the attestation of truth. The position is as follows:[487] since the lawsuit between the aforesaid monks and the previously mentioned cleric had been brought to an end, and since, following many appeals and prosecutions of appeals, they had made the most of their allegations in the presence of many judges and aired their differences as much as they wanted, everything was set out clearly in a report to the aforesaid Pope Anastasius, and the case was decided by him in the following manner. He decreed that the monks were to be put into possession of the said manor and, unless the aforesaid Henry should produce within a year a guarantee of attending and obeying a judicial hearing with respect to this same case, he judged that this same manor should be confirmed as belonging to the monks and their church in perpetuity. And he appointed the lord Theobald, Archbishop of Canterbury and ourselves as executors of the verdict thus given by himself. Obeying the apostolic mandate, therefore, we have inducted them into possession of the estate and because, now that a year has elapsed, we have heard nothing from Henry's side about the guarantee stipulated to him, we confirm that the aforesaid manor belongs to the church of Ely in perpetuity, of apostolic authority, and, by the same authority, we issue the instruction that they are to hold the manor released from every claim by Henry and his successors.

112. Again, a charter of the same Bishop; on what kind of terms he ejected the usurpers from the estate of the monks of Ely.[488]

Gilbert, by the grace of God Bishop of Hereford, to the cleric Henry: greeting. As you can remember, when you were standing in our presence at the command of the lord Pope in opposition to our brothers, the monks of Ely, over the manor of Stetchworth, you evaded the passing of judgement by interposing an appeal to the lord Pope. However, since you have not prosecuted your appeal, we remove you from the position of possessing the aforesaid manor by the authority and command of the lord Pope and put the monks of Ely into this same position of possessing it. If, on the other hand, you refuse to obey[489] our orders, know that you are to be bound by the sentence of anathema. Moreover, we send an official warning with apostolic

---

[487] Lat. simply: *itaque*.

[488] Source: Stetchworth archive, cf. cartularies GM. After September, 1154.

[489] Reading with G: *obtemperare*.

authority to you, Ralph and Roger and William de *Halstede*, who entered into this same estate on the authority of Henry, that you are to depart once more from this same estate without delay. And if you refuse to obey, you shall be bound by the same sentence of anathema and you shall never be absolved from it except on the authority of the lord Pope. Farewell.

113. A charter of Archbishop Theobald about the estate returned to the monks of Ely.[490]

Theobald, by the grace of God Archbishop of Canterbury, Primate of the English and Legate of the Apostolic See, to the cleric Henry and to Ralph and Roger and William de *Halstede*: greeting. In accordance with the tenor of a mandate of the lord Pope, which we have recently received, we invest the monks of the church of Ely with the manor of Stetchworth and we put them into possession, and invest them with possession, of it and we remove you, Henry, by the authority of the Apostolic See, from that manor and its appurtenances, and we prohibit the other men named previously from being intruders from henceforth with respect to that manor and from presuming to bring about any trouble for those brothers. Otherwise we shall bring an anathema against your persons and cause it to be rigidly observed. Farewell.

114. A charter of King Stephen, to the effect that the monks of Ely are at liberty to have possession of their vill of Stetchworth.[491]

King Stephen to Ralph de *Halstede* and Roger and William, his brothers, and William Fitz Baldwin: greeting. I instruct you that you are to let the Stetchworth estate of the monks of Ely be in peace and neither intrude yourself further in any way nor take anything from it and, if you have not done so, my judiciary of Cambridgeshire is to cause it to be done, so that I may not hear a complaint about lack of justice. Witness: William Martel.

115. That someone obligated by debt to the monks of Ely incurred a charge of perjury.[492]

Now, it came to pass that in the 1154th year from the incarnation of the Lord, Stephen de Scalers, because of his father's entitlement, was holding, in

---

[490] Source: Stetchworth archive, cf. Ely, Dean and Chapter, charter no. 82; cartularies GM; printed in Saltman, *Theobald, Archbishop of Canterbury*, pp. 323–4, no. 102. Date: After September, 1154.

[491] Source: Stetchworth archive, cf. cartulary G. Date: 1154.

[492] Source: adaptation of a report on a dispute with a tenant of the monastery, possibly from one of Richard's works; it is included also as a miracle narrative in B (*Book of Miracles*), though with slightly different emphases.

succession to him, two-and-a-half hides and nine acres, with one church, belonging to the monks of Ely in the vill of Shelford, for an annual food-rent of seven skeps.[493] This man had been withholding his rent from the aforesaid monks for two years. And since, when hardship increases, maternal help ought not to be withheld from children, Lord Nigel, who at that time was the holder of the bishopric of the church of Ely, after hearing the complaint of his monks and having recognized the wrong done to them, decreed that the above-mentioned man should be bound by the chain of an anathema, if he had not given satisfactory payment to the monks by the next Palm Sunday. But on the aforesaid day, Stephen, coming before the presence of the bishop in Ely, kept asserting that he had been reduced to such great and overpowering[494] poverty that he was now in no way capable of paying the said rent from past revenue. Moreover, the appropriate amount of rent to be paid was assessed in those days at forty marks. And the monks would have restored his land to him too, at that time, if they or any of their retainers could have determined its whereabouts.[495] But, because the passage of time devours the World itself and the things which belong to the World, {the place and extent of} the aforesaid land belonging to Stephen was utterly unknown, even to the monks, because of obsolescence over a long period: for its marked boundaries had been utterly destoyed and its boundary-stones completely removed from their footings. Wishing, indeed, to make future provision for themselves and for their church, after a consultation entered upon by the bishop and the monks, they made the concession that they would excuse Stephen his whole two years' debt, with the condition specified that <he should> make {the place and extent of} his land clear to them and <swear>, in future, to pay food-rent to the monks annually <and>[496] formalize his tenancy of the land under surety. Stephen agreed, promised and swore the oath. He swore, indeed, with his right hand placed upon the altar of Holy Cross, with the very body of the Lord placed nearby and many relics of the saints, that he would show the monks as clearly as he could, in person and with the help of his retainers {the place and extent of} the land referred to, which he held in Shelford in the name of the monks, namely two-and-a-half hides and a church with nine acres, and he formalized under surety his tenancy of this land on the basis of the annual payment of the food-rent. If there was anything, furthermore, that remained additional to that land which <neither> he nor his men were taking into account, he

---

[493] See Miller, *Abbey and Bishopric of Ely*, p. 40.

[494] Reading conjecturally at p. 363.12, ed. Blake: *vehementem* in place of *vehementer*.

[495] Lat. *internoscere*.

[496] Reading conjecturally at p. 363.21f.: *hac conditione interposita quod terram suam eis manifestam facere<t> et se ipsis monachis firmam suam annuatim redditurum <iuraret et> terram eandem sub fideiussione constitueret.*

himself would pledge this, too, out of a knight's fee which he held at Shelford under the bishop's lordship; and {he made} this {undertaking} with the bishop's agreement. In addition, the oft-mentioned[497] knights, Robert de *Cunigetuna* and Theobald de Scalers and William Fitz Roger, promised to Stephen, with a pledge of faith, that they would give their lord no advice to back out of this agreement and that, if it should be necessary, they would take the part of the monks against Stephen in the establishment of title. And the witnesses of this matter are: Bishop Nigel; Archdeacon William of *Lavantonia;* David, Archdeacon of Buckingham; Richard *de Sancto Paulo;* the chaplain Roger; the chaplain Ingeram; *Ærnaldus* of *Lavantonia;* John *de Sancto Albano;* Richard of Stuntney; Master Roger; *Grælangus de Tenet;*Gilbert, his brother; Ralph the steward; Alexander the butler; the cleric Alexander, in the hearing of the people of the town of Ely. But when the feast of Easter was over, Prior Alexander and Archdeacon William met at All Saints' church at Shelford. Also present was Stephen, with his retainers resident in that vill. So, on the instructions of Stephen himself, the priest Richard and all the villagers[498] of Stephen's vill swore that they would on no account conceal the truth which they had learnt from the talk of their forebears, or by any other means, about the oft-mentioned land. Specifically, the following witnesses were present at the swearing of the oath: Archdeacon William; the chaplain Nicholas of Cambridge; Robert Trencehart;[499] Richard of Stuntney; the prior's clerk, Roger; Peter and Osbert, clerics of Shelford; Robert of *Cunigtuna;* Theobald de Scalers; William *Monachus;* his son Nicholas; Brand and Gilbert of Shelford; Hervey, son of Vitalis of Cambridge; Roger *de Fossa,* of Melbourn; William, a kinsman of the prior; Serlo of Hauxton, and the villagers of Newton and Hauxton; Alfred, the sacrist's man; Adam, a kinsman by marriage of Serlo. Despite the fact that these people were standing by, neither Stephen nor his oath-helpers made a full disclosure of the fief: instead they are caught up in the noxious evil of perjury. As a result the monks to this day have a complaint against him. Without delay, the vengeance of God followed upon the perjury which the same Stephen had knowingly presumed to perpetrate, thereby heaping damnation upon himself. For he fell into a serious and unbearable paralysis of the feet, and from henceforth could not be cured by any of the physicians and thus he grew old in this same illness, his life blighted, and brought to its closure the day of his last light.

---

[497] Not previously mentioned in *LE*: presumably they had figured repeatedly in a documentary source underlying this narrative.

[498] Lat. *tota villatica.*

[499] In ms. B (*Book of Miracles*) the rest of the list is summarized by a formula meaning 'and many others', but much more detail is given about the deception about the extent of the land.

116. How mercifully God acted with regard to a certain sick man cured through the merits of St Æthelthryth at her spring.[500]

Now, all the miracles, and beneficial outcomes of mighty acts, which are known to have come about in Ely by the grace of the Lord Jesus Christ, with the assistance there of the merits of the holy lady virgins in that place <are conducive>[501] to the consolation of simple people. Their purpose is to ensure that such people, on beholding the good works of these same ladies, may glorify the Father who is in the heavens. From amongst these miracles, those, not negligible in number, which have been set down on the written page, are seen to extend to a large volume. The aim of this volume is that the helpful remedies which have been experienced may not be consigned to oblivion in another generation: rather, that children yet to be born and grow up may not be forgetful of the works of the Lord, and may enquire into His commandments. Hence, therefore, from the outset, where our discourse takes its beginning – and let none of the faithful disparagingly decline belief – the hand of the writer will not turn aside from the way of truth: rather, because[502] Queen Æthelthryth in her many mercies has become accustomed to bringing to pass, with the assent of the Divine Clemency, <many things>[503] among the generation of those who seek her, and who seek the face of the God of Jacob, I intend to describe one of the many.

In Northamptonshire there lived a man, very poor but well-known for his meritorious goodness, who, overcome by sickness, for a long time lamented and languished. For a poison, spreading through all his limbs, had distended them by puffing them out like an inflated skin. This had so overwhelmed him that he could not stand or walk, lie or sit. But this illness, as the eventual outcome proved, was not a mortal one. No, it was to put his endurance to the test, so that the glory of God and the merit of the bountiful virgin should be made manifest in him. And throughout the time that his agony was thus being ceaselessly aggravated, its irksomeness to him kept being augmented anew; moreover, his old agony persisted unremittingly.

And when, one night, he had gone to bed for a respite after long groanings, it was with difficulty and pain that he obtained sleep – as is the way with the afflicted, especially those who are in tears. He could have despaired utterly now of salvation, being someone whom the strength of

---

[500] Source: miracle narrative, also included in B *(Book of Miracles)*. The narration of miracles at St Æthelthryth's spring witnessed by the compiler has been promised in *LE* i. 31.

[501] Reading conjecturally at p. 365.5, ed. Blake: *omnia miracula . . . que in Ely . . . evenisse noscuntur ad simplicium consolationem <conducunt>, ut . . . non obliviscantur . . .*

[502] Reading conjecturally at p. 365.10, ed. Blake: *quia* or *quod* in place of *quid*.

[503] Reading conjecturally at p. 365.10–11, ed. Blake, e.g.: *quia regina Æðeldreða in miserationibus multis <multa> . . . patrare consuevit . . .*

pain had reduced to emptiness;[504] it was on Christ alone that he called, with repeated tearful cries. But God, the Hearer of all, did not spurn or despise the pleading of a pauper. He visited him, sick though he was; He encouraged him, anxious though he was; He consoled him in his tribulation and He deigned to make it clear in a vision that he could receive a cure from his illness through the personal intermediacy of a certain venerable woman. She proclaimed the availability of a remedy and cure in some such terms as these: 'O man, believe me, your salvation and the means of expelling your pitiable sickness is in Ely. Hasten with all speed to that place and you will very soon be rejoicing in your longed-for salvation.' On hearing this utterance, the man arose immediately, pondering on the vision which he had seen, wondering whether, maybe, what he had seen in his slumbers were true. Further to her previous utterances, the heroine to whom we have referred added more words of the same kind, giving him encouragement. For what she said was: 'In that place Æthelthryth, the glorious betrothed of God, blooms with body all undefiled, marvellously resplendent all the time amid signs and miracles. She makes well the people who come flocking to that place, suffering from no matter what illness.' Cheered, certainly, by such events, he believed that they were being made manifest to him by God to give him greater hope. Encouraged, he began to exult, and confidently set forth in haste upon the journey which he had been commanded to make, burdensome and painful[505] though it was for his weak limbs.

And it so happened that he arrived at the hall[506] of the aforementioned church at the hour when the brothers were invited to take their daily food and refreshment of the body, just when the entrances and exits are customarily bolted and kept under guard. Yet, none the less, in the nick of time he found at the threshold one of the guards ready and making haste to close it, and about to secure it with bolts. He called out in his direction, emitting a sob rather than an utterance, and asked him to allow him to go in for a little while. The guard refused and was contemptuous of the wretched man for being uncouth and slow-moving; furthermore, approaching him in furious anger, he gave him a slap and told him to go away. The man was insistent, beseeching and begging him with pleas for God's sake and for the love of his lady, St Æthelthryth, and importunately adjuring him to be allowed at least to go up to the spring of the blessed virgin. But that fierce and cruel servant was more stirred to anger than to pity by the poor man's wretched plight. However, because he had behaved offensively to a pilgrim, he became afraid that he would be hard put to bear the losses resulting from

---

[504] Reading at p. 365.23, ed. Blake, with change of word-division: *quippe quem vis doloris inanem reddiderat . . .* (cf. E).

[505] Reading with E at p. 366.2f., ed. Blake: *onerosum et grave . . .* to agree with *iter*.

[506] Lat. *aula*.

such actions, if report of them should reach the ears of their masters, and he said, 'See! The entrance is open, but there is no bucket at the well, nor do you have anything in which to draw water, and the well is deep.' But the man persevered in his plea that he should at least go in to pray and go right up to the well. At last, despite the guard's reluctance, he was allowed to go and went in. He looked all around him and – here was a miracle – this man who had never previously been in this place to pray, then made his way to the well without a guide, as if he were familiar[507] with it. He was looking all around and did not have a bucket. Suddenly, an outlet of the spring gushed forth in front of him by the well-head: it performed its ministry for the servant of God and – to speak more truthfully – offered itself to be tasted. For, flooding the floor-surface of the *atrium* all around with its waters it rendered it an accessible and generous source of medicine. Scooping it up in his hand, he poured it over his whole body, often invoking the name of St Æthelthryth and invoking her help. And while he was tasting it and it was flowing down, having been poured all over his limbs, he immediately felt relieved and began to recover, and indeed all the swollen tumidity deflated. He gave thanks to God and His bountiful virgin Æthelthryth.

But the fierce and good-for-nothing servant banged at the door, announcing his return, urged him with shouting to come out, asking whether, having taken his fill of the spring, he had drunk the whole of it! But he refused to believe what he heard had been brought about. Finally, when the poor man brought a cup of water to him, he understood and believed and, so as to make absolutely sure, ran right up to the spring which he found to have overflowed all around; hence he was himself made a witness of the happening which had been brought to pass. So the man drank from this water, as we have described, bathed and came, now happy and in good spirits, and reported to the aforesaid man-servant of the church what had happened and how, on arrival, he found neither a bucket nor any means of drawing water by the spring. So it was that he went away and everywhere told of the gracious act of God which had been performed for him miraculously through his saviouress, Æthelthryth, in her ever-superabundant piety. Indeed, people coming there with hope have often experienced cures of their ailments. Sufferers from dropsy take a drink from there and are healed. The blind wash and see, as one finds in the next chapter in praise of the most holy virgin Æthelthryth.

117. Another miracle about the spring of St Æthelthryth.[508]

This water is a lively spring and the source of a stream, bringing delight

---

[507] Here *notus* is apparently used in the rare, but classical, active sense.

[508] Source: miracle narrative, included also in B *(Book of Miracles)*.

continually to the city of God which[509] the long repose[510] of the corpse of the blessed virgin Æthelthryth had consecrated. For in the first instance she had not been buried in that place,[511] but where now the bishop's establishment[512] has been created, quite deep in the bosom of the earth in the cemetery, in a wooden coffin, amongst her people, following the order in which they had passed away. There, when her mighty powers were becoming well known, she was observed, in the presence of the blessed Wilfrid and the physician Cynefrith and also a circle of brothers and sisters standing round about, to be totally inviolate with respect to body and clothing, as Bede relates in the *History of the English People*. From there she was translated with great joy by her sister Seaxburh into the church of the blessed, ever-virgin Mary which she had founded, and placed by an[513] altar, where she was reverently entombed for many ages, specifically for four hundred and thirty-five[514] years, until the nineteenth {recte ninth} year of the peaceable King of the English people, Henry. In that year Abbot Richard translated her as mistress and doyenne into the new minster,[515] entombed in a more elevated position

---

[509] Note the bold identification of Ely with the 'City of God', as designated in St Augustine's book-title: the monks would have known that *Heli* meant 'my God' in Hebrew.

[510] Reading with E: *diutina repausatio*.

[511] Lat. *illic*.

[512] Lat. *status episcopi*. If this phrase does not simply refer to the founding of a bishopric at Ely, it appears that, though the spring was approached through the monastery gates, it was within an 'estate' or 'establishment', belonging to the bishop, which was considered distinct from the city of Ely. The wording would suit the bishop's Barton Farm, where Moore's map of the Isle of Ely (*Maps of the Fens*, 1684) shows 'St Aldreth's Well', still locally identified with a pond on what is now the golf course. However, this pond is a disconcertingly long way from the main monastery buildings. We might think of locating St Æthelthyth's spring, and reputed former burial-place, rather, somewhere in the vicinity of the former Bishop's Palace, the area close to the Fountain Inn, and the present St Mary's Church, where the water-table is high and has several outlets. The impression given by *LE* iii. 117 is certainly of a spring that arose within the lockable abbey precincts; but it must have been in a part of them usually open to the public, for in the next chapter a crowd of women is found drawing water there. It does not seem plausible that the spring was actually within the abbey church: *status episcopi* might in another context be translated 'bishop's stall', but improbabilities would result if we adopted this interpretation here. The reference to the spring in the 12th-century metrical *Life of St Æthelthryth* by Gregory of Ely (i. 353) places it within the 'holy precinct of the church' (*ambitus ecclesie . . . sacer*), but is not more specific.

[513] Lat. *iuxta altare*, 'by an altar' or 'by the altar'. In *LE* ii. 146, before Abbot Richard's translation of the lady saints into the 'new monastery', St Æthelthryth is said to have lain by her own altar to the south of the 'tower' and St Seaxburh by hers, to the north. Contrast, however, i. 35, where Seaxburh is said to have been buried, originally, behind her sister (*post beatissimam sororem suam*).

[514] Problematic figure: the compiler of *LE* in i. 28 gives the date of the first translation of St Æthelthryth as 679, but this was the date of her death; the further 16 years of her first burial bring us to 685, and then a further 435 to 1121, after Abbot Richard's time.

[515] Lat. *novum monasterium*.

behind the principal altar, in a bridal chamber which had been made ready.[516]

Furthermore, in the place mentioned previously, where, as we have said before, the virgin of God had reposed for a long time, the monks made a pit like a cistern, continually pouring forth[517] living waters which, on account of her merits, are acquainted with remedies and assiduous in curing the sick in her name. To these waters – this is a true story – neighbours and friends brought a poor little woman who had long been deprived of eyesight. On the strength of the mercy of the holy virgin, displayed to innumerable people, they urged her not to be at all afraid, to have firm hope and to pray with her lips and in her heart. Putting her trust in her neighbours' words, she prayed most intently, and immediately her prayer was heard. She came, therefore, with someone else leading the way; she approached the spring, calling out and invoking the aid of the most pious Æthelthryth; forthwith she drenched her face with tears and then she washed her face and her eyes together with the water of this spring. She saw clearly, and was filled with great joy. And so she gave thanks to God for all His benefactions, and to her lady advocate, Æthelthryth. She who had come as a blind woman, in grief and sorrow, returned home without a guide.

118. Again, a miracle concerning the same spring.[518]

The incident which I am relating happened recently, in summer-time, while the brothers were performing divine service at the first hour of the day, and even I am a witness of this happening.

Well then, there came a certain young woman to the aforementioned spring to drink the water with the crowd of those who hastened there. But they forced her to move back, standing in her way all around her and thrusting her out of the way with their elbows. However, she threw herself into the middle of the throng, albeit by pushing. While she was trying to get in front of the others and, after she had drawn water, to retrace her steps, no less in haste, the vessel which she had been carrying slipped from her hand by accident and, moreover, she herself followed, falling in after it! When this was observed, the people standing around, squabbling with one another

---

[516] Cf. *LE* i. 21 (burial in cemetery); i. 25–6 (translation by Seaxburh to Church of St Mary); i. 35 (Seaxburh herself buried behind her sister); i. 43 (sarcophagus identified as that of Æthelthryth in the ruinous church of the canons); ii. 52 (Æthelwold is reputed to have found the tomb of Æthelthryth near the high altar, where her sister had buried her; apparently St Peter replaced St Mary as the dedicatee of the church where she was buried); ii. 144–6 (translation by Abbot Richard from north and south in the 'tower' of the 'old church', to positions in the 'new'); iii. 50 (positions of the shrines in the new church described: Æthelthryth has Wihtburh to her left and to the north; Eormenhild to the south, and Seaxburh at her feet, towards the east).

[517] Reading conjecturally at p. 367.14, ed. Blake: *manantem* in place of *manentem*.

[518] Source: miracle narrative, also included in B (*Book of Miracles*).

about the bucket, stopped their arguing and fled far away, crying out, 'St Æthelthryth! Help!' They saw her, with her head downwards towards the bottom of the well and her feet protruding upwards. There she remained submerged for quite a long time – two or three hours. No one, meanwhile, arrived to rescue her, until[519] Stephen and Richard, two clerics sitting nearby at their book, came running, <not> doubting[520] that she had been drowned in the water, and lamenting, of one accord, 'Alas! Alas!' They pulled her out by the feet. <They saw>[521] that she had not only not suffered any ill effect from having lain in the pond for such a length of time, but that, on the contrary, through the mighty power of St Æthelthryth, she appeared unharmed. And thus the Lord kept her unharmed at the bottom of the whirlpool, just as He once kept Daniel safe in the lions' pit. He did so in order that the waters sanctified by Christ for the glory of His beloved betrothed – waters from which it is customary for many benefits to arise – should not be contaminated by bloodshed – a mark of shame.

Awesome place, putting to flight as it does various miseries from the sick, through the intercession of our lady propitiator, Æthelthryth, curing bodily illnesses by means of the fullness of her spring – by taste or sprinkling! Tell of its greatness with me, <everyone>,[522] but most of all those of us who 'shall be filled with its goodnesses! The temple of God is marvellous in just dealing.'[523] Let us cry out to God in the innermost recesses of our heart, and say to the Saviour: 'Lord of all, Thou who hast no unseemliness, preserve this house of Thine untainted for evermore, O Lord. AMEN.'

119. With what severity the Lord avenged the injuries inflicted on his beloved virgin Æthelthryth.[524]

Although it was for a long period that the race of barbarians from Denmark,

---

[519] Reading conjecturally at p. 367.35f., ed. Blake: *Nemo qui eriperet interim advenit, quoad Stephanus et Ricardus, duo clerici . . . adcurrunt . . .* (with *quoad* replacing *quod*).

[520] Reading conjectually at p. 367.36, ed. Blake: *illam <haud> dubitantes in aqua necatam fuisse . . .*

[521] Reading conjecturally at p. 367.37f., ed. Blake e.g.: *pedibus extraxerunt, <conspexerunt> non solum de tanto spatio nichil mali in lacu iacuisse perpessam, immo per virtutem sancte Æðeldreðe incolumem apparere.*

[522] Reading conjecturally at p. 368.7f., ed. Blake: *Magnificate illum mecum <omnes> sed potius qui replebimur in bonis eius.*

[523] Cf. Psalm 64.5–6 Vulgate (version according to the Septuagint).

[524] Source: miracle narrative, also in B *(Book of Miracles)*, where, much more appropriately, it follows a brief account of the restoration of the monastery in 970. There is extensive quotation from *LibÆ* 10–13 = *LE* ii. 11. Why this and the next chapter should have been included here, rather than in book ii, with reference to the time of Abbot Byrhtnoth, is very puzzling. They take up a theme treated, certainly, in iii. 115, and their purpose may be seen as discouragement to despoilers, but they have only remote relevance to the land disputes of Bishop Nigel's time.

coming to England, laid it waste on every side with warfare and arson, eventually, thanks to the providence of God's clemency, it ran out of strength, and was in time forced to return to the land of its origin and abandon its occupied territories. This happened, specifically, in the days of the venerable King Edgar, in as much as any Dane, if found, was struck down by swords or subjected to tortures. Moreover, on his instruction and with his authority, the holy pontiff Æthelwold brought the monastery of Ely back to its former religious observance and refounded it and endowed the place richly with estates, obtained both by purchase and by endowment. For he procured the vill of Downham, a vill which is very fertile and close to the monastery. First, he agreed to pay fifteen pounds to Leofsige and his wife Siflæd at Cambridge for two hides, and he paid for it in full, in front of a large number of faithful people, with Leofwine, a monk and provost of the church, as intermediary.

Meanwhile, King Edgar died. Upon his death, the aforesaid Leofsige – an enemy of God and deceiver of men – and his wife, made void the whole agreement they had with the bishop, and sometimes offered part of the money to the bishop, and to abbot Byrhtnoth, which they had received from him, but at other times denied that they owed him anything at all. They also reckoned that, in this way, they would recover through trickery the land which they had sold, but the church continually refuted them in all respects with its witnesses. During that tempestuous time, moreover, when the king, as we have said, had died, and they were keeping us waiting and wearing us down over a long period, nobody ploughed the land in question, nor sowed or cultivated it in any way, and so all the arable land was going to waste. And then, seeing with what great injuries and tribulations that inveigler was burdening his servants, the Lord God had pity on their hardships. Through his mercy, the holy church of Ely recovered what it unjustly lost. For as it is written in a psalm, 'The righteous called out and the Lord heard them and freed them from all tribulations.'[525]

While these things were going on and that wretched man was confident that he was holding the stolen possessions of the holy church and the lawful entitlement of St Æthelthryth with the utmost freedom and security and was not ceasing to beset the servants of God, divine vengeance came to the boil and he died shamefully and miserably, in vindication of the virgin of Christ, and there was fulfilled in his case what one reads in Solomon: 'The righteous shall rejoice but the impious shall fall into woe.'[526]

We have taken this from the *Book of Lands* which they call the *Book of St Æthelwold*, with the object that people who read or see these things may fight shy of alienating or diminishing the properties and goods of the holy

---

[525] Psalm 33.18 Vulgate = 34.17 RSV.

[526] Proverbs 24.16.

456

virgin Æthelthryth; for everyone who did such things incurred judgement.

120. Once more, how God wreaked vengeance on the enemies of the blessed Æthelthryth.[527]

There follows another miracle and it proves to have happened under like circumstances, if with a different turn of events. The brothers, moreover, were involved and acquired the most certain knowledge of the matter and set it out in English in the *Book of St Æthelwold* referred to previously, but now that, in our own day, it has been translated into Latin, we long to bring it to the notice of all, and we believe that it should be related in full as something which if attended to carefully, is a warning to many.

The fact is this: on a certain occasion, when the spokesmen of England had gathered at London, one Wihtgar, a man well endowed with goods and estates, offered for sale to Bishop Æthelwold five hides at Brandon and Livermere. When the bishop and abbot had heard of this, they gave him twenty pounds for the land: fifteen pounds at that time, in the witness of many respectable men, but a hundred shillings at a later date, with the aforesaid Provost Leofwine and Wine of Witchford, a man of the highest repute, as intermediaries; and these men gave him this same money at Brandon in the witness of the whole hundred in which the land is situated. At the time when King Edgar died, however, a certain man named Ingulf forcibly and unjustly took Brandon away from God and St Æthelthryth.

O wretched and unhappy man, contrary to what you think, you will not be capable for long of holding on to what you are stealing! As a consequence of it, you are very quickly to be heavily penalized! For it is written: 'There is no wisdom, there is no prudence, there is no discernment contrary to the Lord.'[528]

For, in demonstration of the power of God and the merit of the blessed virgin, from the day on which he thus usurped the property of the church he tasted no food or drink, for without the slightest delay his heart suffered rupture. And so it came about that he who, when living, unjustly seized what belonged to God, on meeting death, was unable to keep it, but simultaneously lost himself and the property. After he died, his wife and sons also took possession of the same land similarly, but, in line with the fact that they gave honour neither to God nor to the blessed Æthelthryth, they did not spare their souls. So, divine vengeance burst upon them and they all perished miserably within one year. At this moment Siferth, the brother of Ingulf, groaned very deeply at their demise and anticipating the judgement of the Lord upon himself, began to take fright. And, against the wish of very

---

[527] Source: see above on *LE* iii. 119; extensive quotation from *LibÆ* 46 = *LE* ii. 35.

[528] Proverbs 21.30.

many people and particularly against the wish of Æthelwine, styled Ealdorman, he gave the land as an offering to St Æthelthryth and relinquished it freely, so that what is written in the Book of Wisdom: 'The house of the wicked shall be destroyed: the tents of the just shall flourish',[529] should be well fulfilled[530] with regard to these people.

For the Lord destroyed the household of this wicked man, so that his seed would not remain for evermore in his sight, and the reason for this was that he had gratuitously hated the holy church and the most blessed Æthelthryth. Rather, God the Beholder and Judge of all, who speaks of injuries and kindnesses done to his people as being His own,[531] makes it clear that the wicked incur harm from the sources from which they think advantage is coming to them, as, for instance, He has made clearly evident in the case of this man. Moreover, this man is not the only one, but, to speak more truly, it is also widely apparent to all that, ever since the virgin Æthelthryth was taken up from the prison of the flesh, any person[532] of the land of England, whether prince or potentate, who has weakened or robbed that monastery in respect of its dignity or its properties, has always suffered the most dire bodily torments and definitely been seen to end his life with a miserable passing. These are astonishing matters and very greatly to be feared. Let no one, then, hold in doubt or deride what we are relating, and so plan to perpetrate something similar: rather, let him learn, from being punished by afflictions brought upon him by others, not to offend God's virgin by injurious acts, but rather to please her by acts of obedience.

121. About a priest who did not wish to celebrate the feasts of our lady saints.[533]

Just as we are taught by the polyphony[534] of the prophets that the salvation of the righteous is from the Lord, similarly the reverse is true: salvation is far removed from sinners. There was, belonging to the confraternity and number of sinners, a man named Gervase who, by much flattery, obtained the office of priest at Holy Cross – that is, a parish of the town of Ely – from the patron,[535] Ralph, an innocent and ingenuous man. But he obtained it not in order to take care of the souls committed to him: no, it was to exact

---

[529] Proverbs 14.1.

[530] Reading at p. 370.7, ed. Blake: *ut bene de hiis adimpleatur . . . (for adimpletur)* **so BE.**

[531] Cf. Matthew 25.39f.

[532] The Latin moves ungrammatically from singular *quisquis* to plural *cruciabantur*.

[533] Source: miracle narrative; not included in B *(Book of Miracles)*.

[534] Lat. *organum*, meaning 'concerted voices', as in part-singing. Cf. the beginning of *Miracula S. Ætheldrethe Virginis* CD, ed. Love, on the *organum* of the Holy Spirit.

[535] Lat. *yconomus.*

BOOK III

worldly profit and the mammon of wickedness. For the wickedness of that
man arose seemingly from his fat; it transferred itself into the sensibility of
his heart; he thought and spoke evil; he spoke wickedness on high; 'he set his
mouth against Heaven and his tongue made its way to and fro on earth'.[536]
As a consequence, God surrendered him to evil thinking, so that he would
act improperly. The upshot of his doings proved that this was so, for he made
moves to annul and abolish the feasts and praises of lady saints of ours,
namely the blessed Wihtburh, Seaxburh and Eormenhild, so that their
commemoration would not be for evermore and the name of these ladies
would not endure from generation to generation. For this man had given his
right hand to Master Ranulf, the ex-monk,[537] pledging to afflict the servants
of God and St Æthelthryth with injuries, to harass them with insults and to
overwhelm them with losses.

To explain: on one occasion, it came about in the month of July that[538]
the aforesaid priest completely refused to announce to the congregation, on
the preceding Sunday, the feasts of the blessed ladies Wihtburh and
Seaxburh, at the time when they come together in a week: no, he wished to
make no mention of them. But some people, standing nearby and, in
surprise, asking one another why he was not giving any notice of their feasts,
tried to prompt him by telling him in a murmur that he was omitting to
announce to the people the feasts of their ladies. He, however, made a
pretence of not hearing, proceeded in a hurry with the remaining parts of the
mass and was all the more angry with these people and disdainful of them.

But God, in whose sight all things are 'laid bare and exposed to view',[539]
and who is glorified 'in the council of the saints',[540] strengthened His arm
and raised His right hand[541] to avenge the aforesaid sainted ladies by
punishing their abominable enemy, so that people of generations to come
might learn to venerate the rightly glorious feasts and rightly cherished
praises of the virgins who repose in Ely.

And it was not long afterwards, to be precise, within a week, that 'in
consequence of obduracy and an unrepentant heart', he 'stored up evil for
himself on the Day of Anger'.[542] For he went out as a guest to a banquet, ate a
great deal and drank with merriment, and afterwards, all night, he became
enslaved to unchastity and drunkenness. And thus, after having spent a
whole week surrendered to gluttony and temptations, on the day in question,

---

[536] Psalm 72.7–9 Vulgate after Septuagint = 73.7–9 RSV.

[537] Cf. *LE* iii. 51ff.

[538] Lat. *Accidit . . . et* + lit. 'it happened . . . and': a construction characteristic of Hebrew,
familiar to medieval monks from literal translations of it in the Latin Vulgate.

[539] Cf. Hebrews 4.13.

[540] Cf. Psalm 89.7 = 88.8 Vulgate.

[541] Cf. Psalm 89.13 = 88.14 Vulgate.

[542] Cf. Romans 2.5.

in a state of semi-consciousness,[543] he vomited up food as yet undigested. He made everyone laugh by not knowing how to keep to a straight path. Despite this, he made his way fearlessly towards the altar. He had no fear of the judgement of the Lord and made no decision, in the secrecy of his heart, to refrain from presuming to take the life-giving mystery of the body of Christ unworthily.

He arrived, put on holy vestments; in a hesitant state, as if out of his mind, he carried out the remaining procedures, and stood ready in all his priestly array until the introit of the mass, when, fittingly, in accordance with his deserts, as a result of the Lord's punishment in vengeance of His lady saints, before the eyes of the whole congregation, there came upon him a state of helplessness and shame. For, up above, because of nausea, he vomited profusely from the mouth and, down below, he emitted excrement from his privy orifice with a loud noise and let it fall to the ground! But people standing nearby took pity on his misery, carried him to somewhere a considerable distance away, and stripped him of the holy vestments, which would no longer be of any use for altar-service. And thus, in his miserable state of life, he not long afterwards, against his will, eventually recognized his guilt, and made public confession not only for having been reluctant that the feasts of the lady saints be proclaimed there, but for having even forbidden them to be held. May God be praised, therefore, in respect to His saints, who are to judge the nations of the peoples.

122. About the pall of St Æthelthryth: in what a merciful way it was restored to the church of Ely.[544]

It was at this very time that Stephen, the most pious King of the English, fell sick with dysentery and, moreover, died from it. He had by then held the kingship for [[about]] nineteen years, but at the cost of the utmost effort and with great difficulty. His successor as king was his kinsman Henry, whom he had chosen as his heir in succession to him. Henry was the son of the Lady Matilda, the former empress, the daughter of the old king, Henry, his father being the venerable Count Geoffrey of Anjou.

On being received as king and consecrated by Theobald, Archbishop of Canterbury,[545] he prohibited unjust legislation, restored long-lost peace, imposed punishment on transgressors, pulled down illicit castles and expelled insurrectionists from the kingdom. No one prevailed against him: only the hostile region of the Welsh kept causing trouble. He collected,

---

[543] Lat. *vix palpando.*

[544] Source: independent of known chronicles for national events; most likely again Richard of Ely on the episcopate of Nigel; not in B *(Book of Miracles).*

[545] Lit: 'of Kent'.

moreover, much bronze and an exceedingly large amount of gold and silver, for paying soldiers for an assault on Toulouse, a city of Aquitaine; for[546] he wished to add it to his dominion. Bishop Nigel, to be sure, seeing the lord King to be in need of money in an undertaking of such magnitude, accepted a promise from him and bought for four hundred pounds an office among the courtiers – the post of treasurer – for his son, named Richard, educated at the monastery in Ely, a young man of great cleverness and prudence, by whom and through whom that house was damaged by considerable ill-usage. As he – {the bishop} – did not have the resources to pay, he took from the house of St Æthelthryth vestments and vessels, and any desirable objects that were there, saying to himself that the things which were there were always sufficient. To cap it all, he took the pall, with excellent decoration of gold and jewels, an offering which Queen Emma had presented, to be a covering for the tomb of the holy virgin, and he sold it to the Bishop of Lincoln, without the consent of the monks, to raise money. He had on another occasion, as has already been written above, similarly taken it away elsewhere, with other goods of the church, but the monks redeemed it, from their own meagre resources, to prevent an ornament of such importance from being fraudulently removed from the monastery.[547]

Well, it came about at that time that this very <Bishop>[548] of Lincoln was going to Rome in furtherance of the interests of [his] church, during the pontificate of the lord Pope Eugenius, and he wanted to offer him this same pall as a means of gaining his favour. But when the lord Apostolic Father saw it, inspecting it very carefully in bright light, he was amazed at the costliness of such a covering, and realized that it came from some famous and ancient church. Such was the quality of the ornament that he made enquiry as to its origin, and when he found out that it was from Ely, he issued an order, on pain of apostolic anathema, that he was to return his ornament to that place, with all excuses barred.

As a result, after the conclusion of the essential pieces of business by reason of which the bishop was compelled to go to the high places of Rome, he returned to England, taking back with him the pall which he had taken there. Moreover, wanting to remove the gold from it, he found goldsmiths and orphrey-embroideresses, who were to carry out his intention concerning the work. And they put their hands to the task, applied scissors and prepared to unpick the precious gold-embroidery: but it was as hard as stone or bronze against the sharpest iron implements. They tried again and again, but their effort was in vain. Well, we declare and trust that this must have come about

---

[546] Reading with E: *enim.*

[547] Repunctuating at p. 372.16, ed. Blake: *ne tantus ornatus fraudaretur a loco, redimerunt.*

[548] Reading conjecturally also at p. 372.16, ed. Blake: *episcopum* (instead of *ipsum*) *Lincolniensem.*

in accordance with the will of the holy virgin. For the monks were lamenting with groans that the veil of their mother had been taken away from that place and eventually, after payment of a sum of money, they received back what they had wrongfully lost, giving thanks to her for all her benefactions.

123. That Bishop Nigel was suspended by the Pope for the dispersal of the goods of St Æthelthryth.[549]

Hadrian,[550] Bishop, servant of the servants of God, to his venerable brother Nigel, Bishop of Ely: greeting and apostolic blessing. We are seated, with the Lord's authority, unworthy though we are, on the throne of the Prince of the Apostles for the specific purpose that, †as regards offences committed in the churches of God against the order of reason, it behoves us, also, to guard solicitously against them.†[551] For if, in our time, the properties of the Church should suffer dilapidation, there is no doubt but that this redounds to our peril. Hence, certainly, it is that, following in the footsteps of our predecessor, Pope Eugenius of pious memory, we are issuing a mandate to your loving self, venerable brother, by means of apostolic writs, instructing that, within three months after the receipt of our letters, you are to recall the possessions of your church which you are known to have alienated and dispersed, in contravention of the promise made at your consecration, to the state in which they had been when you were appointed to the position of ruler over the church of Ely, and you are not in any respect whatsoever to delay this.[552] But if you should delay putting this into effect up until the prescribed deadline, we order you from that time to be suspended from episcopal office. Given at Benevento, 22nd February.

124. Mandate of the lord Pope to the chapter of Ely concerning this same man.[553]

Hadrian, Bishop, servant of the servants of God, to his venerable brothers, the whole chapter of Ely: greeting and apostolic blessing. We, unworthy though we are, are seated, with the Lord's authority, on the throne of the Prince of the Apostles for the specific purpose that, †as regards offences

---

[549] Source: monastic archives, cf. cartulary G; document printed in Holtzmann, *Papsturkunden in England*, ii, no. 92. Date: 22nd February, 1156; at Benevento.

[550] Hadrian IV, Nicholas Breakspear, the English Pope.

[551] The Latin here is very strange, but must accurately convey the intended text, as there is exact parallel for the wording in the next charter (*LE* iii. 124). One would expect a verb in the subjunctive to complete the sense of *residemus, ut ea . . .* (p. 374.1, ed. Blake).

[552] Slight recasting of this sentence has been necessary for clarity.

[553] Source: monastic archives, cf. cartulary G; document printed in Holtzmann, *Papsturkunden in England*, ii, no. 92. Date: 22nd February, 1156; at Benevento.

committed in the churches of God against the order of reason, it behoves us, also, to guard solicitously against them.†[554] For if, in our time, the properties of the Church should suffer dilapidation, there is no doubt but that this redounds to our peril. Hence, certainly, it is that, following in the footsteps of our predecessor, Pope Eugenius of pious memory, we are issuing a mandate to our venerable brother Nigel, Bishop of Ely, by means of apostolic writs, instructing that, within three months from the receipt of our letters, he is to recall the possessions of the church of Ely, which he is known to have alienated and dispersed in contravention of the promise made at his consecration, to the state in which they had been when he was appointed to the position of ruler over the church of Ely, and you are not in any respect whatsoever to delay this. But if he should delay putting this into effect up until the prescribed deadline, we order him from that time to be suspended from episcopal office. Given at Benevento, 22nd February.

125. Likewise to the archbishop, concerning this same man, on the subject of the recall of the goods of St Æthelthryth to the monastery of Ely.[555]

Hadrian, Bishop, servant of the servants of God, to his venerable brother and friend Theobald, Archbishop of Canterbury and Legate of the Apostolic See: greeting and apostolic blessing. In the course of this year, we gave it to be known, in mandates to our venerable brother Nigel, Bishop of Ely, that he was to make efforts, on pain of losing his episcopal office, towards the recovery of the goods of the church of Ely which had been reduced to a <di>lapidated state[556] and alienated. Now, however,[557] since he makes out that in the absence[558] of our most beloved son in Christ, Henry, King of the English, he cannot put this into effect, we have been swayed, assenting to his entreaties, and have considered it right that he should be given a period of lee-way †from† the next feast of St Luke[559] to do this. In the mean time we are, in effect, relaxing the sentence of suspension which we promulgated against him. Because, therefore, we believe that, for the recovery of the goods which have been alienated, the power of this same son of ours, the king, is absolutely essential, we are issuing a mandate to your fraternal self, through apostolic written instructions, to this effect: you are to induce him by the

---

[554] The strange wording is identical to that at the equivalent juncture in the previous chapter.

[555] Source: monastic archives, cf. cartulary G; document printed in Holtzmann, *Papsturkunden in England*, ii, no. 93. Date: 22nd February, 1156; at Benevento.

[556] Reading conjecturally at p. 374.18, ed. Blake: *que <di>lapidata sunt* (cf. *dilapidationem* in line 3 above).

[557] Reading with Holtzmann: *nunc autem*.

[558] Reading e.g. with Holtzmann: *id in absentia* for *absentiam*.

[559] The text: *a proximo festo sancti Luce indutias* is problematic: one would expect the Feast of St Luke, 18th October, to be the final deadline set, not the beginning of the period of lee-way.

insistence of your exhortation – and your prudence is to endeavour to advise him with frequent urgings – to lavish his effort and cooperation on securing the recovery and restoration of the said goods. He is to act thus with the insight which belongs to piety and for the salvation of his soul. And you are to strive, by whatever means you can, <to . . . >[560] him to do this. Given at the Lateran, 17th March.

126. Exhortatory letter of the Archbishop of Canterbury about the recall of the goods dispersed from the church of St Æthelthryth.[561]

Theobald, by the grace of God Archbishop of Canterbury and Primate of all England, to his venerable brother Nigel, by that same grace Bishop of Ely. It has reached our ears that certain individuals who are violent and oppressors of the poor are for ever attacking the church of which you are in charge with exactions and depredations and – something which we take very seriously – that, <assisted>[562] by you, they have violently and illicitly usurped some estates and vills of the blessed Æthelthryth by forcible expropriations and other malpractices. But since things which are brought about by force or intimidation are considered invalid, and thus the authority of the sacred canons prescribes that sales, purchases, donations and exchanges of ecclesiastical goods made without the assent and written agreement of the clergy are of no validity, and of no moment, we are issuing instructions that goods belonging to your church are to be returned to it and all things which have been extorted by you violently and from an unwilling party, are to be recalled to the aforesaid church, and in particular Rattlesden, Marham, Hartest, which we have heard have been stolen from your church. Indeed, if the oppressors of your church have obtained by extortion any muniments or charters belonging to you or your chapter, we declare them of no validity. The reason is this: in view of the fact that you are not permitted to alienate the goods of your church, it has been even less permissible for you to confirm grants of them for future time, the principle being that they should be kept from being held by despoilers. Indeed, if anyone approaches a secular judge about these matters, with the aim of gaining possession of the goods of the aforesaid church with his authorization, we prohibit you, even if you are summoned to the hearing by the judge himself, to attend the court of any of the secular powers, no matter which, since the goods of the Church, which are the ransom-payment of sinners, the offerings of faithful people, are not at the disposal of the jurisdiction of secular powers, unless the authority of the

---

[560] An infinitive dependent on *enitaris* seems missing at p. 374.29, ed. Blake.

[561] Source: monastic archives, cf. cartulary G; Saltman, *Theobald, Archbishop of Canterbury*, pp. 324–5, no. 103. Date: perhaps 1157.

[562] Reading conjecturally at p. 375.7, ed. Blake: *a te <adiuti> violenter . . . extorserunt*.

sacred canons is disregarded. For the rest, we wish you to keep safe from now on, with the greatest vigilance in your power, holdings consisting of real-estate[563] belonging to your church, preventing them from being forcibly usurped, because it is unlawful to allow them to be dispersed, and Christ has foreordained you to keep them gathered together and to be their custodian. Moreover, if anyone should presume to despoil your church with respect to the estates, holdings and freedoms which are its due: after you have given notice of this once to his bishop, if he does not give satisfaction, you are to deliver canonical sentence on him, whether it is in your own bishopric that he has been, or in that of London or Norwich or Lincoln. We give instructions, furthermore, to our brothers and fellow-bishops that, from the time when you issue a denunciation declaring the perpetrators of malpractices against your church excommunicated, they are to excommunicate them and to issue a denunciation declaring them excommunicated, and they are not to be released from the sentence imposed until they have given suitable satisfaction. Farewell.

127. Another instruction of the lord Pope to the archbishop and bishops of England concerning the recall of goods to the church of Ely.[564]

Hadrian, Bishop, servant of the servants of God, to Theobald, Archbishop of Canterbury, Legate of the Apostolic See, and Roger, Archbishop of York and all bishops in office throughout England: greeting and apostolic blessing. Swayed by the supplications and entreaties of our most beloved son, Henry the illustrious King of the English, we have deemed it right to remit, by apostolic authority, the sentence of suspension whereby our venerable brother Nigel, Bishop of Ely, was formerly held in constraint, and you are to know that, because of intervention both by that same king and by yourselves, he has been restored into the fullness of our grace. However, with a view to the recovery of the properties of the church of Ely which have been alienated, as a result of which he has also deserved to endure the sentence of suspension, remission of the sentence is conditional on his swearing an oath in your presence, brother Archbishop of Canterbury, to endeavour to the best of his ability, and with all his might, to recall them, and on his not presuming from henceforth, for any reason, to hand over as fiefs any estates of this same church, or to alienate them by any mode of entitlement. But since we neither can nor should overlook the usurpation of the properties of the church of Ely without enquiry into it, we give instructions to your fraternal selves, issuing a mandate by means of apostolic writs that, within

---

[563] Lat. *possessiones immobilium*.

[564] Source: monastic archives, cf. cartulary G; document printed in Holtzmann, *Papsturkunden in England*, ii, no. 100. Date: 16th January, 1158; at the Lateran.

four months of receipt of these present letters, you are to endeavour with the greatest diligence to convene the usurpers of the properties of the aforesaid church: William, Earl de Warenne, Earl de Clare, Earl *Albric,* Geoffrey Martel, Henry Fitz Gerold, Robert Fitz Humphrey and John de Port, with a view to their restoring, with all pretext and excuse ruled out, all the properties of the church of Ely which, so it is said, they are presuming to withhold by violence and in contravention of justice. But if they should disdain to do so, you are to bind them, on our authority, from thenceforth by the chain of excommunication, with all right of appeal terminated, and you are to cause them to be shunned[565] by all people in your dioceses as limbs of the Devil, until the providing of suitable satisfaction. Given at the Lateran, 16th January.

128. Again, a mandate of the Pope to the King of England about constraining the malefactors who had harmed the church of Ely.[566]

Hadrian, Bishop, servant of the servants of God, to Henry, the illustrious King of the English: greeting and apostolic blessing. The more we know you to be faithful and devoted to the Holy Roman Church, your Excellency, and the more ready we see you to honour and exalt it, the more do we who[567] exercise our ministry in it, albeit with insufficient merits, wish to grant your entreaties and petitions and desire to give you a full hearing, in so far as we can, with reverence preserved, in respect to your concerns and likewise those of your friends and faithful subjects. For, certainly, it is with true loving kindness in the Lord that we love your person as that of a most Christian king and Catholic prince, and, readily assenting to your royal entreaties, are very glad to honour your Highness in the ways we know to be most expedient. Hence, at all events, it was that, won over by the insistence of your entreaties and your request, we deemed it right to remit, by apostolic authority, the sentence of suspension whereby our venerable brother Nigel, Bishop of Ely, was formerly held in constraint and, because of your intervention, it is our wish that he be restored into the fullness of our grace. Certainly, indeed, this remission is conditional on his swearing an oath in the presence of our brother, the Archbishop of Canterbury, Legate of the Apostolic See, that, with a view to the recovery of the properties of the church of Ely which have been alienated, as a result of which he has also deserved to endure the sentence of suspension, he will endeavour, to the best

[565] Reading conjecturally, with Holtzmann and Blake: *evitari* (p. 376.26, ed. Blake).
[566] Source: monastic archives, cf. cartulary G; document printed in Holtzmann, *Papsturkunden in England* ii, no. 99. Date: 16th January, 1158.
[567] Reading conjecturally, with Holtzmann: *qui in ea . . . ministramus* (p. 377.6, ed. Blake).

of his ability and with all his might, to recall them and will not presume from henceforth, for any reason, to hand over as fiefs, or to alienate by any mode of entitlement, any properties of that same church. But since, with respect to the recovery of the goods, we have confidence both in the power of your Serenity and in the oath of the man himself, in the Lord's name we <exhort> your Magnificence by means of apostolic writs of the Church of Rome, and enjoin you for the remission of your sins, to endeavour, by whatever means befits your Highness, to compel William, Earl of Warenne, the Earl of Clare, Earl *Albric*, Geoffrey Martel, Henry Fitz Gerold, Robert Fitz Humphrey and John de Port, usurpers of the properties of the aforesaid church – seeing that[568] these are men under your lordship and command – to restore completely, with all pleading and excuse-making set aside, all the properties of the church which, so it is said, they are presuming to withhold by violence and in contravention of justice, or else, in the presence of our venerable brother, the Archbishop of Canterbury, Legate of the Apostolic See, not to prevaricate about enacting full justice thereafter. You, indeed, are to grant the aforesaid bishop help by all methods, and support, for the recovery, without diminution, of those goods. But if the malefactors disdain to restore the goods of the bishop which they are alienating, or to bring about what is just, you are to punish them, in what will be a just manner, with the vengeance of royal severity. We make it clear[569] in our mandates to our venerable brother, the Archbishop of Canterbury, Legate of the Apostolic See, to the Archbishop of York and to all bishops in office throughout England that, unless, within four months[570] after receipt of our letters, they restore all the items which have been alienated, or, in the presence of the Archbishop of Canterbury, have enacted full justice with respect to these matters, they are to bind them with the chain of excommunication, by our authority, with all appeal set aside, and they are to cause them to be shunned by all as if limbs of the Devil. In view of this, we issue a mandate to your Highness by the purport of these present writings that, as soon as they are put under constraint by the sentence of excommunication, you are to shun them in all ways, as the most Christian king that you are, and as one grounded in the perfection of the Catholic faith, and you are to beware of feeling affection for them, lest – perish the thought – you should be found to be a sharer in their communion. Given at T'. [571]

---

[568] Reading conjecturally, perhaps, at p. 377.26, ed. Blake: *quippe qui sub tuo dominio et ditione consistunt.*

[569] Reading conjecturally at p. 378.7, ed. Blake: *declaramus* for *dederamus.*

[570] Deleting the comma after *infra* at p. 378.8, ed. Blake.

[571] Only this abbreviation for the place is given.

129. That Bishop Nigel, on the instruction of the Pope, swore to restore the goods of his church, and thus earned release from suspension.[572]

Hadrian, Bishop, servant of the servants of God, to his venerable brother Nigel, Bishop of Ely: greeting and apostolic blessing. Swayed by the entreaties and pleadings of Henry, the illustrious King of the English, our most beloved son in Christ, and by those of archbishops as well as bishops, we have deemed it right that the sentence of suspension by which you were formerly held in restraint should be remitted on apostolic authority and, thanks to their intervention, you are to know that you have been restored to the fullness of our favour: this is conditional, however, on your promising on oath, in the presence of our venerable brother Theobald, Archbishop of Canterbury, Legate of the Apostolic See, that – with a view to recovery of the goods of the church of Ely which have been usurped, as the result of which, also, you have deserved to have the sentence of suspension imposed on you – you will to the best of your ability and with your utmost strength endeavour to recall them and, from now on, will not presume on any account to hand over as fiefs any properties of that same church, or alienate them by any mode of entitlement. And since we neither can nor should overlook the alienation of the properties of that same church without enquiring into it, we command your fraternal self by our issuing of instructions by means of apostolic writings, and we give instructions by our issuing of a mandate, that you are to endeavour to bring to bear all effort and solicitude to recover the estates of this same church, with the assistance and support of our aforesaid son, the king, to whom we have been most careful to give firm advice about this matter – so acting because,[573] with the grace of God going before and with the assistance of the king's resources, you are obliged to recall to the church all the items which have been alienated and forcibly usurped. If, indeed, William, Earl of Warenne, the Earl of Clare, Earl *Albric*, Geoffrey Martel, Henry Fitz Gerold, Robert Fitz Humphrey and John de Port have been the usurpers of the properties of the aforesaid church, you are to endeavour, with the utmost diligence, to convene them, so that, with every plea and excuse set aside, they completely restore all the possessions of the church of Ely which they are presuming to withhold by violence and, so it is said, in contravention of justice. But if they should disdain to do so, you are to bind them from thenceforth, on our authority, with no option of appeal, by the chain of excommunication and cause them to be shunned by all people of your diocese as limbs of the Devil, until suitable satisfaction is given. Given at the Lateran, 16th January.

---

[572] Source: monastic archives, cf. cartulary G; document printed in Holtzmann, *Papsturkunden in England*, ii, no 98. Date: 16th January, 1158.

[573] Repunctuating at p. 379.1, ed. Blake, with only a comma after *adhibere*.

130. A miracle concerning a certain boy-monk healed by St Æthelthryth.[574]

A little monk in our house, named John, a boy of amazing simplicity and innocence, twelve years old,[575] was suffering from an illness. He was smitten by a very bad ulceration which caused itching to spread generally through all his limbs and deprived him of the use of them and their movement. And he was not strong enough to sign himself with the sign of the cross, and was incapable of taking food or drink by himself: instead, his nourishment was given to him by the hands of his comrades and of servants. To be sure, he called continuously, in mental prayer, for the help of the blessed Æthelthryth and God his Saviour. But the people round about him had by now utterly despaired of his restoration to health.

And one day, while his heart was in anguish, on the one hand from bodily affliction and on the other from fear of death, he fell asleep towards noon, as he lay in the infirmary. Suddenly, there appeared to him a woman standing nearby, wearing the veil of holiness, who declared herself to be his lady, Æthelthryth, saying, 'O poor dear! You have been tightly bound up in the knot of sickness for a long time and you are still not recovering! With the help of God you will be able to recover from your sickness and attain your original health, but not entirely in this place. Do not delay[576] to go to Bury St Edmunds. In that place, very close to here, you will soon be cured.' And, coming up to him, as if wiping his sweat away with the edge of her cloak and removing all the dust from upon him, she subsequently withdrew to the church. Carefully watching her, he followed at a distance until, coming right to the shrine, he began to keep vigil there, in order to pray, And when – so it seemed to him – he bowed his head to make supplication, he vomited up all the poison by which he was being inwardly tormented and afterwards, on waking up, he was made well and then related in sequence the things which he had seen, in praise of God and of his bountiful virgin Æthelthryth. And, not long afterwards, coming to Bury St Edmunds, he made earnest prayer to God's martyr, St Edmund himself, so that by his merits he might obtain the remedy revealed to him, one, furthermore, that had been made manifest to him in a vision.

131. About a demoniac rescued by the blessed Æthelthryth.[577]

We are recalling to recollection a marvellous thing which the faithful congregation knows well enough and remembers. There was staying in Ely a

---

[574] Source: miracle narrative, also included in B (*Book of Miracles*).

[575] Reading conjecturally at p. 379.15, ed. Blake: *duodecennis* for *duodennis*.

[576] Reading conjecturally at p. 379.26, ed. Blake: *tardes* for *tardas*.

[577] Source: miracle narrative, also included in B (*Book of Miracles*).

young foreigner called Richard. He showed the virtue of gentleness and patience in his facial expression, so it was thought. But, being in urgent need of nourishment for his mental processes – a complaint which the human race scarcely guards against, or does not guard against at all – he incurred, in the course of much bodily discomfort, the loss of his mind's sanity. He became a complete demoniac, he broke chains and fetters, could not be held by any means of binding him. And why or how this happened to him, we do not know, but we declare that it was by a judgement of God, and a just one. And for a very long time he kept disturbing and terrorizing people all around, day and night, with the misery of his madness, hiding in pits all through the country districts, now that he had spurned human society.

Then, lo and behold, one night, while he was being very seriously agitated by the goad of his insanity, he roused everyone all around from their night's sleep by shouting in the market-place[578] and running around, and thus it was, while he was wandering in the street in the shades of night, that there stood in his way a nun with a most fair face, whose incandescence lit up the darkness of the shadowy night by its splendour, and she said to him: 'Poor man, how you are exciting yourself and others, causing a disturbance with your most pitiable raving. I am full of compassion for your weakness.' In reply he said, 'Who are you, lady? Let me know your name and, for Christ's sake, help me in this most disastrous crisis.' Marvels followed upon marvels. She replied, 'I am Æthelthryth, the lady of this place, whom you for a long time have been calling upon to help you in your prayers.' And, approaching, she wrapped the head of the sick man in the sleeve of the virginal robe of the nun's clothing which she was wearing, signing him with the sign of the Holy Cross, and she said: 'Go your way and give thanks to God, who has rescued you from this infirmity and from the power of the Enemy.' And immediately that personage disappeared. But the sick man, confident in the salvation mercifully granted to him, ran to the church, spent the remaining part of the night in prayer, keeping vigil throughout, and, magnifying and praising God, waited with joy for the congregation which would come there in the morning. He related to everyone how the blessed and most forgiving Æthelthryth had come to meet him, and how he was snatched away from the Enemy and from the danger of death.

132. About sailors in peril on the sea saved by St Æthelthryth.[579]

There came about a miracle which should by no means be suppressed in silence: rather it should be brought into common knowledge for the glory of God and the glorious virgin Æthelthryth.

---

[578] 'Market-place': Lat. simply: *platea.*

[579] Source: miracle narrative, not included in B *(Book of Miracles).*

Well then, one day, as some merchants were sailing across the sea, a raging storm arose which was whipping the whole sea up in peaks and tossing the ship hither and thither in a pitiable manner, so much so that, what with the winds assailing it and the waves buffeting it too, the ship had been shattered on all sides and the waters were flowing in. The wretched men, exposed as they were to so many dangers, realized that they were on the brink of death and deprived of all human means of escaping, so they had recourse to divine aid and called for it, over and over again and as often as they could, through the merits of the most clement virgin Æthelthryth, and pleaded with tearful voices that she should come [to their assistance].

And, immediately, the raging of the winds subsided, the swelling of the sea abated and the gaping ship itself was made whole by divine agency, and thereafter gave the water no way of coming in. And so, now that the waves had been calmed and the winds were blowing with moderation, the sailors breathed again and, proceeding with their voyage on a direct course, they made as speedily as possible for the shores they had longed for.

Furthermore, on making landfall in England, they soon went to the church of the blessed virgin, gave manifold thanks to God and St Æthelthryth, their saviouress, and they gave the timbers as well,[580] to correspond with the fact that they had brought them to land in the ship, as an offering to repair damaged parts[581] of this same church, as a sign of their deliverance, and with joy they returned, praising God and glorifying Him in respect to the saints.

133. [[A mandate of Bishop Nigel for the estate of Bawdsey.[582]

Nigel, Bishop of Ely to Hervey de Glanville and his son Ranulf: greeting. I instruct you, as you love me and the fief which you hold from me, that you release to the monks their estate of Bawdsey, exempt from ties and in a peaceful state, and free from all harassment, just as they were in possession of it in the year and day on which King Henry was alive and dead and when our lord the King, on the last occasion, crossed the Channel. And if you claim any right in respect to it, I will uphold what is right in consequence of this. Farewell.]]

---

[580] Translating the reading of F: *ligna quoque*, as printed by Blake (p. 381.2).

[581] Lat. *ruinas*. N.B. The word for 'church' could refer to the whole monastery, not just what we would term the 'cathedral'.

[582] Source: monastic archives, cf. cartularies DGM. Date: episcopate of Nigel, 1135 X 1169. Blake argues that this charter dates to King Stephen's time, thus earlier than its position in *LE* suggests. This chapter is a marginal addition in E, in a later hand; it is in O but not in F.

134. A charter of Bishop Nigel to the effect that the monks of Ely should hold their churches freely and in peace.[583]

Nigel, by the grace of God Bishop of Ely, to all children of holy mother Church:[584] may you abound[585] in the spirit of wise counsel and boldness. Whatsoever expenditures or grants have been made by bishops most holy, with divine insight, for the benefit of holy religion, ought to be conserved and venerated by their successors, so that it may not be overturned from its foundation, or diminished by misinterpretation. For to detract from the privileges of a venerable church is like sacrilege. And indeed, any one of the bishops who, on some pretence of authority, attempts to appropriate for himself grants made out of religious devotion by himself or by his predecessors, becomes devoid of charitableness and does not avoid sacrilege, as he is maltreating a benefaction. Wishing, therefore, to provide for the peace of our beloved sons, the monks of Ely, for evermore, we renew, on the authority of the present document, the grant set down in writing by us long ago, concerning the churches which are on the lands of these same brothers. We lay down, therefore, and, in so far as it is recognized to concern us, we give instructions, that these same aforementioned churches, along with the estates in which they were founded, should belong to the jurisdiction and demesne of these said sons of ours and, in so far as it pertains to the duty of our charge, it is our wish that they be assigned to the purposes of the aforementioned brothers, with all their benefits and revenues, for all time in the future. Moreover, in future, from the time when they have become vacant, they are to accrue to their advantage in all respects, unless they wish, of their own accord, to bestow any item <from them>[586] to honourable and suitable persons. However, the priests or clerics who will minister in the oft-mentioned churches are to be appointed by the aforesaid brothers, following as they do an estimable way of life. For indeed, it is thus that we interpret the wording concerning our grant, written by us long ago, and we order that the wording subject to this interpretation be adhered to in its entirety. May any person, indeed, who is a faithful preserver of this state of affairs, receive recompense from almighty God. But may violators, if they do not come to their senses again, not avoid the damnation of the judgement that lasts for ever. With the following as witnesses: Hubert the cleric; Master Malger;

[583] Source: monastic archives, cf. cartularies DGM. Date: perhaps 1162 X 1169. Blake suggests that this charter might have been written in response to an extant letter from Archbishop Thomas à Becket (MS Cotton Titus A i, fo. 53).

[584] Lat. *matris ecclesie filiis*: an alternative to a formula meaning 'to all faithful Christian people' (see next chapter) and hence to be interpreted generally, rather than to Ely minster as mother church.

[585] Here, and in chapter 135, Bishop Nigel replaces the normal formula, *salutem*, with wording dependent on an infinitive.

[586] Supplementing the reading of the LE mss. with *inde* (from cartulary D).

Geoffrey the chaplain; Master Peter; Ralph, son of Alexander; the clerics Henry and Bartholomew; John the physician; Master Ærnald; Master Robert *Christianus,* and many others.

135. Another charter of the bishop to the effect that none of his successors should harass the monks of Ely with respect to their holdings.[587]

Nigel, by the grace of God Bishop of Ely, to all faithful Christian people to whom these letters may come: may you be comforted anew by the consolation of the Paraclete. Those who are continually applying themselves to acts of divine service ought to be fortified by fatherly consolation. Hence, by virtue of[588] the office of bishop enjoined upon us by God, we are compelled to provide sufficiently, by means of the most vigilant actions <and>[589] the utmost diligence, for the upkeep of our sons, the monks of Ely, and for their quietude. We decree, therefore, no, rather, we confirm, in renewal of what has previously been made statutory, and by this present document, at God's instigation, issue a general prohibition: that no one of our successors in the bishopric of Ely shall dare to take for himself or usurp any commodity from the lands and possessions assigned for the purposes of the aforesaid brothers except with their assent, or try to demand it on the pretext of some aid-requirement. But let all the revenues from their properties, in future, provide for their purposes for evermore. On the other hand, if at any time, due to pressing need, we have taken any commodity from the aforesaid possessions, we declare by this present writ that this was not on the basis of any customary right. In addition, we also reiterate something already made statutory: no one is to dare personally to meddle with the court of the oft-mentioned brothers in respect of any cases, greater or lesser, whatsoever, which are recognized as pertaining to our church. Rather, let all cases, greater or smaller, which shall have arisen in regard to their holdings or as a result of their holdings, be always, without any exception, subject to their jurisdiction and power. For the authority of our predecessor firmly established this and the tenor of our charter written long ago confirmed it. Indeed, whoever in future attempts to infringe or abrogate this written statement of our ordinance, unless he regains his senses, shall experience vengeance from the Eternal Judge. With these witnesses: Hubert the cleric; Master Malger; Geoffrey the chaplain; Master Peter; Master Roger; Ralph Fitz Alexander; the clerics Henry and Bartholomew; John the

---

[587] Source: monastic archives, cf. Ely, Dean and Chapter, charter no. 55; cartularies GM. Date: perhaps 1162 X 1169.

[588] Reading with E at p. 382.18, ed. Blake: *Unde ex iniuncto nobis . . .*

[589] Supplying from Dean and Chapter, charter no. 55: *<que>* after *summa* at p. 382.20, ed. Blake.

physician; Master Ærnald; Master Robert *Christianus* and many others.

136. Again, another charter of the bishop, concerning the estate of *Ærnethern*. [590]

Nigel, by the grace of God <Bishop>[591] of the church of Ely, to <all faithful Christian people>[592] present and future, nearby and far off, known and unknown: greeting and prayer. Your fraternal selves certainly <are to> know[593] that I have never given to Adam of Cockfield, or to any person, St Æthelthryth's estate of *Ærnethern*, on terms whereby our beloved brothers, the monks of Ely, would lose any of their legal entitlement, whether in respect to the revenue from herrings or anything pertaining to herrings, which used to be paid by that place to the church of Ely on the day on which King Henry was alive and dead and many years afterwards, at the time of the war.[594] Hence, we earnestly entreat all lords and all our friends that, if ever there shall be any opportuneness[595] of time <for hearing>[596] the case of the aforesaid brothers, they should give their complaint a diligent hearing and take it in hand with justice, and defend them. With the following witnesses: Hubert the cleric; John the physician; Master Peter; Master Roger; Stephen de Marisco; William Muscat; Goscelin of Terrington.[597]

137. How Bishop Nigel became ill, and about his demise.[598]

In these days, however, Bishop Nigel, paterfamilias of Ely, fell sick and his weakness was so extreme that scarcely any breath remained in him. But I will first give[599] an idea of the calamitous nature of this very great sickness and later I will make clear what a sad outcome for us resulted from it.

---

[590] Source: monastic archives, cf. cartularies GM. Date: 1139 X 1160.

[591] The word <*episcopus*> is missing at p. 383.12, ed. Blake.

[592] It seems that specification of the addressees, e.g. *cunctis fidelibus Christianis*, as well as the word *episcopus*, is lacking between *ecclesie* and *presentibus* (p. 383.12, ed. Blake).

[593] Assuming that the usual formula for giving notice, *noverit* (not *novit*) . . . was the original intended wording of the charter at p. 383.13, ed. Blake.

[594] Or, 'in war-time'. Lat. *tempore guerre*.

[595] Taking *opportunitatis*, in the charter-text at p. 383.19, ed. Blake, to be a partitive genitive.

[596] Reading conjecturally in the charter-text at p. 383.19f.: *causam predictorum fratrum <audiendi>* . . .

[597] There follow, in O, eighteen further charters of Nigel not printed in Blake's edition.

[598] Source: first paragraph (on Bishop Nigel's sickness) probably Richard of Ely on the episcopate of Nigel; remainder of chapter: separate miracle narrative. The chapter is paralleled in B (*Book of Miracles*).

[599] Both Latin main verbs in this sentence are in the present tense.

A certain very poor woman was living in Ely, supported by a living-allowance supplied by the monks. Living under a semblance of religious discipline, she was taming her body by vigils and much abstinence to set aside its libidinousness. Well then, one night in her slumbers, it appeared to her that she was in the church near the entrance which faces the altar of the blessed Æthelthryth and she went in to make supplication to the Lord and His saints resting there. There, at the shrine of the lady saints, she caught sight of a nun coming forth from above the altar and, step by step, making her way right up to her. She saw her head and her eyes up above looking in her direction, as she spoke to her: 'Do you see, good woman, how everything here is going to ruin and there is no one who gives it a thought?' And she had been carrying under her cloak a staff, which she raised up high and said, in her presence: 'By means of this staff, I extinguished the enemies and the destroyers of the goods of this place and forthwith, at the command of God, I will similarly beat down with it those who remain, in vengeance for the bountiful queen, the virgin Æthelthryth.' In answer to these words the woman said: 'My lady, please say your name and who you are, so that I may know truly from whom I have heard such things.' And she said: 'I am Wihtburh, with whose virginity the Lord, the Heavenly Bridegroom, deigned to unite – the sister of the most holy Æthelthryth. But as for what you have heard and seen: tell of it truthfully, and when you come here in the morning, you will encounter the monk Augustine. It is to him that you are to reveal my latest secrets.'

Thereupon, the woman, extremely frightened, woke from her sleep and, just as had been indicated to her, she found the aforementioned monk confronting her as she was going in, and related the order of events in her vision. On hearing it, he was utterly astounded and said: 'These things I believe without a doubt, trustworthy, and I think it no wonder if things are turning out badly for us, because we are for ever attending to the losses of this house.' And not long afterwards, at the beginning of the feast of Easter, the bishop, while seated in the church, was smitten by severe illness, and could scarcely be given relief to the slightest degree by the compounds[600] of physicians. And thus for three whole years he used to be carried in a chair by the hands of his retainers, utterly deprived of the functioning of his body. He persevered continuously in confession and prayer to God right until the very end of his lifetime but, even so, he was not 'turned, so as to bless' Jacob and 'the house of Judah'.[601] And he died in the 1169th year of the incarnation of

---

[600] Lat. *pigmentis*.

[601] Cf. Zechariah 8.15 Vulgate, with Genesis 27.27. In Zechariah's prophesy it is God who turns and blesses the house of Israel, but Latin does not normally change subjects in mid-sentence, so presumably the meaning is that Bishop Nigel to the end of his life failed to bring blessings upon the prior and community.

the Lord, in the thirty-sixth year of his episcopacy, on the 30th May, a Friday, at the ninth hour,[602] and on the Sunday afterwards he was buried by the venerable monk William, Bishop of Norwich, and was honourably buried in the church of St Æthelthryth near the altar of Holy Cross, in the seventeenth year of Henry the Younger, King [of the English].

But the monks bewailed in that place their orphaned state, they wept for the death of a father and were exceedingly grieved, with one accord calling upon God with prayers and tears not to leave them orphans, but to send them the Holy Spirit as their Counsellor and Champion, and to provide for their house a pastor and someone suitable to preside over them.[603]

138. With what severity God avenged the injuries done to His virgin Æthelthryth, and how Robert the chamberlain gave Denny to St Æthelthryth.[604]

So it was that when the Lord had struck him down, bold and strong, proud and arrogant as he was, He consigned all the enemies of His beloved virgin Æthelthryth, at one and the same time, to stupor and unknowing, to whispering and abusive talk[605] on the part of everyone all around. These were the enemies who, as has been explained in a previous chapter,[606]

---

[602] The day and hour also of the death of the Lord Jesus, cf. Matthew 27.45ff. Bishop Nigel's burial near the altar of Holy Cross would therefore have seemed apposite.

[603] In ms. O there follows here the further additional chapter, printed in Blake's edition, p. 385, n. *d*: **On the ornaments which the said bishop bestowed upon the church of Ely and about the priors there were in Ely in his time.** The bishop referred to bestowed upon his church one alb with decoration, embroidered with gold with wonderful beasts and birds, with an amice which belongs to it and is surrounded by stones and excellently ornamented in the manner of a collar with one stone of white colour which is called 'Camau'. He gave in addition two chasubles, one black, encircled all around with gold; another of saffron colour, embroidered with red birds. He also gave one cope which is called 'the World's Glory'. In his time there were four priors at the house of Ely: William, Thembert, Alexander and Salomon, who was later abbot of Thorney. He gave to the church of Ely a decorated alb of which the decorations are of Saracen work, and two white copes, ornamented all around with orphrey, with silver fastenings. Prior Thembert gave a cope of black *purpura*, decorated with orphrey, with gold circles and flowers all over, and two copes without ornament.

[604] Source: the chapter is paralleled in B (*Book of Miracles*), but probably originated in Richard of Ely's account of the episcopate of Nigel, picking up as it does the theme of the punishment of those perceived to be enemies of St Æthelthryth (cf. chapters 78, 89, 92). The present chapter takes up the narrative from where the bishop has fallen sick (chapter 137, first paragraph) and presents an alternative account of his last years and demise to the one presented in paragraphs 2–4 of that chapter. The narrative in the present chapter extends beyond Nigel's death. Its last paragraph (found in E, but not F) takes us, awkwardly, back to Nigel's life-time, and the acquisition of Denny.

[605] The Latin alludes to e.g. Jeremiah 19.8 Vulgate: *et ponam civitatem hanc in stuporem et in sibilum.*

[606] Or 'the previous chapter': if we assume that the compiler is simply taking over his source material word for word, as he often seems to have done; but the reference is not to *LE* iii. 137.

devised iniquity and carried out a very bad plan of action against her. These men I have delayed mentioning by name, with the consequence that I am charged by some with untruthfulness. I have delayed because I have been exceedingly bitter in the indignation of my spirit: <I have been grieved>[607] at presenting, in my recollections, the continual miseries of men, incurred because their guilty acts have demanded it – although it is to groaning that they move me, rather than to contempt. However, so that we may not be judged to have received the grace of God unworthily, we present an account, relating both to monks within the house and to laymen outside it, who had acquiesced in the very bad plan, as the virgin of God had made clear through a dream.[608]

Prior Thembert and Ralph the sacrist, whom the Lord had given as watchmen over the house of Israel, were, in fact, the first to go; then Adam the constable died, just as the blessed virgin had predicted, and horrible visions about him were made manifest after his death. Alexander the butler followed him in facing peril, smitten at the time of his espousal[609] by a serious illness, so that for a long period up to his death he had neither voice nor use of the senses. No one doubted but that he had been struck down by the lady saint. Then there was William of Shelford, whom we have already mentioned above; Henry *Peregrinus*, too, afflicted in the midriff, lived for three years in a sufficiently dire condition. Next, to be sure, was Ralph Fitz Olaf, who deprived this house of a very fine pall, valued at forty pounds, and was a persuasive advocate and constant supporter of the ruination and misappropriation of many estates and goods of the monastery. Now, indeed, by the judgement of God, he was overtaken suddenly by illness: a cyst which the physicians call a carbuncle swelled up under his nipple; he had it excised but could not be cured of it. Then Richard *de Sancto Paulo* came up against the stumbling-block of affliction: he became so amazingly feeble that he was abandoned altogether by his kinsfolk and people known to him. But Archdeacon William was in the church of St Æthelthryth itself one day, pleading a case against his lord himself, when, in the presence of everyone assembled, he suddenly became deaf and dumb. What need for many words? He was carried by the monks into the infirmary; all week he was without movement of his body, exhausted by the strain put upon him in many ways by his illness; on the ninth day, he breathed his last. Thus, we report on a great many of those who wronged this house: so as not to importune the reader, we omit mention of those whom the common people unceasingly

---

[607] Reading conjecturally at p. 385.15, ed. Blake: *Fui enim amarus nimis in indignatione spiritus mei: <merui> iuges hominum miserias . . . reminiscendo proferre.*

[608] Reading conjecturally at p. 385.19, ed. Blake: *sompnium* for *sompnum*, or taking *sompnum* to have the equivalent sense.

[609] Lat. *desponsationis:* this term seems usually to refer to literal betrothal.

call to mind.

Finally, indeed, the bishop likewise, sitting in the same church, had a business-matter in hand with the people into whose hands he had wrongfully dispersed the possessions of the lady saint; he began to be seriously ill; with the breath of life scarcely remaining in him, he was carried outdoors in an unconscious state, so that the hearer ought[610] not to doubt but that truly the Lord takes vengeance against enemies of his holy virgin Æthelthryth. But many people had flocked together to visit him and, as a consequence of the bishop's seizure, made in a keen impulse of devotion the due acknowledgements to God in respect of his saints.

Finally, when he was snatched away from the prison-house of the flesh, the monks consigned the body of their father, with very great sorrow and weeping, to most honourable burial in a fitting position within this very hall.[611]

When he had been buried, his son Richard, who has been mentioned above, continually an enemy to the church of Ely, quickly went up to the king, across the sea, fearful that evil was being prepared for him, supposing the envoy whom the church was sending were to arrive there ahead of him. By accusing them of many things in this man's presence they made the lord King so angry, relating many sinister and dishonourable things about them, that, on dispatching him to England, he gave orders through a cleric of his, the ex-priest Wimer, that Ely's prior should be deposed from his position of ministry and the monks banned from use of all their goods.[612] And so it came about.

But indeed, it was in these days that a certain nobleman, Robert the chamberlain of the Count of Brittany, fell mortally ill. When he foresaw that death was upon him, he asked to become a monk and received the habit of holy religion, as he had requested, from the monks of Ely. In addition, he handed over to them, along with himself, the daughter-house at Denny, which the monks themselves had founded under his purview, so that they might take possession of it with right of ownership for evermore. And he made the grant in the presence of the public[613] and of all his kin, as the charters set out below intimate.

---

[610] Reading conjecturally at p. 387.1, ed. Blake: *ut qui audit diffidere non debeat* . . . (instead of *debet*).

[611] Lat. *aula* = 'hall', 'nave'; evidently the nave of 'St Æthelthryth's Church', cf. chapter 137, p. 385.1f., ed. Blake.

[612] For interpretation of this report see Blake, Appendix C.3 (pp. 407–8) on: 'The possessions of the priory during a vacancy in the see.'

[613] Lat. *plebe*.

BOOK III

139. A charter of Robert the chamberlain to the effect that he gave Denny to St Æthelthryth.[614]

Robert, chamberlain of the Earl of Richmond, to all children of Holy Church, present and future: greeting. You are to know that I have granted and given and confirmed in this present charter, as an act of permanent almsgiving, to St James and St Leonard and to Reginald, monk of Ely, and the monks of that same church serving God and St James and St Leonard [on][615] the island which is called Denny: two parts of Elmeney, together with[616] the land which I gave in the vill of *Beche* to the church of St James and St Leonard of Denny in the presence of the lord Bishop Nigel for the salvation of my soul, and that of my wife, and for the soul of my father and that of my mother, since that place was consecrated by that same bishop, namely: nine acres, three in any one field, and one curtilage,[617] to be held freely and quietly and without any customary obligation for ever. In addition to this donation, I made other grants to them as well, namely: that messuage in *Beche* which Godric, son of Rafrid *Brito* used to hold, with all the land which this very man Godric held in the fields, which is assessed at a half-virgate, and I made this gift so freely to them, that they shall be quit for ever from all scutage-payments and aid-payments and all customary dues which pertain either to me or to my heirs or also to our lords, from whom we hold our tenancy, with the single exception that they are to pay for the last-mentioned half-virgate the taxes which pertain to the king's crown and which are current thoughout the whole county. After these, moreover, I gave from my demesne a ninth part of Wilbraham, and of Wendy, and the church of Wendy and everything pertaining to this same church to God and to St James and St Leonard and to the brothers serving God for evermore on the aforesaid island. I also confirm the grant to the aforesaid church of Denny which I made in the presence of the lord Bishop Nigel, namely all the churches of my land, as they in future become vacant, wherever they are, specifically: the church of Wendy and Wilbraham and Kirkby,[618] and I wish and instruct that the aforesaid church

[614] Source: monastic archives, cf. cartularies GM. Date: episcopate of Nigel, 1133 X 1169. On the basis of the fact that Robert uses the style of chamberlain, Nicholas Karn (pers. comm. 17.6.02) argues for a date no later than 1158 and notes the existence of a papal bull as early as 1160 initiating a process whereby Denny passed out of the control of Ely and into that of the Templars (see Holtzmann, *Papsturkunden in England* i, nos. 79, 109). The positioning in *LE* of the charters relating to Denny is therefore very odd, as is the omission of any mention of the Templars.

[615] Reading with F and cartulary copies: *in insula*, not the reading of E (p. 388.1, ed. Blake).

[616] Reading with F: *cum terra*, in view of the parallel passages in related charters (p. 388.3, ed. Blake).

[617] A curtilage is defined as 'a small court, yard or piece of ground attached to a dwelling-house and forming one enclosure with it' (OED).

[618] Kirkby Fleetham in Yorkshire.

479

is to have them and hold them freely, and exempt from obligations, as a gift of alms for evermore. Moreover, my heirs, namely George and Nigel, allowed these grants of mine in the presence of the lord Bishop Nigel in a public audience.[619] I wish, therefore, and vehemently desire, and as a father to his most dear sons, I give instructions, that they augment and expand both the aforesaid island and the land in *Beche* which pertains to the aforesaid island, to the advantage of this same church and for their soul, by whatever means they legitimately can. Furthermore, I have done all this so that perpetual remembrance of me and of my parents may be kept there before God. But if, by chance, after these transactions, any of my heirs steals from the aforesaid church of Denny any item from these gifts of alms, may he be cursed by my lips in the sight of God and condemned in the fearsome Judgement, unless he regains his senses. AMEN. Witnesses: Walter *Pilatus*; Martin, Dean of Bottisham; Ralph, Dean of Whaddon; Peter, Dean of Histon; Dean Baldric; Master Malger; Bernard, Priest of *Beche*; Robert *Christianus*; Ærnald *de Laventonia*; Henry, a cleric; Ralph the steward; William, his clerk;[620] Everard of *Beche*.

140. A charter of the Count of Brittany about the same matter.[621]

Conan, Duke of Brittany, Earl of Richmond, to all children of Holy Church, both present and future, and all his bailiffs and all his men, French and English: greeting. May it be known to you all that I have granted, and in this my charter confirmed, for the salvation of my soul and the souls of my ancestors, all the gifts which Robert, my chamberlain, has charitably given to the church of St James and St Leonard on the island which is called Denny, and to the monks of Ely serving God in that place, with the object of pure and permanent almsgiving. For this reason, I wish and instruct that the aforesaid monks are to have and possess these grants as well, and as peacefully, and as completely, as the charter of the aforesaid Robert testifies to them, because this same aforementioned Robert has petitioned me on this account, orally, and I have made the grant to him. Witnesses: Countess Margaret; the constable Alan; the chamberlain Ralph; Robert, the Count's brother; Brian and Reginald, brothers of the Count; Henry Fitz Hervey; Walter, son of *Acarus*; Nigel, son of the chamberlain; Henry and Bertram, two twins; Nicholas of *Muletune*; Wimer, son of Warner; Master *Drui*; Alan *de Bass*;[622] Henry *de la Camera*; John *de Camera*; Blanchard; Bartholomew, a

---

[619] Lat. *in communi audientia*.

[620] The same Latin word, *clericus*, can be translated as either 'cleric' or 'clerk'.

[621] Source: monastic archives, cf. cartularies GM. Blake's dating, 1160 X 1169, is deemed too late by Karn (pers. comm. 17.6.02); see above on chapter 139.

[622] Most probably = 'of Bassingbourn'.

monk; *Gord'* Pinchard and very many others.

141. A charter of Aubrey Picot about how the monks of Ely bought his part of Denny.[623]

Aubrey Picot to all children of Holy Church both present and future: greeting. Having heard the frequent complaining of the monk Reginald and the brothers of Elmeney, specifically because, on that same island, they are very seriously troubled by influxes of water and impeded in their service of God, in sympathy with their inconvenience and wishing to help this same man and wishing to make an improvement to my almsgiving, specifically so that it may be possible for divine service to be freely and consistently attended by them, I have given to God and St James and St Leonard and to the aforesaid monk Reginald, and his aforementioned brothers and their successors, with the object of perpetual almsgiving, free, moreover, without ties, and exempt from all secular service and customary obligation or taxation in perpetuity, whether in respect to the king or in respect to me or in respect to my heirs or anyone else: four acres and a half on the island which is called Denny, that is to say, in a higher position, because of flood-waters and in a position more suitable for the construction of a church and its buildings and for the making of gardens and coppice-woods. The object of this is that they may transfer their abode to this more suitable island from the first-mentioned island which is unsuitable, as has been said, because of influxes of water. However, the aforesaid island, namely Elmeney, is to remain available for their purposes, together with the land which my father Henry gave them in the vill of *Beche,* that is six acres, two in any one field, and one curtilage. And I did this with the agreement of my wife and my brothers and my heirs. Indeed, the aforementioned men, the monk Reginald and his brothers, wishing to provide support for my needs, have given me in exchange, from the wherewithal of their church's benefice, two-and-a-half silver marks and twelve pence. I desire, therefore, that this grant of mine should remain firm and stable, for the honour of God and the aforementioned saints, and for the convenience and peace of the aforesaid brothers, and for my salvation and that of all my kin. Witnesses . . . [624]

---

[623] Source: monastic archives, cf. cartularies GM. Date: see above on chapter 139.

[624] The witness-list is not given in the *LE* mss. but a partial copy of it occurs in cartulary M, viz.: 'With these witnesses: Jonathan, priest of Cambridge; the priest Nicholas; the priest Herbert; the priest Absalom; the priest Robert and others.' See also Blake's note *ad loc.* on a charter-fragment in which some of the same names occur, but not in the same order.

142. A charter of Bishop Nigel about the same matter, to the effect that his monks are to hold Denny freely and in peace.[625]

Nigel, by the grace of God Bishop of Ely, to the children of the whole Catholic Church, present and future: perpetual greeting in the Lord. It pertains to our office, undoubtedly, to be glad to further the pious endeavours of good people and to sanction with episcopal authority the arrangements salutarily made by these people for the honour of God and for the healing of their souls. In view of these considerations, we give thanks for the pious act of devotion of our beloved sons, Robert, chamberlain of the Earl of Richmond and Aubrey Picot. We ratify, and decree by episcopal authority to be firm and stable for evermore, the grant which they have made to God and to the blessed James and the blessed Leonard and to Reginald, our monk, and the monks of Ely, our brothers, serving God on the island which is called Denny – both in this island itself and in another island which is called Elmeney – a grant relating to the churches of Wilbraham and Wendy with all the tithes belonging to them, and also to a ninth part of {Robert's} own demesne[626] of Wilbraham and Wendy and to lands outside the aforesaid islands, and some revenues and alms assigned to the aforesaid monastery, with a view to increasing the frequency of divine service in that place and for the sustenance of the brothers living there, in accordance with what is contained in the charters of the same men, namely Robert and Aubrey. If, additionally, <from> henceforth,[627] these aforementioned men or any other faithful people, prompted by a God-sent impulse, shall have contributed benefactions to the aforesaid monastery from the moveable goods conferred on them by God, we confirm no less, by the aforementioned power of the office which we hold, the grant of those benefactions for divine service in that same place, and for the use of these same brothers both future and present. And so that no one may rashly dare to unsettle or disturb them and presume to take away or diminish the possessions or liberties of that place, we prohibit this by an edict of excommunication. But we decree that venerators and benefactors of this monastery are sharers in God's blessing and mine. Witnesses: . . .

143. The passion of the most holy Thomas the martyr, Archbishop of Canterbury.

For a long time I had been feeling fatigued by the burden of my studious endeavour and had almost collapsed in a state of prostration and, this being the case, I made up my mind to rejoice in the attainment of a longed-for objective. Storm-tossed though I had been over a long distance by the waves

---

[625] Source: monastic archives, cf. cartularies GM.

[626] Lat. simply *dominii sui*, 'his own demesne'.

[627] Reading with MO: *de cetero* (p. 391. 8–9, ed. Blake).

of this expansive labour, I was making speed to the haven of rest at last. And I would have thought that I had rid myself of the encumbrance of my prolix task, and it had been my desire to have reached the bosom of perpetual rest. However, the thought came into my mind of the most holy Thomas, confessor of the Lord and beloved martyr of Christ who, recently, and now in our times, is seen to have met his death. And I have resolved to extend my work by including him, so that my labour, entered upon in a holy beginning may, by the mercy of God, be allotted a joyful ending. But, since many people abhor prolixity and obscurity of speech, it will be in a succinct and nimble style that I will touch briefly upon the martyrdom of this most blessed athlete of the Lord.

At the time when Henry II was first presiding over the monarchy of the English and over also the many overseas regions comprised within it,[628] this blessed confessor of Christ, descended from citizens of London of no mean standing, was charged with the archdeaconry of Canterbury under Archbishop Theobald, in succession to whom he was elected as archbishop – with the king's consent, furthermore – and received consecration. But – and this was a miracle – no sooner was he anointed sacramentally with holy unction than his mind became replete[629] with the reality of the sacrament, that is, with the manifold grace of the Holy Spirit. And since for a steward of the Church it is permissible to cultivate and increase the things which pertain to the Church, and not permissible to neglect and diminish them, he began to make efforts to wrest from usurpers estates of his church which had most unjustly been given away or ceded by his predecessors, and to restore the legal position of the church to its original state. Moreover, because he used to find fault with negligent behaviour of the clerics who belonged to the court, they[630] provoked the king and all his household to bitter anger against the Lord's saint.

Retreating, as a consequence of this, for no small while and, as it were, awaiting his hour, he bore adverse circumstances patiently, but endured an exile and harsh proscription which lasted into a seventh year. Finally, after peace had been restored between them through the intervention of the Pope and the King of the French and a number of archbishops and bishops, he returned to his church, this being the will of God, and spent his time so intent on prayers and preaching, acts of almsgiving, vigils and fasts, that even those familiar with his religious devotion when he was in the lands of Gaul, were amazed.

---

[628] Lat. *et interiacentibus transmarinis etiam multis regionibus.*

[629] Interpreting, conjecturally, as if the reading at p. 392.2, ed. Blake, were *refercitur* rather than *refertur.*

[630] This sentence does not hang together grammatically: the subject of *exasperaverunt* must be assumed to be *clerici* (nominative).

But he had not yet been reinstated in his church for a month when – behold! – four courtiers, arriving from overseas, addressed him in the following manner: 'We bring a mandate from the king according to which you are to make your way to his son, the new king, to do what you are obliged to do for him: to restore to communion the bishops who have been excommunicated.' The sainted Archbishop Thomas replied, 'I have received a command from the new king not to travel through his cities and towns, and not to come to him. Moreover, it is well known that the bishops to whom you have just referred were excommunicated not by me but by the lord Pope, since they presumed to consecrate this new king without my consent.' At this the courtiers burst into abuse and threats. The blessed archbishop answered, 'Look elsewhere for the kind of person who would fear your threats! For your swords are no more at the ready than my mind is ready for martyrdom. Look elsewhere for the kind of person who would flee from you. For you will find me prepared to confront you, foot to foot, in the battle of the Lord! Far be it from me for ever that I should flee because of your swords or depart from justice!' As he was saying this, they laid hands upon him as fast as they could, dragging him along so that they could carry out the sacrilege outside, as they were instructed, but, as he had been grasped by one of the clergy, he could not be easily moved away. So, one of the aforesaid sons of Satan, with the sword which he was holding raised aloft, almost cut off the arm of the aforesaid cleric and with the same blow struck him on the head, an unblemished lamb for God. He murdered his own father in the womb of his mother, extinguishing him around the eleventh hour of the day. Eventually, after another blow received to his head, the martyr bent his knees and forearms, offering himself to God as a living sacrifice. But, as he was falling forward, the third man inflicted upon him a heavy wound. The fourth so sliced from his head the crown, which was of considerable breadth, that blood made white and brain-tissue reddened with blood adorned the face of the church, virgin and mother as she is, with the colours of the lily and the rose, at the death of a confessor and martyr.

And thus the priest of God, making his passage from the temporal World, had his birth in the heavens on {29th December} the fourth day {inclusive} preceding the first of January in the 11{7}1st[631] year from the incarnation of the Lord. And the next day, the monks, in the customary way, stripping the most pure body of the martyr to wash it, found that, beneath the habit of a canon regular, he had by now long been in the habit and order of monks, secretly, so that this was unknown even to his close associates. Finally, they found next to his flesh a hair-shirt so full of fleas that anyone would reckon his martyrdom of the previous day a lighter matter than this, and that his larger enemies had done him less harm than his smaller ones.

---

[631] The numeral is given incorrectly in EF.

His under-breeches, too, were found to be of hair-cloth, down to the knees, something which used formerly to be the custom among our men.

Truly, in the place of his martyrdom and the place where he spent the night before the high altar awaiting inhumation, and the place where, finally, he was buried, the leprous are made clean, the blind see, the deaf hear, the dead rise again, demoniacs are set free, and the sick are cleansed of various ailments as, by virtue of this very martyr, these and very many other feats, which would take a long time to recount, are brought to pass by Him who alone is blessed for evermore and is triumphant in respect to His saints.

LIBER ELIENSIS

Note on the Appendices

For the convenience, especially, of readers using this translation in conjunction with Blake's edition of the *Liber Eliensis*, translations are given below of the texts printed in his Appendices A and B, and of a Latin poem, cited in a note at the end of *LE* ii, which describes visual representations of four episodes in the life of St Æthelthryth.

APPENDIX A

Libellus Æthelwoldi: translation from the Latin text in Blake's Appendix A, pp. 395ff. from Trinity College, Cambridge MS O.2.41: preface; chapters 1–3; poems found in the *Libellus,* but not included in the *Liber Eliensis* transcripts.

A LITTLE BOOK ABOUT CERTAIN OUTSTANDING WORKS OF THE BLESSED BISHOP ÆTHELWOLD

Here begins the prologue to certain outstanding works of the blessed Bishop Æthelwold.

Since the knowledge of past things can come to be enveloped in the darkness of ignorance and, with the interposition of changed circumstances, can easily have slipped from human memory, it is worth the labour to entrust to diligent penmanship that which has been done in such a way as to be worthy of record, so that what would be consigned to oblivion, were it not written down, may thus be set forth for remembrance. And since we see the fictions, or absurdities, of the pagans set out in all seriousness and adorned and, so to speak, painted, with the colours of rhetoric, strengthened and supported by syllogisms and presentations of proofs, celebrated in public, and recited with praise in seminaries and schools, we have considered it fitting that the words and deeds of the saints be written out and, once written out, made into a contribution to the praise and honour of Christ so that, through them and in them, He Himself may be glorified and may be declared a worker of miracles, it being through Him that they become glorious and perform their marvels. For the Lord Himself spoke thus: 'Let your light shine forth among men, that they may see your good works and glorify your Father who is in Heaven.' The blessed Æthelwold, truly one of their company, was in his time eminent as a chosen bishop of God, whose life, gloriously renowned for virtues and miracles, blazed forth a shining light. If this is less than clear to anyone and he wishes to gain a fuller knowledge, he should read the book which was composed about his ancestry, life and death, and he will discover plainly how meritorious and holy a man he was. However, some of the notable things which he had done during his lifetime are not included in that book, nor were they written down in the Latin language. When Hervey, the venerable bishop of the church of Ely, a judicious and distinguished man, discovered that these matters were worthy of report, at the request of some of the brothers, he assigned me the task of translating them from the English language into Latin prose. In no way venturing to go against his instruction, I obeyed and undertook the work assigned me and, to the best of my ability, took pains to carry it through to the finishing touches. If there is anything set down in it which is acceptable to God, let it not be attributed to the burgeoning of arrogance, but set to the credit of the virtue of obedience.

1. How the blessed Æthelwold restored the community at Ely.

During the time when King Edgar, in the exercise of royal power, held control over the kingdom of the English, the blessed and outstanding Bishop Æthelwold, a man of special virtue and great holiness, shone as a brightly burning lamp among the people of God. After this man, endowed as he was with the adornment of all the virtues and with an exemplary record of good works, had undertaken to rule the church of God, he emerged not only as an energetic leader, but also as a noble founder of a great many communities. Some, indeed, he took from their beginning and developed through to their finishing touches, but others, which had been destroyed or abandoned, he rebuilt with painstaking restoration: he established a household of the High Paterfamilias in all respects under the rule of the holy monastic life, and supplied to them most generously revenues and landed estates, and other things of which they had need. Among these, he restored the monastic house at Ely. This monastery was very famous: of the highest repute for its relics and miracles. But pagans, assailing it long before in a cruel invasion, had set fire to the monastery and, after having cruelly put to death the numerous contingent of nuns there, and having seized all the goods from all around[1] departed, leaving the place, along with the relics, more or less a total ruin. And so afterwards, in its desolated state, the place had been added to the royal estate or treasury.

2. How King Edgar refused to give this same monastery to certain men who were asking for it.

At the same time, moreover, when the blessed Æthelwold, as we have said, was in his prime, two of the king's magnates, namely, Bishop Sigewold, a Greek by nationality, and Thurstan, a Dane by race, made a request to the king that this same monastery should be given to them. And as they were rivals of one another, panting after it with gaping mouths, and each of them reckoned

---

[1] Interpreting *undeunde* as equivalent to *undecumque* (p. 396.19, ed. Blake).

to achieve this object, a huge dispute and altercation arose between them, as to which of them would have his wish fulfilled. So, while these men were quarrelling with one another, a man called Wulfstan of Dalham who was a privy councillor of the king, a prudent man, full of good sense, received Heaven-sent inspiration, approached the king and said: 'Lord King, whereas we are all duty-bound to make provision for your safety and your authority to rule, there is no one of us who wishes to give you the advice that you ought to assent to their request. For if you knew, lord, how famous the house is and what precious relics are kept in the place about which they are disputing, you would certainly not wish to entrust the place in question to such men.' Then he gave an explanation to the king in an ordered fashion about the dignity of the place and the fame of the relics in question; for previously this was unknown to the king. When the king heard this, he was enflamed by divine fervour and not only kept refusing to give to the aforesaid men what they had asked for, but also kept saying that he would contribute to the greatness of the monastery in question.

3. How Æthelwold installed monks in the monastery of Ely.

And it was done. After those men, who said: 'Let us possess the sanctuary of God by right of inheritance', were thwarted and cheated of their desire, the glorious King Edgar, after summoning the blessed Æthelwold, entered into consultation with him, and having revealed to him his intention, began to ask the blessed man to gather together monks in the aforesaid place, to perform service to God, saying that he did not wish that such great relics should be kept any longer without anyone to promote their cult, and without suitable veneration. He also promised that he would make this same community rich by means of lands and grants, and that he would confirm this by a privilege of eternal liberty. The man of God realized immediately that the Holy Spirit was operating in the king; he gave thanks to God, in whose hand are the hearts of kings, and he did not hesitate to bring the good work to fruition that the king had enjoined upon him to bring to pass. He was mindful of the scripture which says: 'While we have time, let us do good to all',[2] and in another place: 'It has always been harmful to delay things which have been made ready.'[3] Why am I prevaricating? The blessed Æthelwold, then, always assiduous as he was in the furtherance of holy works, restored the aforesaid monastery, as we have said, on the instruction of the king; he adorned the site of the monastery in distinguished fashion with monastic buildings, he installed monks there and appointed a man of religion by the name of Byrhtnoth as their abbot, and he assigned the whole

---

[2] Galatians 6.10.

[3] Not scriptural, but from Lucan, *De Bello Civili*, i. 281.

to God and St Æthelthryth, this grant being confirmed by a privilege given by royal authority.

> Then were there truly golden ages in the World,
> Eternal Spring, then too, gleam'd forth a heav'nly grace;
> Then e'en had bramble like sweet rose-bush bloom'd;
> Then rivers rich with milk and honey flow'd;
> The earth then proffer'd fruit at will and on demand;
> Pure faith and peace, true love were then pre-eminent;
> Fraud, pride and envy, perjury then slunk away;
> Then liberty sat down upon a settled throne;
> Then in the church was Martha glorious and Mary, too;
> Good order then prevail'd, when this our patron throve.

Verses following *LibÆ* 4, equivalent to *LE* ii. 4

> O wealthy founder, blessèd wilt thou ever live!
> For earthly gifts bestow'd, heav'n's gifts thou hast receiv'd.
> Lo! Thou attainest Heaven: thither guide our sail,
> So we may reign with thee for aye, thy fellow citizens.

Verses following *LibÆ* 5, equivalent to *LE* ii. 7

> The custom of the ancient Enemy is oft-times thus:
> To break the peace of holy men, disturb the good.
> He arms the thievish World thus 'gainst the saints,
> To ensure defeat of just men's cause by villains' might,
> Unless the Lord's compassion deign to call a halt,
> Lest, put to testing, they endure too hard a trial.

Verses in the middle of *LibÆ* 7-9, equivalent to *LE* ii. 10

> How great a man he was, with such great grace imbued
> That, in this World, unworldly life he led for Christ!
> That blessèd father whom no sprite of darkness knew,
> Beneath whose breast the power of this World had no hold!
> O glory of the Church! Wisdom's receptacle renown'd,
> By imitating whom, O man, thou wilt become Christ's shrine!
> O Æthelwold, good father, patron, pious saint!
> Thy thirst was for Heav'n's joys 'midst riches of this age.
> Cheap grows the World: for thee, meanwhile, Heav'n's dow'r accrues.
> May we be dow'r'd likewise: deign, blest one, so to pray.

489

LIBER ELIENSIS

Verses following *LibÆ* 7–9, equivalent to *LE* ii. 10

The man I deem most worthy of good augury
Is he who serveth Christ whilst living in this World,
As Æthelwold the venerable prelate did.
Once parted from his mother's womb, black deeds he shunn'd;
With healthful aim, from birth-pangs on, throughout his days,
He set about a life school'd in the law of God;
His habits set in order like so many flowers.
Refined by boiling, purified in purging fire,
A most pure extract, gleaming: so his action was.
Steering an upward course, too, t'wards the heav'ns above,
He came through life's last haven to eternal birth.

Verses in the middle of *LibÆ* 10–13, equivalent to *LE* ii. 11

On Little Downham

'A place there is where liquid honey drops like dew.'
So people say: its namers called it by the name
Of Downham – a delightful place, rich, fertile, glad,
Where ploughland freely gives fertility enough.
Rivers of fish are noticed as at hand nearby.
A green wood stands, convenient for frequent hunts,
Adorn'd with flowers and set about with bank'd up turf,
Enclosing in its ramparts every kind of beast.
Here, while a sweet breeze wafts around, sings every bird:
The chatting magpie, blackbirds, thrushes, turtle-dove
And nightingales evoke harp-music as they sing,
Competing with each other in loquacity.
A palace shines where beauteous woodland yields a space;
Within its cloister-garths the wind blows from the south;
There dwells abundance; opulence rejoicing laughs.
Here is fair country: lovely are the verdant groves;
Compared with here, Thessalian Tempe's glades seem naught.
A garden grows, capacious of all kinds of fruit.
'Golden' they call the garden of the Atlantid race;
Golden enough the apples of the Hesperides,
So I believe, likewise: for apples, to be sure,
Are said to grow, in that place yonder, all of gold.
Either that once-gold garden was transported here
Or things are so contrived that this resembles it!

APPENDICES

Verses following *LibÆ* 34, equivalent to *LE* ii. 24

He who was faithful in his work and in his stewardship,
Christ's devotee: that man wert thou, O father Æthelwold.
Thou dost not covet silver's beauty, nor the show of gold;
A pit thou dost not dig: in heav'n thou knowest how to store
Riches and wealth, where thieves by wickedness achieve no harm,
Where, following thy goods dispatch'd ahead of thee,
Of which thou madest such a fine apportionment around,
Thou rulest now in safety, dwellest in the midst of wealth
That lasts for ever and amidst supernal treasuries,
Rejoicing in the peace of Christ, whose worshipper thou wert,
Wise man! So, our undoubted patron, come, have pity on us.

APPENDIX B

A translation of the opening chapter of the *Book of Miracles* from British Library MS Cotton, Domitian A iv, as printed in Blake's edition of the *Liber Eliensis*, Appendix B, p. 400f. The portions of the text omitted by Blake are italicized.

How King Edgar, divinely inspired, restored the church of Ely with the help of the holy bishop Æthelwold.

It remains now to write about the restoration of the church of Ely. Among the innumerable miraculous benefactions which the Lord has deigned to bring to pass through his venerable virgin Æthelthryth †<which indicate>† that this church was remarkable and excellent, †<is the fact>† that Edgar, the most powerful of the kings of England[4] prompted by a divine oracle, restored the church of Ely, adorned it with gifts, enriched it with estates, surrendered it to eternal liberty and commended it in its entirety to God. Its frequent overturning by pagans invading it in times gone by caused the place to be without worship for a hundred years less one, those offering worship having been killed.

This watery place, rich in fish, wooded and fertile, while it is seen as providing a satisfactory and quiet dwelling place, deservedly acquired as the first mistress of its monastic discipline the holy, venerable and glorious virgin and queen Æthelthryth who, founding a monastery of handmaidens of God, placed there a second Paradise and, bringing Heaven to the regions of Earth and the regions of Earth to Heaven, so altered the place that the one

---

[4] There seems to be a missing verb, at least, to be inserted, probably after *dignatus est* at p. 400.5, ed. Blake, where a lacuna should be marked.

the other.[5] As spiritual mother there succeeded her into the position of spiritual leadership her sister St Seaxburh, the wife of Eorconberht, King of the Kentish people and the mother of the holy virgin Eorcongota. Her successor was her other daughter, Eormenhild, the wife of Wulfhere, King of the Mercians and the mother of the holy virgin Wærburh. When, indeed, Eormenhild was taken up to Christ from the flesh, her aforementioned daughter Wærburh undertook to rule in the monastery, as I remember ascertaining from records written down long ago. After her death, blessed mothers and women whose names the knowledge of God alone knows, but they are utterly unknown to us, observing a mode of life guided by a rule, kept the place in honour and sanctification up until the times of the Danes. These were the men who overthrew their dwelling-places, having killed some of the women who lived there and put the rest to flight. The desolation of this place, bringing about the extermination of the former religious observance, had made a transition from heavenly liberty to human servitude *and, right until the times of the glorious* King Edgar, it was subservient to the royal[6] treasury.

But God, who all the time, and for everything, provides what is suitable in His sight, did not allow either that the monastery should be subject to contempt or that the lady saints should be without a cult for very long. Rather, the glory of those who repose there made supplication by virtue of the fame of their mighty feats, and summoned up a most suitable king for the time, and a most suitable bishop for the king, both of them most suitable for its deployment. So then, Edgar, the peaceable king of England, and Æthelwold, the outstanding pontiff of Winchester, who in different capacities, certainly, but with an identical end in view, were walking in the law of God, had subjugated the whole country to religion as much as to domination, King Edgar by ruling, Bishop Æthelwold, by preaching. In these circumstances, kingship and priesthood were in the aptest correspondence one with the other, in that what one decided, the other confirmed, and, as they had consulted together over the whole state of affairs, neither had differences of opinion, but rather they both agreed. Thus, raised to an exalted position by the favour of his king, the magnificent Bishop Æthelwold harnessed all the strength of his spirit to varied activity of his holiness, now initiating and carrying through to completion new undertakings, now completing projects begun, but not finished, by others, now restoring in various places monasteries that had been destroyed.

In his time, the house of Ely, famous for its miracles and glorious for its relics, was an adjunct to royal finance[7] and, being not a religious

---

[5] Reading conjecturally at p. 401.14, ed. Blake: *dum alterum alterius cives possideret.* Perhaps also emend to *possiderent,* though the form *cives* can be singular.

[6] Reading conjecturally at p. 400.25, ed. Blake: *regio fisco.*

[7] Reading conjecturally at p. 401.13, ed. Blake: *regio censui.*

community-house but a public minster, devoid of ceremoniousness and reverence, was open to everyone passing through. Two of the king's magnates, namely Bishop Sigewold, a Greek by nationality and Thurstan, a Dane by race, having seen the disposition of the place, asked for it from the king more out of acquisitiveness than devotion. As they were at rivalry in their shared ambition and a lawsuit between them was frequently in contention, *a certain man called* Wulfstan *of Dalham, who was a privy councillor[8] of the king, intervened, so that the one should not behave insolently towards the other in contempt, nor one be envious of the other on his acquisition of the property. He was motivated by divine approval rather than led on by human feeling. To the end that the king should not grant them the objectives of their petition, he approached him with this speech: 'Lord King, whereas we are all duty-bound to make provision for your safety and honour and for the whole kingdom, none of us has given the advice that the request of these men of yours be complied with. For it is a holy and famous place, and undeserving of owners such as these and, so that you may not be pressed unwittingly into sinning against its ancient dignity, I will, if you command it, not hesitate to supply you with a brief account of it.' And he gave the king an ordered account of the dignity of the place and the sanctity of its relics and whatever other things,* hitherto unknown *to the king, had either been written down by Bede or spread around by word of mouth.* And so weightily did the Holy Spirit stimulate the mind of the wise man in his speaking, that neither of the men desirous[9] of it was deemed the possessor of the desired possession, but envious avarice and avaricious envy suffered one and the same rebuff. *Now that these presumptuous individuals had had the expectation of gaining their objectives* cut from under them, *the glorious King Edgar forthwith summoned the blessed Æthelwold and conferred with him about the restoration of Ely monastery, saying that his inward desire was for the gathering together in that place of brothers by whom the most high Lord and the holy relics might be revered with worthy veneration. And, promising that he would endow the monastery in question with lands and gifts and a privilege of eternal liberty, he asked that man of God to be his colleague in the accomplishing of this very important undertaking, and to make a concerted effort with him regarding the establishment of monks in that place. The man of God, consequently, understood that the Holy Spirit was at work in the king and, giving thanks to God, in whose hand are the hearts of kings,[10]* he made no delay in bringing the good work to maturation, but carefully built anew the aforesaid monastery. Having expelled the clerics, he formed a congregation of monks there, and he also granted in their entirety to God and St Æthelthryth many lands, not only some bought by himself from the king, but also others received *gratis* from the king, these lands being accompanied

---

[8] Lat. *a secretis*; Bishop Æthelwold is also so described.

[9] Reading conjecturally at p. 401.21, ed. Blake: *neuter cupidorum* . . .

[10] Cf. Proverbs 21.1.

493

by various gifts and ornaments and confirmed by a privilege having royal authority. He also bought a great number of other lands from other people and bestowed them upon the church, which it would be otiose to enumerate individually because they are to be found elsewhere contained in their own volume. For the rest, so that the scale of the king's benefaction may be made known to readers the following privilege of his will tell forth what devotion and liberality he had towards his holy church of Ely. This[11] it seems to be right to place here to the end that it may be clear to all with what firmness the house of God rests upon its foundation.

Here, in the *Book of Miracles*, there follows the charter of Edgar recorded in *LE* ii. 5, and then two miracles derived from *LibÆ*, which are transcribed in *LE* iii. 119, 120.

APPENDIX C

Poem from the end of the account of Abbot Richard's translation of the Ely Saints in British Library MS Cotton, Domitian A xv (Blake, pp. 235–6, n. *g*).

Four scenes from the life of St Æthelthryth.

> *Here* Etheldreda, pious virgin, begs her wedded lord
> That he allow her to be called henceforth 'betrothed of Christ'.
> The king *here* pledges to the bishop for his wife's return
> Rewards, should he in holy wedlock bind her to himself.
> These orders of the king he to the blessed lady brings:
> She, Etheldreda, says: 'Let him allow me to serve Christ.'
> She, with the bishop, to her puissant lord brings her demand,
> Who also, though unwilling, sadly gives assent thereto.
> The longed-for royal edict learnt of, she, the virgin, seeks
> This temple, with a troop of virgins as her retinue,
> And *here* the queen is sanctified as spouse to God on high,
> Despising empty show and pomp of royal consort's rule.
> To Ely with her congregations comes the blessed maid,
> Forthwith the consecrated abbess to a blessed flock,
> The kindly lady Etheldreda, beauteous and strong
> In holy merits and in honour ever permanent.
> And she it was had built the citadel of this our shrine:
> The kindly virgin's flesh, untainted, lies disclosed to view,
> As four-times-four years in the tomb beneath the earth it's lain.
> The surgeon marvels at the wound heal'd over in her throat.
> The virgin's venerable corpse is carried to the church;

---

[11] Reading conjecturally at p. 401.30 Blake: *quod* in place of *quid*.

APPENDICES

The walls of this our holy temple guard the mausoleum
Of her who ruled it seven years, in chaste virginity.
Here, at the sight of miracles, the people praise their King:
The Lord Christ prais'd and honour'd be throughout eternity.

LIBER ELIENSIS

Note on the Indices

In the Index of Names and Index of Topics which follow, references are given to book- and section-numbers rather than to pages. One aim of this method of numbering has been to ensure that the Indices may be reusable, no doubt with many refinements, by future editors of the *Liber Eliensis*. The system of referencing should also facilitate cross-reference to Blake's Latin edition, which is followed exactly in the ordering of chapters. The three prefaces at the beginning of the work, on the history of the Isle of Ely, on the situation of the Isle and on the life of St Æthelthryth, are referred to as i pr. H; i pr. S and i pr. Æ respectively. All other references should be self-explanatory. The indices refer exclusively to the text of the *Liber Eliensis*: the introduction, footnotes and appendices accompanying this particular translation have not been indexed.

The Index of Names is heavily indebted to Blake's indexing. Hence the decision to list people chiefly by Christian names, regularizing but not modernizing Old English names, while giving place-names in their modern form, where this is known. Subdivided entries are given for many of the more important personages mentioned in the chronicle, including all the abbesses, abbots and bishops of Ely, and the kings of England from Edgar onwards. These longer, biographical entries are arranged in chronological order as far as possible. For the interest of local historians, the Index of Names presents, within square brackets, samples (not an exhaustive list) of the Old English and Latin place-names in the *Liber Eliensis*, as they appear in Blake's edition of the Latin text. Where English towns and villages are assigned to counties, 20th-century changes in county-boundaries, notably the amalgamation of Huntingdonshire with Cambridgeshire, have been disregarded.

The Index of Topics, which has no counterpart in Blake's edition, takes into account the likelihood that this translation will be read, or dipped into, by people with a wide variety of interests and backgrounds. It has also seemed appropriate to highlight the topics which the compiler himself clearly considered most important. The long list of the attributes of God reflects the fact that the *Liber Eliensis* might be termed a theological chronicle. Cross-referencing of every tiny item worthy of a place in this index would not have been practicable, so it seems sensible to note here that there are particularly elaborate entries on: Agriculture; Endowment of Monasteries; Land; Jurisdiction; Meetings (a term used to cover anything from a national assembly to a meeting of conspirators); Music; Occupations (of men, boys, women and girls); Ornaments of the Church (comprising church plate, vestments and other church furnishings); Tools and Weapons; Travel and Transport. Within a few of the longer entries, alphabetical sequence is abandoned in favour of other principles of arrangement, for the sake of clarity. The Index of Topics is not a simple index of word-use: rather, its longer entries list passages worth consulting for a variety of reasons, should one be enquiring what the *Liber Eliensis* has to offer of relevance to a particular topic.

INDEX OF NAMES

Ælfsige *(cont.)*
  Abbot of Peterborough, ii. 117;
  Cild, ii. 25;
  son of Wulfsige, ii. 15.
Ælfstan, ii. 30, 33;
  ---, son of, ii. 21;
  Bishop of London, ii. 31;
  brother of Leofsige and Wulfgar, ii.
    33;
  brother of Æthelstan, the priest,
    and of Bondo, ii. 33;
  of Ely, ii. 16;
  of Fulbourn, ii. 11a;
  subsacrist of Ely, iii. 50.
Ælfswyth, wife of Wulfwine *Cocus,*
  ii. 7.
Ælfthryth:
  matrona, ii. 39;
  noblewoman, ii. 31;
  Queen of King Edgar:
    joint donations of, ii. 37, 47;
    brings Æthelred to Ely, ii. 11;
    commits murders, ii. 56.
Ælfwaru:
  Lady *(domina),* iii. 50, 78;
  widow, ii. 61.
Ælfweard, ii. 10;
  of Stodham, 49a;
Ælfwine, ii. 30, 82;
  Bishop of Elmham or Thetford, ii.
    75, 80, 86, 118; iii. 50;
  brother of Ecgfrith, King of
    Northumbria, i. 23;
  father of Leofsige, i. 11;
  husband of Siflæd, ii. 17;
  Retheresgut [Reðeresgut], ii. 135;
  son of Ælfwold of
    Mardleybury, ii. 10;
Ælfwold, ii. 25;
  Abbot of Holm, ii. 116;
  brother of Eadric *Longus* of
    Essex, ii. 27;
  brother of Ealdorman Æthelwine

  and Æthelsige, ii. 11a, 34, 51;
  of Mardleybury, ii. 10;
  ---, sons of. *See* Ælfwine,
    Æthelmær;
  Grossus, ii. 11a;
  ---, wife of, ii. 11a;
  magnate of England *(optimas
    Anglie),* ii. 7.
  See also Leofstan, son of Ælfwold.
Ælfwyn:
  Abbess of Chatteris, ii. 71;
  grand-daughter of Ealdorman
    Byrhtnoth, ii. 88.
Ælgetus, i. 23, iii. 94.
Ælla:
  King of the Deiri, i. 8;
  King of Northumbria, i. 39.
Æneid {of Virgil}, ii. 110.
Ælred, ii. 130.
Ælric, monk of St Albans, ii. 103.
Ærmeswerch. See Cambridge.
Ærnaldus:
  de Laventonia, iii. 115, 139;
  magister, iii. 134–5.
Ærnethern, iii. 136.
Æsop, ii. 131.
Æscwig, Bishop of Dorchester, ii. 29,
  34; iii. 50.
Æscwyn, widow, of Stonea, ii. 18, 24.
Æsgar, the Staller, ii. 96.
Æthelberht, King of Kent, i. pr. S; iii.
  pr.
Æthelburh, daughter of Anna,
  King of East Anglia, i. 2.
Æthelferth, father of Leofric of
  Brandon, ii. 8, 35.
Æthelflæd:
  sister of Leofric of Stretham, ii. 10;
  wife of Ealdorman Æthelstan, ii.
    64;
  wife of Leofric of Brandon, ii. 8,
    10;

Canterbury *(cont.)*
  archbishops of. *See* Ælfheah;
    Ælfric; Æthelnoth; Anselm;
    Augustine; Dunstan; Lanfranc;
    Oda; Stigand; Theobald;
    Theodore; Thomas; William;
  archbishopric of, controlled by
    Ranulf Flambard ii. 140;
  St Augustine's Abbey, ii. 78–9,
    98;
  martyrdom of St Thomas à Becket
    at, iii. 143.
Carthage, Council of, iii. 51.
Castle Holdgate, Shropshire, [Castrum
  Helgoti], iii. 7, 8, 14.
Catiline, iii. 47.
Ceadda, Bishop of Mercia, i. 7, 8.
Cecilia, St, i. 33.
Cenwold, priest of Horningsea and
  kinsman of Wulfric, *prepositus* ii. 32.
Cenwalh, King of Wessex, i. 7.
Charybdis, i. 11.
Chatteris, Cambs., [Chateriz, Chaterihc],
  Abbey of, i. pr. S, ii. 71; iii. 6,
    17–19, 25, 56, 85.
Chedburgh, Suffolk, [Caedeberi,
  Ceaddeberi], ii. 68.
Chelles, [Cale], monastery at, i. 2, 7.
Cherchewere, Chirchewere, 1 pr. S;
  ii. 54.
Chertsey, Surrey. *See* Wulfwold,
  Abbot of.
Chester, Cheshire, [Cestra], i. 37.
  See also Robert, Bishop of;
    Hugh, Earl of.
Cheveley, Cambs., [Chefle], ii. 63, 82,
  86.
Chichester, Sussex, [Cicestria]:
  Bishops of. *See* Hilary, Ralph.
Chippenham, Cambs., [Cipenham,
  Cypenham], ii. 11, 11a.
Christ, Jesus. *See Index of Topics.*

Cirencester, Gloucs., [Cirecestria], iii.
  60.
Clac of Fulbourn, ii. 33.
Clare, Suffolk, iii. 43;
  Earl of, iii. 127–9;
  Gilbert de, (Earl of Pembroke, 12th
    century), iii. 69, 73–4, 88;
  Richard Fitz Gilbert de (regularly
    referred to in *LE* as Gilbert
    de Clare), ii. 29, 108–9, 111,
    116, 121–2, 140–1.
    See also Rohais (Richard's
    wife).
  Richard, son of Richard Fitz
    Gilbert de Clare. *See* Richard,
    Abbot of Ely.
  For Osbert of Clare, Prior of
    Westminster, *see* Osbert.
Clayhithe, Cambs., [Cleie], ii. 11.
Clement, St, i. 28.
Cliffe (King's Cliffe), Northants.,
  [Cliva], iii. 24.
Clinton, Northants., [Clinton]. *See*
  Geoffrey.
Cluny, monastic order of, iii. 43.
Cnobheresburch, i. 1.
Cnut, King,
  his comrades kill Bishop Eadnoth
    and Abbot Wulfsige at battle
    of Ashingdon, ii. 71;
  marries Queen Emma, ii. 79;
  orders consecration of Abbot
    Leofric, ii. 80, 118;
  appoints Abbot of Ely as one of
    three chancellors, ii. 78;
  orders institution of food-rent
    system, ii. 84;
  visits Ely at Candelmas, ii. 85;
  a song attributed to him, ii. 85;
  crosses ice from Soham, ii. 85;
  has church built and dedicated at
    Ashingdon, ii. 87;

England, [Anglia, regio Anglorum] or
    English people, the, [Angli],
    i. pr. H, pr. S, 1–2, 6–8, 15, 26, 34,
    38–40, 42–3, 49–50; ii. 7, 11, 28–9,
    35, 50, 53–54, 62, 72, 78–80, 82,
    85, 90–3, 95–6, 99–101, 104–5,
    107, 110, 113, 116–8, 120–8,
    133–5, 140, 147, 149; iii. pr., 5–16,
    18–24, 33, 39–40, 42–46, 49–50,
    62–3, 65–6, 70–2, 75–6, 79, 81–3,
    85, 87–8, 90, 92–3, 97, 103–4,
    106–7, 113, 117, 119–120, 122,
    125, 127–129, 132, 137–8, 140,
    143;
---, annals of, iii. 5;
---, church of, ii. 134–5; iii. 103.
English Ocean, ii. 53.
    See also Index of Topics, under
        Languages: English.
Eni, father of King Anna, i. 1.
Eorconberht, King of Kent, i. 2, 7, 17,
    25.
Eormenburh:
    Queen of King Merewald of West
        Mercia, daughter of King
        Eormenred, i. 17;
    second Queen of Ecgfrith, King
        of Northumbria, i. 11.
Eormenhild, St, i. pr. S:
    daughter of St Seaxburh, i. 7;
    married to King Wulfhere of
        Mercia, i. 7;
    mother of St Wærburh, i. 7, 15;
    successor to St Seaxburh as Abbess
        of Ely, i. 36;
    succeeded by St Wærburh and
        other abbesses, i. 37–8;
    enshrined in Ely i. 43; ii. 53, 82,
        105, 145, 147; iii. 50;
    translated by Abbot Richard, ii.
        145–6;
    vision of, ii. 133;
    her feast, iii. 121.
Eormenred, King, i. 17.

Eorpwald, King of East Anglia, i. 1.
Eowils, i. 39, 42.
Ernulf, *medicus*, iii. 89.
Esgar. *See* Æsgar.
Essex. *See* East Saxons.
Estona, Estune, ii. 128; iii. 38.
Eu. *See* William.
Eucharistus, i. 5.
Eulalia, St, i. 33.
Euphemia, St, i. 33.
Eudo, the steward, ii. 114.
Eugenius III, Pope, iii. 98–110, 122–4.
Eustace, Sheriff of Huntingdonshire, ii.
    116.
Eve (in Book of Genesis), i. 33.
Everard of *Beche,* iii. 139.
Evreux, iii. 12.
Exeter, Devon [Exonia], iii. 20.
Exning, Suffolk, [Exninge], i. 3; ii. 11a.
Eye, Cambs., [Eie], ii. 32–3.
Eynesbury, Hunts., [Henulvesberi], ii.
    29, 108.

Fambridge, Essex, [Fanbrige,
    Fanbrege, Fanbruge], ii. 81, 92.
Felix, St, Bishop of East Anglia, i. 1, 6, 7.
Feltwell, Norfolk, [Feltewelle], ii. 74,
    84, 92.
Fen Ditton. *See* Ditton.
Ferentino, iii, 100, 102.
Finborough, Suffolk, [Fineberge], ii.
    62.
Fincham, Norfolk, [Fingeham], ii. 92.
Folcard, ii. 16.
Fordham, Cambs., [Fordeham,
    Fordham], 11a, 31; iii. 82.
Fotedorp, Norfolk *or* Suffolk, iii. 26,
    54, 56, 85.
Fourches. *See* Herbert.
France. *See* Gaul. *Also:* Aquitaine,
    Britanny, Burgundy, Maine,
    Normandy.

S., Bishop, ii. 128.

Sæthryth, step-daughter of King Anna, i. 2.

St Albans, ii. 98, 103; iii. 108;
  abbots of. *See* Ecgfrith; Paul; Richard;
  monks of. *See* Ælric, Semannus.

St Augustine's Abbey, Canterbury. *See* Canterbury.

St James in Galicia, iii. 42.

St Neots, Priory of, ii. 29.

St Paul's, London. *See* London.

St Pierre sur Dive [Sanctus Petrus super Divam], iii. 11, 18.

Salisbury:
  bishopric controlled by Ranulf Flambard, ii. 140;
  Roger, Bishop of. *See* Roger.

Salomon, Cantor of Ely, iii. 103;

Samson (in Book of Judges), iii. 72.

Santiago de Compostela. *See* St James in Galicia.

Sapphira. *See* Ananias and Sapphira.

Sarah, wife of Tobias (in Book of Tobit), iii. 35.

Satan. *See Index of Topics under* Devil.

Sawtry, Hunts., [Saltreda], iii. 21, 22.

Saxons, i. 1. *See also* East Saxons, South Saxons.

Scalers:
  Hardwin de, ii. 114, 116, 121, 134; iii. 26, 54, 56, 85;
  ---, heirs of, iii. 26, 54, 56, 85;
  Hugh de, iii. 71, 76;
  Stephen de, iii. 71, 76, 115;
  Theobald de, iii. 115.

Sceppeia, Scepeia, Suffolk, iii. 26, 54, 56, 85.

Scotland, ii. 102, 134–5.
  See also David; Malcolm, Kings of Scots.

Scots, *Scotti* (including *Scotti* from Ireland), i. 14; ii. 5, 102, 134; iii. 46.

Scule, Earl, ii. 36–7.

Scylla, i. pr. Æ.

Seaxburh, St:
  daughter of King Anna of East Anglia, i. 7;
  Queen of Eorconbehrt, King of Kent, i. 2, 7, 17, 25;
  mother of Hlothere, King of Kent, i. 21;
  mother of Eormenhild, i. 17;
  grandmother of Wærburh, i. 17;
  founds Sheppey Abbey and takes the veil. i. 36;
  Abbess (of Sheppey), i. 18;
  later, nun at Ely, i. 15, 18;
  succeeds her sister as Abbess of Ely, i. 25;
  arranges first translation of St Æthelthryth, i. 25–28; ii. 144;
  her death, i. 35;
  succeeded by St Eormenhild, i. 36;
  enshrined at Ely, i. pr. S, 35, 43; ii. 82, 105;
  translated by Abbot Richard, ii. 145–7;
  position of new shrine, iii. 50;
  appears in visions, ii. 132–3;
  her feast, iii. 121.

Seaxferth, ii. 11;
  Oscytel, son of, ii. 33;
  ---, son of, ii. 11.

Seaxwulf, Abbot of Peterborough and Bishop of Mercia, i. 17.

Sebaste, iii. 35.

Segni, iii. 104–5.

Semannus, monk of St Albans, ii. 103.

Serlo of Hauxton, iii. 115.

Sewara, i. 11, 13, 15.

Sewenna, i. 11, 13, 15.

Shechem, son of Hamor (in Book of Genesis), i. 12.

INDEX OF TOPICS

INDEX OF TOPICS

541

INDEX OF TOPICS

INDEX OF TOPICS

Evidence *(cont.)*

factual, iii. 47;

from learning and morals, iii. 2, 4;

God-sent, iii. 60;

historical. *See* Historical, aims, methods, use of evidence;

legal, ii. 124–5; iii. 96–7; 100, 108;

material, i. 28; iii. 58;

of divine activity, ii. 129, 131, 133, 147; iii. 27, 29;

of holiness , i. 22, 26 37;

of illness, iii. 60;

of miracles, i. 12, 43; iii. 33, 57–8, 60, 93;

spoken, i. 12;

written, i. 2, 12; iii. 48.

See also Witnesses.

Exchange-rate. *See* Money.

Excommunication, ii. 9, 39, 58, 93; iii. 26, 54–6, 68, 79, 85, 126–9, 142–3.

Exemptions, i. pr. S; ii. 85, iii. 12–13, 15–16, 19, 21–2, 56, 84, 141.

See also Liberty of Ely monastery.

Ex-monk, iii. 47.

Ex-priest, iii. 138.

Facial expression, iii. 93, 131.

Famine, ii. 104, 109; iii. 50, 82.

Fathers of the Church, i. 5; ii. 141.

See also Index of Names under Benedict, Gregory.

Fasting and Abstinence, i. 7–8, 14, 16, 18; ii. 53, 100; iii. 44, 51, 137.

Feasting, ii. 52–3.

Feasts of Ely Saints. *See* Church's year.

Femininity, iii. 60.

Fens. *See* Marshland.

Ferthing. *See* Hundreds.

Fetters, miraculous, iii. 33–5.

See also Chaining of captives.

Feudal tenure. *See* Land.

Fighting:

criminal offence, ii. 49b;

in resistance to Norman Conquest, ii. 101–2, 104–7, 109–111, 134–5;

against Bishop Hervey, in Welsh rebellion, iii. 1–2, 4.

Fihtwite and *fyrdwite. See* Customary Rights.

Finance:

of archdeaconry, ii. 54; iii. 25, 37;

of bishopric, iii. 25;

of monastery, ii. 136; iii. 27, 37, 105. *See also* Endowment of Monasteries.

Fining, as punishment. *See* Punishments.

Fire, destruction by, i. pr. Æ, 6, 14, 27, 33, 33–9, 40–1, 48–9; ii. 52–3, 106–7, 134, 138; iii. 28, 50, 82, 97, 119.

Firewood, ii. 7.

Fish i. pr. S; ii. 24, 105:

burbot *(burbutes)*, ii. 105;

eels *(anguille)*, i. pr. S; ii. 5, 21, 24, 105; iii. 26, 54, 56, 85, 136;

herrings *(allecia)*, iii. 26, 54, 56, 85, 136;

lampreys/water snakes *(murene)*, ii. 105;

perch *(percide)*, ii. 105;

pike *(luceoli)*, ii. 105;

roach *(rocee)*, ii. 105;

salmon *(isicii)*, ii. 105;

sturgeon *(rumbus)*, ii. 105;

water-wolves *(lupi aquatici)*, ii. 105.

Fisheries, ii. 18, 20–21, 23–4, 60–1, 93; iii. 90.

Fleas, iii. 143.

Floods, iii. 141.

Flowers:

flower seen in girl's dream, iii. 60;

'flower of the hay', ii. 58;

Processions *(cont.)*
welcoming king, ii. 85;
--- bishop, iii. 44;
--- recipient of miracle, iii. 33;
--- relics, iii. 33;
with carrying of crosses and relics,
ii. 111; iii. 69;
--- carrying of staves, at festivals,
ii.139;
--- carrying of tower-pyx, iii. 89.
Professions of monks, written records
of, ii. 65.
Property qualification for *proceres*, ii.
97.
Prophecy, i. 14–15, 18, 19, 21, 39, 49; ii.
39, 79, 87, 92, 100, 133.
Prosae. See Sequences.
Priests. *See* Occupations of men and
boys; Priesthood.
Prisoners, i. 23.
Protection:
from consequences of
misdeeds, ii. 32–3;
from enemy attack, ii. 62.
Protection-money. *See* Money.
Psalms.
See Music: singing.
Psalters, ii. 139. iii. 43;
Punishments, ii. 93, 95–95a;
amputation of limbs, ii. 101, 111;
anathema, ii. 112; iii. 1, 68, 90–1, 112–13,
115, 122;
arrest ordered by king, ii. 96;
blinding, ii. 101, 111;
corporal punishment by
schoolmasters(?), iii. 35, 93;
curse. *See* Cursing;
ecclesiastical censure, iii. 83;
excommunication. *See separate*
entry;
death-penalty, ii. 32; iii. 52;
demotion or expulsion from

priestly office , ii. 32, iii. 77;
deprivation of honours, ii. 101;
distraint, iii. 71, 76;
exile, ii. 107; iii. 52 (perpetual);
feet of knights tied beneath
horses, iii. 69;
fining, ii. 111; iii. 62;
forfeiture of property, ii. 7, 19,
24–5, 34, 43, 49b; iii. 62, 65,
68, 86;
hanging, iii. 52;
harassment, ii. 112;
imprisonment, ii. 107, 111; iii. 52;
--- for remainder of life, ii. 96,
--- in dungeon, ii. 90, 96; iii. 33,
52, 96;
--- in guard-house, ii. 106
101–2;
just punishment of royal severity,
iii. 128;
payment of compensation,
--- to value of *mund*, ii. 11;
--- to value of *wergeld*, ii. 11;
payment of fine, ii. 18, 24;
perpetual custody (of monks), ii.
108;
reproof from king, ii. 96;
rod and correction, iii. 60;
torture, ii. 101, 138.
See also Bodily injury, deliberately
inflicted; Chaining of captives;
Excommunication.

Quarter-days, iii. 106.
Quasimodo geniti. See Church's year.

Rationality, how manifested in deaf
and dumb persons, ii. 130.
Recluses, ii. 134.
Reed, eucharistic. *See* Ornaments,
under Straw.
Reeds. *See* Vegetation, wild.

Wine. *See* Food and Drink.

Wisdom:

  biblical conceptions of, i. 2, 3, 12,
    28; ii. 55, 85, 87; iii. 36, 60, 74,
    120, 134;

  character-trait, 9, 49 ii. 5, 11a, 25,
    60, 62, 77, 112; iii. 1–2, 4, 42,
    46, 62, 74, 93, 101, 108.

Witan, Witenagemot. See Meetings.

Witchcraft, ii. 56, 106.

Witnesses:

  in legal disputes, ii. 124–5; iii. 100,
    108, 110;

  of character, i. 8; iii. 93;

  of historical facts, i. 9, 49; ii. pr.,
    65, 91, 144;

  of inventories, ii. 114; iii. 50;

  of king's decision, iii. 46;

  of land-transactions ii. 7–8,
    10–12, 16–17, 19, 25, 27–31,
    33–38, 46, 48–49a, 59, 65–7,
    69–70, 75, 92, 95, 120; iii. 7,
    14, 49, 90, 139–40;

  of miracles, i. 11, 27–8; ii. 147; iii.
    36, 43, 118;

  of saint's virginity, i. 5, 12, 27;

  of saints' translation, ii. 144;

  of written documents, ii. 5, 65,
    93, 97, 114, 117, 126, 128;
    iii. 7–8, 10–16, 18–25, 40,
    49–50, 63, 70–1, 75–6, 87–8,
    134–6.

Women:

  as inheritors, purchasers and
  bequeathers of land; ii. 8,
    10–11a, 18, 24–5, 31, 37, 47, 59,
    61, 64, 81, 83; iii. 60;

  education of. *See* Education;

  occupations of. *See* Occupations;

  participating in meetings, ii. 10;
    11a, 34, 60; iii. 140;

  petitioning king, ii. 25, 39; ii. 88.

Wooden:

  artefacts, ii. 6;

  coffins/burial cases, i. 20, 30;
    ii. 145; iii. 117;

  church, iii. 43;

  fortress, iii. 62;

  staff/ stake, i. 13, 48;

  statues (with precious overlay) ii.
    6; iii. 50;

  tower, ii. 107;

  tower-pyx (with precious overlay),
    iii. 45.

Woodland, i. pr. S; ii. 7, 9, 11, 19, 26,
    28, 55, 58, 61, 82, 92, 105–6, 126;
    iii. 55, 90. *See also* Coppice-woods.

World, Worldliness, Earth, Earthly
    Things, i. 3, 4, 7–12, 15, 17–19, 21,
    23, 26–7, 32–3, 41, 43, 46; ii.
    4–6, 9, 11a, 28, 39, 51, 58, 64,
    67, 74, 76–7, 82, 87, 92, 97,
    100–1, 108, 112–13, 129, 131,
    145, 148; iii. 2–3, 5, 17,
    28, 31, 33, 41–3, 52, 60–1, 82,
    93, 115, 117, 121, 143.

Worship. *See* Liturgy *for references to
    separate entries.*

Wounds, i. 21, 23, 27, 48; ii. 18, 56, 60,
    79, 106, 110, 132; iii. 1, 58, 69, 86,
    92, 143.

Writs. *See* Charters, Writs and
    Privileges.

Lightning Source UK Ltd.
Milton Keynes UK
UKHW031836280420
362465UK00005B/216

9 781843 830153